Kingston: City on the Hudson

KINGSTON

City on the Hudson

Alf Evers

The Overlook Press
Woodstock & New York

First published in the United States in 2005 by
The Overlook Press, Peter Mayer Publishers, Inc.
Woodstock & New York

WOODSTOCK:
One Overlook Drive
Woodstock, NY 12498
www.overlookpress.com
[for individual orders, bulk and special sales, contact our Woodstock office]

NEW YORK:
141 Wooster Street
New York, NY 10012

Cataloging-in-Publication Data is available from the Library of Congress

Book design and type formating by Bernard Schleifer
Manufactured in the United States of America
ISBN 1-58567-732-9
3 5 7 9 8 6 4 2

Contents

Part 4

A Dutch Company and then the Commercially Driven British Further Profitably Colonize the Land and People of Kingston under Changing Rulers 1661-1700

Part 5

Life in the Colony of Kingston as Oppressed by British Colonial Rule in the 18th Century up till July 4, 1776

Part 6

An Independent Nation is Born in Battle with the Help of Kingston 1776-1783

Part 7

The New Nation Begins to Take Shape

Part 8

Kingston Develops its Character in Peace and War
1813-1865

Part 9

A Multi-Ethnic and Historic City Faces a Restless World
1865-1890's

Part 10

Kingston Makes Progress Toward Becoming Accepted as a Truly Historic City of the U.S.A. 1890s-Present

List of Illustrations

Preface

THERE ARE OVER THIRTY INHABITED PLACES ON EARTH WHICH ARE IN ONE way or another important enough to get listed in gazetteers or shown on maps under the place name of "Kingston." Most, including the one with which this book is concerned, are in the United States, several are in England, one is in Australia and two in Canada. One of the British Kingstons is known because of its location on a famous river as Kingston-on-Thames, another on the coast of Yorkshire is called Hull in common speech but is known officially as Kingston-on-the-Hull. Transplanted Yorkshireman, Ralph Radcliffe Whitehead in 1903 described his new arts and crafts colony of Byrdcliffe in Woodstock, N.Y. as lying twelve miles from "Kingston-on-Hudson" but could not persuade his colonists or their neighbors to follow this example. Europe has its Frankfurt-am-Main and its Frankfurt-an-der-Oder while Holland can boast a Bergen op Zoom and Russia a Rostov-on-Don. Such compound names do very well in preventing confusion between riverside places sharing the same basic name. Yet in spite of a number of successful attempts to transplant the use of similar hyphenated place names to other Hudson Valley places all attempts to riverize and hyphenate the name of Kingston, Ulster County, New York, have as yet withered as Whitehead's name change did.

The most memorable try at changing the name of Kingston to Kingston-on-the-Hudson was made in 1920 by Kingston watchmaker and jeweler, Charles Safford. On July 30, 1920 Mr. Safford sent out to each of the twenty-seven American Kingstons which then had a post office, a leaflet headed "Kingston U.S.A. Kingston-on-the-Hudson." The leaflet contained a brief chronological history of Kingston and much other material aimed at presenting the myth of the city. This myth, as the word is used here, consists of the body of beliefs about their home place, held by its inhabitants. The myth concerning Kingston which combines factual and imagined local and universal elements has never been more persuasively given shape than it was by Safford. And that was not all. Mr. Safford also included an advertisement for "a sterling tribute" to "Our Fine Old Colonial Town" in the shape of a "souvenir Stuyvesant-Clinton spoon (price, two dollars). The spoon honored the memories of two men who rank high in the Kingston myth. One was Peter Stuyvesant who had planned, laid out and supervised construction of the stockaded village which was to grow into the City of Kingston. Sharing honors on the spoon with Stuyvesant was George Clinton, Revolutionary War general, first Governor of the State of New York, Vice-president of the United States who maintained a close tie to Kingston until the end of his life in 1812 by clinging through thick and thin to the job of clerk (maintained by deputies chosen by Clinton from his wife's family) of the Court of Common Pleas of Ulster County!

In a two-page folder which supplemented his leaflet Safford expanded his detailing of the Kingston myth. He praised the beauty of the city's scenic setting as seen against the Catskill Mountains and on the beautiful Hudson River, the patriotism of its men in the Revolutionary and Civil Wars, and the courage of its people when faced with the "barbaric burning" of their town by British soldiers in 1777. In only one way did Safford depart from the accepted Kingston myth. That was when, instead of portraying the Native predecessors of the white colonists as cruel enemies he complimented them by describing them as "connoisseurs of nature." Safford wrote with fervor of Kingston's attractiveness as an industrial and transportation center and a tourist mecca; he praised the then new bridge across the Rondout Creek as "a Dream-Bridge." He gave evidence that the world recognized the magnetic power of Kingston even to international post office clerks by asserting that letters sent from Europe and addressed to no more than "Kingston U.S.A." reach their destination and that a postcard from Holland once found its target although it was merely addressed to "Kingston" plus a little image of an American flag. Safford concluded in a fine burst of soaring into the stratosphere of local pride that Kingstonians had a right to boast that while "there are 27 Kingstons in the United States there is only one Kingston-on-the-Hudson and but one 'Kingston U.S.A.'."

The city of Kingston and the succession of communities which have occupied the same space on our planet have been known by many names. The Native Americans of early historic times referred to the fertile flatlands along the Esopus Creek on which their wigwams and gardens stood as Athar-hacton which is thought to mean a fertile, cultivated plain. Then the place under white rule became Esopus, then in 1661 Wiltwyck, then Kingston, if very briefly, then Swanenberg, then Kingston again (as village, town and at last as city). Each change of names marked a change in self-image or myth by the people of the place as they found their way through challenging times to the right to be called a historic city of marked individuality. But a change to either Kingston-on-the-Hudson or Kingston-on-Hudson although considered, never officially happened. During the final decades of the nineteenth and early decades of the twentieth century and with the approval of the U.S. Post Office, a number of other Hudson Valley riverside places added "on-Hudson" or "on-the-Hudson" to their official names as recognized by the Post Office Department. Croton, Hastings, Cornwall, Malden and Annandale are among them. In 1926, Castleton became the last to make the change. These changes were rooted in a desire not only to set a place apart from others with which they might be confused but also by an urge to profit by asserting that their spot of the earth's surface shared in the romantic glamor of the famous Hudson River. And that river and its valley ever since the early years of the nineteenth century had stood in the top rank of America's almost "sacred places" for its scenic beauty, its historic interest and its economic use to industry and business which sprang from the river's great value as a means of transportation of goods and people.

The Kingston-on-Hudson with which this book is concerned deals with a mere one-twenty-seventh of the nation's ample stock of Kingstons. And by whatever name Kingston has been known and whatever names have been considered and then dropped, Kingstonians like dwellers in other cities have evolved the distinctive set of beliefs about the character of their city which inspired Mr. Safford and which gives rise to a pride in the place they call home. It has been well said that, "No city or landscape is truly rich unless it has been given the quality of myth by writers, painters or association with great events." Kingston's eminent early American painter John Vander Lyn has given the city a secure place in the history of American art not only by his portraits of Kingston and other American worthies of the past as well but also by his efforts in historic panoramic painting and his great nude *Ariadne*. And the City has been the scene of a significant event in the American Revolution. And while Kingston has not affected the course of American literature it has made up for that by being set in a landscape given distinction by its combination of mountains (chosen by Washington Iriving as the site of Rip Van Winkle's twenty year sleep), streams, fertile farmlands and the noble Hudson River whose mythic quality has made it the goal of generations of admiring travelers. It is Kingston's myth—the set of agreed-upon beliefs about their city—which sets the place apart not only from all the other Kingstons of our planet, but from all other American communities whatever their names might be.

For over a century and a half Kingston's charm has tempted a succession of local writers as well as a few outsiders, to try to snare in a net of words the special flavor of Kingston and its history, and to hold their trophy up for public inspection.

How the immigrants of varied ethnic and cultural backgrounds to the place which some geographically precise people have called Kingston-on-the-Hudson related to each other and to the land on which they lived—and how that land responded to them, that is the aim of this book about historic Kingston-on-the-Hudson.

Alf Evers
Vosburgh Mill Complex
Shady Post Office, in the
Town of Woodstock, Ulster County,
New York

PART 1

Men, Women and the Spirits They Believed in Share the Remarkably Fertile Place Where Three Valleys Meet until Dutch Traders and Colonizers Intrude from Beyond the Sea—about 12,000 B.C.–to about 1652

1.
The Fertile Place Where the Three Valleys Meet

IN 1862 ABRAHAM LINCOLN ASSURED HIS FELLOW CITIZENS THAT "WE CANNOT escape history." In the City of Kingston N.Y., escape from history may not be impossible yet it certainly is difficult. Most of the Kingstonians whom I queried informally as I started work on this book in 1989, as to what was the outstanding feature of their city did not hesitate to answer, "its history." One uptown businessman went so far as to express the opinion that "Kingston has too damn much history for its own good." The man was referring to the waves of protest that arise these days whenever someone proposes tearing down or modernizing one of the fine old buildings which stand as resolute witnesses to Kingston's fascinating past—and in the opinion of a very few, as barriers to a more prosperous commercial future.

Yet to many Kingstonians it is all too easy to escape the local earth history and the pre-history of the time before human efforts left their first visible but unwritten marks on the landscape. We must turn to find a useful base for the pre-history of Kingston (before white peoples' written records were kept) by using such things as surviving ancient articles of daily use or visible changes on the face of the earth left by human effort.

Long before the earliest written records were kept in what was to become Kingston the true human pioneers of the place, the Native Americans, who could neither read nor write nor erect lasting buildings, were drawn to the site of the Kingston-to-be and its surroundings because the place had certain advantages for Native Living. These advantages were described with enthusiasm in the following words by an anonymous writer in the Kingston periodical called *Olde Ulster, An Historical and Genealogical Magazine,* of April 1905, page 97: "Here (at the site of the future Kingston) converged three great valleys through each of which flowed a magnificent stream between wide and fertile lowlands. Here the Indian trails came together; here on these broad and open savannahs were the cornfields and gardens of the red men; here in the forests was an abundance of game; here in their season were the waters of the Hudson alive with shad and herring for their food supply." Ancient deposits of discarded fresh water mussel shells found today where the Esopus Creek joins the Hudson tell us of the wide use long ago as Natives' food of the fresh water mussels which lived above the point at which the tidal Hudson was not salty enough to support the oysters which were a favorite food of the Natives before the great River's waters lowered.

The unknown writer of 1905 was correct in sensing that the harbor-endowed place where the valleys of the Rondout (after it had been joined by the Walkill), and the Hudson come together, with the Esopus flowing through what is now uptown Kingston on its way to joining the River at Saugerties, has marked advantages as a place where Native Americans might live and live well. But the writer of 1905 did not point out that it was also a place where the white intruders who would arrive in the 1600s from the part of Europe known as The Netherlands would also believe that they too might live even better than the Natives. However, because the white intruders and Natives did not understand their different sometimes competitive ways of relating to the land nor each other's ways of living, the two groups could not live in peace together like brothers and amicably share the advantages of the favored place. For that reason the beginnings of the little settlement of white intruders that was to grow into the present City of Kingston would be stained by bloody conflict. In the struggle in which intruders from European nations were to impose colonialism on much of the globe, the simpler stone and wood tool dependent American natives along the Hudson and the other streams were ill-prepared.

Until some eleven thousand years ago, human life, for Natives or whites, as far as is known, even at its most primitive level, could not have existed on the land on which Kingston would rise. And this for a very understandable reason. For about a hundred thousand years much of North America (including the site of Kingston of today) had been covered by a slowly moving mass of ice up to a mile thick which because of a lowering of local planetary temperature was grinding, crushing and scraping the land beneath. With a warming of the climate the ice slowly receded northward and a damp, desolate and visibly lifeless landscape appeared. Then visible life, so long impossible on the ice-covered land, slowly returned to the warming surfaces of the earth. And for the first time, human beings, those we call today Native Americans or Indians were known to have been attracted to the region. The pioneer immigrants to the place where the three valleys meet were of Asiatic emigrant origin and may have been ancestors of those we know today as Native Americans or Indians. The first to arrive, to remain and to make their homes there earned their living by hunting large mammals such as mastodons which fed on the scant returning vegetation, using stone-tipped spears and darts as they hunted in groups, by fishing and by gathering edible parts of wild plants on the recently tundra-like land from which the ice was drawing back. During thousands of years other Native Americans with somewhat different ways of making their livings displaced the pioneers in response to the evolving of a landscape slowly becoming more like the one we know today. More than three thousand years ago, Natives with ways of life adapted to the milder region made their appearance. These people's women grew beans and squash at first, and later, as white intruders arrived, also mingled these with maize or "Indian corn," on the fertile lowlands along the Esopus and other streams. Their men had removed the encumbering trees and bushes to make these usually stone-free alluvial flatlands fit for use as gardens. In search of materials for food, clothing and shelter, these mobile people, the earliest met by Europeans, explored their region as they moved or sent out work parties over trails leading from their bark-covered wigwams and garden plots, some on the fertile flat lands which had appeared beside the Esopus Creek (gently tilled by Native women with digging sticks and other crude tools of wood and bone) to the bank of the Rondout and Hudson to catch spring runs of spawning shad, herring and other fish. In the fall they left their wigwams for the shallow rock shelters of the lower slopes of east-facing Catskill Mountains to hunt the deer, bear and turkeys attracted by falling chestnuts, beech and other nuts while their women prepared the skins of deer and bears for winter clothing and bedding. By midsummer the Native families spread out to the sunny sides of the nearby mountains and harvested huckle and other berries to be dried for winter use.

To the Native Americans, as the white intruders arrived, everything in their material world had its counterpart in the world of spirits. Sky and earth, stone, fire, trees, deer and fish—each had its spirit. And men and women had to be on good terms with these strong spirits with which they shared the land if they were to live well. And so it was felt reasonable to propitiate the spirits by prayer and other rites when hunting, harvesting or trying to gain help in such landmark events as birth, reaching adulthood and dying.

John Bierhorst reports in his *Ways of the Earth* that Munsee or Esopus Native Americans, some of whom lived in the Kingston area, also believed that plants and animals were of similar descent. So did many other Native Americans who were also speakers of the great Algonquian group of dialects (including the Esopus or Munsees of the Kingston area), who had among them shamans who believed they could detect this kind of relationship between humans, animals and plants as hinted at in the mythologies and cosmologies of the North American Natives as orally handed down.

The evidence of archaeological studies of 1983-1986 revealed that among the first of all humans to inhabit what is now Kingston had been a small village of native

Americans of the late Woodland period dating to about 5500 B.C. up to before the arrival of explorer Henry Hudson in the Hudson Valley, within what are now the limits of the city of Kingston. The Native village was situated at Ponckhockie on a bluff then located nearer to the surface of the Rondout Creek than the site is today because of the lowering of Lake Albany which once filled this part of the Hudson Valley and received the melting ice water of the great ice mass, into which the creek once flowed during the retreat of the most recent Ice Age, so that back then the village was almost at the broader Lake Albany or creek's edge. The worked pieces of such hard stone as chert, quartzite and other stones into spear points, scrapers and knives, have taught archaeologists that these natives descended from emigrants from northeastern Asia who had found the place to be good to live on, with its plentiful fish and mollusks, its water birds, and bears and other large mammals to be able to furnish food and clothing when captured, and the many kinds of river and creek fish swarming upstream in the tidal water in season to spawn, furnishing their contributions to native fishermen. All of this left behind traces of the Natives' way of life on the land, especially in the middens or rubbish heaps left behind by the Native Esopus or Munsee people. The land which the Dutch intruders who followed Henry Hudson thought of as almost an empty wilderness for them had long been used in their own way as a good living space as far back as the time when many parts of Europe were still densely forested. And its small human population had moved on to a European way of life more sophisticated than that of the Native Americans with a greater development in ways of making tools for war and in ways of daily life by use of the land and its water resources.

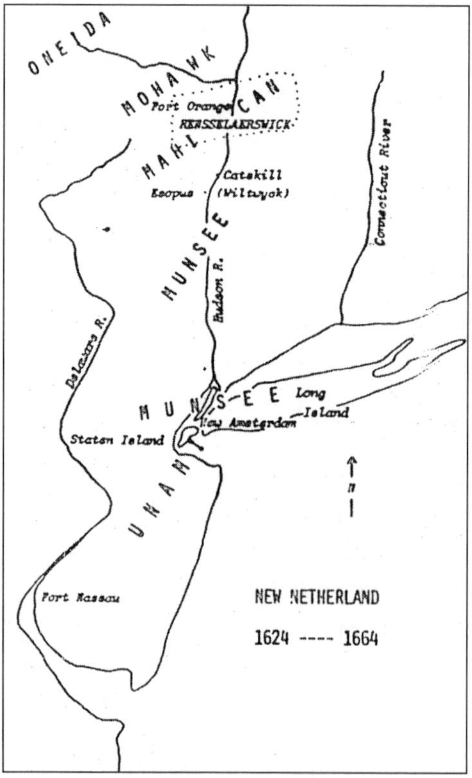

Map of New Netherland, 1624-1664, from *Proceedings of American Philosophical Society*, 1977

2.
Natives and Intruders Try to Live Together Like "Brothers"

But the way of life of the Native Americans beside the Hudson River Valley with its strong sense of being part of an integrated natural world in which the Native Americans usually felt themselves (except in winter) to be comfortably at home with the help of their usually benevolent spirits, began to unravel some three and a half centuries ago with the arrival of the trading and business like intruders from across the Atlantic whose ways of thinking and living had evolved into those which were very much at odds with those of the Native Americans. These European ways flourished well in the homeland of the intruders and especially in the booming commercial city of Amsterdam. There, innovations in the design and operation of ships and new methods of doing business had so combined as to increase the accumulation of wealth and exert pressures to find uses for that wealth or capital in doing profitable business especially at the expense of the inhabitants of the new lands being explored beyond the seas by daring seamen on board their improved ships. No longer was European energy and acquisitiveness being confined within its own ancient shores. Trading with distant places and colonizing their people were not a new way of life for humans. From far back adventurers had left their homes to visit or settle down on European lands which promised better ways of life for them by trade or by conquering their inhabitants and colonizing their societies and lands. Ancient people of Mediterranean lands, of Central and Eastern Asia, Vikings and others had all left marks of their lives on distant overland and coastal parts of the European earth, its adjoining land masses and their varied people as explorers, peaceful traders and then as aggressive colonizers of the lands they had come to covet.

Now in Europe a powerful urge to explore and colonize beyond the old limits was rising among owners of ships and saved-up wealth and would not be resisted.

In response to the discovery by European sailors of the distant Spice Islands of the South Pacific Ocean, the States-General (the governing body of the Netherlands) had chartered the Dutch East India Company and authorized it to traffic in the pepper and other spices (in high demand in Amsterdam) which grew to perfection in the Islands. Because such spices are high in value and low in bulk they are ideal commodities for very profitable trading with the people of distant corners of the globe. Spain had already set a spectacular example of how very profitable dealings with distant parts of the earth might be by colonizing and enslaving the Native Americans of the parts of the New World they had seized and forcing their Native people to lead short and miserable lives digging silver and gold from the mines of Central and South America. The era of global Colonialism had dawned and was about to move ahead from continent to continent, island to island, until it reached the more subtle form of the global colonialism which exists today. Now colonialism was ready to enlarge its scope to include the last yet unexplored inhabited lands remaining.

In September 1609, in the hope of finding a route that might shorten the long and often hazardous way to the Spice Islands (now part of eastern Indonesia), Captain Henry Hudson, aboard the eighty ton yacht the *Half Moon* sailed up the estuarial river that now bears his name in a vain search, on behalf of the already-incorporated Dutch East India Company, for a rumored shorter route from the Atlantic to the Pacific Ocean. Hudson found that the rumored short so-called Northwest Passage was often blocked by ice. But he also found that the river he explored and its tributaries might be made to yield wealth from a very different source than the spices or silver mines which were enriching the investors of the Netherlands and Spain. As the *Half Moon* rode at anchor, not many miles above the site of the Kingston-to-be, Robert Juet, who was one of Hudson's ship's officers set down in his own private journal a fine word picture of the event including this significant detail, "the people of the Countrie came flocking aboord . . . many brought us Bevers skinnes and Otter skinnes, which wee bought for Beades, Knives and Hatchets."

This was Hudson's good news, the Natives of the mid and upper valleys of the River basin and its back country were eager to trade pelts of fur bearing animals and other products of their land for European toys, tools, glass beads and cloth. Especially promising to the Dutch was the prospect of trade in beavers' pelts.

In northern Europe in 1609 the glossy, brown fur of beavers which the American Natives used for warm winter clothing, was also in high demand as a source of the felt used in making the immensely fashionable beaver hats which had come to symbolize by their shape and quality the social status of the wearer. With Captain Hudson's good news in mind, the West India Company was chartered by the States-General in the hope that it would accomplish wonders similar to those

Henry Hudson's Half Moon near Yonkers in 1609 surrounded by Indian canoes, from E.M. Ruttenber's *History of the Indian Tribes of the Hudson Valley*, Albany 1872

with which the East India company had delighted its stockholders. The Company (or Corporation) was given the broad powers of virtual proprietors in managing lands in North and South America, the west coast of Africa, and in harrying treasure-carrying Spanish shipping by means of the Company's own private but authorized land and sea's armed forces. And, more relevant to the founding of Kingston, it was given through the political influence of Company owners a monopoly of the fur trade in North America. Trading posts were built at what are now Albany and Manhattan Island and it is likely that there was soon activity in trading for furs at the mouth of the Rondout (where a "redout" or small fortified enclosed defensive place was constructed and gave its name to the kill or creek) on the Hudson River where Company-authorized traders' sloops might readily anchor or canoes be pulled ashore and where well-trodden Native trails from the ponds of beaver-rich back country conveniently converged on the Hudson River at what was to become Kingston's busy Rondout Harbor.

Before their first contact with white traders the neolithic Native Americans had worn beaver furs only for the sake of their winter warmth and beauty. Now stimulated by the lure of European novelties in trade goods, including hard liquor and firearms as well as steel knives, glass beads and warm woven duffle cloths for making blankets by Native women, they pursued beaver relentlessly and with a lessening of their former concern for propitiating the animals' spirits (lest they be punished by beaver spirits) to the point where they no longer bothered to think of pleasing the spirits by maintaining a thriving beaver population. Yet despite the Natives' zeal in taking beaver the Company managers and stockholders saw the expected profits, while good, fail to soar as high as desired because of slack management. The short, inner layer of beaver fur had been valued in Amsterdam as a basic ingredient of the felt of which the finely crafted and currently fashionable beaver hats were made. The rage for beaver hats had its ups and downs as such fashions always do. Vigorous competition in fur-trading from the French and Natives of Canada to the north and northwest and, worst of all, illegal trading on their own by independent non-Company merchants of New and Old Amsterdam and by men brought to New Netherland by the careless Company as their own indentured servants all combined to temper the dream of working what might be called a furry gold mine. Instead, Company managers tried to wrest a better profit from their New Netherland investment by attracting colonists to the Natives' scattered tracts of superb, already cleared alluvial farmlands while continuing to do their best with the fur trade. But this effort was not enough. Nor was the Company's new business of introducing captured black natives from their African holdings to sell as slave laborers in New Netherland (including Esopus) as profitable as the Spanish had made their combination of slave dealing with silver mining, due to the Dutch Company's failure to locate similar mines in their holdings. An attempt by the none too well managed Company to grant vast tracts of land to wealthy Dutch individuals or partnerships with the understanding that the grantees or patroons would finance the settling of diligent tenant farmers as colonists on their acres to obediently grow readily marketable crops of wheat was not at first a great enough success. Only at the patroonship of Rensselaerwyck forty miles to the north of where the City of Kingston now stands did a new kind of patroonship become fairly well established in the Upper Hudson Valley under the none too watchful eye of the major absentee partner, a rich Amsterdam jeweler named Kiliaen Van Rensselaer. And it was in Rensselaerwyck that a group of lease-holding men from adjoining Beaverwyck and fur-trading Fort Orange made plans to settle as farmers of land of their own or perhaps invest as speculators on the very fine lowlands which lie beside the Esopus Kill or Creek in Kingston. What stimulated these people who were dissatisfied with their conditions as tenants on leased Rennssalaerwyck farms to take action may have been a decision of the Directors of the Dutch West India Company intended to cause the added peopling by whites of their proprietorship of New Netherland. One result of the Directors' action was the first attempt by whites to settle on the rich, dark-soiled

Esopus Creek lowlands (already long before cleared of forests and then cultivated in a garden-like way by Native women) within easy access to a strand or landing place on the Rondout Kill close to the great Hudson River near the place where that river and Redout or Rondout Kill converged. This was near the "Indian Crossing" of the Hudson River at the convergence of a widely-used system of Native trails which made possible close relations between the Valley's Native people. The Esopus creek-side lowlands were already demonstrated by long and gentle Native American use to be an extremely productive place where a rich alluvial soil had been built up over a long time from repeated flooding of the silt-bearing Esopus Creek. The soil of the Indian fields long cultivated by women with simple digging sticks and stone and bone hand tools would be expected to yield fantastic crops when given the more violent treatment by horse-drawn tools of the white men.

The early white colonists of the favorable region to become the settlers of Kingston were not quite as Dutch as is generally believed. They were led by a man of English birth and included, through the earliest decades of colonizing, natives of a variety of the people of the small states which ringed the Baltic and North Seas in northern Europe. Under the influence of their striking New World landscape, the new Hudson Valley colonists evolved a culture usually thought of as decidedly Dutch, and given a New World tinge by such additives as an addiction to the Natives' tobacco and maize. One writer about the white people of the Hudson Valley has suggested that the Dutch, usually being thought of as a phlegmatic and unimaginative people (despite their outstanding skills in the arts), nevertheless moved from the uninspiring level plain of their homeland to a part of the New World featured by a landscape rich in striking contrasts. The writer credits the Dutch with having brought the Hudson Valley "more glamour, more of the supernatural and of elfin lore" which Washington Irving seized upon as literary sources. In 1646, Jesuit missionary Father Jogues found eighteen different languages being spoken in New Amsterdam at the mouth of the Hudson. And a similar situation must have prevailed in early white Esopus on a smaller scale as indicated by the Church-and-government recorded birthplaces of its inhabitants. Most of New Netherland, as well as the City of New Amsterdam, might be characterized as polyglot and gradually evolving a provincial Dutch flavored character.

On the sixteenth of February 1650, the Directors of the West India Company had written a significant letter to Peter Stuyvesant, the former Company soldier who had become the Director-General of New Netherland. They wrote among other things, that "formerly the name of New Netherland was seldom mentioned and now heaven and earth are, as it seems, moved by it and everyone wishes to be the first to select the best part of it." The directors went on to urge, in a letter dated March 21, 1651 the Director-General not to grant any land to anyone without his "acknowledging properly the authority of the West India Company." And the Directors made it plain that grants of land should be made only to those patroons "able to populate, cultivate and bring into a good state of tillage" the lands granted. By 1651, the ailing Company had given up a bit of the concentrating on trying to enforce its attempted monopoly of the fur trade in the Hudson Valley and abandoned their dreams of capturing Spanish treasure ships after no more than a single spectacular success by its marine hero Piet Heyn. Its managers were seeking instead to aim more sensibly at what profits they might coax from the leaky fur trade under better management and from luring new colonists to plant crops of wheat and other marketable grains on the most fertile native-cleared parts of the Company alluvial lands (most of which was still in the hands of the Natives). The response to this policy was vigorous and evidently helped cause the attempt by the upriver white tenant farmers led by Thomas Chambers to settle at present-day Kingston (as yet unexploited by whites) on tracts long before cleared by the Natives.

It was in the land rush to which the Directors referred that on June 5, 1652 the colonist leader named Thomas Chambers became the first white man to take the initial step required by the Company to gain ownership of one of the "best parts" of New Netherland. It adjoined a cleared tract of fertile farmland being taken from the Natives by land-hungry Director Peter Stuyvesant for himself. What Chambers did that day in Fort Orange or Beverwyck, close to Rensselaerwyck, was to persuade two Esopus or Munsee Native sachems named Kawachhikan and Sowappekat to make their characteristic Native marks on behalf of themselves and other Esopus Natives on an "Indian deed" to a fertile tract of land described as lying on the Esopus Creek flatlands, and including a path leading down to a good Native landing place or Strand on the shore of the bustling Rondout Creek of more recent times, close to the joining place of the Rondout and Hudson, which would become in time part of the busy Rondout Harbor.

The two Natives made their marks during a lull in Native-white tensions which had taken the place of the initial hope for a "brotherly" relation between whites and Natives of New Netherland. In 1637, Connecticut land-hungry militiamen had burned a large palisaded Pequot village and slaughtered its several hundred inhabitants including women and children. In this way an American version of total war as it had evolved in Europe during centuries of dynastic and religious conflicts came to the northeastern part of what is now the United States. By 1643, this kind of war, much more ferocious to civilians and bystanders than the milder variety to which the Native warriors had been accustomed in pre-white invasion, "pre-contact" days, soon reached the Hudson Valley. That happened when Peter Stuyvesant's predecessor as Governor-General of New Netherland (he was Willem Kieft) in a true total war spirit, ordered the killing of a group of Native civilians who were quietly sleeping on the shore of the Hudson opposite New Amsterdam. The killing was followed by widespread resentment by the Natives of the whole Hudson Valley. And by some of the whites some of whom expressed disapproval of the harsh and unbrotherly treatment of the Natives. This resentment was given strong expression in 1650 by the Council of Nine Men who acted as advisers to Stuyvesant. In a reluctant concession to a demand for a touch of democracy for New Netherland people grown restive under autocratic Company control, the nine men spoke up.

In the document called a Representation the Nine did more than tell of their unhappiness at the way Kieft and other company officials had behaved toward the Natives. They added a touching personal statement of regret at the manner in which the whites as a whole had mistreated the Natives. The nine wrote, "We are also in the highest degree beholden to the Indians, who not only have given up to us this good and fruitful country, and for a trifle yielded us the ownership, but also enrich us with their good and reciprocal trade, so that there is no one in New Netherland or who trades to New Netherland without obligation to them. Great is our disgrace now, and happy should we have been, had we acknowledged these benefits as we ought, and had we striven to impart the Eternal Good [Christianity] to the Indians, as much as was in our power, in return for what they divided with us." The Nine begged God to forgive them, "and so direct our hearts that we in future may acquit ourselves as we ought for the salvation of our own souls and of theirs."

The sense of guilt, springing from a moral and religious conviction could hardly have been more forcefully put. Yet the appeal of the Natives' superb, gently tilled fields, already cleared of the heavy burden of trees, like those beside the Esopus with their potential easy access down the Hudson River to an assured and profitable market for their wheat and other crops in New Amsterdam and also in the West Indies was strong enough to overcome any religious and moral qualms which prospective colonists of New Netherland might have felt. But seductive as the rich and level creekside land was (and already gently tilled by Native women and their digging sticks), its colonists would have to pay a steep price in the burden of anxiety that would inevitably come with the land. For danger had come to threaten Esopus as well as New Amsterdam from every direction. The nearest help for Esopus white colonists in case of a flare-up of ever-possible conflict with the surrounding badly treated Natives would be at the Company's ill-kept fur-trading outpost of Fort Orange, forty miles up the Hudson from Esopus and weakened by disputes among the sharers in the huge adjoining patroonship of Rensselaerwyck. Some eighty miles to the south was New Amsterdam with its fort, like that of Fort Orange, allowed to fall into disrepair and its autocratic governor reluctantly yielding to pressure from his commonalty for a few minor reforms. Holland and England were at war based on commercial rivalry on the high seas. Belligerent Connecticut was eager to help its mother country and itself by attacking the Dutch of the Hudson Valley to which England strongly asserted its own claim. To the North the Mohawk allies of the Dutch were members of the Iroquois Confederacy which their Fort Orange traders had supplied with firearms, ammunition and plentiful hard liquor in return for furs. The Mohawks were rumored to be urging all the Hudson Valley Natives to turn back the wave of white settlers which was washing into the Valley in response to the Company's increased zeal for settlement of the Natives' best improved lands by Dutch farmer-colonists. The fertile lands of Athar-Hacton with their excellent landing close to the place where the Hudson River and the Rondout Creek join were certainly attractive enough. Yet exposed as they were in the critical state of the times these tempting lands were not for timid souls. And pioneer Thomas Chambers and other men from Rensselaerwyck and adjoining Beverwyck, who began actual settlement at what would become Kingston with Chambers, probably in 1652, were far from timid.

3.
A Trio of Very Bold Men

THOMAS CHAMBERS ON ONE OCCASION HAD BEEN TAKEN BEFORE THE Beverwyck court on a charge of having spoken abusively to the judges. His bold defense was that he knew nothing at all of the matter because he was drunk at the time. The judges expressed understanding of his problem but fined him anyway. Two of the Esopus colonists of about 1652, Jacob Jansen Stoll and Kit Davitz, like Chambers, were aggressive, notably bold, enterprising and willing to take present risks for the sake of a chance of future success. We know of no evidence to suggest that the three were hampered by the kind of qualms to which the Nine men had given utterance in their Representation of 1650 although they too may at times have felt them.

Chambers, Stoll (who hailed from Germany) and Davitz who was English by birth formed a trio who were conspicuous in the first days of the settlement in Groote Esopus or Great Esopus as the vicinity was called, for their occasional appearances in the court records of Fort Orange and Beverwyck, which had jurisdiction over the settlement at Esopus during its infant years. There Chambers was often officially called "Thomas Clabboard" a nickname derived from his frequent use, as a carpenter, of clapboards. These are the kind of boards within whose protection millions of suburban and rural Americans live today but which were unusual in old brick-built Netherlands and not yet widely accepted even in the timber-rich Hudson Valley. All three of these bold men when they lived in Beverwyck (separated from Rensselaerwyck in 1652) before founding Esopus fitted well into the rowdy frontier society of their time and place with its heavy drinking, its frequent brawling over trifles and its quickness in resorting to fists, knives or swords as first impulse arguments when offense was suspected. Stoll was known by the nickname of Hap which meant "mouthful" or "bit" and may well have had reference factually or whimsically, to his size. He was a frequent boozer and brawler and was also closest of the trio to the established Dutch Reformed Church which the Dutch West India Company was pledged to support and encourage. The earliest known services of the church in the infancy of the Esopus settlement would be held at his house close to the Strand Gate in Esopus. The available evidence strongly suggests that the third of the trio which helped give shape to the new colonial settlement may well have been a Fort Orange trader with the Natives—he was Kit or Christoffel Davitz (or Davis) who knew the Native languages well enough to serve as an interpreter and go-between.

Fort Orange had been founded by the Company to function as a defensive trading post in a place fearful of Native intentions. Its people and those of adjoining Rensselaerwyck and Beverwyck, whatever other interests they may have had, were at least part time legal or illegal fur traders. Some went into the woods to dicker more sharply for furs with the Natives without Company permission. These were known to the Dutch as "bosch loopers" or to the Canadian French as "coureurs du bois," meaning forest runners or rangers. Natives also often brought their furs illegally to the homes of Beverwyck or Rensselaerwyck colonists and there made better deals sometimes with the more easy-going women of the families.

Traders with the Natives had not had the best of reputations even before the 1630s when trader Thomas Morton had scandalized the other New England Puritans by frolicking with his Native customers around the maypole he erected at his base which he renamed Merrymount (originally Mt. Walliston). And the Fort Orange traders, at least until some grew into sufficient wealth to be seen as respectable, were looked at askance. Davitz has left behind a record which has its discreditable side. After his first wife died, for example, he was found guilty of having acted badly in caring for the couple's children and the childrens' assets. Custody of the children was taken away from him by court order and awarded to the dead wife's parents. Like so many other New Netherlanders, Davitz was a brawler with a readiness to flash a threatening knife. He was among the Fort Orange traders by sloop using hard liquors as persuaders in dealings with the Natives whose trails touched the shores of the Hudson River between Fort Orange and the Highlands some twenty miles below the juncture of the Rondout Creek with the Hudson.

This part of the River was trading country for those Albany traders who routinely and illegally carried hard liquor and firearms aboard their vessels for use in trading. The possible future usefulness of alcoholic liquors in trading with the Natives had been clearly hinted at by Henry Hudson's officer, Robert Juet, on September 20, 1609. That day Juet wrote in his private journal (not a log book) that as the Half Moon lay at anchor not far above the mouth of the Rondout Creek, "the Master and the Mate determined to trie some of the chiefe men of the Countrey whether they had any treacherie in them." To do this they resorted to the old European strategem of loosening tongues with liquor. They took the chiefs down into the cabin (of the Half Moon) and "gave them so much wine and Aqua vitae (brandy), that they were all merrie . . ." In the end one of them was "drunke . . . and that was strange to them, for they could not tell how to take it."

In a state of alcoholic exaltation the chiefs gave no sign whatsoever of treacherous intent. And they showed that the effects of alcohol were the same for Native Americans, unaccustomed though they were to alcohol, as they are for white people.

It did not take long for traders with the Natives to discover that once they had befuddled the Natives with brandy, wine or rum they could easily persuade them to hand over their furs in trade at delightfully bargain prices even at a cost to the Natives of the loss of months of work—plus a hangover which made the Natives irritable and at times hostile. But very soon alcohol was playing a part in Native life which gave serious alarm to both white and Native leaders and helped cause bloody conflicts which threatened the very existence of the colony at Esopus—and its still profitable liquor-using fur trade. Alcohol, unfortunately, had an especially strong appeal to the young men among the Natives who had been well trained to act as a warrior class in the inter-tribal little wars and raids which were quite common among many groups of Native Americans. In their newly experienced bouts of drunkeness the young warriors, unlike their wiser elders, saw enemies lurking behind almost every rocky outcrop. They quarrelled among themselves and brooded over the insults offered to them by whites. They asserted their martial manliness to which they had been trained by behaving violently toward their white neighbors and toward white property in an unbrotherly fashion. In vain did their chiefs try to reason with the young men. In vain did they protest over and over again to leaders among the whites in an effort to have the use of hard liquors forbidden in dealings between Natives and whites. All these attempts at first were no more effective than similar ones intended in the 1960s to curb the rise of the use of marijuana and LSD among young Americans of a later time. Or in the 1920s of ending the use of all alcoholic drinks then strictly outlawed by the Volstead Act of 1919.

In what had come to be a chronic state of uselessness despite belated Company ordinances forbidding the use of hard liquor in trading with Natives, the Dutch West India Company did little to enforce their well known regulations. And the way was cleared for modifying the Native way of life. So alcohol began to play a significant and even essential part in the loss of the land on which their people had lived for many centuries and in the evolving on that favored spot of what is now the City of Kingston of bloody conflict over ownership of land.

In the beginning of their relationship, both whites and Native Americans had asserted a sincere desire to live together as "brothers," as the Natives put it, beside the winding Esopus and the great River. But even as the two sides continued to talk of brotherhood, living side by side in peace was proving difficult. The ways of life of whites and Natives would soon prove to be incompatible. Differences in ways of thinking and working gave rise to frequent disputes which were magnified in importance when both the parties concerned were tipsy. The first fields of European wheat which the whites tilled with the aid of horses, harrows and plows, lay close to or adjoined patches with bean and squash vines shallowly tilled clambering up the cornstalks which were tended to by Native women with hand tools of wood and bone. When the Natives asked the whites to help them by more deeply plowing their vegetable patches, the whites were reluctant. Irritated Natives threatened to burn the white's farm buildings to compel brotherly (if soil-harming) cooperation. When the Natives walked on their traditional trails even after all traces of them had been swallowed up by the whites' deeply plowed wheat fields, the farmers resorted to blows as Natives did when the horses of Clappord strayed into the Natives' garden patches and damaged their soil and crops with their iron-shod hooves. Settlement on the hoped-for brotherly basis had hardly begun to be attempted when white colonizers of Esopus complained that "they suffered great annoyance" because of the sale of "some beavers (a recognized high monetary unit of value) worth of brandy to the savages of Esopus," by Jacob Clomp, a Fort Orange skipper of a Hudson River trading boat and that Kit Davitz shared in the "troubles and difficulties that arose" as a result. Complaints like this directed against both whites and Natives multiplied into an almost perpetual mutual irritation.

Even before settlement began people with sharp eyes for possible future profits and who had considerable weight in New Netherland affairs had obtained more and more choice bits of the limited fertile alluvial land in what would some day become Kingston. Peter Stuyvesant was one of them. Commissary or Magistrate and Vice-Director Dyckman, of Fort Orange, was in possession of the strategically placed bit of land long used by Native canoeists and called The Strand on Rondout Creek—an area of pebbled beach sometimes partly under water at high tide and destined to function well because of its location and character, as the chief landing place for the new colonial settlement and on which sloops could easily be hauled ashore at high tide for repair. Dyckman turned over his speculation in Rondout real estate to Kit Davitz who also bought one of the tracts adjoining Thomas Chambers' on the Esopus and close to one of Peter Stuyvesant's pieces of prime farmland (with a history of good care by Native women) which the Director worked at a distance of more than eighty miles by employees or slaves. In these varied ways and by a variety of people, the fields once cultivated by Native women and known as Athar-Hacton and the excellent and essential landing place on the Rondout began to take shape as those of a successful colonial farming community with a good route to its logical markets at the Hudson River's mouth on the Atlantic ocean and beyond. The region known earlier as "the Groote (or Great) Esopus" now lent half of its name to the budding settlement which was being called Hysopus, Esopus or other variants. One of these popular variants, "Sopus" hung on in the daily speech of some Kingston and Ulster County people who were still alive a few decades ago. "Kingston-Sopus" was a variant used in his writings to avoid confusion by eccentric preacher Lorenzo Dow about two centuries ago.

In June 1653, a couple who would play a significant part in the growth of the colony or settlement of Esopus in its cradle days arrived in Beverwyck. They were accompanied by their four children, a number of servants, and brought with them some capital to invest. Johan and Johanna de Hulter were no run-of-the-mill pair of colonists beguiled into emigrating by the West India Company's seductive enticements—far from it. Johanna de Hulter was the daughter of the learned and respected Leyden historian Willem de Laet, one of the West India Company's directors who had owned a one-fifth share in the huge Rensselaerwyck patroonship until his death in 1648 and had been embroiled in a lengthy dispute with the Van Rensselaers over how the vast tract of their land should best be managed. De Laet had written published material on the wonders of the Dutch possessions in the New World and while some of his output was the result of careful research, taken as a whole his writings served well as effective and not always realistic promotional enticements for the Company in its efforts at luring shareholders' money and colonists' labor to its far-flung possessions. Once in Beverwyck, de Hulter plunged into the business life of the place. He bought or leased farming acreage. He acquired a brick making and a tile making venture and a residence in Beverwyck which caused him trouble when it developed that the former owner did not have a clear title. He was ordered to vacate the place after rebuilding a wall he had torn down and filling up a well he had ordered dug.

And, very relevant to the history of Kingston, de Hulter bought (by an Indian deed) the Native American rights to one thousand acres including much of the best of the moist, lush Esopus Creek flatlands which had been tilled by the Native women's hand tools such as digging sticks for many years, and which would serve as much of the economic heartland of Kingston because of its ability to produce profitable crops of wheat and other grains.

It is unlikely although possible that de Hulter aimed at creating a traditional landed estate over which he might preside as the landlord of productive slaves and tenants. More likely he hoped to profit as the other Company officials may have suspected, by holding the land until settlement nearby by others would cause his own investment to grow in value. But he did neither of these during his brief and not entirely happy fling at life in the New World of which his father-in-law had written with so much gusto but upon which he had never set foot. About this time de Hulter became a judge of the Beverwyck court, and so became by this Company appointment entitled to be called "The Honorable." There is no record of his actually serving on the bench because he died soon after his appointment, and shortly after enigmatically petitioning the Governor's council at New Amsterdam "to pass and cause to be published a certain ordinance to inhibit, restrain and control the insolence, opposition and disobedience of his servants in particular and others in general" the Honorable or Monsieur Johan de Hulter as he was sometimes known, died after leaving his possessions to his widow. The Juffrouw (or Madame) de Hulter, as she would be known for a few years, sold her late husband's brick and tile making ventures at auction but was able to cling to the Native deed to the thousand very fertile acres on both sides of the Esopus. De Hulter had died before he had asked for or received the patent for the acreage which would make his land his property in the fullest legal sense of the word.

Part 2

Living Side by Side Like Good Brothers Proves Difficult as the Intruders Succumb to the Lure of Cleared and Fertile Land and Valuable Furs and the Natives are Seduced by Trade Goods such as Colorful Glass Beads, Steel Knives and Mind-Bending Liquors— an Ambush at the Indian Tennis Court Strikes a Hard Blow to Brotherhood

1655

1.
When Natives in 1655 Attacked New Amsterdam, 80 Long Miles to the South, the Colonists at Esopus Flee to Fort Orange, Forty Miles to their North.

THEN, IN SEPTEMBER 1655, TERROR SEIZED MANY OF THE PEOPLE OF NEW Netherland and those at Esopus who had been hopefully trying to establish farms on the provinces' scattered and scarce and therefore very valuable resources of alluvial and easily worked (and already cleared) flatlands as they heard that Native warriors had attacked their capital city of New Amsterdam. The terrified new white colonists at Esopus abandoned their cherished fields, their buildings and their livestock and fled to the protection of the none too trustworthy palisades and guns of the Dutch West India Company's Fort Orange in the hope that the Valley Natives would confine their rumored attack to New Amsterdam alone.

By the time the white colonists only recently settled at Esopus fled in terror from their plantations in 1655, hopes of good friendship with the Natives seemed to many to be threatened. The immediate cause of the colonists' flight from the scattered homes and creekside flatlands on which they had built high hopes for prosperous and safe lives took place when rumors of bloody attacks were verified on far away New Amsterdam some eighty miles away down the Hudson—attacks which sent a shiver of fear racing throughout New Netherland as the news of it spread. The attacks had come as an effective example of the kind of surprise in which the Natives were skilled and which formed part of their traditional art of war.

The well-informed Natives (via swift runners on their excellent trails) had taken advantage in May 1655 of the temporary absence from New Amsterdam of Director-General Stuyvesant and the Company soldiers under his command. These Company men had all gone to the Delaware River with the intention of ousting

Swedish colonists from farmable and fur-producing land the Dutch Company also claimed.

Members of half a dozen Hudson Valley Native American tribes, some Esopus, Munsees and others from adjoining New England then sensed an opportunity and had rendezvoused over their trails outside New Amsterdam in the dimness of an early morning and then stormed into the city as the sun rose. They broke open doors, dumped the contents of chests and smashed furniture in revenge according to tradition for the killing of a Native woman who had helped herself to some of the colonists' ripened peaches. This was before many peach pests had followed the fruit to America from across the Atlantic and the peaches had grown in such quality and abundance in the colonized peach pest-free parts of New Netherland, including Esopus, that they were even fed to hogs. But once inside the city the Natives were joined by fellow warriors many of whom were equipped with firearms. An assault on the farms surrounding the city then resulted in many colonists' deaths, the taking of many prisoners and the widespread destruction of crops and buildings. Stuyvesant hastily returned from routing the Swedes. In full awareness that he then lacked the military force required to counterattack, he ransomed the captives with a payment of gunpowder and ball which the Natives usually claimed (in peaceful times) they needed in order to hunt deer and so supply the Dutch with venison in return for trade goods but which more and more often would serve them well in battle against the invading colonists. And Stuyvesant agreed to a treaty of peace.

Once word of the agreement on peace reassured the Esopus colonists who had taken refuge at Fort Orange, the colonists gladly returned to their cherished and unharmed creekside plantations. Before long as hope was restored for a good future rooted in the rich, very easily worked soil beside the Esopus, fields were plowed by horses and grain planted and the work of white settlement once again carried forward. With her inherited thousand acres once more promising to become marketable, Juffrouw de Hulter resumed efforts to have the tract of very fertile land petitioned for and properly granted in order to put her in full legal possession of the now more valuable than ever thousand acres. In language of the inflated and pompous sort often used at the time in similar petitions to officials, she wrote, "The Lord has taken out of the world the Husband of your Honorable Worships' petitioner and leaving her as an afflicted widow with four fatherless children in this vale of tears, she is compelled to turn to your Honorable Worships so that her young children may have some hope to reap evenings and mornings, some advantage of the great and excessive expenses and labors her late husband has had in a rather excessive manner." Soon, however, the Juffrouw emerged from her sad state of widowhood to marry Jeronimus Ebbingh, a merchant said to be one of the six richest men in all New Amsterdam. The couple then lived on New Amsterdam's Hooge Straat (High

Street) in a neighborhood of other moneyed people. Ebbingh as "husband and guardian" took over the management of his wife's lands, had them patented, and had most of the thousand acres subdivided. He arranged for their sale at auction. And so the largest white-owned tract of exceptionally fertile and already Native-cleared farmland in Esopus seemed about to become open to settlement and cultivation by more and more white colonists with the aid of slaves, plows and horses rather than the simple digging sticks of the Native women. Although the late Johan de Hulter had only an "Indian deed" which gave him no more than permission to apply for a patent from the Governor which when granted would make the land his in the equivalent of the English and American term of fee simple, he had proceeded just before he died, it was said, to fence the thousand acres, including those on which Johan de Hulter had already built houses and barns. This fencing infuriated the Natives because they believed they had given de Hulter in trade no more than the right to use the land, pending patenting, and not the right to fence the unused acres in order to keep others from sharing in the land's use. The West India Company officials were also annoyed because they granted land in Esopus only on condition that a good start of settlement and the sowing of crops should begin within two years after the granting. And the land had not yet been granted, let alone tilled by de Hulter, by the time of de Hulter's death. (The Company granted the afflicted Juffrow de Hulter's petition to be given an additional two years during which to put the land into cultivation.)

Even so, with the fate of the thousand acres no longer in doubt, the settlement seemed now poised for a period of growth. And grow it did as the Juffrow allowed her new husband to manage her thousand acres at Esopus. And the Juffrow's new husband plunged into caring for his wife's unsold part of the thousand acres with considerable success even at one point in defiance of official orders (when he hauled his land's products, "six wagon loads of grain," to the Landing at a time of Native unrest when such activity was forbidden.)

2.

The Two Cultures Start to Mingle and the Colonial Farming Community of Esopus Begins to Take Shape

IN THE NEW SETTLEMENT SOME LITTLE SENSE OF LIVING AS A COLONIAL FARMING and trading community had gained among the colonists scattered on their own land along the Esopus Creek with a very few beside the none too fertile Rondout Landing Place. A good indication of this was the employment of Andries Van Der Sluys to teach the colonists' children to recite the catechism of the Dutch Reformed Church, in the lack of a Dominie. The precentor, as Van Der Sluys was called, also read from the Bible to a congregation and led the singing and praying on Sundays at Stoll's house. And he also acted as a "krankenbesoeter" (Dutch for comforter of the sick) who read comforting Biblical passages to ailing colonists and especially to those on their deathbeds, and he probably gave Esopus children instruction in reading and writing.

Thomas Chambers (no longer as he settled down in prominence in Esopus referred to merely as "Clabbord" or "Clabbort") and Stoll, as leaders in the little community, appealed to the West India Company officials to send them a qualified minister and the impressive ecclesiastical machinery needed to produce a minister was set in motion far away in old Amsterdam. But before a candidate for the post of minister could arrive and a church be organized much happened to change the straggling haphazard settlement into a carefully planned village enclosed for protection against the Natives by a wall of stout tree trunk palisades.

Fortified communities were no novelty to the colonists of New Netherland. In their homelands, centuries of bitter warfare had resulted in the construction of stone walls or earthen ramparts around many communities. West India officials by now realized that their colonists in outlying parts of New Netherland could not be expected to live unprotected side by side with the sometimes restless and often resentful Natives. They urged the colonists to give up living on scattered farms no matter how fertile the soil but to settle as New Englanders had done in villages surrounded by walls of palisades from which workers and livestock might go out by dawn to till their fields and tend their pasturing stock and return at dusk to the safety of their stockaded village homes. Today what are advertised as "gated communities" from which white collar and some blue collar workers sally forth to their jobs each morning and return after the day's work is over, carry on the same method of living in what is seen as a dangerous world.

However it was not easy for the colonists to make up their minds to give up living beside their rich soil to take up a new way of life in a village protected by a wall of stout wooden palisades. Making the decision did not become possible until the arrival at Esopus of no less a person than doughty and persuasive one-legged former soldier, the Director-General of New Netherland, Peter Stuyvesant, who reached Esopus by sloop with a body of armed Company soldiers. At the Director's strong urging the settlers on their Esopus Creek-side fields all signed a bond which committed them, under a harsh penalty in case they failed to comply, to taking down their dwellings and re-erecting those surviving the moving to within a stockade which they agreed to help build, or building new structures for living and farming inside the stockade if needed.

By the time the first white colonists began to plant fields of wheat and other easily sold European grains beside the Native women's inter-mingled corn, squash and bean patches on the flatlands known as Athar-hacton, whites and Natives had already begun to influence each other's ways of living. The largely ritual smoking of tobacco by the Natives was giving rise to a recreational, addictive and potentially harmful habit of the Dutch and other Europeans even as the traders' dreaded infectious diseases like smallpox, venereal diseases and a sometimes fatal form of measles were afflicting the Natives and the drinking to excess of strong white men's liquor by the Natives' young men of military age (known to colonists as Barebacks) was starting to undermine Native society. Maize or Indian corn was becoming a welcome addition to white diet. Durable European-made brass kettles obtained in exchange for beaver and other furs were taking the place of fragile Native-made clay cooking pots or were cut up by Native men and the pieces fashioned into points for arrows and for tomahawk heads. Useful steel hatchets (also worn as ornaments) became status symbols of Native men. Wampum or sewant, long used for personal ornament and in dealings of an official or occasional trading nature by Natives, were becoming currency used in everyday transactions by both whites and Natives with beaver pelts also serving as measures of higher value. Wampum was made from shells, including those of the large coastal clams known as quahogs by natives of the coasts of parts of Long Island and southern New

England. The unstrung beads were known as seewant and those strung into chains of the purple, black or white beads might be fashioned into swatches or belts known as wampum. In Kingston a man named "Hendrik, the sewant reyger" (or stringer) appears in tax records. Whether Hendrik was white or Native is not known, but the whites would before long take over and speed up into an industry most of the wampum-making.

The pelts would be eagerly traded for muskets and the later flintlocks once these weapons and the gunpowder and lead they required were illegally available from traders. Firearms began slowly to displace bows and arrows. Not only maize (also called Indian corn), but also squash and kinds of beans new to whites were soon entering the whites' diet and Native herbal lore was not slow in becoming valued in the treating of white people's diseases. In winter white children wore fur caps and deerskin jackets made by Native women and whites of all ages took to moccasins. Whites and Natives learned a few commonly used words from each others' languages.

So with the two ways of life beginning to infiltrate each other the Natives and whites' ways appeared to be slowly moving toward each other. But the two groups were also becoming more formidable as enemies even while they adopted some features of each other's ways of doing daily business and killing game and people more efficiently.

Inscribed rock face just over Esopus line showing Indian of trading days, no longer existing. The original was from an early book by an Indian archaeologist. E.M. Ruttenber copied it from that book for his *History of the Indian Tribes of the Hudson Valley.*

3.
A Protective Stockade against the unhappy Natives is Built, a Prospective Minister Comes and Goes, and an Ambush at the Indian Tennis Court or Katsbaan Leads on to more Conflict

THE SIGNED BOND (SIGNED LARGELY WITH MARKS) OR COMMITMENTS TO build a stockaded village similar in some ways to those of the Natives as well as to those of their European homelands would come after a series of shocking events had demonstrated once again that the hope of living with the Natives as good friends or brothers had been stretched beyond its limits at Esopus—many incidents made this increasingly obvious. In 1657, a drunken Native attacked one of the white colonists near the Strand (or Landing) on the Rondout Kill and caused him to see his son killed and himself to lose the use of an eye. The next year as the flow of intoxicating liquor from Fort Orange traders' sloops to Esopus Natives by the Hudson River continued, tension between whites and Natives reached a pitch that seemed to demand action.

On the night of May 1, 1658, one of a group of drunken Natives shot and killed Harmen Jacobson (nicknamed Bamboes, which means "deceit" in Dutch), as he stood on the deck of a sloop on the Rondout waterfront. Bamboes was a Beverwyck tavern keeper and tax collector who also ran an Indian trading sloop on the Hudson. Earlier it had been testified in the Beverwyck court that he was "hiding out" in Esopus as a "fugitive from justice." That same night drunken Natives burned the Rondout Creek-side house and farm buildings of Jacob Andriensen—the same man who had lost his son and an eye the year before. Andriensen and his tenant, Precentor Van Der Sluys with their families fled from the Landing.

The Native sachems (as noted earlier) had often complained without result that they could not control their young men, once the men became drunk. They urged that the selling and trading of liquor to them be ended. Some intelligent leaders of the white colonists even joined the Natives in this urgent plea. The unrestricted selling of liquor to Natives, they alleged, tended "to the ruin of the whole country" as well as to their own loss of capital and labor and the risking of their lives. Restrictive ordinances were passed at last but in vain—the rules were not obeyed or enforced—because that would not show an immediate profit on traders' or Company books.

Governor-General Peter Stuyvesant and the Company directors in old Amsterdam had for some time insisted in vain that colonists in outlying parts of New Netherland (like Esopus), give up living beside their isolated farmlands and instead take up life in fortified villages—and at last the Esopus colonists seemed ready to agree to do so.

With a reported surge of hostility rising among the Natives, Stuyvesant sailed up the Hudson for Esopus bringing with him from New Amsterdam a detachment of about fifty Company soldiers and a determination to convert Esopus into a safe and therefore consistently profitable colonial farming and fur-trading community. He brought with him, too, a fund of experience gained as a Company soldier, demonstrated creative and diplomatic ability and the reputedly silver ornamented wooden leg which was doing its best to replace the real one which he had lost in the Company's service in an attempt to drive the competitive Portuguese from the island of St. Martin in the West Indies. He must have left behind in New Amsterdam much of the testiness and bigotry which at times flawed his character. For the work of creating the new stockaded village went smoothly at Esopus and Stuyvesant had little difficulty in persuading the colonists, cowed as they were by their recent bloody experiences with the Natives, to sign the bond which committed them to living as villagers within a stockade, as many of the Natives did. The Native sachems who feared the proposed stockade as an inevitable menace were reluctantly persuaded to fall in with Stuyvesant's plans. After protesting that the killer of Bamboes had been none of theirs but a footloose Native who belonged to a tribe to the south they agreed to make reparations for the other damage done at Rondout and settled on a treaty of peace. Even as the two sides were making peace and once again sometimes speaking of one another as friends or brothers, however, Stuyvesant and the Directors in Old Amsterdam were quietly looking forward to launching a war of virtual extermination against the Esopus Natives once the Company achieved a stronger financial and military position.

Stuyvesant himself chose the site for the stockaded village which was to become the heart of the future uptown Kingston. And he chose well. The village would overlook the rich farmlands strung out along the Esopus Kill's long-productive alluvial flatlands and which had been crossed by ancient and still often used Native trails. It was well placed for access to the vital landing place called The Strand and to the Kingston hilltop to its south called the Kijkuit, or Lookout from which enemies approaching down the converging valleys might be observed—the hilltop thanks to the efforts of a real estate subdivider of the early 1850s is now called Golden Hill.

The site of the stockaded village would be convenient to the landing place by way of the level Plains and the difficulties of the harsh and rocky Armabowery that intervened between the Stockade's Strand Gate, the Plains beyond and the Rondout Creek. In the journal covering his trip to Esopus of May 1658, which he kept for the information of his employers back in Old Amsterdam, Stuyvesant told the story of how he had planned and supervised the construction of the village and its surrounding wall of upended logs. In efficient military fashion he had organized colonists and soldiers alike into squads with each assigned specific tasks—some to cut trees of specified size for making the palisades, others to haul the trimmed tree trunks to the chosen site, and still others to sharpen the tree ends and to plant them firmly at a certain depth in the earth, and to dig a sort of moat (in imitation of those of medieval Europe) at the marshy foot of the slope leading down from the stockaded village to the flatlands. He told of going to Fort Orange by sloop and bringing back carpenters to help assemble the houses, barns and other buildings taken down and brought to the village site and to build new ones where needed. He saw to the providing within the stockade of a stout guardhouse and barracks to house the Company soldiers who would be stationed there, he promised, for the protection of the villagers and their property.

At the end of more than a month of effort under the Director-General's close supervision the stockade-encircled village of Esopus became a bustling reality. Lots had been assigned to each of the colonists. Widow de Hulter's lot was number five. Houses had been fashioned of planks with roofs thatched with reeds from the village's community reed beds growing beside the Esopus. The "old stone houses" of today would come a little bit later. In the exhilaration which accompanied the building of the village the dread that had hung over little Esopus showed some signs of being about to be replaced by a return of hope for the future. Yet it soon became apparent that the stockaded village could not provide an entire answer to the settlers quest for prosperity, expansion and security in an insecure and dangerous country. For the Esopus Natives viewed the stockade as an indication that the white invaders were determined to remain on the precious fertile creekside flatlands which they too valued as highly as the colonizers did.

Stuyvesant's plan and its carrying out mingled Old and New World precedents.

It owed some features of its design to the simple stockades fashioned from the trees in the surrounding forest, which were traditional among the Natives.

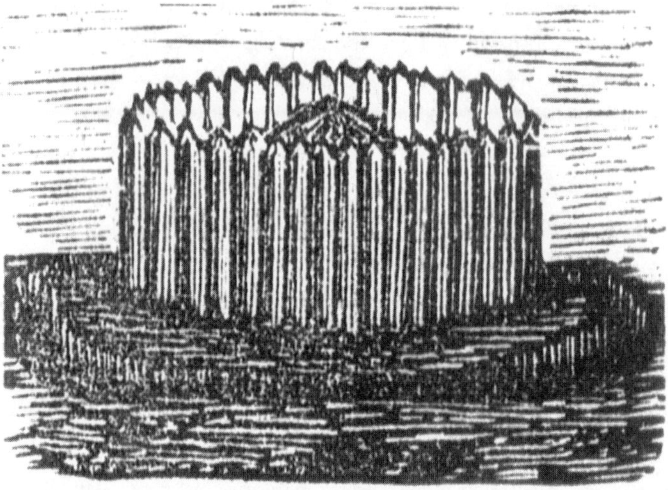

"Maringoman's Castle, Chief of Waoranacks," woodcut by Philip Smith, from his *History of Dutchess County*, 1878.

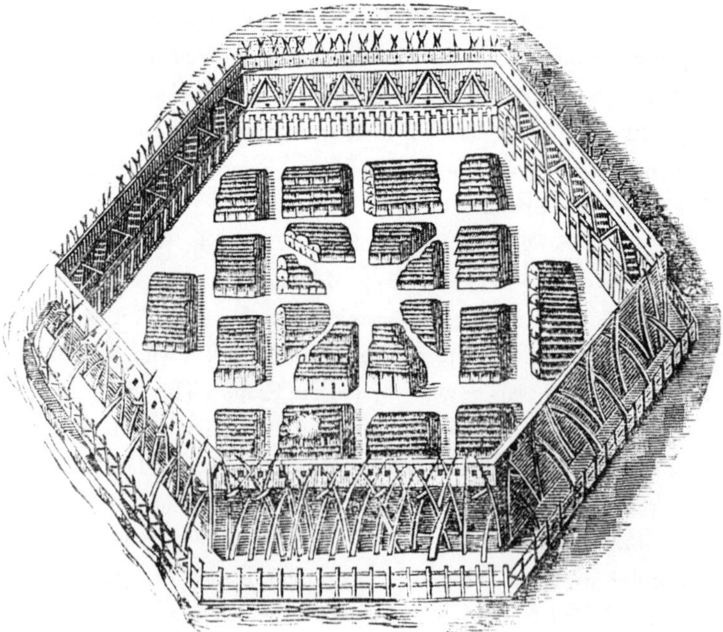

"Indian Fort, Onondaga, the Capital of the Five Nations—1609," from E.M. Ruttenber's *History of the Indian Tribes of the Hudson Valley*, 1872.

And it had features that were reassuringly familiar to the old Netherlands-born whites. The plan of the Esopus stockaded village which Stuyvesant drew for the benefit of the directors in old Amsterdam has been lost. But a sketch of the stockade as it looked to a travelling clergyman in 1695 after being enlarged several times shows arrowhead-shaped salients projecting from each corner. Before the mid-sixteen hundreds features like these had become popular in Europe. And they had decided advantages. Marksmen might use these bastions or "hornworks" as they were called to protect the walls or "curtains" and the gateways against attackers. One gateway was called the "Strand gate" because it gave access across the level Plains over the rough road leading down and across the despised Armabowery to the Landing Place which was as vital to the economic well being of the settlement as the fertile fields themselves. Another gate gave access to the Esopus Creekside fields—already the source of bountiful crops for many generations of Natives.

Within the stockade was a secondary one which surrounded the guardhouse and barracks for the soldiers to be stationed there. Inside the major stockade a rugged blockhouse of logs stood ready to serve as a final defensive position should the outer stockade wall ever be breached. In many features the Esopus fort followed the design of the Fort Orange and New Amsterdam forts. The rows of lots assigned within the Stockade for the colonists' houses and barns determined the location of most of the streets of the present historic Stockade District, listed on the National Register of Historic Places for many years. When completed the fortified village inspired some confidence on the part of the whites. But the Natives continued to view it with uneasiness as directed against their safety—as indeed it was.

The transition from a shapeless straggle of streamside houses and fields interspersed with Natives' plantings of intertwined corn, on which beans and squash climbed, and of bark-covered wigwams plus colonists' fields of wheat and other European grains to an orderly village with precise bounds, reasonably straight streets and defensible walls for the farmers of the corn, wheat and other foreign grains brought a conviction that the place was now mature enough to deserve a dominie (the Dutch common word for a minister) and the church for which Chambers and Stoll had asked. Not just a church of any Christian denomination but one of the Dutch Reformed Church as established by law in the Netherlands and vigorously supported by the Company and its New Netherland Director.

A candidate for the post of dominie appeared in the shape of a young and advanced divinity student, Hermanus Bloem, who had been considering a future as a chaplain in the Dutch navy under the younger Admiral Tromp. Giving up a chance at the hazards of life on the warring seas for those of the equally hazardous New Netherland frontier, Bloem crossed the Atlantic and inspected the new village of Esopus, or Wiltwyck as Stuyvesant was to name it (in 1661). There, Bloem

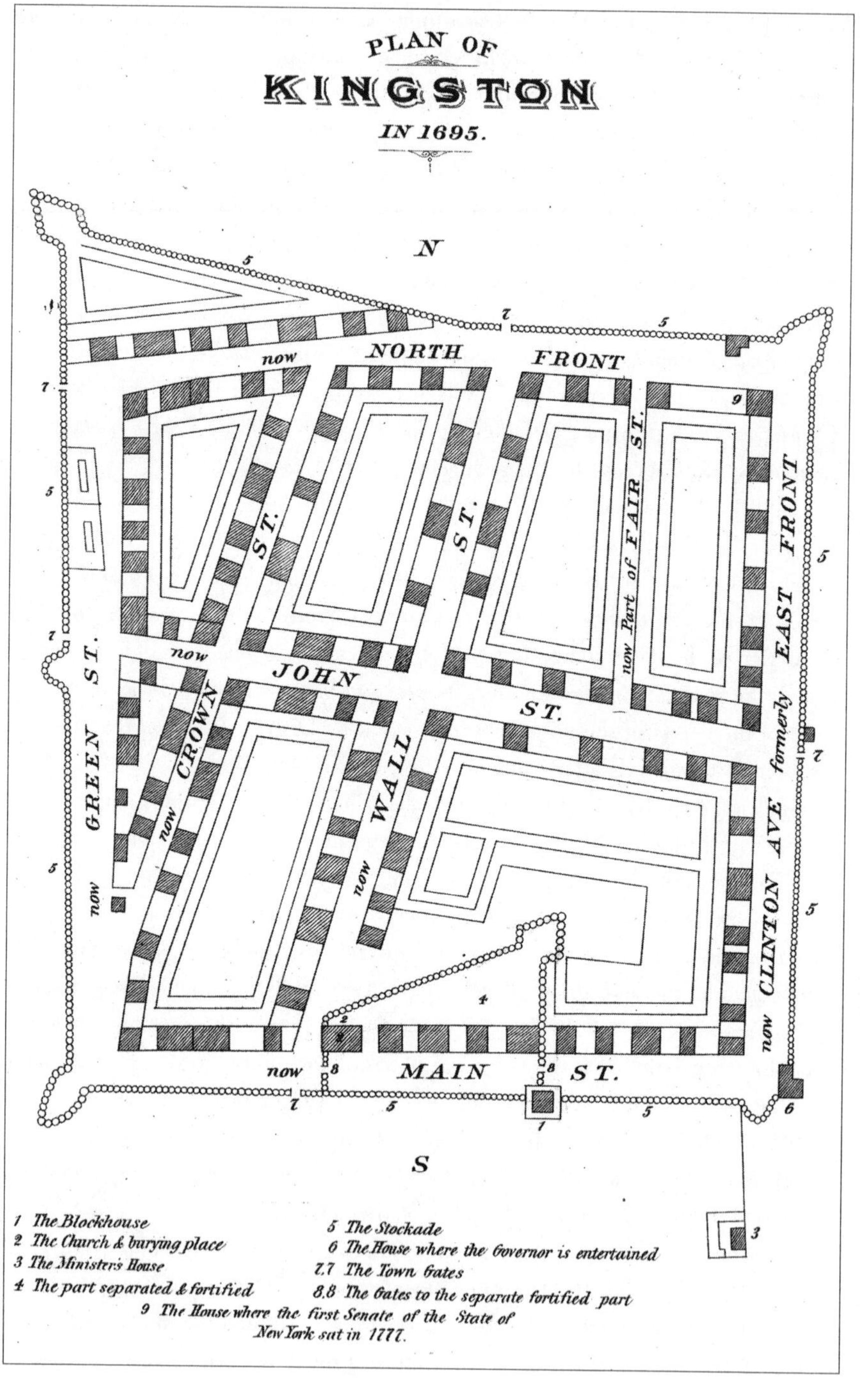

Kingston Stockade, 1695, from Vol. 13, *Documents Relating to the Colonial History of New York*

preached two sermons to the colonists who were in the process of adjusting to snugger lives as protected villagers. The villagers approved of Bloem's trial sermons. After helping organize but not build a church Bloem returned to Amsterdam to complete his studies and be ordained. By March 1660, the freshly ordained Bloem landed in New Amsterdam with a new wife (which made a difference because a married minister would expect a higher salary from his congregation). But the new dominie was not permitted to proceed to Esopus and begin his ministry. The unhappy fact was that Esopus, new houses, new name, new stockade, fertile old lowlands, inhabitants, and all, was in trouble—in such serious trouble that it was judged no fit place for a minister.

Not very long before the first appearance of the whites in their new country the Esopus and other Native peoples of the region had been humiliated in battle by the increasingly powerful members of the Iroquois Confederacy in its strong push eastward. They still felt the hurt pride that followed the occasional decisions of the Dutch whites to deal with them indirectly through their new Iroquian overlords, the Mohawks (who were the most eastern of the five [later six] tribes of the strong Confederacy.) In a movement that may have been realistic considering their weak position with respect to the Esopus colonists the Esopus or Munsee Natives had sought to mollify the whites by making a present to them of the chosen stockade site. Some say it was no longer the Natives' right to give the land because it was part of the big but vaguely bounded de Hulter tract. The Governor antagonized the Natives by failing to make a gift in return for the land. A reciprocal gift in trade goods like that would be in strict accordance with Native customs.

Much documentary evidence shows that it was becoming clearer than ever to the Company that war lay not far ahead. On the Natives part (in their unhappiness at watching the building of the stockade) there were dreams of bringing together, by negotiating over their convenient trails, Hudson Valley and New England Algonkian-speakers (as at New Amsterdam in 1655) and joining forces to drive the Dutch intruders from the Natives' cherished homeland. While Director Stuyvesant had effectively planned and supervised the building of the Village and its Stockade, he had bungled, it was said, when he shamed the Natives with an impulsive offer to match his soldiers in a fight to be staged by pitting his soldiers against the Native Barebacks, or young braves, even at a ratio of two braves to one soldier. An offer which could not fail to bring up unpleasant memories of the Esopus Natives' recent defeat at the hands of the Mohawks. And this, according to the Esopus sachems, at a time when their young braves were not present to take up the challenge. In addition to yielding up the stockade site, the sachems swallowed their pride still further by being willing to give up their rights to much of the cherished lowlands which they had relied on for many centuries to furnish corn and beans to feed their families through the winters.

The Natives' increasing distrust of the whites quickly became obvious. Some stated that what they wanted was for the whites to withdraw altogether from the garden plots and former wigwam places they had occupied and restrict their holdings to such simple but very welcome trading posts as the one the Dutch had established on the Rondout Harbor before the surge of white passion for growing grain on the very fertile, mostly cleared banks of the Esopus had increased tension between Natives and invaders. The Natives by this time had been trapped into a hopeless addiction to European trade goods including hard liquor, steel knives, cloth and trinkets and would not willingly live without them.

Records of the new Court of Wiltwyck, the governing body of the place, began on July 12, 1661 with the newly appointed young schout or Sheriff Roeloff Swartwout presiding and schepens or commissaries (unnamed) on the bench. Swartwout had been appointed to his job by the Amsterdam directors, although Stuyvesant did not approve of the appointment on the grounds of Swartwout's youth and inexperience (he was not yet twenty-one), yet he had the backing of important Company members in old Amsterdam and with their strong approval proposed taking up farming in the new Dutch agricultural colony with the aid of some "servants" and other young men he had brought to the colony to work at farming. The schout quickly asserted command when he filed a charge against important colonist Thomas Chambers of attempting to knife a man, and on a second try of succeeding in wounding him.[79] The charges were made in writing. Chambers' reply to these charges was also made in writing, apparently, because Swartwout had not been aware until his arrival in Esopus that few of its colonists could read and write and relied on oral communications alone.

And so Chambers was denied the chance of defending himself orally before his fellow colonists in open court. To remedy this, Swartwout appointed a man named Jousten to the post of court messenger who would communicate orally with the people of the place, the charges, evidence and decisions of the court. Much of the business of the court consisted of demanding the payment of debts owed by one person to another, payable in either seewant or Dutch guilders.

A good many of the court records dealt with the keeping intact of the newly palisaded walls of Wiltwyck where posts were burned (in one case burned where the wall touched a piece of land owned by Thomas Chambers). Others dealt with replacing palisades which were lacking, and of closing up two exits cut for an unspecified reason by a Wiltwyck man. The court also dealt every now and then with infractions of the ordinance forbidding leaving the stockade to work the land without having a convoy of Company soldiers for protection. One woman when charged with this infraction explained that she had gone out unguarded because her ripened wheat had suddenly been threatened by an approaching storm. There were disputes requiring court settlement over the use of a canoe to cross the Esopus Creek in order to take advantage of tempting fertile acres on the other side. There was a case involving the paternity of a child of Grietje Westercamp when the wisdom of the court under its young schepen held that as Grietje had performed a "sexual service" to the father she deserved to be paid for that service.[82]

A case which occupied pages in the court records was an indirect result of the oncoming of the Esopus War. When Wiltwyck people were forbidden to sell liquor to members of the militia being assembled to battle the Natives, they sent Jousten the court messenger to warn the militia not to buy drink. The messenger for no given reason presented a paper notice to Aeltje, wife of militia member Roeloffson, and the apparently illiterate Aeltje advised him to "cleanse his fundament with it." (So her retort was set down in the court record by the translator from the Dutch.) But since Aeltje denied using these words, a number of witnesses were summoned, each one giving his own slightly different version of what Aeltje had said in his hearing.[83] Thus was recorded other variants to be heard today of the disputed vulgarism which has gone down the years to our own time.

The published court records of 1661-1664, translated though they are from the Dutch by Samuel Oppenheim of the New York City Bar, give the modern reader a good idea of the system of government brought across the Atlantic from Dutch villages, with some elements of Roman law, and flourishing on the banks of the Esopus (and later to be replaced by a version of the Common Law of England.)

And the records of the Village often have much to say about the ever present danger of fire in a community of thatched-roofed buildings (with roofs made from reeds cut from community reed beds along the Esopus) where plentiful straw was used for both human and farm animal bedding and then was hastily and carelessly discarded in ways that too often favored ignition.

If the dwellers in the Village of Wiltwyck expected their threatening wooden walls to force the Natives into submissiveness, they soon found that they were mistaken. As earlier, incidents of misunderstanding of each others' ways erupted and swelled into hostility and open, brutal and often fatal conflict which came to be known as the Esopus Wars.

4.
The Rondout Indian Tennis Court and Its Place in Native Life

THE AMBUSH HAD BEEN CARRIED OUT CLOSE TO THE ONLY HUDSON VALLEY place with special uses and meanings for the land-sensitive Esopus Natives. This was the Natives' "tennis court" or Katsbaan (as the Dutch called it), a smooth, level and fairly narrow plateau which interrupted the steep and often rocky slope of the Armabowery that lay near the end of the Stockade's Strand road and the Rondout landing place not far above the lower end of the Strand Road. Old deeds and maps tell us of its existence; the name by which it was known shows that it was used by the Natives as the place where they played their traditional racquet-and-ball game which has given rise to the fast modern game of lacrosse, now the national game of Canada. The racquet-and-ball game was no ordinary one played to while away an otherwise empty hour nor was the place where it was played a lightly chosen one. To the spirit-conscious Natives, such level courts had an almost sacred character which we may speculate that the Esopus Natives felt may have contributed to the success of their ambush. None of the early white colonists or explorers of the region has left behind details of such features of Esopus Native life as the rich variety of games the people played, or the songs and dances or the strong spiritual beliefs which were essential features of their life style, in which spirits played a very important part, and in which the stick and ball game might be sometimes played with a human skull instead of a ball. These songs, dances and expressions of spiritual faith have often been lumped by the Christian white invaders with the Natives' religious practices as "Devil worship," as in one famous site on the west bank of the Hudson River above Newburgh.

We do not know at present the exact size of the court on which the Natives once played the game of "Indian Lacrosse" but we do know that the courts on which the game was played might extend as long as a mile and a half or two miles, depend-

Early writers spoke of Indian dancing as "Devil Worship." From E.M. Ruttenber's *History of the Indian Tribes of the Hudson Valley*, 1872

"Ball-Play of the Choctaws," by George Caitlin, 1824, showing a version of Lacrosse.

ing on local customs and the lay of the land. For a fascinating account of the game published in 1994 you should read Thomas Vennum, Jr.'s authoritative book, *American Indian Lacrosse, Little Brother of War*, whose author, however, was clearly unaware of the existence of Rondout's "katsbaan." Vennum was very much aware of the part played by medicine men or conjurers and spiritual ideas in choosing the site, and influencing the outcome of games on the spirit-haunted grounds. Thomas Vennum showed by his book his understanding of the relationship of the fiercely fought game to the preparation for war.

As late as 1909 a short book on State and Kingston history, by Mary Isabella Forsyth, could refer (in error) to the Rondout Katsbaan as a traditional place where the 17th century white colonists played tennis while the Indians looked on. Yet a vast amount of correct information about the racquet-and-ball game as practiced by Native Americans in general is now available.

Edward M. Ruttenber of Newburgh in his *In the Footprints of the Redmen; Indian Geographical Names*, published in the *Proceedings of the American Antiquarian Society*, for 1906, was probably the first to mention the Esopus "tennis court" in print. Ruttenber expresses doubt about the exact location of the "tennis court" near the Strand and doubted also that the Dutch would have had a tennis court or Katsbaan as they called it so early in the history of their settlement. He suggests in a footnote that the "tennis court" may have been an "Indian football" field and refers to such a Native recreational facility as having been described as observed in Virginia in 1609. The only place in Rondout that fits the requirements of the racquet or stick and ball game which has become modern lacrosse, and which was played by Algonkian Natives who inhabited the Esopus of the 17th century and earlier, is the long level plateau on the land that slopes down abruptly below steep irregular rocks from the Weinberg to the Rondout Creek, and is identified as the Katsbaan or Tennis Court on old maps and in official deeds. It forms a land class name in the dividing up of the Kingston Commons.

Part of the Court is now largely covered with neat houses, a church and lawns. And part of the Tennis Court is located at the corner of Hoyt and Pierpont Streets of today. This naturally almost rectangular area at the base of the precipitous ascent of the Armabowery to the crest of what was once known as the Weinberg (for its once abundant wild grapes). From its eastern border the plateau drops off abruptly to the Rondout Creek where the sachems who took care of the spiritual aspects of the game might perform the ceremony of "going to water," which was often performed to bring success to the side that practiced it.

In "going to water" the participants waded into the creek in order that the strength of the flowing water, so Natives believed, would be imparted to their muscles.

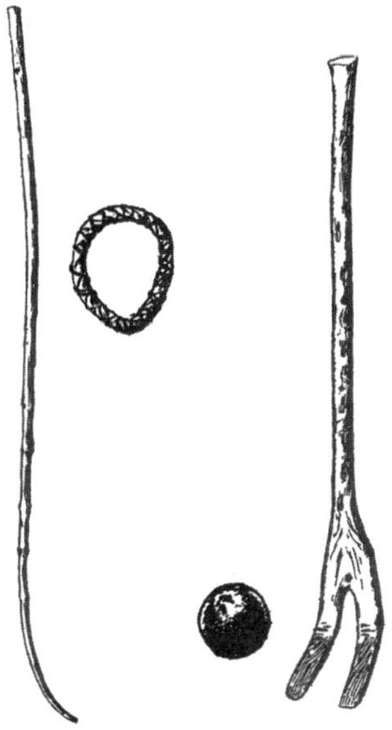

Drawings of racquet and ball as used in the game by Native women of the Sierra Madre in Mexico in the 1890s, from Carl Lumholz, *Unknown Mexico—Explorations in the Sierra Madre and Other Regions, 1889-1898.*

We know that the game was played under the directions of shamans or medicine men. Rites and ceremonies intended to transfer to the chosen players the swiftness of a bird or deer or the strength of a bear were also performed. To give themselves keen vision and aggressiveness the players very often wore feathers of a hawk or eagle. Some day the site of the "Indian tennis court" may reveal its secrets of a rich Native life when studied by ethnologists and archaeologists. Meanwhile, we have reason to feel that the plateau held a special meaning in the minds of the land sensitive Natives because of its being the site of the organized invoking of spirits by shamans as an essential feature of a very fast game which may be classed, like our football, as one giving young men training for war, and on which heavy wagers, as in our football, were placed. Like war, it demanded courage, violence, competitiveness, strength and cunning. A mild version was sometimes played by women.

While there is no evidence that the Natives chose the place for their ambush with an eye on its connection with their tennis court with all its powerful and mystical associations, the possibility remains a tantalizing area for speculation in our present scanty knowledge of the deeper side of local Esopus Native American life.

What is perhaps beyond the realm of speculation is this—that by late September confidence in the likelihood of victory in war (perhaps strengthened by the success of the ambush at the tennis court), was growing. A report that the Natives were busy by day and night making bows and arrows was seen as evidence. In the flush of war-like energy which followed the triumph of the ambush a siege that could test the strength of the stockade was planned and put into sudden execution by the Natives. The unprepared, besieged colonists then realized that now they were trapped within their own log walls—which were intended to protect them.

To those on the inside of the walls, a siege is among life's most unpleasant experiences. The loss of freedom of movement, the possibility of running out of food and water, the pain of seeing enemies destroying crops and even human prisoners outside the walls joined to cause a feeling of powerlessness and frustration. We know nothing of what went on in the minds of the men, women and children imprisoned in the stockade by the surrounding Natives. We do know that an estimated four to six hundred well-armed Natives used their system of trails to come together and do their best to breach the stockade walls. Natives were not often successful in such attempts at mass assaults against such walls—this way of attack was not among the Natives' special skills. They relied most often on man-to-man fighting. But they sent burning arrows over the walls and succeeded in destroying by fire Stoll's barns and hay barracks but not his probably plank-roofed house near the Strand Gate of the stockade which lacked the usual inflammable roof of reed or straw thatch. Casualties on both sides were not great—but tension was.

Bits of traditions hint that the colonists felt abandoned by the Company, by Stuyvesant and by their fellow colonists at Forts Orange and New Amsterdam. On June 15, 1758, Tory Cadwallader Colden of Orange County (a notable disliker of the Dutch) wrote to his son Alexander some harsh words that suggest a then persistent sense of grievance still kept alive after the passage of a century: "While the Christians were besieged the Indians burnt some of their prisoners alive in sight of the fort and while the Dutch of Esopus were in their distress several of their countrymen from Albany came to a place called Sagertie, about ten miles from the fort (the Kingston stockade) and supplied the Indians with all sorts of ammunition. Such are the effects of having no other principle of action but the love of money. The Dutch of Esopus to this day remember the behavior of their countrymen of Albany and speak of them with the greatest indignation!"—so Smith wrote in 1758.

Just before the tennis court ambush took place, Stuyvesant had ordered Ensign Smith to sail from Esopus for New Amsterdam with eighteen of his men. The colonists were thrown into a turmoil at the prospect of losing the few soldiers they had when, as it developed (and as the Natives may have learned), they might need them most. The Governor at the time had worries on his mind and was not functioning well. He admitted as much in a report to the Company Directors back home. For one thing he was concerned at a threat by the English in New England to assert their claim to the Hudson Valley by setting up a colony of their own people near Fort Orange and so, said Governor Stuyvesant, "cutting off our fur trade." For another he had sent the soldiers he commanded to the Delaware colony where the Swedes again threatened Dutch possession—leaving only a half dozen ill or otherwise unfit soldiers at his disposal in New Netherland. But once he became aware that the new stockade at Esopus was under siege and that the Natives were waging war against it in ways that suggested serious planning and preparation, he summoned his council but found the members unenthusiastic about raising volunteer troops to rush to the aid of the faraway and beleaguered Esopan colonists. Several generations earlier the Dutch had rallied heroically to throw off the Spanish grip on their homeland. Now as sharers in a commercially oriented colony of their homeland the stockholding Company superiors hired foreigners to perform defensive functions—Thomas Chambers is said to have once belonged to an English company of mercenaries in the Dutch Company service. The best the council of burgomasters, schepens (magistrates) and captains of trainbands (militiamen) could offer to Stuyvesant was the thought that the enlisting of volunteers might have a better chance of success if Native warriors were to be awarded as prizes of war to any volunteer who could capture them (and who might then sell them into slavery).

However, the resolute side of the Governor took over. Although not yet entirely recovered from an attack of an epidemic which had prevailed in the city of New Amsterdam and handicapped by his wooden leg, Stuyvesant had himself hoisted into the saddle and did his best to rouse the citizens to do their duty. When the citizens refused to be roused, Stuyvesant fell back on choosing men by lot from the pool of citizens each of whom would have the right to avoid service by paying for a substitute (if he could find one). Or a citizen might avoid service by paying a fine of fifty guilders.

By adding some Company clerks and half a dozen of his own house and farm servants Stuyvesant managed to scrape together a body of thirty-six men augmented by about fifty Long Island Englishmen (Connecticut Yankees who by then had crossed Long Island Sound and made English-speaking settlements on the Island) and added some Native Americans from Long Island. At the head of this motley and not notably enthusiastic little army, Stuyvesant finally reached the Esopus stockade only to find that after a fierce final attack by night the Natives had admitted defeat and had dispersed.

The ill-kept Esopus stockade had passed its first test. With no adequate garrison of Company soldiers and with only the inhabitants to defend it, and possibly despite active help to the enemy by the Fort Orange traders (as would be claimed by Cadwallader Colden), the Wiltwyck people had demonstrated with relatively little loss in lives and property that they had become a community which might with good luck stand on its own. As for the Natives, they could only have felt a deep disappointment and apprehension for the future. And in Amsterdam the Company directors were talking more seriously of planning to virtually exterminate the Esopus people altogether to safeguard what was left of their substantial investment in the New World's Hudson Valley.

Part 3

The Esopus War Begins Which Tested the Stockade, and as Martin Kreiger's Journal Shows, Was Aimed by West India Company Officials at Exterminating, if Possible, the Esopus People

1.
The Esopus Wars Drive the Natives from their Homeland

ONCE THE STOCKADE WAS BUILT AND THE BETTER OUTLYING BUILDINGS removed to within its protective walls and new buildings added, it remained for stockade dwellers not only to keep the log walls in repair but also to test the Stockade's efficacy in bringing safety to the daily lives of the colonists. And that test was not long in coming. It arrived as the culmination of a series of abrasive incidents which led to an explosion of violence on the night of September 20, 1659 which has become known as the beginning of the First Esopus War. That night a party of corn harvesting Natives made high by liquor supplied by their employer, Thomas Chambers (who was licensed as a wholesaler to deal in liquor), staged the kind of joyous and noisy revel known to the colonists as a "kintacoy"—a word derived from the Natives' word for a lively party. The Natives' whoops and happy shouts greatly annoyed those within the stockade and prompted a small detachment of soldiers stationed in the guardhouse and a few colonists including Jacob Jansen Stoll and Thomas Chambers to sally from the stockade to put an end to the disturbance. Stoll, it was said, had undressed for the night. He became furiously angry at the sound of the Natives "kintacoying," joyous though it was from the celebrants' point of view. And Stoll was a man in whom anger led on to violence—so his past court record plainly shows.

Beverwyck and Fort Orange, which Stoll had left to take up life in Esopus, were noisy and rowdy frontier places of frequent trading of shouted insults, of fights and drunken frolics and brawls. In this frontier-oriented life style Stoll had proved himself to share abundantly. He had been charged with wounding a man by striking him on the head with a mug, of threatening all comers with a sword, of speaking abusively to magistrates, of beating his wife and then hurling a firebrand at her with such force as to send it through his open doorway and strike the house of a neighbor. The court had found it had no jurisdiction in this last case because it was "between man and wife." But in other cases of charged violence Stoll was found guilty.

Sergeant Lourissen of the Company's soldiers who was in command of the little detachment which had left the stockade to investigate the racket outside acted with the restraint ordered by Lourissen's superior, Ensign Smith. But not so Stoll—in defiance of the Ensign's orders, he aimed his gun at the group of kintacoying Natives and fired. Within a short time two of the four Natives were dead and another was taken prisoner. The Sergeant and Ensign Smith felt it necessary quickly to inform Director Stuyvesant of the savage attack of a kind which the two officers had not ordered and which might have serious consequences in the tense situation which prevailed.

The next day with a band of colonists headed by Thomas Chambers and a guard of soldiers for protection, Lourissen went to the Strand and sent a report by sloop down the Hudson to the Director. On their way to the Strand the band had met no opposition but on the way back they stumbled into an ambush of the kind which the Native warriors used with great skill and for which the rough road to the Strand as it moved down the Armabowery presented ample opportunities.

The Strand Road while necessary, was not the most favorable feature of the stockade's location. After a level start from the Stockade and across the Plains the road sloped up and then sharply downward at the Armabowery which was beset with rocks, bogs and dense undergrowth all of which could be put to effective military use by a people as sensitive to the subtleties of the landscape and as skilled in the art of ambush-making as were the Natives of the Esopus country. The ambushing of the band of colonists, soldiers and Stoll, from the Natives' point of view, was a smashing success. Thirteen colonists were surprised and taken prisoner of whom seven are believed to have been later tortured to death. Among the prisoners mortally wounded was Jacob Jansen Stoll who was to die after a short time as a prisoner. Thomas Chambers was also captured but he was quickly exchanged for one of the Natives. Exchanges of prisoners was not a very common custom of the Esopus Natives. They may have made an exception in Chambers case because he, like Kit Davitz, spoke their language and showed a better understanding of their ways than did the other colonists at Esopus. So he was qualified to serve as an interpreter and intermediary in difficult situations. And the situation that September day was indeed difficult. Stoll's attack on the carousing Natives, excited by Chambers' liquor, with which he may well have paid his Native workers, into holding their kintecoy, acted as a catalyst that set off a burst of further violence. Word of the bloody ambush carried along traditional Native trails by swift Native runners and alerted Natives of other Hudson River tribes.

There was no doubt that Stoll had been the aggressor. Observers among the stockade-dwellers emphatically reported to the Governor that Stoll had disobeyed the order of the Sergeant to withhold fire. Native Americans of the Mahican tribe living at Catskill submitted a very detailed report in which they laid all blame on Stoll. Efforts at bringing about a peaceful solution failed even when urged by the Esopus Natives' overlords, the Mohawks. Attempts by Chambers to clear Stoll were made. They were awkward and unconvincing.

2.
Times of Peace, Times of War are Cause for Gains in Land for Whites and Temporary Destruction of their Society for Natives

By the time the Natives successfully sprang their trap at the tennis court and the colonists proved the value of their stockade, the Dutch West India Company had less than four years more to cling to its North American possessions which included Kingston. Already the Directors (although still making money) were showing some feeling of insecurity. The English who had already successfully defied the Company's claim to Connecticut were boldly re-asserting the right to use the Hudson River as a means of access to proposed colonies of Yankees near the present Poughkeepsie and Albany. The proposed new colonies of Yankees, director Stuyvesant realized, would further jeopardize the Company's upriver fur trade but also its Company's cozy understandings with the Iroquois Mohawks which was essential to the very life of the fur trade.

As long as the Company had relied on the fur trade alone as the major source of hoped-for profits it had usually been able to get along reasonably well with the Natives of the Upper Hudson. But once the extremely fertile creekside fields used by the Native women in growing their own basic foodstuffs of maize, beans and squash came to be coveted by the Dutch for growing their people's own basic and saleable bumper crops of wheat and other European grains in the dark and fertile Esopus-side soils, conflict erupted. By the winter of 1659-1660, the Natives' hopes of driving the Dutch out of the productive fields and restricting them to a few riverside fur trading posts, reached by Native trails, had become unrealistic. The Company directors contemptuously dismissed the Esopus or Munsee Native people as "this barbarous Esopus tribe" from which "neither the Company nor the inhabitants (the Dutch colonists) derive the least profit or advantages." Yet these Native people, economically worthless as they seemed to the Company had the potential of dealing Company investors a crippling blow by triggering a disastrous war by the use of their trails that might well draw in the other Algonkian-speaking Native peoples of the Valley and the Mohawks to boot. The Company officials urged Stuyvesant to head off this calamity by "persuading and instigating" the other River tribes to join them in smiting the Esopus. Stuyvesant replied that he'd tried that tack but it hadn't worked. As the winter of 1659-1660 slowly moved along the Valley, the Mohawks to the Esopus Native's northwest and the Company officials in New Amsterdam and Fort Orange and even in far off Old Amsterdam talked once again of bringing about a kind of peace. Not a lasting or real peace, of course, but one which might hold long enough for the Company to become prepared for the war to extermination which had long seemed to them to be desirable for the Company's profit. Late in October two Mohicans appeared at the Esopus stockade and offered wampum on behalf of the Mohawks and their own people in token of their desire for the feigned armistice which Stuyvesant had instructed Ensign Smith to arrange. The Mohicans left but returned with two prisoners they had taken from the Dutch, but not with the son of Esopus brewer, Evert Pels, his wife and his mother who served as the Esopus people's midwife. He had been captured at the tennis court ambush and, in accordance with a Native custom, adopted to replace one of theirs killed in battle. The young man had married a Native girl who had become pregnant. Young Pels refused to leave his wife and expected baby and as far as is known never returned to his own people but lived on as a born Native.

That winter of 1659-60 was a hard one for the colonists and the Company soldiers huddled together in the stockade at Esopus or Wiltwyck and who were confined there because this was a winter of unusual fierceness and heavy snow. Colonists and soldiers alike were cut off from easy communication with New Amsterdam and Fort Orange by the icing of the Hudson River and the covering of the river's rough ice by deep snow. Few Natives made their way through the deep snow to the stockade in order to trade the maize and the deer, bear and turkey meat which Ensign Smith needed to feed his garrison of seventy hungry soldiers. The Directors in old Amsterdam had advised Stuyvesant to treat visiting Natives with a feigned goodwill but to be on the alert for a chance to seize and imprison them. Stuyvesant dutifully handed on this bit of advice to the Ensign and the Ensign did his best to pretend good will toward his few winter visitors but was unable to trick the wily Natives. For the Natives were adept at this little game of deceit long sanctioned as a useful feature of the art of war on both sides of the Atlantic.

In February, 1661, after much discussion of the legality of such a move, Amsterdam directors passed a resolution declaring war on the Esopus Natives.[120] The resolution was not to take effect until the following fall. But Ensign Smith jumped the gun by leading forty of his men from the stockade at Esopus in an attack in mid-March as the harsh winter unexpectedly relented, on a group of Natives encamped some three Dutch miles to the south of the stockade at Esopus. Four or five of the Native inhabitants were killed and the rest scattered. Twelve young and vigorous men were captured. These men were destined to play a significant part in the turn being taken by what has come to be called the First Esopus War.

It was on this expedition in March that the Company soldiers came upon a revered aged sachem who was fishing—his name was Preumaker. They captured the old man and when on the way to the stockade at Esopus he proved too feeble to undergo the rugged march, gave him a blow on the head with his own hatchet. And in this way killed him. A stream and part of the present Town of Hurley now bear the name of this remarkable and beloved Native leader.

As March moved along it brought with it the melting of the Hudson River ice and the snow that had covered the land. It also brought with it a compelling urge by both Natives and whites to make preparations for the spring planting of corn and beans, or wheat and oats. In order for both Natives and Dutch to sow, sachems of the River people and the Mohawks journeyed to Forts Amsterdam and Orange, drew on their impressive stocks of woodland eloquence and laid down much wampum at the feet of "brother" Stuyvesant and other white sachems in token of the proposal for peace they were making on behalf of their Esopus brothers. But where, Stuyvesant asked, were the Esopus sachems if they were so desirous of peace? Why did they not come to him in person to make their wishes known? The sachems were afraid (because they had learned not to trust the whites), was the reply. Stuyvesant refused to consider peace until he could meet the cowed Esopus sachems face to face.

The evidence we have strongly suggests that the Esopus (also called Munsee) sachems were indeed afraid. The elation over their successful ambush at the tennis court had soon yielded to a fear that the stockade they had been unable to capture even with the help of various Hudson River allies, was indeed there to stay. The hope that the Dutch could be driven from the silt-enriched creekside fields tilled by the hands of women and confined to simple trading posts on the Hudson or Rondout (to supply Natives with their still ever welcomed trade goods) grew even more dim. It seemed likely that the stockade would remain as an intimidating symbol of Dutch domination looking out over the fields the ancestors of the Native Esopus women had tilled for so many centuries in their earth-gentle ways.

While the First Esopus War had pursued its sometimes quiet and subtle, sometimes violent way, young Dominie Harmanus Bloem was confined to New Amsterdam by the orders of Stuyvesant and his Council. September of 1660 saw Bloem petitioning the Company officials for compensation for the expenses he had incurred for board and lodging while he had "waited with sincere desire for the time and opportunity of being forwarded" to his agreed upon post at Esopus. His petition had its effect and before September was over Bloem and his wife had been forwarded to Esopus. And a very different Esopus it was from the one Bloem had visited in 1659. Then it had just ceased being a scattered assemblage of colonists' fields, houses and farm structures, mixed with patches of tangled Native corn and beans and squash, and bark wigwams all strung out in an unplanned fashion beside the buildings and the wheat and lesser European grains of the colonists along the Esopus Creek flatlands.

Now while the whites' fields remained as scattered as before and the Native women continued to tend their own crops beside those of the colonists, the colonists' houses and barns had been moved and then set on a somewhat diamond-shaped elevation as close neighbors within the strong stockade walls on a little irregular grid of streets. The place was clearly working its way after the testing of the stockade toward becoming a village of Dutch elements grafted on the haphazard frontier venture begun in 1652. Very un-Dutch were the rough houses made of easily available timber planks instead of the neat reddish bricks of villages in the motherlands. Even less Dutch were the Natives who were admitted within the stockade to peddle their furs and deerskins and their corn, beans and venison which by then filled important niches in the domestic and commercial economy of the village. As his first eight months in the village went by, Bloem saw the name of the place changed by Director Stuyvesant from Esopus in the Groote Esopus to the Dutch Wiltwyck of uncertain significance. It is generally held to mean "a wild or savage retreat." Or it may have reference to the voluntary retreat from the stockade site by the Natives after their offer to make a gift of the site. As far as is known colonists had not been consulted in the change to a new name, but many of the colonists knew they did not especially like it. The old name Esopus or Sopus remained in oral use by some oldtimers in Ulster County until half a century ago.

Wiltwyck was taking its first steps toward a merger of old and New World features at a time of semi-official peace between colonists and Natives. It is true that during this nervous period occasional incidents of conflict erupted and that some colonists expressed a conviction that a future war of virtual extermination of the Natives was inevitable. Or that, among the Natives a strong sense of having been ill-treated simmered as did resentment against the sending by the Dutch of prisoners, including those of the 1660 ambush episode to harsh slavery on the island of Curacao in the West Indies. Natives resented the suggestion of Stuyvesant that the release of the rest of their twelve enslaved fellows might result from their own good behavior. What the Director was really trying to do was to hold the enslaved Natives as hostages. Yet at the same time a kind of cheerful almost boomtown feeling took over among some of the Dutch. The prosperity of farmers on their fat creekside acres drew more and more ambitious men to the place. Lack of sufficient room within the stockade for more houses, shelters for night-dwelling livestock, barns and other farm buildings forced an expansion of the stockade. A group from Beverwyck applied for permission to found another stockaded village to be known as the Nieuw Dorp (the New Village), and today as Hurley. Their petition was granted. Hermanus Bloem's church also shared in the expansive and at the same time nervous mood of the time. In his report to the church authorities in old Amsterdam, dated June 18, 1663, dominie Bloem reported the state of his church as of his three year pastorate to be "somewhat prosperous—its membership had increased from sixteen to sixty." He added that "all was well ordered in Church matters. . . . The newly rising community was beginning to grow and to bloom right worthily." At this time officials of the Colony and leaders in Esopus were trying to establish a local government more like those prevailing in villages in the Netherlands. With this in place dependence for court and other local governmental functions on distant Fort Orange and Beaverwyck would be greatly lessened. But progress toward this goal was slow. The Directors in Amsterdam, and Director Stuyvesant and his council members agreed that Esopus (as it was then still commonly called) lacked a sufficient pool of qualified (and literate) men from which to appoint a schout or headman who could be relied on to preside well over a board of three magistrates called schepens or commissaries in whose hands judicial and other governmental matters would rest subject to appeal to the Director in New Amsterdam. Under this system the officials of Fort Orange and Beaverwyck some forty miles away would end their power over little Esopus. In order to achieve a stopgap solution to the lack of properly qualified candidates for official jobs in Esopus the Directors in Old Amsterdam proposed a solution in the shape of a provisional schout named Roeloff Swartwout, a Fort Orange man then visiting the Netherlands. Swartwout had good connections by marriage with the upper level of Company administration in Amsterdam. He proposed soon returning to Esopus and aiding the Company by farming there with a group of men he would bring along. However, he had no experience in public administration and worst of all he was not yet twenty-one years of age. A howl of protest against this appointment went up from Stuyvesant, as well as from other leading Esopan colonists. Before Bloem's first year in Esopus had ended, the Company had granted the colonists the right to name a slate of choices for schout and schepens from which the Director would make a choice to serve for a year, and Swartwout got the top job.

We know that of the eight leading members of the church who offered Bloem a salary of seven hundred guilders a year plus a farm only two were literate enough to sign their names. We know that "a minister's house" was built—a list of its costs payable in wampum (by then the seashell-derived currency of the place). From these humble beginnings would arise Kingston's Dutch Reformed Church which was to dominate Kingston's cultural, religious and sometimes public life until the early years of the nineteenth century in spite of divisions among its communicants and the rivalries of the new ethnic people who reached Kingston and brought with them their own different ways of life and religious practices.

3.
Horror in the Stockade

If Dominie Bloem's two early years at Esopus have left cheerful traces, his third year in contrast was marked by a bloody tragedy which was clearly recorded by the dominie with deep feeling and sympathy. That horror can be shared and lamented by Kingston people of today as they look backward on their own history. For the dominie left in writing a shocking account of what he saw and felt on that never-to-be-forgotten day of violent death.

The three year spell of new peace had not been altogether worth calling entirely peaceful. From time to time rumors of Native unrest had filtered through the walls of the stockade. The Natives continued to be resentful over Stuyvesant's failure to keep a promise to pay them for their stockaded land, the harsh enslavement of their captured brothers in Curacao in the West Indies, the continued incursions of the whites' farm animals (The Natives had none) into the Native garden patches, the Natives' ever watchful presence in the dark woods which eerily hemmed in the stockade and the thriving Esopus creekside fields all worked to keep the new settlement from taking on the quiet glamor of the little overseas Eden as hinted at by the Company's promotional writers. Yet life went on among the stockaders in a lively and even sometimes confident fashion.

Natives were permitted to enter through the gates of the stockade to trade or peddle their corn, beans, venison, deerskins, furs, crafted objects of skins and wood, as the Rondout trading post was neglected. More and more families were drawn to Esopus as the excellence and ease of working of its flat, stone-free and mellow farmland became known throughout the province. Beer had begun to be brewed and brandy distilled. Ordinances for curbing excessive drinking by both colonists and Natives were enacted (and largely ignored), and a system of local government as similar as possible to that in force in Dutch villages in the Netherlands (largely based on

Roman law) was granted and gave Esopus people a modest sense of having a community of their own and some measure of control over their public affairs.

Every morning the locked gates of the stockade were opened and the eager cows and other livestock which had spent the night within in cramped safety were led to pasture by a community herdsman. And the men of the village trooped out to spend the day at work in their fields (for a time under the protection of armed Company soldiers who after a while of uneasy peace were ordered back to old Amsterdam by penny pinching Company officials). As the three years of peace rolled by a certain amount of carelessness became apparent and the stockade was not kept in good repair. And so confident were the Wiltwyck people that the authorized sister settlement of the Nieuw Dorp was created to take care of eager new colonists such as those from Beverwyck. It was planted on the fine soil of what is now Hurley. Hurley so became the first of the satellite settlements which would develop into a flock of many offsprings of Old Esopus to appear in Ulster County. Governor Stuyvesant approved of the new village even in the face of Native displeasure at a time when an uneasy peace had lulled the whites both in New Amsterdam and Wiltwyck into an acceptance of things as they were. Then on June 7, 1663, the blow long pondered in secret by the Natives as they watched from their garden patches and from the shelter of the dark woods around, fell with a devastating suddenness after the able men had left the stockade in the early morning for work in their fields.

That fine summer morning some Natives had been admitted through the gates to trade or peddle their wares in a way that had become a routine part of stockade life. Suddenly a horseman rode into the stockade shouting that Natives had attacked the Nieuw Dorp, set the place ablaze and were carrying off many of its inhabitants as captives. At this signal the apparently peaceful bean and corn and pelt traders became transformed into murderous demons striking right and left with hatchets, killing or maiming every white person in sight. Other Natives who carried guns also joined the slaughter in the Stockade.

The horror of that sunny summer morning was vividly felt and vividly reported by grieving dominie Harmanus Bloem. To the governing board of the Dutch Reformed Church in old Amsterdam Bloem wrote, that up to June 7th, "this newly rising community" had been doing well. But as of June 7th he could tell only of a "cruel blow at the hands of the heathen, who intended to destroy this church altogether and to devour it alive had not the Lord our God wonderfully protected it and they fled having taken a fright in their hearts, when no person drove them away. . . . Mens' help was far from us for the Company soldiers whom we had before were discharged and sent to the Netherlands. There lay the burnt and slaughtered bodies, together with those wounded by bullets and axes. The last agonies and moans and lamentations of many were dreadful to hear. The burnt bodies were most frightful to behold. A woman lay burnt with her child at her side as if she were just delivered, of which I was a living witness. Other women lay burnt also in their houses, and one corpse with her fruit still in her womb, most cruelly murdered in their dwelling with her husband and another child. The houses were converted into heaps of stone. We are made desolate. The Indians have slain in all twenty-four souls in our place, and taken forty-five prisoners . . . (as of September 18 when Bloem's report was dated). And about the same number of theirs are in our hands. . . ."

In that time of sorrow dominie Bloem did his duty conscientiously. He visited the wounded and comforted the bereaved. He preached on an appropriate text, "Who gave Jacob for a spoil and Israel to the robbers?" And every evening for a whole month Bloem, in a rite that had pagan as well as Christian antecedents, "offered up prayers with the congregation on the four points of our fort (that is on the four bastions) under the blue sky."

On June 10, the magistrates of Wiltwyck wrote to beg Stuyvesant for help, "We doubt not, your Honor's utmost pity will be extended to us and we will speedily be succored by soldiers, with ammunition and clothing for the inhabitants have been mostly robbed of it and are almost naked in consequence of the fire and robberies."

Stuyvesant was faced with the necessity of making hard decisions. A first step in helping the Wiltwyck white people would be to ransom the prisoners believed to be held by the Natives in scattered locations back in the Catskill mountains. But ransoms would come high and Stuyvesant had little Company money to spend—he set about raising a loan of four or five thousand guilders pledging the credit not only of himself and the Company but also of the members of his Council. The stockade at Fort Orange which would normally have been a base from which Esopus might expect help had been allowed by the Company during the time of so-called peace to deteriorate and the soldiers formerly stationed there had been ordered to leave. The Company in its concern with the profits of its more guilder-promising holdings in Brazil, the West Indies and its promising slave-trading business on the west coast of Africa, had been niggardly with the expense of soldiers for the protection of New Netherlands—and more soldiers had to be found. The many Native tribes of the region, the Mohawks, the Mohegans, the Haverstraws and the rest had to be placated lest they join the Esopus Natives in a fearful general uprising.

As the people of Wiltwyck recovered from the shock they had received and began rebuilding their sorely shattered lives, Stuyvesant as in 1655 put great energy into enlisting soldiers—but as before recruits came forward reluctantly even when bills were posted in public places in New Amsterdam offering "free plunder" and the possession by each volunteer soldier of the "savages" he might capture. Also posted in public this time as a new inducement was a grisly list of indemnities to be paid, so much for the loss of an arm, a leg or an eye. At the same time supplies needed for the dreamed-of war of extermination against the Esopus Natives which had in effect now come out of hiding and been openly declared by the Director and his Council had to be piled up in Esopus. Almost daily, sailing vessels made their way up the Hudson laden with ammunition, military hardware, swords, clothing, and food-stuffs for use in the war. From the landing at Rondout Harbor the supplies were hauled up to Esopus by the horses and wagons requisitioned from reluctant farmers who protested they needed the animals for their farm work and made disrespectful remarks about the negligent Company. From among the rocks and stunted trees that lined the rough road crossing the Armabowery and linking Rondout and the Esopus stockade above, lurking Natives watched the convoys of wagons but because they were guarded by well armed and alert soldiers usually restrained the urge to attack. But the Natives passed on word of the white preparations by speedy and frequent runners over the many miles of trails which linked the centers of Native activity throughout the Hudson Valley and beyond.

In October 1663 all this effort at getting ready for a vigorous attack aimed at the virtual extermination of the Natives was reported to Director Stuyvesant in the form of a detailed journal running to some twenty-five thousand words. The journal writer and head of the whole military operation was Martin Krieger, a captain in New Amsterdam's burgher guard, a burgomaster of the city since its inception as a city in 1653 and a tavern keeper (an occupation then of much greater consequence than it is today). In his journal Krieger demonstrated an ability to write clear, straightforward and business-like prose which brings to life his campaign aimed at the extermination of the Esopus Natives. The journal is seldom pleasant reading as it preserves the details of the series of military actions which was to break the strength and the spirit of a people already weakened at the hands of their Mohawk overlords as well as by white-trader-obtained alcohol and the European diseases to which they had no inherited resistance.

First, as Krieger tells his superiors, there were minor forays into the forest in search of Native groups who might be holding prisoners to be rescued and used as sources of information about Native plans. Native prisoners might be coerced by whites to act as guides to the Natives' fortified places. On September 3 the expected exterminating thrust against the Natives began with ample military supplies stored within the stockade, and despite the continuing unwillingness of Esopus men (except for Thomas Chambers) to supply horses, the first expedition took off. The soldiers dragged two heavy cannons known to be objects of terror to the Natives and struggled the cannon across rain-swollen streams and up and down rocky slopes sometimes with help from horses. With Wappinger Natives captured in an earlier raid across the Hudson as guides and Christoffel Davitz, the Rondout trader as interpreter, a large stockaded Native log-built fort was reached and attacked. The

Natives' chief was killed as were fourteen of his men, four women and three children. The few Native survivors melted away into the forest.

At this point Krieger had a critical choice to make. Should he decide to follow the instructions of the Directors in old Amsterdam and of Stuyvesant and pursue what was to come to be known in the twentieth century as a scorched earth policy and destroy the Natives' stocks of food, their growing crops, their dwellings and everything else that might make life possible for them? Or should he heed the pleas of his volunteers to turn back and permit them to get ready for their spring planting?

During April of the year after Krieger's initial searching of the Natives' lands, Director Stuyvesant reported to the Company directors that the Esopus Natives were so discouraged and scattered that it wasn't possible to find even five or six together at any place in the vast woods. And Krieger noted in a smug business-like style that his soldiers, hoping to find further Natives to loot and punish, found only unburied bodies scattered in the woods.

But six of Krieger's men were wounded and needed attention they could not get in the woods and besides the expedition did not have enough horses to get the wounded and the plentiful booty or plunder back to the stockade at Esopus with any comfort. The members of the Esopus Council of War, including Captain Chambers, who had accompanied the later expedition, agreed with Krieger to postpone the work of destruction of the now deserted forts and Native villages and get back to Esopus with one badly wounded man carried in an improvised litter. But before burning them they had first plundered the Natives' shelters "wherein was considerable booty" in furs, wampum, firearms, skins and other objects of value. They smashed pottery kettles and "took the best of the booty along and resolved to set off" and returned to the stockaded village. On October 2, Krieger and about two hundred men went back on their trail of attempted Native extermination. They found the big unburned fort and the cluster of remaining Native shelters beside it eerily empty and desolate. The dead of the struggle of September 5 had been buried and wolves had already dug up some of the bodies and gnawed at them. All this and more Krieger related in his chillingly business-like factual way. On September 5 he had revealed admiration in his journal at the skill with which the Natives had built their log fort, now he directed his men in tearing the fort apart, piling its heavy palisades in heaps and burning them. Burned too were the Native wigwams of bark-covered poles, the stocks of corn remaining from the previous year's harvest and skillfully stored in pits in the ground. The soldiers pulled up the Natives' newly growing corn sprouts and threw them into the stream and did the same at another smaller fort a few miles away. For weeks after that the soldiers sought out every homestead and campsite of the Esopus Natives however small, humble and isolated and burned and otherwise destroyed and looted everything of use or value. On

December 31 with his work accomplished Krieger returned to his New Amsterdam tavern to again serve his customers. The War was over, the Esopus Natives so thoroughly demoralized as to have ceased being felt as a serious threat to white colonization plans and profits of the West Indies Company. The few surviving Esopus Natives hid in the forest and felt that even their once helpful spirits had vanished.

On May 15, 1664 a few saddened surviving sachems representing the Esopus people met the Council of New Netherland in New Amsterdam to make a final treaty of peace with their white brothers. Thomas Chambers was said to have been there, representing the Colonists. While persistent tradition tells of the ending of the Esopus Wars by the agreeing "under the blue sky" at what is now Kingston's Academy Green or Park, records prove that the treaty was concluded at the council chamber at New Amsterdam by Native participants unarmed and accompanied only by women and children present to indicate the peaceful purpose of the meeting. Present were surviving sachems of all the Native groups which had taken part in the war.

By the terms of the treaty signed that day the Natives would give up all claim to the lands occupied by the whites in the Esopus country. As the treaty of peace was being concluded, dignified old sachem Sewackenamo of the Esopus Natives held up a stout stick and expressed a prayer that the peace being made would prove as firm and solid as the stick. He folded his arms and expressed the hope that the peace would be as binding as his intertwined arms. On this note embodying the kind of eloquent oratorical and histronic skill which the whites respected in their Native opponents, the Esopus War ended.

A belt of wampum laid down by Sewackenamo in token of peace, took its place as a significant element of the official chain of records of the white colony of Ulster County. It was filed away among the Dutch and English manuscript documents and is still in the custody of the present County Clerk.

From time to time Native delegates visited Kingston during the 17th and 18th centuries, accompanied by successive generations of a few young men whom they could trust to carry on in their brain cells the memory of the text of the treaty and of having seen the belt. For the Natives, lacking a written language, had cherished a way of handing on their evolving history and the terms of treaties in the memories of successive generations of their people and so signifying the ratification of treaties to be renewed from year to year by the "laying down" of belts of wampum.

This treaty of 1664 was marked not only by the Esopus sachems presenting the wampum belt but also by the giving by the trustees of the colonists' village in return knives, strouds (a kind of coarse cloth of which blankets were made), and other trade goods.

The treaty was renewed from time to time by successive groups of Indian sachems and others. Notable renewals were made and recorded during 1710, close

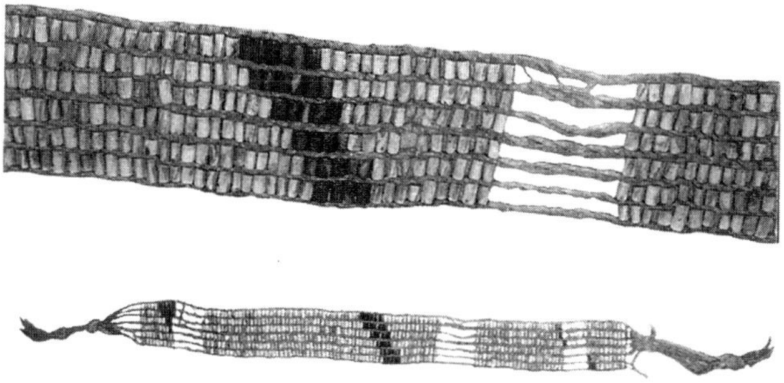

This is the Wampum belt which ended the Esopus Wars and which was used by the Natives to periodically renew the peace. The upper image is a closeup to indicate the structure of the belt. The Belt is maintained at the Ulster County Hall of Records on Foxhall Avenue in Kingston.

to the end of Queen Anne's tenancy of the British throne, 1741, and the final known colonial renewal in 1774. All these renewals left marks (just as valid as signatures on paper documents) in the official records of Ulster County, Kingston or the province. And there were probably others which failed to be recorded or otherwise passed down to us.

The whites appointed—as peace treaties were made—an official to act as special agent in Indian relations and to see to it that disputes over boundaries or claimed abuses of one side or by the other should be settled amicably if possible.

As the white people of what would become the United States were chafing under their final bonds of colonialization, in 1774 the Esopus sachems appeared at Kingston having still managed to retain their own tribal structure enough to bring along a new generation of eager young officials, listeners and memorizers, and probably women and children as well to emphasize the peaceful purpose of the occasion, to hear recited the treaty's provisions for peace agreed upon more than a century before. This resulted in the last recorded renewal with the trustees of colonial Kingston.

During the years of struggle for independence from Britain and for the end of colonial oppression, some Native Esopus people dutifully obeyed the treaty obligations and supported in a brotherly way the people of Kingston and Ulster County in their struggle for independence, except for a few who chose to follow the leadership of white-educated Tory Joseph Brant.

At a recent historical celebration in Kingston plans were made for a modern renewal of the treaty accompanied by the presentation of a new wampum belt but this could not be carried through when making a new belt proved too difficult because no one could be located who knew how to make such a belt.

4.

Wiltwyck Comes out of its Stockade—a Poem about Esopus is Written

WITH PEACE CONCLUDED, WILTWYCK FELT READY AT LAST TO BURST OUT of its confining, if badly maintained, stockade of past history. It could now take full advantage of its rich flatlands and its favored position by land and navigable water, and could hope to grow into a prosperous if still no longer colonial community.

The scattered remnants of the Natives carried on life, as best they could, sometimes in small groups, a few on their old hunting grounds near the base of the Catskills, some on the flatlands of the upper Walkill Valley. Some lived beside small and lonely streams or ponds considered not worth taking by the whites before merging with neighboring tribes of Native Americans or other more distant ones in the Midwest.

Some wandering remnants of the Esopus or Munsee people eventually came together and settled in a community now named Munseeville in Canada's province of Ontario, and their descendents maintain a good deal of their old tribal structure and carry on their people's culture as well as that can be done today.

During Kingston's years of Native wars its colonists as well as the Natives had shown the effects of the cruelty, the hatred and the lowering of standards of decent behavior which have usually marked war ever since its beginnings. Early recorders and commentators on the Dutch white colonists of the Hudson Valley in Company days had seen them as a rough, tough lot. And they had to be in order to deal with the harsh facts of demanding frontier colonial existence in a country they had invaded. The court records of the Village of Wiltwyck between 1661 and 1664 have survived many threats to their existence and remain today as do the earlier records of Fort Orange and adjoining Beaverwyck to tell us of how very rowdy life was in the days when the people of Wiltwyck were still reeling from the effects of the massacre of 1661 and when dominie Bloem was seizing every opportunity to remind his flock that their troubles were often caused by God's determination to punish them for their own sins. The dominie requested the Wiltwyck Court to prohibit all revelry on what he called "the public sinful and scandalous days of Fastseen (or Mardi Gras) coming down from the heathen from their idol Bacchus, the god of wine and drunkenness, also leaven of popery, inherited from the heathen . . . the sword of war still threatens us. . . ." as the dominie warned. The sword of poverty threatened them too, as slow recovery from the human and property losses of the Esopus Wars added to grief at the loss of friends and relatives at the hands of the Natives darkened spirits and sharpened tempers. When Tryntjie Slecht was brought to court on a charge of having slandered that dignitary Johan de Decker who was a member of Peter Stuyvesant's Council and Vice-Director of Fort Orange by calling him a blood sucker she admitted making the charge but explained that she had made it because she was "depressed and discouraged because of the many misfortunes which had befallen her through the savages." Tryntjie was fined twenty-five guilders in sewant by the sympathetic judges to be paid not for the benefit of the Village but for that of the church.

Depression and discouragement led many another Wiltwyckian to appear in the court records as drawing a dagger or unsheathing a sword in the course of an argument over the ownership of a pig, the making of what was taken as an insulting remark or nothing at all that could be determined with accuracy. The haze of alcohol hung over the courtroom as it did over trader deals with the Natives, as frequent cases of offenses induced by drunkenness, or selling liquor on Sunday or to the Natives, smuggling liquor or evading the excise tax imposed on the wholesale selling of liquor were tried and penalties imposed. Of the Wiltwyck people arrested, Thomas Chambers was arrested the most often.

When his congregants did not pay the shares of his salary as required by the Company, dominie Bloem regretfully resorted to taking them to court. Some pleaded the "troubled times," some that as (indentured) servants of the Dutch West India Company, they were not required to pay.

And as the whites rebuilt and the Natives nursed their wounds and sorrow as they carried on their battered society, dominie Henricus Selyns of New Amsterdam, a good friend of dominie Bloem, was ushering Wiltwyck and the Esopus wars which it had survived, into the world of poetry. Cotton Mather wrote of Selyns that he had "a nimble fancy" and that he "sent poems, on all occasions to all sorts of places." In a celebration of the bethrothal and marriage of his friends Aegidius Luyck, rector of the Latin school in New Amsterdam and Judith van Isendoorn, Selyns managed a neat poetic trick. He told the story of the First Esopus War set in the framework of a bit of classical mythology (as favored by the Dutch humanists of the period) and at the same time conveyed his congratulations to the newlyweds.

Cupid, the god of love, Selyns writes, happened to be in Wiltwyck the morning of the attack in 1663. He noted that the corn and bean peddling Natives "show a friendly smile, but cloak a hostile mind." He saw the sudden murderous assault, the roaring flames, the bodies lying here and there. In the confusion Cupid and the white survivors fled, Cupid to the summits of the Catskill mountains from which he could look down on the holocaust. His bow and arrows had been snatched by the attackers. As peace returned and prisoners were exchanged the Natives restored Cupid's bow and arrows and he hastened to New Amsterdam where he shot a belated arrow which united Lucyk and van Isendoorn in love and marriage.

In the poem Cupid scolded the New Netherlands Dutch people. As the nine men had scolded them in their "Representation" of 1650 for living sinful lives, for which they had been punished by God, now they had ignored nature's God-given signs of the coming doom from comets in the sky and in the shaking earth and by an epidemic of smallpox which should have warned them to change their ways. And then Cupid denounced the:

> "Uncleanness, drunkenness and base and sordid pride;
> The land's three crying sins,—this ruin have effected,
> And driven happiness and peace your land aside
> For gross debauchery, and punishment's inflicted;
> Whose warning often giv'n did little heed command."
> "Remember," he continued, "the earth how it was shaken,
> How fires fell from the sky, and small-pox scourged the land;
> And then seek for those lives, whose lives had now been taken.
> Insensibly all trade and pleasure go to naught,
> And daily wickedness produces daily evil."

(Which would have had stern John Calvin's approval.)

Selyn's "Bruydtoft Toorts" or "Bridal Torch" cannot be classed among the great poems of the world yet to those to whom the history of Kingston matters it can be felt as marking the point at which the rough frontier outpost of Wiltwyck was becoming a thing of the memorable past and the village despite the sinfulness detected by its dominie and his poetic friend was taking shape as a place which might even stir the imagination of a poet.

Part 4

A Dutch Company and then the Commercially Driven British Further Profitably Colonize the Land and People of Kingston under Changing Rulers

1661-1700

1. When Changing Loyalties Were Expected of Kingston

The people of Wiltwyck had been well aware that the Netherlands and England were bitter rivals as aggressive traders and colonizers, and for control of the seas and world wide trade, that the claims of the Netherlands and England to territory in the northeastern part of what would become the United States overlapped and were in conflict, that the settlers of New England were increasing mightily in number and in strength and were pushing hard against the eastern boundary of New Netherland, and more and more of them were moving into Dutch-claimed Long Island from Connecticut. To the north, the Wiltwyck people knew, lay French Canada, a land—as they saw it—of energetic Jesuit missionaries for the Protestant-hated Papacy and of traders who were cutting off a flow of upper New Netherland and Canadian furs which otherwise might have helped enrich the dissatisfied Dutch West India Company's investors.

Against this disturbing background Protestant King Charles II of England had handed over in March of 1664 to his Catholic brother James, the Duke of York, the proprietorship of a straggling collection of lands in North America, including both New Netherland (with its Wiltwyck) and New England. The Duke who was also High Admiral of the Royal Navy, soon asserted his new rights by speeding four sail-propelled warships to feebly Company-defended New Amsterdam to demand—and to receive—the City's surrender from a very reluctant Peter Stuyvesant. Soon, English Colonel George Cartright, in obedience to the orders of the Duke of York, received the surrender of Fort Orange. He then appeared at the Strand gate of the Wiltwyck stockade and was given possession of the place by Wiltwyck officialdom. Soon afterwards in a little binge of attempted Anglicization, New Amsterdam was reborn as New York, Fort Orange became Albany but not until September 25, 1669 was Wiltwyck given the English name of Kingston. And in a gesture of conciliation toward the Dutch people of the now English colony, the Dutch Reformed Church would be permitted to exist and the people allowed to speak Dutch. Native and Dutch titles to land would be confirmed and old Dutch customs allowed to continue being observed. All this was by way of an attempt to smooth the way to an acceptance of English colonial rule (and soon taxation) in the Dutch-speaking communities of what was no longer New Netherland but New York.

The new Governor under the Duke of York—he was Richard Nicolls—issued orders requiring the members of his small occupying force at Kingston of regular English soldiers under Captain Daniel Brodhead to treat well the Dutch inhabitants. Yorkshire-born Captain Brodhead proceeded to carry out his job at Kingston with a kind of intensity and casual brutality which often accompanies the holding of conquered territory by occupying invaders. Marius Schoonmaker, a lawyer descended from an old Kingston Dutch and German family, later put in words the old local tradition of the resentment which rose up in Kingston against Brodhead and his men, and British colonial rule, when he wrote in his *History of Kingston* of 1888 a burning denunciation of the British for perpetrating "one of the most cowardly and dishonest stealths of a neighboring nation's unprotected territory in the history of any civilized nation on the globe." Governor Nicolls, however, had written in his instructions to his underlings that the Dutch were "not malicious" as some said and so deserved justice in the settling of disputes between English and Dutch.

Captain Brodhead in his disregard of the Governor's orders seized and imprisoned in the Kingston guardhouse Tjerck Classen DeWitt, a leading burgher of the place on a charge of improperly celebrating Christmas. In DeWitt's official complaint DeWitt complains that Brodhead "abused him because hee would keepe Christmas on ye day accustomary with ye Dutch and not ye day according to ye English observation." And the day "accustomary" with the Dutch was not December 25 as with modern Americans and English, but December 6, St. Nicholas' Day. That was an important day with Dutch-speaking children and was celebrated with enthusiasm in Kingston. On the Dutch Christmas morning Sinter or Santa Claus appeared bringing gifts to all children who had been good throughout the past year. He was accompanied by an assistant named Black Peter who carried a bouquet of bare whip-like twigs, one of which he presented as a token to each child who had not been well behaved during the year—this to suggest that the child deserved (but was not given) a whipping.

The Calvinist Dutch Reformed Church to which all but a very few church-minded Kingstonians adhered, paid little heed to Christmas celebrations which it regarded as mere relics of the "Popery" against which their forebears had struggled during the Reformation. But on the home level Kingston children and their parents clung to their old pre-Reformation Christmas ways. That was why Captain Brodhead's action which seemed to deny the childrens' rights to their traditional Christmas pleasures touched them deeply. But this charge, touching as it is to all lovers of Christmas, was as nothing compared to many others involving Captain Brodhead and his English soldiers.

So many complaints poured in from Kingston to Governor Nicolls and other officials that a special court was convened to sit in Kingston and judge the merit of the offenses charged against Brodhead and his soldiers. The list of these was long. They ranged from beating a man when he objected to having his hens stolen, stealing a ham, laming a man whose goat the soldiers had taken and eaten, ill treating Cornelis Barentsen Sleght in his own house and then locking him up in the guardhouse (Sleght was an important person; he was the village brewer and his wife Trintje was equally important—she was the Kingston midwife). Sleght accused the Captain of throwing a keg of liquor on the floor in a fit of temper when he was refused a free drink by newly arrived Huguenot immigrant, Louis Dubois and of manhandling citizens going quietly about their business on the streets or enjoying the comfort of their homes. The Captain readily admitted later on having juggled the dates of Christmas in favor of England but he and his men denied having committed many other offenses charged. Yet the evidence against the soldiers and their Captain was so compelling that Brodhead was to be quietly deprived of his command. On another and more serious charge, that of having taken part in a mutiny against Brodhead, a court convened to try the case found many of Kingston's militiamen guilty because about sixty or seventy of them had assembled, angry and armed, with the purpose of rescuing their brewer from the grip of Captain Brodhead when the cries of Sleght's wife and children resounded as Sleght was hauled off to prison. Mutiny was punishable by death but the ringleaders of the protest were sentenced to no more than banishment from Kingston; a few years later they returned home. Brodhead however lost his position in the army and died shortly afterward and the lot in Hurley to which he was entitled went to his widow.

Until the end of the 1600's and even beyond, the people of Kingston continued to remain in a state of confusion and doubt as changes in their government, pressures to alter their Dutch-colored way of life and ambivalence as to what loyalties were expected of them swirled about them. At first the Duke's rule seemed reasonably benign, and under it representatives to an elected Assembly legislated on many matters. English common law was substituted for the Dutch Roman-based kind and such English innovations as trial by jury were grudgingly accepted in Kingston. Dutchness remained strong although elsewhere and especially in the fast growing cosmopolitan city of New York, Dutchness was being diluted and the English language and culture were getting ever more evident to visitors. A climax came, helped along by a slowdown in the economy and higher taxes imposed by the British colonial government on behalf of the mother country. Then the King William who had married Catholic Princess Mary Stuart and became the father of a son who might in the normal course of events one day reign as a Catholic king of England.

People of Kingston were disturbed at this present and prospective shuffling of the throne and religious pressures, as they felt the waves they created. They had felt agitated too when the proprietorship of the Duke gave way to their membership with New England in a Dominion of New England. Some of their more aggressive and sharp-witted people took advantage of the turmoil. Among these was Thomas Chambers who rode rising and falling political waters with remarkable agility and survived the transition to British rule even within a joint Dominion as he rose in the ranks of local society, thanks to his British birth, and was no longer disrespectfully nicknamed Clabbord, in memory of his youth as a simple carpenter.

In the "Certaine Place called Kingston" as it came under British colonial rule there were few colonists of elevated social status either for reasons of wealth or ancestry. Most upper class European persons could do very well in their homelands in the prosperous Netherlands or the other countries of northern Europe including Britain; they had no reasons for exposing themselves to the risks inherent in life on the North American frontier where they would be exposed to the Natives who remained stubbornly unreconciled to being colonized except when under the spell of alcoholic drinks and trade goods brought to the New World by their colonizers. One of the very few people of more elevated rank to be associated with early Kingston, as we have seen, was Johanna de Hulter. After the death of her husband Johanna lived as Mrs. Jeronimus Ebbingh, wife of a rich New York City merchant, on the Hooge (High) Straat, a street favored by the very rich of the City of New York. She appears in a quaint family history snobbishly studded with the names of related upper crust old New York families, called *The Making of New York*, by Mary de Peyster Rutgers MacCrea Congers (Vanamee), who describes Johanna Ebbingh as a friend of her de Peyster ancestors who followed her father's interest in Native languages. She spoke several and was on friendly terms with Native families—or so Mrs. Congers tells us.

Whenever Esopus in its early years had a resident dominie, he was respected, although usually of low social origin, as being in a special social class since he had studied Latin and probably Greek and Hebrew. But some dominies lost respect when they became topers or engaged in sexual excursions outside of marriage. The first doctor to appear in Esopus was Gisbert van Imborch, who came there as a by-product of the Esopus Wars. In 1660 Peter Stuyvesant had sent the doctor at Fort Orange to treat a company soldier named Domenicus who was suffering from fifteen severe wounds received in the Native wars at Esopus. The doctor was credited with 50 guilders in beavers for treating the man successfully, suggesting that he was competent. By 1661 Dr. van Imborch was established as a member of the upper layer of Esopus. Rachel his wife was captured by Natives, escaped and served as a guide for Dutch soldiers to the Native fort at which she had been held prisoner.

Doctors in Western European society are often classed, on account of their learning, with the gentry and in a place like Esopus or Wiltwyck and early Kingston a properly educated doctor would surely be looked up to, unless he were one of the ill-educated quacks who were known to have been at work in colonial society. An examination of an inventory of the belongings van Imborch left behind made in 1665 after his death shows that he owned good medical books, many medical implements and drugs. Like other doctors of his time he was also a barber. His inventory includes two barber's chairs, fourteen razors, and barber's towels and other barber equipment. He also owned a collection of books, not only on medicine but on several other subjects including mining, religion and gardening. His inventory also included small objects used in Native trading, as well as fur hats and children's leather jackets described as "made by the Savages." Dr. van Imborch may have been a trader on the side with the Natives as nearly all the inhabitants of Fort Orange and Esopus were, as evidenced by the listing of substantial numbers of small mirrors, combs and other trade goods. The doctor served with Thomas Chambers as an Esopus magistrate. However, he could not have used his medical and barbering skills for long in Wiltwyck, for both he and his wife were dead before 1665.

The plant resources of the new world—to the eyes of the white colonists—were rich in those properties of which the Native Americans alone knew the medical uses. Hence practicing physicians like Van Imborch and the many generations of the Kiersted family who followed van Imborch in caring for the health of Esopus and Kingston people, took the trouble of learning the native dialects of the Algonkian language. The once popular Kiersted Ointment, prescribed by five generations of doctors of that family, eventually became a popular over-the-counter household remedy in Kingston—it was compounded in part of Native botanical ingredients, so said Mrs. Louise Hasbrouck Zimm.

2.
In a Time of Conflict, Captain Chambers Becomes Lord of Foxhall Manor

AFTER THE DEATH OF DR. VAN IMBORCH CAPTAIN CHAMBERS STOOD OUT even more clearly as the top man in the society of Wiltwyck. He had already been a militia captain, a commisarie (magistrate or schepen), and a leader in most community affairs—for by this time Esopus had evolved into what might justly be called a settled colonial community not altogether pleased with its colonial status. Among his fellow colonists, he was outstanding already as the first owner of land in Esopus, energetic leader of the first band of Beaverwyck colonists to settle in Esopus, Captain of the Esopus militia, and because he spoke Dutch, English and Native, was inevitably relied upon (in the polyglot peace) by the English provincial authorities and so confirmed in his strong position with the Kingston people of British origin and accepted by the Dutch.

While the various positions he held and his high standing are all matters of record, nothing that can be proved is known about Chambers' life before his arrival in New Amsterdam as a simple carpenter. He has been said, by local historian J.W. Hasbrouck to have been red-haired, tall and lean—but there is no known portrait or other evidence to bear this out. He is said to have been "a soldier of fortune" in the service of the Dutch West India Company but here too there is no hard evidence. He is usually said to have been of English birth but some called him Irish—here too without producing any evidence. Nothing Chambers wrote or is quoted as having said, sheds any light at all on the mysteries surrounding his early life before he reached New Amsterdam. It is possible that he was the Thomas Chambers who is mentioned as arriving in Philadelphia aboard an English ship. In New Amsterdam he first worked as a carpenter and so acquired the nickname of "clappord" from his frequent use of clapboards as wooden house siding. He once had leased farm land on the Van Renssalaer manor.

About the granting to Chambers of the Manor of Foxhall, however, there is no mystery. Preliminary steps seem to have been taken in 1669 and the reasons are plain, from the wording of the confirmatory grant of his manor at Kingston made in 1672.

Colonel Francis Lovelace was the initial grantor of the Manor on behalf of the British Crown. The manor consisted of 250 acres including a foothold on the Rondout close to that stream's junction with the Hudson, connecting it to a fine tract of the fertile arable Esopus Creek-side flatlands a little to the north of uptown Kingston of the present day, at the place known to the Natives as Athar-Hacton, which means a tract of good, fertile land in the Esopus people's Algonkian dialect. This elevation of Captain Chambers, alone of all Kingstonians to reach the position of lord of a manor was made in recognition of his part in the "Indian wars" and to his having already built a "mansion house," as well as having accumulated much land. Foxhall was unique by being the only manor ever to be granted to the west of the Hudson between the vicinity of the City of New York and that of Rensselaerwyck. And this at a time when the granting of manors was no longer being done in England.

Chambers' life as lord of the manor of Foxhall was pretty much of an open book until his death on April 8, 1694. Then for well near two centuries Chambers remained a dim figure in the minds of all Kingstonians except for lawyers sniffing and prowling in the dusty pages of old land records. It would not be until a few years before the celebration of the hundredth anniversary of the signing of the Declaration of Independence in 1876 that he began to emerge from the shadows—and have many questions asked about him and only a few correctly answered.

Thomas Chambers was appointed surveyor-general of the earliest roads of Esopus which badly needed attention. We know that in 1646 he had leased farmland across the Hudson River from Fort Orange. He had been chosen as among the men who took part with Arent Van Curler, a useful Dutch negotiator with the Natives, and according to tradition led a few others to join him in leaving the Fort Orange vicinity for the fine flatlands beside the Esopus. Official records document Chambers playing an important part in the community life and in the struggle by white colonists to take over the Natives' land. As the settlement at Esopus grew, records show Chambers as interpreter with the Natives, a signer of numerous letters to Company officials asking for favors for little Esopus, as reporter on conflicts with the local Natives and in an appeal for Esopus to be sent a minister. When King Charles II gave his brother, the Catholic Duke of York and Ulster, the proprietorship of New England, New Netherland, New Jersey and other possessions he claimed in North America, Dutch officials were confirmed in their jobs. Chambers was confirmed as Captain of the Kingston militia. He took care to avoid choosing sides in most of the episodes of Esopus anti-English expressions of disagreement with their British colonizers.

The new English authorities obviously found English Chambers very useful in Kingston where they had a hard time—as Brodhead's experiences showed—in becoming acceptably established, so it was hardly surprising that as they sought to consolidate their rule over what was now part of the Province of New York in the New England Dominion, they appointed Chambers to positions of influence. And Chambers was bountifully rewarded for his services to King and community. On October 16, 1672 Governor Richard Lovelace confirmed in detail that the previous governor had raised Chambers to the status of lord of the Manor of Foxhall, and in words which amply spell out reasons for this action:

> "Whereas Captain Thomas Chambers, a Justice of the Peace at Esopus hath been an ancient inhabitant in those parts, where he hath done signal and notable service, in the times of the wars against the Indians, and having by his industry in time of peace, acquired considerable estate, of which he now stands possessed, among the rest having a mansion house not far from the town of Kingston, commonly called Fox hall, with a great tract of land thereto belonging, which said house is made defensible against any sudden incursions of Indians or others. In acknowledgment of the services heretofore done by the said Captain Thomas Chambers, I have thought fit to erect the said mansion house, called Fox hall, and land belonging to it, into a manor, to be known by the name of the 'Manor of Fox hall;' the which shall for the time to come be held, deemed, deputed, taken and be, an entire enfranchisement manor of itself, and shall always from time to time have, hold and enjoy like and equal privileges with other manors within the government, and shall in no manner or any wise, be under the rule, order or directions of any town Court, but by the general Court of Assizes, or as from time to time the said Capt Chambers shall receive orders or directions from his Governor and his council."

The "mansion house" already standing in 1672 probably conformed in design to that of the fortified small manor houses of England's late middle ages. It probably had strong stone walls forming a defendable cubic shape. Structures like these were no longer being built in England (nor were similar manors being granted there), but were appropriate enough for a British colony liable to be attacked by Natives or the French of Canada. There is no known record of the negotiations leading up to the granting of the manor.

It is unusual for an English manor to consist of a tract of land on which, as far as is known, only one tenant house stood besides the mansion. But it is reasonable to suppose the English authorities saw Chambers as a man of substance on whom they could depend to fight off possible attacks, and otherwise support the new English government. As to English-born Chambers, the role of lord of a manor, equal in rank although not in area or wealth to Hudson Valley magnates like the Van Renssaelaer and Livingston manor lords across the Hudson, evidently had great appeal. This supposition is borne out by the fact that in 1672 Chambers' rights to the manor were officially confirmed and the privileges which accompanied then were spelled out, similar to those of other lords of manors. These included the right of advowson, which is the right to name the manorial minister of the established Anglican church. Also included was the right to hold certain courts for the people of his manor of Foxhall as well as certain traditional controls over his manorial tenants, and he was not subject to control by Kingston courts. But his manor was too small to justify following up on these and the other rights he was given such as holding his own courts. In his will, probated in the spring of 1694, Chambers conclusively showed that he wanted the manor to go on indefinitely into the future. To achieve this he wanted to entail the manor, i.e. limit future ownership to his descendants—but he had no children of his own. And so he entailed Foxhall manor on his stepson, Abram Van Gaasbeek, son of his wife by a previous marriage to Laurentius Van Gaasbeek, the one time dominie of the Wiltwyck Dutch Reformed Church. The stepson was to meet one condition—that was that he assume the name of Chambers and that the name would be assumed by eldest son after eldest son and passed on with the manor to eldest sons indefinitely. In case of the failing of sons the manor would pass to the husband of a daughter provided that he live in the manor and assume the name of Chambers. In 1752 the entail was legally broken by a Van Gaasbeek heir and so Thomas Chambers' wish to have his name continued endlessly tied to the land he had owned was thwarted.

And it would not be until the last years of the nineteen century that the first lord of Foxhall Manor came to be recognized by the people of Kingston as the founding father of their community. This after new materials on his life would be made public in print.

3.
A Time When Britain Gains Ground in the Life and Land of Kingston

After the Duke of York took possession of New Netherland as proprietor he had shown no haste in beginning to put an English spin on the very Dutch settlements of the Hudson Valley. First he imposed what were called the Duke's Laws, which seemed appropriate enough, in parts of the Province which had large English populations. These parts were in Westchester, Long Island and parts of New Jersey. He also allowed very Dutch Fort Orange and newly named Kingston and other Hudson Valley Dutch settlements to go on living much as they had done before. Serious Hudson Valley Anglicization began for Kingston with the stationing there of Captain Daniel Brodhead and his English soldiers in the Village. The Duke's governor by then had confiscated the assets of the Dutch West India Company. Residents of the Province had been expected to take an oath of loyalty to Catholic King James II but after a year or so some were threatened with confiscation of their property if they did not comply. These demands were results of the second Anglo-Dutch war, then beginning. To further confound already confused and rumor-ridden Kingston word reached the Village of the appearance of a Dutch fleet heading toward New York as an Anglo-Dutch war measure. In New York the Dutch Company had by then allowed the fort which was the Dominion's chief defense to become neglected and virtually useless. Militia soldiers were summoned to New York from the Hudson Valley—some were from Kingston—to help defend what was now a port of New York in the Dominion of New England. The rumors of impending attack were judged unreliable. The fleet of Dutch ships arrived and took the city without much effort and held it for a short period during which the city and Esopus became Dutch once more until, under the Treaty of Westminster of 1674, about a year later (negotiated in far off London), the Anglo-Dutch war ended and Kingston, to the surprise and disappointment of its Dutch people, became English again. But this was not the only change to be imposed upon the people of Kingston as the 17th century drew near to a close and faint glimmers of the 18th century appeared on the horizon.

By 1683 King Charles II had been persuaded to make some sweeping changes in his American possessions (including those managed by his brother the Duke of York). These included enlarging the assembly in New England as well as New York and New Jersey which was proposed in a Charter of Liberties. Before the Charter could be signed the Duke's brother King Charles II died and the Duke became King James II. As King, he bore down more heavily on what was now called the larger Dominion of New England which stretched from Maine along the Atlantic coast to the mouth of the Delaware River and included New Netherland. He refused to sign the Charter of Liberties. Kingston had not been pleased at being changed from being a Dutch colony to becoming a small part of a Dominion of New England, in which, they feared, New England (of which they did not approve) would seek to take precedence over them. The Dutch people of the Hudson Valley had learned to take fairly well to such English innovations as trial by a jury of their peers and the calling of representatives of their own to attend a provincial assembly, in which Kingston had two representatives and which over many tumultuous years would develop into an Assembly elected by qualified white male freeholders with the power of imposing taxes and other essential powers today guaranteed to the representatives of American citizens.

The final two decades of the 17th century were marked by episodes of not always pleasant feeling between English and Dutch business people of the Province of New York. Religious tolerance was practiced even to Catholics and Jews but Anglican church goers (of the established church) and those of the dissenting Calvinist Dutch Reformed church were in competition for the better off and more powerful people of the colony on into the early years of the next century. And Quakers and other non-conforming Christians were scorned.

In 1679 two European visitors inspected Kingston and found the place to be doing well thanks to its fine fertile wheat fields and its good landing place on the Rondout Creek close to the Creek's junction with the navigable Hudson River. And in their *Journal* the cultist-visitors wrote a good report on the Village and found that it was doing well, even under changing colonial rulers and confused loyalties, and while still feeling the heavy losses inflicted by the two Esopus Wars and the terrible massacre.

4.
The Labadist Cultists Come and Go and Report Favorably on the Condition of Kingston in 1679

Death had compelled Captain Chambers to relinquish his position as lord of the manor of Foxhall by only five years when two very unusual religious zealots turned up in Kingston and left behind after they departed in a journal eventually published a fine informative account of the Kingston from which the manor of Chambers had been detached.

In 1679, Jaspar Dankers and Peter Sluyter, agents of the Labadists religious cult reported on the colonial village as already a well settled place, no longer having the look of a frowzy frontier outpost struggling for a foothold in a hostile land.

The two Franco-Dutch agents were seeking out Kingston among other attractive American places as a possible site for a community of their fellow cultists known as the Labadists, from their founder, ex-Jesuit, charismatic and at the same time eccentric, French Jean de Labadie. Thanks to his remarkable eloquence in preaching and the aura that came of his onetime claim to be a kind of reincarnation of Jesus Christ, De Labadie attracted many followers who contributed their worldly goods to the common stock of the community they formed. They dressed plainly, prayed in silence and tried to conform to Labadie's belief that true marriage was possible only between two of his believers and that all other sexual relationships didn't count. The sect met with opposition in France and charges of bizarre sexual practices and so they considered (after a stay in Holland) moving to the New World. After considering an attempt at settlement in Dutch Surinam where the two agents reported that snakes were as common in the houses as mice were in the houses of Holland, the two men landed from a sloop at Rondout and left behind in their *Journal* a succinct account of the place, to encourage their followers, and they hinted at the lively economic life of Kingston. "At the mouth of the creek on the shore of the river, there are some houses and a redoubt together with a general storehouse, where the farmers bring in their grain, in order that it may be conveniently shipped when the boats come up here (from the City of New York), and wherein their goods are discharged from the boats, as otherwise there would be too much delay in going back and forth." This was an early mention of Kingston Landing by the time the place had recovered in many ways from the effects of the massacre and the Esopus Wars.

The Labadists mentioned the existence of a "redoubt," but have nothing to say about trading with Natives taking place there or elsewhere on the Creek. Although the two Labadists mentioned that the people of Kingston had borne the largest part of the cost of the Esopus wars, they gave the Labadists an impression of a place that was doing well and growing.

In Kingston the two Labadists had planned to meet an acquaintance, young Gerrit Duykinck, son of a glass-making and painting New York City family who was busily installing the glass in the new stone Dutch Reformed Church (60 by 45 feet in size we know from other sources). Duykinck left his work to act as the Labadists' guide to the remarkably fertile Esopus Creek flatlands which stirred their enthusiasms. "We found here exceedingly large flats which are more than three hours ride (on horseback) in length, very level, with a black soil which yields grain abundantly." The Labadists sampled the Kingston beer and concluded that it and that made at Albany, "were the heaviest beer we have tasted in all New Netherland and from wheat alone, because it (wheat) is so abundant." (The malt from which beer is made is usually derived from cheaper grains, most of it barley.) The two Labadists inspected the stockade and estimated that it then held fifty houses. And although Kingston clearly appealed to the explorer-agents they realized unhappily (as Governor Andros confirmed to them later on) that it had no large, fertile and forest-free tract suitable to their purposes which was available by grant or was on the market.

By the time their thoughts were turning to the New World, the Labadists' unusual beliefs had modified but a disapproval of the use of tobacco and of slavery remained. The governor of the province of New York had told the Labadist explorers of other New York places with the very best agricultural land. (Kingston was referred to in 1684 as "being the fats of the land by tillage" in the minute book of the Council of the City of New York.) After visiting other promising flatlands along the Mohawk and upper Hudson Rivers and finding nothing on the market that suited their desire for superior farmland they had arrived at Kingston to be delighted by the fertile flatlands which the Esopus Creek generously fertilized and had required no white men's clearing of forest growth. But here too they found this land which roused their enthusiasm for New World possibilities "already taken up." They went on to Maryland where they obtained and worked a 10,000 acre plantation and in spite of their objections to tobacco smoking and slavery they successfully and profitably raised tobacco with slave labor.

A year or two before the Labadists had come to Kingston a people of a different ethnic background and a different religious sect were beginning to arrive and to remain. These were the French Calvinist Protestants known to the Dutch of the Province of New York as Walloons and to us today as Huguenots. Many Huguenots had left their homes because of religious persecution during the reign of Louis XIV culminating in the 1685 revocation of the Edict of Nantes which had guaranteed them freedom of religion. Huguenots then fled to many parts of the world where Protestants were not discriminated against and some turned up in Kingston and Hurley. A group of these left Kingston and obtained from Governor Andros a large grant of land in southern Ulster County (almost as fine as the Athar-Hackton flatlands) and there settled down as Kingston's third satellite community, following Hurley and Marbletown, and known as New Paltz.

Some of the Huguenot immigrants remained in Kingston and Hurley where they merged into the Dutch culture of the place while those in New Paltz clung for many years to their French language dialect and French Protestantism. They had reached New Paltz after the Natives of the neighboring regions had been vanquished in the bloody Esopus Wars with the whites and so began the settlement under circumstances very different from those of the Kingston people. They lived in peace with the few remaining already pre-vanguished Natives and so prospered on the Wallkill flatlands long before cleared of trees and gently broken to use by Native labor.

5.

The Boulting Act Angers Kingston, Leisler Steps Forward as the "Glorious Revolution" Places William of Orange and Queen Mary Stuart, Eldest Daughter of King James II, on the Throne of England

After the Dutch had briefly retaken New Amsterdam the British seized possession again (they held it as the Labadists came) for a tenure that would not be successfully challenged until after 1776. Kingston people were disturbed by the changes in the colonial loyalties expected of them, as well as by their inclusion in a New England Dominion which yoked them tightly with a people they did not at all like. They were perhaps even more upset by living under the burden of the Boulting Act which substantially cut the profits from the processing and shipping by sea of the fine wheat they grew and sent to New York City—some of it probably for export in baked form as bread or ship's biscuit (a mainstay of a sailor's diet which we know as hardtack). Under pressure from New York traders formed as a committee, an act of government restricted the rights to the boulting (sifting), baking and exporting of wheat and flour in and from the City of New York to a monopoly of New York City traders as the sole bakers for exporters. This caused consternation in Kingston because of the loss it would inflict on growers of Esopus creekside wheat and on local traders.

As Kingston people fretted over the Boulting Act, The Glorious Revolution of 1688-1689 took place in England resulting in the abdication of Catholic King James II (the former Duke of York) and James' replacement by invading Dutch Protestant Prince William of Orange and his wife Mary Stuart, the oldest daughter of James II. Prince William ruled as William III of England. The by-product of the British

Navigation Acts of 1651 called the Boulting Act was then agitating the citizens of New York City and Kingston. This Act, intended to improve British colonial profits and sea power against the Dutch. This processing and baking was to be restricted to the Port of New York and to be forbidden to be undertaken by Kingston and elsewhere in the Hudson Valley and Long Island where wheat was also becoming a significant source of income, while Albany, with its good relations with the fur-trapping Natives of the upper provinces and Canada, had been given a monopoly of the fur trade in the upper part of the Valley.

On December 12, 1688 a body of sixteen Hurley men signed a pledge of allegiance to former Protestant prince William of Orange and his co-Sovereign Queen Mary Stuart for the "good of the country and the Protestant religion." Kingston had already gone on record publicly and orally by proclaiming the ascension to the throne by William and Mary.

Jacob Leisler of New York City had been keeping a sharp eye on the changes taking place in New York as the seventeenth century neared its end. When word of the Glorious Revolution of 1688-89 reached him Leisler stepped forward as a militia captain who scented serious trouble brewing behind all that was happening.

Jacob Leisler, son of a German Calvinist pastor, had immigrated as a youth to New York, married a rich widow, and had done well as a merchant. He came to be a close friend of such New York Dutch-descended upper class people as the Van Cortlands, the Bayards and the Lockermans. Upon the success of the Glorious Revolution Leisler took possession as a militia officer of New York's Fort James, to ensure the city's continued allegiance as he said to William and Mary and the protection of Protestantism.

During Leisler's tenure, another source of fear and doubt, besides the Boulting Act, agitated the upper part of the province bordering French and Catholic Canada as the French allies, the powerful Iroquois Confederacy of five nations (later on six), had been rumored to be hatching a plot to invade the province in the interests of both the Papacy and the French fur trade. The rumor was shown to have some basis in fact, when late in 1690 the Iroquois burst into the ill-defended Mohawk Valley white settlement of Schenectady and massacred many of its inhabitants and carried others away as captives. Leisler organized a counter-expedition aimed at the French stronghold of Quebec in which Kingston militiamen and supplies were employed—the campaign, under the command of General Winthrop of Dominion-member Connecticut and Leisler's son-in-law Jacob Milbourne, was a complete failure. This dismal event was soon to be cited among other anti-Leisler and Milbourne charges of high treason.

Leisler siding against his rich fellow New York merchants and suspecting a "hellish plot" to increase Catholic strength in the Province, favored the abolition of the Boulting Act which was causing such losses to Kingston. Under Leisler's tenure as self-appointed Lieutenant Governor the hated New York merchant favoring Boulting Act was revoked by the Assembly created by the Duke's Laws only to be restored later on following the downfall of Leisler.

After newly-appointed Governor Henry Sloughter finally arrived belatedly from London as the legitimate Governor of New York, the weak Sloughter, under the thumbs of the City's anti-Leisler merchants, caused Leisler to be tried, convicted and sentenced to death by hanging, together with his son-in-law Jacob Milbourne and other adherents to changing the Boulting Act (who were later pardoned). The ancient and barbarous punishments for high treason were said to have been invoked, among them quartering while alive, culminating in burying the mangled remains in unsanctified ground to prevent the victim's soul from ever entering Heaven.

Though the act soon came back into force, the British Parliament found the sentence of Leisler and Milbourne on a high treason charge invalid and ordered their property, which had been confiscated under a Bill of Attainder, to be turned over to their heirs.

William Andros had been governor-general of the newly-created Dominion of New England (which included the Province of New York) before the change of monarchs. He had been tending to his job in Boston when news of the invasion of England by William caused Bostonians to question Andros' right to go on as if the "Glorious Revolution," which set William of Orange and Mary Stuart on the English throne, had never happened. The Bostonians seized Andros and thrust him into prison. In New York Andros' deputy Francis Nicollson aroused the same doubt as to the legality of his position after the passing in England in 1689 of a Bill of Rights which brought to an end the old belief in the divine rights of British monarchs and strenthened those of the Parliament. Violent arguments on the subject of Leisler's behavior had arisen and threatened old friendships and close family relationships in Kingston and elsewhere in New York.

Lieutenant-governor Nicollson had returned to New York, seized and carried off the governmental records and other government materials and had taken them to Boston which he seemed to regard as the Dominion's capital.

Leisler then had declared himself acting governor of New York, as the place was in a tumult and rumors of an impending French invasion from Catholic Canada were being circulated.

A letter from the Privy Council in London arrived ambiguously addressed and Leisler understood this ambiguity to give him the right to become governor in place of Lieutenant-Governor Nicollson.

In Kingston meanwhile the burghers had petitioned the Governor to grant them the right to choose their own local judges. For this the petitioners had been imprisoned in 1684 on a charge of rioting for which the penalties were severe. After they had meekly submitted the charges were dropped and the two leading petitioners were released. But they still quietly clung to their own opinions.

The execution of Leisler and Milborne had done nothing to quell the dissatisfaction of either the Dutch or English or mixed factions of their province. A long period of contention between pro- and anti-Leisler followers continued and kept pro-Leislerians of Kingston agitated as the 17th century moved to its end and the contention continued well into the 18th.

The English rulers after the Glorious Revolution had restored Protestantism to the throne of England, discouraged too the increase of Catholics in the province and cleared the way to an Anglican established church in New York and, it was hoped, in Kingston as well. The people of Kingston resisted vigorously the slightest sign of an English government intention of setting up an established Anglican church in their village. They stood by their own Calvinist Dutch Reformed Church, the only organized church in their village. The Dutch church remained a stalwart symbol of the continuing Dutchness of the place.

Dominie Bloem had reported in 1664 that the Kingston church was "growing right worthily" despite the absence from among its members of enough literate men to furnish a full quota of deacons and elders. Some Dominies following Bloem did not rise to the heights Bloem had reached at the time of the massacre but sought escape from the trials of frontier life in drink or a neglect of their duties. Episodes in the history of the struggles between official determination to impose an American version of the Anglican church on Kingston took place. One was in 1702 under the Governorship of Lord Edward Cornbury.

Shortly after Cornbury began his term as Governor in 1702 he protested against the post-mortem cancellation of the death sentence of Leisler and Milborne and their re-burial in holy ground—this cancelling, Cornbury hinted, had been done under pressure from Leisler relatives whose confiscated property had been returned. In the revision of the original Bill of Attainder against Leisler and Milborne which had been approved by the English Parliament, Cornbury believed the Parliament members had been misinformed into passing the bill and he also believed that revising the bill would do more than anything else to quiet the disturbance caused by pro-Leislerites. Cornbury's letter was confused, but so are many other claims, charges and alleged facts which confirm the lengths to which factional confrontations were leading New Yorkers at this trying time.

Cornbury as Governor brought to the job vigorous efforts at establishing the Anglican Church and so made himself heartily disliked in Kingston. He was successful in parts of the province like much of Long Island where New Englanders had settled. But he met with stubborn resistance in the Dutch part of the Province.

Dutchness was at that time nowhere more determined than in Kingston. There the people of the Dutch Church refused in every imaginable way to accept an Anglican priest to fill the pulpit of their stone Dutch church.

By 1695 a Dominie named John Pieter Nucella had come to serve at the Dutch Reformed Church. Following the Glorious Revolution King William decided to set up a Dutch Chapel Royal at his court in London. To preside over the Chapel he reached over the Atlantic to the no longer stockaded frontier village of Kingston for Dominie Nucella. And in 1704 Nucella abruptly left Kingston to take up his new duties at the Royal Court in London.

It was at this point that Lord Cornbury saw and seized a chance to advance a favorite aim of his—the placing of an Anglican minister in the pulpit of the Dutch Church in Kingston.

What happened when Anglican minister Hepburn arrived in Kingston was recited in October 1704 by the Reverend William Vesey of the Anglican Trinity Church of New York City, "Mr. Nucella being lately called home, left them destitute of any person to officiate among them, which His Excellency (Lord Cornbury) was pleased to take under consideration, and has appointed the Reverend Mr. Hepburn to preach and to read Divine service to them, whereby the English (of Kingston) who never had (an Anglican) minister among them have the benefit of public worship and are in hope of bringing them to a conformity (to the established Anglican church). The Reverend Mr. Hepburn has, at present, small encouragement from the people but chiefly under God, depends on the Kindness and Bounty of His Excellency the Governor of the province."

The Dutch people, however, had also added to their hostility to the English government and their governor a very passionate and even increased devotion to their own church which came under the guidance of the overseas Classis of Amsterdam in the Netherlands. The earlier ministers of the Kingston church had been trained in the Netherlands in the Dutch language, ordained in the Netherlands and their colonial Dominies preached in Dutch and the congregation sang in Dutch (until 1809). Children were taught Dutch in their church school.

Lord Cornbury did his very best as some said to "foist the establishment on Kingston." When he permitted them to have a Precentor to teach school, this olive branch or mere twig did nothing to soften the Dutch Reformed followers. They still refused to attend Hepburn's services and they gave Hepburn as a dwelling place a house he called "too mean for a man of his character (as an Anglican priest)," however well suited to a "dissenting minister." After two years of vain struggle Mr. Hepburn left. The Governor then gave in. He appointed a Dutch Dominie named Henricus Beyl to serve the Kingston church. For two years Beyl served well. Then he left after having been accused of having had improper relations with his servant girl. Later the accusation was withdrawn but Beyl by then had yielded to pressure from above and had become an Anglican priest and passed from the Kingston scene. Beyl was followed by the eminently satisfactory (to Kingston) Dutch Dominie Vas who served the Kingston congregation well until 1758.

During the years after the Cornbury threat had been removed, peace did not reign among the members of the Kingston church nor in the other Dutch Reformed Churches of North America. A new cause for dispute had arisen. This was the Coetus (pronounced Ceetus)-Conferentia controversy.

PART 5

Life in the Colony of Kingston as Oppressed by British Colonial Rule in the 18th Century up till July 4, 1776

1.
18th Century Kingston People Endure British Colonial Rule

After England had seized its final possession of New Netherland in 1674 and a slow creeping tide of attempted Anglicanization moved up the Hudson Valley, the tide lightly buffeted Kingston and Albany beyond. One symbol of this tide was the changing of the great seal of the province from the one used in Dutch days. Then the seal had shown as its centerpiece a rampant beaver which emphasized the hopes of the Dutch West India Company for a high degree of beaver-derived wealth which might rival even that which Spain had extorted from mining the precious metals of their American colonies by the forced labor of the enslaved natives.

The New York State seal when the beaver wealth was high; and the State seal after the beaver was less profitable, and replaced with Native Americans from Edgar A. Werner, *Civil List and Constitutional History of the Colony and State of New York, 1888*

Under English rule, although the English were still active in the fur trade, the beaver was tossed aside and his place on the official seal was taken by colonized Natives kneeling in token of abject submission while presenting a tribute to the English monarch of the time. And more significant changes affected the daily lives of the Kingston people. In the days of Dutch Company power the new medium of exchange to come into use (because of a shortage of standard currency) had been the little beads once used as personal adornments by the Natives and made from parts of seashells and called sewant; when strung on cords for convenience in counting them for use as currency in trading they were known as wampum. About 1701, wampum had diminished for use as currency in Kingston commercial transactions and was often replaced by pounds, shillings and pence, when available. Vanished was Hendrick "sewant reyger" or stringer and no one took his place. The beaver, deposed from his place on the provincial seal, began also to make his slow exit as a measure of value. From the satellite farm settlements of Hurley and Marbletown along the rich dark-soiled flatlands of the Esopus valley (now that the Native threat was ended) reached by newly built roads, wagon loads of wheat, oats, rye and other European grains, as well as millstones fashioned of Shawangunk (pronounced Shongum) grit, continued to make their way to Kingston merchants. Shingles, barrel staves, headings and hoops and other forest products made by up country farmers when other work was slack also moved in, following the roads in creaky and bumpy wagons to the stone houses now freed from their stockade walls but in which the merchants still lived with their families, journeymen, slaves and apprentices, and did business both wholesale and retail, especially in wheat and other grains as well as furs. From there the products not consumed locally made their way to the Rondout Landing and thence down the Hudson to New York with some to be shipped from there to England and the West Indies.

In the years following the ascent of the Catholic Duke of York to the English throne as James II, the arrival of invading Protestant William of Orange and Mary to succeed him, then on the death of childless Dutch William and English Mary Stuart the reign of Queen Anne which extended to 1712, Kingston people had reason again to be confused as to the changing loyalties expected of them by their rulers. Except of course for some like ambitious colonist Thomas Chambers who until his death in 1694 rode the rising and falling political waters to good effect for himself.

Kingston people from the days of the Company rule and then pre-English New Netherland had not been accustomed to much self government, but they accepted from the Duke of York such English innovations as trial by jury. Nevertheless they clung through the eighteenth century onto their Dutchness of Company days in language and many little long familiar customs. Kingston was increasing in population and in the number of satellite back country farms from which its merchants might draw farm and forest products for sale at a reasonable profit for mere colonials. By 1700 the stockade had deteriorated and the remnants were taken down, as the Native American threat lessened, to the encouragement of builders of houses and barns and cultivators of new fields now well outside of the old stockade bounds.

The nearing completion of the solid-built stone Dutch Reformed Church building reported by the Labadists in 1679 had shown that Kingston people were rallying from the trauma and loss of income brought on by the two Esopus Wars and the dreadful massacre and were advancing toward the goal of secure prosperity envisaged by their first colonists of the 1650s. There are traces in the official records that show that the people of Kingston were still upset by the Esopus wars. For example, when an occasional man or woman convicted of using such derogatory terms as "blood sucker" to characterize a schepen to his face might explain that they had used the term in a spell of dejection caused by lingering effects of the massacre in the stockade or the fear-ridden days of the terrible clashes with Natives. But many obstacles lay ahead before the goal of secure prosperity could come near realization. For one thing those who used slaves profitably to till their fields or do household drudgery may have been shown that slavery was a corroding moral evil harmful in the long run to the master as well as to the slave. The masters occasionally freed a favored slave in their wills but this did not prevent Kingston slaveholders from fearing a slave uprising while the slaves continued to dream through the 1700's of freedom from bondage if only they might find a chink in the armor of their masters.The existence of this dream stimulated masters seeking to find ever more repressive means of keeping the blacks firmly enslaved beyond any hope of freedom by means of a violent uprising.

In 1741, fear of a slave revolt panicked the whites of the City of New York and this fear made its way up the Hudson to terrorize Kingston people. There an enlarged night watch roamed the streets and stricter control over the movements of blacks was enforced. Uneasiness on the part of whites continued to increase until it became obvious that the local uprising they feared had no immediate basis in fact. But during these same years and later, to add to whites' uneasiness, rumors of impending attacks by the French of Canada and their Iroquois allies seemed to make Kingston's growing prosperity seem less secure. That was why in 1759 Royal Governor James de Lancey directed the Kingston trustees to build a defensive blockhouse 32 by 24 feet with two fireplaces and other necessities. De Lancey also had directed the trustees to arrange for the quartering when required of His Majesty's soldiers among Kingston householders, and to provide a hospital for those soldiers who might be wounded or ill. The provincial Assembly authorized the raising of several thousand troops in the Province of New York and when that seemed not sufficient the Assembly drafted militiamen from Kingston as well as other places. And so some Kingston men saw service in the wars which had their causes in the national dynastic and commercial rivalries of European powers which had or hoped for profitable colonial outposts in America. Before these wars ended in 1763, some settlers in Kingston's back country were killed or others watched their houses and barns burned by raiders but the Village remained intact and largely untouched by the border struggle. Some Kingston militiamen however were detailed to patrol the back country. They returned with tales of mountains interspersed by valleys in which a rough sort of farming was managed by tenants of absentee landlords, but in whose clear and rushing brooks trout abounded, with here and there a squatter's cabin whose rough inhabitants lived in a state of primitive yet enjoyable independence too far away from settlements to be often troubled by landowners. In Kingston these were nervous times, yet an occasional Kingston man, often an escaped slave, took off to find a cherished freedom in the lonely backwoods. Mink Hollow in Woodstock was named, oldtime whites believed, for one of these runaway slaves from Kingston.

2.
Slavery for Some and Prosperity for Others

DURING SLIGHTLY MORE THAN A CENTURY OF SERVING AS A COLONY OF Britain, Kingston grew in population and prosperity in spite of existing under a system called Colonialism under which a colony was planned to be so managed as to bring a profit to the mother country even if the white colonists as well as the remaining native inhabitants suffered in the process.

Lord Edward Cornbury, a cousin of Queen Anne, filling the post of Governor of the Province of New York, beginning in 1702, had something to say about the relevance of monopolistic restrictions like those of the Boulting Act. In 1705, Governor Cornbury wrote in a report to London officials that of the colonies he managed, including New York, "all these colonies, which are but twigs belonging to the main tree (England) ought to be kept entirely dependent upon and subservient to England," to prevent their people from trying to detract from England's dominance in trading, in transportation on the seas and in manufacturing. All of which they did if they could because his Lordship stated, "they are not very fond of submitting to English Government."

Cornbury has been presented by many historians as having been in the habit of appearing in public in New York dressed as a woman and explaining that he did this in order to emphasize that he represented his cousin Queen Anne in the Province of New York. Recent histories of the period have attributed charges of Cornbury's transvestitude more likely to have been been the attempts by political antagonists to denigrate him. But in his likening of Colonial places like Kingston to little twigs on a great imperialistic tree of England, he made sense at a time when the white people who were being colonized as the Natives had also been were beginning to arrive at the eventual determination of 1776 to embark on the great adventure of independence and struggle to success in a much more glorious and signifigant revolution than that of 1688-89.

Slavery which had been a good source of profit to the Dutch West India Company and Kingston farmers and traders continued to flourish among Kingston whites under English rule. Owners of large plantations had ten or more slaves, small farmers two or three; these worked as either field or domestic hands or at skills which they had been taught by way of increasing their value to their owners.

In 1706 the New York Provincial Assembly passed an act entitled, An Act to Encourage the Baptism of Negro, Indian and Mulatto Slaves. The Act stated that "a Groundless opinion . . . hath spread itself in this Colony that by the Baptising of such Negro, Indian or mulatto slaves they would become free and ought to be sett at liberty." The act further provided that "all and every Negro, Indian, Mulatto and Mestee Bastard Child & Children who is, are , and shall be born of any Negro, Indian, Mulatto or Mestee [a variant of Mestizo], shall follow ye State and Condition of the Mother & be esteemed reputed taken & adjudged a Slave & Slaves to all intents & purposes whatsoever." And finally the Act provided that "no slave whatsoever in this Colony shall at any time be admitted as a witness for, or against, any Freeman, in any Case matter or Cause, Civil or Criminal whatsoever."

In the Province of New York as the number of slaves increased so too did a fear of uprisings of slaves who had a natural dislike of their lowly station in colonial life.

In Kingston in 1732 a shocking episode rising out of the burning alive, according to law, of a slave on a charge of arson caused an annoying problem to the County Board of Magistrates. This episode was recorded in 1930 from contemporary sources by a meticulous student of Kingston history, Chaplain R. R. Hoes (pronounced Hoose) of the United States Navy and son of a dominie of the Dutch Church, in his *The Old Court Houses of Ulster County, New York.* The Provincial Assembly had passed an act dealing with the building of a new courthouse and jail. The act also contained a report of an incident "of startling and sensational character—one it is to be feared, in no way creditable to the county,"[217] wrote the historian-chaplain.

"And whereas," reads the act, "in the year one thousand seven hundred and thirty, a negro called Jack being convicted of burning a barne and Barrack with wheat in the said County was Condemned to be burnt for the same, but the Justices not being able to procure an Executioner to performe the sentence at the rate Limited in an act entitled An Act For the More Effectual Punishment, for the Conspiracy and Insurrection of Negroes and other slaves, for the better Regulating them.... were obliged not only to hire one at a much greater price but likewise to pay the price so agreed upon for and the same being as yet not paid . . ." The Act authorized the supervisors at their next monthly meeting be added to that to be raised by money to be raised by a levy "such sum of money as has been actually payd by the said Justices in and about the execution of the Said Negroe. . . ."

It was said to be believed by blacks that death by burning was especially to be dreaded because it destroyed the soul as well as the body an so kept the soul from any hope of ever returning to Africa.

Chaplain Hoes gives details of Jack's execution by Sheriff Johannnis Low's slave named London at Marbletown where Jack had confessed to the crime of arson and where his execution was carried out after his conviction by the Kingston court. Hoes relies here on a manuscript note by historian Jonathan W. Hasbrouck which may rely in part on traditional sources, but no documenting material as far as is known. But we are not clear from the records Chaplain Hoes was able to find, or any others, whether the twenty shilling fee which loomed so large in the case of Jack was paid to London, the actual executioner, or as is more likely to his owner, the sheriff, who had a right under law to the earnings of his slave—yet life went on and became less frontier-colored as some vestiges of Dutch West India Company-imposed slavery ceased to be part of Kingston daily life.

The middle years of the eighteenth century were often lived under a cloud caused by apprehension resulting from activity of the French and their Iroquois allies as well as what their own slaves were up to. Years later, Professor Myers-Williams of SUNY New Paltz in his thoroughly documented book, *A Long Hammering*, a penetrating view of the history of Afro-Americans in the Hudson Valley (not including Kingston) in the days of slavery and beyond, tells of the final attempt at an uprising of slaves in 1775, on the eve of the American Revolution as reported in a New York City newspaper and no where else.

As the agitation toward what was about to become the Revolutionary War against Great Britain grew ever hotter, some African-Americans held in slavery felt a similar agitation of their own against still being kept enslaved. In and around Kingston some slaves shared the rebellious spirit of their masters and behaved in ways that showed an unwillingness to obey orders and submit to oppression as slaves. Among them were two men known as Jack and Joe.

According to a dispatch credited to the New York City *Weekly Mercury* of March 6, 1775, cited by the SUNY professor, Jack and Joe were overheard by their masters while planning the details of a slave uprising in Ulster County, by organizing bands of slaves who were to set fire to the Kingston village's houses and kill the fleeing inhabitants. For their part in the plot the two black men were hanged. The firing of a good deal of Kingston, said to have been by accident, happened the next year. And then the burning of the whole village as an act of war by the British army took place on October 16, 1777. It was this third fire that gave Kingston a permanent place in the history of the United States—the other two fires have been largely forgotten.

Life in the early years of British Colonial Kingston also had many episodes of panic caused by fears of French or black hints of attack. And every now and then militia troops were alerted for protection against French and Indians to the north, and this as well as fears of black uprisings helped keep rumor-plagued Kingston people (especially those who could not read and so were more dependent on rumors) from feeling that they were living safe and unthreatened lives.

In 1933 Kingston lawyer Augustus H. Van Buren, author of *Ulster County under the Dominion of the Dutch* looked back and wrote an informal brief on slavery in the city. He brought together much information drawn from old laws and records, and official Dutch letters all of which tended to make a case for a reluctance at first on the part of the Dutch colonists of Esopus to accept the institution of slavery which was at the same time not imposed in the Netherlands itself by the Dutch. That company, Van Buren argued, became concerned in 1625 that their colony of New Netherland could not meet the competition of other Dutch, Spanish and Portuguese colonies in the New World unless it had "servants" in the form of slaves. Lawyer Van Buren tells of attempts made in Dutch Company days to encourage the conversion of black slaves and Natives to Christianity, and to a belief by some, as hinted at in a law, that baptism might cause the legal freedom of a slave.

Nowhere does Van Buren in his otherwise thorough brief ever mention the attempts at slave uprisings, or fatal conflicts between white masters and black slaves. He does tell of manuscripts or recorded lists of the names of many Kingston slaves borrowed from the Bible and the Roman and Greek classic literature. In contrast to what Chaplain Hoes had been turning up about slavery time in Kingston, the Van Buren brief presents slavery as a much milder part of colonial life in which the search for profit, first by the Company and then by the British colonists was a predominating factor in earning many Kingston livings, and causing Kingston doubts and fears as well.

The history of slave-holding days in Kingston awaits careful study. Also, the fears of Monster Brant as planning murderous raids on Kingston do not have any basis in fact. That Brant conducted raids during Revolutionary times on other places is true but not on Kingston.

3.
Life in 18th Century Kingston Among White Colonists

THE MERCHANTS WHO FORMED THE BULK OF AN UPPER CLASS NOW MORE often kept their books in English, although often with a decided Dutch accent, and more local people made their wills in English, while a few owned popular English books like Milton's *Paradise Lost* and Addison's *Spectator.* Young men and women increasingly followed English fashions in dress if they belonged to the more prosperous merchant or plantation class. Well established families kept in their big brass-clasped illustrated Dutch language Bibles careful and reverent records of family births, deaths and marriages, some in Dutch, others more recent in English.

Relics like these of the Dutch past gave a more mature color to the village. People from Kingston's growing satellite towns and lonely farms at the edge of the unbroken forest came to enjoy social pleasures with friends in their homes or in the village's numerous jolly taverns. The annual or semi-annual Netherlands Festival called kermis (and later in Kingston called a kirmess), combining market fairs with jollity while leaving slight footprints in old Kingston records, have their place in Kingston's oral history and would be revived in the 1890s in a way that then aroused great interest.

Recalled in the nineteenth century when the rough gangs of New York City were being heard of in Kingston were the gangs of young men who sometimes roused Kingston sleepers with their shouts and brawling. These were the youths and apprentices of the Village. Two gangs of the 1700s, the Kinderhookers and the Wolverhookers, one named because its members lived as apprentices in the homes of their masters in the part of the village rich in children. The other because its apprentices to various trades lived on the Village's edge where the howling of wolves living in the forests beyond the fields across the Brabant (creekside fields) might be heard by night.

When County courts were in session the village hummed with life; then litigants and witnesses came to town and there many lawyers practiced. The court of piepowder was ready to settle small disputes arising on market days and was given its name (derived from the French "pied" and "poudre") because it had jurisdiction only over cases arising while the dust of the market was still fresh on participants' feet. In the solid stone houses of the merchants in which they "traded and trafficked" still lived their apprentices and journeymen, with slaves housed in their dank cellars. Now and then a showman appeared outside a tavern with a dancing bear or some other source of entertainment, perhaps a human juggler. The taverns or inns had each a "long room" usually on the second floor where music of violins often played by talented enslaved black men furnished music for dancing. In the taverns men who had nothing better to do played such board games as chess or backgammon.

On the streets piglets sometimes followed their mothers as they searched for an occasional tidbit in the litter of the roadways, chickens cackled and ducks quacked from puddles or ponds. Men selling freshly caught shad or herring or ready to sharpen knives by their characteristic street cries made their presence felt and the hubbub of a busy village rose in the air given urgency now and then by the insults hurled at each other by the rude words reported in the village court records when such brawls came to the attention of the village magistrates. On Sundays the village was likely to be still, for ordinances of the court prevented all unseemly activities and noise, especially while the sermon was being preached (although interruption of the Sunday calm could not be prevented from farm animals).

To support all this the steady flow of wheat, rye and other grains continued to flow in season on weekdays through the place on their bumpy way to the safe harbor of Rondout at the Kingston Landing or Strand on the Rondout Kill close to the Hudson and from there down the big river aboard sloops, schooners or barges to New York. And afterward perhaps to be moved on to Europe, other British colonies or the British West Indies. At the outermost fringe of Kingston's satellites, trees were felled by brawny axemen to be processed by hand or in water powered mills into products such as white pine house siding, shingles, joists, oaken ships' timbers, barrel staves, hoops and headings, plus ground bluestone, destined to follow the same path to market as the grain. Fresh shad were consumed locally or shipped downriver in season. Many barrels of salt fish also went downstream, plus fruit, nuts and passenger pigeons shot or netted on the Ponckhockie Heights around the base of the Vleit Berg, and much else followed the same convenient River route to a profitable market. Every time these products were handled by the Kingston people, a certain modest amount of profit stuck to Kingston hands in spite of the village's twig-like status on the English colonial tree.

Captain Chambers in 1652 had chosen well the place where the streams and valleys meet at the Hudson River to serve agriculture. Commerce was also paying off, even though the clinging of many of the Esopus Dutch inhabitants to the ways of their grandparents gave them a conservatism that sometimes blocked advance into the new American age that was taking shape step by step in the American colonies of the royal Georges on their thrones across the broad and often stormy Atlantic.

The traders of the village maintained large households in which children, unmarried relatives, and employees shared space with slaves—until most slavery ended by law on July 4, 1828—with slaves being housed in the gloomy cellars and apprentices sleeping in attics. There were few neighborhoods in 18th century Kingston where only poor people lived by themselves. On the fringes of the village, however, occasional misfits of mixed ancestry lived as outcasts in makeshift structures of their own making. These outcasts, including an occasional suicide, were denied burial in sanctified ground and were without much ceremony laid to rest beyond the village bounds. Slaves were buried in cemeteries of their own. One of these cemeteries, as Kingston expanded, gave way to a lumberyard on the extreme edge of Academy Park on Pine Street. An area of misfits on the upper edge of Jacob's Gat, now known as Jacob's Valley, yielded to urban growth as the village expanded about 1850.

Such workers as tailors and dressmakers measured and fitted in the homes of their customers. Door to door cobblers were relied upon to do their work at the same houses in the years before they might set up their shops. There were few shops—when the court was in session people from all over Ulster County came to Kingston by boat, on foot, on horseback or in wagons, and the taverns did a brisk business. Lawyers thrived trying cases involving boundaries of farms and debts owed. Natives still were allowed into the village to peddle corn, deer skins, beans, or craft objects they had made.

Yet Kingston on what came to be called "the poor man's bank of the Hudson" had its relationship with the "rich man's" or "manorial" bank less than two miles or so across the great Hudson where it narrowed at the former Indian Crossing at the meeting of Native trails. In winter after the river froze to ice strong enough to bear the weight of a man and a horse, the Hudson was more quickly crossed and it became possible for a man to walk or skate across in what seemed almost no time at all compared with that taken by horsepowered ferries bearing passengers across in the summer.

By midwinter horse drawn sleighs whisked Kingston people across the Hudson's ice at the old Indian Crossing with a merry jingling of sleighbells.

Gilbert Livingston, a younger son of the first lord of the huge east bank Livingston manor, married Kingston's Cornelia Beekman, daughter of William Beekman, who owned a huge amount of Ulster County land. He and his wife had 14 children, as Gilbert functioned as Ulster County Clerk while his cousin Henry filled the same office in Dutchess County on the manorial side of the Hudson. And in the absence of a church on the east bank, east bank babies were carried across the Hudson to be baptized at the Dutch church in Kingston where marriages of east bank people had been solemnized.

Judge Livingston of Clermont's 13,000 acres, (separated from the Livingston manor of 165,000 acres, with Clermont's land known as the Lower Manor), built a road opposite Clermont at what is now Saugerties, to lead to his settlement at Woodstock, first known as Livingston's Mill (at which logs from the cleared lands were turned into usable timber). Judge Livingston laid out farms for tenant farmers at Woodstock, with strict leases lasting for three lives, modeled on those on the manorial side where German or High Dutch people were the tenant farmers tilling the land, in contrast to the Low Dutch farmers on the west bank who came from the coastal Netherlands.

The Judge, who had heartily favored the Revolution, died and after that his west bank land holdings were divided among his thirteen children in tracts of around thirty thousand acres each after which, the Judge hoped, his progeny might live in a somewhat manorial fashion.

Following the burning of Kingston by the British in 1777 Chancellor Livingston (son of the Judge) gave to each owner of a Kingston house which had been burned a tract of 50 acres each located in his Hardenbergh Patent lands in the pleasant countryside northwest of Margaretville. (In gratitude the Kingston people named the Chancellor's gift New Kingston.) He also built a mill for grinding limestone which was coming into use as an agricultural amendment on the edge of the Kingston Commons near Saugerties for the use of his tenants and others. And he presented his Woodstock tenants with a ram from the royal flock at Rambouillet in France (in order to improve the breed of local sheep). He had written a book titled "An Essay on Sheep."

In the spring of 1777 Kingston ceased being merely a provincial village of New York when the sophisticated framers of the new State government gathered in Kingston to write the Constitution of New York State and set up the machinery of its government, amid the high hopes of the village of Kingston to become the permanent capital of the State. John Jay, Chancellor R. R. Livingston, Pierre Van Cortlandt, and General George Clinton were chosen as the first top officials of the state.

That fall, when the village was burned by the British, it was briefly abandoned, and then rebuilt, but Kingston's hopes of being the national or state capital were dashed.

In 1804, upon his return to Kingston after a period serving as our distinguished minister to France, the Chancellor was given a rousing welcome, like a favorite son, by the people of Kingston and after a parade through the streets of the village was the guest at a sumptious banquet of Kingstonians at which he was highly honored in speeches and toasts.

Chancellor Livingston died in 1813 at Clermont, and Kingston mourned the loss of their generous neighbor who had given them so much.

4.
The Huguenot Touch

Huguenot refugees had arrived in Kingston late in the 17th century because of religious persecution in France. These refugees were trickling into many parts of the world including America. In 1675 the first of these Calvinist Protestants found his way to Kingston and many others followed. While many of the other earliest immigrants to New Netherland had been misfits of various sorts, the Huguenots were often adaptable and capable people who took life seriously and were likely to do well in places like Kingston, and get along well with the Dutch. As late as the 1880's it was recalled that earlier in that century it was customary at the funeral of a person of an old Kingston family for the sexton to step forward at the end of the burial ceremony and thank those attending. He began with the words of greeting, "Vreind en Meesieur" in mixed Dutch and French in token of the successful mingling of the two ethnic groups in Kingston.

A group of Huguenots which came to Kingston and Hurley obtained a grant including much fertile lowland similar to that at Kingston but higher up the Wallkill Valley. They named the place New Paltz in commemoration of a town in the Rhineland where they had taken refuge for years before coming to America.

It was not uncommon for the Huguenots who were very family oriented to keep interesting family records or histories. In some cases these records were simple family genealogies and in others they contained much material preserving details of life as once lived in their communities. Such details of Kingston life sometimes cannot be found anywhere else. The family records contain also hints of people's beliefs of their time and place, and sometimes clues to their intimate religious convictions as well as details of floods, fires and the appearance of such natural phenomena as earthquakes and insects or floods destructive to crops.

The very informative Abraham Hasbrouck family record of life in Kingston was begun shortly after the marriage of the grandson and namesake of the immigrant

Abraham Hasbrouck on the 5th of January, 1738. The records' first keeper was the Colonel Hasbrouck who would tangle with rigid Dominie Mancius of the Kingston Dutch Church in 1758 and who would take Ann Moore's part in her struggle with the Dominie (as will be seen in the next chapter). Both the missionary activity in Kingston of Ann Moore and the account of the final days of Catherine Hasbrouck would happen as the religious revival known as the Great Awakening was stirring minds and emotions in New England under the influence of Jonathan Edwards, and in New York under that of Dutch Reformed preachers Theodore Freylinghusen and Gilbert Tennant.

After the Colonel's death the Record was kept by Abraham's descendants until well into the nineteenth century. Hasbrouck's account of his daughter Catherine's death apparently owes much to the atmosphere of the coming Great Awakening.

A few pages into the records, Hasbrouck gives this touching account of his daughter's deathbed scene of a sort once popular among deeply religious people, but rarely found today in a world of changing religious tastes.

After a detailed account of the symptoms of the "measles distemper" which had affected his daughter, Hasbrouck wrote, "her words or short account thereof I shall write down in this book; here below. She was very beautiful and comely counted by all persons; she was very tall for her age; and well proportioned and accordingly; had a high breast & fine waist, a fair skin with a blooming colour; a great deal of hair of a brown colour, a handsome full round face or visage, dark blue eyes, looked almost a light-brown. She was ingenious in learning, very good natured with a great deal of agreeableness. She was an obedient child to her parents; very charitable and meek hearted to those in need. In a word, she was adorned with a great many good qualities which can't all be mentioned here."

Hasbrouck continues with "A true relation or short account of the last words of my daughter Catherine Hasbrouck. She spake a few minutes before her death. I write it down here that I might call her dying words to mind all the days of my life, that my children and children's children may read this after my decease, how she took her leave of us and the world and may be taken for a truth. I shall use her own words as she spake as follows: —the fifth day of December 1747, it seemed as if she had some more ease than she had for some days before. The Doctor Hans Kierstede came about 7 o'clock and she expired about 9 o'clock. He was in hope, then, that with God's blessing of her recovery. But about 8 of the clock she grew much worse as it appeared. Her mother sitting upon the bedside, she said to her mother or asked her, 'what noise there was in the house?' The mother replyed that there was none and bid her to lay herself easy down, as she did. But a little after she asked her mother the same question—her mother answered as before and she lay a little while again. Then she said 'Mammy I hear and do but hearken for I hear the sweetest noise I have ever heard, all the days of my life,' though there was nothing heard by us in the room. But we believed by the marks she gave, that she had heard anthems and singing of the Blessed Angels who were hovering over or about her—So it seems she had some small glimpses of that glorious estate she was about to inherit which was prepared for her from Eternity. She then said her prayers aloud and ended her prayers in these words." (Here she repeated the Lord's Prayer.) "And then I and she kissed one another said 'Good-nighty, Daddy, good nighty Mammy, good nighty Uncle Severyn, (and others for there were many in the room) . . . Then she said 'Daddy, give me some wine. I answered her, 'I will for I believe this will be the last wine I shall give you and that you shall drink in this world; but the next shall be of the New Wine in the Kingdom of Heaven. . . . She then drew herself down with her head on the pillow and so expired and resigned her soul to Almighty God who gave it."

Throughout the Record, until Colonel Hasbrouck ceased to keep it, were contained careful descriptions of the physical appearance of many relatives together with estimates of their characters, sometimes conventional but at other times showing sharp observation. In contrast to the accounts of births, marriages and deaths were businesslike entries very relevant in a society in which the economy was based on the buying and selling or "trading and trafficking" as Hasbrouck puts it, in productions of the field, Hudson River and forest. In the same book of records appear brief notes of times when unusual weather flooded out crops on the Esopus-side fields, froze fruit blossoms, or dried up crops; the appearance of comets and occasional earthquakes are mentioned without the moralizing that we might have expected at the time.

In the Hasbrouck Record we have materials for forming a picture of the Huguenot immigrants in Kingston unsurpassed by any similar clue to the daily lives of other immigrants who turned up in early Kingston. It deals with the thoughts and activities of only the middle and upper class of Kingston's immigrants, their religious beliefs and suggest how these helped shape Kingston.

A revealing entry is that concerning the unfortunate member of the Hasbrouck family of whom we are told only that he died while confined in the Kingston debtors' prison. While we sympathize and wonder by what route this member of a fortunate and prosperous family should have reached so ignominious an end—as ignominious as that of an occasional member of the lower class of the same society. We are helped to realize that Kingston society of the time was not always so thoroughly organized into classes as we might have suspected.

5.
Ann Moore, Quaker Missionary
1758

IN 1758 ANN MOORE, A QUAKER PREACHER FROM THE CITY OF NEW YORK arrived in Kingston on a blustery winter day and insisted on presenting the Quaker point of view, and succeeded in that over many obstacles. And so she supplied evidence that the old devotion to Dutchness of the Village was showing signs of crumbling and new ways of understanding religion were emerging.

Quakers, since their arrival in the New World in the 1630s, had usually been given a hard reception except in Pennsylvania. In New England Quakers had been savagely persecuted. In New Amsterdam they were permitted and once the British were in control had been given grudging tolerance. But in Kingston the Dutch Reformed Church had a monopoly of acceptance in religious matters (for one thing, it was the only organized church in the village).

In the southern part of Ulster County small groups of farming Quakers had even established themselves and set up their plain unsteepled meeting houses.

Throughout southern Ulster County Ms. Moore felt the benefits of the growing acceptance even of Quakers, whose men would not serve in the military forces or take oaths on the Bible when giving testimony in court. She and the little group of fellow Quakers who accompanied her were well received in New Paltz and other southern Ulster towns and were encouraged to proceed on horseback through the bitter January snow and cold to the Village Ms. Moore knew as Esopus. On arriving, Ms. Moore asked the sheriff if she might use the courthouse (the usual place for such meetings as the one she had in mind) and the sheriff gave permission. But soon a storm broke loose.

After the "hour was appointed and the people acquainted therewith," Ms. Moore wrote in her journal, "the priest and the deacons (of the Dutch church) hearing thereof, were offended, and caused the sheriff to come and tell us, we must not have it, for which he (the sheriff) expressed his sorrow, and strove to get a private room; but all being bribed by the priest (Dominie Mancius), made some excuse. . . . But God who loves man's welfare better than doth man himself, moved on the minds of several young men, who were so sorry to think we were like to go away without having a meeting, and they sent one who had a sword by his side to tell us there were several sober young men of the town, and several soldiers who would be very glad to have us." The young men suggested the use of the newly re-built market house "as that could not harm any body."

Lt. Colonel Abraham "Horsebrook" (Hasbrouck) of the militia was applied to for help and "he seemed surprised to find that any should be against our having the courthouse . . . unless they were bigots." The Colonel offered the use of his own barn instead, and there the meeting was held with a large and attentive audience including the sheriff and the Colonel himself.

The Moore incident illustrates a change that was taking place in Kingston. The Village still had enough of the conservative spirit of its Company days to make it stand out among other Hudson Valley places with populations of less Dutch flavor, where the Dutch church reigned almost supreme. But young people and some of the influence of people like Colonel Hasbrouck and the sheriff were showing a kind of open-mindedness that was growing.

6.
1747-1772:
"Coetus and Conferentia"

VICTORY OVER LORD CORNBURY AND MR. HEPBURN AND CONTINUING submission of the few remaining Esopus Natives which followed the ending of the Esopus Wars in 1659 did not mean that Kingston people could relax and enjoy in peace the bountiful products of the fertile lowlands they had wrested from their Native predecessors. To the north the Catholic French of Canada and their partners in the fur business, the Iroquois Natives, long remained a threatening presence as the traditional enemy of Britain. Kingston was not too far from the frontier where a series of armed confrontations were taking place between the British and their Native allies and the French. These confrontations were caused by squabbles resulting from the struggling of the occupants of European thrones, of religious hostilities and disputes over colonial spoils such as those of New York.

Kingston men for long years into the future would be drawn into these British-French-Indian military actions as soldiers or as rangers along the long, weary frontier which separated French Catholic Canada and Protestant British America. Memories of the Schenectady massacre of 1690 (where Iroquois had massacred 65 inhabitants and carried off many others before burning the settlement) were kept alive and every even slight rumor of impending Iroquois or French threats caused shivers to run down Kingston spines. Kingstonians also long remembered the horrors of their own massacre of 1663.

During these years the division of loyalties that prevailed in many parts of the Province when English rule was new and Leisler was at his height of attempted power, another sort of loyalty was gaining strength or losing strength as new rumors or new personalities fanned the flames. In the Dutch-speaking parts of the Province of New York this was what was known as the Coetus (pronounced "seetus") Conferentia controversy. The question at stake was this: should American ministers of the Dutch Reformed Church be trained, ordained, and licensed by the Classis of far away old Amsterdam or should all this be done in America?

The church was more than the center for the religious life of the people of Dutch background. It was a dominating force despite Kingston's relations with the "manorial bank" while keeping a fairly strong Church-maintained Dutch culture under English rule. Its congregations still sang their psalms in Dutch, listened to Dutch sermons and approved when their dominie taught their children in Dutch or in the absence of the dominie when the vorleezer read the sermons and did the teaching in Dutch. There was no common school system until well into the 1700s. Schooling while regarded as needed in order to enable Kingstonians to read the Dutch Protestant Bible and avoid being cheated in trading was neither regular nor thorough and it was most often in Dutch until after the 1700s were half gone. It was over the question of whether their church and village should remain as a center of Dutch culture under the influence of the Mother Dutch Reformed Church in The Netherlands or become an American organization that, between 1747 and 1772, turmoil split the churches of Dutch New York into the two groups, the Coetus people and the Conferentia people. The Coetus people believed that an American board should control the American churches. Kingston became a notable battleground of the conflict.

Sermon after sermon was preached and vocabularies were ransacked to their bottoms by battlers for each side; Kingston dominie, the learned Dr. Meyer, who succeeded Beys, was unable to make up his mind on which side he stood. A group of his congregants, with Lt. Colonel Abraham Hasbrouck in command, took the dominie to court in a desperate effort to help him decide. The court ordered tendered to the dominie the oath of allegiance to King George of England which included a renunciation of "all dominion or authority ecclesiastical or spiritual" to any foreign prince or potentate. This renunciation was originally aimed at the Pope but was now interpreted also as including the home church in Amsterdam. Reluctantly, Dr. Meyer obeyed the court and signed and so put himself on the side of the Coetus party; soon by marrying Col. Hasbrouck's Coetus-minded daughter he brought the conflict to a boil. A century later, Kingston's respected historian Marius Schoonmaker, captured the passions of the time by quoting the words of a member of Meyer's flock in which Col. Hasbrouck was characterized as aspiring to become a pope holding a kind of papal power over the dominie. Into this confusion a proposed arbitrator intruded in the person of a dominie from across the Hudson. He too was tendered the oath of allegiance but when he refused to sign was unceremoniously seized and thrust in jail until more sensible heads brought about his release after the hopeful arbitrator yielded to pressure and signed.

Soon on an otherwise normal Sunday morning the Conferentia believers of the Dutch church congregation turned up in their pews with clubs in their hands and a determination in their hearts to compel Dr. Meyer to resign his post. Faced with the threat of force Meyer descended from the pulpit with an appropriate text from the Bible on his lips to signify his resignation. After that for seven years Meyer conducted services and performed baptisms and marriages in the homes of his congregants while the Classis of Amsterdam stubbornly refused to recognize his dismissal or to appoint a successor. Meanwhile the church stood empty.

It was not until 1772, a quarter of a century after the Coetus-Conferentia struggle began that peace returned to battle-scarred Kingston after it had been agreed that the Dutch Reformed churches in America might train, ordain and appoint their own ministers.

It is obvious today that during the years of the Coetus-Conferentia struggle the people of Kingston as well as those elsewhere in the Province were undergoing a process of Americanization which would help make possible their enthusiastic joining of the rebel side in the American Revolution which lay ahead.

By the 1770s the schism that had rent the Dutch church in America had been settled. The church in Kingston was still the only one in the village. Yet a willingness to consider other denominations was beginning to be noticeable even while many of the Dutch living there were clinging to their culture with all their strength. This growth toward tolerance became evident when Ann Moore brought her devotion to Quakerism to Kingston and there found a divided reception, but a willingness on the part of many people to be informed about views which differed from theirs.

In spite of these changes one feature of life under Company rule had persisted —this was the use of the Dutch language in the home and on the street by slaves and poor people, by many mothers in lullabies, in polite conversations or by workers uttering profanity, although not in official records and communications. As late as the 1820's Severyn Hasbrouck, a descendant of one old Kingston Huguenot family, and a student at Yale College in New Haven wrote home in Dutch to his Ulster County family explaining that no one in New Haven understood the language and he was using it in order not to forget it. Until 1808 sermons were given and psalms sung in Dutch at Kingston's Dutch Reformed church so the church served as an anchor of Dutch culture in the community. Until the period of English rule was more then half gone the wills filed in Kingston were most often written in Dutch. On the streets and in the homes, among the slaves and old people the Dutch language struggled to maintain its hold. And since the church was a cultural anchor even for many of those Kingstonians who did not attend the Church and whose ancestors were German, Irish, French or any of the many other ethnic groups which would make up Kingston's population the church was a positive force in maintaining Dutch ways against the strong official English tide.

The retreat from Dutchness which was becoming visible in Kingston as Ann Moore arrived there slowly strengthened as the years passed by. In the mid-nineteenth century a wave of romantic nostalgia was sweeping into Kingston as the Dutch colonial past of the place acquired a rebirth of glamor. Their sense of Kingston's Dutch past as something to be cherished was given fine expression in a New Year's Day Carrier's Address of 1851, and in an article printed on June 10, 1891 written by a reporter using the pseudonym of Van der Sluice. The report told with obvious regret of the "passing of the Dutch" language "seldom heard now in Ulster County." He told of the struggle by local people of the past to cling to their Dutch after 1808 when it had ceased its use in their old church. Then Henry Ostrander, a dominie who was still eloquent and fluent in "sonorous" Dutch was coaxed to go to the Dutch church at Hurley once a month to deliver a sermon in the old language to which Kingston people flocked. "And what a fat feast of things was enjoyed there by the Dutch-starved worshippers." A dozen years earlier Reverend Abram Lansing of Blue Mountain, a few miles to the northwest, had announced a sermon to be preached in colloquial Dutch every now and then for the benefit of the people of Dutch stock in the vicinity. The reporter for the *Leader* urged the Holland Society which by then had members in Kingston to learn enough Dutch to use it at their meetings to keep the language alive. But this suggestion was never accepted.

As late as the 1920s, it was customary after Sunday services were over for the elderly Dutch descendants to linger outside the Church doors at New Paltz, Woodstock and Kingston and try to converse in what they could retain of the Dutch of their ancestors.

The use of "veiling" for mopping a floor and that of "blozzard" for the puff-adder which inflated its neck to alarm those it sees as threatening its safety were in use in the Ulster County of the author until almost 1920 or so. "Veil" (pronounced *file*) is Dutch for a mop and a blozzard is a blower or puffer. A New Paltz plowman of village gardens named Roosa is remembered as urging his horse to greater effort by shouting at him in a strange language which oldtimers identified as very colloquial Dutch profanity.

PART 6

An Independent Nation is Born in Battle with the Help of Kingston

1776-1783

1.
George Clinton and the Prelude to Revolution

As the French and Indian Wars ground to an end in 1763 a little more than a century had elapsed since Thomas Chambers had "made his pitch" on the fine Native lowlands bordering the Esopus Creek with a pathway to the Landing Place near where the Rondout joins the Hudson.

By 1763 the white invaders, in intervals of peace, had worked out a horse and plow way of using the fertile flatlands they had won from the Natives with a modified method of their traditional Netherlands way of farming. They had adapted too, growing the Native staples of maize, squash and Native kinds of beans as well as becoming addicted to Native tobacco. The Esopus "Indians," now thinly scattered in the back country, had in exchange adopted the whites' use of trade-obtained alcohol, steel and cloth.

The whites of Kingston had no doubt that they had the better of the exchange and so felt very much superior to the Natives.

They felt superior too, if in a different way, to the English colonists across the Hudson River to the East. Their English neighbors to the east were (so the Dutch believed) aggressive and motivated by what the Dutch saw as "low cunning" and bigotry. The Yankees of New England returned the compliment by regarding the Hudson Valley Dutch as stingy, narrow-minded and overly profit-driven. On many levels Dutch and English did not get along well together—not very much better than the Dutch had gotten along with the Natives. A forerunner of a willingness to get along on the part of some Kingstonians, as shown in the outcome of Ann Moore's adventure in Kingston in 1758, was an indication of the possibility of changes to come. This kind of understanding of the role in life of compromise with those of different views was obviously intruding into the very Dutchness of Kingston.

Kingston people of the present day, when they look back on the Revolution, think of George Clinton as one of their outstanding heroes. His larger-than-life bronze statue stands within the limits of the old stockade near the former gates from the stockade to the road leading to Kingston's landing on the Rondout. Clinton's bones are now interred inside an impressive monument in the churchyard of the Old Dutch Church.

Kingston people like to humanize Clinton by telling the story of how he came to hold a life long grip on the office of Clerk of the Court of Common Pleas of Ulster County (or as mistakenly sometimes said the County Clerk) as a result of a favor to himself and his father Charles Clinton, a farmer and land surveyor, from Cadwallader Colden, who was then Surveyor-General of the Province of New York. When George Clinton was only a lad of nine, Colden proposed recommending the boy's father to the English Governor for some government office. This Charles Clinton turned down. Then Colden, still bent on showing some sign of good will, recommended young George for the office of Clerk of the Court of Common Pleas of Ulster. This was to take effect upon the death of the then present incumbent. So, in 1741 twenty-two-year-old George Clinton was sworn into the clerkship to which he clung by means of deputies, usually members of his wife's family (the Kingston Tappens), until his death in 1812. Such complicated acts of favoritism were not uncommon in the days of British colonial rule.

George Clinton became a hero to Kingston because he had the competent politician's talent for being able to feel the pulse of his public and to act accordingly while at the same time being able to use his own judgement and persuade his followers to follow his lead when he thought this best. His job record before achieving the rank of general in charge, with his brother James, of fortifying the Hudson River at the approach of the Revolutionary War was one of pleasing his Ulster backers and gaining their confidence. During the period of stress that preceded the Revolution he served as a member of the Provincial Assembly where he voted with the faction headed by the great Hudson Valley landholding manorial Livingston family, which was popular in Ulster County, and not the faction headed by the more business oriented de Lanceys. He had set off on his career as an elected Assemblyman with careful, almost cautious steps. But as the pace of the American march toward declaring independence quickened, he became bolder and more confident as an accepted leader of Kingston's people. He was a yeoman of English and not Dutch descent, a distant cousin of the George Clinton who had been a British Governor of New York and the Sir Henry Clinton who would be a British general. But he married a Dutch-descended woman. His wife's family were decidedly Dutch and part of the Kingston community which had become very much one in which family relationships were close and influential. And his marriage helped Clinton become seen as one of the village's very own.

In 1764 as Clinton was practicing law, surveying and farming, events that would change the course of his life were stirring Britons and their American colonists. In order to pay the debts incurred by their long series of North American wars (which some Britons saw as having been beneficial to their American colonists) and in order to lessen taxes on Britons, Parliament passed Acts imposing much of the war-caused indebtedness on their American colonies. Nothing like this "taxation without representation" (for the Colonies were not represented in the British Parliament) had ever been attempted by earlier Parliaments. A storm of protest arose in the American colonies. In the City of New York the radical Sons of Liberty demonstrated around the Liberty Poles which they had erected under the leadership of fiery Alexander MacDougal.

A post-French and Indian war economic slump was harassing the Colonies which felt doubly angry at the action of Parliament, as their businesses sagged while higher colonial taxes were threatened. Charles De Witt of Greenkill in the Village took notice of the gloom felt in Kingston after the people heard of Parliament's new taxes and their severe restrictions on many areas of trade.

De Witt wrote to a friend in the spring of 1764, "Nothing but darkness, I cannot say Egyptian darkness, for the great source of light continues its wonted course, and nature once more, in all probability, will adorn this earth. . . . I mean the times, which are so bad, that I am often doubtful whether or no things will not return to their primitive frame; trade being so discouraging that I see nothing but destruction for many, who in all likelihood would do well in case those unheard of prohibitions to trade had never existed. Will not America tumble into confusion, I hope not. . . ." Colonial Kingston was indeed very deeply concerned as Parliament seemed bent on piling added burdens on the already shaky colonial trade from which the British economy had come to owe so much.

The half century of French wars with only one substantial period of peace had cost much in levies of colonial troops and money which had balanced the usual boom of wartime years. When Parliament passed the Stamp Act in 1765, anger in the Colonies rose to a fever heat. The Act required that stamps bought from official agents be affixed to all such objects as playing cards, legal documents, all manner of printed materials except books, to insurance policies, marriage licenses and so on and on. This, added to a currency shortage and quartering acts, brought riots by radicals to the streets of Boston as well as by Alexander MacDougal's Sons of Liberty in New York. The first shipments of the hated stamps were seized and burned by irate citizens. Colonists refused to use the stamps and some influential Parliamentary leaders supported the Colonists. Colonists called a Stamp Act Congress which demanded an end to the Stamp Act. Parliament saw the light and repealed the hated Act. But this did not end the growth of tension between American colonists and British officialdom. Acts followed which further manacled Colonists in their trade with Britain and the rest of world and so did other results of a Parliamentary determination to keep the Colonies in their proper place as exploitable economic subjects of the sort that Lord Edward Cornbury had written of in the time of Queen Anne.

In Kingston, George Clinton stood for election to the Assembly in full confidence that he had earned the support of Kingston people in opposing the recent acts of Parliament. He was however opposed in the election to his surprise by Cadwallader Colden, Jr. Young Colden's father was then the provincial Surveyor-General who had been responsible for Clinton's appointment to his Ulster County clerkship at the age of 9. The elder Colden asked George Clinton to withdraw his candidacy. This put Clinton in a hard place, for Clinton was by then on the opposite side politically of the monarchy-supporting Coldens. He chose to stand by his beliefs in the rightness of the American cause and refused to withdraw.

2.
The Years of Revolution Begin

After election to the Assembly with his fellow Ulster Whig, Charles De Witt, at first Clinton did not draw much attention. The Assembly was still dominated very strongly by the Parliament-supporting conservative Colden-De Lancey family. In 1769, however, Clinton supported the right of Alexander MacDougal to express his radical views in a pamphlet. The pamphlet was denounced by the conservative Assembly and Clinton was one of only five Assemblymen to support MacDougal's right to express his views. And Clinton went on gaining the good opinion of Kingston people who were now beginning to think, if somewhat cautiously, of a future independence from Britain. Clinton, it was said, boldly stood up in the Assembly and stated that "the time was coming, when the Colonists must have recourse to arms, and the sooner the better." He may have been misquoted, yet he made his radical position clear in other Assembly words and actions. Because of this he was chosen by the Ulster County freeholders to be a member of the Second Continental Congress and so emerged as a leader of a larger constituency than that of Kingston. The Committee of Safety of the Continental Congress next moved Clinton into a new field of activity by naming him Brigadier-General of the combined brigades of the Militia of Ulster and Orange Counties. Clinton had served briefly in the army during the French and Indian war. Yet he was not enamored of the glamor of a military man's life. In later years he disparaged that life by writing that military life required deception and strategems which were obviously distasteful to him. Yet, as events showed, a strong current was leading American minds to a future marked by armed struggle. And soon Clinton became willing to play his part in military life. His continuing support of radical American action brought him membership in the Continental Congress which passed the Declaration of Independence and before long appointed him Brigadier-General of the military forces not only of Ulster and Orange but also of Westchester and Dutchess Counties. He was ordered by the Congress to take charge of guarding the Highlands of the Hudson against British attack. This was an assignment of critical importance to the cause of the Americans as the Revolution got under way.

The British clearly planned to seize the Hudson Valley by sending troops up the Hudson River from New York harbor to meet St. Leger's troops from Fort Niagara and troops under Burgoyne including Iroquois allies via Lake Champlain—all these to meet near Albany. If the plan succeded the rebellious New England colonies would be cut off from the rebellious middle Atlantic and southern Colonies. The revolutionary forces planned at first to counter the enemy by holding New York City and the lower Hudson and blocking the middle Hudson to British ships. Even as George Washington was struggling to hold the City of New York and George Clinton was fortifying the Highlands, the British sent a very large troop-laden fleet of warships from England to the harbor of New York City where they bombarded the place but delayed taking possession until they could force passage up the Hudson and meet the British forces pushing down from the North and northwest.

Clinton had the double task of building forts on the steep and craggy slopes of the Highlands which constricted and twisted the Hudson near West Point and at the same time he had to take advantage of his popularity to rally the men of 16 to 50 years old who were liable to militia service but were not quick in coming forward prepared to fight. While the region had its small upper class of suitable men who could afford to take time from their work or leisure to accept commissions as officers of the militia, most men of the right age were poor farmers and had families dependent on them. And farming required sowing and harvesting to be successful, to be done in acceptance of the whims of weather and the changes of seasons. Absence of a farmer at critical times can mean the failure of a crop of corn or wheat and that might mean starvation for a farm family with no other resources to keep them alive.

Most of the people of the four county region over which Clinton had military command favored the American cause, many with obvious enthusiasm. When the agreement to maintain the new American Constitutional rights was presented to Ulster men in the summer of 1775, 564 signed and only 33 are known to have refused. Recruiting militiamen, even those so much inclined toward an independent America was a vitally important task facing Clinton. And so too was the guarding of the Hudson River against the expected invasion by strong ever-increasing British naval forces which remained another. Forts and batteries commanding the River had to be rushed to completion (with the aid of Kingston men). A mighty iron chain was forged at Sterling Forest and hauled to the River from Stony Point to be put in place a little under the Hudson's surface to foil passage upstream by the British fleet which remained anchored in readiness to act at the River's mouth. As preparations for thwarting British attempts to move up the Hudson and as British forces were being piled up around New York City in preparation for capturing the city, which the British were planning to make their base for major military action in North America, George Washington recognized that his forces were no match for those of the British. He evacuated the City of New York.

With the city closed to the Americans, their new revolutionary government agencies were forced to move upriver. After brief stops at Fishkill and Poughkeepsie, the agencies of the new State of New York settled upon Kingston as the Capital of the new State. Kingston was chosen largely because it had adequate quarters for housing and caring for the revolutionary delegates to assemble in the selected Capital, and because of the Village's geographic position in relation to the expected military action.

Kingstonians have based much of their pride in the place on the historic accomplishments of their new government while Kingston was the state capital. In Kingston the first New York State Senate met. There the State Constitution was adopted. There George Clinton was inaugurated as the first Governor of the new state while he still remained a very active general of the American armed forces under George Washington. There the first Supreme Court of the State of New York held its first session. There John Holt, the official printer of the new State government, set up his very helpful press in cooperation with the new government which Holt vigorously supported.

Yet the British forces both above and below on the Hudson remained day and night a continuing threat to the safety of the village which had become the proud and more vulnerable State capital in which important history would be made.

3.
General Vaughan Forces the Hudson and Attacks Kingston 1777

IT HAD BEEN RECOGNIZED BY BRITISH STRATEGISTS IN THE OPENING DAYS OF THE American Revolution that possession of the Hudson Valley would give a great advantage in the war to the side holding it, so the British sent their troops from east and west and north hopefully to meet at Albany. And the village of Kingston had become a special target now that it was functioning as the State capital.

The rebellious colonies, once they became aware of the British plans, had done their best to counter them. The Americans under General Clinton hastily built Forts Montgomery and Clinton at the entrance to the reaches of the Hudson at the place where the high and rocky Highlands narrowed the River. A chevaux-de-frise consisting of heavy logs from which sharp spikes and barbed wire projected was thrown across the Hudson in addition to the heavy iron chain.

George Clinton, in whom General Washington had expressed great confidence, had already been placed in charge not only of fortifying and guarding the Highlands but also of protecting the entire mid-Hudson region. At the same time, Clinton had the urgent task of persuading militiamen from the four mid-Hudson counties to join his forces at a time when eligible men of 16 to 50 had to fit military duty against British oppression into their farm work. Militiamen came and went or served short terms before leaving. And Clinton, himself a part time farmer, understood, yet continued his mobilizing efforts. He was given strength by a faith in the backing of Kingston and Ulster County people. Already Kingston militiamen had been sent to join General Montgomery's expedition against Montreal and Quebec in 1775. They had worked at building the forts and other obstructions to Hudson River assault by the British. Kingston men had taken a part in the building of fire ships and upstream militiamen, in a campaign in which fire would play a major role, had constructed fire rafts along the middle and upper Hudson. These disposable vessels were made as inflammable as possible by loading them with dry pine twigs and trains of gunpowder strewn upon their decks.

In the summer of 1776 the *Phoenix* and the *Rose* of the British fleet became the targets of two American fire ships while both British vessels were at anchor a little above Yonkers, New York.

Under cover of darkness the two fire ships approached the *Phoenix* and the *Rose* and their men fastened their highly inflammable crafts by means of grapnels to the hulls of these vessels. Then they ignited the trains of gunpower, cut loose their whaleboats from the fire ships and so tried to make their escape. The crews of the whaleboats were daring New England sailors accustomed to difficult work at sea. The fires blazed up and were visible 22 miles away. But no great amount of damage was done to the big British fleet anchored in New York bay. New Yorkers watched the conflagrations with amazement at this grand pyrotechnical display which did so little harm to either side except for the death of three of the New England sailors who never made it to shore in their whaleboats.

Lord Howe who was in command of British forces at New York and of the ever increasing number of troops reaching there from Britain, was waiting for the right moment to "force" the Hudson and meet near Albany with the other British troops coming from the north and from the west. In 1777 Howe judged the time had come for sending a squadron in flatboats loaded with British and necessary Hessian troops up the Hudson River. At the same time George Washington was fighting his way through defeat at the battle of Long Island and the modest victory at Harlem Heights but the constant building up of British strength around him caused him to abandon New York City once he reached it rather than risk having his army risk being entrapped on Manhattan Island.

For a time Washington considered setting fire to New York City before leaving it as a not uncommon military step to take in order to prevent an evacuated position from becoming a valuable base to the enemy. A great fire raged for days. Britain claimed that one-fourth of the buildings of New York were destroyed. The British who blamed the Americans and Americans or New Yorkers who blamed the British as the arsonists are said to have tossed people of the opposite belief into the flames as having deliberately caused the conflagration. Abraham Hasbrouck of Kingston lost the house he owned in Manhattan with all its contents to the flames. In his family record he clearly attributed the fire to "the enemy, that is the British."

The taking over of New York by the British was followed by a sometimes confused de facto government. The Americans's temporary governing body, or "Association," fled from New York City to White Plains, then to Fishkill on the Hudson and on to Poughkeepsie in succession. In the spring of 1777, on learning that Kingston could offer very acceptable accomodations for working and living for its officials and delegates, the center of Revolutionary government had moved there and Kingston became the State Capital. And on April 22, 1777, after two years of de facto government of the province, largely by committees, the people of the State had a legitimate revolutionary government which has endured with many modifications ever since. The Legislature had already sent the records of the new state to the inland Ulster County Town of Rochester for safekeeping. Now, under their new Constitution adopted in Kingston, they were enabled to take care of such matters as the electing of state officials and the enacting of temporary laws.

George Clinton was chosen both Governor and Lieutenant Governor of the State. Clinton resigned the Lieutenant Governorship in favor of downstate Pierre Van Cortlandt but kept the Governorship in which he would serve for eight terms. He was inaugurated in a festive atmosphere in front of the Courthouse on Wall Street in Kingston and ended his acceptance speech, not with the once familiar words of "God save the king," but with the new and exciting "God save the people!"[5]

The British had hoped that once they had established their base in the City of New York, many loyalists from the former Province would rise up to aid them. But this was not to be. While British agents were active behind the American lines in recruiting young men for their army, the recruits did not result in any substantial addition to their military strength. To build up their forces they employed Hessian mercenaries. The need for fresh meat to feed the many thousands of armed Britishers on land and sea was not easily met. Men known as "cowboys" or "cowjockies" worked often by night driving cattle, hogs and sheep from Westchester into British-held New York. Sailing vessels were sent up the lower Hudson to fire upon riverside houses of both the poor and the rich and to send out landing parties on foraging expeditions for livestock, grain and vegetables. Many local men in their rage at the British fired at the ships with their muskets even when the ships were too far away to be hit. The looting and burning and ineffectual musket fire produced only annoyance to both sides and a heightening of the demonization of each side by the other. This was made evident by the reference of each side to the other in opprobrious terms. Among these were rabble, cowards, scoundrels, rascals, banditti, royal hirelings, damned rebels or Tories, and traitors. Prisoners of war have seldom been treated well by either side. In Kingston prisoners of war were crammed in the cellar of the Kingston courthouse with the new Legislature meeting on the floor above. Legislators petitioned to be allowed to smoke while in session in order to mask the foul odor arising from the cellar prison with its almost nonexistent sanitation. One prisoner who petitioned to have the chain which had been placed on his body be removed, "in order," as he put it, "that I might cleanse myself." Another prisoner who denied any guilt complained bitterly of being locked up in a foul "dungeon." The conditions prevailing in British prison ships in New York harbor were no better. The tide of mutual demonization was rising to a peak. And Governor Clinton was accused by the British of being especially cruel in his treatment of the opposite side. British forces in New York kept in touch with the forces of Burgoyne and St. Leger to the north by means of spies and intercepted letters. Clinton relied on members of the Ulster Light Horse to serve as an express to carry letters from his command along the Hudson to General Schuyler's northern militiamen.

By October 6 as British were ready to move, a substantial squadron of flatboats carrying about 1,100 British and Hessian soldiers under General John Vaughan accompanied by a variety of other naval vessels moved up the Hudson burning and looting as they went. Word of this movement came to Clinton who passed it along to Albany's General Schuyler who would soon under New England pressure give up his command to Yankee Horatio Gates. The British squadron reached the Highlands and there came face to face with the obstructions which Clinton's engineers had devised to thwart them. They made short work of storming and taking undermanned Forts Montgomery and Clinton. They laboriously chopped a gap through the logs of the chevaux de frise; they conquered the mighty chain. Ahead of them on the river there lay no obstructions all the way to the State Capital of Kingston and beyond. A junction at Albany with the British northern army and their Native allies seemed virtually certain after that.

General Clinton had been in charge during the struggle to hold the obstructions at the entrance to the Highlands. The fighting had been bitter and the casualties substantial for his greatly outnumbered forces. He escaped over a parapet and made his way from the east bank of the Hudson to the west. From overwork and lack of sleep he plunged into the task of rallying his men for a 40-mile twenty-four hour-a-day forced march to hopefully save Kingston, which now had become endangered. On October 10, Clinton had written to the Kingston Council of Safety, which conducted business of the Legislature when the Legislature could not form a quorum. Clinton urged the Kingston people to make preparations for a possible assault on their village by the British who were then trying to force the Hudson. He wrote, "I wish some small works could be thrown up toward the Esopus Landing so as to cover the Landing and secure the Defiles leading to the town. Every man that can fire a gun should immediately be embodied and employed at the works."

According to a letter, with date not given, from Clinton to engineer Captain Machin in a footnote to Benjamin Lossing's account of the burning of Kingston, Clinton had once considered "enclosing" Kingston (with a wall) as a defensive measure but had rejected the measure because being made of stone, with the window spaces filled up, Clinton wrote, would provide defense enough. This conversion of the village into a fort, however, was never carried out.

In Kingston Clinton's urgent letter of October 10 had a quick reply. Pierre Van Cortlandt wrote him at 5 pm on October 15: "Just received from the Landing that about 30 sail of the enemy's Vessels have appeared opposite to Esopus Island and standing up the river. Some Works have been thrown up below in accordance with your Excellency's wishes. The alarm gun just now fired. . . . Will contribute all in our power. The militia officers who command here to make the best possible Defence here at this Post during your Excellency's absence."

Kingston, plunged into a war against its colonialism, must have been aware from time to time of the part which fire played in the struggle. There was a general fear of fires as part of Native or black uprisings—a threat of one having appeared in a New York City newspaper in February 1775. The disastrous fire of 1776 had been recorded as causing severe damage to Abraham Hasbrouck's Kingston house in 1776, as graphically recorded in Hasbrouck's journal. All had rendered Kingstonians well aware of fires both accidental and as an essential tool of war.

The extensive destruction of part of New York City, the fires set along the lower Hudson by the American fire ships—all these helped make Kingston people take precautions to remove all valued property to their back country as the threat of a British attack loomed, with a strong possibility of fire forming part of that attack.

4.
Trial by Fire
October 16, 1777

Once their alarm gun had sounded warning of General Vaughan's approach on the Hudson, the people of Kingston plunged into a whirl of activity. The members of the Council gave up their dealing with the welfare of prisoners of war. They ordered men to hitch up horses to the twenty-four wagons already brought together in readiness to haul to safety the large stocks of war stored in Kingston for military and civilian use and to remove them to the back country to keep them from falling into the hands of the enemy. Although Kingston had just received the good news that Burgoyne, hampered by a lack of supplies and his ignorance of forest warfare, had offered to surrender after his loss of the Battle of Bemis Farm, preceding the Battle of Saratoga, there was little time or taste for rejoicing in Kingston. The enemy was preparing to land at Ponckhockie. Kingstonians who had not already fled were rushing out of the village, along with some refugees from New York City who had fled to Kingston in houses of safety there, to take shelter in Marbletown, Hurley, Woodstock and other more distant settlements where they had friends and relatives. Men, women, children, and mothers with babes in arms all carried with them whatever portable assets they could. In the case of upper and middling people this meant the silver spoons, tankards and teapots in which savings were invested in a village which had a silversmith or two but not yet a banker.

Cattle, sheep and hogs were being driven to safety. Chickens and ducks were being placed in crates and loaded on wagons to go to Marbletown, Woodstock and other satellite settlements. Poor people with only a pewter teapot or a bundle of blankets were doing their best to save that. Bewildered dogs and an occasional cat tagged after their masters.

At about 10 o'clock on October 16, cannon shot from British vessels had been hurled against the Americans' armed galley, the *Lady Washington.* The damaged vessel was then run upstream on the Rondout and scuttled. The two batteries which Clinton had asked to be "thrown up" were taken by the initial landing force of four or five hundred soldiers who very quickly routed the American militiamen from their batteries. They at once spiked the guns and moved on.

Among the Americans who had manned the batteries were the three sons of Abraham Hasbrouck—Jacobus, Abraham and Daniel. Their father proudly noted in the Hasbrouck family record that his sons had been among those in the "opposing of the enemy from landing." And that they also opposed the enemy "from coming to Kingston and showers of shot flew on every side of them." The Ulster militiamen, thought to number about 150, whom Clinton had asked to be mobilized to defend the village, retreated up the Rondout Creek. They were greatly outnumbered by Vaughan's many hundreds of redcoats and mercenaries who continued to pour ashore. (The militiamen for whom Clinton had asked Yankee General Horatio Gates were anxiously awaited but had not arrived.)

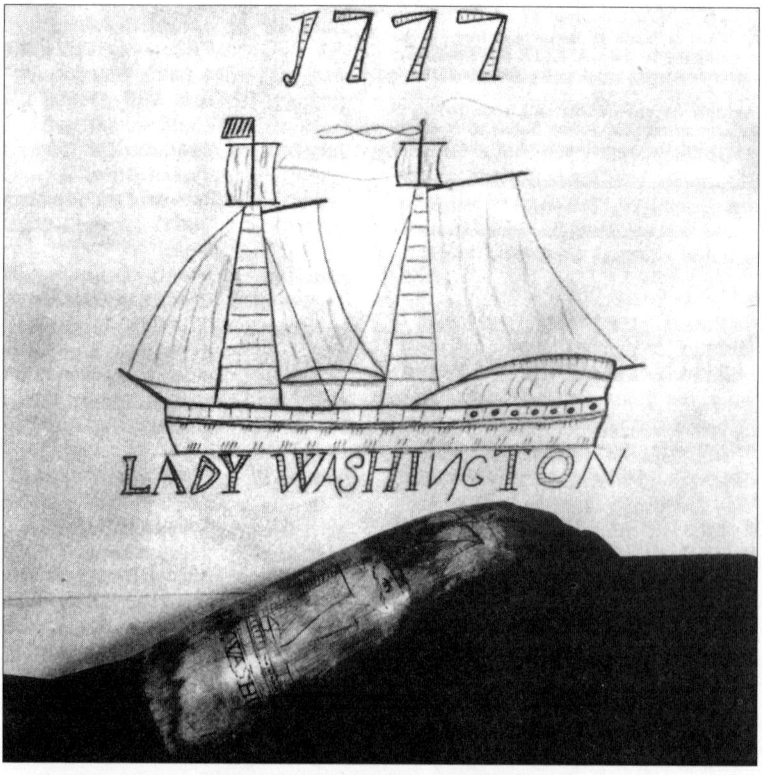

Powderhorn engraving of Revolutionary Galley, *Lady Washington,* sunk in the Rondout during British invasion of 1777, from the *Ulster County Gazette,* 1966

After setting fire to the ships of the Fleet Prison to which prisoners had been sent from the Kingston jail and elsewhere and to the few buildings then standing along the Rondout Landing place, the invading troops marched up the steep hill toward Kingston, guided, it is said, by a local slave. They met with no more resistance than a scattering of musket shots near the site of the present City Hall and Kingston High School. At Kingston the troops marched to what appeared to be an abandoned village but according to General Vaughan's second-thought official version Kingston men had been "drawn up with Cannon and we drove them out of the Place. On our entering the Place they fired from their Houses, which induced me to Reduce the Place to Ashes, which I accordingly did." (This was permitted under the rules of war should a beseiged town offer resistance; and it was put into the report to justify harming the village although almost all other evidence denies it.)

Vaughan was aware that Clinton and his men were on their grueling forced march to Kingston to get there before Vaughan and his men could arrive. With all possible speed Vaughan had his troops set fire to Kingston. According to the Tory New York *Gazette* of November 3 they burned "three hundred and twenty six houses, with a barn to almost everyone of them, filled with flour, besides grains of all kinds, much valuable furniture and affects, which the Royal army disdained to take with them. Twelve thousand barrels of flour were burnt, and they took at the town four pieces of Cannon, with ten more upon the River with 1,500 stand of Arms and a large quantity of Powder were blown up. The whole Service was effected and the troops re-embarked in three hours."

The *Gazette* was a Tory newspaper so that a very liberal discount must be made for their account of the triumph of the Royal troops. Yet the destruction was great. Abraham Hasbrouck made this plain in detailing his own losses, "My dwelling House and barn, cider house or store house and another barn (and) wagon house at my late dwelling house, also a small out Kitchen which was left standing when my dwelling House was burnt down (by accident) the 25th of October, 1776."

Vaughan's men, Hasbrouck noted, "Carried off with them one Negro man (of his) named Harry, two Negro wenches named Janey and Flora, and destroyed my household goods and furniture and my Library of Books—my loss I sustained this time I compute at no less that 5,000 pounds at least. The house I had in New York burnt last year by the enemy . . . 1,000 pounds." Hasbrouck's total loss by the three fires he estimated at nine to ten thousand pounds. The losses to less fortunate Kingstonians by the British conflagration can only be guessed at. About 1950 Kingston fire chief Murphy reported to City Historian W. C. de Witt that according to his family tradition the Chief's great-great grand-aunt had been an eyewitness to the burning of Kingston on October 16, 1777. She stated that some British officers had tried to restrain the Hessian mercenaries who were burning the Village.

But there was an intangible gain to the dreadful blow delivered against Kingston. In addition to the fact that no one was killed, the devastation to the village by fire caused shocked reporters throughout the rebelling Colonies to write about the firing of Kingston as an example of "British barbarity." Contributions poured in for the relief of Kingston from as far away as Charleston, South Carolina. The burning was denounced in the British Parliament and Chancellor Robert R. Livingston gave a 5,000 acre tract in his part of the Hardenbergh Patent to those whose property had been destroyed in Vaughan's fire. All this helped arouse Americans to a pitch of anti-British emotion that played its part in the winning of the Revolutionary War. For the conversion of your enemy into the semblance of an incarnate devil is a superb propaganda weapon in war.

And it rested heavily on the conscience of George Clinton as is made apparent by the number of times he returned in his letters to the cause of the failure of his military forces on their desperate forced march which was hoped to save the village of Kingston, in a war in which burning was playing an important part. In one letter he attributed the burning to failure of New England's General Horatio Gates, who had just replaced Albany's General Schuyler to fulfill his promise to send additional militiamen to the help of the Hudson Valley.

An important factor in the fire, however, was the fact that Clinton and his battle-tired troops, after their loss of the defense of the Hudson works at the Highlands, had made a harrowing forced march with heavy packs to Kingston, so that they and their General were in no physical shape to help the beleaguered village which had done the best its people could do under the circumstances.

Colonel Samuel Blanchley Webb was a young man still in his twenties, of Weathersfield, Connecticut engaged in the promising West India trade (sugar, rum and molasses) when the Revolution began and he distinguished himself by his courage at the Battle of Bunker Hill. First an aide to George Washington, and then a Colonel in the army commanded by George Clinton, Webb was assigned the defense of the Highlands against British attack. There Webb took part in helping Governor George Clinton and his brother James escape after the British had taken Fort Montgomery. Colonel Webb then himself escaped with his battered men to Shongum (Shawangunk).

On October 17, 1777 thirty British sail moved up the Hudson bound on a mission to destroy the thriving village of Kingston. From Shawangunk Colonel Samuel B. Webb and his men began a "force'd march" with heavy packs on their back toward Kingston. They reached the vicinity of Kingston 6 hours after the British had completed burning the village, and took up quarters at Marbletown. "This savage kind of War," the Colonel notes on page 31 of Volume 3, *Correspondence of Samuel Blanchley Webb*, "destroying defenseless towns, and making War against Women and

Children seems peculiar to *Britons* and *Savages.*" Webb hastened to view Kingston by horseback and commented that "to appearances was one of the most beautiful Villages I ever saw—the inhabitants are now scattered all over the country." The Colonel thought less highly of the beauty of the Village ladies, but made an exception of Miss Betsy Elmendorph and the Ten Eyck sisters, plus a few others, whom he invited to tea at his quarters in Marbletown, and whom he met again, on their invitation, at a social occasion with band music.

The Colonel left behind in his *Journal* the first eye witness account of what the Village of Kingston looked like after what Webb called "such cursed Barbarity . . . not equalled in History, Revenge for Burgoyne's misfortunes seems their darling object." Webb was referring to Vaughan's burning of Kingston and other Hudson Valley places.

5.
Clinton-Sullivan, Tories and "Monster" Brant

FOLLOWING THE BURNING OF KINGSTON CAME THE DETAILS OF SUCH SUCCESSES as the surrender of the British under Burgoyne at Saratoga and the decision of France to join the war on the American side and to keep fighting their traditional enemy Britain until American Independence was won. All this good news did not give a sense of strategic safety to Kingston or the Hudson Valley, although the center of military action was moving southward and away from them.

Had the undated note from George Clinton been authentic (as it may have been) and had it been written after and not before the British fire and had engineer Machin agreed with Clinton's suggestion the old stone house Stockade district of present day Kingston might have had a very different look than it now has. But the people of Kingston got to work raking the ashes of their buildings to recover such handmade objects as iron nails and hinges, door latches, melted silverware and surviving parts of their cast iron German stoves. With winter not too far ahead those who could not afford better shelter elsewhere patched together huts by running up lean-tos against the surviving stone walls of their ruins or improvising roofs across parts of their blackened walls. Building materials were very expensive as they usually are during times of war. There was some temporary resentment against rich Madame Livingston, mother of the Chancellor, who could afford easy access to materials and labor to rebuild her family mansion of Clermont across the Hudson. The mansion had been burned by Vaughan's troops after they had burned Kingston and raided Saugerties and other nearby valley places.

According to historian Marius Schoonmaker, some of the walls of the Village had an extraordinarily strong mortar—so strong that after sixty years of exposure to the weather some of those burned out by the British "were taken down finally with great difficulty, the stones themselves breaking and giving way before the mortar yielded and when, finally, the walls were brought down by scores of men pulling at the ends of ropes fastened to the walls, which had been previously undermined, the walls lay on the ground broken up in large chunks, which required the free use of the sledge-hammer to break in pieces." (These obdurate walls may have been caused by the clay which was used as mortar between the stones to harden into a hard ceramic because of having endured such great heat, perhaps because of oil or paint being stored within them, as in the paint and oil dealing Vander Lyn's big house.)

Kingston was far enough away from New York's frontier with Canada to feel fairly safe from the kind of warfare with the Native British allies that had ended after the conclusion of the Esopus Wars. Yet the village was close enough to the country still occupied by hostile Natives allied with the British to be subject to having their isolated farms scattered in the still largely forested back country still at the mercy of the enemy. A few Native raiders accompanied at times by Tories often disguised as Native Americans were terrorizing the fringe of white settlers in the border country and thought to be led by "Monster Brant." Kingston militiamen ranged these western border lands but were unable altogether to control the raids. Supplies that might have fed the mobilized American forces were burned, as were houses, crops and barns, and panicky white settlers along with friendly Natives retreated closer to the older and safer settlements.

An expedition under General John Sullivan and Governor Clinton's brother General James was carefully planned by George Washington. As the expedition was being organized, the British were becoming active in the City of New York and were once again threatening to gain control of the Hudson. They sent troops up the River and succeeded in seizing the not yet restored forts at the Highlands and Stony Point. Americans led by Anthony Wayne succeeded in retaking the Point, and it may have been at this perilous time that George Clinton may have thought of fitting up the burned out house windows of Kingston with stone to form a stony fort. The situation may have seemed threatening enough to warrant so unpleasant a remedy as one which would cement their houses with all their associations of warmth and family into parts of a grim fort.

And to add to the woes of Kingston people, British troops were sent across the Long Island Sound from the Connecticut shore in a doomed effort to make good the old British claim to the Island. The prospect for Kingston in 1779 did not look promising yet the people of the Village went on restoring their homes.

As they were providing temporary shelters for themselves in their burned Village, they were at the mercy of the British and their Iroquois allies all the way to the Susquehanna Valley where the Senecas were members of the Confederacy and the Senecas were called the Keepers of the Western Gate, while the Oneidas and the Tuscaroras of the Confederacy were trying to remain neutral. George Washington planned an Expedition in the summer of 1779 to remove this threat to Kingston and the rest of the Hudson Valley. Washington wrote to General John Sullivan, who was to head the Expedition, "The immediate objectives are the total destruction and devastation of their [the Iroquois] settlements, and the capture of as many prisoners of every age and sex as possible." This contrasts with the motivations of the Dutch Company in the Esopus War when the then Directors sought to exterminate the Natives and made no bones about it.

Meanwhile the Sullivan-Clinton expedition leaders arranged for troops from eastern Pennsylvania, the Mohawk Valley and Wawarsing in Ulster County to come together at Tioga in the valley of the Susquehanna River and there build a base for an attack that would devastate the home country of the border Native raiders. Some of this was a level country of rich riverside alluvial soil where Natives were living an almost white American style of life. Some were Christians who had built white men's kinds of neat houses, farmed and gardened as white Americans did, and appeared to be assimilating into what might be thought of as American culture.

During the Esopus Wars Kingston defended the lands they had taken over from the Natives by crippling the Natives in their attempts to recover their lands with the help of an old tool in the art of war which had been successfully used against the Esopus Natives by Captain Krieger. This consisted of destroying not only villages but all means of subsistence. Washington's plan now called for the pulling up of growing corn and the burning of barns and dwellings, and of crops that had been stored in pits in the ground left there in the care of the earth's ground spirits the Natives had trusted.

As in the Esopus War, the campaign was not one that could be carried out easily. But it was well coordinated. Soldiers were well prepared and supplies were seldom lacking. However, people who were unaware of the difficulties of warfare in partial wilderness criticized Washington. They did not realize that this kind of warfare demanded the felling of giant trees to make way for roads for the movement of heavy cannon, loaded wagons and the movement of pack horses and stores of food to make their way over unsettled and rough back country. Boats had to be built to be used in crossing rivers and floating supplies and troops down the waters of the Susquehanna. General Sullivan is said to have carried out this Expedition with a ruthless efficiency, which was to give Joseph Brant the name of "Monster" because of American zeal. In planning and execution the campaign was recognized as a military triumph. But its barbaric features such as the slaughter of unarmed Natives in their houses instead of capturing them as advised by Washington and the destruction of the foodstuffs and the plundering of the Natives' possessions were not in later years features to be rejoiced at.

It was not until 1923 when Kingston lawyer Augustus Van Buren in his *Ulster County Under the Dominion of the Dutch* could present the American Natives as other than cruel barbarians worthy of whatever barbarism was inflicted on them in return that at last there was recognition of how very barbaric the white Americans had been. In the early 1930s State historian Alexander Flick wrote an account of the Sullivan-Clinton Expedition in which he could treat the Natives allied with the British in a manner that showed an understanding of the inhuman aspects of both sides of colonial war.

With Kingston's western borderlands becoming more secure George Clinton had set to work at overseeing the reconstruction of Forts Montgomery and Clinton and the other obstacles the British had managed to pass and damage on their way to Kingston in 1777. And he also added the new fort at West Point.

Neither Clinton's nor engineer Machin's solution to Kingston's trial by fire was carried out. And when, in 1783 George Washington visited Kingston he congratulated its inhabitants on having already achieved so much in restoring their village as a trading and dwelling place, even though it had lost the honor of being the State's capital.

Kingston was known during the Revolution for having few loyalists (or Tories as they were then called by their opponents). This was what General Vaughan was getting at when he called the town the "greatest nest of villains in the country." In the super-heated mood to which each side had ascended when referring to the other, Vaughan's "rascals" referred to what his opponents called "patriots."

Among the loyalists or Tories who once played a part on the British side in the march to war, was an extraordinary man named Charles Inglis. He is not known to have ever lived in Kingston but he owned a large number of village lots and other pieces of Kingston real estate. He probably spent time in Kingston as other Tories did as war neared to protect family members sent there for safety and provisions sent upriver from seriously threatened New York City. He has a place in American literary history because he wrote a forceful attempt at a refutation of Thomas Paine's great *Common Sense* which in 1776 stirred thousands of Americans to join the effort to throw off the colonial chains placed on their minds and fortunes by Britain. Charles Inglis was once the rector of the established Anglican Trinity Church of the city of New York under British rule. So devoted to the British was Inglis that (after the Revolution had begun) he once read the collect asking God to bless King George III to his somewhat Americanized congregation, and a tumult followed.

Inglis was attainted by the American Congress and his Kingston lands were accordingly confiscated and sold at auction. Like many other loyalists he fled to Canada. There he eventually presided as bishop over the see of Nova Scotia.

An event that stirred passion was the circulation in Kingston of a pamphlet labeled *Free Thoughts on the Resolves of the Late Congress,* being Under the Signature of A.W. Farmer. The Farmer was actually Samuel Seabury, an Anglican clergyman of Westchester County, but among those suspected of being the author was Charles Inglis. A meeting of indignant Ulster County men assembled in Marbletown with a purpose of expressing support of the Articles of the Congress. They also listened to a reading and a denunciation of the pamphlet, suspected to be the work of Inglis, and a demand that it be burned as a sign of their disapproval and this was immediately done. In other places on the American side of the war, the pamphlet was tarred and feathered and treated in other disrespectful ways to express disapproval.

Another loyalist supporter—who however is not known ever to have set foot on Kingston soil was Native "monster" Joseph Brant. Why and how he is remembered in Kingston is made clear by the letter of British spy Isaac Davis of Woodstock to George Clinton written from Kingston in May, 1779 as what is known as the Sullivan-Clinton Expedition (to destroy back country settlements) was in progress: "These are the Intelligences I Can give from the Indians after they Returned from Shandaken; they was too go to fitch Bradt (Brant) with his company to come down this Quarter. Burn & Distroy where Ever they Come Down." Their first attempt was to be at "Schohery from Butter (Butternuts), that, they Supposed would draw the militia their." Brant would come down the Quarter to Marbletown, Hurley, Kingston, Churchland (now part of Saugerties) "& a Report that I have heard that They want to gether all the Tories they can fron fear if they should be Beaten off & the Indian's should turn their arms against them. These Informations I have received from my wife; from Who she has it I don't know. But the whole to Remain a Secrit. Isaac Davis."

Hanging on a wall in Fenimore House Museum in Cooperstown, NY, many visitors to this museum pause to admire a striking portrait by American painter Gilbert Stuart painted in the late 1780's. His subject is Joseph Brant, wearing an extremely picturesque headdress of plumes and leather, unmistakably meant to seem Native American in design. He had earlier enjoyed a lively social success even among upper class Britons who regarded him on his visit to them as a splendid example of that Romantic hero, "The noble savage," held up as a role model for the colonized native people of the world. In his own New York State Brant was causing shivers to afflict the backs of American revolutionists who saw him as a "monster," "cruel barbarian" and a relentless enemy of American freedom. He was a brother of Molly Brant, the Iroquois live-in companion and later the legal wife of Sir William Johnston, the Superintendent of Indian affairs under British rule. Brant had been given a white man's education and a good start in life as a loyal subject of King George, and also as a Mohawk of the Five Nations Confederacy he worked toward steering the Oneidas (one of the five) toward support for King and Parliament. He realized that the largely tenant population of such great absentee landlords as those of the Hardenbergh Patent were none too fond of their landlords. The usual absentee landlords sided with the American Congress but a fair number of the tenants were Tories. And when British recruiters found their way into the Patent, some sons of tenants enlisted and were secretly conducted through American lines to New York City to serve as British soldiers. Others, with Brant as Colonel, served in their own borderland in ragged uniforms and with poor equipment. They were often disguised as Indians. It was these men who terrified the borderland colonists of the older settlements and Kingston just as more than a century earlier settlers who had moved out from Kingston were terrified of the Esopus Natives with whom they remained in conflict for many years until they agreed on a workable peace treaty. Some settlers fled to Kingston and other older settlements whenever acute danger threatened.

Under the Treaty which ended the Revolution in 1783 provisions for good relations with loyalists who had not served in arms against the Americans were not always strictly carried out. In Ulster County returned Tories are remembered to have been tarred and feathered and otherwise treated with violence, but Joseph Brant in 1797, although a few years earlier regarded as the terror of Kingston and its back country, was in the United States. There he was associating with leading citizens in connection with land deals. In New York City he was asked to dinner by Aaron Burr. Burr's daughter Theodosia as she planned the dinner told William Leete Stone, a New York editor, in her whimsical way, that she had thought of sending to a hospital for a human head and properly dressing it as a main course of the dinner to help Brant feel welcome at home.

As late as the 1860s, tourists to the Catskills were being shown a ruined encampment or fortification said to have been Brant's near the top of the Platte Clove on the eastern wall of the Catskills, and not very far from Kingston. From there Brant, it was said, once kept an eye on the Mid-Hudson Valley and made his choice as to which communities would become his "prey." The Clinton-Sullivan expedition, although it did not entirely end fear of border country devastation, as helped by Brant, was a success in sending the final years of Revolutionary military activity to the southern colonies. And as a base for American claims to Native-held lands in the Great Lakes and Upper Middle West areas. American soldiers of the Sullivan-Clinton Expedition who had coveted the fine lands of the Natives in the Susquehanna and Mohawk Valleys now returned as civilians to lay claim to the lands from which they had cruelly expelled the Natives.

And so the Susquehanna Valley filled up as did much good potential valley farmland to the West and beyond. And all this played a part in the "Conquest of the West" by the United States and its loss by the Natives. In addition, the "scorching" of the British Native allies in the Susquehanna Valley and the British burning of

Kingston (and its borderlands to the west by Natives and Tories) were both contributory factors, each in its own way, to the American victory in the Revolutionary War. The Susquehanna valley formed part of the homeland of the Seneca Natives, members of the Iroquois Confederation. These "Keepers of the Western Gate" of the Confederacy remained deeply resentful of the injury done them as a result of George Washington's plans for the Clinton-Sullivan campaign. They gave Washington a name which means "destroyer of villages" in their language.And the fertile land devastated in the Sullivan-Clinton campaign was settled by Americans some of whom had been soldiers in the campaign.

6.
George Washington Visits Kingston 1782

NEWS OF THE SURRENDER OF BURGOYNE NEAR SARATOGA IN 1777 WHICH would lead to the recognition by pre- French Revolution Bourbon France of the Independence of the United States had set off a period of rejoicing by the people of Kingston; and then early in 1781 the string of victories by American armies brought even greater rejoicing to Kingston. And on November 16, 1782, before the official treaty of peace with Britain had been signed and sealed at Versailles, Kingston was honored by a friendly visit from George Washington, now relaxed from his arduous wartime labors. The General had reached Kingston from New Jersey after a round-about ride including visits to Stone Ridge and Hurley where he had spent a night in the imposing two-story gambrel-roofed stone dwelling of Col. Wynkoop in Stone Ridge, and so set that handsome house in the class of future "Washington slept here" memorials.

The Kingston trustees greeted Washington with a reverent tribute to his services to the nation and to his fine character. Washington replied by praising Kingston people for their devotion to the cause of Independence and their sacrifice in gaining it. Mutual good wishes and congratulations passed from and to the General and the minister and elders of the Old Dutch Church. There were traditional festive meals and it is said a lively dance during which all Kingston celebrated their hero with enthusiasm and spirit. And until not-so-long-ago many Kingstonians boasted that Washington had danced with their grandmothers—although without good proof of this beyond showing a worn old slipper of 18th century origin, claiming that an ancestor had worn this when dancing with Washington. During the visit, along the widespread borders of the town, militiamen were still ranging through the war-deserted settlements in search of Tories and hostile Natives still unaware that the war for American Independence had been won and who were still seeking enemies to conquer.

Colonel Wynkoop as a boy, with the sword he used in the Revolutionary War attached to his portrait, from Holland Society publication in 1886.

Many years ago, in the 1930s, as George Washington's two hundredth birthday anniversary—1732-1932—was being celebrated, a summer resident of the nearby art colony of Woodstock, Clowry Chapman, studied the just-published expense account records of Washington and the accepted rationale of the reasons for his tour to Kingston. Chapman theorized on this basis that the reason for a gap in Washington's recorded expenses was this—that the General was meeting and making arrangements for peace (and land deals) with those Natives who had fought for the British. Thus Chapman expounded in the form of a college master's thesis. He deposited a copy in the Woodstock Library because he had theorized that Woodstock was the place of the meeting with the Indian representatives with whom Washington had made a treaty of peace. A copy still remains in the Woodstock Library and is well worth reading as a bizarre contribution to the story of Washington's visit to Kingston long ago. Yet there may be more than a grain of truth behind Chapman's theorizing. Both Washington and George Clinton have left behind some evidence to suggest that both, once the actual war was ended, went back to the speculation in land of their pre-war days, but were not eager to have this known. George Washington is known to have bought tickets for Catskill mountain lotteries of land which came into white possession as a result of the Sullivan-Clinton Expedition which he had planned.

PART 7

The New Nation Begins to Take Shape

1.
After the War was Won

THE REVOLUTIONARY WAR HAD BROUGHT BOOM YEARS TO SOME SHARP business oriented Kingston Americans, and once peace appeared to be in sight, the Kingstonians were suitably optimistic. The war had played a substantial part in moving some old fashioned Kingston minds out of a constricted corner in which conservative Dutchness lingered on. They were now faced with preparing to play their parts as energetic and aggressive American citizens freed from colonial shackles. When the Constitutional Convention of 1788 decided to redeem the Continental currency (which had helped finance freedom but which had sunk in value) at full value, the news was leaked. And by means of fast horses and daring riders word of the decision was rushed to favored speculators. Such men found it easy to buy up from former Revolutionary soldiers the supposedly almost worthless currency in which they had sometimes been paid and make large profits once the paper was redeemed at full value.

By August 1793, Charles De Witt could announce that nature herself was cooperating in creating prosperity for Kingston and its agricultural surroundings. "We have the greatest crops here that we have had for many years past, and the most fruitful that I can remember to have ever seen. I am in hopes the poor laborers will be better able to rub along this year, and wheat, rye, corn etc. are vastly cheaper than they have been in a long time."

Even before the new treaty with Britain was finalized in 1783, George Washington, George Clinton, and other former army officers had traveled northward to the Mohawk (and Susquehanna) Valley to inspect the lands from which the Natives had been forcibly expelled and to choose promising tracts of farmland for speculative ventures. The United States, thanks to the rolling to the Mississippi of the boundaries the nation claimed, and thanks to the work of Kingston's neighbor Chancellor Robert R. Livingston in negotiating the great Louisiana Purchase with Napoleon for less than four cents an acre, would now lay the groundwork for an extension of white settlements to more than halfway across the continent. But war is an expensive activity and wasteful. The Americans had incurred national debts. Many demobilized soldiers were finding it diffficult to "rub along" as Charles De Witt would put it. And some of them were becoming rebellious.

Thc wavc of cuphoria that accompanied peace was brief indeed. In 1784 and for several years after, prices of the farm and forest products on which Kingston people depended for a living dropped as Charles De Witt observed and Americans had a sharp taste of what would become a recurring phenomenon in their lives—the first of their series of economic depressions following periods of speculation and prosperity.

The ending of the war brought with it the emergence of what were seen as fresh opportunities, however, for doing profitable business for the "traders and traffickers" who continued to form the upper crust of Kingston's social and commmerical life, and served the village as trustees. What had been sparsely settled back country, recently at the mercy of Iroquois Native and Tory raiders, was showing signs of becoming a productive source of saleable crops, timber and potash, a saleable by-product of clearing the land. The settlers required roads to link their productions for marketing to Kingston with its convenient landing place on the Hudson River at Rondout.

The Kingston trustees were perceptive enough to hire a surveyor named Hynpaugh (who was a black man) to explore the back country and determine the best routes that might serve Kingston's trading purposes. Hynpaugh came up with two routes—one crossed the Esopus Creek at Kingston and thence went on to and over the steep Pine Hill and thence on to the west branch of the Delaware River; the other, judged at first more promising by the trustees, led to the still Livingston-dominated hamlet of Woodstock, and up Mink Hollow to the Schoharie Creek and down its valley to the Mohawk Valley and Creek which would empty into the Hudson River above Albany. The Kingston projectors of the road began in the fall of 1783, by sending employees and slaves to wield axes, picks and shovels on the road building job. Elias Hasbrouck, only recently a quartermaster (usually a post of considerable profit) in the American armed forces, who also owned a shop in Higginsville on the edge of Kingston, saw a bright enough future in the Schoharie road to cause him to leave Kingston and buy land at the entrance to Mink Hollow (named after a black man who settled there) on the new road. There he set up a store and proposed the entertaining of the numerous travelers he expected. The travelers, however, were few, for the road was not a success. There were good reasons for the failure of the Schoharie Kill Road. It was a daring pioneer step in a period of competition by three communities on the west bank of the Hudson to link themselves commercially to a back country now about to be available for exploitation. Newburgh and Catskill, before long, would send turnpike roads westward on which settlers from New England and elsewhere could travel to make their "pitches" on land they preferred and strip the forest from the land. But in this movement of prospective tenants and settlers Kingston was laggard.

As the Kingston men built their road, the back country it led to was still in the first stages of settlement, not by independent owners, but by tenants who paid rents (according to manorial customs) in bushels of wheat, labor, maple sugar or bacon to the absentee landlords of the Hardenbergh Patent who let their holdings to tenant farmers on leases for three successive lives, as did the lords of manors across the Hudson. The land through which the new road made its way was described by a rent-collecting observer as a "land of rocks, roots and beggars." Its primary advantage of having a relatively mild upward slope from the Hudson was not enough to overcome its slowness in becoming productively settled by non-owners who sometimes skipped leaving back rents unpaid.

During the years of the anti-Colonial War there could have been no very stable government for the rebellious colony of New York. They had rejected that of the British crown, and had managed to patch together an adequate wartime system of government by congresses and committees under the Articles of Confederation. It was not until 1781 that an attempt to revise the Articles of Confederation led the way to the formation of the Constitutional Convention, to improve the generally admitted shortcomings of the Articles. The struggle to create the Articles had made it plain that there was a substantial division of its New York delegates into two groups, one largely dominated by rich Americans who favored a strong central federal government, and the other made up of members less favored in material things, who preferred facilities such as taxation in large measure left to the states. Governor George Clinton, like most Ulster County people, belonged to that second group, and when he criticized with decided harshness the views of federalist Alexander Hamilton, bitter controversy followed between those advocating a strong central government under a new national Constitution and those who argued for relying on a mere revision of the Articles of Confederation and so for less centralization.

Kingston and the rest of Ulster County strongly favored the anti-federal group. Governor Clinton and Cornelius C. Schoonmaker were notable battlers for retaining the Articles of Confederation with some amendments added to favor somewhat less centralization.

On July 25th, 1788, Ulster County delegate Schoonmaker reported to anti-federalist politician Peter van Gaasbeek of Kingston "after a long and tedious discussion," in which he stated he was opposed to the Articles, but voted for them "and the proposing of amendments thereto, the result of the New York delegation will be an adoption of the Constitution on the grounds of expediency." And so the people of Kingston, by means of their delegates, reluctantly adopted the Constitution under which, with Amendments and interpretations, we now live.

Those Kingstonians who clung to the Articles or had espoused Federalism did not take their defeat lightly. In his *History*, Marius Schoonmaker, a relative of delegate Cornelius, tells of the bitterness that marked the political life of Kingston between Federalists and anti-Federalists. "Party feelings in the early days of the republic between the Republicans and Federalists became extremely bitter and personal. Many a fight in Kingston was the result of a canvass, and the Court House yard and the street at the corner of Maiden Lane and Fair Street, were witnesses of many a bitter fray and pitched battle. The headquarters of the contending parties were located at the opposite corners of those streets." These headquarters were in inns where liquid stimulants added to the fury of the political battlers. "This spirit had its ferment and expression at the periodical returns of caucuses and elections; at other times quiet reigned," wrote lawyer-politician-historian Schoonmaker.

As late as 1804 the Federalist trustees in expectation of being followed the next year by an anti-Federalist village board, unanimously voted the amount of village funds on hand amounting to over three thousand pounds to be paid to the churches of the village, all four of which were Dutch Reformed, to be used as ministers' salaries. They did this to embarass the incoming anti-Federalist board—so anti-Federalist Schoonmaker reported in his usually reliable history.

Among the noticeable later breaks of quiet from time to time was the work of Ferdinand Augustus de Zeng, energetic son of a German baron who was High Forest Officer to the Elector of Hesse-Saxony. An expert on the then-booming German interest in forestry and forest related industries, young de Zeng had come to America as an officer of the soldiers whom the Elector had hired out to Britain to fight the rebellious Americans. He soon took the American side in the Revolution, became an American citizen, married an American woman, and following a brief spell in Red Hook, Dutchess County, he took to living in Kingston and operating, in 1795, a sawmill on the Esopus Creek, about 10 miles above Kingston.

In Kingston, he shattered the usual quiet of the place by scolding the trustees of the village for mistreating the timber they had bought for building a new bridge across the Esopus Creek. De Zeng is also said to have introduced Kingston to the use of picket fences. After a period of involvement in Mohawk Valley canal and road ventures and as superintendent of a glassmaking factory at Sand Lake near Albany, de Zeng dazzled Kingston people with his proposal of a toll-paying turnpike road to follow the southern Hynpaugh survey from their village, to the Catskills and the east branch of the Delaware River and beyond. He invited Kingston investors to share in his turnpike project. In a letter about this time to Chancellor Robert R.

Livingston, outspoken de Zeng characterized the Kingston citizens as "a parcel of old Dutchmen, heretofore remarkable for doing nothing." Now he galvanized the Dutchmen into subscribing to his turnpike, which in his enthusiasm he proposed extending eastward from Kingston Point by means of a ferry to an addition that would reach across Dutchess County to the Connecticut line. This was to be called the Delaware, Ulster and Dutchess Turnpike and which de Zeng expected would take, if completed, the flow of settlers coming from New England to the Catskills.

The proposal of the road stimulated Kingstonians to look forward to having a thriving center of population at Kingston (then Columbus) Point. Large stone houses were built, a stone building at the landing from which the ferry would take off, were actually built (by Moses Cantine) before it became obvious, first that the plan to cross the Hudson would have to be dropped after a short trial. Then the whole plan went into bankruptcy, leaving a bleak little settlement of substantial stone buildings to form a ruined cluster of relics of the scheme at Kingston Point to hang on for many years while New Englanders reached the Catskills through Catskill or Newburgh.

The failure of their Schoharie Kill road venture of 1783 into western road building had chilled Kingston entrepreneurs. They had allowed their commercial rivals of Catskill and Newburgh to become infected with the virus of turnpike building, then beginning to afflict the state. Turnpike roads leading to hitherto lightly settled regions, were planned, built and operated by corporations like de Zeng's, which charged tolls and hopefully would pay dividends. The immensely successful Susquehanna Turnpike from Albany to the northern Catskills and beyond had also contributed to siphoning off many of the emigrants from New England to the West, bypassing Kingston's offering. The Delaware and Hudson Turnpike of Ferdinand Augustus de Zeng, taking off from Kingston, had been heavily invested in by the Kingston trustees who found this stock rejected when they offered it later on as security in deals to help finance the Kingston Academy they hoped to enlarge.

Catskill and Newburgh in the mid 1790's began to hum with proposals aimed at making possible the settlement of the back country, which they hoped would reject Kingston and accept Catskill and Newbugh as their ports and markets on the Hudson. Kingston subscribers, with the aid of the village trustees, took the first early substantial steps toward bridging the Esopus Creek to replace the former fording place or rift and earlier flimsy bridges destroyed by floods. And after much delay, the bridge became a fact. This bridge, in the mind of de Zeng, would become the first bridge on a turnpike road that might tie Kingston to the farming country being then settled in the southern Catskills and beyond.

By 1802, the road, chartered as a turnpike, was under construction and its planner was vigorously trying to dispose of its stock. A bit later roads floored with hemlock planks following a Russian example became popular but the planks proved not durable and these roads ceased being built. De Zeng's fertile imagination at the same time was aglow with a private project. He proposed making glass on a large scale in nearby Woodstock. There, he assured Kingston prospective investors, everything needed for glassmaking could be had in abundance—sand, waterpower, thousands of acres of hardwoods such as beech needed to feed the hungry furnaces of the factory. And his turnpike would pass through this ideal location as it made its way to Kingston across the now-bridged Esopus Creek, and so down to the Kingston Landing or Strand or even by way of the slippery clay road that led to Kingston Point. But in order to enable the turnpike to live within its means, it became necessary, he found, to straighten out its route by passing close to his glass factory at Woodstock, and changing the glass factory's Kingston shipping point. Instead the road would end at a landing place on the Hudson River at bit above Kingston which soon came to be named Glasco, from its connection with the glass company. In expectation of a fine future for Glasco, a map of the place dividing it into building lots was prepared. The road, Glasco Turnpike, is still in existence today as a part of the Ulster County highway system, but Kingston was by-passed.

With the glass factory launched on half a century of reasonably successful business by others, ebullient de Zeng had sold his Ulster County possessions and gone off to make glass with his Ulster County profits at Sand Lake near Albany and in the Mohawk Valley and to immerse himself in a variety of ways of hunting for further profit. He moved to Canada where his pioneer attempt at glassmaking failed dismally, due, he claimed, to local hostility by ethnic Canadians. For several years he and his wife, who had been raised as a Quaker, were members of a Shaker Community, with its emphasis on celibacy, crafts, dancing and its own sort of music.

Kingston, encouraged by the initially profitable behavior of the Ulster-Delaware turnpike, thought up others, most of which accomplished little beyond losing money for the subscribers. One of these has its place in Kingston memories because it gave its name to a street called Lucas Avenue, in honor of its fellow projector, Lucas Elmendorf, who is still better remembered as the ingenious lawyer who continued to keep a not very important lawsuit before the courts for forty years.

Also among the memorials of the days when Kingston was still getting its breath after its holocaust of 1777 and the great fire of 1804 are a number of massive cube-shaped buildings standing in or near the Stockade area of the present city. In these outwardly plain, yet imposing structures members of the upper stratum of traders did business in their shops and counting rooms built in a style that approached positive luxury within, and still continued to house their apprentices and families. And in their basements or down in their cellars provided a minimal kind of housing for their slaves.

Kingston, no longer a colonial outpost and with the promoting energy of Ferdinand de Zeng at work, gave most travelers who passed through it the impression of being a pleasant, wealthy community. There in the early decades of the nineteenth century the Reformed Church still dominated the religious scene as far as organized denominations with buildings of their own were concerned. Yet other sects such as Baptists and Methodists were active. And by the 1820s the village had its first Sunday School in a building on North Front Street to which it is said black children were also admitted. In Dutch churches, of which there were five in the township, sermons were no longer preached in Dutch, nor hymns always sung in that language after 1806.

Yet, Washington Irving traveled to Kingston and the surrounding part of Ulster County shortly after 1830 and set down in his journal his impressions of a decidedly Dutch flavor in the lives of the farmers living in houses of the Kingston area inherited from their forebears and still carrying on Dutch ways. Yet even here as in the village of Kingston the culture of colonization days—both Dutch and English—was slowing to an Americanization which would affect most parts of the United States, whatever the culture of their first white settlers might have been. It was the slaves who often continued to speak only Dutch into the middle of the 19th century after their enslavement ended.

One slave who lived for a while in Kingston and who spoke Dutch as a child—we do not know exactly where—shares today with George Clinton and painter John Vander Lyn the honor of being the most written about and talked about resident of Kingston of the past. She was the remarkable black woman known to us as Sojourner Truth, but during the 3 years she spent in Kingston, and earlier, her name was Isabella Van Wagenen.

2.
The Beginning (and the Ending) of the Kingston Commons

THROUGH ALL THE MANY CENTURIES OF NATIVE OCCUPANCY OF THE LAND which was to become part of the Dutch and British colonial possession of the Kingston to-be, the personal and private ownership of portions of it was unknown. A group or tribe like the Algonkian Esopus or Munsee people, it is true, might claim chief rights to the use of designated tracts of land and would fight to keep out interlopers. But the land and all its useful features and products were there for the use of all the members of their group subject to their cooperation with their pantheon of spirits.

With the reluctant yielding by the Natives of the possession of their land destined to come under the control of what was to become colonial Kingston, many radical changes came to the place. But one feature of life and the land in England as well as among the Esopus people was retained. This was the retention in a form slightly modified of the ancient feature of community life known to white colonists as the Commons. The Commons gave every inhabitant of a community an equal right to share in the use of the products of the uncultivated parts of the community lands. In Britain, long subject to deforestation, marked restrictions on the use of the Commons had crept in, notably on manorial grants. But in almost universally forested northeastern America, restrictions on the cutting of trees, the use of stone and the taking of game, nuts and fish, or the pasturing of livestock, were not at first imposed by the colonizers on their colonists. Only the appropriation of discovered mines of "royal metals"—(gold and silver) were reserved for the European monarchs who ruled over the colonies and its people.

The earliest white attempt at organizing the colonial settlement of Esopus was made by Dutch Governor Pieter Stuyvesant in 1661. Precise boundaries of the place were not given—the land was left afloat and otherwise vague except for the West bank of the Hudson. As for Stuyvesant's proposed organization of Esopus, it was only as a judicial district separated from that of Beaverwyck which adjoined Fort Orange. So there is no mention of a Commons in the Stuyvesant document of 1661 granting to the "settlement's inhabitants" of a Commons. That had to wait until 1687 when Esopus had come under British control and was no longer officially called Esopus, but Wiltwyck or soon Kingston or Kingstowne. The word Commons as applied to land use in 1687 also meant land open to use by all who shared in the right to use a certain designated part of that land for specific uses such as pasturing their cattle or sheep, or cutting wood for use as fuel, fencing or building.

In 1687 the Patent was granted by the British governor to the "Freeholders and inhabitants" of Kingston in trust to a Board of Trustees for the possession not only of the land which we know today as Kingston, but for a vast vague tract of surrounding wilderness to the north and west to serve as a Commons. In addition to a long enumeration of landscape features are included the right to the use of woods, timber, feedings, common of pasture, swamps and marshes.

The word "ffeedings," as mentioned in the Patent refers to foodstuffs such as nuts and berries gathered on the common lands for human and domesticated animal use. For many years, into the nineteenth century, swineherds in Kingston would go from door to door collecting a little army of hogs which they would take to the commons to permit the hogs to feast and fatten on the acorns strewn under the trees of the oak forest. This was at the time when fat pork and lard were in high demand.

Here is the exact wording by which Governor Dongan in 1687 granted to "the ffreeholders and Inhabitants of a Certaine Place or towne called Kingston" a long list of rights in the land granted, including the right to use the Commons for "Trees, Timber ffeedings, common of Pasture, Marshes Swamps" and so on and on, according to the Patent. In later years the rights of all inhabitants to a common use of the timber and pasture resources of the Patent were called the "rights to the Commons."

The Patent granting the right to use the part of the earth's surface upon which the City of Kingston was to rise as a white living space, and the surrounding forest, was held under English colonial law by the "freeholders and commonalty" of Kingston.

The Patent covered the wilderness thrust outward into the surrounding forests from the part beginning to become inhabited by white colonists. Their way of life required far larger and sturdier shelters against the often bitter cold of winter than did the wigwams of their predecessors, because they used large, jambless and very inefficient Dutch fireplaces sending most of the heat produced by fuel cut on the commons up their big chimneys as if in an attempt to heat the clouds above. Hence the value of the forests of the commons which the colonists cleared and on which they could then pasture cattle and plow for growing grain while using the trees they cut for fuel and building. To the Native Esopus people whom the colonists had supplanted, the whites' kind of magic in using the soil made little sense at first when compared with their own magic which made great use of the invocation of the spirits of the earth, the sky, the water and the spirits of the earth's non-human living things. Yet as the axemen and plowmen pushed them ever farther from their old homes and garden patches, they adopted something of the whites' farming methods.

The recital of the boundaries of the Patent of 1687 began with the Albany (now Greene County) line, ran down the Hudson to the Little Esopus Creek to the bounds of Hurley, thence along the bounds of Hurley to Mothar Creek, then northerly to Preamaker's Creek, and so on "as the mountains range" to the Albany County line. The first attempt at giving more precise boundaries to Kingston had taken place in 1661 when the judicial district had been created to remove Kingston from being subjected to the Court of Beaverwyck and given a court of its own, its bounds still vaguely defined and no mention being made of commons which were not yet needed.

In 1687 however, Wiltwyck, as the place was then known, was a fast growing community needing to reach out farther and farther for supplies of wood as fuel and as timber. The Wiltwyck white people by the peace treaty of 1661 by which the Esopus Natives had yielded as reparations for war damage the lowlands on both sides of the Esopus Creek for a distance of two to three Dutch miles (four to six English miles) already used as Kingston wood-cutting and grazing resources.

Now in 1687 the Provincial authorities looked ahead and gave Kingston the generous grant of larger wilderness commons. The commons part of this grant in the years ahead would be put to uses which would have astounded its grantees and grantors.

But first the Kingstonians' right to the land called the Commons sometimes needed defending. At one time in the eighteenth century the Kingston trustees had leased some land along their supposed northern boundary to emigrants from the Rhineland brought to the Hudson Valley in a doomed venture intended to supply naval stores to the Royal Navy and made from the sap of certain kinds of pine trees. The survey on which the boundary relied had proved defective and the trustees reclaimed the land. The question of title was litigated. One witness produced was a mature lady who testified that when she was a girl, her father had taken her to a large boulder known from its shape as the Steene Hert, or Stone Heart which stood on the disputed line. The father had pointed out to the girl certain marks within the heart on the Albany County side and given the girl a "smart whipping." Then on the Kingston

Commons side he had drawn the girl's attention to a set of marks made to record that side as the Kingston Commons side. Then the father repeated this ancient adaptation of "beating the bounds" by beating or whipping the girl. This was accepted in evidence in court. In 1783 as the peace treaty which would cut the United States loose from its former colonial master was being written, a much more potentially significant event than the whipping of a girl being placed in evidence was underway.

As preparations for the birth of the United States as a free and independent nation were being made, the question of the location of a national capital was being vigorously discussed. And the Kingston trustees drew up a paper offering a square mile of their Commons for that purpose. The presenting of their offer was put into the very capable hands of their neighbor across the Hudson, Chancellor Robert R. Livingston who was expected to use his proven powers of persuasion to obtain its acceptance.

The Committee in charge was clearly impressed but suggested they would be even more deeply impressed were the Kingston village fathers to increase their offer to two square miles of their Commons. This increase was made at once by the trustees. Then, a period of seven years followed before the suspense of Kingstonians was relieved by word that Maryland had won the prize and the present District of Columbia would become the national capital. During the period of suspense, the trustees had so seriously joined in the hope that their community would profit should the capital come to their commons that they had joined the "freeholders and commonalty" for whom they held the lands of Kingston, including the Commons, as to ways they might prepare for sharing in the increased value the coming of the national capital should confer on their village.

Accordingly the trustees caused an undeveloped part of the village, including the present Academy Park or Green, the site of the "plains" and "water ploss" where boys swam or skated, to be surveyed into building lots. These they offered for sale to Kingston people, under bonds to be forfeited unless the buyers built upon the lots. Most purchasers failed to build as the hope of a national capital eluded them. In addition, 1784 began a period of economic slump and prolonged litigation followed between the lot purchasers and the trustees. After 1790 the year of the collapse of the final shred of Kingston's hope of becoming the capital of the nation, in a mood of snatching a kind of victory from defeat, the trustees offered the same tract of their Commons to the State as a site for a college or a university and this too was turned down, leaving as a memento a tract which came to be known as the Promised Land.

With the rejection of their offer to the State there came an understanding that changing times had made the Commons no longer possessed of their values of frontier days, and the process of getting them into private hands began.

Perhaps with Britain, where the remains of old commons were being "enclosed" or put into private hands (because of the profits of the wool trade to great landowners and raisers of sheep), furnishing a precedent, the Kingston trustees by 1804 took steps to end the old method of using the Commons. They had all the Commons, except a few hundred acres for an Academy, surveyed into lots. These lots were distributed upon payment of small fees to men born in Kingston, possessing specified amounts of property, and so being entitled to specific numbers of acres of the old Commons, to be held in fee simple, with no commitment in the later document as with some earlier sales or leases of Commons acreage to inhabitants "to preserve the timber." And so the many acres of what had been Commons went into private hands.

And their way of distributing the old Commons will explain why present day owners of parts of that old tract, in searching their title deeds, may find their acres described as having once formed part of the Binnewater class or the Supplies Hook class or some other class (such as those title searches of Saugerties land as part of the Pansie Bergh [Violet Hill] class—Saugerties became a separate town from the Commons in 1811). To make official the transfer to qualified Kingston men of the Commons it was divided into about 36 "classes," among them Binnewater, Huzzy Hill, and of "Catsbaan (Indian tennis court) classes." First several hundred acres were dedicated for the benefit of the Academy, plus a ferry base across the Rondout, then publically owned and operated, and now sold to make it clear that the Trustees were no longer holding much of Kingston in trusteeship, and that they were transferring it to private ownership.

In this way there happened a quiet American version of the final ending in Britain of the commons system under indusrial pressure for factories and workers' housing, by transferring the land to private owners after hot controversy, and several disappointments in attempts to set aside parts of community commons for national or local public use in the 18th and 19th centuries.

3.
Kingston Academy's Success

Back in 1774 as the tense years that heralded the leading up to the proclamation of the Declaration of Independence were bringing many uncertainties to Kingston the upper and middle levels of the village people took a bold step forward. A step that had nothing at all to do with the stirring events then leading to the cutting of their colonial ties to Britain.

It was a first step toward setting up for themselves a Latin School or Academy —the kind of institution we now use as a high school or school for secondary education. A school like this already existed in the City of New York. Its purpose like that of similar schools in the Netherlands and Britain was to prepare the sons of the more privileged classes for careers in the professions, government service or the ownership and management of land or business or to go on to university education.

The earliest hint we have that such a school was being discussed came in a letter of April 1769 from the Reverend Chauncy Graham who had been a pioneer schoolmaster in Fishkill in Dutchess County. A tutor of manorial Livingston children across the Hudson, Graham had gained some notice by publishing in 1761 a sermon in which he strongly denounced the use of "profane cursing and swearing" by members of the armed forces of the Hudson Valley engaged in the French and Indian War. Now he wrote to Charles De Witt, a trustee of Kingston, that he had been considering "opening an academy in either Albany or Kingston, provided I meet with substantial encouragement in either of those places."

Encouragement had come from Kingston when Graham heard that a "gentleman of that place had been in Fishkill making it his business" to inquire about Graham's fitness for founding the Academy. It was true enough that interest in having an academy for Kingston was stirring. By 11 October 1773 interest would reach

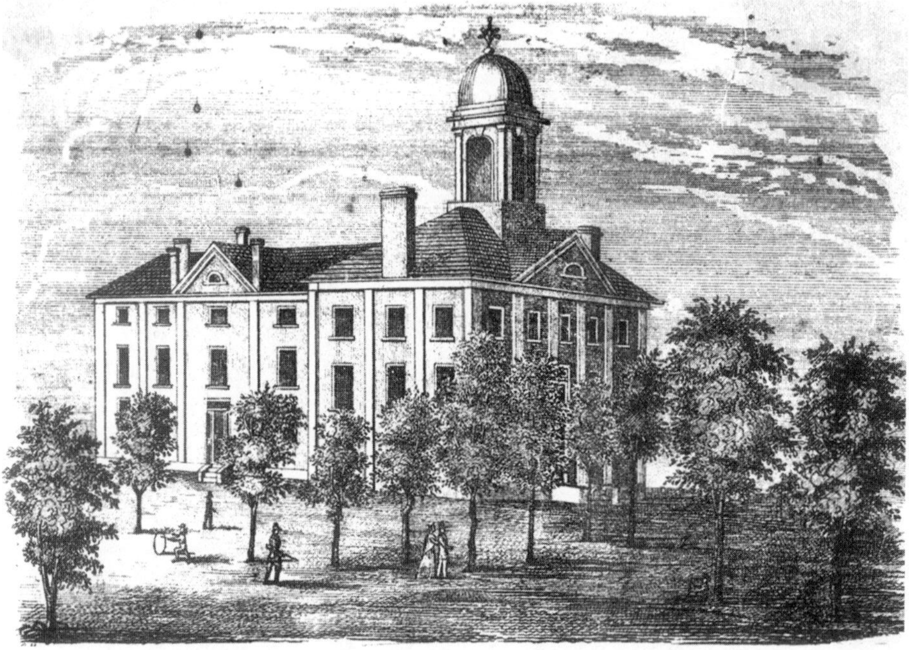

Two images of Kingston Academy:
Above, from the Tillson & Brink 1854 map; *below*, an 1896 postcard in the collection of Alf Evers.

the point at which trustee Johannis Sleght could propose to his fellow Kingston trustees that "in consequence of frequent conversations in regard to the building of a school or academy" in their town for the education of children, the Board "must make it a matter of the utmost moment." Sleght moved that they get on with this "laudable business for the public good." And the Academy was voted into existence on paper. It was voted also to take such steps as soliciting the advice of some eminent New York City men with connections to that city's Latin Academy. Notable among them was New Yorker Rev. Dr. John Henry Livingston (from an east bank manor family), to advise on such matters as the choosing of masters and ushers.[372] But Graham was ignored while financing and student fees were arranged for in the Village. Each student was also required to contribute as part of his fee two loads of firewood.

Students were assigned seats in the Dutch Reformed Church (still the only church in the Village) and penalized if they did not attend services. Latin and at times Greek were the cores of the instruction as were mathematics, history and "moral philosophy." The school day began with a reading from the Bible and a prayer.

An existing stone building, of by then familiar local design, well within the stockade area, was chosen to become the Academy, with a cupola added for the bell. It still stands at the corner of Crown and John Streets, a solid structure of local limestone now lacking its bell cupola. In appearance it is very much a typical part of Old Stockade Kingston. But as it began its career, it enjoyed backing from the great landowning Livingston families, with huge stakes in Ulster County wilderness and by marriage to the land rich Beekman family of Kingston.

From its beginning the Academy proved a success, not only for Kingston but for the Mid-Hudson Valley as well. Even as the fire and bloodshed of war moved close, while the students translated the prose of Cicero and extracted square roots in the manner of Euclid, the British fleet was assembling in New York harbor, the Declaration of Independence was read in front of Kingston's courthouse, the government of the new state had been established in Kingston, and the Academy students studied on. It was not until General Vaughan's men approached to make a dreadful bonfire of Kingston that the students put down their quill pens and their books and fled.

With the embers of their Academy barely cool, reconstruction of the building began. By the spring of 1778 the student body reassembled with a sufficient supply of equipment to justify returning to their studies.

Even before the Revolution ended in a treaty of peace, the trustees of Kingston had petitioned their new State Legislature for a charter to enable the Academy to incorporate as a college or even a university and they had been turned down. The hot Revolutionary climate had turned chilly for the Academy. The president of the Academy resigned yet sufficient faith in the institution remained to justify keeping it alive. The trustees solicited the learned Dr. John Witherspoon of Princeton College for advice about choosing a new master; their only stipulation was that he "not be young, and unmarried, as young gentlemen are fond of making experiments."

Dr. Witherspoon unhappily, in spite of his long and meritorious services to mankind, did not in this instance come up to expectation. The school came close to closing. Parents had petitioned for the discharge of the new principal, charging that their sons were not receiving the instruction they had paid for. Kingston's mood of pride turned to one of grim disappointment. Yet the trustees struggled on to restore life to the Academy which had already survived so many trials.

In 1795 the trustees applied to the state for a charter which would turn over control of the Academy, under state supervision, from the trustees of Kingston to a board of the Academy's own. The new board of the Academy was made up of local men of mostly Dutch and Huguenot ancestry with a Kingston man largely of English ancestry, law-trained John Addison, presiding as he had done earlier. Under the leadership of Addison until his death in 1800, all went well and the Academy regained its former momentum. Although Addison was in some ways very conservative (for example he favored the retention of slavery) in others he was in keeping with progressive movements of the time. Under his reign a room made its appearance on the second floor of the Academy for uses unrelated to instruction in the Latin School subjects. An occasional singing school under a New England master was held. There an English School (minus Latin), offered more practical courses; there women were first welcomed and classes in painting and embroidery and "other arts" were presented for a short time. One girl student was Catherine van Gaasbeek who achieved some reputation as a poet and who married a Yankee Kingston Academy teacher and went on to become the mother of a professor of mathematics at Yale.

The greatest feature of life at the Academy in its heyday and also an object of village pride became the semi-annual public examination days of students which were also treated as public holidays by the villagers. Here is how Marius Schoonmaker tells of these days of celebration, perhaps with the over-enthusiasm of an Old Grad. How "these days were looked forward to with great expectations of delight by the citizens of Kingston and the surrounding country both old and young. Every house was thrown open for the reception and entertainment of strangers and visitors on these occasions." With nostalgic relish Schoonmaker recounted the events of the days of academic and civic celebration—the gathering of the trustees at a public house where they met the Academy trustees and shared a glass of wine with them, and "their being escorted thence by a body of students and distinguished visitors, preceded by music and the merry ringing of the village bells to the Academy Hall where the rigorous and thorough examination took place." Next there was a public dinner in which trustees, students and distinguished visitors shared.

In the spring the literary exercises of the day closed with declamations in the church; in the fall there were scenes from "tragedies, farces and comedies" popular on the English stage. Among the plays were Dryden's Cato, and Home's Douglas, The Road to Ruin among them. Kingston on these cheerful days had the air of a true college town. But these plays were forbidden by the trustees after Yale's head Timothy Dwight forbade them at Yale in 1805 during an uprising of Calvinism, and Kingston followed Dwight's lead. Thereafter "dialogues, dissertations, and disputations on questions proposed" were substituted as "being more fit and proper for being better to train students in public speaking." The festivities received their climax with a Commencement, or ball "at Bogardus or de Wall's," public houses where Schoonmaker tells us "visitors and students united in the merry dance and thus joyously the rest of the night went."

By 1810 the public dinner and some other celebratory features began being abolished as the Academy's role in the community dwindled. The role of the English school had never been such that it was regarded as a true part of the Academy's place in the Village. Now the Latin School was beoming secondary to the English and was given up. The old school building within the Stockade area was judged inadequate to the needs of the new secondary school aspirations and was being remodeled to meet them. It was eventually sold and the proceeds applied to the cost of building a new frame Academy of contemporary design on the trianglular plot now known as Academy Green or Park.

One feature, shared by town and gown, continued. That was the Academy Library set up in 1795 with funds provided by the Board of Regents of the State of New York and open to the public. In 1864 the Academy became the High School of the free public school system of Kingston.

During its career covering 91 years the old Academy had played an important part in giving the people of Kingston a stronger sense of community as well as a broadening of their cultural and intellectual horizons.

And it had educated a remarkable number of leaders in many phases of the life of New York State—legislators, lawyers, jurists, diplomats, and some of the Livingstons and othe Hudson Valley magnates of the east manorial bank, and let us not forget painter John Vander Lyn, who brought resounding fame in American art to his native town.

4.
John Vander Lyn Contributes to Kingston History

In a book in French on his travels in the United States during 1795, 1796, and 1797, the Marquis de la Rochefoucald-Liancourt tells of visiting Peter Van Gaasbeek, a wealthy merchant and politician of Kingston, and a descendant of the second Mrs. Thomas Chambers's family. The French author's admiring attention was drawn to a portrait hanging above a fireplace in Van Gaasbeek's house. The subject, the Marquis' host explained, was Aaron Burr, then a lawyer, well known in Kingston and a member of the State Assembly. The painter, said Van Gaasbeek, had been a remarkable young man. Mr. Burr, having discovered in the young Kingston man as a child "a great talent for painting" had seen to it that he took all the best lessons in the art which America offered, and recently had sent him at Burr's expense to France and Italy to study the works of the old masters and there to receive the best instruction from modern ones. The French author does not mention the name of this talented prodigy but there are not many Kingstonians who cannot guess what it was. The boy was Kingston's great contribution to early American art—John Vander Lyn.

Vander Lyn (so he and his portrait painting grandfather sometimes spelled the family name) was born in Kingston in 1775 in a massive two-story stone house then standing at the intersection of John and Wall Streets of today. Grandfather Peter (himself a descendant of Dutch painters) at the age of 90, according to family tradition, made the 26 mile trip afoot to refuge with relatives from the dreadful British fire of 1777. Young John grew up in a lean-to against the ruins of the family house burned in 1777 and wagon painting and paint selling shop, amid the clutter and clatter of a neighborhood of old stone walls in the process of regaining their interior fittings and roofs. Painting of one sort or another seemed to have come down in the family. John's father Nicholas painted wagons, signs, houses and before the fire dealt in paints and oils. Grandfather Peter, the sprightly nonagenarian, had been a portrait painter of merit.

John had an excellent classical education for the time at the Kingston Academy. He began drawing early and in his teens was sent to New York where he studied painting and worked in a shop where artists materials were sold. Along the way he met clever, ambitious Aaron Burr, and under Burr's patronage studied with Gilbert Stuart who was widely aclaimed in Britain and the United States for his elegant portraits. Sent by Burr to Paris, he became a student at the Ecole des Beaux Arts under Andrei Vincent who in turn had studied with Jacques Louis David who had led French painters into a cool, classical kind of history painting. In reaction to what in the days of the pre-Revolution Bourbon monarchy was regarded by some as the frivolous and entertaining, if elegant work of pre-French Revolutionary days. Under Vincent, Vander Lyn worked hard, drawing from plaster casts of ancient Greek sculptures, he made copies of sober and voluptuous Renaissance masterpieces in the Louvre and painted from living nude models. This emphasis on the classics currrent in the second half of the 1790s came easily to Vander Lyn after his instruction in the world of the classics at the Kingston Academy.

As he worked away in Paris and Rome, he made friends, especially with the American painters beginning to visit Europe. Robert Fulton, who was a painter before his steamboat-improving days, Matthew Pratt, and especially Romantic Washington Alston were among them. He traveled when he could afford it to Switzerland and Italy; he tried out his Esopus Dutch in Holland and found it was not easily understood by real Dutchmen. In spite of no great skill in European languages, and a limping leg, he lived a pleasant social life in Paris of the 1990s and early 1800s.

Faithful to his master's teaching Vander Lyn worked on two paintings to demonstrate his arrival at mastery of his art; one was a historical work named *Marius Amid the Ruins of Carthage.* This painting shows the vanquished Roman general seated amid ruins far more imposing than those of Vander Lyn's native village, soberly meditating on the transitory nature of fame and glory while planning revenge against his Roman enemy Sulla. *Marius* was exhibited as one of 1200 paintings brought together at the order of Napoleon Bonaparte at the Louvre. Ribbons of the Legion of Honor were awarded to six of the painters shown who were French citizens and sixteen gold medals to foreign winners. Vander Lyn was awarded one of these medals. This marked a high point in Vander Lyn's life. He seemed on the verge of a decided success in Paris. The demand by the French for portraits by him soared. Yet a success in Paris while gratifying, was not what Vander Lyn dreamed of. He had set his hopes on returning to his native land and there taking a part in leading the United States to a high place in the world of art equal to that which he felt his people had earned by battling against colonialism.

After being delayed in returning to the United States until the War of 1812 was ended, hopeful Vander Lyn landed in New York. The American cognoscenti expressed admiration of his *Marius* while others showed little interest. It was otherwise with Vander Lyn's *Ariadne*, a masterly work showing the nude daughter of Minos, king of Crete, in a landscape setting. Ariadne is asleep on the island of Naxos where Theseus had abandoned her after she had rescued him from her father's labyrinth and the dreaded half bull half man Minotaur. And while *Marius* bored many Americans who took little interest in European myths, classical learning and history, glorious Ariadne shocked a great many of them. In the largely still Calvinistic nation a nude human figure was something to be ashamed of. A painting of a nude woman, even when so superb as that of Vander Lyn's, was no more than a pornographic trap of the Devil. Only a slightly draped version of the work by an engraver, perhaps Asher B. Durand, pleased proper Americans. It was after the rejection of his work and hopes that the painter began a long period of spells of despondency from which he sought relief by drinking, and giving strong expression in conversation and letters to his conviction that the arts in America were in a sad state of neglect.

John Vander Lyn's *Ariadne.* Courtesy of Pennsylvania Academy of Fine Arts.

In Kingston over the years their famous painter has been regarded with ambivalence. He had been spoken of with pride, his works had been collected by rich Stockaders and are proudly displayed today in the Senate House Museum in Kingston. But when in the 1950s a new school was being built it was strongly suggested it be named for Vander Lyn. To this there were vigorous objections. A member of an old Kingston family explained why. "Mr. Vander Lyn," she said, "drank too much sherry wine and he painted naked ladies." The school was named for that impeccable hero George Washington, who drank sherry and madeira in gentlemanly moderation and painted no ladies at all.

Until the final years of what had become a frustrated existence, Vander Lyn struggled to support himself by painting excellent portraits which work he did not enjoy, devising other ways of earning money by his art and never missing a chance to contribute to that national and public understanding of the high place he believed the arts deserved in American life. In this, he agreed with John Adams who had written to his wife Abigail as the Revolution had raged that his days were being taken up with Revolutionary War matters in order that their children, when the war was ended, would be able to enjoy the arts in peace.

Because Americans were beginning to take pride in their distinctive scenery and such wonders as Niagara Falls, he painted large and imposing landscapes showing whites and Natives giving a sense of history relating to the great Falls. He went to London and there arranged for engravings to be made from his Niagara painting. The engravings were first shown in Paris at a reception given by the American minister to France, that good Hudson Valley neighbor of Kingston, Chancellor Robert R. Livingston. He made sketches for paintings of scenes of the highlands of the Hudson and of the Palisades which were then rising in status in American minds as natural wonders. But all in vain. The public refused to become excited and pressured Vander Lyn to turn out the portraits in which the artist caught likenesses and at the same time gave his subjects a dignity they might not have possessed in reality.

In London and Paris Vander Lyn had been impressed by the panoramas of places of historic and scenic interest which were doing well there. Striking panoramas were realized by means of an invention in 1787 by an Irish painter of a means of displaying them in a way that gave them an almost magical quality. Vander Lyn began making sketches in the royal gardens of Versailles for a panorama of his own. He borrowed money to build a simple classical building in New York's City Hall Park. There he would exhibit a few panoramas of other artists, while working in Kingston on the one of his own showing the glamorous palace and gardens surrounding it at Versailles. Once he had finished his work on the panorama with a Kingston barn as a studio, he unveiled it for the pleasure of the people of New York. It was painted with skill and spirit largely from sketches Vander Lyn had made on the spot. He also exhibited his own paintings. However, patrons did not enthusiastically rush to the Rotunda in which his panorama was shown.

About 1803 during his first return to the U.S. from Paris, Vander Lyn made a trip to Niagara Falls on which he made sketches for a painting of the stupendous falls as a first step in the glorifying of the magnificent scenery of his native land by a native born American painter. A masterly view of the Falls hangs today in the Kingston Senate House Museum. Vander Lyn's Niagara paintings and the engravings made from the 1804 examples did not arouse the American interest for which Vander Lyn had hoped at a time when the more emotionally charged works of what would come to be called the Hudson River School were winning public favor. Vander Lyn's huge painting however captures Niagara Falls at a time when the use of part of its once unblemished form for industrial purposes and the deforesting at the demands of farmers has lessened its once pristine appeal.

Vander Lyn fitted easily into the custom of his time of forming relations with patrons who sometimes helped him to proceed with his work. He now waited upon the great men of the national government in an effort at being commissioned. He was commissioned to prepare illustrations for the Hartford wit Joel Barlow's widely heralded attempt at a proposed multi-volumed national epic called *The Columbiad.* This Vander Lyn never finished, but it led him to paint a striking historical work based on an incident used in Barlow's turgid volumes. *The Murder of Jane McCrae* presents the lovely young woman begging for her life from the two extraordinarily brutal and demonic looking Natives as one poises his deadly tomahawk which is about to descend upon her head in a whirl of Native arms and legs. As commissions for painting further historical subjects eluded Vander Lyn in a nation which failed to rise to the heights of glorious devotion to the arts for which he had hoped Vander Lyn made it plain in his letters and conversation that he had become morose and embittered. He went on painting portraits and copies of his *Ariadne* no longer entirely nude but wearing bits of costume suited to the tastes of the patron. In 1832 the Congress after much debate commissioned him to create a full-length figure of George Washington but here there was a catch. Vander Lyn was required to copy the famous head painted by Gilbert Stuart and equip it with a body and background which were to be Vander Lyn's own original work. This pastiche, thanks to Vander Lyn's skillful craftmanship, managed to gain the satisfaction of the Congressmen and the public, but perhaps not of Vander Lyn himself. But he was better satisfied with a commission which finally arrived in 1838 which seemed to be exactly the painting he had hoped all these years to get a chance to do. It was offered him by Congress to fill one of the panels of the Rotunda in the national Capitol, and Vander Lyn chose the subject the *Landing of Columbus.* Today Columbus is not quite the unblemished hero he was in the 1830s because of his cruelty to the Native

Americans. But in those years he was regarded as an American hero to be extravagantly admired.

Vander Lyn visited the site of Columbus' landing at San Salvador in the West Indies and made meticulous sketches of local vegetation and landscape. As usual he was careless in money matters. While working on the *Landing* he managed to run through the substantial payment for the 11 feet 10 inch by 12 feet mural and lapsed into his usual state of near-poverty before the painting was finished. Yet finished it was in a manner that gave credit to his training in Paris and to his lifelong passion for creating important historical works which would inspire his patriotic fellow Americans. The painting has been faulted by some recent art critics as reflecting the by-then unfashionable French Directoire tastes. Yet in design, execution and color it reflects the less-chilly design of his Paris masters of the school of David in his own impressive personal way.

Vander Lyn had been unfortunate in many aspects of his life. For one thing his generous patron Aaron Burr, after barely missing becoming President of the United States (which would surely have brought success and fame as a painter to Vander Lyn) and serving as Vice-President under Jefferson, had killed Alexander Hamilton in a duel. He had been acquitted of a charge of treason after he became involved in a murky scheme to set up a new nation from parts of the southwestern United States and Mexico. Bankrupt, he took refuge in Europe where he is remembered to have been helped by his grateful friend Vander Lyn. In 1852 Vander Lyn, then ill and tormented by the addiction to alcohol of his namesake, returned to Kingston and promptly died at 77.

In Kingston which had never given him a great deal of support, the Village authorities declared a day of public mourning. The old church bell and all other bells in the Village tolled together and great and small citizens attended his funeral. In the wave of appreciation of their departed famous son there was talk of erecting a handsome stone memorial to Vander Lyn. But this rmained only a hope until a friend, Kingston poet Henry Abbey, supplied a modest headstone.

Shortly before his death, Vander Lyn had been dealt a final blow of fate. A tale was circulated which claimed that being too old to paint his *Landing* he had hired a young Frenchman to do the work. Vander Lyn made no secret of the fact that he had employed an assistant or two to sketch costumes of the Columbus period in the museums and libraries of Paris and to attend to some other details as other helpers of other mural painters are in the habit of doing when faced with large commissions. The rumor has persisted to this day but the difference in quality in sketches made by the assistant and the master is obvious to anyone studying them today.

John Vanderlyn the Nephew, as he is called in Kingston, was by no means the equal of his uncle yet he painted portraits which are sometimes accredited to the elder Vander Lyn. He painted fruit pieces and scenery for a local amateur theater group. A Kingston newspaper praised him for a feat of painting which would be regarded with horror by present day art lovers. He overpainted two old Kingston family portraits of Jacob Bruyn and his wife. Bruyn is shown wearing a Ramilly wig which has a pigtail with two bows and went out of style about 1760. Vanderlyn added a landscape background showing the Shawangunk mountains which rise above a farm the Bruyns owned near New Paltz. While the reporter was ecstatic about the improvement in the painting, people of today who suspect these two paintings might have been by Vander Lyn's forebearer Peter are far from ecstatic. But the whereabouts of these "restored" paintings is not known.

Today Kingston realizes that Vander Lyn was one of the greatest of all early American painters and holds him in high esteem. One of the major buildings of the Ulster County Community College bears the name Vanderlyn Hall. The Senate House Museum owns a large and excellent collection of Vander Lyn's works and of Vander Lyn's memorabilia. In New York City his Versailles panorama, splendidly restored, is admired every year by thousands of visitors to the Metropolitan Museum of Art as well as the painter's superb self-portrait hanging in the same great museum. His *Landing of Columbus* long ago achieved indisputable respectability by appearing, as it still does, in a variety of forms on national currency and postage stamps. And a diligent art historian writing of the stamp bearing an engraving of Vander Lyn's *Landing of Columbus,* has calculated how many millions of American tongues have licked the backs of the postage stamp. This is a distinction which no other works of American art can match. But a far greater distinction was to be given to Vander Lyn many years after his death by his magnificent *Panoramic View of the Palace and Gardens of Versailles* which will be dealt with in a later chapter.

PART 8

Kingston Develops its Character in Peace and War

1813-1865

1
Sojourner Truth
1830

IT IS KNOWN THAT ISABELLA VAN WAGENEN WAS BORN IN THE VICINITY OF Kingston. Recent scholars who have probed her life story accept 1797 as the most likely year of her birth. The place of Isabella's birth is not known to be noted in town records although the birth of black babies was required to have been recorded, but most scholars now agree that she was born in the low and damp cellar of the old house of the Rutsen and Hardenbergh families, which stood until it was picked out for destruction on July 5th, 1911 by a bolt of lightening with no respect for historic landmarks.

The house stood beside the old fording place or rift in the Rondout Creek in the northern part of the hamlet of Rosendale not very far from the Kingston line. A few years before Isabella's birth, another distinguished person is known to have had a different sort of relationship to the house. It was in this already old stone house that Martha Washington and Governor George Clinton breakfasted with the Hardenberghs on the 21st of June, 1793—so a letter of General Washington's aide testifies.

Confusion as to Isabella's birthplace is all of a piece with many of the printed details of the story of her life. At the age of about 30, she left Kingston where she had lived for three years, and left its satellite settlements which had been her home from her birth. She had learned to relate satisfactorily to her early owners, who worked her hard and often treated her with cruelty. She had become a valued possession, as is a mare broken to the bit and bridle, and willing to do what is required of her for a ration of hay and oats and a heap of dry straw to sleep upon.

The Ulster County of Isabella's birth and youth saw freedom newly won for whites from the British, but with slavery continuing to be built into the economic and social fabric of the free country for black Americans. In Kingston and its vicinity, substantial populations of slaves did not always accept their fate easily, involving as it did the State's repressive legislation which permitted the use of the slave whip and forbade slaves gathering in groups of more than two or three. Yet gather they sometimes did.

This prohibition and many similar restraints were the result of a pervasive fear of a slave uprising which was never entirely absent. Throughout the years since the Dutch West India Company had realized that there was money to be made in the cruel slave trade by snatching up black people in Africa, transporting them as mere cargo crammed into the holds of ships for the dreadful voyage to the colonies in the Americas, the residents of Kingston had their periodic upsurges of acute fear of their slaves. But the slaves were welcomed as profitably exploited laborers, especially by the owners of plantations in the south and by such farm owners as those who prospered with black slave labor on the fertile Esopus Creek flatlands.

Kingston historian Jonathan W. Hasbrouck wrote that black slaves used to gather under a big oak tree on the road leading from Kingston to Hurley. And there, under the leadership of a black man almost seven feet tall named Prince Terry, said to have been the son of a British officer, occasionally played games of strength and skill. This may have been a feature of the celebration of Pinkster (the English Whitsuntide), a holiday, as Marius Schoonmaker and others tell us, celebrated with special gusto by the black people of Kingston and Albany. Yet side by side with an acceptance of the black peoples' sometimes unrestrained celebration was another and very different aspect of their lives.

In the 1790s three slaves were convicted of arson and hanged in Albany four years before Sojourner's probable birth and the memory of these events lingered among Hudson Valley slaves as did the accidental killing of Colonel Wynkoop of Kingston by a slave. This was a feature of Sojourner's girlhood in which whippings formed an ever dreaded part.

In an edgy atmosphere both for blacks and whites, Isabella grew up to be tall and strong. She recalled in later years that she could once do as much hard field work as a man. She endured much as a slave, not only hard work and an occasional whipping, but sexual abuse and being treated as saleable property when a master died and his son inherited her. She witnessed much cruelty to fellow slaves. She was mated with another of her master's slaves, and probably bore five chldren. Such children became the property of her masters just as the offspring of the master's pigs and chickens did.

Isabella took to smoking and drinking, and taking part in the permitted revelry of the black people at Pinkster. However, in the 1820s, a change overtook her—she became a member of the Holiness Branch of some Methodist believers, then making converts among the whites—and a few blacks—and meeting in their homes in Ulster County. Isabella ran away from her masters and found refuge with a white family named Van Wagenen, who were Quakers living in Poppletown adjoining Kingston and like many of their religious beliefs did not believe in slavery.

By the late 1820s, the time when Isabella began living and working for the Van Wagenens, Kingston's conservative Dutchness in its culture was somewhat weakening. Several denominations of Christian believers such as some of the Methodists and Baptists now challenged the long-held monopoly of the Dutch Reformed Church. When eccentric self-appointed circuit-rider Lorenzo Dow, who was known sometimes to preach while sitting in a tree was on his way to Kingston to preach shortly after 1800, he found that he could not cross the Hudson River to get to Kingston. He was lacking the shilling needed for the Rhinecliffe ferryman. Dow paced up and down the river's eastern shore in prayer. His eye was caught by a glistening object on the sand. He bent down and picked up for his fare a York shilling (worth one half of an English shilling) which a stranger had lost. In Kingston, Dow was not welcomed with immediate enthusiasm; neither had Quaker Ann Moore been many years earlier. He was also denied the Courthouse as a meeting place for preaching. But when he returned about ten years later, so hospitable had Kingston become to what they thought to be offbeat religious people that he was cheerfully offered the use of the Courthouse, and there delivered his eccentric sermon to an interested audience.

Abolitionists by then had begun to make small inroads against the strong Kingston opposition to ending slavery and to other reforms. Bills aimed at abolishing the institution of slavery in New York state had been introduced and defeated in the New York legislature for some time. Then a bill providing for the freeing of the State's slaves in the year 1828, but requiring babies born to slave mothers to remain in slavery, if male, for 28 additional years, and if female, for 25 years, was introduced. It found Kingston's John Addison opposed. Addison was the respected Principal of the Academy in which Kingston took great pride, and he was a lawyer to boot.

In an address to the members of the Legislature, Addison based his opposition to the abolition bill on his belief that slaves were a "species of property," for which the owner had paid, and whom their masters were obliged by law to feed, clothe, and maintain in sickness and old age, in return for their labor. The Constitution forbade the taking away from citizens of their property. Whites were citizens and black slaves were not. After the bill became law effective on July 5th, 1828, Isabella was no longer a slave, but her son Peter, born to her as a slave mother, would have to remain a slave until his 28 years had expired, and only then would he be free. In order to get around the loss in value to their owners of slaves in Peter's predicament, their owners often disobeyed the new law and sold them into slavery as children in southern slaveholding states, which had no abolition statute. Although this was illegal in New York, there the abolition law was often disobeyed without incurring any penalty.

As the late spring of 1828 neared a close, July 5th approached, when Isabella would become free from slavery. She then underwent a transforming inner religious experience as she was looking forward to the secular pleasures of Pinkster. Suddenly and without warning, she was overwhelmed by a sense of the presence of God in everything, so she explained, and the role of Jesus as her friend and helper. In Isabella's case the experience marked the beginning of a new phase of life. She had become a free human being, ready to apply all her energy and talent to advocating the national abolition of slavery and to urge the reform of many aspects of American life as a whole. As an advocate of a greater freedom not only for blacks but also for all Americans, including women, she later became famous under the name of Sojourner Truth, thanks to her natural eloquence, her singing and her extraordinarily arresting personality. First of all her projects during her new life as a free person was the rescuing of her son Peter from slavery, in which he had been illegally kept. Isabella found her black friends not at all sanguine; the wife of her former owner John Dumont ridiculed the hope, but Quakers like the Van Wagenens with whom she was still living, and the other Quakers settled in Poppletown (named for the then almost worthless poplar or popple trees which had followed clearing the native woods), on the southern fringe of Kingston, not only approved but gave her help in money. In Kingston, where she did housework for a living, she was able to get legal support from the firm of Ruggles and Hasbrouck. This help, which was vital to Isabella's hopes for her son, had to begin in secret owing to the persisting Kingston anti-abolitionist feeling, which had been given form by John Addison of the Dutch Reformed Church and the Academy. She joined the newly organized Kingston Methodist believers in helping support the newly founded Sunday School of Methodist John O'Neil to which both black and white children were admitted.

Isabella's lawyers were both able men, destined for successful careers, Ruggles as a judge and A. Bruyn Hasbrouck as longtime President of Rutgers College. They managed to steer the freeing of Peter to his appearance at the Kingston Courthouse as a free person. Here, however, Isabella's joy was tempered by the instant if temporary refusal of Peter, traumatized by his cruel treatment as a slave in the deep South, to recognize and accept her as his mother and so to shrink from her in terror.

Shortly after this, Isabella under the influence of a powerful impulse to communicate her religious and reformist beliefs to others, left for the city of New York. She left behind her older children, who were still bound by the chains of slavery. Her daughter Diane stayed behind in the keeping of the abolitionst Van Wagenens and, witnessing the power of the religious thrust that was sending her to New York, having arrrived at a good understanding wth her son Peter, Isabella arranged for Peter to go to work for a lock-keeper on the Delaware and Hudson Canal, where other boys, white as well as black, from Kingston would go to work in the years to come, and sometimes arouse sympathy because of ill treatment. Later Peter went to sea and vanished forever from his mother's knowledge.

Once in the city of New York, Isabella worked as a domestic in the bizarre establishment of a religious charlatan called by its owner Matthias Kingdom. Here she is thought to have gained added skill in her already considerable skills at exhortatation and singing of religious songs and others advocating a variety of freedoms from conventional burdens. And here, when another inmate of the Kingdom was believed to have been murdered, Isabella was given a favorable character endorsement by her Kingston lawyers.

It was from a beginning at the Kingdom into which she had stumbled that Isabella began to launch herself into her career as a traveling evangelist and advocate of reform. She came more and more not only to speak in her own distinctive and impressive manner of the kind of emotional Christian faith we often call today the Pentecostal, but to urge her audiences to adopt such reforms, then very much in the public mind, as temperance, the national abolition of slavery, and giving women both black and white equal rights wiith men. She aimed, as she liked to phrase it, to "set the world right."

And then as she advanced in finding recognition as an accepted figure in some of the most advanced reformist movements in the hectic decades of her time, she learned from experience that her appearance and manner seemed to attract favorable attention. Tall, rather gaunt and with a strong, rugged face, and a voice that may have been given volume and a distinctive color by her days as a field hand needing to speak up to be heard in the open. And perhaps given a distinction in the ears of English-speaking audiences by remains of the "sonorous" Dutch which was the daily speech of Ulster County slaves of the period. Sojourner learned to take advantage of the unexpected touches of wit and humor with which she was apt to please audiences and to modulate her voice to express emotion and so stir those who heard her to respond by sharing in her feelings.

One of Sojourner's hands was deformed, probably by a working accident in her days of slavery. She made no attempt to hide it. Neither did she make an attempt to ape the speech of the white reformers with whom she came more and more closely associated, nor did she try to correct her homespun and often ungrammatical yet effective way of speaking with its noticable moulding by the style of the King James version of the Bible. She remained true to herself while strengthening her power to influence the thoughts and conduct of others—a simple aging black woman who was difficult to analyze yet hard to resist.

About 1840, Isabella gave up her former name in favor of Sojourner Truth. The name suggested her mission of wandering from place to place after leaving the Kingdom, and pleading her vision of reformist ideas, which she regarded as embodying truth as she understood it.

During the two decades that were leading up to the Civil War, Sojourner moved about the country advocating among other reforms a variety of spiritualism which took the form of the ideas of Swedish Immanuel Swedenborg as Americanized by A.J. Davis, known as the Poughkeepsie Seer. She took up residence with a Northhampton, Massachusetts group of enthusiasts for the simple life who hoped to support themselves by making silk (a popular delusion of the time). When this project like so many similar ones failed she moved on, having enriched her life experience by making friends with activists, among whom was Frederick Douglas, a popular and progressive black leader who had escaped from slavery, as well as many other leading reformers white and black.

In 1846 Sojourner began dictating the story of her life which was to be published in 1850 as the *Narrative of Sojourner Truth*, and this little book she sold at the many conventions and reformist meetings she attended. She sold photographs of herself. In her photographs she appeared dressed very respectably in a gray gown, a white turban and a white tasseled shawl. Sometimes she was seen in the act of knitting. The caption "I Sell the Shadow to Support the Substance" explains with imagination the practical purpose of distributing the photos.

Then, as the Civil War entered its second year, President Lincoln signed the Emancipation Proclamation, which freed all slaves in the seceding states—national emancipation would come later. It was in this historic year for the triumph of the Abolitionists that the *Atlantic Monthly* carried Harriet Beecher Stowe's lengthy article on Sojourner, whom she presented as the "Libyan Sibyl" to emphasize a fancied resemblance of the Sibyl to Sojourner, as known to the public in a popular statue by William Wetmore Storey. The Sibyl in Mrs. Stowe's essay is described as born in the deserts of northern Africa amid palm trees and tropical exuberance, but this portrayal of Sojourner served to give her the kind of respectability and exotic glamor which she had not heretofore enjoyed on the the more genteel levels of American society. By that time, the real Sojourner was in Washingston, sponsored by public organizations for the relief of the thousands of freed and escaped southern slaves who had fled there. She was also proving a relentless foe of the public stage drivers who failed to obey her newly granted right to a seat on their public vehicles. She pursued the drivers through the courts as she had during the kidnapping of her son Peter long before in the Kingston court house. Like Rosa Parks in Montgomery, Alabama in 1955 she insisted on her rights and as she had done in Kingston in 1829 she resolutely pursued the stage drivers until she triumphed, temporarily at least.

The meetings of Sojourner Truth with Abraham Lincoln at the White House and later on with President Grant were given wide publicity.

Her later years in retirement among the spiritualists and diet reformers of Battle Creek, Michigan were the crowning ones of her career, which had taken her from birth to slave parents in a rural cellar to becoming welcomed at the White House.

As Sojurner's reputation grew, and her skill in pleasing audiences with her homely wit and her ability to present the case for controversial causes, an often confusing fog of legend and lore came to surround her. Her pungent phrases were shaped into even more pungent forms to suit the purposes of fellow reformers who admired her and came to envy her ability to captivate an audience.

The question of why obviously intelligent Sojourner never learned to read or write remains unanswered. She was certainly intelligent enough and possessed great determination, but she may well have had a physical or emotional difficulty, perhaps related to her injured hand, which played a part. Yet in spite of all the confusion which surrounds her life, Sojourner, by the time she died in 1883 in Grand Rapids, had become an enduring heroine of the great wave of reform which was a feature of her life span and which did much to shape American life for the better.

Following her death the memory of Sojourner was respected among black people and whites sympathetic to the extension of civil rights to all Americans. But in Ulster County and in Kingston she was largely ignored until the reformist spirit of the movement for civil rights of the 1960s at a time of growth in Kingston's black population. After that scholarly methods began to be used in exploring her career. Pride in her achievements grew. This recent movement caused a Sojourner Truth Institute to be founded in Kingston and there was talk of naming a public school for her, but the thought was rejected. And the Institute's ambitious goals faded. After much debate, however, a plaque paying tribute to Sojourner was placed in front of the Kingston Courthouse. The plaque reads:

SOJOURNER TRUTH
CA. 1797–NOV. 26, 1883

FAMOUS SLAVE OF ULSTER COUNTY. BORN IN
HURLEY, N.Y. THOUGH ILLITERATE, THIS WOMAN OF
INDOMINATABLE CHARACTER AND INTELLECT LEFT HER
INDELIBLE MARK AS AN ELOQUENT CONDEMNER OF
SLAVERY. FROM THIS COURT, BY WINNING HER
LAWSUIT—THE FIRST EVER WON BY A BLACK PARENT—
SHE SAVED HER SON FROM SLAVERY IN ALABAMA.

A STAUNCH ABOLITIONIST AND A FERVENT CHAMPION OF HUMAN RIGHTS, SHE MET PRESIDENT LINCOLN AND SUBSEQUENTLY SERVED AS ADVISOR AT FREEDOM VILLAGE IN VIRGINIA. HER OWN WORDS EXPLAIN HER TRIUMPH: "I TALK TO GOD AND GOD TALKS TO ME."

2.
Steam, Scenery and the Effects of Rumors of a Canal to Come 1825

IN MID-AUGUST 1807, KINGSTON PEOPLE HAD A CHANCE TO OBSERVE IN ACTION a form of energy which would for many years play a large part in transforming their village and its landing place at Rondout. Up to that time, these people had relied for doing work on the muscles of white people and black slaves, horses and oxen. They had relied on the power of falling water and like their ancestors had relied on wind to move boats and the wings of mills. For Kingston people the new and transforming energy source of 1807 was steam, which might have been seen at work from the parts of Kingston and Rondout bordering the Hudson. That August day, engaged in moving up the Hudson River, a strange looking vessel without sails or oars called the *North River Steamboat*, or the *Clermont,* was making its trial trip for Robert Fulton in partnership with Kingston's neighbor and good friend across the Hudson at the 13,000 acre estate (also known as the Lower Manor) at Clermont, Chancellor Robert R. Livingston. It was remembered years later that a small boy in Kingston, when he saw the boat in action on the Hudson, shouted, "Ma! Ma! Come and see the wagon go through the river without any horses!" Marius Schoonmaker who reported the reaction of the boy on the Kingston River bank also wrote that the passage of the Clermont up the Hudson "gave rise to many curious surmises and ideas."

A startled observer elsewhere on the Hudson is remembered to have described the *Clermont* on its historic trial trip as looking like "the devil going up the river with a tea kettle on a raft." The boat was powered by an English Watts engine fueled by burning wood, that made possible the harnessing of the expanding steam latent in boiling water to furnish power for engines of a kind already used in industry for a century and a half, and now in steamboats which would render obsolete the wind-powered sails of the past of Rondout on the Hudson as well as those of windmills.

A very different kind of power was soon also put to use to bring additional change to nineteenth century Kingston minds. This was a recognition that an aspect of the village, long praised by travelers for the fertility of its placid creekside fields, its pleasant pastoral valleys, its majestic mountain background and its easy access to the world by way of the Hudson, had an additional kind of power—that of its scenery.

The first to urge travelers to visit Kingston (leaving dollars behind as they left) was travel writer William Darby in his *A Tour from New York to Detroit in 1818.* Earlier writers had set down figures as to the number of bushels of wheat, the number of Shawangunk grit millstones, the Esopus Valley-bred horses, salted fish, the grain that had been sent down the Hudson on Kingston wind-powered sloops and schooners to be sold. The economics-minded Duke de la Rochefoucald-Liancourt in 1799 had given very meticulous statistics of the barrels of salt fish and of bushels of ground limestone produced and shipped to New York. The clerks of Peter van Gaasbeek and other Dutch-descended merchants had covered countless pages of their daybooks with records of transactions in grain and in forest products. William Darby paid less attention to Kingston as an economic unit. Instead, influenced by the wave of romantic feeling which had crossed the Atlantic and been altered to fit the American landscape and culture, he emphasized and dramatized the local scenery and stirred his readers with an account of one striking episode in the village history, the burning of Kingston by British troops in 1777.

Darby had reached the west bank of the Hudson on the ferry from Rhinecliffe. He wasted no time in telling of the horse-powered ferry trip across the River, but plunged with contagious gusto into presenting the bleak three mile drive up from Kingston Point in a way that would heighten the charm of the looks of the Village of Kingston that lay above, this by contrast with the sterile wildness of the Road, "which winds up amid broken fragments of rocks. The heights above the road are clothed with stunted pine, cedar, and oak; everything announces sterility. Nothing is seen that can give the slightest anticipation of the fertile and beautiful Valley of Esopus" toward which Darby was headed. Then, as if he were a skillful showman raising a curtain on a scene which sharply contrasts with that of the Armabowery (the Dutch word for a stretch of land, hardly fit for human habitation) Darby writes, "I do not remember ever to have enjoyed a more agreeable surprise, or hope to have seen a more rapid transition than in passing from the sterile and shapeless Hudson Hills to the fine and extensive plains upon which stands the romantic village of Kingston."

Here, Darby, first of all writers, effectively shifts from the beautiful landscape to Kingston's major historical event—its burning by the British troops. By incorrectly presenting the British troops as creeping upon unsuspecting Kingston without any advance warning—as evidence of this he omits any reference to the hastily "thrown up" batteries at Rondout where American soldiers bravely tried to stem the British advancing human tide after landing from crowded troop ships and flatboats. He writes of the Kingstonians taking refuge in the back country as having been the scene of a sudden "tumultuous flight" as the British arrived (without warning) and began to burn Kingston homes. He concluded that destruction of Kingston was an act of "blind rage"—as it was called by the Americans. And the author implies, without actually saying so, that "a factor in bringing about the surrender of Burgoyne on the 16th of October 1777, was a result of the indignation of the Americans of Kingston and elsewhere." So, as Darby moralized in error upon his spirited and not entirely accurate excursion into revolutionary history, he turned to what may well be the earliest recommendation of Kingston as a worthwhile goal for tourists "in making the tour of this part of the country, no traveler ought to pass without visiting Kingston and every stranger will be pleased with the soft beauty of its scenery, and with the plain, but affable manners of its inhabitants."

A stranger arriving in Kingston in 1826 after being led there by Darby's reccomendation would have found that much had happened since Darby's visit to enrich the appeal of the place. By 1826, the Hudson Valley and the Catskill Mountains had taken a prominent place in the minds of Americans as national treasures because of their scenery and romantic literary and historical associations.

These changes were imposed by such widely read and persuasive writers as Washington Irving in his tales of Rip Van Winkle and his Knickerbocker history; and the *Headless Horseman of Sleepy Hollow*, by James Fenimore Cooper in his Leatherstocking series of novels and especially through Natty Bumppo of the "The Pioneers" of 1823, and, very recently, by painter Thomas Cole, whose Catskill Mountain landscapes were breaking new and more glamorous ground in the appreciation of American art history and scenery.

And this was not all that was being added to the attractions which Darby had found to stir him in the Kingston area. By the mid-twenties one of the fellow travelers impressed by Darby's enthusiasm to visit Kingston might have picked up a sense as to what was going on there had he read the recent copy of the available *Ulster Sentinel* as he sipped his evening drink in the barroom of the new Eagle Hotel of J.H. Rutzer. An advertisement of Mr. Rutzer in the newspaper would inform his guests that his host offered service by stage not only to the steamboat landing three miles away, but to "the Catskill Mountain House, at a distance of 24 miles through a pleasant and romantic country," and as a bonus, Rutzer promised "that savory article green turtle soup to be served at 11 a.m. and 8 p.m." at his hotel. In the same newspaper, rival Kingston hotel keeper W. Prince made it known that steam power and scenery were now working in cooperation. His hotel "was newly furnished in genteel style for the accommodation of steamboat parties of pleasure, and travelers in general." And he added that he offered stages to run "from his house along the Delaware and Hudson Canal (which would not be open for another year or two)." From fellow drinkers in the barroom the traveler we have imagined could learn that the Delaware and Hudson Canal had been planned in Pennsylvania to connect the Delaware and Hudson Rivers with the primary purpose of transporting anthracite coal from mine to consumer, and that Kingston business people had tried in vain to persuade the canal's projectors to run the canal through uptown Kingston and down the Esopus Creek to join the Hudson River at Saugerties. Another group of Kingston men had bought up lands close to the junction of the Rondout Creek and the Hudson River because they expected that this would be the spot where the Canal people would inevitably have to build their Hudson River terminal. But the speculators lost out when the terminal was sited at the Kingston Landing higher up the Rondout Harbor.

Undiscouraged by the failure of the canal to yield the speculators their expected profits, when shares in the canal were offered, Kingston men oversubscribed their alloted quota. Abraham Hasbrouck, owner of the strategically placed more than eighty acres which was to become the heart of many of the Canal Company's activities at its terminal and those of the extractive mining efforts along the Rondout Harbor, plus former Ulster County Assemblyman Garret Abeel (for whom Abeel Street was named) and clever Kingston lawyer John Suydam were among the Canal Company's local trustees. They and Abraham Hasbrouck guarded the interests of Kingston investors in the Canal. Visible to the observant traveler of 1826 were the effects made under the pressure of a romanticizing of the region and the expected approach of the canal to their shipping point right on the Rondout Harbor. Had the Kingston visitor of 1826 brought with him the *Northern Traveller* guidebook, just published, he could have informed himself of the planning of the D&H Canal and of the stir about visiting the Catskills and putting up at the new elegant Catksill Mountain House which was a current public enthusiasm. Said the *Northern Traveller*, "An excursion to the summit of these mountains (the Catskills) is performed by great numbers of travellers; and indeed has become so favorite an enterprise that it may be very properly be ranged among the principal objects in the great tour which we are just commencing." The attraction of the Catskills and its adjacent and newly discovered scenic wonders "are increased by the presence of agreeable and refined society."

To turn this happy situation to profit, Kingston historian Marius Schoonmaker would recall sixty years later that "at that time the village (of Kingston) was not deficient in talent, training or men of note, but they had sunk into a lethargic slumber, satisfied at enjoying themselves, and caring little for the outside world; seemingly satisfied with what they had, apparently wanting nothing more." But the time had come "when they were to be aroused from their slumbers." Not however to the kind of efforts to welcome travellers which Darby had urged but in efforts to stimulate commerce and industry made possible by the arrival of the boom in neighboring Rondout of new extractive, if not earth-friendly, industries aroused by the completion of the canal and its cheap means of moving freight.

The observant traveler could see one result of the awakening to commercial and industrial efforts on nearby Wall, North Front and John Streets. In anticipation of the completion of the canal in a few years, a fury of "tear down and build up again" struck part of the Stockade district, centering on John and Wall Street to be wondrously transformed to suit the whims of the boom which the opening of the canal was expected to produce.

Kingston men in whom a speculative fever had come at last to burn were then being seized by an urge to convert a central part of the former Stockade district into a primitive and ahead-of-its-time sort of business and shopping district. Its backbone would be Wall Street, given emphasis by its already central status by the Dutch Reformed Church with its ancient burying ground edged by Lombardy poplars. The trees had been furnished by the Kingston trustees in 1804 when these quickly growing trees were becoming fashionable. Across the street was the handsome, recently-completed stone Courthouse, on the site of the one burned by the British in 1777. Other buildings were of stone.

A formidable obstacle to the kind of commercial development its promoters aimed at and which confronted the advocates of what would be called today a modern business center was that the area contained too many of the old stone buildings combining homes and businesses that had been reroofed and otherwise restored (or neglected) after the fire of 1777. By the 1820s these were thought to be hopelessly out of style and could not be expected to seem attractive to a newer and very different generation of clients or customers who were being made newly sensitive to changing fashions. Some of the old buildings stood to the right and left of the new and much admired courthouse, rebuilt in 1818-1819. Others were on Wall Street on the Dutch Reformed Church side. So down some old stone veterans went, to be replaced by buildings of local brick or frame, so much more fashionable and healthful, it was believed by newcomers to Kingston and even some old Kingstonians, than the now mouldy old stone houses typical of the outworn Dutch days in the Hudson Valley.

The chief barrier to progress was the stone Van der Lyn house which resolutely barred the entrance of the block of present day Wall Street extending from John to North Front Street. This was the very massive stone house in which painter John

Vander Lyn had been born and in which he had spent his early babyhood. After the British fire of 1777, the remains of the big house, in which John's father and his grandfather had painted wagons and whatever else had come along, had sheltered the Van der Lyns in improvised lean-tos and partial reroofings, but its thick old stone walls had remained. Now they had to go. It was long remembered as having put up a valiant resistance to being wrecked. But at last the walls crashed down. The three old stone houses of Marius Groen between John Street and the Reformed Church yard were allowed to remain for only a short time longer.

A leader among the men active in bringing the new business center into being was Militia General Joseph S. Smith who did wholesale and retail business for a time on John Street just off Wall. His new building was of local brick, as were many other new ones. Ever since his youth, General Smith, as he carried the mails from Kingston to Delhi, had made many friends and had risen to a position of authority in the village. He was not of Dutch or Huguenot ancestry, but like Governor George Clinton of Scotch-Irish and English background. By its modernizing of the 1820s, Wall Street made a bid for attracting business men not only from the older Kingston but from outside. And it welcomed new people eager to take part in the opportunity for profit being newly opened up, especially among the inhabitants in the surrounding country which continued to depend economically on their Ulster County seat of Kingston.

Wall Street, ca. 1830, from a print in the author's collection

The old custom of having the slaves, journeymen, and apprentices all living togeher in a single building now began to come to an end after 1828. The "traders and traffickers" took up residence on such fashionable places as Fair Street, and the apprentices and others dwelt wherever they might find places on side streets, and slaves freed in 1828 were likely to leave Kingston for better opportunity elsewhere.

And General Smith was making a contribution to the future attractiveness of the commercial center by digging up saplings of trees from nearby woodlots and planting them beside Wall and adjoining streets, to give shade by summer to future generations of horses, lawyers, litigants, churchgoers, traders, and of course shoppers.

After General Smith was no longer living, when one of the wild saplings he had planted gave over to old age, Kingston newspapers gratefully noted that the tree had been one of the General's plantings.

3.
An Army of Diggers Advances on Rondout

THE YEAR 1761 HAS BEEN MARKED IN BRITAIN BY THE CREATION OF A landmark in the rise of the British Industrial Revolution. This was the completion of the first of many coal canals constructed to carry bituminous (or soft) coal from coal mines to factory centers such as Birmingham and Manchester. This pioneer of all coal canals ran from the seaport of Liverpool to what soon became known as the "Black Country" after its air was polluted by smoke and soot resulting from the burning of bituminous coal to power factories. The English canal was dug—as the Delaware and Hudson, or D and H canal was also to be—by an army of young men from troubled Ireland. Now, in the 1820s, a similar American coal canal (the D and H) was being dug by a similar little army of soldiers of the pick and shovel, which was to bring a striking transformation to Rondout and a lesser change to Kingston and its old Stockade District. But the D and H Canal would carry a different kind of coal from that of British coal canals, which carried the soft, easily ignited kind known as bituminous which burned with the aid of tall factory chimneys and with a very polluting smoke. In the United States in northern Pennsylvania lay vast deposits of the hard, shiny, slow-to-ignite and less polluting variety of coal called anthracite, which was once known from its problems in easily igniting as "stone coal." An occasional gardener was said to have used crushed anthracite as a novel surface for garden paths. Some Native Americans had broken up surface deposits of this coal and added them to their campfires with some success. A few Pennsylvania gunsmiths had learned from the Natives' experience that if given a good enough supply of oxygen, the stone coal used in a forge could produce a hot and cleaner fire. Early in the 19th century, with the design by white men of grates to allow enough oxygen to reach the coal and enable anthracite to burn well, the fuel became tamed enough to become a reliable servant.

Hearing of this, the two Wurts brothers, who had done well in dry goods in Philadelphia, caught fire in their imaginations at the thought of what seemed a bright future for the up to then generally despised stone coal. They proceeded in fair weather and foul to ransack the wilds of the northeast Pennsylvania mountains and accumulated at very low prices much potentially anthracite-producing land.

By 1825, the Wurts brothers, Maurice and William, had obtained the legislative action and private financial backing needed to put them in the business of mining anthracite coal and so soon were planning on sending it to market on horse or mule pulled barges on a coal canal like those of England. Surveys were first made of the canal's proposed route of a hundred miles or so plus the steep 16 miles that intervened between the proposed canal head to their first actual coal mines. Plans were made for the more than 100 locks needed to compensate for the up and down nature of much of the route, bridges had to be made by men who had learned their engineering skills in the building of the great Erie Canal, and were now acting as officers in the army of diggers. The Canal route as first planned would run between its head at Honesdale, named for the president of the D and H, to an outlet on the Hudson River. There coal would be unloaded to be transhipped on larger company barges pulled by company tugboats to Providence, RI; Albany, Poughkeepsie, and the greatest seaport in the western world, that of New York City.

To the dismay of Kingston speculators like General Joseph S. Smith, the Hudson River terminal of the D and H canal had first been planned to end at Newburgh on the Hudson. At this news a little boom seized Newburgh and gloom pervaded Kingston. But after it was decided that tunneling the Shawangunk Mountains that stood between the canal route and Newburgh would prove too expensive, the spirits of the Newburgh people drooped and the Newburgh economy suffered. Substantial involvement in the canal by Kingston men as board members of the D and H, included prominent lawyer John Suydan, and former Ulster Assemblyman Garrett Abeel, for whom Rondout's creek-facing Abeel Street was named, and Rondout's sole resident pre-canal bigwig Abraham Hasbrouck, operator of a line of two sloops plying on schedule between New York City and Rondout—these local men gave reassurance to Kingston investors that their interests would not be neglected in canal matters.

Kingston people learned from the *Peoples Advocate* that an army of a cheerfully over-estimated 20,000 men and 200 teams of horses and mules had been recruited and were advancing on Eddyville at the head of Rondout tidewater and were digging and blasting the canal as they proceeded. As the army marched on, it became clear that the workers were suffering casualties. Strained backs and hernias were not uncommon. And injuries from misplaced strokes of fellow workers' tools plus premature blasts occurred. Agues and fever felled many men. James Quinlan, of Irish Catholic ancestry, in his *History of Sullivan County*, of 1873, tells of another problem that afflicted the workers, most of whom were Catholics. Quinlan wrote that canal workers "sometimes became destitute souls" when they felt about to die "unhousellc an unnancalcd with no priest closer than 100 miles away to give last rites." Quinlan also tells that "the native population was unanimously Protestant and loudly derided rites and observances which the newcomers revered as sacred. Very often the Protestants whose houses were filled with Catholic (canal army) boarders caused their tables to groan with an extra supply of pork and beef on the days when the Church commanded her children to fast and openly sneered when an untimely food was taken away untasted."

The invasion of a Protestant countryside by a predominately Catholic army could not help exacerbate the already strong Protestant-Catholic feeling. "In time," Quinlan adds "these and other aggravating annoyances . . . terminated." They did, indeed, but not until the veterans of the invading army slowly and at times painfully had merged within the regional population, by marriage and otherwise, after the beginning of the 20th Century.

As they began their campaign against a rough and often resistant terrain it was not all smooth digging. There were many places where hard rocks blocked their advance and needed a good blasting, there were ponds and brooks which needed to have their water coaxed to flow as feeders for the canal, there were areas of mucky marshes, buzzing with disease-carrying mosquitoes, to be drained, there were rivers to cross, there were places where blasters or "blowers" as they were called, were brought in to interrupt any thought of steady digging. Then there were shouted warnings of a blast to come, some workers showed bravado at times like these, and merely held a shovel over their heads to ward off showers of fragmented rock. And sometimes they suffered nasty or fatal consequences from ill-judged blasts, but for all the difficulties of the shoveling campaigns, there was a traditional source of solace as on other digging projects it was customary to pleasantly punctuate hard working days with the administration of an occasional free slug of whiskey. When a contractor became aware that the date on which he had agreed to complete his contract for a section was too close for comfort, the number of slugs of whiskey might be increased as part of a speeding-up process and the length of the working day increased from twelve to as many as fifteen hours. The men at these times worked in a not unpleasant alcoholic daze.

It should be remembered that these soldier-diggers, like the rank and file of a regular army, formed a selected body. Mostly young, unmarried, alien Irishmen in a foreign land, nearly all Catholics among Protestant strangers, they possessed a sense of comraderie because of their forming a body of young men of a common origin, common religion, and common culture engaged in a common method of earning their livings as a group. So they could not escape making a strong impression on the people of the foreign land into which they had been plunged by the misgovernment, the vagaries of weather, epidemics and over-population of Ireland, and to arouse Kingstonians' frequent hostility by their different ways of daily life. The newspapers of the region through which they advanced toward their objective of the Rondout Creek tidewater harbor at Eddyville, about three miles above the junction of the Rondout Kill (or creek) with the Hudson, did little to prepare the people of Kingston and Rondout for what lay in store for them on the completion of the canal. Nor did they take advantage of one of the most significant features of the time when the D and H Canal and its diggers reached its goal and began transforming that goal to enable it to take part with energy in the American phase of the Industrial and Technological Revolution and the Age of Steam, which would transform much of the American landscape and life.

4.
The Stourbridge Lion Takes a Ride on the D & H Canal as a Trial

MOST TROUBLESOME TO D & H ENGINEERS HAD BEEN THE PLANNING OF the means of moving the anthracite coal, mined at Carbondale, Pennsylvania, over the top of Moosic mountain which lay between the mines and the canal head. It was planned at first to raise the loaded cars during their initial four miles on their tracks some 900 feet upward across the mountain by using horse power or the power of stationary steam engines—gravity would take care of the remaining miles sloping down to Honesdale where the canal began.

But when word came of the availability in England of a novel steam-powered hauling device called a locomotive, plans were changed. It was decided to give the locomotive a trial. The steam locomotive had been invented in England by George Stephenson, and never till then put to work as a means of transportation anywhere in the western hemisphere. Chief D & H engineer John Jervis asked his assistant Horatio Allen who was going to England anyway to buy two locomotives, after watching competing locomotives at work. Allen ordered the two, including one called at first the *Stourbridge Lion.* This tall locomotive was said to be of the kind called "the grasshopper type" because of the resemblance to a grasshopper's legs of the rods which rose above the horizontal boiler and connected its steam-generated power to its oaken wheels. On its front, the twelve foot long locomotive bore an image of a lion's red face, hence the name of the zoologically confusing machine.

The *Lion* and its anonymous companion made their way up the Hudson on the wood-fueled steamboat *Congress,* which had been among the first regularly scheduled steamboats ever to have entered the Rondout Harbor. It docked at Wilbur, formerly called Twaalfskill, originally named for the 12 striped bass which abounded there in season—"twaalf" in Dutch equals twelve in English. The *Lion* was transhipped to a canal boat and reached Honesdale without creating any known comment at the passage of so strange a beast making its way through or past the cornfields and forests, locks and hastily built canalside grogshops, stores and dwellings.

Rumors of the coming of the strange beast called the *Stourbridge Lion* were spread about. The Dundaff, Pennsylvania *Republican* of July 23, 1829 gave a "spirited" account. "Imagine to yourself the appearance of that animal of, the body at least twelve feet in length and five in diameter, traveling at the rate of four or five miles per hour, together with a host of young ones in train, and you will have some idea of the scene before us."

At Honesdale, the *Lion* found everything in readiness for a trial run, and a hopeful crowd eager to observe the novel event. The pair of tracks on which the *Lion* was to perform its trial was probably made of unseasoned local hemlock topped with iron strips. Hemlock was the most easily worked and cheapest timber to be had in the region. The day when the *Lion* reached the canal beginning at Honesdale and was placed on the tracks was a gala occasion, marred at the outset by the explosion of an overloaded cannon fired to celebrate the event. No serious injury to the cannoneer, and neither the *Lion* nor Allen were discouraged. Away they went on August 16, to the admiration of their cheering audience. Soon, however, admiration changed to apprehension as the locomotive visibily quivered as it rode ahead with Allen holding the throttle. But the engineer boldly guided the quivering *Lion* across unsteady bridges, around treacherous curves and trestles until it returned from the mines to Carbondale. It was a fine display of courage by man and *Lion*, but not a good omen for a successful future for the *Lion*. After a second trial run, the *Lion* was left to rust at Honesdale. Horse and steam power furnished by stationary engines took the place of the *Lion*. Why the trackway prepared for the *Lion* proved not equal to its task was not agreed upon by the Canal's many historians. Some believe that the trackway and its supporting structure had been designed to support a locomotive of not over 4 tons in weight, but the *Lion* as delivered weighed almost thrice that amount. Another factor in bringing about the failure of the trackway may have been the underrating of the costs of the project. In his Annual Report for 1828, the company president hinted at this when he wrote that "the loan of the credit of the state on two occasions rescued your board of managers from the pecuniary difficulties with which they were threatened, and assured the completion of the great work in which you are engaged." This report suggests that the track and its structure were built under a determination to make the work done as cheaply and hastily as possible. Even so it could not be denied that the *Lion* had performed the very first run on a railway track in North America and thus had made history.

In 1825, President Hone had turned the first shovelful of earth at the place then

The *Stourbridge Lion,* from *The Story of Anthracite,* 1932

called Summitville, a section where the digging was easy and the stockholding public would be assured of seeing quick progress. In the fall of 1826 (and before the Canal was completed), the tidewater location at Eddyville was dedicated, to the accompaniment of the firing of cannon, the blaring of a band, and Masonic rituals peformed by the Kingston chapter of the Masonic order of Kingston, which had been founded in 1774. From the day when the first laden boats arrived at Rondout, until 1899, when the canal died, the Delaware and Hudson Canal would remain a strong influence on the land it traversed and which it had transformed almost beyond recognition.

An accurate model of the *Stourbridge Lion* may be seen on display in the Smithsonian Institution in Washington, D.C. to help illustrate the part the energy of steam when properly harnessed played in the Industrial Revolution. And some of the rusty bones of the *Stourbridge Lion* locomotive itself are there reverently preserved. Although the *Stourbridge Lion* failed in its purpose, other locomotives, steamships and many other applications of steam which were developed during the Industrial Revolution would share in supplying transportation in many American places—as they did in Rondout and along the route of the D & Canal, where they were used for the first time on the American continent.

5.
Temperance, Abolition, the End of Time, and the Reign of Peace

In Kingston as in the rest of the United States strong drink was once very much an ingredient of daily life (as it had been in Colonial times and during the digging of the Canal). It formed an essential part of the diet of men like the D&H Canal workers. Whiskey was strong and plentiful—it was made from grain which was not then as easily transported as it later became to centers of population or export. It was easy (and often more profitable) to convert it to whiskey (or fruit to brandy) in little breweries and distilleries close to the fields or orchards. In Kingston distilleries for making brandy from grapes were at work even before the first church was built. More expensive sources for malt than the usual barley made Kingston beer, like that of Albany, "the heaviest beer we have tasted in all New Netherland," as Dankers had reported in 1679, because its malt was made from the more expensive Esopus wheat.

In many shops a barrel of whiskey stood ready to provide a free drink to customers. A drink of liquor was used to seal a bargain on the street, or perhaps in a lawyer's office; few social occasions could be allowed to pass by without the aid of liquor in raising spirits and loosening tongues. Kingston in the two first decades of independence from Britain was known as having a wealthy upper class of people with frugal habits and at the same time conservative Calvinistic religious views. And, according to an observant and journal-keeping nephew of painter John Vander Lyn, Henry Vanderlyn, as he looked back on his Kingston boyhood in the early 1800s, recalled that even haughty ladies of good families were sometimes notable drinkers and otherwise rebels against their straitlaced Calvinistic elders. "Kingston at that time abounded with young men," Vanderlyn wrote, "whose appetite for pleasure and amusement knew no bounds & all of whom have died at an early age, victims of their improvident, inordinate habits." Henry's brother Nicholas "was much attached to this company," especially to a reckless lawyer who would become known as the Congressman Barent Gardenier who fought the duel in Maryland in 1804 which would lead to a Federal attempt to ban dueling by law. Nicholas, according to his brother, followed this man (with whom Henry had tried to study law) "in his irregularities with a fascination that shut off from his sight the ruin that awaited them—"only to have his brother spurn his advice. Years later Henry wrote, "in writing these memoirs of my youth, my griefs are again remembered at his untimely fate but I will recollect the pain I felt on giving him my hand on parting with him at his door in Kingston in August, 1807. But on bidding him adieu I thought as I looked on his melancholy face that I would never see him again. He died in July 1809 in the 26th year of his age. Such is the lamentable consequence of intemperance in our enjoyments."

As Nicholas died a movement for restricting or prohibiting heavy drinking was gaining speed in the nation following changes in social thinking in Britain and in France and in the United States of the harmful effects of excessive drinking given publicity nationally by eminent Dr. Benjamin Rush. A year after the untimely death of Nicholas Vanderlyn, New York State's first Temperance Society was formed and a flock of others followed. The movement culminated in 1919 with the passage by Congress of the Volstead Act, which ended as a failure and was repealed in 1932.

While the army of canal diggers was moving and drinking its slugs on its way-toward Rondout and Kingston, people had many other new subjects to occupy their minds. As the canal which was transforming the place and while the events that were to shape Americans' acceptance of their Civil War moved ever closer, they were being more heavily bombarded by reformist notions than in any previous time in their experience. Some of the notions proved to be fruitful, others would vanish. Some, like the Temperance Movement, had some beneficial results in setting reasonable limits to the making and distributing of hard and softer alcoholic drink in Kingston and throughout the nation.

It was a period too when natural assets hitherto not valued were found to have values that made them sought after for pleasure and for profitable use even in the Industrial Age which was being ushered in.

Kingston people, in the days of struggle between whites and Natives for the possession of their favored tract of land, which we know as Kingston, had been much concerned by the effects on the Natives of addiction to liquor. That concern, however, had vanished after the Natives had been expelled as disturbing factors in the life of Kingston. Kingston beer continued to be praised and consumed for its quality and strength throughout the Hudson Valley.

In 1828, as rumors of the near approach of the D & H Canal alerted Kingston people to the glittering changes looming in their future, they were also hearing tales of heavy drinking being a habit of the canal diggers, many of whom would soon (after the Canal was dug) become shovelers working in Rondout at transhipping coal. The canal carried anthracite brought on the small barges of the D & H Canal, from their Pennsylvania mines to Rondout and Port Ewen for transhipment on larger barges to New York City and elsewhere. Kingston men then organized an Ulster County branch of the New York State Temperance Society. General Joseph S. Smith, who in 1832 signed the "Old Pledge" which called for total abstinence, became the zealous president of the Society which had a special zeal for curbing the reported drinking of canal men.

As the Ulster Society flourished, a spirited debate arose among its members. At first they had worked toward total abstinence from "ardent spirits," while permitting the use of wine and beer, which had long been the favorite tipple of many Kingston drinkers who now refused to give them up. Rondout canal workers, on the other hand, were whiskey drinkers by choice, as they had been in their homeland. Their many illegal stills making potato whiskey testified to that. A battle between the two factions within the ranks of Temperance Society members took place. With General Smith sticking to his total abstinence guns, his faction triumphed, although hard liquor drinkers continued to abound.

In Rondout, as in Kingston however, the temperance movement was growing, as it was in much of the United States. Clergymen were especially enthusiastic promoters of the cause, largely on moral grounds. When Rondout's Roman Catholic St. Mary's Church was dedicated in the 1840s, a feature of the proceedings planned for the occasion was the appearance of Father Matthew of Ireland, famous for forming temperance societies in his native land in which a temperance movement parallel to that of the United States was underway. Father Matthew was to receive in person from church members a pledge of total abstinence from hard liquor. But for some reason never explained, the Father never made his appearance. However, an active Temperance Society sponsored by St. Mary's soon did well.

These beginnings of the temperance movement were a significant part of American life in the 1830s and 40s and did not soon die out, even as the Wild West flourished.

Another wave of a different kind of reform had been an early symptom of the stirrings among religious Americans, one of which came to be known, even before Lorenzo Dow's coming to Kingston, as the Second Great Awakening. Then the fiery exhortations of such powerful preachers as Charles Grandison Finney had so inflamed parts of upstate New York as to give the region the name of "the Burntover District." Revival meetings, marked by tears, shouts, rolling on the earth and public declarations of acceptance of Jesus as Saviour were memorable features of meetings, often held in the woods and fields. These came to be known as camp meetings.

In Vermont and upstate New York, William Miller studied his Bible, and made out passages which, to his mind, spelled out the ending of the world in flames, to be foretold as happening in the year 1843. Thousands of Americans, known as Millerites, accepted Miller's belief that with the cleansing as foretold in Revelations, of the world by fire, and with the coming down of Jesus from the heavens to judge all humanity, a Millennium, a new world of love and peace would emerge and last for a thousand years.

Millenialism was a part of the beliefs of the Shakers or "Shaking Quakers" who had been led to America by English Mother Anne who claimed to be a sort of re-incarnation of Jesus. The Shakers developed a culture of hard physical work, celibacy, and a characteristic kind of music and dancing of their own, with the sexes kept apart, and an elegant and simple design and making of physical objects used in daily life. (These objects, by their simple, functional style, compel admiration and high prices in antique shops today.) Yet by the 1790s an observer of the Hudson Valley had written that Shakers indulged in nude dancing, and naked whipping of one another, as well as in occasional bouts of drunkenness. They believed in the coming of The Millennium during which their own actual rather Spartan way of life would prevail.

Very different was the shape and color of the Millennium world of Kingston's intellectual John Lillie D.D. of first the Dutch Reformed and later the first Presbyterian Church.

In Kingston, the Rev. John Lillie was not backward in letting his congregation at the Dutch Reformed Church in the 1840s know that he was a pre-millennialist, who believed, unlike Miller, that the Millennium would not fully get in motion until the scattered Jews of the world would return to their homeland. Mr. Lillie left his Kingston pulpit for writing and promoting pre-millennialism in the city of New York, where he edited a publication called *The Jewish Messenger*, and worked diligently on books of biblical exegesis which he believed revealed hints of the details of pre-millenialism. For one of his works of biblical scholarship, Lillie's alma mater, the University of Edinburgh, at which he had been an outstandingly brilliant student, awarded him the degree of Doctor of Divinity. A few years later, when the Millennium and Millerite excitements had subsided, Lillie returned to Kingston as the minister of the First Presbyterian Chuch. After his death, it was said of Lillie that "he was a firm and outspoken opponent of Southern slavery a generation before it was outlawed and when it was universally and disasterously unpopular, and hardly safe to be an abolitionist. He was a millennarian in his views. This struck the key notes of his preaching, colored his conversation, and tinged his fervent and heavenly prayers." Until the early 1830s the Dutch Reformed Church alone had openly held religious services for the people of Kingston, but during that decade people who preferred other Christian denominations felt free to organize congregations which reflected their own beliefs.

After the years 1843 and 1844, when William Miller had predicted the end of the world, (and as some called it, "the end of time" and the descent of Jesus from heaven), the Millerite excitement died down, leaving destitute some of its believers, who had given away their farms and other possessions, in the belief that the end of time was at hand. Resurgent varieties of millennialism and those of Millerites have been with us to this day, and are found in the beliefs of Jehovah's Witnesses among others.

By the 1830s, another clergyman far less learned and respected than Lillie was active in Kingston and the vicinity during the reforming ferment of the time. He was the eccentric Rev. William Boyse, who was sent to Ulster County by the New York Dutch Reformed Church's commitee for sending missionaries to weak churches of their denomination. After serving as pastor of the church at Woodstock, Boyse launched on a career, like Lorenzo Dow before him, as a wandering preacher. He put into print a succcssion of booklets which offered sermons he had delivered, prayers to be read at home, folklore as remembered from his boyhood days in the Carolinas as well as in Woodstock, and rules for playing baste and town ball and other games which gave rise to our baseball. He collected witch lore, and told of a Woodstock person suspected of practicing witchcraft being dumped into a mill pond to test if he were truly a witch.

If they were actually witches they might be protected by the devil and not drown, if not they might be left to drown. While professing to disapprove of slavery, Boyse saw southern slaves as greatly enjoying life, and expressing their joy in music of "bangos" (meaning banjos) and dancing. He expressed a belief that the colonization of freed American slaves in Africa might have the beneficial effect of spreading Christianity throughout Africa, and so in all this he was supported by the anti-abolitionist view of conservative Kingston as expresssed by men like John Addison.

In the late 1830s, as the Millerite storm was rising toward its peak and breeding bizarre behaviour on the part of its devotees, Boyse was also playing a regional role in the universal peace movement which was widely being agitated ever since the end of the Napoleonic Wars which ended in 1815. He was giving his vision of world peace in a booklet circulated in Kingston, in which he urged his readers to do what they could to hasten the great day's arrival. The goal of universal peace had soared among reformers of Napoleon's time and decline and had many vigorous advocates in the United States. Peace was much in Mr. Boyse's mind, as it was in that of a Connecticut man named Elihu Burritt, often called "the learned blacksmith." Burritt, from a beginning in life as the son of a cobbler, had become a blacksmith after only the rudiments of education, and demonstrated amazing skill as a self-taught linguist. In the spirit of reform which was gripping so may Americans of his time, Burritt devoted himself to campaigning in Britain as well as the United States for universal peace.

William Boyse, probably influenced by Burritt or other peace advocates of the time, took up the same cause and proposed in 1839 that all the nations and sects of the earth choose delegates to be sent to a meeting at St. Peter's in Rome, and there on the second of July, 1840, pray together for the promised millennium and era of peace, with all the blessings attending it. Boyce granted that the delegates would bring with them to St. Peter's the cultural prejudices of the people who had sent them. But these they would shake off for the occasion.

For this, Boyse had what he offered as a simple solution. "I would say," Boyse wrote, "as a general would say to his army, 'Stack your arms! Put them all up in one stack! Make a mountain of them, as high as Mt. Ararat! To St. Peter's let us go!'"

"If it (St. Peter's) is a den of thieves," (wrote anti-Catholic Boyse) . . . "let us make it the house of God." Then to strengthen his proposed effort at universal disarmament and peace, Boyse offered a lengthy description of the architectural wonders of St. Peter's. Yet, quirky as he was, Boyse acquired a following in the Hudson Valley, Kingston and on Long Island during his years as a wandering preacher. This is evidenced from the list of subscribers to his "writings" which he printed in his pamphlets and booklets, and which give lists of names and the hometowns of those who bought them. Or perhaps these people bought Boyse's works just to get rid of him.

The names listed as purchases by the minister as he tramped up and down the Hudson Valley amount to about 1700. Kingston is represented by several hundred names. Pre-millennial Dr. John Lillie, is listed, and representatives of old Kingston families, Du Bois, Van Keurens, van Gaasbeeks. Abraham Hasbrouck is the only person given as of Rondout, then feeling the effects of the boom of population which the canal would bring them as well as Kingston and surrounding communities. A bound book of Boyse's writings which turned up in West Hurley some years ago bears witness to a division of opinion as to the value of the Boyse collection. Someone in the 1840s had thought well enough of the pamphlets to have them bound into a very handsome red leather volume, richly gilt and elaborately tooled or stamped. Someone else, obviously someone other than the one who paid for the binding, had had a go at the book, and scrawled his conclusions on the flyleaf by writing "this book owes all the connection in it to the binder." That may have some truth, for Mr. Boyse's mind indeed skipped about in often disconnected and disconcerting ways, yet he served well in demonstrating for us that the Kingston people were being subjected to the torrent of new and often upsetting ideas which were a feature of several decades and which played a part in the preparation of Americans for the emancipation of slaves, greater civil rights for women and blacks and more sensible ways of dressing and eating. Many reformist lecturers came to Kingston and Rondout to peddle their reformist wares; among them was Orson Fowler, who had two reforms on his mind. One was the building of octagonal houses as healthful and convenient of which Kingston's Broadway still has an example. Another on which Fowler spoke about in Kingston was the pseudo-science of phrenology. Wilbur storekeeper Nathaniel Booth after having heard Fowler lecture invited him to his house to "read" the configuration of the heads of a half dozen male friends. Some of the results were convincing to Booth, but others not.

And Booth in his diary has left us an insight into the presence in Rondout of a group of followers of cultist John Humphrey Noyes and of a Yankee self-called right hand man of his named Abram C. Smith, involved in a Wilbur limestone mining and cement production venture. Smith was the object of mob hostility as a practicioner of "Free Love" and a belief in what was called Perfectionism.

6.
"Free Love" on the Rondout

Some converts to Charles Gradison Finney's ideas went on to elaborate a sect called Holiness, and a later variant of Holiness known as Perfectionism. These enthusiasts did not believe that they shared in the innate sinfulness of man but were capable of living sinless lives on earth. One of these believers who had followers along the Rondout was John Humphrey Noyes, a former divinity student in New Haven. Noyes had acquired a license to preach but the license was revoked after he let the public know of his Perfectionist views which included before long a remedy for the problems associated with the relations between the sexes. He advocated "multiple marriage" in which all Perfectionist Group members would be equal in sexual rights to all others. Added to this was a provision of Noyes that reproduction be so ordered as to improve the quality of the human race (Noyes called this stirpiculture), by forming a committee of his sect whose members would choose mated pairs of what they judged to be of good genetic constitution to become parents. Others might marry (with Noyes' approval), but would have no offspring because of using a method of birth control (coitus interruptus), which in their practice seemed to work.

Noyes in 1838 founded a community at Putney, Vermont, in which his way of life was carried on by his otherwise devout Christian followers. This way included requiring members to work together and own their property in common. These and others were among Noyes' Perfectionist ideas which were tried out at Putney. Noyes' eugenic innovation, stirpiculture, was put into practice. The people of Putney were openly outraged at stirpiculture and multiple marriage. Threats of violence were heard in Putney and warrants for the arrest of Noyes, and George and Mary Cragin were issued. These three would later become the center of hostility in Rondout.

After receiving threats of tarring and feathering, the three Perfectionist leaders on the advice of their lawyer took off in the dark of night for Brooklyn where a branch of the Perfectionists was thriving and issuing publications advocating their views. They occupied a building given to them by Abram C. Smith who then worked in Wilbur on the Rondout. Noyes himself spent part of the winter of 1837-38 within the stout stone walls of a gloomy pre-Revolutionary farmhouse on the east bank of the Rondout Creek. The house was owned by a Rondout relative of Smith. While George Cragin exhausted himeself trying to work the farm with the aid of a blind horse, his wife Mary who had been a talented teacher and an ardent Noyes follower, did her best as housekeeper in the very sparsely furnished house. Smith went on with his work with the Wilbur limestone company—and as "strong right arm" to Noyes. He traveled up and down the Hudson as master of the sloop *Rebecca Ford* which was laden with local limestone. While in Rondout he kept in touch with the Brooklyn-based Perfectionist group to which he had given the building which they used as headquarters. Smith at this time liked to show Rondout friends like Nathaniel Booth a document in which John Humphrey Noyes named him his substitute and surrogate in all Perfectionist matters. Mary Cragin was often plagued by convictions of her own unworthiness and fell into spells of melancholy.

After Noyes had left to return to a somewhat less agitated Putney, Mary consulted Smith on her problems. Smith invited her to visit him in his bed by night for "spiritual advice." Mary complied and so began a sexual relationship unsanctioned by Noyes and his committees. It rendered Mary's devoted husband exceedingly unhappy yet he appeared to have felt reluctant to object to the relationship because it involved Abram Smith who claimed to be second in command of the Perfectionist group at Rondout and under Noyes's Perfectionist belief Smith had the same right to Mary as he did. Smith's wife complained bitterly to her Rondout relatives. And so was set the stage for the growth of an angry and theatening period of rage by the *Rondout Courier* and "Rondout hoodlums." Rage rose to the exploding point when Smith returned from Pennsylvania after advising a new group of Perfectionists there. He had taken Mary Cragin along to help with the good work. The couple spent a week along the way in sexual dalliance. On their return Mary, who was intelligent yet subject to emotional ups and downs, confessed everything to George, and George was understandably upset.

Soon Noyes himself arrived in Rondout, excommunicated Smith and censured Mary, but later restored her to favor. Smith's wife was deeply hurt by her husband's behavior, and told her Rondout relatives about the goings on in the bare and gloomy old house. Word quickly spread throughout Rondout. After the Rondout "hoodlums" demonstrated and rioted against them, Smith, Noyes and the Cragins hastily left for Putney. For a few years Perfectionism in Rondout seemed to have died out, but in the 1850s Perfectionism began to play a new part in the lives and in the deaths of some of the members at Rondout and the Brooklyn station, and brought a tragedy to the Hudson River near Rondout.

Abram C. Smith had presented the Perfectionist movement with his apparently profit-making sloop, *Rebecca Ford*, and the Brooklyn-Rondout Perfectionists had greeted the gift with cheers. The sloop promised to provide a means of helping finance their movement and besides it would be used as a "school" for their "navigators" who tended otherwise to rely much on divine guidance for other nautical help. During the almost ice-free season of 1850 the *Rebecca Ford* seemed to be fulfilling the Perfectionists' hope by making successful trip after successful trip between New York and Wilbur to deliver limestone to customers. In April of 1851, the sloop made its last trip for the Perfectionists and ended the lives of two of them. Aboard the sloop were three men working as "navigators," and two women. One woman had come to Rondout to work at keeping house for one of the navigators. The other was Mary Cragin. Mrs. Cragin had been sent down from Noyes's new and soon to be celebrated colony known as the Oneida Community, in the founding of which Mary had played an important part. Her mission at Rondout was to persuade navigator Francis Long to stick with his recent conversion to the movement about which he was now showing signs of having doubts. All accounts as to what happened as the sloop headed north off Hyde Park agree that a sudden flaw of wind had struck the vessel, that Francis Long whose watch it was, took the helm as the sloop heeled, and somehow mismanaged things (as he confessed later on), so that the sloop went to the bottom, taking with it the two women, who had been trapped in the cabin where Mary Cragin was reading aloud from the Bible's chapter 8 of *Romans* (which has Perfectionist suggestions). All three navigators escaped with their lives.

New York City and Hudson Valley newspapers reported the tragedy with varying degrees of accuracy and the official Perfectionist publication the *Circular* presented the version in which tributes to Mary Cragin abounded.

Mary Cragin and Eliza Allen, the *Circular* reported, were buried in the cemetery of the Church of the Ascension in Esopus (on the Hudson). They were buried wearing the short dresses, the pantelettes, and the short hair which had been adopted by Noyes's Perfectionist women to help assert the belief of their movement in the equal rights of men and women.

The *Circular* on November 6 reported that "the two bodies were buried with appropriate exercises in a cemetery belonging to the Episcopal Church of Esopus whose "obelisk" (steeple) rises on the west bank of the Hudson nearly opposite Hyde Park. A monument of white marble was erected over the grave. Beside the inscription which gave the life statistics of the two women were the words: "Gilbert Johnson, a resident of Esopus, kindly gave the strangers a grave." In present day Rondout, however, it is believed that the two women were buried in "a pauper's grave." The New York *Tribune,* had reported the tragedy under the headline, "Sloop sunk and two women drowned." John Humphrey Noyes had responded with a vigorous correction of some details of the tragedy that he believed the *Tribune* had misstated.

The Rondout Courier edited by usually judicious editor John A. Hageman published an account of the drowning in which the scanty group of Rondout Perfectionists were called "sinners" whose community is one "in which all the vicious and corrupt inclinations of man have full sway." Until this incident the editor had believed that the "cage of unclean birds had been scattered, never to pollute our shores again, but the dog will return to his vomit and the swine to the mire."

New York City's *Observer,* a leading religious paper, denounced the Perfectionists whom they confused with the then-polygamous Mormons or Church of the Latter Day Saints. The *Observer* suggested that the New York Legislature should take action to stop the activities of the followers of Noyes. So vigorous was the paper's attack on the Perfectionists' struggles for a new place in life for women, that other papers up and down the Hudson Valley took it up.

The Oneida *Circular* responded by publishing a manifesto in which they appeared to be giving ground on their policy regarding sexual relations, and especially complex or multiple marriage. Henceforth there would be a change. The change came but not for many years after the association for reconstruction of society had become a stock company engaged successfully in making silver plated tableware and with no interest in social or sexual changes.

In 1977 with the appearance of Constance Noyes Robertson's very informative *Oneida Community Profiles,* Mary Cragin's image begins to gain sharpness. Yet Mrs. Robertson, granddaughter of John Humphrey Noyes and great granddaughter of Mary and George Cragin, tells us that we do not have the whole story of this remarkable woman. Many source materials have been destroyed for fear of rousing the kind of hostile emotions that so often accompany proposals dealing with changes in sexual conduct and by scholars who have not been able to use the very large amount of contemporary manuscript source material which is privately held and not available, according to Mrs. Robertson, but which have implications for our own day.

Meanwhile we have good reasons for regarding Mary Cragin as a talented if fallible woman born ahead of her time.

7.
Rondout Transformed

THE MAJOR ASSETS WHICH FIRST MADE KINGSTON WITH ITS APPENDAGE OF the Landing or shipping point on the Rondout Harbor on the Hudson River a desirable place for human habitation remained its rich Esopus creekside alluvial fields and their convenient outlet to the world's markets by navigable water. But by the 1820s the gentle way of growing crops by the hand-held digging sticks of the Native American women had long before changed to the more intensive and masculine horse and plow farming method used by the white colonists. The more thoroughly loosened soil of the more deeply tilled fields made them an easier target for the occasional flooding waters of the Esopus kill or creek, and for sheet erosion following rainfall. European pests had followed the introduction of European food plants and profitable yield for the market had become a little less assured. As settlement moved westward a network of turnpikes and canals opened the way for competition from western farms, especially on or near the Erie Canal, to the markets of eastern consumers. With the American phase of the Industrial Revolution now touching Rondout, the Kingston Landing and Twaalfskill would be chosen as the hearts of the D & H Canal's furious impact on the regional landscape. It brought the cutting of trees and the use for growing food crops of land not well suited to that purpose. European plants and insects had begun also to do battle with native species such as maize and the South American potato.

Used for centuries, ever since the recession of the most recent Ice Age, first by Native women and then by whites was the Landing on the Rondout Kill, so convenient to Kingston's productive fields above. The Landing, as the map of 1814 shows, had been well adapted from its natural state of early Native days to the needs of a fishing and a shipping point for Kingston agricultural, fishing and forest-derived crops (timber, shingles, staves, barrel heads and hoops, potash, fur, livestock, etc.). Now it was adapted to suit the additional needs of the Canal. The 1814 map

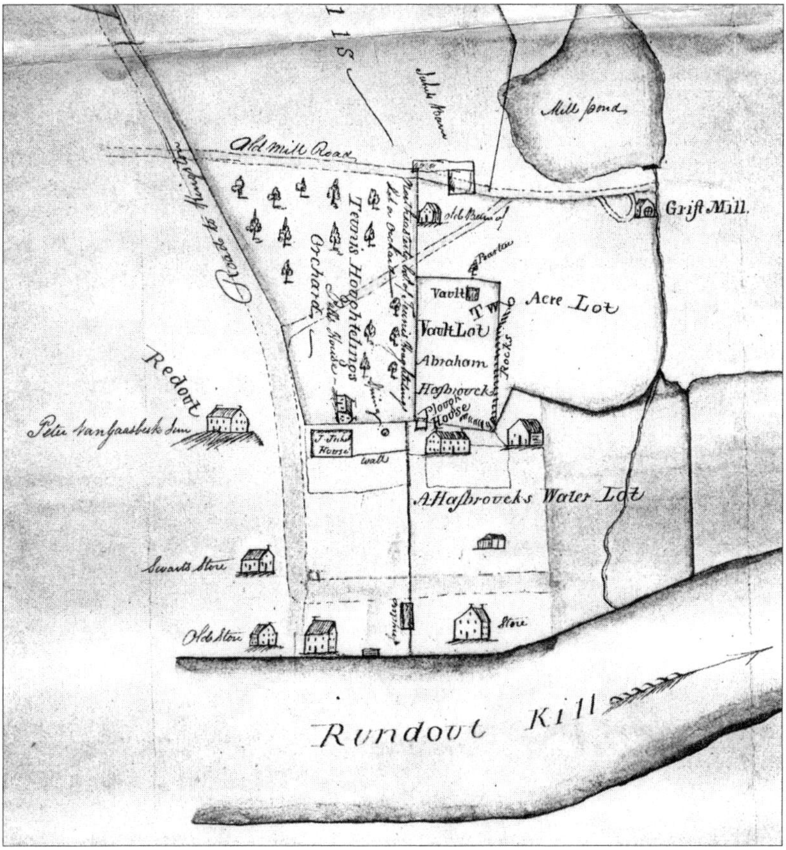

Map of Rondout, 1814, Senate House Museum Library

shows the pre-Canal Hasbrouck farm and the grist mill and its mill pond fitted in among the rocks along the Rondout Kill. It was a partly farmable tract of about eighty acres where fields, orchards, a grist mill and other uses might be carried on near a sometimes marshy shoreline, and which might be adapted to shipping or storing purposes. On this tract, close to the Vault Lot, or cemetery, stood until about 1850 two stone farm houses built by Abraham Hasbrouck in the 1790s. The 1814 map also shows the little collection of storehouses in which grain and forest products and so on were stored, while awaiting shipment in the sloops owned by residents Major Swart and Abraham Hasbrouck. "Hasbrouck's Water (or Tidal) Lot" appears on the map—this was the pebbly and partly sandy shore or Strand on which Native canoes and then white colonists' sloops could be hauled up when the tide was in for repairs. There was the house of the first colonist Thomas Chambers's heirs, trader and politician Peter Van Gaasbeek, and the site on a rise of a "Redout" of Revolutionary days or even earlier. (A "Redout" mean an enclosed fortified space of the seventeenth century or of Revolutionary days or possibly used at both periods. The uptown stockade when newly completed was sometimes referred to as a "Redoubt" in the Esopus Village minutes.)

The road to Kingston is shown coming down across the bleak Armabowery and the steep slope to the kill, or creek as it was now often called, and making a sharp turn to the Strand or Water Lot. All this was fair game for the needs of the D & H Canal Company's managers, and the limestone and cement people of the future, as they began to transform Rondout. An exception to this was the two acre "Vault Lot" in which the body of pioneer Thomas Chambers had been buried in 1694, beneath a modest gravestone of native bluestone; and the old pear tree beside the grave, the tree which Chambers, according to tradition, had planted perhaps with his own hands. But even that too was later built over. The vault's integrity was respected until Chambers's remains would be removed in response to the Canal's boom, to Kingston's Montrepose Cemetery about 1850. Although the village of Rondout would be dominated by the requirements of its thriving extractive industries and its Canal, the ancient pear tree lived on until past the end of the 19th century. It was photographed, as was Chambers' gravestone, by or for R. L. de Lisser for inclusion in his *Picturesque Ulster* of 1897.

It was not until the D & H Canal had been dug that it was realized that the Landing and Ponckhockie had certain less obvious assets of value now made visible in the light of the urgent needs of the Industrial and Technological Revolution.

One kind of extractable asset discovered in the digging of the canal was the wealth of ledges of limestone rising along the Rondout. They were now seen not only as obstructions to travel, as Darby had found them to be, but had positive values in the marketplace. The rocky ledges which stood out rough and in places forbidding along the three miles of the tidal Rondout Harbor had once indeed given the look of sterility on which Darby had commented in 1818. Yet these ledges were no longer seen as altogether sterile but by the Wurts brothers time would have acquired value in cash for their stone and in the making of the "Rosendale" cement which had recently come on the market to be used in the building trade.

Underlying the Esopus creekside part of the Kingston region on which Natives and whites had made their first settlement also lay limestone which was recognized by the early white colonists as having a local use as a readily quarried building material for the fine old houses of which Kingstonians are so proud today. Hydraulic limestone was also burned or calcined in the 19th century in primitive kilns and then put to a variety of uses. (To the Natives the stones had no value.) Another stone asset long hidden lay ten miles or so inland. It was the bedded Devonian sandstone, first picked up as smooth irregular-edged fieldstones, which was to become known and highly valued under the trade name of North River Bluestone. Later on it was quarried and used lavishly for urban sidewalks, sills, lintels, fireplaces, hearths and mantels. Still another asset to be used locally and moderately in the Colonial past, were banks of clay very suitable for brick-making, which were found in abundance especially along the Hudson River shore at Kingston Point and northward to beyond the Kingston line. Many of these additional assets once had been found to have modest local uses. The clay had been found by the late Woodland Natives who greeted the first colonists to be a good material for making pottery. It was used by the white colonists mixed with oat straw for laying the masonry of stone houses and for the plastering of interior walls. Many of the brick walls faced with brownstone in New York City usually owed their bricks to Kingston and other Hudson Valley brick-yards.

The bluestone found within the surrounding suburban regions served as flaggings for local walks and cellar floors. It was worked by craftsmen into troughs for feeding hogs, bowls for salting cattle and vessels for feeding domestic pets. Kitchen sinks were sometimes carved from bluestone and "potlids" were split for covering crocks. In addition, fine grained bluestone could be made into whet-stones for sharpening tools, and it was the smooth material from which many early gravestones were made. And squares of the stone did duty imitating those of black marble tiles in the checkered tile floors of entry halls of New York City brownstone houses. Sculptors of the Woodstock Art Colony would find bluestone of use. The statue of the Virgin Mary standing on the west bank of the Hudson at West Park to bless the sailors of river tugboats is of bluestone—the work of Thomas Penning, a notable user of the stone in the arts. And at High Woods the great work of Harvey Fite known as Opus Forty, (which includes a collection of old bluestone working tools), is a monument which now dominates the surrounding once-quarried countryside as a noble tribute to bluestone workers of the past by means of this great work of art.

During the 18th century, millstones of Shawangunk grit, shaped in the Rondout Valley, were used in local grist mills to grind grain or when placed on edge to grind cement or shipped from Kingston Landing. All of these early products put together could not for many years come close to equaling the economic sustenance given to their community by its fertile fields and its forests and the furs of its four legged inhabitants. This had to wait until the great surge in technology, which became a shaping feature of the Industrial Revolution which brought the D & H Canal to the very door of Rondout and Kingston. The great value of hydraulic limestone for industrial use as cement was discovered for intense exploitation by canal engineers overseeing the removal of a rocky obstruction, which was being blasted away at High Falls, in the town of Rosendale, only a few miles above the terminal at tidewater Eddyville. It was found that the stone was similar to the hydraulic limestone found as the Erie Canal was being dug more than a decade earlier at Chittenango. This stone, when crushed and burnt (or calcined) in a kiln at a high heat, produced an excellent cement. The "Rosendale cement," after being mixed with water and sand, could be used by masons for cementing stones and bricks together and as the binding ingredient of concrete. The Rosendale cement set well and hard even under water. Up to the discovery at High Falls, upstate Chittenango cement had been used in building the extensive stonework of Delaware and Hudson locks. Now it became possible to economize by making what came to be widely known around the world as Rosendale cement and using it in all D & H masonry as well as throughout the nation.

In 1870 a Children's Church was built on Abruyn Street in Rondout to serve the children of the community of whatever Protestant denomination. It was presented to Rondout by Calvin Tompkins of the Newark Limestone and Cement Company as a gift. The building, of Gothic Revival style, is a pioneer architectural example of the use of concrete reinforced by steel rods and plates, and still remains in use as a Sunday School under the name Union Chapel. Like many other experimental structures, it suffered minor damage from time to time but these were usually restored and now it is one of the City's most notable buildings. It is listed on the National Register of Historic Places.

The same hydraulic limestone found at High Falls was later also found to be present in the ridge rising along much of the Rondout Creek between Eddyville and the elevated mass that formed the now destroyed landmark once known as the Vleitsbergh above Ponckhockie and close to Kingston Point. The making of Rosendale natural cement in Ulster County began in 1826. It moved closer to Kingston when a plant was opened at Lawrenceville, and before very long its manufacture had crossed the Rosendale-Kingston line and the mining had become active along the creek for cement stone, at the point at which the stream known as the Twaalfskill, which rises close to Kingston's Greenkill Avenue, tumbles down the limestone ridges into the Rondout.

In the first century and a half of domination by whites, forests blanketed much of the area under the economic sway of Kingston as the forests had during the time of their Native predecessors. Here and there along the Rondout under white rule trees had vanished to make way for the white settlers' occasional pastures and tilled fields wherever they might be squeezed in among the rocks. Rondout rocks and tidal flats remained for years not too different from what they had been in the time of the Natives, except for the signs of Rondout's use as a landing place for Kingston.

The coming of the canal brought great artificial hills of anthracite coal to await shipment piled up on the banks of the Rondout Creek and on the long man-made Island Dock. The moving of coal barges, sloops, schooners and steamboats stirred the water of the Rondout Creek, as they had never been stirred before.

The process of producing cement was hard on the land and its people. It began with the mining of the proper stone from the layers of varying thickness of the ridges that look down on the Rondout Creek. Here miners with their picks, shovels and explosives drove tunnels in pursuit of the wanted kind of limestone until, here and there, from the Vleitsbergh south, the ridges came to resemble the tunnels driven by ravenous maggots in an unprotected cheese.

As the demands for Rosendale cement in flush times increased, horses and mules instead of men were employed to pull the carts, and later stationary steam engines were installed to bring the stone to daylight and to the kilns placed on the sides of the steep ridges. Here, weary men kept vigil as the hydraulic limestone was burned or calcined for about fifty hours. Then the crumbled stone went to hillside mills where it was ground by Shawangunk grit millstones to a powdery state. To ready the cement for sale, it was packed at first in barrels made on the spot by coopers, banging out in one Ponckhockie (a word of uncertain but likely Dutch origin) plant at the height of Rondout's Rosendale cement boom hundreds of barrels per day. By then, cement making facilities had pockmarked the slope at suitable areas from the waterfront at Ponckhockie and at Wilbur up the ridge, with overhead bridges and hilllside roads tying together a confusion of processing facilities, sending cement dust to pollute the air, injure human lungs and coat surrounding neighborhoods and their vegetation. Gone were the days when the slope formed an idyllic entrance to Rondout Harbor. And gone, too, were the immense flocks of passenger pigeons which had seasonally haunted the woods on top of the ridge from which the Vleitbergh rose above Ponckhockie and were shot or netted to supply profits to a few, and as one local newspaper put it, cheap food for the poor.

Once the canal was in full operation, ever greater artificial hills of coal patiently awaited transhipment on the Hudson, along the western bank of the Rondout. The huge spindle-shaped artificial island, a mile long, called Island Dock, appeared in the Kill at the foot of what is now Broadway, and on this, additional mountains of coal were stored until transhipped. The waterfront at Ponckhockie and at Twaalfskill was busy with the piling up of barrels of cement with sloops, barges, schooners and steamboats, (among them a vessel named the *Cement Rock)* being loaded. This business only stoped when winter freezing of the Rondout brought the labor by men and horses to a halt.

Cement-making was not the only extractive industry of its kind to exert a transforming influence by drawing capital and workers to Rondout, Ponckhockie, and Wilbur (once called Twaalfskill). Several smaller cement making operations and quarries for building stone were giving competition to the major Newark Lime and Cement operations at Ponckhockie and helping pollute land and water. Workers for the bluestone quarrying and coal shovelers lived in hastily put together huts or simple rented cottages of standard design beside the quarries and owned by the quarry owners. Those mining limestone, quarrying bluestone or working on the canal dwelt beside the mines and quarries in minimal comfort. And others ran up skimpy shelters for living between the ridges of the banks of the Rondout with each enjoying such conveniences for life as a pig or two and a few chickens and perhaps a few ducks which enjoyed the pools which kept damp the slopes beside the quarries on the creek. In ancestral Ireland a family pig had helped make life possible for the victims of absentee landlords. In Rondout the same benefit to life was possible and could be fed on table scraps and whatever might be found by foraging pigs and piglets in the neighborhood.

The introduction of industry to Rondout brought profits to some and labor at low wages to many who suffered the blasts of limestone mining and an atmosphere rich in cement dust and the green of trees often turned gray by the same dust. It also brought the noise of traffic on ill-made roads, and the loss of a natural picturesque feature, the Vleitsberg (or Vlightberg), jutting skyward from the Ponckhockie Ridge and forming a welcome landmark which helped Hudson River boatmen tell when they were nearing the mouth of the Rondout and Kingston Landing or harbor. A brook which once trickled down from the base of the Vleitsberg furnished a name for the landmark (from a Dutch word for such a stream). Such a "Vleight" or brook might well have been easily visible from aboard a sloop or some other vessel on the waters of the Hudson River.

8.
"Where is the Vlight Berg?"

On October 12, 1831 a great mass of rock close to the top of what we know as Overlook Mountain in the town of Woodstock spontaneously detached itself from its position on the precipice known as the Minister's Face and crashed into the valley far below. The Minister's Face lost much of the brooding profile which had caused it to become a landmark for Hudson River boatmen.

Sometime in the fall of 1849, a change was also to occur at the summit of the bald peak known to Hudson River boatmen who valued it as a landmark for guiding them to the entrance to Rondout Harbor with its Landing Place for the Village of Kingston and that village's productive alluvial fields above. The summit of the Vlight Berg was destroyed not by any natural force but by determined human effort. The peak had been found to be largely made of the same kind of limestone of the Niagara and Helderberg formation which may be coaxed to yield a useful and valuable cement for the use of masons—and so it had to go.

John Vander Lyn had included the Vlight Berg in an early landscape. The Vlight Berg had also been represented as it was in the act of being destroyed. This was shown in a lithograph of 1852, made in Newburgh, and is reproduced on the following page.

The Rondout *Courier* of February 11, 1848 carried a story called "Where is the Vlight Berg?" The story explained that the Berg was then being torn down by the Newark Limestone and Cement Company. The paper predicted that in the future this prominent landmark to boatmen approaching Kingston (around which immense flocks of passenger pigeons roosted from time to time) might be remembered only by a glimpse of its image in one of Vander Lyn's paintings. And the Vlight Berg once guided Hudson River pilots to the location of Kingston Landing, much as the Tarpein Rock (as one writer of 1849 put it) once marked the way to ancient Rome

The one time landmark which marked the entrance to Rondout Harbor from the Hudson, destroyed through converting it to cement. Image courtesy of the Friends of Historic Kingston.

and from which, as graduates of the Kingston Academy may have learned, criminals had been flung to death.

No one however was known to have been flung to death from the Vlight Berg. Many hikers had admired it from a distance. And young and even old people had climbed it in order to enjoy the glorious view from its top once such views became fashionable.

The Vlight Berg had come to be thought of as a place on the landscape of sufficient romance to become the subject of an anonymous so-called legend printed in the Rondout *Courier* on February 18, 1848. Here a tale of villainous Tory doings on the Berg had been stitched together telling how British troops under General John Vaughan landed at Ponckhockie and passed the Vlight Berg on their way to burn Kingston. The account was partly based on fact but contained much fancy. This fabricated legend is an example of those produced by lesser writers than Washington Irving to fill a public demand for such tales of the Hudson Valley.

There was an exciting view to be had from the Vlight Berg top of the Shawangunk mountain range all the way across Esopus Meadows on the Hudson, beyond Krum Elbow. Now, in 1848 the Vlight Berg was doomed to annihilation—and doomed by the very blessing that was to make some Rondouters rich and furnish employment, if at low pay, and with possibly damaged lungs, to thousands of immigrants.

Years before 1848 Calvin Tompkins of Tompkins Cove on the Hudson River opposite the east bank Village of Peekskill had discovered in the Cove's ledges a vein of the kind of limestone suited to the making of cement. The vein ran along the rocks marking the shore of the cove or shallow bay which bore the Tompkins name. Tompkins had gone about mining the stone, burning it and converting it to the cement which was coming into profitable demand. Later Tompkins was to learn of the Vlight Berg and the extensive nearby ledges which were easily worked from the outcrop at Rondout to the landmark called the Vlight Berg because a stream started from near its base. Tompkins bought the surrounding land once part of the Hasbrouck acreage and set up a dusty and noisy operation of combined quarrying and mining the Vlight Berg and carrying the results at first to his Tompkins Cove works on sloops or barges which docked at his Rondout Creek waterfront below the Vlight Berg. Later on, with the Vlight Berg destroyed, Tompkins acquired more land nearby and set up making cement there on a large scale.

Earlier, when the presence of the appropriate kind of hydraulic limestone had been discovered while digging the D & H Canal at High Falls, manufacturing cement had begun in Ulster County. Before the late 1840s the Newark Company had mined the limestone in Rondout and also at Calvin Tompkins' works lower on the Hudson and had shipped it on barges, schooners and sloops to their home base in Newark for processing. Later the whole process was carried out in Rondout.

Within a few years, shafts and tunnels were well underway on the very body of the Vlight Berg and a mill for processing the rock burned in hillside kilns was at work. Most of the upper part of the Vlight Berg began to disappear as a first step. And before many years the very name as well as the landmark itself disappeared from Rondout conversations. The mining was accompanied by occasional loud and roar-

Newark Lime & Cement Company, from *County Atlas of Ulster, New York*, F.W. Beers, NY 1875

ing, passenger pigeon frightening blasts and rock slides which Rondout people found hard at first to became used to hearing.

The network of underground tunnels dug and blasted to bring the stone out eventually formed a vast system reaching hundreds of feet down to the level where it was invaded by the water of the Rondout Creek. The surface of the great ridge became to the eye a disorderly arrangement of dirty buildings of many discordant shapes and sizes tied together by huts and other connective structures, yet all this having its use in cement making. Lower down were thickly crowded houses of workers standing amidst a few once impressive older buildings of pre-cement days.

At the foot of the slope which was known as Ponckhockie were warehouses and docks of the Newark Company. Then with the development of an improved variety of artificial or Portland Cement, Rosendale Cement, which took longer to set was forced from the market after vigorous attempts to maintain its sale were made under the direction of Samuel D. Coykendall.

Many Kingstonians of today have never heard of the peak which was once the landmark of their harbor. And most signs of the once prosperous industry at Ponckhockie vanished from human sight in a vast dark lake formed underground where a few rusted relics of the mining machinery remain, not to mention the silent miles and miles of shafts and tunnels and other excavations dug by long dead workers at the risk of their lives from premature blasts and falling rocks—in the ghostly lake area of the present day above which recreationists stroll in the sunshine in ignorance of what chapters of Kingston's industrial history lie beneath their feet.

Entrance to mines in Vlight Berg. Image courtesy of Friends of Historic Kington

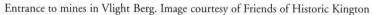

Near where the Vlight Berg once stood is a new industrial park to which, it was at one time hoped, new and properous industries would be attracted. And Hasbrouck Park now offers views of the surrounding country similar, if less exciting, to those which drew Kingstonians to scramble up the Vlight Berg, and where later on the Knaust family had had a flourishing mushroom-growing business in the dark mines (now flooded) left by the limestone miners.

The question "Where is the Vlight Berg?" had been asked as far back as the 1840s. The only answer today can be, "Nowhere, it is gone forever." And the Legend of the Vlight Berg exists only in a yellowed old newspaper read only by delvers into local history tidbits or genealogy, and very few of those at that. For extractive industries exact a lasting price from the earth, and leave marks on the land which are not always easily interpreted, yet are worth thinking about as steps in the rise to the status of a historic city such as Kingston's.

The former landmark called the Vlight Berg has long passed out of the memories of Rondout people. So too have the now extinct passenger pigeons which once settled around it as they migrated. The pigeons, once a wonder of North America and a source of food, became extinct. The last lonely individual, a pigeon named Martha, died in 1914 in an American zoo and their association with the Vlight Berg gave them a place in the history of the conservation movement which their vanishing helped start.

9.
North River Bluestone

THE NORTH RIVER BLUESTONE INDUSTRY, BASED AT THE TWAALFSKILL (ALSO known as Wilbur), was firmly tied, like an extractive suburb, by roads to sources of supply outside the boundaries of Kingston but owned or under contract to the Wilbur, Rondout or Kingston owners of the bluestone sales, finishing and shipping yards on the Wilbur and other waterfronts at which economic shipping by barges and sloops awaited to carry the finished stones away for use in endless American towns and cities.

Kingston owners or leasers of quarries, in industrial suburbs located up to sixteen miles inland, entered the lists as transformers of the virgin bluestone lands and effectively put them within the Kingston orbit as they financed and managed the

Coal from Pennsylvania in Rondout on the Long Canal

Stacks of bluestone in Rondout. Postcard from the collectionof Alf Evers

quarries of their layered Devonian sandstone. This stone was shipped via the Hudson River, and by canal and to some extent by rail to many parts of the United States and sometimes even to foreign places. According to the U.S. Census of 1880, the stone would eventually be used for the remarkable number of 60 miles of Kingston sidewalks (in that city alone), as well as many, many crosswalks, curbs, and hitching posts of varied designs on its streets.

Much bluestone was processed in dusty sun-baked stoneyards by derby-hatted, red-shirted workmen spread out along Rondout Creek shipping points concentrated at Wilbur. The derby hard hats were used to protect workmen's eyes and heads from flying bits of stone (known to them as spalts) by their use of chisels, hammers and mallets.

The stone was used not only as flagging for the sidewalks of New York and many another American city, but was sold to masquerade as the black flooring tiles to be used alternating with white real marble tiles to form checkered floors in New York City entrance halls. It was used for sills, lintels, hearthstones, mantels and sometimes for entire building facades in cities along the Atlantic coast. It was also widely used for sewer heads and curbing. It had been used in many buildings, including New York's elegant Tiffany House and government buildings throughout the nation.

The bluestone industry, from a small beginning in the 1830s, underwent an astonishing expansion until about 40 years later. It left large regions of Kingston's hinterland resembling hard fought battlefields given a desolate quality of their own by irregular mounds and walls of quarry waste with here and there a quarry pool in which frogs spawned and children bathed—these pools marking the places where a promising ledge had led a quarryman to strike a spring. It also created around the quarries settlements of sometimes shanty homes slapped together by quarry workers of rough hemlock boards, or in a very few cases neat cottages built by the owners to a standard design and rented to workers.

Adding to the changing looks of Kingston and its suburbs were the brickyards. Most of these—the big ones—were located where huge banks of clay between Kingston Point and past the northeastern Kingston boundary line gave jobs to seasonal often black or Italian workers, except in the winter months. Later on, in the 1890's, owners brought young black Southerners to work in the brickyards in the spring and returned them in the fall. Other brick workers were emigrants from Italy who remained. The clay banks, when wet and after being tinkered with, were unstable and gave the landscape a hard time when huge masses of disturbed clay slid down, sometimes covering the brickyards almost to the very bank of the Hudson.

The clay for the brick was hauled from the pits to the facilities for moulding and there mixed with coal dust. The wet bricks were then trundled out on hand-pushed trucks to drying fields resembling vast clay tennis courts, and were there allowed to dry in parallel breast-high walls until they could be moved to the shed-protected kiln areas and burned in piled-up masses of bricks serving as kilns.

The growth of the bluestone industry as it responded to the rapid growth of American cities and towns reached by water on boats able to bear the bluestone weight forced Kingston to reach out beyond its official boundaries. It reached out to localities such as Jockey Hill, Hallihan's Hill, Stoney Hollow, Lewis Hollow and the huge California Quarry above the base of Overlook Mountain in its search for saleable upper strata stone. In the ledges located about a thousand feet above sea level along the base of the mountain and known as the Quarrybank (pronounced "bonk"), erosion of softer deposits of red shale had left shallow caves once known to the Dutch as "jadg houses," (meaning hunting houses or shelters) in which Natives had camped out on autumnal hunting trips. Now some of these former Native and Dutch hunting shelters were recycled as small blacksmith shops for sharpening and repairing quarry tools using huge bellows to fan the fires of their forges. All the above quarries usually shipped their products via Rondout's waterfront stoneyards. Each had its "Irish Village" or "New Dublin." The Irish Village in Lewis Hollow had an outdoor wooden dance floor for parties and houses that functioned as shebeens (where liquor was sold). In Kingston the using of Wall Street and North Front Street for transporting of bluestone to the Wilbur or Rondout waterfront was favored for many years.

The uptown Kingston stockade area had not required the kind of violent treatment that was needed to fit Rondout for the reception of an industrial age existence.

The impact of heavy industry and its accompanying onrush of workers as well as degradation of the landscape fell on Rondout almost alone. Kingston remained as Darby and later visitors noted a place of visual charm and much surrounding pastoral and mountain beauty (except for the quarry-ravaged suburban lands) now that scenery was coming into fashion.

The site of what is now uptown Kingston was high enough to prevent invasion by the floods to which the Esopus was then addicted. It was high enough to permit pleasant glimpses of the surrounding country, and close to the lookout or Kijkuit (now Golden Hill) to permit a stirring panoramic view from its summit. The shopping center of General Smith and his fellow business people was also as well adapted to the purpose of selling merchandise in its day as the site had been for defense in the days of the first white colonists. In only one way was uptown Kingston ill adapted to playing a working part in the bluestone industry. In order to haul the very heavy and often large stones to their waterfront yards for finishing and shipping, the shortest and most convenient route had to pass down a bit of North Front Street and down much of Wall, the center of uptown's business, legal and municipal activities. In the early years of the industry, permission for the occasional use of these streets by the heavy stone wagons was readily granted.

But as the industry grew in size, there were second thoughts as the heavily loaded and frequent wagons ravaged the surfaces of the streets and there were clouds of irritating dust in dry weather and muddy slop when it rained. Besides, the racket caused by the passing of stone laden wagons was said to cause so much annoyance

Heavy wagon broken down in Higginsville, from *Picturesque Ulster*

in the Courthouse on Wall Street that proceedings there had to be halted until the noisy bluestone wagons had rumbled and rattled by. On some roads heavily used by bluestone wagons parallel tracks were laid (of bluestone) for the wagons to run on, and the wagons wore deep channels in the tracks.

In Rondout, on the other hand, the land bordering the creek below Eddyville was ill adapted to becoming a site for the operation of several of its extractive mining, manufacturing and transportation ventures under the relentless energy of corporations, some huge for their place and day, and financed by stockholders, and sometimes when that proved insufficient, by the state of New York. It took much blasting and considerable ingenuity to devise sites for offices, manufacturing, and storage and shipping facilities, docks on the shore from which sloops, schooners and barges might load and carry to market finished bluestone flagging, barrels of limestone cement, and other products, coal and brick, or to await the transhipment of anthracite at Port Ewen (a base on the River of the Pennsylvania Coal Company) to New York and elsewhere on the Hudson. The Pennsylvania Coal Company, builder of Port Ewen (named for a Pennsylvania Coal Company president), was the largest customer of the Canal Company. Most of its coal-carrying barges would be made in the numerous shipyards along the Rondout Creek as the stream ran just below Eddyville. These barges were not sold as were the D & H barges to captains who understood how to manage the craft until they aged beyond repair. The Pennsylvania Coal Company owned its own barges on the Hudson and hired their own crews.

The people of Rondout as they transformed the place found no housing prepared when workers began to pour in to take up industrial jobs. They lived at first in hemlock shanties they built tucked in on rocky slopes between the industrial structures and reached by crooked paths and lanes. The workers whose energy and muscle would play a large part in the Rondout boom which was being born had been induced to come from lands in which poor workers such as they might have hoped for happier lives than those that faced them among the rocks of Rondout. The abdication of Napoleon in June, 1815 had been widely expected to result in an outburst of prosperity in Europe. This was not to be, and workers were faced with such economic tribulations as high prices and unemployment. 1816 ushered in several years of remarkably cold weather, which resulted in crop failures. Ireland was already long plagued by an archaic system of land tenure, absentee Protestant landlords and Catholic tenants, and placed too great a reliance on the ailing potato crop, and conflicts between Catholics and Protestants arose. Altogether this set the stage for tragedy. As Maurice Wurtz and his brother William were going about the mining of anthracite coal in Pennsylvania, the first serious disease-caused potato crop failure—that of 1822, caused famine to engulf much of Ireland. A worse famine struck in the late 1840s.

The British state had continued to accept the Poor Law of the first Queen Elizabeth. Under this law, families of the poor were crowded into local poorhouses. Some received meager help from charitable Britons and landlords, who realized that tenants caused them a loss by not being able to pay their rents, but few landlords found it beneficial to lower them. Landlords and parish officials sometimes reacted by shipping many of the suffering Irish off to America in order to get rid of them. A host of European economists, amateurs or professionals, including the Rev. Robert Malthus had foretold that dire consequences were about to plague Europe as a result of overpopulation especially, some said, when trusting too much to a single crop or a single industry. This added to the number of schemes for helping the starving poor to leave. In New York City, the Society for the Prevention of Pauperism was well aware that their city was becoming jammed with Irish immigrants. The Society set up soup kitchens as the first of all these institutions to be put to use in America.

By 1825, Maurice Wurtz and his associates had obtained legislation for constructing their canal from State authorities of both Pennsylvania and New York. Stimulated by the near approach of the completion of the Erie Canal, many a dream of profiting from "internal improvements" was buzzing in many American brains. All such dreams to be realized would require a vast amount of unskilled labor. And in Ireland and in the German principalities, the stage was being set for the "Great Migration" to the United States of 1830-1850. Many hundreds of thousands of manual workers, aroused by shipping agents and ship masters, would embark as passengers under the sharp spur of poverty to land in New York and Boston. Some of them had already served apprenticeships on British coal canals.

The immigrants drawn to Rondout as demand for labor got intense were largely Irish. But in the German case, the movement was largely aimed at Brazil, the American midwest and even at Russia. Otherwise the immigrant rush to the D&H Canal might have had a decided German rather than Irish flavor.

In Ireland, oppression by the often absentee Protestant English land owners had caused the Catholic Irish tenants to form secret societies, often with the help of their priests. These societies helped the Irish (and so did their strong sense of social solidarity) to devise means of doing battle against the oppresors. In the 1830s and 1840s, the Rondout Irish emigrants lived as best they could in ways they had brought from their homeland, adapted to those of a new country.

There is no evidence that the owners of the Rondout industries in a day of meager means of public transportation gave any thought to where their workers would live, or how they would travel each day to their jobs—all that was left to chance—on an inhospitable terrain amid a foreign people.

At first no road linked the centers of work and living along the northern shore of the Rondout. If a Ponckhockie man wanted to go to Twaalfskill by land, he had to go up the rough road over the Armabowery to Kingston and then down the hill by another road to his goal, or else travel by boat. Eventually, the resistant topography was overcome. By dint of much blasting of bedrock, a road tying together the settlements on the higher shore of the Rondout became a reality. When the first church was built, ("on the rocks," it was said), Rondout people often reached it by boat instead of by walking.

The Delaware and Hudson Canal Company officials, as if to stamp Rondout as their "company town," proceeded to name the place Bolton, in honor of the president who had followed first president Phillip Hone, and was the financial expert of the company. This was when the establishment of a post office for Rondout made a choice of a name necessary. Other streets were given the names of other company bigwigs—Hone, Wilbur, and others. A howl of protest arose from residents who resented becoming known as the company town of Bolton, and the old name of Rondout (derived from redout, a space cleared and protected by walls for defensive purposes) was restored. But many roads went on bearing the names of company officials; some do to this day. President's Place, on which the company President Bolton dwelt, also keeps that name.

With frequent bangs and muffled explosions giving evidence of limestone mining, and clouds of dust thickening the air and coating the landscape and nearby human lungs, with the harsh rumble of bluestone wagons hauling stones of up to 12 x 15 feet in size on Kingston Streets, shrewd Yankees poured in from New England and other places in search of business opportunities. They opened stores where food, shoes, ropes and other marine supplies and boatmen's clothing, tackle and boats went on sale. Workers turned up from neighboring regions, often from parts of New York state. These were usually willing to work at any job providing it paid the 80 cents to a dollar a day that might keep their particular wolves from the door.

Kingston businessmen had hoped to benefit from the opening of the D & H Canal, yet General Smith and his associates, who had prepared to profit from canal-related business, could not have forseen the kind of transformation which was overtaking once quiet, thinly populated neighboring Rondout. It was true that when Rondouters required legal or medical help, they had at first to go up the hill to Kingston for it. If they needed banking services they had to seek them after 1832 in Kingston's first bank. No longer did Kingston passengers and freight destined for New York City patronize the weekly service of Rondout's Abraham Hasbrouck and Major Swart, who had long almost monopolized the Rondout transportation business by water. Steamboats and tow barges were nosing out the sloops. And while some of the steamboat lines were controlled by proper Kingstonians of Dutch and Huguenot ancestry, newcomers to the Kingston-Rondout region were pushing their way into the lucrative if competitive steamboat or other businesses.

Kingston, faced with the taking over in what had long been little more than their Landing or shipping point for the field, fishery and forest products which had supplied so much of the village's income, became uneasy. Until then, for example, their apprentices and journeymen had lived in the homes of their employers. Now Rondout was setting them an example by the way the upper level employees of the industries were living. While the workers were gnawing away at the bedrock of Rondout for shanty spaces, their betters were living on choice sites on the scenic slopes above the shores of the creek. At the same time the 88 cents to one dollar a day shovelers of coal, blasters of limestone, convertors of rough bluestone into saleable flagging were tucking themselves into whatever nooks and crannies they could find on the ridge that rose above the creek that could be spared from extractive industrial and commercial needs, with the lungs of their families assaulted by stone dust.

As the bluestone industry grew in size and profitability, shabby settlements of workmen made their appearance right beside the suburban quarries from which they wedged and split their stone. Bluestone quarry villages, such as those in Woodstock, Jockey Hill, Stony Hollow and West Hurley featured shanties or rough boardinghouses for single workers. Married men might add to their incomes with the help of a wife and children by doing a bit of hillside or mountainside farming on the steep rocky slopes above the quarries, and hunting and trapping to eke out a meager income. The quarry settlements were outposts or suburbs socially and economically of Kingston and would eventually become the scene of battles for political control.

In Kingston, the conflict between Catholic Spain and the Netherlands following the Reformation had left scars on three-fourths of the Dutch who accepted the Dutch Reformed Church as their religious body. Until the preaching in Dutch in Kingston's Dutch Reformed Church came to an end in 1809, the daily ways of life of the Village had been heavily influenced by Kingston's only church, with no competing sects to appear in Rondout or Kingston for two decades. In Rondout, traveling Catholic priests occasionally said mass, performed marriages, baptisms, and comforted believers and the bereaved. Until the massive arrival in Rondout of the demobilized members of the canal-digging army, Catholics had been few indeed in Rondout or Kingston and were viewed with suspicion. As Catholic workers under Protestant employers began to pour in and change the look of the place, Kingston people could not help being even further disturbed. Maurice Wurtz, himself a Presbyterian, gave some comfort to Kingstonians by donating a piece of land "on the rocks" close to the Rondout to be used as the site of a Presbyterian Church (a denomination not very different in practice from the Dutch) and sites for other Protestant denominations, but not for a Catholic place of worship. Dutch Reformed church members discussed setting up a chapel in Rondout, but the proposal was voted down as likely to weaken their Kingston church.

Among the predominantly Irish shovelers, bluestone and limestone and cement workers there were few Protestants. In nearby Saugerties, a large Catholic population had been imported to work in the 1820s in the attempt of Henry Barclay of New York City to convert Saugerties to an industrial center with the help of its fine Esopus Creek waterfall for power and its harbor on the Hudson for transportation. There, a Catholic Church was built. The Irish Catholic workers of Rondout, as they grew in numbers, met and contributed thirty-two dollars and two cents to make a beginning of a fund to build a church of their own. Abraham Hasbrouck sold them, for $300, to be paid in installments, the high and commanding site where St. Mary's now stands. This church came to serve not only Rondout, but the predominantly Irish quarry workers whose rough products their teamsters moved from suburban quarries down Wall Street and other dusty roads to the stoneyards beside the Rondout at or near Wilbur, where other Irish workers finished the stones for sales and shipment at waterfront stoneyards or docks. All this helped strengthen the ties that bound Rondout to the Kingston quarry suburbs at the foothills of the Catskill Mountains.

And quarry workers liked to live in neighborhoods favored by previous fellow emigants from their own homelands, insulated from American culture and slow in adapting to American living patterns.

Not all of the Irish who dug the D & H Canal went on to labor in Rondout, but a good many became "bark peelers," who felled and then stripped the Catskills hemlocks of their tannin-rich bark, which was needed for turning rawhides into leather, and relied on the tanneries for a variety of other jobs once the Canal was in operation. Loads of malodorous rawhides alive with flies, often brought by sea from such places as South and Central America and California, were unloaded along the Rondout Creek, on consignment from New York City tanners, from sailing vessels by Rondout's usually Irish dockhands. The hides were returned to the Rondout waterfront following their tanning inland, no longer fly-ridden and stinking, but smelling with the pleasant odor of new leather. They were then loaded on ships by the Irish dockhands to be sent back to their consignors in New York's tanning center on Gold Street at what is now the west end of the famous Brooklyn Bridge.

Other Irish ex-canal diggers worked at the many odd jobs available in the rapidly-growing river port. And many worked their ways up into skilled positions of responsibility on land or on the boats of the Hudson River.

Workers from the early tanneries of the forests of the Catskills frequently walked their way down to Irish Rondout to celebrate their days off in the shebeens and brothels which arose in the place. Street fights became common, and the deaths of drunks by stumbling into the Rondout Creek happened from time to time. A report of a local Temperance Society told of the presence in Rondout in the 1830s of more than sixty illicit stills for making whiskey. Often quoted of this period by local historians describing the character of Rondout, was that it had become a veritable "Natchez under the Hill." This referred to a famous blowing-off place for the habitues of the dens of iniquity of a Mississippi River town which openly flaunted the current code of morality. But we must remember that Militia General Erastus Root, who so described Rondout for the information of the Washington officialdom, in the usually sober American Biographical Sketchbook of 1848, was called "a little uncouth in his manner, and rough, and I fear somewhat rude in his expressions. His wit was keen and his sarcasm biting."

The General was also a shrewd politician, ever ready to coin phrases that would ring bells for his benefit in the popular ears. In addition, he was himself a notable toper.

Certainly the ears of many Kingstonians were pleased with what the Congressman had to say about the many floaters and members of the brash new community of workers which had shot up on their waterfront from which they themselves were doing business by water with the entire country and beyond.

It was not easy for the people of Kingston to adapt to having as neighbors a noisy community of the sort which was a not unusual by-product of the Industrial Revolution. The new Rondout complete with poverty and slums was one which only Abraham Hasbrouck and Major Swart and a few old-time hangers-on from Rondout's slimly-peopled past profited by. At the same time a tentative center of a Kingston industrial area of its own was attempted, where Division Street (now Broadway) and Pine Street joined at the edge of what would become the Academy Green. It was centered about the successful Baldwin Machine plant which made farm machinery and other products of cast iron, but the closer shipping and cheaper labor facilities of Rondout limited growth of most large industries to Rondout.

As the Rondout workers grew in number, and more seemed to be landing from every immigrant ship docking at New York and hastening up the Hudson, Kingston people viewed the newcomers with more suspicion than ever. The immigrants had been crowded into cramped quarters in the immigrant ships' ill-ventilated steerage, poorly fed on the long voyage, tormented by seasickness, sometimes suffering from typhus (called "ship fever.") They did not always as they landed make an attractive entrance into Rondout life. Epidemics of yellow fever, cholera, and other contagious diseases, which now and then afflicted Rondout and spread to Kingston, were usually thought to have been (and sometimes were) to have been carried in by recent immigrants. Kingston people who had to do business in Rondout sometimes held handkerchiefs steeped in camphor over their noses and lower parts of their faces, and hastened back to the safety of Kingston.

In the 1830s, an epidemic of fever was attributed to the eating of pineapples brought to Rondout from the West Indies on board the schooner *Vanda.* Eating

Rondout waterfront with the schooner *Vanda,* which was thought to have brought an epidemic to Rondout and Kingston. The print once belonged to Franklin Roosevelt. Courtesy F.D.R. Library

fruit was often seen at that time as a source of illness. Modern understanding of such epidemics makes it much more likely that the fever may have been conveyed by enterprising mosquitoes which had stowed away on *Vanda.* When epidemics of Asiatic Cholera first swept the northeastern United States it 1832, it raged with a special fury in Rondout, causing doctors from New York City to arrive and set up an emergency hospital room or two and write a lengthy medical report.

Poor sanitary conditions in Rondout came to be a cause for concern, and thought of as the focal cause of the spread of epidemics. It was not until after Rondout became a separate village in 1849 that a beginning could be made at conquering the haphazard disposal of sewage which had marked Rondout from the days of the arrival of the canal and had invited epidemics.

People were coming and going to and from Rondout and Kingston at a lively rate and spending money there. The Rondout *Courier* warned parents to keep an eye on their children because the paper reported the canal was a means of channeling "rogues" to the town. Yet most of the new people who were drawn to shovel coal, quarry limestone or bluestone and work in the shipyards and shops or to crew canal barges or river boats were decent people. And so many arrived, including rapidly increasing numbers of Germans, that in 1849 the population of Rondout had grown beyond that of Kingston and that year the Village of Rondout came into being in order to make the management of the place the responsibility of those who lived in it rather than that of all of the people in the old Town of Kingston which included those two Villages. In Rondout there was little popular enthusiasm for the new order and officials were slow in tackling the many problems caused by the rapid, unplanned and uncontrolled growth of the past twenty years. Yet a few years later Rondout's sometimes rowdy mining camp atmosphere began to move toward becoming a thing of the past, and many changes took place as the 1850s came. For one thing, the bank of the Rondout, however convenient for Canal and limestone and shipping purposes had proved far from ideal as a place for workers to live. Ledges of steep rock protruded through the scanty soil; springs fed by rainfall on the heights above burst out of the steep hillside above the creek banks. In Rondout, Wilbur and Ponckhockie hemlock shanties had been placed without much regard, in the haste of the times, to esthetics, convenience or good drainage. The pigs, chickens and ducks which were a normal part of this and other similar settlements ran as they pleased, scavenging as they went. After rains, paths and lanes became filthy torrents and carried down accumulated sewage and garbage. The various clusters of dwellings along the creek as they grew had no means of communication with each other except via creek—until after Rondout became a village (and so empowered to make improvements), a creekside road was blasted into being. Drainage was then provided for the major roads. Pigs, chickens and ducks were deprived by village ordinance of much of their old freedom.

If the major industrial powers of Rondout—the Canal company—the limestone and cement firms which dominated the Rondout waterfront, the bluestone and shipping men played any part in the agitation that led to the organizing of the Village of Rondout, it was not obvious. But through the 1840s J.P. Hageman, editor of the Rondout *Courier*, had strongly advocated the formation of the Village in order that sanitation, police and fire protection and care of streets might be better handled. Hageman was the first booster of the place and his vigorous championing of local business and industry suggests some understanding with the community's commercial and industrial giants. When the Village finally began operating the voters were slow in giving it backing and did not enthusiastically support even measures to deal with epidemics among the immigrant population. In 1851 however when the *Courier* reported that a "Shelter for the Sick" had been provided in a Rondout basement where a family of six new arrivals ill with ship fever were installed. The six were "of wild western tribes" (of Ireland) who do not talk any variety of English, the *Courier* reported. A few days earlier the *Courier* had urged the provision of a hospital to care for the "influx of pestilent-smitten victims of long voyages." In 1852 as the first epidemic of cholera struck, the trustees of the Village leased a house to be used as a hospital but the voters voted against the action and only accepted it "on the third try" as Stuart M. Blumin wrote in his *The Urban Threshold.*

Other measures intended to improve the quality of life along the Rondout were spurred by the holding of unofficial public meetngs, as one in 1850, because Rondout had become "the theater of so many riots and outrages that its citizens became justly alarmed" and "discussed measures for the preservation of the peace and the security of life and property," so said the *Ulster Republican*, a conservative Ulster County paper. By the time of the Civil War Rondout had established police and fire protection and other services normal in a village of its time but which had not been possible until it acquired the legal powers of a village.

The Rondout Creek and its almost three mile long harbor lost the purity of the creek's waters that had welcomed early white explorers. Darkened by topsoil washed down from upriver forests now transformed to cultivated fields, downstream came the litter and rubbish of a new brand of culture with a new way of making a bargain with the earth. The Rondout, however, had other uses of value to those who lived along its banks, and those who sat in offices where they financed and provided a necessary management for the industries which had become the economic and therefore the social dictators of Rondout.

Each one of the bluestone quarries which sent its products to the Rondout stoneyards was located within a distance from a shipping point on the Rondout Creek or Hudson River which made economic sense. Those which shipped to Wilbur, were from Woodstock's part of the long ledge called the Quarrybank or from West Hurley. The hauling by horsepower of stone, which is very heavy and sometimes cut into very large saleable slabs, made the trip to the stoneyards a major part of the cost. It also made a frequent breaking of bridges and caused damage to the roads along the way, and this found its way into the law courts. On one occasion old time quarryman Ben Snyder recalled the day when an exceptionally large stone slab was on its way to installation as part of a Fifth Avenue sidewalk in New York. The event took on the look of a holiday, said Ben, with children riding on the slab holding flowers and singing. The teamsters stopped their vehicle at every tavern on the way to the waterfront to "drink the stone's health."

Among the largest of the Rondout-related quarries were those of Lucius Lawson of West Hurley whose men once broke down a bridge with damage to a valuable piece of stone, and to a wagon and leading to the death of one of his horses. As was testified in the lawsuit of Woodstock versus Lawson, teamsters were in the habit of stopping for refreshment here and there, culminating at Higginsville on the edge of Kingston. From there they made their way down Kingston's Wall Street and on to Wilbur wearing down the pavement and raising clouds of dust.

On Sundays the quarry workers marched in formation, by fours to St. Mary's Church in Rondout for mass, passing down the same Wall Street route past the Dutch Church. These processions were sometimes met with hostility when tipsy local anti-Irish-and-Catholic toughs lay in wait at Higginsville at the end of North Front Street and threw stones at quarrymen, resulting in very active brawls and much injury. A piece of land on which it was once hoped to build a Catholic church at Higginsville (close to the edge of Kingston) and so avoid the ethnic conflict which the march to church of quarrymen incited, was planned. But the project was never carried out and instead the Church of St. Anne was first built at Sawkill very close to the quarries, and was welcomed by the quarry families. This church stills holds its position in the community.

Kingston officials, after taking protracted legal action managed to have the use of bluestone wagons on Wall Street forbidden.

By winter the quarrying of bluestone was shut down as was traffic on the canal and usually the iced-up Hudson. Then it was that workers resorted to whatever jobs they could find. Some workers scattered to chase rumored jobs elsewhere. Other unemployed men found work for a time at harvesting a crop which usually only became available in mid-winter. This was ice to be cut from the Rondout and the Hudson beginning in the 1830s when a demand for it rose from New York and other cities (and even some cities in the tropics). The ice was cut, stored, and packed in sawdust in huge ice houses made of rough unpainted hemlock boards which rose on the banks of the lower Rondout and the Hudson above Poughkeepsie where the River was less salty. The ice was shipped to urban markets on tow barges as needed.

The ice industry was unlike any other in that it involved the harvesting and storing of a most perishable substance. This industry had one decided advantage to a place in which winter unemployment was high. Nathaniel Booth, with his keen sensitivity to the look of the landscape, has left us two excellent word pictures of the icecutters in action in 1849.

"A lively scene is presented on the ice today—more than one hundred and fifty men and horses are occupied in filling the three large ice houses on the creek—some are ploughing large furrows up and down, others transversely, others sawing through—others conducting the blocks down a Canal (cut in the creek's ice) and so into the houses into which they are hoisted by horsepower—all are busy as interest and a certain degree of fun can induce. The ice is but seven inches thick and the weather having turned warm promises to spoil the business for the present." And then having given this succinct and accurate account of the ice cutting on the Rondout, Booth adds, "The scene is a rich one for the painter."

On January 15, 1849 Nathaniel Booth again lit up in his diary with a jolly scene on the ice of the Rondout: "The snow is going fast—it is now raining. The Ice houses are filled and the workmen are having a glorious carouse on the ice—liquor is abundant and they are yelling like wildcats." In this painting in words Booth has nothing to say about the less picturesque side of the ice business. He does not tell us that workers at the harvest earned only 88 cents a day. These workers for the most part were shovelers of coal or workers on the canal through most of the year but were unemployed and so without pay during the winter. Then they had to compete with back country unemployed men who drifted into Rondout harbor when freezing weather began and tanning slowed to a crawl. But Booth also saw and recorded more cheerful aspects of winter unemployment. He gives for example a very lively picture of the captain of a coal barge on the canal, made unemployed by the ice of winter, who had become a dancing master: "The company at the (dancing) school was made up of extraordinary materials—good, bad and indifferent, old and young, wed and single. While a half drunk white and black orchestra played, the Professor-captain was wonderful—almost sublime. Two-thirds of the night he passed between the floor and the ceiling, he would spring from the ground like a rocket—his long legs in half a dozen knots... and then send them flying about like the spokes of a wheel, he would bounce like a ball and then shuffle over the floor like a Terrapin." And the diarist ends his extravagant but comic picture on a characteristic note of ambivalence: "Everybody said it was pleasant—perhaps it was."

Auxilliary enterprises to the extractive industries of Rondout multiplied—ship chandlers, a dry dock, machine shops and many shipyards for making their river sloops as well as barges for use on the canal. A large steamboat, the *James Baldwin*, was made at Ponckhockie, although its fitting was supplied in New York City. (The *James Baldwin* was named to honor the owner of the big foundry at the beginning of Broadway at the Strand Gate.) Sail lofts for sloops and schooners continued in business long after the arrival of the steamboat. Other shops supplied clothing and boots for boatmen, run by Yankees and New Jerseyites. Machine shops of various sizes supplied not only steam engines but replacement parts for such engines, boats and farm equipment. Jewelers, doctors and optometrists appeared. And grog shops were frequently undertaken, each usually serving a different ethnic group for which they also served as social centers. Street musicians and other ambulatory entertainers were frequent visitors to Rondout's shores. Rondout came to have a community of its own character and color, distinctly different from more staid Kingston on the heights above.

An elaborate office building of Renaissance-derived design for the D&H was soon built. James S. McEntee of the Canal company built and for a time ran the Mansion House which before too long would surpass in size and quality any similar venture in Kingston. Rondout was becoming a busy, bustling and undeniably vital settlement of newcomers, different in occupations and character from the well-organized village of Kingston above.

And while Kingston was conservatively Whiggish, Rondout became the target of New York City Democratic politicians with a special eye on the immigrant Irish. These politicians in 1848 made a first bold bid for Wilbur and Rondout voters to the surprise of the people of those communities, unused as they were to such attention, and somewhat flattered by it.

10.
Politicians Appeal to the Irish of Wilbur

In 1847 Nathaniel Booth described his part of the hamlet of Wilbur (then not yet a part of either Kingston or Rondout) in very unflattering and surely exaggerated terms. No matter that Booth had his prejudices, or that his impetuous style of writing sometimes was carried too deeply into whimsy, he often shows awareness of these faults by recognizing that there is another side to the questions he is addressing. Here he is describing the store he began operating as a new arrival in the hamlet of Wilbur, still known to oldtimers as Twaalfskill: "The store and the place deserve more than a passing notice. The form of the former would puzzle Euclid to describe. It has three compartments which may be classed—small, smaller and smallest—irregular in shape and possessing more angles than a starved cow." His neighborhood, Booth suggests, matches the store. Close by stood a large ramshackle rooming house known as the Astor House, in mock honor of the elegant New York City hotel of that name. But it was known to Booth as the Madhouse because of the quarrels, fights and even the recent ax-murder which had drawn brief notoriety to the building. The hamlet of Wilbur, Booth wrote, "Was in the same order as my store—namely disorder. An imaginative man might say that a wagon load of houses had been dumped on the lovely landscape helter-skelter."

The landscape before the Canal's arrival had indeed been lovely. The road up the rocky valley of the Twaalfskill to the Village of old Kingston had been improved until it became the shortest and best of the three that led from the Rondout shore up to Kingston—the one from Kingston Point, the one from the Landing at the Strand and the one from Twaalfskill. The Twaalfskill Road ended at the sloop and steamboat docks of the Wilbur waterfront. The heavy hand of industry had just begun to bear down hard upon Wilbur. "A painter would say that the scenery was wild and romantic," Booth noted. And at this season (September, 1847) also entirely beautiful yet the diarist (himself an amateur painter and versifier) could not avoid seeing that the Irish immigrant life that bubbled around him had elements of the roughness we associate with mining camps and American communities of the sort spawned by the unplanned rising of a new order of extractive industrial enterprise and its resulting kind of unplanned housing for its workers. He notes examples of conflicts between ethnic and religious groups which would then disturb Americans in response to wholesale waves of Irish and a few German immigrants who were willing to work long hours at low wages with pick and shovel if need be to escape the hunger and insecurity which threatened the poor of the Old World.

Booth's neighborhood was decidedly indigent and rough, yet by March 1847 it had become enough of an attraction to draw the attention of ambitious politicians including some from the City of New York. Tammany Hall's Democratic politicians had already drawn Irish immigrants of their large city into becoming pawns in politics by means of their recently (and not always legally) acquired votes. Now even ramshackle Wilbur was worthy of their efforts. The right to vote was easily obtained by recent immigrants, often by a mere statement of intention to become a citizen, often by mass naturalizations. Such votes were then rarely questioned at the polls where contending parties both used similar methods.

The Wilbur men, whether demobilized veterans of the D&H army with a decade of struggling to adapt to American civilian domesticity or very recently arrived immigrants, appeared worthwhile to those with political ambitions.

Many of these Wilbur men were under the difficulty of adapting to a new environment which marked their neighbors living in what storekeeper Booth called "The Madhouse."

In 1848 Democratic politician Lewis Cass captured the Democratic nomination for the Presidency after a vigorous struggle. His opponents referred to him as a "dough-face" or a Northern man of Southern anti-Abolitionist principles. And his supporters advertised a pro-Cass meeting in Wilbur. The Democratic Party those pre-election years was favored in the South and by those in such parts of the North as were agitating for the digging of "lateral canals" (These sprouted out from the very successful Erie Canal) and they were plausibly said to be favored by Irish voters who wanted more of the pick and shovel work involved. The Abolition of slavery would throw on the market many thousands of black competitors for such little-better-than-nothing work, or so it was being rumored. Cass, a shrewd and cunning man, was making a strong bid for the Irish canal digger vote.

Up to this period not any great attention had been paid to getting out the Irish vote of Wilbur or Rondout by the opposing Whig or Democratic parties. That was why when a notice of a meeting of local Democrats to boost Cass's candidacy was posted in Wilbur, Booth dismissed it at first as a hoax. But it was no hoax. And that evening of March 31, 1848, when Booth heard the sound of distant drums and saw the flare of torches he knew from this "that something real was going on." What was happening was that "the Democracy of Wilbur was assembling with the purpose of making a demonstration in favor of General Cass."

In his very lively, perhaps over-lively diary report of the demonstration Booth plainly showed a disgust at the raw vulgarity that was then and still is a part of American political campaigning. By the light of the torches of cotton soaked in turpentine and while standing outdoors on planks supported by barrels which formed the dais, orators did their best to cajole the hopefully more or less naturalized Irish voters-to-be and pointing out what the orators presented as the wicked nature of the Whig supporters of their presidential candidate, slave-owning General Zachary Taylor. A supposedly local politician named G.B. Craig (marshal of the parade) led off the proceedings with a plea for votes for the Democratic Party and General Cass, especially by what he called the "patriotic sons of Erin." He showed "our beloved country to be on the verge of destruction through the evil designs of the opposition party" whose character he exposed—proving that party to be "selfish and unprincipled." He alluded to "the noble Irish heroes Emmet and Caroll" and others, and besought their countrymen now assembled to show their love of country and justice at this particular crisis. "And now, gentlemen, to turn to another infamous black hearted falsehood that has been uttered against our illustrious candidate, General Cass—would you believe such an atrocity could exist—would you believe a heart so blackened could beat with life—a heart so blackened—could you believe that a man could be found to publish or to utter or to listen to so infamous so atrocious a *Lie* —so damnable in its character, as this, that General Cass voted against the Irish Relief Bill. Yet such a charge *has* been made, fellow citizens and (is) now engaged in imposing the minds of the noble sons of Erin with a belief of its truth!!!"

Here Booth reports shouts from the crowd: "'Arrah, don't let it trouble you sir, says a good natured fellow in the crowd. 'Sure we don't believe it.' 'Divil a ha' p' worth, says another man, 'surely any man in his senses knows better nor that'—'Hurrah for Cass, Hurrah for Matthews, Hurrah for Taylor, to hell with *you*, Hurrah for Cass (prolonged cheering)."

Next Booth told of the rising on the platform of a New York City politician named Michael (Mike) Walsh, "a large gross looking man with much superfluous fat about his face." Walsh launched into a series of anecdotes. One was designed to sneer at ex-President Martin Van Buren's son, as favoring "practical amalgamation between whites and blacks."

John Van Buren had become known as Prince John ever since he had danced when in England with Queen Victoria who was heartily detested by the impoverished Irish who resented the Queen's rumored failure to give substantial aid to the starving Irish. Next Walsh, who had a reputation for "extemporaneous singing," sang in tribute to local Democratic politicians, one of whom was a German tavern owner, John Klein, and Walsh sang "When I get back to the old South (sixth) Ward (center of Irish Democratic political activity in New York City), I will tell how I spoke on this board, how the Irishmen, free hearted souls, are blasting rocks and are shoveling coals." Here Booth notes that the uproar of applause was great as "the allusion was understood by all."

The political rally at Wilbur on March 8, 1848 was being staged at the prompting of the political machine known as Tammany Hall which was dominated by Irish emigrants who had carried across the Atlantic the protest organization of their native land known as the Whiteboys from the way of its members of wearing a white shirt over the usual garb in order to make it easier for the Catholic tenant farmers to recognize one another in their nightly protests against their oppressive Protestant absentee landlords.

The speaker, the able Mike Walsh, was the Tammany leader well characterized in recent times as one of the most efficient of the Tammany organizers, "a combination of clown . . . and authentic leader of the people." The Sixth District of Manhattan was on the Lower East Side where Tammany strength was greatest. The 1848 political foray on Wilbur was an early example of the extension of New York City political machinery to the mid-Hudson Valley as an arm of the Democratic Party's Tammany Hall.

In the second half of the 1840s the Temperance Movement, spurred on by Kingston lawyer John Romeyn, a Whig politican, was dominating local and state elections and Ulster County with both issues of local options of selling liquor and anti-immigrant feeling growing stronger among its supporters especially in the village of Kingston. It was not by accident that a German Rondout saloon-keeper was active in the pro-Cass rally which descended upon Wilbur and drew a Democratic-claimed attendance of 800, including many from Rondout as well as Wilbur. And it was no accident that the Whigs' candidate, "Old Rough and Ready" slave-keeper and military hero Zachary won the presidency in 1848, and carried both Kingston and Rondout.

Eighteen forty eight was a pivotal year for both western Europe and the United States. For failed revolutionary movements in Europe, and the issuance of the Communist Manifesto played parts in starting a flood of immigrants to the United States where within the next half dozen years legislation such as the Fugitive Slave Act and the Nebraska-Kansas Act passed Congress and the publication of *Uncle Tom's Cabin* by Harriet Beecher Stowe shook the Whig Party to its roots. And so the party members defected and made possible the Republican Party which in time would elect Abraham Lincoln.

But first for a few years the Know Nothing Party, strongly devoted to anti-immigration and against such features of the Catholic church as parochial schools, came to capture the political affections of a majority of Kingstonians. They were able to fill many local and regional offices for two years while the Know Nothings did little to change the Kingston and Rondout ways of government. And after 1855 the Know Nothings no longer dominated the local scene but remnants of their followers managed to perpetuate their policies in secret organizations. One of these, called the Junior Order of United American Mechanics persisted locally until well into the twentieth century. Yet the days were over when native Know Nothing leader Daniel Bradbury, pioneer Rondout photographer and later on Kingston postmaster, according to the Rondout *Courier*, "strode the streets of Kingston like a cock o' the walk."

11.
A Utopian Dream for Jacob's Valley

Rondout by 1849 when it became a Village had been thoroughly transformed from its use as a thinly inhabited rural landing for the village of Kingston. It had become a well functioning part of the investment of several profitable individuals and corporations. One other part of what is now Kingston, watered by the Twaalfskill as that stream splashed its way to the Wilbur waterfront, at the same time had endured a remarkable series of changes from a wild area fit only for "outcasts," as the Rondout *Courier* once said, to a place of a few small water-powered industrial ventures. These ventures had been stimulated into growth through use of the falls of the Twaalfskill, which drains Jacob's Valley, by the boom years of the late eighteen twenties and early thirties, but were dealt what seemed to some a death blow by the national economic crash of 1837-1838.

The first years of boom that followed the opening of the Erie and the Delaware and Hudson Canals had flowed by to the accompaniment of a growing interest on the part of many Americans in the natural world around them and in creating more aesthetically pleasing houses and gardens. Now, thanks to the energy and talents of landscape designer Andrew Jackson Downing of Newburgh, as well as Washington Irving's Rip Van Winkle, J.F. Cooper's Natty Bumppo, and General Morris's poem, "Woodman Spare that Tree," Americans in Kingston as well as elsewhere took a second look at their landscape and discovered fresh and newly exciting values in it.

When Peter Stuyvesant chose the site for stockaded Esopus he had no notion that the elevated place would be seen generations later as having not only defensive advantages but esthetic ones as well. Marius Schoonmaker in reminiscing about his early nineteenth century boyhood wrote with warm appreciation of the walks which young people of his youth enjoyed outside Kingston's stockade borders as well as on the way to Jacob's Valley. There, and in the valley, limestone ridges carrying mysterious fossils, hilltops giving stirring views of far-off woods, meadows and mountains, impetuous streams dashing down steep and rocky gullies and springs and ponds all gave an excitement to the American landscape now that it had been touched by the magic of the arts by such masters as Irving, Cooper, Cole and General Morris.

Rondout and Kingston bulged under the thrust of the Canal power and more housing was needed. Many new arrivals, even married couples, were taking to unsatisfactory boardinghouse existence. The Dutch barns which had stood beside old Kingston stone houses came down to be replaced by frame or brick houses and housing moved beyond the old stockade limits and was pushing, for example, beyond the part of the Plain (now the Academy Green) across what is now Pine Street and almost as far as the old ring fence to the Armabowery or poor lands, converting in its course the old black people's Pine Street burying ground into a lumber yard. Early in the nineteenth century Kingston's trustees had conveyed some of their lands held in common to tenant farmers and sold some to new people and so enlarged the area within Kingston's close influence. After A.J. Downing's popular books on landscape gardening and rural architecture appeared in the 1840s some Kingston people were sufficiently aroused to the Downing enthusiasm for country life to build a few board and batten dwellings beyond the stockade limits. In Rondout the steepness and roughness of the Creek bank on the Kingston side made building there by the poor difficult yet it was done. But not until after efforts in breaking up rocky ledges, in diverting springs and re-shaping the face of the land.

There were some who were sensitive enough to the growing feeling for the natural landscape to protest. By February 18, 1848, the Rondout *Courier* lamented the vanishing of the "rocky peak called Vleightberg" (more often spelled Vlightberg) under assault by the "pick axes and gunpowder" of the limestone miners.

Not everyone saw the expansion of stockade Kingston and Rondout as a cause for rejoicing. A writer in the Rondout *Courier* in 1848 deplored the slaughter of a grove to make room for a dwelling in terms that verged on the tearful. "Spare Those Trees," his lament was headed. The "axe has begun its destructive work in the beautiful fragmentary grove on the hill back of the Mack House. It was fondly hoped by some lovers of the green-wood that this spot would have escaped the havoc which has desolated all its vicinity. . . . Couldn't that miniature park be preserved as an evidence to posterity that woods once crowned the hills. . . . In pagan times it might have been saved by consecration to some popular divinity . . ." Now, the writer adds, "the grove's fate is being decided by the present divinity of these regions—the almighty dollar." (Which was also driving the destruction of the landmark peak of the Vleitberg.)

On December 25, 1863 as the Civil War raged, the Rondout *Courier* looked backward thirty years to the time when Jacob's Valley had been "a secluded place" with two log huts on the edge, the huts "inhabited by negroes and coffee colored squatters," and holding the "outcast grave of a suicide."

Speculators saw the waterpower "of the Twaalfskill going to waste. But the dreams of the flush times of the early 1830s were unfulfilled" although a dam was built and "lager bier brewed at" the Twaalfskill's "head spring" close to Greenkill Avenue of today. The *Courier* continued, "the ledge of rock known at that time as the Devil's Pulpit excavated into lager bier vaults . . ." All this fell into ruin and quickly gave way in that shady and well-watered valley to a mini-forest as the fearful depression beginning in 1837 took hold.

Kingston lovers of the natural world were cheered for a time by the efforts of local entrepreneur Abijah Smith to save the remaining beauty of Jacob's Valley (which lay between Kingston and Wilbur) by turning it into a combined real estate development, cemetery, park and lake according to ideas given currency in the books of A.J. Downing and since the 1830s by the proliferation of American landscaped cemeteries such as Mount Auburn near Boston which were also serving Americans as pioneer municipal parks (the need of which had not been felt earlier).

Until it felt the pressures of the Canal-powered boom plus that of the flush speculative times of the 1820s and 1830s which prevailed nationally, Jacob's Valley had reverted to being a natural enclave too rough for farming. As the boom made itself felt the waterpower of the Twaalfskill, the stream which dashed and sparkled down the Valley was curbed by dams and drew small water-powered industries to its many artificial as well as natural falls. There were a mill making wood turnings, a tannery, a flour mill, a mill making gunpowder kegs and others, plus the brewery above which took advantage of the very pure water of one of the springs (lager beer making requires pure water) which were the sources of the Twaalfskill. The depression beginning in 1837 put an abrupt end to all these industrial adventures and at once nature began returning "natural purity" to the very well-watered Jacob's Valley. By 1850 the Valley was once again a picturesque and romantic spot enriched by its now romantic industrial and vine clad ruins. Young couples walked there again and pointed out such features as the Devil's Pulpit, Moses Rock from which a spring again trickled, and other striking rock formations.

And there distinguished painter Asher B. Durand sketched and exhibited the finished results in New York's National Academy of Design Gallery and for the city's thriving Art Union. It was then that Abijah Smith, brother of Perfectionist and surrogate to John Humphrey Noyes, Abram C. Smith, entered the picture. He published a lengthy prospectus in Kingston's the Rondout *Courier* phrased in language fervent, extravagant and persuasive enough to have done credit to a twentieth century public relations wizard.

Moses Rock, in one of the upper layers of rock near the top of Jacob's Valley, from which a spring gushed and which may have been the source for beermaking, which requires very pure water. Stereograph, circa 1880

Smith extolled the reborn natural beauty of the place, its closeness to Kingston, Rondout and Hudson River tidewater, "a spot as secluded, and almost as wild as any to be found among the Catskills. Here are found in miniature almost all the beauties of nature. . . ." A "great improvement was about to take place" in the Valley, the prospectus stated—two New York capitalists were about to survey and offer for sale building lots with frontage on the Twaalfskill. There would be a cemetery distinguished by the kind of serpentine walks and drives favored by Downing, ponds to supply water not only for ornamental fountains and a water supply for the houses to be set along the Twaalfskill but hopefully also for Kingston as well. The lot-buyers would have the use of the Valley and it would also serve, should Kingston be agreeable, as a park for that Village. The development would give Kingston "a public promenade and place of rural resort exceeding anything of the kind in America" surpassing the parks of New York, the Commons of Boston and the "most celebrated parks in Europe." And there would be still more.

The Jacob's Valley development would embody some of the most advanced social planning ideas of its day: "it would be a practical demonstration of the beauty of Free Soil Doctrines as held by the projector of the scheme who was a citizen of Kingston—known to everybody, whose system for the division of lands, and whose method of equalizing property, and spreading money equally among the people, is unrivaled by Fourier, Ledu Rollin, or by any of the Agrarians, ancient or modern." Or, as Smith might have added, Horace Greeley, editor of the *New York Tribune*, who had many readers and followers in Kingston.

Here Abijah Smith in a manner not too unusual at his time was stirring together a variety of current enthusiasms, some getting space by *New York Tribune* editor and publisher Horace Greeley, into one tasty dish containing almost all currently palatable ingredients and omitting only a few like temperance and women's rights. Kingstonians of the time were aware that Free Soilers, in whose ranks were communists who believed in common ownership of all land, also believed that slavery should not be extended to territories or new states and some Kingston people enlarged the belief to include a variety of other freedoms. Charles Fourier and the others mentioned were influential advocates of the communities holding all property in common. Such utopian settlements—about forty of them—were springing up (many only to wither quickly) around the country—Brook Farm at Concord, Massachusetts was a notable example. Agrarians were strugglers for the rights of farmers. Included among them, some enthusiasts even asserted, were the recent Anti-Rent tenant rebels of the huge Hardenbergh Patent in the Catskills.

Abijah Smith was not satisfied with merely proclaiming the proposals outlined in his prospectus—he took vigorous action to implement them by means of a sales campaign for his building lots—and by staging a gala picnic.

Nathaniel Booth's diary entry for August 3, 1850 describes the picnic as held against a background of the partly finished mortuary chapel and receiving vault with gingerbread, lemonade, assorted cakes and other goodies being served. Celebrants were brought to the scene aboard a special stagecoach. Booth tells of a discordant brass band blaring while a hurdy-gurdy competed and young ladies sitting on beds of white pine branches added their charms to the scene. In the midst of it all Abijah Smith was clearly visible darting about as Booth put it, "now here, now there as if he had discovered the secret of ubiquity."

Smith's Jacob's Valley dream was never to come down to earth sufficiently to take the form of more than a few houses, winding drives and ponds. Kingston people soon referred to the whole vision as Smith's Folly and freely predicted that failure would overtake it—and so it did. Yet the project aroused people with more interest in dollars than in Free Soil doctrines, serpentine drives and picturesque scenery, to plan less structured housing attempts on their own. A notable one crowned the height known as the Weinberg overlooking smoky and dusty Rondout with a fine panorama of land and water visible beyond. The Weinberg (or Grape Hill) had once been covered by a fine natural stand of woods in which noble old American chestnut trees were conspicuous with grape vines clambering everywhere. Eager builders had seized the tract, cut some of its trees and vines, probably to enhance the fine distant view, leaving a clump of isolated trees or bushes here and there. On this tract, with some care taken to preserve the remnants of the old wood, houses and gardens came to be built by prosperous Rondout people, among them James S. McEntee, who was a promoter of the housing development as well as chief engineer of the Canal Company and active in many other engineering ventures. His son Jervis McEntee N.A., the distinguished landscape painter lived on the Weinberg by summer in a romantic studio designed by his brother-in-law Calvert Vaux, and in there also was General Samson whose wealth had come from tanning in the Catskills, Dr. Abraham Crispell and other outstanding people who valued living on landscaped acres. Some of their places survive after years of being admired as among the most distinguished of all Kingston residences.

To the south of the old stockade area a hill long known as the Kijkuit, or Lookout, from its use in early Native and Dutch days as a place from which approaching Native or white enemies might be observed was divided into building lots advertised to be sold for from fifty to two hundred fifty dollars, many commanding views of the Village of Kingston, the lush Esopus Valley and the blue Catskill mountains. The old Dutch name of the hill was rejected and a new one—Golden Hill—more appropriate to the tone of the times, substituted. This was an appropriate name at the time suggesting the current preoccupation with California and the gold mines to which some Kingston men were hastening in search of wealth and from which a few were sending home an occasional sample of gold dust.

By the late 1840s buildings had begun to cluster around the point between the Broadway and Albany Avenue intersection of our day. This was a convenient home place for workers in the foundries and machine shops like James Badwin's, steam sawmill and foundry and other industries which had sprung up nearby. To serve "people of small pecuniary means" banker Henry H. Reynolds and some of his New York City relatives built the Reformed Protestant Dutch Church of the Comforter or Wiltwyck Chapel—in its earliest years it was used as a Sunday School. From the appropriation by the Chapel sponsors of the old name for stockade Kingston the name "Wiltwyck" came to be applied to the entire neighborhood much to the confusion of some later purists in the study of local history. Wiltwyck even appeared on the signboard of the local grog shop and on the side of the fourteen seat horse-drawn omnibus of Joseph P. Davis which began running through the place every hour beginning in 1851. This first means of public transportation in Kingston made it to the landing at Kingston Point and was before long joined by a rival connecting Kingston with The Strand or Kingston Landing. The omnibuses did much to encourage buildings to rise along the level parts of their routes. So quickly did the new Wiltwyck grow that it was being predicted in 1840 that "The Plain" was ready for division into a grid of "blocks and village lots . . . with space reserved for a public square or park."

By the time the Canal boom had passed its twenty-first anniversary Kingston people who took the trouble of looking into their municipal future were having pleasant dreams. One of these dreamers, in October 1851, stood on top of the hill known to his forbears as the Kijkuit and looked toward Abijah Smith's development and cemetery in Jacob's Valley, the new settlement at Wiltwyck and the grid of newly made streets at Ponckhockie and at a similar grid across the Rondout Creek brought into being by boatbuilder Morgan Everson and named South Rondout (now Connally) and saw a prophecy and a vision which were put into words for the *Courier* of October 1851:

> "If it (Kingston) continues to improve and expand as it has for the past five years it will not require half that time to see the borders of our village mingle with those of our sister village, Rondout, in one common city and extend in other directions in the same proportion. No person was so visionary five years ago as to believe that all that extensive plain south of St. James Street as far as Jacob's Valley would now be cut up with streets and laid out in building lots, which are rapidly becoming occupied."

Kingston and Rondout during these years were expanding and bursting out of old bounds in more ways than one. There was talking and thinking being done about new things. The first attempt to incorporate Rondout as a Village failed in 1841, but by 1849 another attempt succeeded. However, for several years little was done to take advantage of Rondout's new governmental condition. More Kingstonians and Rondouters were reading New York City newspapers and subscribing to national magazines. More were discussing national issues and fewer could understand Dutch in Kingston or Gaelic in Rondout.

12.
Know-Nothings, Soft-Shells and Hard-Shells

THE ATTEMPTED TRANSFORMATION OF JACOB'S VALLEY AND THE AWAKENING of many Kingstonians to the charm of their natural environment were not alone in stirring local emotions between 1848 and 1855. This was also a time when the political struggle between the white native-born Kingston people and recent immigrants had brought a rally to Wilbur in 1848 to signal the beginning of a tough political tussle which reached a temporary triumph in Kingston and Rondout. The factions known (among other names) as the Know-Nothings then advocated the exclusion of foreign-born people, and especially Catholics, from the holding of all public offices and a refusal to permit Catholics to have their own parochial schools.

In the preceding local elections the anti-Catholics and anti-immigrants had won the town of Kingston, including the villages of Kingston and Rondout. They had then filled town of Kingston appointed offices with their own people but had made no anti-Catholic or anti-immigrant changes in town or village government. Now, with a new town election of 1855 coming up it became obvious that there were influential people in Rondout among the Soft-Shell Democrats whose party would share before long in helping form the new Republican party which would elect Abraham Lincoln.

On Thanksgiving day 1854 the Reverend Benjamin T. Philips of the Rondout Presbyterian Church delivered a remarkable Thanksgiving Day discourse called "The Benefits of Foreign Immigration" which was published by request. It filled a 23-page pamphlet put into print by J. P. Hageman, editor and publisher of the Rondout *Courier*. The minister's text was the familiar Biblical one taken from Leviticus XIX 33-34 and interpreted here so as to have a striking bearing upon the coming election of 1855 in Rondout, "and if a stranger sojourns with thee in your land ye shall not vex him. But the stranger that dwelleth with you shall be unto you as one born among you and thou shalt love him as thyself. . . ."

The pastor states that Rondouters as well as all Americans should be thankful on this Thanksgiving Day, November 30 for the continued prosperity of their nation as a whole. And that they should be thankful to those who had been the agents of that prosperity. In response to expanding America's need for stalwart young men to wield picks and shovels to create such great works as canals, railroads and turnpikes, the sojourners had come out of poverty at home in Ireland. They had been sent to America to rid their parishes of them and to clear their local almshouse. Mr. Philips cites recent census figures and a study in the respected *Edinburgh Review* to back up his arguments.

The sojourner-workers, said the pastor, deserve credit together with Maurice Wurts and the other D&H managers for turning Rondout into the prosperous bustling village it had become. They had done this by causing the anthracite of the distant Pennsylvania mountains to be shipped to Rondout and then to the many great steamboats of the Hudson for use as their fuel instead of wood, and to float anthracite in immense quantities to wherever it was needed to heat buildings or power industry.

Philips statement of indebtedness to the digging and shoveling workers might have recalled to a few listeners and readers the expression in 1650 of shame at the way in which the Dutch colonizers had treated their Native predecessors. This had been expressed poignantly in the "Remonstrance" of the nine men of New Amsterdam.

There were likely to have been many skeptics among the readers of Philips's discourse. It was known that the Rondout Presbyterian Church occupied a position of authority in Rondout similar if lesser to that held in Kingston by the Dutch Church. Maurice Wurts had contributed the land on which the Presbyterian Church was built and with other board members of the D&H had backed the Presbyterian Church and other Protestant Rondout churches with land and money. They had set up a Sunday School "on the rocks" where Wurts Avenue begins at the present Rondout Creek bridge. When a Catholic church was organized a site was not given but was sold to the Catholics by board member Abraham Hasbrouck. In many ways although most of the Irish and many of the German sojourners were Catholics the company which dominated Rondout continued to treat the place as a company town in which pressuring Catholic workers into Protestantism was to be expected.

For Catholic Nathaniel Booth as for many others also, 1854 seemed to have been a year of decision. By then Booth had sold his store, bought the bluestone quarry of suburban Jockey Hill, remarried and taken a step before ending his diary forever that seemed to indicate a decision to become an active member rather than a mere sceptical observer of Rondout life. On the 17th of March, 1854 he made one of his final entries in his diary:

> "Got naturalized—Americanized—civilized—by law my having been since 1828 not being sufficient without it—I have therefore foresworn all allegience to her majesty Victoria in particular and turned Yankee!"

In his "The Benefits of Foreign Immigration" Philips treated the question of parochial schools which was a very hot issue at the time, because there was an election coming on which the question of public funding for parochial schools would be voted on, by simply saying that public schools had been provided for both Protestant and Catholic students, and then he went on to state, "I am not now an advocate or even an apologist for the Roman Catholic church. I heartily pray for its speedy downfall." And Mr. Phillips adds that "let each man be a Jew, a Christian, Mohammedan, or Buddhist, Papist, Protestant, 'a man's a man for all that.' And upon this truth our government rests. In America every man who obeys the law deserves equal protection." Enough voters agreed with this sentiment to sway the election against the anti-immigrant Know-Nothings and their radical supporters.

The Saugerties bard Henry Backus at the same time wrote a ballad published as a broadside in which he favored treating immigrants more kindly.

From the joining of the thirteen North American colonies of 1776 to form a nation to 1861 the union of the United States had withstood many threats. Its flag formed an excellent symbol of that unity—thirteen stripes stood for the original members and the number of stars increased by one as each new state was added. It was when a new territory became a state that the differing of the states in language, ethnicity and the sources of their incomes caused most tests of the national unity. These had usually been settled by compromises. In 1858 Senator W. H. Seward of New York had declared however that the question of continued slavery was at the root of "an irrepressible conflict" between North and South. And many Americans in awareness of the gap between the slave and cotton-based economy of the South and the low wage-based manufacturing economy of the north were in hearty agreement. The State of New York owed its past prosperity in part to its farmers' use of slavery, and in the 1850s a strong sympathy with the South lingered on. This was made evident by many episodes in Kingston cultural life.

When the American flag was fired upon on April 12, 1861 at Fort Sumter in the harbor of Charleston, South Carolina, and when the new electric telegraph at once brought the news to Kingston, the response was a nearly universal sense of an almost electric shock. A "spontaneous" gathering assembled at the Kingston courthouse and was fervently addressed by prominent and persuasive Kingston leaders. In Rondout the American flag was raised above Mr. Philips's church. A group climbed to the church's cupola and sang patriotic songs as they unfurled the American flag.

While many saw armed conflict lying ahead, Kingstonians were ill prepared for it, with many pro-Southern sympathizers known to live among them. Yet Kingston Copperheads who would later raise their voices in protest against the Civil War remained temporarily silent as the first shot of the Civil War startled the nation.

The election of 1855 had seen the beginning of a few years when the once sharp edge of the anti-Catholic and anti-immigrant passion was dulled in Kingston and Rondout as the apparently growing gap between North and South absorbed national political attention. In 1861 that gap widened beyond all hope of bridging peacefully.

Yet Kingston church goers continued to carry on their "trading and trafficking" while on Sundays they nodded approvingly at the high standards of morality being advocated by their respected dominies. And for a while life went on much as usual.

13.
Canoes to Sloops to Steamboats

Among the advantages to human habitation of the place on which the City of Kingston was to rise were its resources of flowing water. These had evolved as the meltwater of the most recent Ice Age fell to the point at which it could provide successive waves of wandering Native American hunters and food gatherers with an attractive living space. These pioneer people and the more settled Natives who followed them on the ever-changing landscape, had developed a kind of water-borne vehicle which we know as the canoe. The canoe used by Native Americans on the Hudson and parts of suitable stretches of its tributary creeks was nothing like as sophisticated in design as the kayaks of the ethnically-related Aleutian Islanders, yet it was well adapted to the needs of the Natives of what is now Kingston in supplying themselves with a major part of their diet of fish and shellfish, and to speed them in getting about in peace and in intertribal war and raiding.

The first Native Americans to be recorded by whites as seen by them using the Hudson River for transportation used canoes "made of one piece of wood" and shaped with fire and with stone knives. Eighteenth century Natives are sometimes said to have made and used canoes of elm bark, easily stripped from tree trunks during springtime flows of sap.[516] The traders from Europe who first entered Rondout harbor probably rode in small ships' boats from their anchored sea-going ships rather than trusting sailing into the then inviting but uncharted harbor. Dutch colonizers called to their minds the sloops and shallops developed for use in the shallow inland and coastal waters of their homeland and found these sloops or shallops to be admirably capable after some modification for carrying freight and passengers on the waters of the Hudson. Shallow of draft, broad of beam, in proportion to length, with

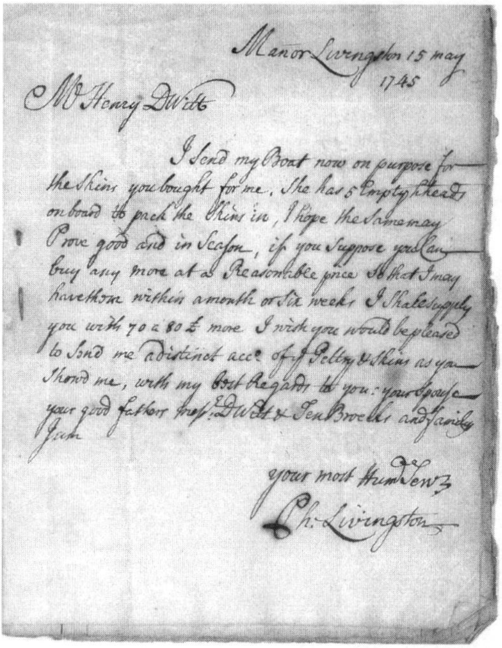

Manor Livingston 15 may 1745

Mr Henry DWitt

I Send my Boat now on purpose for the Skins you bought for me. She has 5 Emptyhheads on board to pack the Skins in, I hope the Same may Prove good and in Season, if you Suppose you Can buy any more at a Reasonable price So that I may have them within a month or Six weeks I Shall supply you with 70 a 80 £ more I wish you would be pleased to Send me a distinct acc. of ye Peltry & Skins as you Shoud me, with my best Regards to you: your Spouse your good father Mess. DWitt & TenBroecks and family I am

your most Humble Servt

Ph: Livingston

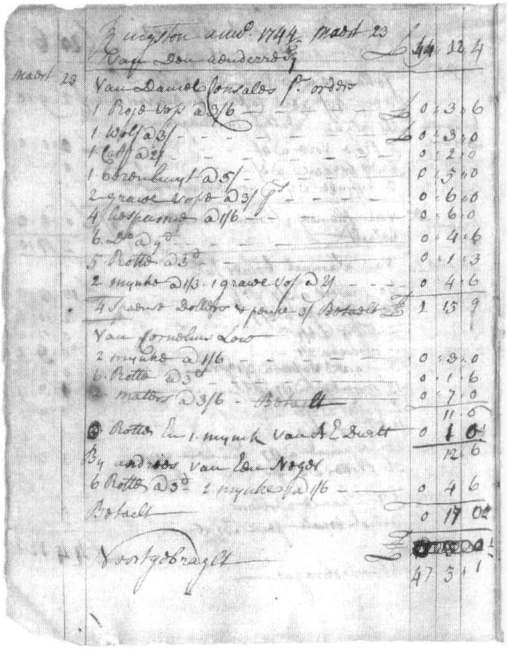

Records of account of trading in furs between Philip Livingston, of Livingston Manor, and Henry DeWitt of Kingston, 1745. Courtesy of Morris Rosenblum collection.

a topmast of up to ninety to one hundred feet and a main boom of seventy-five to eighty-five feet, a Hudson River sloop could carry three to five thousand feet of sail.

The sloops could sail closer to the wind than any other vessels of any rig or model, so wrote H.H. Pitts, the nineteenth century Twaalfskill sloop owner and postmaster. So popular were the sloops that it has been said that close to a hundred at a time might often have been seen spreading their sails on the Hudson on summer afternoons. Ulster County farmers often sent their farm products, including livestock (which included draught horses bred along the Esopus Creek), to market in the City of New York on sloops. They often trusted sloop captains to drive a good bargain for their products with smart city buyers. Kingston people looked forward with pleasure to the trips of two days or more to the big city and when tide or adverse wind forced anchoring to pleasant rambles ashore, picking flowers or gathering nuts or berries to while the time away. Manors and riverside estates often had each its own sloop to do business and help them enjoy social life. In 1745 Philip

Livingston, of "the manor of Livingston" wrote to trader Henry de Witt of Kingston and sent the letter aboard his own sloop with payment for a shipment of pelts to be sent back as agreed upon. Livingston wrote that he was sending on sloopboard materials for packing the pelts, each of which was identified by its Dutch name, in order to make the Ulster County "low Dutch" understand exactly what he meant (as distinct from the "high Dutch" [or German] working people of the east bank).

A large and fascinating body of sloop lore arose to be repeated by Kingston and Rondout people—of lucky and unlucky sloops, of the bewitched sloop *Martin Wynkoop* (successfully treated by witch doctor Jacob Brink of Ulster County), of sloops that could find their way home even in the dark without a human hand on the tiller to guide them.

When steamboats began to use the Hudson after the *Clermont*'s (better known in New York City as the *North River Steamboat*) successful beginning in 1807 it was feared that they would prove cheaper for shipping freight and so displace the sloops which had come to add so much color to the charm of the River in the eyes of both Americans and European tourists—even of those who could find little else to praise in the United States. Yet this did not happen. Sloops had a price advantage. Instead of using free wind to keep them moving, the steamboats although speedier had to burn many cords of purchased wood or tons of Pennsylvania anthracite and used larger crews and hence sloops could charge less to shippers. After many decades the sloops finally yielded to the more economical riverside railroads and to the long, long lines of barges, many moving merchandise down from the Erie Canal to be hauled to New York City by steam-driven tugboats or towboats.

However, the appearance of the first railroads in the Hudson Valley lay a quar-

City of Kingston steamboat constructed in 1884. Courtesy of Gerald Mastropaolo Collection.

ter of a century in the future. Then the railroad offered its challenge to the prosperous river port of Rondout. Until then steamboats, schooners and sloops would work together to help Rondout grow into a thriving community third in importance as a river port to Albany and New York City.

Steamboats, serving both as the palatial excursion boats which were the largest and most luxurious in the world, or carrying cargoes of diverse products and which made the Rondout harbor their home port sometimes demonstrated the excellence of their construction by spending their old age in distant parts of the world. One of them, the *City of Kingston*, made its way around the difficulties of both stormy Cape Hatteras and even stormier Cape Horn to the Pacific Ocean and up along the coast of South and North America to Seattle—this before the days of the Panama Canal which was to ease the once so arduous voyage around the often hazardous coasts of the two Americas.

14.
The Supreme Court Frees the Steamboat

THE STEAMBOAT BEST KNOWN TO MOST VALLEY PEOPLE AS THE *CLERMONT* which had made its first appearance before astonished Kingston and Rondout eyes in 1807 had been greatly improved by recent inventions. By then, it was an example of the state-of-the-arts version of the application of steam propulsion which had been the subject of endless experiments in England and Europe, and especially on the Seine in France. This ever since a primitive version had been given a trial in 1775.

There had already been many difficult problems solved in adapting a steam engine

Replica of the *Clermont,* or *North River Steamboat* built in 1884, courtesy of Gerald Mastropaolo Collection

for use on a craft designed to move and float in the water. The weight of the engine and its placing in order to guarantee a boat's stability had been solved, for example, by a series of experimenters who had brought the steamboat into the kind of practical reality capable of earning profits and assuring passengers there was no serious danger of explosions.

Robert Fulton's *Clermont*, also called *North River Steamboat*, was the earliest example of a steamboat that could be trusted to work well. It had been helped along by the financing, encouragement and scientific knowledge of Chancellor Robert R. Livingston, Kingston's helpful neighbor on his 13,000-acre estate of Clermont on what had come to be called the "manorial" or "gentleman's side of the Hudson." A monopoly on the use of their steamboat on American rivers and lakes had been granted to the two in 1807. It was not until 1824 that the Supreme Court of the United States decided as urged by the eloquence of lawyer and Senator Daniel Webster, no longer to tolerate the restrictive monopoly. The effect of the decision was the almost immediate proliferation of steamboats on American waters and the rise of rigorous competition. And the cutting of rates of steamboats boomed trade by water at Rondout as well as elsewhere. In spite of an artificial monopoly cooked up by hopeful groups of steamboat owners and only partially successful, an ever more fierce competition went on raging on the Hudson and steamboat skippers often threw caution aside. Exploding boilers, as steamboats recklessly raced, were pushed beyond safe limits, and speed related disasters brought deaths on the Hudson from scalding, burning and drowning. As this happened rates dropped and schedules improved. From all this Rondout steamers stood a little bit aside, thanks to the development of an innovative steam engineless kind of vessel newly put into service on the River—this was the "market barge" as towed by a steamboat.

Kingston and Rondout newspapers proclaimed that Rondout steamboats with barges attached at a safe distance were the safest on the Hudson. And this was recognized as a fact that led to a liberal Rondout use of market barges, although they were a bit slower than steamboats.

Because of its linkage with the D&H Canal with its already good ties to the farm and forest freight resources of Kingston, and to the huge Hardenbergh Patent

The Winne Market Barge, collection of Alf Evers

then being partially and recklessly cleared of its forests by hard-working tenant-farmers, there were shipments not only of timber, shingles, barrel parts, bear meat and bear grease (used as a hair dressing) but also of industrial quality potash (a component of wood ashes) which resulted when forested land was cleared and the debris burned and the potash separated.

Rondout and Kingston shipowners and captains enjoyed a period of profitable years. With freight-users and passengers multiplying they chose using market barges to further increase the shipment of both—and so increase volume of business in booming Rondout.

Let competing lines of steamboats risk the lives of their passengers and crews by racing rivals to make cutting rates possible—Rondout people like Mr. Winne would use a market barge strategy to stress safety.

The loaded barges were lashed often to the sides of Rondout steamboats or towed behind. This slowed them just enough to take the mother vessel out of competition as a racer, (as any other pregnant mother would be). If the mother steamboat got into trouble it would be a simple matter for passengers to scurry to the untied barges where moderately comfortable quarters awaited them, beside the cattle, hogs, horses, farm and forest products and Shawangunk grit millstones which were then their fellow passengers. And to reassure even more cautious passengers barges were designed to be towed behind a steamboat which had only passengers aboard. A popular "safety barge" out of Twaalfskill on the Rondout was called *The Lady Clinton.* And on the other hand, the truly adventurous passengers who scorned losing a few minutes of their passage time by docking on the Rondout harbor landings, the faster Albany-New York City boats made available what steamboat historian Donald Ringwald knew as a "harrowing contemporary maneuver" called the "fly-by." To perform this risky feat (which was regulated by an act of Legislature intended to minimize its risk) the speed of an approaching steamboat on nearing the Landing at Kingston Point was checked. As it continued moving on, but at a slower rate, a small ship's boat was lowered at the steamer's landward side. Into this boat passengers who hoped to land at Kingston Point were helped. One end of the painter was held by a skilled member of the steamboat's crew who remained on the steamboat's deck. By skillfully maneuvering the painter he was able to guide the ship's boat as it moved toward the landing with the passengers anxiously gripping the gunwhals. Then the passengers and luggage (if all went well) would be unloaded. And the boat with any waiting new passengers hastily hauled aboard would be guided to the still-moving steamboat to be dumped with little ceremony on deck.

Then in April 1829 a memorable event took place when the sidewheeler *Congress* became the first steamboat to operate on a regular schedule from Wilbur (or Twaalfskill) to the foot of Liberty Street which was then in the heart of New York

City. The *Congress* was described by an observer as looking rather like a catfish because of its narrowness leading up to its broader forward section like the big head of a catfish.

The *Congress* docked where it did for a very practical reason. This was at Theron Skeel's Twaalfskill or Wilbur wharf because that was at the time at the end of the shortest, best maintained and least steep road leading from the creek to Kingston, and so gave Skeel's place an advantage over the old traditional Kingston Landing but close to which the D&H canal company had set its fine Italianate office building and other facilities.

The *Congress* was followed as a Twaalfskill boat by many others, among them the famous *Norwich* which came to be known because of her or his unusual ability at breaking through ice as the "Ice King." As the old Kingston Landing area was built up, the elegant hotel called the Mansion House, with a view-catching and ornamental cupola and then fashionable cast-iron balconies, was improved and enlarged until it became known as belonging to the top class of Hudson Valley hotels. And many other ships soon took to docking here rather than at Twaalfskill, now Wilbur. In 1852 the opening of a Rhinecliffe station for the new railroad (eventually to reach Albany) from New York with a ferry connecting the station to the old Kingston Landing at the foot of Division Street (now Broadway) revived the old Landing as the more convenient for most Kingston people.

In 1845 Twaalfskill had given to the Hudson River one of the most extraordinary and flamboyant river steamboats in all the River's history.

The 1840s were a decade when the modern Christmas with its emphasis on jollity, lavish gift giving, and commercialism, with Santa Claus presiding over it all in the minds of children was on its way to acceptance into American life. Charles Dickens's *A Christmas Carol* of 1843 was delighting readers on both sides of the Atlantic. The new steamboat was appropriately named *The Santa Claus.* The Hudson River valley even before the launching of the *Santa Claus* in 1845 had already benefitted much as a romantic region. American and British writers had already seen to that. And the Reverend Clement Clark Moore had claimed authorship of "A Visit from St. Nicholas," popular as "The Night before Christmas," first published anonymously in a Hudson Valley newspaper in 1823, and in 1844 in Moore's *Collected Poems,* had given Christmas a merrier feeling than it had enjoyed earlier, even after Washington Irving in his *Sketchbook* had extravagantly praised the English Christmas. (The true author of "A Visit from St. Nicholas" was later found to be Henry Livingston of Poughkeepsie.) About 1840 the Christmas tree and Santa Claus had arrived from Germany and the first Christmas cards had been sent. In Kingston the old Dutch sort of Christmas was waning under English pressure—this was the kind of Christmas which Captain

Brodhead had tried to bring in by arresting a Kingstonian for celebrating the holiday in the Dutch fashion. In the decade of the 1840s Hudson River steamboats were entering a stage in which the boats were being given names which suggested happy times aboard rather than merely efficient transportation and the quick movement of freight.

In response to all this, Ezra Fitch of Kingston had commissioned the steamboat *Santa Claus* and was also responsible for commissioning its remarkable decoration. Fitch had expected to call the boat the *St. Nicholas.* But, another boat builder with a similar ambition, it was said, chose the same name. Fitch thereupon named his boat the *Santa Claus*, derived from the Hudson Valley Dutch "Sinter Klaus," which had been widely used by the children of the early colonists of the Valley. Fitch's new steamboat celebrated the joys of the secular Christmas more bounteously, especially during the ice-free months of the year when no one else had given thought to celebrating the holiday at all. For during the Christmas season most Hudson River steamers were laid up by river icing. And so Fitch gave the boat a year round sense of the Christmas spirit. The painter whom Fitch is believed to have employed to decorate the boat was said to have been none other than the nephew of Kingston's greatest artist of the brush. The nephew was John Vanderlyn, Jr., then at the height of a modest Kingston career as a painter of portraits of people, apples and of scenery for an amateur theatrical offering in his home town. It is likely that his commission from Fitch, as described by Donald Ringwald, was the largest Vanderlyn Jr. had ever attempted.

And no one could deny the suitability of the name of the 185 foot, 5 inch long paddle wheel steamboat. One of the covers of its paddle wheels bore a realistic painting of Santa Claus, with a pack on his back filled with gifts and a face filled with gaiety. He was caught in the act of descending the chimney of a tile-roofed Dutch house while his sleigh and reindeer were shown waiting for his return. On the other paddle wheel cover was shown the interior of a Dutch house with bounteous Santa about to exit via the fireplace after stuffing the hanging stockings with gifts. A similar scene decorated a large wall of the ship's grand saloon, and there was more. The figurehead of the craft was a carved Santa Claus. But atop the pilot house was a carved cupid with wings outstretched and bow and arrow in readiness.

The steamboat itself had been built to Ezra Fitch's order at the New York City shipyard of Thomas Collyer. Whether the decoration was applied in New York City by an unnamed artist or in Rondout by Vanderlyn Jr. is not known. It is not certain either whether the figurehead of Santa or the cupid on the pilot house roof were his work, but they may have been Vanderlyn's because he is believed to have had enough skill at handling carving tools to have made some still existing ornamental butter molds of a local traditional sort. Younger Vanderlyn, like his famous uncle, was known in Kingston, from references to him in the elder Vander Lyn's letters, for his notable addiction to drinking.

The *Santa* at its initial docking at Wilbur in July 1845 was loaded with free passengers and was greeted by the music of the Kingston Temperance Brass Band. Several days later to send it off in style it carried invited guests on a party-like celebratory cruise. The *Santa* made its maiden voyages at a favorable time in one way. Hudson River steamboats were indeed sharing abundantly in the veil of romance which by then had come to hover over the River. And the new steamboat, while it served well as a day boat and then as a night boat on the Wilbur-New York City run, was not the crashing kind of success Ezra Fitch evidently expected. He had encouraged the ship's decorator to lavish Christmas artwork upon it of a sort which before long would achieve great seasonal popularity as a decided source of marketplace profits as applied to a great variety of objects being sold in December.

The *Santa* may have owed its failure to find a public to its celebration of Christmas at the wrong time of year, as Ringwald suggested, or for a more arcane reason. But once its novelty wore off it was apparently simply taken for granted.

Sooner than might have been expected the fine steamer entered the class of riverboats which had outlived their youthful glamor—a fate which was so poignantly to be expressed in *The Sloops of the Hudson*, by William Verplanck and Moses W. Collyer, whose brother Thomas had been the Santa's builder. With her name changed to the *A.V. Valentine* and "stripped of cabins, saloons and upper decks, a mere skeleton of a boat, wearily drawing a huge assemblage of barges, scows and down east schooners and Erie canal boats on the river . . . , a melancholy sight indeed." The Santa had been converted into a towboat—one of the early trophies of canny Thomas Cornell in his successful drive to become the virtual monopolist of the towing industry of the Hudson above New York harbor. Yet in one notable way the pioneering effort of the *Santa* of putting symbols of the new kind of Christmas on the Hudson was followed by other river steamboats until well within the twentieth century. For it was on these boats as winter approached that the first Christmas trees to be sold on New York City streets were shipped down river from the ports of Rondout and Catskill.

The trees had begun to be harvested by Mark Carr in the early 1850s on the "cold lands" of the higher mountain hinterlands of Rondout and Catskill. They were largely young and fragrant wild balsam firs. These trees when shipped aboard the river steamboats gave off their pleasant, pungent Christmasy fragrance to the delight of the passengers aboard the chilly vessels.

The *Santa* was also among the steamboats which helped establish Hudson River steamboats as places where political groups, church and other organizations took pleasure in using for events ranging from a few hours to an entire day. Ethnic and

The A.B. Valentine, formerly the Santa Claus, courtesy of the collection of Gerard M. Mastropaolo

religious brawls occasionally marred these festive occasions in an atmosphere that sometimes smelled of peace on earth Christmas.

The *Rip Van Winkle*, built about the same time as the *Santa Claus* and being decorated with paintings inside and out of Washington Irving's old Rip hero of the twenty years sleep among the Catskills was a sort of sister (or brother) ship of the *Santa Claus.* Its artwork was done by James Ackerman and Edward A. Miller, partners in a NewYork City firm which produced signs and banners as well as hand-colored lithographs of flowers used as book illustration. The *Rip* was notable for its excellent sleeping accomodations and so appropriately named for the hero of a world record sleep. The *Rip* enjoyed a long life as a night passenger boat, unlike the *Santa.*

The *Rip Van Winkle* evoked of course the romantic veil drawn over the mountains and the River by Irving. As Donald Ringwald suggested the *Rip* could exert its charm every day of the sailing year while *Santa* could do similar tricks only on one day of the year, Christmas day, and that a day when the vessel was likely to be laid up for the winter. Yet the *Rip* was long a popular night steamer on the New York-Wilbur run.

Steamboats continued to be built as pleasure craft even as the Civil War convulsed the nation and shipyards along the Rondout Harbor were kept busy turning out barges and small craft for war use. Some former passenger and excursion Hudson River steamboats were sold to the Union government to carry troops or war supplies.

And as pleasure cruises on the Hudson lost popularity, the big boats made salt water voyages over many parts of the world's oceans. Steamboats which once made the Rondout Harbor their home port sometimes demonstrated the excellence of their construction by spending their old age at work in distant parts of the world in search of employment. The steamboat, *City of Kingston*, rounded turbulent Cape Hatteras and stormy Cape Horn and began a good career on Puget Sound. And other oldtime Kingston steamboats did good service as they made their way on tropical rivers far from their Hudson homes while the former *Santa Claus*, operating as a towboat under a number of names, hauled barges of coal and other mundane merchandise such as ice on the Hudson with the colorful laundry of the captain's family flapping in the wind as it dried. Or in the case of ice-carrying barges, there were little miniature brightly painted windmillls which gently whirled above bringing up the melt-water when the ice that formed the larger cargo melted in the hot weather of mid-summer.

Above: Post card of ice barges in tow on the Hudson, note windmill to draw out water, courtesy of G. Mastropaolo
Left: Ice house at Wilbur, stereograph in Alf Evers collection
Below: Ice harvesting on the Long Canal, from *Picturesque Ulster*

15.
A Competition in Church Building
1850s

THE GROWTH OF KINGSTON POPULATION FOLLOWING THE DIGGING AND successful functioning of the D. & H. Canal, and extractive industries as well, helped cause some devoted members of the Old Dutch church in Kingston to urge the need of a chapel in growing Rondout to be established by their church—others held that this would weaken the parent church. The proposal was voted down. In Rondout, a Presbyterian church had already appeared as early as 1835 sponsored in part by the Canal's Wurts brothers who belonged to that denomination. It was explained that some of the Irish workers in Rondout were from the North of Ireland and so already Presbyterians. Rondout Catholics were served at first by occasional visiting priests. In November 1839 the building of a Catholic church of their own was proposed. A collection had been taken for that purpose from among the poorly paid Catholic workmen in September and it amounted to $32.02 Because the church would serve a scattered congregation, some members living in Rosendale on the canal and others at the new suburban bluestone quarries, it was planned to place Catholic St. Mary's on the commanding site high above Rondout where it still stands in a larger and much more elaborate form than originally conceived. Plans for new churches in Kingston and booming Rondout continued to be agitated, Baptist, Methodist, Episcopalian and others.

All this rush to build new churches was taking place against a background of tearing down the simple earlier church buildings of the United States and substituting newer ones which reflected not only ethnic backgrounds of new immigrants, but also the changing aesthetic notions of their congregations in behavior, beliefs and their changing architectural tastes. The editor of the Rondout *Courier* put it well in 1853 when he wrote that the older churches were going, "not because they were inadequate to the needs (and beliefs) of their congregations, but purely and plainly speaking, because they were out of fashion." Editor Hageman believed that present congregations had entered into a contest of "display and outlay" in a "spirit of sheer rivalry." He suggested that trouble lay ahead for congregations which failed to accept sober, "ideas of church building" and "common sense views of debts." Hageman as it turned out was correct—troubles did indeed lie ahead in which human frailties combined with harsh blasts of the breath of nature joined together.

Newcomer from England and Catholic Nathaniel Booth viewed the church building rivalries with some amusement and bewilderment and besides he enjoyed making fun of the Kingston establishment so long safely centered around their Dutch church once within the old stockade bounds. "The honest Dutch burghers of Esopus," he wrote, could not permit the second Dutch church then being planned to surpass their own old one. The old Dutch church, wrote Booth, had been judged too large for all, "now it was judged too small for half."

By this time many of the members of the old Dutch church were convinced they had outgrown the brick structure they had built in 1833 to replace the stone one (across Main Street) restored after the fire of the Revolution and judgd too small for the growing congregation as the Canal and extractive industry boom struck. Statistics of membership and attendance were flourished and interpreted in various ways. In 1849 after much hesitation twenty-two members were permitted to leave the old Dutch church and organize a new one. After this events followed thick and fast as believers in other denominations newer to Kingston looked on in wonder. The new second Dutch church began to rise close to the old one but on Fair Street. It was first also planned to be of brick with a tin roof. But as the old church members in the brick building of 1833 decided to build a new larger and grander church of stone on their old graveyard site and retained talented and well known church architect Minard Lafevre of New York to design it, the plans for the church on Fair Street were changed to call for local cut limestone and a slate roof with cornices of stone instead of wood—this meant a doubling of the cost.

The brick church built in 1833 was offered for sale as building of the Fair Street one began. It was being said that the old brick one might be used as a town hall, a concert hall, a place for lectures and entertainment by singers, dancers and actors. In mock horror Booth wrote that the brick church was "being taken and put to the service of the Devil." Booth reported with interest that "a private movement has been made to quietly purchase the building for the use of the Catholics . . ." The good people of Esopus-descendants of the Huguenots would sooner see it in ashes or with a Jim Crow jump within its walls. (The black song and dance act known as Jim Crow had recently become popular in minstrel shows.)

A few months after the death of architect Lafevre (who had been too ill to give

Old Dutch Church minus steeple, from *Olde Ulster*

much personal attention to the construction of the stone Dutch church he had designed to replace the brick church opposite the graveyard), the steeple of this Reformed Church crashed to the ground on Christmas Eve, 1853 in a gale. This did so much damage in its fall to the body of the building that services could not be held there for many months. On St. Patrick's Day, 1854 the steeple of the new church on Fair Street followed the example of the first Dutch church and toppled to earth in the churchyard as a horrified crowd watched it swaying in a storm. And as if to suggest that Providence was not playing favorites in the village's Protestant-Catholic division the steeple of St. Mary's above Rondout tumbled down in the same storm.

As the Second Reformed church began existence its pastor was the Rev. Henry W. Smuller who resigned in 1853 after having given rise to a scandal which kept gossips' tongues busy. The Rev. Mr. Smuller acquired a band of supporters who believed that he was "being persecuted" as Nathanial Booth observed. The charge which brought Smuller before an eccleciastical court summoned by the consistory was that he had been sexually involved with a member of his flock although the evidence submitted did not go beyond a kiss of more than pastorly quality. The decision was ambiguous, that while Smuller was not guilty as charged his conduct was unsuited to a minister. Under pressure Smuller resigned and was immediately followed out of the Fair Street church by twenty-seven devoted members who proceeded to found Kingston's First Presbyterian church (similar in its services, but not in its organization, to the Dutch Church) with one time Presbyterian Smuller as pastor.

The church on Fair Street was deeply in debt and the loss of so many members worsened the situation. General Joseph S. Smith who was said to have personally supplied one-third of the capital, put his entreprenurial skills to work to solve the church's financial troubles by a variety of stratagems. In spite of Smith's efforts the church seemed to be on the verge of disaster when it was rescued by a substantial loan from the prosperous Collegiate Dutch Church of New York City and went on to play an important part in Kingston life.

Kingston and Rondout too came to be admired for their many unusually attractive church buildings. Observors who climbed from the old Indian Kaatsban and up the Weinberg in later years to take in the fine view expressed admiration of the many church spires ornamenting the land above and below, even in the poorest parts of industrialized Rondout, but especially on Wurts Street where Congressman Thomas Cornell also lived in splendour.

In 1870, an addition to the City's already large collection of churches was made with the opening of the Union Chapel or Children's Church on Abruyn Street in East Rondout which is now listed on the National Register of Historic Places. This building was built as a pioneer demonstration of the use of concrete reinforced with steel rods and plates and to accomodate the Protestant children of Rondout. It was financed by the owners of the Newark Limestone and Cement Company as a community gift, in the Victorian Gothic Revival style of the period, still being used in churches. Despite some deterioration to its concrete steeple, now well mended, the building still stands as an important architectural monument and is used to this day as a Sunday School.

And by the time the century came to its end Kingston had even more churches, one and then two for Afro-Americans and two synagogues, plus by the 1890s a church for Christian Scientists—and a Bethany Chapel as a benefaction of the Forsyth sisters located in once but now no longer rowdy Higginsville, which is today no longer regarded as a separate community. In addition there had appeared two German churches, one for Protestants and one for Catholics. And at one time a Polish church appeared to reflect a new addition to the City's increasingly mixed population, plus a few neighborhood Dutch Reformed churches which reflected an increase in the Dutch-descended population.

16.
Business Ethics and a Vanishing Judge

Until the period of Canal and extractive industry influence the Dutch Reformed minister had been an "awe-inspiring personage" who moved among the people in a "stately and imposing way" and wore "a long black gown, high three-cornered hat and a long black wide-sleeved gown." When the minister entered his church the congregation rose to show their respect. For he was a "virtual autocrat," who largely shaped by his personal force the opinions and life of the community," so wrote Dutch Reformed minister Dr. J.G. Van Slyke as he looked back from the end of the nineteenth century. All this was true enough yet ministerial influence had to contend with another powerful force, recognized by Nathaniel Booth.

At times, Nathaniel Booth had pondered the ethical state of the business community of which he was a part and found it not always to conform to the strict code of morality and honesty proclaimed from the pulpit. He had learned well enough that Kingston even before its stockade days had been a trading place where goods were bought and sold and handled for the sake of profit and where the kind of honesty advocated by the ministers did not always lead to wealth. Nathaniel Booth was disturbed by this and set down his thoughts on the subject in April, 1851. "It was once said of me," Booth began, "that I was too scrupulous, too honest to make a fortune by trade—I laughed at the time but now I realize the truth to a certain extent of the remark. The difficulty of making a profit by fair means amounting almost to impossibility—the degree to which this petty swindling is carried out is frightful, by the community it is winked at and tolerated." Booth went on to give examples. Along the Rondout waterfront where the hundreds of hard-working horses and mules required many thousands of bushels of oats each year to feed them, methods of cheating on the measurement of oats had been worked out. Sprinkling with water and salt swelled the oats' bulk as did the ways in which the oats were put into a measure. When oats were put in a measure in a straightforward way more grains were required to fill the measure than if a man tossed the oats in the air above the measure. Then the air rushing out of the measure separated the oats and fewer oats could fill the container. "Here," Booth wrote, "knavery is reduced to a science or rather science used for perfect knavery." As merchandise passed through the hands of producers, middlemen and retailers, adulteration and substitution were rife and, "the poor consumer ignorantly received beans and peas for coffee, sloe (blackthorn) leaves for tea, chalk and marble dust for sugar, etc. Such is the business world at present."

Booth's problems in running a small store probably led him into exaggerating the sins of his competitors. Yet the dishonest practices he mentioned existed, and on a different scale penetrated even the exalted level on which Judge James C. Forsyth lived. In 1850 Booth was beginning to make his entrance into Kingston's uppermost level of society. He had a chance to inspect that level at first hand when he was invited to a party at the Judge's grand new house on Pearl Street in Kingston. The house had been designed by Richard Upjohn, a leading New York City architect. Booth said it "was the handsomest house in Kingston which threw all others in the shade displaying elaborately carved marble—the rich carpets—mirrors—paintings and furniture (which) would rather astonish the honest Dutch who built old Sopus." (The house survives as a Masonic temple.) At the party there was music, champagne and oysters.

"Judge Forsyth," Booth wrote later on, "was a very great man—very difficult of approach—very pompous—very dignified, etc." Well this fine gentleman a few days since suddenly disappeared, and the news came that he had been seen on board the steamship *Africa* on his way to Europe. "People wondered but the excitement rose when it was found that over 200,000 dollars worth of stocks in the various railroads lately consolidated and entrusted to him had been sold out and appropriated, besides \$100,000 in other items as loans, discounts, overdrafts on banks, etc. The heaviest losses fall upon his own and his wife's relations, his father-in-law particularly."

It was during the final four months of 1853 that information came to light and was blazoned abroad in Hudson Valley newspapers which confirmed what Booth had written about Judge Forsyth in almost all its details. It then became evident that the once highly respected judge had indeed become an embezzler.

Forsyth had come to Kingston in 1838 as a promising young Sullivan County lawyer of respectable Newburgh birth. A year later in the economically improving atmosphere he married Kingston's Mary Bruyn who was said to "have singularly resembled her father, banker Severyn Bruyn (of Norwegian ancestry) in appearance, character and temperament." The bride's mother was a daughter of Jonathan Hasbrouck who like Bruyn was one of the richest, most powerful and socially eminent of all the old stockade families. Young Forsyth's people in his native Newburgh were "respectable" but not the equals in wealth and social station of the Hasbroucks and the Bruyns.

For years especially during the busy 1840s (as the echo of the 1836-1837 crash faded) Forsyth did well in Kingston. He was elected county Judge, he ran for New York State Secretary of State as a Whig (the conservative party) and did well but missed election. He was regarded as a model of rectitude worthy of his tie by marriage to the Bruyns and Hasbroucks. He paid his debts on time and was scrupulously correct in money dealings and in attendance at church. But by the late 1840s another James Christie Forsyth was taking shape. This Forsyth was being drawn into a heady trend of the unsteady and speculative times.

After the nation had slowly recovered from the traumatic economic shock of 1836-38 it had been seized by a speculative fever soon urged on by the discovery of gold in California, the flowing into the United States of European and British capital and a boom in often shaky railroad projects. Wall Street was then arriving at its eminent position in money matters and speculation. While Kingston people were regarding the judge with complacency, Forsyth was active in Wall Street speculating with money he borrowed from his own and his wife's families. He was forging names of endorsers and turning to his own account railroad obligations entrusted to him by his brother-in-law, A. Bruyn Hasbrouck. Hasbrouck was the longtime president of that bastion of Dutch culture, Rutgers College, and a man renowned for both probity and shrewdness. Lack of success in speculations led Forsyth to gambling, to fast living, to prolonged absences from Kingston and leisure days in Newport, R.I., then attracting New Yorkers to join the rich Southern planters who had long spent summers there in the pleasant seaside climate while their overseers saw to it that their slaves worked hard and profitably.

It had been in September 1853 that Kingston people were first startled by the news that Judge Forsyth had been seen on his way via Liverpool to safety from extradition on the continent of Europe. His affairs it was soon reported were in chaos with debts running over several hundred thousand dollars and no adequate assets. The Ulster County sheriff seized the contents of the elegant house on Pearl St. and proceeded to advertise them for sale at auction.

The auctioneers, Henry Leeds and Co. of Wall Street, in New York City, used the most enticing language available to them in their advertising to rouse public desire to buy. Many of the articles to be disposed of, they proclaimed on the front page of the conservative Ulster *Sentinel*, "are among the most elegant and luxurious that the present age of luxury and refinement afford," and which would suitably adorn the "kingly palace or the lordly hall." Among the items listed were a silver punch bowl weighing fourteen pounds, "twenty-nine exquisite and valuable oil paintings, superb hand painted dinner, dessert, breakfast and tea sets, marble urns, curtains costing $300, (matched) gray horses, six carriages made to order at great expense, a very costly piano forte, a real Axminster carpet made to order in Europe, superb parlor furniture elegantly carved in Egyptian, Elizabethan and other styles, a six hundred volume law library," and "all the innumerable paraphernalia of a vast and aristocratic mansion," so auctioneers Messers Leeds & Co. ended their sales appeal.

As Kingston and other people bid at the sale of the Judge's household and personal belongings rumors about his whereabouts and the extent of his embezzlements flew about. What seemed certain was that the chief sufferers were his father-in-law and other relatives including his own people in Newburgh. Beyond the fact that he was known to have fled to Europe little was known about the Judge's whereabouts until after his death in England in 1855. Soon after that the Newburgh *Telegraph* brought together the story of the Judge's European and English wanderings and published it on April 3, 1856, and then the details reached Kingston.

Until 1855, the year of a Wall Street financial panic which also ruined many of the Judge's fellow-speculators, his whereabouts had remained largely unknown to the public. Then gossip about him burgeoned and many stories about him began appearing in Hudson Valley newspapers. What has come to light tells us that after traveling in Europe and North Africa, Forsyth settled down to live as a Canadian under the assumed name of Captain Rashleigh. Until his death he lived at the Green Dragon Hotel in England close to the Welsh border. There, with an occasional excursion away, he passed his time in reading and having pleasant conversation with people of the city of Hereford where his hotel was located. He appeared to have substantial means but after a time appeared to suffer from illness and a lessening of his resources to the point at which he paid his hotel bill with his gold watch shortly before his death. He was buried in the churchyard nearby. After news of his death trickled into Kingston with extravagant embellishments, his wife and father-in-law and other relatives maintained the dignified silence with which they had greeted his disappearance in 1853. A more detailed account of the Judge's sojourn in England has never been made public except for occasional bits in Valley newspapers.

What seems beyond dispute is that the Judge's collapse into dishonesty came when a brief contraction in easy credit at a time of frantic speculation might have forewarned him of the depression that would strike after 1855. Prices then shot upward while business stagnated. In Rondout bluestone sales shrunk for a season to almost nothing.

Mary Forsyth and her brother, banker Augustus Hasbrouck Bruyn lived on in the fine house, or "aristocratic mansion" on Pearl Street as the auctioneers had called it. The four Forsyth daughters and the son grew up there in comfort and even luxury. Mrs. Forsyth did not remarry, her brother Augustus remained single; the three daughters did not marry, the son did but had no children.

Above: The Forsyth sisters and friend

Below: Delegates to an historical meeting in Kingston enjoying lunch at Miss Forsyth's house, from a magazine illustration

The judge's widow and three daughters lived for many years (thanks to Hasbrouck family wealth) in the elegant Pearl Street house set in its landscaped grounds and with a household staff, it was remembered, of five under the efficient management of a dignified black butler—all the daughters learned to sketch, to embroider and to develope a desire to help those less fortunate than themselves. The eldest, Mary Isabella Forsyth, became an outstanding leader among Kingston women, devoting her life to good works as if to make up for the sins of her father. Miss Forsyth, with help from her sisters, took part generously in every charitable effort known to Kingston, especially for aiding orphaned and otherwise disadvantaged children, in the Industrial Institute which was largely a Forsyth donation, the Bethany Chapel and with other family members giving to the city Forsyth Park with its zoo and tennis courts. The zoo was started after a bear showed up in the early 1920s in Kingston and it was taken to the Forsyth Park where it was the first animal in the zoo. Mary Isabella was active in civic historical celebrations for which she wrote poems and songs (both words and music) for use at patriotic events. She also wrote a brief history of the City of Kingston and New York State. In addition to being an active member of the local chapter of the D.A.R., she became its first regent. She and her sisters took into their household a youngster named Ralph Forsyth whom they educated at Princeton and whom they explained only as a relative. When City historian, Judge Alphonso T. Clearwater, in his big *History of Ulster County* of 1907 paid tribute to the Judge, it was without any mention at all of the scandal that had once shocked Kingston to its roots. In her own way of restoring credit to her family Mary Isabella and others like Judge Clearwater have succeeded in almost, but not quite altogether, clearing the Judge's name, and have served their city well in the process.

The years of Nathaniel Booth's diary keeping had been unlike any previous period in Kingston's past. The urge to build more imposing churches and private mansions, the widespread enjoyment by the public of the charges and suggestions dealing with the Rev. M. Smuller's sex life, the knocking down of three church steeples by what some probably saw as the hand of an angry God and Judge Forsyth's demonstration that the kind of dishonesty which Booth saw as prevailing behind the counters of shopkeepers had penetrated even into the elegant living rooms of the stockade set itself—all these signalled the emerging of a new Kingston loosened somewhat from its Dutch Calvinist heritage and accepting more and more of the features of mainstream American life of its day, with its emphasis on national expansion and the pursuit of personal wealth, and a greater interest in enjoying life in other ways which earlier generations would not have approved, and which their ministers went on denouncing.

One way in which Kingston life might be enjoyed by families in a quiet way, would be through making use of Kingston's unusual history, centering for a time around family genealogies contained in old leather-bound and brass clasped family Bibles featuring engraved illustrations and ample space for family histories, where they were safe from outsiders' prying eyes. These Bibles occupied the place of highest honor on the center table of the parlors of Kingston's upper and middle class families and gave members of these old families a sense of ownership of the history of the place. So much of which they owned was what their ancestors had been responsible for and in which people like the local Holland Society members looked upon with pride—a pride which, as the years went by, a larger and larger number of Kingstonians of various ethnic backgrounds felt that they too had a right to share in because of their stake in the place in which they too had put down srong roots, although more recently.

And newer families of differing non-Dutch or Huguenot ethnic backgrounds came themselves to feel a pride in what they saw as a historic city, which was given public recognition by the work of Mary Isabella Forsyth and her relatives.

17.
Railroad Hopes
1830s–1850s

A CENTURY AND A HALF AGO THE COUNTRY WAS A-STIR WITH RAILROAD dreams (in which Judge Forsyth shared). Modest dreams of small branch roads, ambitious dreams of large railroads connecting the smaller ones to various parts of the nation; of large railroads connecting other large railroads into systems. Of forming networks that would surely gloriously transform the nature of American industry and daily life, and the look of the land.

No hamlet, however small and insignificant, was altogether without railroad hopes—hopes that by the magic touch of rails and the whistling and puffing of locomotives they might rise into greatness. Not even little Woodstock (no longer under Livingston control after about 1850, and ten miles or so within the influence of Kingston) was immune to a modest ambition to become blessed by a railroad. And in Kingston the fever flared. That there was a dark side to the life of a railroad dream might not be given thought at the time by those Kingston people in the grip of railroad fever. The creation of shabby neighborhoods for the poor to become known as "the wrong side of the tracks," the destruction of landscape beauty and the arrival of smoky air and polluted water, as well as the setting of fires from sparks thrown out from the wood burned by locomotives before coal became the accepted fuel were not anticipated. Neither were incursions into the pleasant place of farming in traditional Kingston life, not to mention the frightening of horses by these rivals on wheels instead of hooves into breaking out of human control and running away.

Woodstock was spared becoming a railroad town and so retained much of the beauty of its clear streams, wooded mountainsides and verdant meadows. These would, in the spring of 1902, attract the founders of the arts and crafts colony of

Woodstock's Byrdcliffe and help cause arts and crafts enthusiasts to settle there and bring the little town world fame without any help at all from a railroad in their midst.

It was quite otherwise with Kingston. There because of its favorable location and natural endowment of remarkably fertile soil close to a navigable arm of the Atlantic Ocean (the Hudson River), and at the meeting place of several valleys had not been able to escape the sharp eyes of European traders and their energetic colonizers and later of railroad dreamers. The arrival of the D. & H. Canal in the 1820s, combined with the industrial use of a valuable limestone and bluestone bedrock, had transformed Rondout (and in a lesser way, Kingston). And so ushered the two places into the age of extractive and steam-powered industry and railroads. The arrival of the Stourbridge Lion at the port of Rondout in 1829 had given a hint of what was to come—the eventual death of the long prospering canal as the railroad would force most coal-carrying waterways out of business. The D&H Canal's place in the region's life and economy would crumble at the sound of the locomotive's whistle.

The railroad which would for a time lead the way into a period when Kingston boosters would proudly call their home town "a railroad center," was the Ulster and Delaware. This line, over-ambitiously named at first the Ulster and Oswego, was aimed at first all the way to Oswego on the shore of distant Lake Ontario.

The line was referred to by local historian J. E. Quinlan with a good feeling for the fantasy railroad-dreaming of the day, in this way: "In 1836 efforts" were made by a Kingston group which had begun dreaming of a railroad running "Westward from Kingston ever since 1831" to get a charter for a line from Rondout to "Chenango Point, Oswego or some other place no matter where it was, provided it blessed Kingston with the magical railroad touch." The Rondout-Lake Ontario vision faded only to revive and refade in others heads for decades.

In the meantime the New York and Harlem line (later the N.Y. Central) was slowly inching its way from New York City up the East "manorial" or gentleman's bank of the Hudson, and by 1852 had a station doing business directly across the Hudson River from Kingston Point to which passengers could cross by ferry. Another set of railroad entrepreneurs were busily promoting a competitive "West Shore" line to link Hoboken and Weehawken opposite New York City with Albany to tap along its way the profitable Ulster County tanning, bluestone, limestone-derived cement, farm and forest products, and other freight sources and the growing summer travel to the romantic Catskills. The Wallkill Valley line by using a number of shorter lines made it to New Paltz, about fifteen minutes by rail from Kingston—and there halted for a rest. And still another line reached Kingston—the Delaware & Ontario from Sullivan County.

Once the Civil War was over the revival with variations of the 1831 dream and the pushing northward of the Wallkill Valley railroad line from New Paltz achieved real substance.

In both of these Hudson Valley adventures in Ulster County railroading the driving energy of Yankee-descended Thomas Cornell who had begun his rise to fortune by trading at canal-boomed Eddyville was very evidently at work.

The period of railroad boom between the end of the Civil War to the end of the 19th century was the height of the time when aggressive American capitalism enjoyed its own almost unfettered way in the minds and hands of such men as Jay Gould lording it over the Erie Railroad, Cornelius Vanderbilt over the New York Central, Erastus Corning over the Hudson and Mohawk. Battles for control among these competing tycoons did much to astonish and entertain the public. The principal man dominating Kingston's hopes for railroads was Thomas Cornell. Cornell was once described by Judge Gilbert D. B. Hasbrouck as having been the "overlord" not of railroads alone but also eventually of virtually all industries of Ulster County. Among the regional transportation industries he came to boss were both of the Kingston trolley lines, and the ferries across the Hudson which served Kingston plus the towing by steam tugboats of the entire Hudson River above the harbor of New York City.

So vigorous was Cornell's passion for acquisition of money makers that moved on wheels or pushed over water that in 1869 the *New Paltz Independent* in an item about the buying of another ferry by the transporation wizard included a whimsical addendum to the effect that Cornell was rumored to have also bought a Rondout wheelbarrow or Irish velocipede factory. (Or this last may have been intended as an angling for or against the critical wheelbarrow-pushing Irish vote.) Cornell was then in the process of acquiring a very useful seat in Congress as a Republican.

As a politician Cornell was active in keeping his name before the public. One of the highest peaks in the Catskills was given his name, he bought the Rondout *Freeman* to provide a channel for presenting his views and the praise of his deeds. He presented a Rondout fire company (the Cornell Hose Company) with an ornamental, wheeled hose carriage used to good effect because it had Cornell's life sized portrait painted on either side. His fine home set on Rondout's Wurts Street—a street which could also boast an unrivalled display of the most splendid churches in the Village—was the scene of gaudy receptions for Republican national dignitaries up to the level of Vice-President Schuyler Colfax. During these revels, a newspaper reported, every light in the Cornell mansion was ablaze. Rolling downhill from the Cornell house were flower beds openly visible by day and night to all passersby and guests and described as positively "dazzling" in color.

Most treasured of all the Cornell many possessions were his steampowered towboats, and new to the Hudson River. Of these (later known as tugboats) he eventually had a monopoly on the mid and upper Hudson, towing vast quantities of anthracite from D&H barges from Rondout and Port Ewen to coal using ports on the Hudson and far beyond. Anthracite came into use as a domestic and industrial fuel, a use which Cornell industriously promoted, as well as, after the 1830s, when it displaced wood as fuel on river steamers. (Railroad historian Gerald Best was to claim that Cornell's railroad collection served primarily to haul anthracite to his Hudson River steamboats and steam-powered towing fleet.)

Cornell became for a while president of the Wallkill Valley Railroad which he helped push from Orange County through New Paltz and Kingston, hopefully aimed at Albany. He was also owner of a rail line that spanned Dutchess County from the Rhinecliffe ferry dock to the Connecticut border, and he was active in the affairs of other regional lines. It was for the key role he played in the rough, contentious early history of the Rondout and Oswego under its changing names that he pulled the most weight in Kingston's railroad history. He was able to leave this long profitable road to his descendants. Under its final name of the Ulster and Delaware the line was to experience a long span of profitability and do much to help the Catskills into the position of a leading American summer resort, and to pay fat dividends to the members of the Coykendall family (the heirs of Thomas Cornell) until well into the Twentieth Century.

This prosperity under Samuel and Edward Coykendall emerged from fierce struggles reminiscent at times of those which titillated the public in battles by such names as those of Jay Gould and Cornelius Vanderbilt for control of the Erie and other railroads of their time.

The proposal to build the U & D was objected to at first by many including influential General George H. Sharpe on the grounds that it would ruin the profitable teaming by horse power of back country products to Kingston traders and Rondout shippers. These objections were overcome and a most promising method of financing the road at little cost to its entrepreneurs was accepted. It was urged that the railroad would surely bring great prosperity to the towns through which it would pass and to which it would distribute its golden blessings. Why not then graciously sell shares to the residents and units of government which would be blessed so plentifully by the new railroad operation? Let everyone share in the profits to come by offering them shares. Salesmen of these securities, headed by Thomas Cornell himself, therefore invaded the territory to be so bountifully enriched by the presence of the Ulster and Delaware. The arguments seemed persuasive in the late 1860s and the bonds and stocks were taken up with the hidden help of local politicians—Kingston's share of bonds was $600,000.

It was not until November 1910 that the historical and genealogical magazine,

Olde Ulster, would make public a reasonably sober account of what would come to be known as the bonding scandal under the title of "Bonding Towns and Corrupt Politics." The years of the birth and rise of the U&D were a period unrivalled until then in American history for political corruption, much involving railroad and municipal management (and sketchily traced in regional newspapers). Political Boss Tweed of New York would be sentenced to prison for his misdeeds in 1871. The administration of President Ulysses S. Grant had been cursed by a number of corporate scandals, some of which came close to good friends of the President himself. It is enough to say that the fierce battles in which reputations were destroyed in newspapers and when regional buyers of stocks in the U&D lost their equity by some clever reorganizing schemes were no novelty in the 1860s and 1870s. These schemes were boldly presented in *Olde Ulster*. The railroad line that was to link Kingston with Lake Ontario emerged with the new name of the Ulster and Delaware and with Thomas Cornell and after him his descendants in control. Another result was the passing by the state legislature of an act to make illegal such tricky methods of financing and manipulating railroads as those experienced to their sorrow by municipal investors in the R&O (or U & D) and the Wallkill Valley Railroads in their early years. (While many of the stockholders lost their entire investment, the bonds, as *Olde Ulster* explained in 1910, continued and the different towns paid the interest on the bonds they had bought till well into the 20th century.)

The first step toward actually constructing the U & D raiload had been excavating and blasting the rough and rocky way up the steep slope that led from the dock on the Rondout Harbor which was the home dock of Cornell's greatest steamboat, the *Mary Powell*. This proved a slow job.

In 1869 construction had been stopped by the failure of the shipment of steel rails to arrive on time from England.

It was not until the spring of 1871 that the diggers and blasters had readied the way from the base of the first slope in what would prove to be an exciting S-shaped curve for thrilling future passengers to a spot just before the tracks would be about to enter a brief tunnel beneath Hasbrouck Avenue. Here excavating was brought to a sudden halt by peremptory action of the Kingston Common Council.

On January 1, 1871 the *Journal* reported that the Common Council of Kingston had voted to instruct their clerk to notify the president of the Rondout and Oswego Railroad (who was Thomas Cornell) to halt all excavations at the point at which the railroad right-of-way skirts the "Sharpe Burying Ground." This was just before the railroad would go under Hasbrouck Avenue by means of what was to be the only tunnel on the line. The digging for the railroad had resulted, the clerk protested, in the "exposure of the remains of corpses and parts of coffins" on the "sacred ground" of the cemetery. A committee of Council members was appointed to see to it that a proper (retaining) wall be built at the foot of the cemetery to hold the cemetery's slope and prevent further exposure of the dead, and this was done.

Native American skulls and other human body fragments had turned up before in previous Rondout excavations, and had caused little comment, but these were the bones and coffins of well known people related to stockade family members, and so had to be restored to their proper places in the sanctified ground before work could proceed.

When the remains of Native Americans had first turned up in Ponckhockie, they had initially been treated at best as no more than interesting curiosities. In recent years professional archeological digs have disclosed the well preserved skeletons of Native Americans of Late Woodland culture and some of these have been gladly accepted as contributions to science and stored for safekeeping and the information of future researchers in the archaeology department of the State University of New York at New Paltz, which had sponsored some of the digs.

With the sacredness of Sharpe's Burying Ground thoroughly restored, the railroad workers spiked the delayed shipment of English rails into place, and the U & D moved on. Thomas Cornell's hope for a quick junction between the coal-carrying Susquehanna and Albany Railroad to the U & D and the coal mines at Carbondale was not to be realized for another quarter of a century. But the U & D went on all the way to Oneonta. In the years of the railroad's decline after many years of building up the resort business of the Catskills, the spacious Oneonta station served well as the bunkhouse of the crew of the freight cars which carried no passengers but only needed food to the county's numerous milk cows as a final valuable service to Delaware county.

18.
Bloody Civil War Years

WITH THE CALL TO ARMS OF THE CIVIL WAR, HOWEVER, THE VERY PLACE to which all the Village's steeples were thought to point seemed threatened. For neither Kingston nor Ulster County were well equipped for the bloody and hate-filled kind of war which now faced their people and was foreshadowed by the *Ulster Republican*'s "Carrier's Address" of the year 1860. The annual "Carrier's Address" was usually a rhymed summary of events of the previous year, printed each year for half a century to be handed out by the newsboys who delivered the paper from household to household, in expectation of a tip. Sometimes the address was also separately printed as a broadside with the name of the newsboy who was expected to distribute it imprinted at the end of the Address (as was the 1860 Address).

The following was the beginning of the copy of the "Carrier's Address," imprinted with the name of the *Ulster Republican* carrier Samuel H. Schepmoes, for delivery on January 1, 1860. Schepmoes, as he delivered the broadside, could not have been aware that before too long he would be a volunteer in the Union Army. The address began:

> And first, it cheers his (the carrier's) heart to state
> That spite of abolition hate
> Intestine feud and foreign foe
> Our land remains "in *statu quo*;"
> That o'er our loved forefathers' graves,
> The flag of Freedom proudly waves,
> Flashing its starry radiance free
> In living light, o'er earth and sea.
> —"'Tis true, and pity 'tis, 'tis true,"
> That abolition's sombre crew,

Their sable hearts with treason rife
Have sought to sow the seeds of strife,
And offered weapons to the grasp
Of hands which brothers' hands should clasp.
But mad the effort, mad the will—
And madder, doubly madder still,
The foul fanatic zeal which made
Its victims martyrs. . . ."

All this was put into the mouths of boys who delivered *The Republican* to its subscribers, after John Brown, the fervent abolitionist, had been seized at Harper's Ferry, and then hanged on December 2, 1859, a martyr and hero of the Abolitionists and a hero to most Americans of today.

The paper's editor takes for granted that its diatribe against abolitionism and John Brown was generally shared by its readers and its newsboys. Kingston, it was true, was by no means ready to understand an event of the magnitude or meaning of the Civil War which was soon to set Americans in strife against one another. For one thing its militia, which had managed to do so well against British professional soldiers in the Revolutionary War, was not at the ready, in spite of Colonel Pratt's effort.

Marius Schoonmaker, the Kingston lawyer-historian deserves our gratitude for occasionally lightening the pages of his very solidly written history with delightful patches of nostalgia. One of these patches tells how the once highly useful colonial institution of an annual training day of militiamen had become a kind of jolly and relaxed annual festival to which people of Kingston and the surrounding country flocked by the wagonload for a day of alcoholic conviviality at the conclusion of which, as Marius puts it, many revellers weren't "certain which end of themselves was uppermost." The militia clearly was not well prepared for the challenge or significance of a war.

Military training there was of course, but it was often secondary to the display of gold braid and pomp by the officers and a gorging with molasses candy, hard cider and even harder alcoholic stuff by both militiamen and their friends and neighbors. One cause of the Revolution of '76, Marius reminds us, had been the maintenance by George III of a standing professional army, with some of its soldiers being hired foreigners. His American colonial subjects preferred to depend on the kind of citizen army called a militia. The militia units of Americans after they had been freed from British rule, however, were degenerating into peacetime excuses for display and revelry. The militia was even being ridiculed at times by parades of men known as the "fantasticals" or in Ulster County as "jobunckers" who parodied the pompous militia officers with their "handles" of "colonel" or "general" attached to their names.

(Some of these officers were also known as "rattlesnake Colonels" because it was said that any man who had ever killed a rattlesnake but done nothing much else was entitled to receive such a title.)

One of the officers who seemed to have the notion of parodying the parodists was Col. Zadock Pratt, the rich and eccentric tanner who used the militiamen of a regiment he financed and commanded in pre-Civil War years in neighboring Greene County to stage such audience-delighting displays as the blasting down of tattered old barns by artillery fire and a noisy mock re-enactment of the Napoleonic Battle of Lodi. The Colonel's son, who was a remarkably intelligent young man and an officer of Ulster County's 120th Volunteer Regiment took seriously the work of such a military unit in protecting the nation. It was Zadock's son Colonel George W. Pratt who had already demonstrated his grasp of historical military matters by researching and writing the excellent paper on the burning of Kingston in 1777 for the new Ulster County Historical Society. This account was the first well researched and well written work on Ulster County and Kingston history ever to be undertaken. His published account stands unchallenged up to the present.

The Secessionists of the "slavocracy" had put to use their bloc in the national Congress. They were helped by Northern political groups (including the former Know-Nothings). By January 7, 1861, young Col. George W. Pratt had shown that he grasped the fact that war lay ahead and he had by then seen the necessity of preparing troops to preserve the threatened unity of the Nation.

When the flag of the United States was fired upon at Fort Sumter by secessionists from the South Carolina shore batteries on April 12, 1861, Kingston received word of the event over the "electric telegraph" installed at Winter's store in Rondout. And there is little doubt that the news struck Kingstonians, even anti-Abolitionist readers of the *Republican* like an electric shock. Before that Kingston had had its share of "copperheads" who sympathized with the South and upheld slavery. Newsboys like Samuel Schepmoes felt no sympathy for the abolitionists who had been so harshly treated in his newspaper's "Carriers' Address" but news of the insult to their flag struck him and many other Kingstonians with a force that caused many of them to change their minds. Kingston people gathered "spontaneously," it was said at the time, at the Courthouse and at Washington Hall in Rondout. Leaders of all political parties in the two villages addressed the meetings with contagious emotion and proposed strong resolutions condemning the insult to the flag. "At times like these, when a great national crisis exists," proclaimed one local speaker, "members of all political parties" must forget their party distinctions and allow them to sink into insignificance.

A Resolution was passed at both Kingston and Rondout meetings which began, "Whereas a base and infamous conspiracy has been formed by traitors and designing men to overthrow the Union and Constitution which our fathers made and subvert and destroy our government. . . ."

For the first time in the history of Kingston the power of the American flag as a symbol of national unity was accepted by people of varied political beliefs. The author of the anti-abolitionist "Carrier's Address" had even named the stars and stripes in denouncing abolitionists. Later newsboy Samuel Schepmoes was moved to enlist as a soldier although he did not approve of President Abraham Lincoln and his letters home would make it clear that he felt that he was doing his duty to the "good old flag," as he put it, even though the flag as commonly used was not actually very old in the 1860s.

As the Southern rebellion against the Union spread President Lincoln called for the raising of 75,000 enlisted troops to put down the insurrection. In Rondout, Pastor Phillips of the Prebyterian Church who had been very active in helping escaped southern slaves reach freedom in Canada via the local underground railroad, gave up his pastorate and enlisted as a chaplain in the United States Army to play his part in the war that seemed to lie ahead.

Even before the passage of the Kingston and Rondout Resolution, leaders of the 120th regiment (including by then ailing George F. Von Beck of Rondout's Harrison Guards) had agreed to ready their troops. They had met in a parlor of Rondout's Mansion House and heard Col. George W. Pratt state that open war was imminent and to give assurance that his 120th Regiment or Ulster Guards was being offered to the State's Governor for three month's service. It was the first unit in Ulster County to offer its services.

The leaders of Colonel George Watson Pratt's 120th Ulster Volunteer Regiment, the 20th Regiment and other military groups, having agreed to make ready their members, were soon occupied in organizing and supplying with what equipment might be found, and drilling Kingston and Ulster County militiamen. Thus they had already made a beginning of preparations for the military action they were certain was coming.

Kingston banks at this time of crisis offered $8000 for uniforms and other supplies. Governor Morgan promised state help in providing equipment. The men of the 120th Regiment or Ulster Guard, after a brief final attempt at training at Camp Sampson above the head of Jacob's Valley on Greenfield Avenue, were mustered in on the Academy Green. A huge gathering of flagwaving well wishers saw them off with speeches by political leaders of both major parties and prayers by the clergy. The troops were not yet well equipped yet martial feeling ran high.

Amid enthusiastic applause and band music and much further flag-waving the troops marched in good order down to the Rondout Creek. There they boarded Thomas Cornell's Hudson River steamboat *Manhattan* to the sound of bands, and cheers and sailed down to New York City with crowds waving flags at every landing.

In New York a series of bungles by New York State officialdom in the confused and emotional atmosphere of the time led to the rescinding of the previous promise of equipment and in a comedy of errors, to an order to return to Kingston and disband. This tangle having been straightened out, the men were ordered to Washingon and Baltimore for guard duty.

With no more active duty having been performed the 120th returned to Kingston at the end of its three months enlistment and was given a most tumultuous welcome before disbanding.

The 120th, although its men had been willing and eager for active service against the rebels had little to show for their three month's service beyond a large national flag presented to them by the ladies of Pougheepsie, and the satisfaction of having ferreted out some civilian secessionists lurking in Baltimore and seizing their hoards of weapons and Confederate flags which had their own symbols not of unity but of rebellion against the Union.

With the war increasing in intensity and in casualties, Colonel George H. Sharpe of the 20th Regiment relentlessly combed Ulster County in search of recruits to enlist for three years or the duration of the war. And the marching men of the two regiments—the 120th and the 20th—took off for the now bloody battlefields of the war amid cheers, speeches and prayers.

The Kingston and Rondout men, some eager and some reluctant, met their obligation by marching into battle. Among the battleworn Civil War battle flags preserved in the War Museum in Albany was one on which is shown the list of battles in which local men fought and died. Among these battles were Gettysburg, Bull Run, Manassas, the Wilderness, Chancellorsville, Fredericksberg, Antietam and others. (The 20th Regiment by now was renamed the 80th.)

And in the many letters sent home by volunteers and draftees many hints of what day-to-day army life was like speak to us. Samuel H. Schepmoes, a volunteer of August 1862 in Company I of the 120th left behind almost one hundred carefully preserved letters to his parents and other family members. Twenty-year-old newsboy Schepmoes, of an old Kingston Dutch family, shows in his letters that he was a member of a loving and united family which approved of his enlistment. He gave greetings to brothers and sisters (to whom he sent kisses and asked to be remembered to "all enquiring friends.") He mourned the death of "little brother George" and showed deep concern at an illness of his mother. Not realizing that he would have been exempt from the expected draft because he was a Kingston fireman or "a fire laddie" (as he phrased it in one of his letters to his parents, Samuel enlisted, but disapproved of any abolition of slavery, and also disapproved of President

Lincoln, but holding fast to his willingness to help preserve the Union. Yet he was determined to follow his father's admonition "to do my duty" to what he called "that good old flag."

Samuel never relaxed his dislike of black people or his devotion to the Democratic party, strengthened by the Ulster *Argus* which he urged his family to send him and which was regarded by many Ulsterites as copperhead in its sympathies. He hoped, he said in one letter, to get a job on the *Argus* once the war ended. Often in depressed spells he repeated his belief that this "war will last until the officers have made enough money and enough men have been killed." Yet Samuel never ceased doing his duty as a soldier.

Army life during Samuel's first two months experience of it seemed to agree with him—he gained 14 pounds and seemed always hungry. His was an irregular and what would be regarded today as a none too supportive diet in which foraged foods, foods irregularly issued by the army, foods sent from home or bought from sutlers were cooked by a mate in the tent they shared.

He wrote, "When I get back home I want you to have a whole hog killed for me. I think I could eat head, body, legs and tail and even all the insides." And one Sunday he wrote of thinking of his family eating chicken while he was eating boiled mackerel—but that the mackerel wasn't too bad.

And he wrote much of mud, not only on his boots but in his flimsy tent and on his clothes and under his oiled groundcloth. And he wrote of endless muddy muddy marches for no reason that he could discern.

Never questioning his officers reasons for giving him orders without explanation, he simply obeyed. Samuel told of marching through cold rain, and of resting to sleep on sodden ground under a tent of "six-penny muslin" while being expected to sleep with "one eye open" in expectation of being suddenly called to duty—all left their marks on kidney function and digestion—problems which the "mean" surgeon dismissed as "a little cold." He marched and endlessly marched through already war-battered country where buildings were ruined and the once abundant old dry rail fences had been already burned for heat and cooking fuel by previous waves of shivering and hungry soldiers. He did picket duty at the limits of his unit's line and learned from personal experience that Union and Rebel pickets often met and peacefully exchanged newspapers, conversation and tobacco.

A new captain of his company named Reynolds astonished and pleased him by visiting every one of the ninety or so men under him to shake hands and exchange a few words of friendly talk with everyone. Of most officers, he wrote with barely suppressed dislike—when General U.S. Grant reviewed his regiment he told his parents, he found the General to be round-shouldered, cigar-smoking, bandy-legged, "a real Hoosier." For General McClellan, a fellow Democrat who was criticized by many civilians for endlessly drilling his troops rather than leading them into battle against the rebels, Samuel had only admiration. When McClellan ran for the Presidency, Schepmoes wrote, "The Chicago Convention brought good news . . . and I hope the people of the North will next November roll up such a majority for McClellan as no president ever received." And yet under all officers he followed his father's advice, and "did my duty." By the time on one of his wearying marches he came upon the grisly bones of an unburied predecessor-soldier he was hardened enough to the horrors of war to describe the sight calmly. It was when he was plunged into the life-and-death struggle of his first battlefield that he could not bring himself to tell his parents of his experience there. He promised to do that after returning home. He managed to give a warmth to his letters by his expression of love for his family and his concern for their well-being.

Now and then Samuel's mind flashed back home across the winter and the warm Virginia spring and reminded him it must be time for his uncle to be getting the canal boat he commanded out of its winter sleep and back into action on the D&H Canal.

As the war neared its end Samuel's opinion of Abraham Lincoln became higher as to his role in the Presidency. When word of Lincoln's assassination reached him he expressed profound shock and anger. He wrote to the folks back home that if he could get his hands on the assassin he would see to it that he had a slow and painful death. Not long after, the bullet of a Rebel wounded him as he was on picket duty.

From a military hospital in Baltimore Samuel reported the city to be crammed with Southern blacks come to the city to enjoy their first experience of freedom. They were often being seized by the Union military police and set to digging defensive ditches.

Before he was wounded and sent to the hospital Samuel had pointed out in his family letters that should any of them become seriously ill a letter to officials might result in his being sent home on furlough. From the hospital he did his best to bring about as he recovered, a return to civilian life. Finally he was ordered to a hospital in Albany, N.Y. Then he was demobilized and vanished into civilian life in Kingston soon afterward. He wrote no more letters that can be located.

In his surviving letters home Samuel never touched upon a side of the war which he obviously didn't feel comfortable in writing to his family about. A Kingston correspondent of the *Argus* who served in the 20th Regiment had no such scruples. This soldier-reporter wrote a series of dispatches to the *Argus* under the heading of "The Ulster Guard (of the 20th Regiment of Ulster) on the Potomac." On April 9 1862 the *Argus* printed one of these (dispatch number 22) which made up for Samuel's reticence about a rough side of Army existence. "Whatever can tempt the military eye is enticingly displayed (at Bailey's Crossroad near Alexandria). The streets are filled with soldiers while the pavement rings with the sharp clatter of horses' hooves. In front of many buildings, armed guards pace their monotonous rounds proclaiming that military law is supreme here and that for 'secess' or brawlers who defy it the guardhouse is waiting to welcome its prisoners. The festering vices which cling like barnacles to ships and to every large army reveal their unsightly visage scarce kept down by the gleaming bayonets set to announce order and terror to evil-doers. The reeling and cursing soldier meets the eye frequently in spite of the grim guardians of the law who should frighten him into decency—while shameless Cyprians (prostitutes) from the large cities are present to drag down the easily tempted to their own abased level and while emptying his purse, inflicting incurable wounds upon his soul. Such is war, and such its inevitable consequences."

While Samuel was doing his duty to defend the unity of the States symbolized by what he continued to call the "good old flag," back home in Kingston the village was adjusting to the demands inevitably made upon it by war. There were higher taxes to be met in order to pay the costs of war. There was the shortage of male labor and the necessity of women doing jobs once performed by men. There were shortages of foodstuffs and an increasing reliance on those that came in cans, originally developed for military use in the Napoleonic wars. Never before had so many women done so much knitting of warm shirts and socks to help their men to fight off cold and damp while they were fighting off the enemy.

There were women making jams and jellies as never before, often from wild fruits gathered by children and intended to relieve the often grim army diet of far away family members. Women who had skill as herbalists stirred stovetop kettles of wild plants believed to be able to relieve digestive and muscle pains of which many other soldiers as well as Samuel complained. Increased numbers of prayers for the safety of their distant battle-threatened soldiers were offered at home and at church. Sometimes the efforts made to relieve the sufferings of members of soldiers' families in an inevitably inflation-ridden economy were unsuccessful and resulted in reports, printed in the newspapers, of women and children being found starved to death in the streets.

"Sanitary Fairs," intended to help raise money by women for soldier's dependents as well as soldiers appeared in larger cities such as New York. Kingston women of higher social standing such as Mrs. Abraham Bruyn Hasbrouck helped in the Sanitary Fairs of New York City. There Mrs. Hasbrouck demonstrated in a "Dutch Kitchen" set up by Kingston women the craft of weaving on a big old-fashioned Kingston loom while two small black Kingston boys made music in a corner.

Draft and casualty lists published as extras by Kingston newspapers were eagerly read and the sale of county newspapers carrying reports of the war and its casualty broke all circulation records.

The harbor of Rondout bustled with the coming and going of sloops, schooners, barges, scows, ferries and freight and passenger steamboats, all carrying a great variety of farm, forest and manufactured products useful in war as well as at home. A deputation of local buusinessmen journeyed to Washington to lobby for the establishment of a Federal foundry or arsenal in Rondout, but without success. The many gunpowder mills of Ulster County which shipped their product from the port of Rondout greatly increased their activity—and the possibility of producing accidental explosions similar to deliberate ones on the field of battle. And the traffic in gunpowder produced its home-front heroes through injuries or deaths in plant explosions by hasty production by new and ill-trained workers. Among these heroes were the Booth Brothers, who were by then in the bluestone business, with a quarry at Jockey Hill and a stoneyard at Wilbur. They had bought two sloops, the *Rebecca Ford*, which had been raised from the river bottom after causing the death of Mary Cragin and one other woman, and the *Hoaxer*. Both of these had come to have the well earned reputation of being unlucky, and hence were on the market at an extremely reasonable price, as such ill-omened vessels often were. The Booth brothers, Jonathan and the others, bought them to do the rather rough work of carrying flagging stone from Wilbur to market, and occasionally also freighted limestone in various forms.

On one Saturday afternoon in July 1862, Mr. Rand, a partner in the overworked wartime gunpowder plant at Saltpeterville on the Wallkill (below Rifton), approached the captain of the *Hoaxer* to ask if he could take on board a rush job of 100 kegs of gunpowder. The *Hoaxer* was already pretty well loaded with ground Wilbur limestone in barrels. The captain agreed to do the job and the gunpowder was placed on board. When it was time for the *Hoaxer* to leave the dock, the tide had turned out to be remarkably low and the heavily loaded vessel could not leave and was obliged to stay there at the dock until the turn of tide the following morning. The captain had given his crew of four men shore leave and later on was asleep in his berth when he was awakened by the smell of smoke. Somehow water had gotten into the hold, and the unslaked lime got wet and was beginning to heat. It could heat to a degree which would cause the gunpowder to explode, so it was feared. The Booth brothers were quickly summoned and they set to work. They took turns going down into the hold and moving out the kegs of gunpowder to safety on shore and when one brother was on the verge of being overcome by the fumes of the slaking lime and charring wood he was helped out and revived while another brother took his turn at the place of danger.

As this was going on, the people of Wilbur had become greatly alarmed in fear of a devastating explosion on board the *Hoaxer* and they were racing up the surrounding hills for safety. But the Booth brothers kept on removing the powder until there was only one keg left. This had become wedged because of the swelling of the moist limestone barrels and required opening and dousing with water before it was safe to take it out, and the danger of a catastrophic explosion was averted—so W.W. Pitts, a sloop owner and the postmaster of Twaalfskill recounted Twaalfskill's close call in Judge Clearwater's *History of Ulster County* of 1907. The incident, however, went unreported in the newspapers.

Their Civil War experiences brought many changes in the lives of Kingstonians who served in the army and at sea. Their exposure to a wider world than the one they had known made them more tolerant than they had been of people of backgrounds different from their own. More tolerant than they had been when their voters had been swept into Know-Nothingism in 1855. Women often obliged to undertake the work once done by men then away in military service took a step forward in the gaining of social equality for which feminists had struggled in the pre-war decades. During the Civil War, because of shortages, canned goods would become familiar to Americans and housewives "put up" fruits and vegetables in glass jars year after year as part of the annual household routine. Other household time-savers being invented and manufactured for military use such as improved can openers and apple peelers increased.

Railroads had demonstrated their value in warfare and now were undergoing a great expansion in the peacetime speculative post-war world. Kingston's Thomas Cornell was adding to his towing fleet on the Hudson a railroad project named at first, back in the 1830s, the Kingston, Oswego and Erie—a railroad aimed in pre-war days to go from Kingston across the State to Lake Erie and Ontario and even farther. This railroad would do much to affect the future of Kingston for years after the Civil War had become no more than a memory kept alive by the presence of crippled veterans and those who had lost arms or legs, some of whom peddled apples on the streets of Kingston.

Part 9

A Multi-Ethnic and Historic City Takes Shape in a Changing World

1865-1890s

1.
Thomas Cornell Thinks Big After the Civil War

THOMAS CORNELL WAS AWARE OF WHAT LAY AHEAD WHEN THE D&H CANAL concluded its early flash of prosperity (after the conclusion of the Civil War). He was looking forward to the eventual obsolescence of the canal by railroads. He let it be known in a newspaper that the Lake Ontario dream of the Rondout and Oswego would form a junction at Cooperstown (in Otsego County) on to Albany. He was also planning a Dutchess & Connecticut railroad line to run from the Rhinecliffe ferry landing on the east bank of the Hudson to Connecticut, with coal-carrying barges ferrying the coal to it from the Rondout end of the canal and so on across the Hudson.

The construction contractors, Saterlee & Company, were surveying a railroad route past Kingston along the Esopus Creek, across a planned bridge over the Esopus Creek and following the creek till they reached Phoenicia and a joyous celebration of mountain people. The State Legislature had been appealed to for a loan to pay for a tunnel to pierce the steep Pine Hill which rose ahead but the Legislature refused and the line was surveyed to be carried up the mountainside in a series of bold curves. Of one of these curves, it was said later to summer boarders by joking mountain people, that if the engineer put out his hand at the right place he could shake hands with the man in the caboose.

At the top of the Pine Hill one of the very largest resort hotels in the entire Catskills had been planned and built with the railroad in mind. It was called The Grand and would be operated by a member of the Cornell family, with a carriage road leading from its entrance down semi-landscaped terraces which dimly hinted at a poor man's Versailles gardens to its Ulster and Delaware railroad station. There was a fountain of water from the Crystal Spring (artfully rumored to be similar in quality to that of the famous spa of Saratoga), playing in the hotel's Rotunda.

Advertisement for Grand Hotel in E. Coykendall's 1903 book celebrating the Ulster & Delaware Railroad

The long hotel, it was said, straddled the borderline between Delaware and Ulster Counties, two counties which had different ordinances with respect to the sale of liquor, and it was said that when the liquor ordinance was changed in one county, the bar could be cannily shifted from one part of the long, long hotel to another to conform to (or avoid) the profit-making (or losing) possibilities of the new regulations. The railroad line went down the western mountainside and up the smiling valley of the East Branch of the Delaware River to West Stamford, stimulating dreams of booming summer boarding business in every hamlet and farmhouse along the route and serving the great Stamford hotel which was to become a favorite of still Calvinist Christian religious groups and of Anthony Comstock who waged war against near-nudity on the stage and in the use of altogether nude models by art schools.

Kingston business people had long hoped to see that Kingston would become the Gateway to the Catskills by railroad magic, and it was the Ulster & Delaware (no longer called the R & O), with a Hunter branch going on from Phoenicia through the Stony Clove to the great Catskill Mountain House (with its famous and exciting Hudson Valley view from the Pine Orchard in which the hotel was perched), which made this dream come true. Kingston to this day has an unusual number of businesses dealing in restaurant and hotel supplies and other goods used in the resort business.

In April 1890 Cornell died and business buildings of Kingston were sorrowfully draped in mourning and the streets and faces of Kingston people took on a funereal aspect. The whole city held its breath in expectation of Kingston receiving a magnificent bequest from Cornell. Cornell's lawyer, Judge Alphonso T. Clearwater, withheld the details of Cornell's will day after day and when he did speak up, the will revealed that Cornell had left nothing to the city but had divided his estate among his daughters, their husbands and other descendants. The Cornell railroads continued to remain a good and useful Kingston asset under the efficient management of Thomas Cornell's sons-in-law Samuel Decker and Edward Coykendall, thus assuring the city its place as the profitable Gateway to the Catskills until into the age of the automobile. Edward Coykendall was an enthusiastic collector of the works of John Vander Lyn. His very luxurious stables across West Chestnut Street from his fine house eventually, after his death, became adapted as the elegant home of Kingston's talented amateur theater group named the Coach House Players whose excellent productions added much to their City's cultural life. And so in roundabout ways the fortune amassed by Thomas Cornell had some beneficial effects on the City he ignored in his will and helped the City develop the special character which gained for it recognition as a historic city with more than commercial and industrial values in the minds of many people as well as in the eyes of outsiders who were induced to visit the City by the Coykendall collection of John Vander Lyn's works.

Right: Thomas Cornell, courtesy of Ulster County Historical Society; *Below:* The *Mary Powell*, known as the Queen of the Hudson, owned by Thomas Cornell at one time. It was first docked at the foot of the Ulster & Delaware Railroad on the Rondout

2.
The Schoharie and Other Ethnic Mixes

In the social mix of Colonial and Post-Revolutionary Kingston those of Dutch and Walloon (Huguenot) ancestry with a later mixture of British tended to form a stable layer of people who were well placed in the scheme of things—they owned much land and were able to engage in trading and farming ventures on the remarkable fertile creekside acres. But those who were Native American, African or mixed (plus a few near whites) gravitated to the lowest rank of the society and often lived on singly as outcasts or in groups of squatters on unpromising land their betters did not want.

The ethnic mixture of the Village of Kingston during the early and middle 19th century is not easy to determine with accuracy. The statement by lawyer and amateur historian William Lounsbery that by 1856 the population of black people in the Village had diminished and the popular saying that in Kingston every other house is a barn and every other white man is a negro is suggestive of something but proves nothing. By the middle of the nineteenth century these statements became obsolete. But of one group of the middle years of the 1800s (and earlier) we have a good many mentions which demonstrate their existence and tell us what was thought of them at the time. These were of the people of mixed white, Native American and black ancestry known as the Schoharies who sometime before 1850 were beginning to appear as strangers with a characteristic look on the streets of Kingston seeking odd jobs as farm hands or manual laborers and the women as domestic helpers.

The Schoharies were most often dark of hair and somewhat swarthy of complexion. At times they entered uptown Kingston to shop, to do domestic labor or to peddle wooden bowls, baskets or other craft objects of their own making. The

Schoharies known to Kingston lived at the "Binnewater," a marshy tract of the Kingston Commons on the Hurley-Kingston-Rosendale border too inhospitable for others to crave. A reporter for the Rondout *Courier* of 1861 had described the area under a heading of "The Binnewater Class" as a once forested area of small ponds. (It had been officially known for close to half a century as that part of the Kingston Commons (see chapter on Kingston Commons) recorded as "The Binnewater Class." A reporter of about 1850 had suggested that a Christian missionary be sent to work among the Schoharies to reform them from what he saw as their almost uncivilized and un-Christian ways.

The Schoharies were thought to have once been emigrants from the northwest, presumably from the valley of the Schoharie Creek which drains the northwestern slopes of the Catskill Mountains. Their genes, as we would describe them today, were hand-me-downs from a mixture of those of Native Americans, whites and Afro-Americans. As such they were regarded by most proper Kingstonians as virtual outcasts. The appearance in uptown Kingston of the 1870s of Schoharies lacking a good reason for their presence caused many Kingstonians to be on their guard against them. People of visibly mixed ancestry in many parts of the colonized world were and are likely to be avoided socially by their colonizers as half-castes or mongrels who were not to be trusted. In Kingston the appearance of the Schoharies who squatted on the soggy and infertile area called the Binnewater (from the Dutch "inner (or lesser) water") was not always welcome.

A "binnewater" was the frequent Dutch name for an sometimes unusually lengthy and narrow body of water left behind after the flooding of a creek such as the Esopus, and sometimes becoming permanent.

Until the 1960s a large truckload of outdoor furniture was peddled by people of apparently similar white, Native and black ancestry in and around Kingston. These people, similar to the Schoharies, but with rather more of a white background, lived, they said, in an isolated community in Orange County. They made the well-crafted furniture themselves, the peddlers said, from peeled arbor vitae wood supplied to them by another similar mixed ethnic group based in Michigan.

Not far away, people also similar to the "Schoharies" had settled down in the "Vly" or low swampy tract at the eastern end of Yankeetown Pond in Woodstock. (The "Vlyonders" sometimes visited Kingston.) Their Mrs. Stewart made much admired baskets, large and small, for farmers' use, by weaving together thin strips of wood split from blocks cut usually from red maple trees which grow well in damp locations. Alternate squares of the basket's surface were colored or decorated in contrasting colors.

Mrs. Stewart claimed "Seneca Indian" ancestry and appreciation of her skill as a basket-maker brought recogition of her talent. Her popularity caused her funeral to "be largely attended" wrote a Kingston newspaper reporter. The baskets woven by Vlyanders, or Vlyonders, are believed to owe their painted ornamentation to borrowing from the craft as practiced by the Swedish colonists along the Delaware River.

A fine example of the sort of large baskets woven by Mrs. Stewart (and often used by white farmers) once belonged to the Woodstock Historical Society but was stolen from its museum in the 1970s and has not been recovered.

The "Vlyanders" seem to have gotten along fairly well with the Woodstock people; the mixed people of the settlement of Lapala (which had its own mixed character), in the hills to the west of the Kingston line also got along reasonably well. The Binnewater-dwelling Schoharies, however, had their troubles with Kingston. Newspapers denounced them as drunken brawlers and their women as prostitutes—perhaps there was some logic behind the frequent descents of police officials on the Binnewater Schoharies. And the Binnewater area came to be called "the Isthmus," which meant a neighborhood of heavy drinking and unauthorized sexual license. The word Isthmus was perhaps derived from the Isthmus of Corinth, once famed for the sensuality of its people. This is familiar to readers of St. Paul's Corinthians in the New Testament.

The Schoharies managed to maintain their identity until into the twentieth century but with occasional mixing with Kingston people by marriage (like those between blacks and whites). Such marriages were reported by Kingston newspapers as shockingly bad examples to be avoided by the virtuous.

In Kingston as in the rest of Ulster County, there are families of blacks and mixed people having the same last names as the old Dutch and Huguenot white families. Some of these explain their surnames as having been those which slave ancestors of theirs assumed when freed. There are also other explanations, including mixed ethnic marriages and irregular matings.

A descendant of an old regional Dutch family liked to remark in the 1950s that the population of the world of the future would be "all kinds mixed together"—and there was nothing one could do about it, the man added with an air of being reconciled to the prospect.

In November of 1880 a stir was aroused in Kingston by the news that a man described as a "rich farmer" of Gardiner in Ulster County had taken steps to stop the proposed marriage in Kingston of his ward, Ada Deyo, descendant of an old Ulster County Huguenot family, to one of the rich farmer's farm hands named Wesley Sampson who was black (and not accepted as a Schoharie) and wore a red shirt. The rich farmer when he learned that his ward and the black farmhand had visited clergymen in Rondout and Kingston and asked them to marry Ada and himself and had been refused marriage, summoned his ward and, getting out a trunk, proposed she fill it with clothing and other personal belongings, because he was going to send her to a boarding school in New York City to separate her from her black lover. She was at the time believed to be engaged to a young white neighboring farmer of whom her guardian approved. Ada affected that she was willing to leave for New York, but at the first opportunity slipped away and joined her lover Wesley.

The two visited friends in the Town of Marbletown where they found encouragement in their hopes especially from a white man named James Cantine, of an old Huguenot white family and his black wife. The Cantines gathered together all the available bottles in their household, removed the corks, and charred them. With this charred cork they annointed all the visible body parts of Ada, her arms, legs and face, and thus disguised the couple called upon the Dutch Reformed minister of Marbletown, who suspected no deception and married them. The Kingston *Freeman* printed this story and commented (with no reference to the apparently happily married state of the James Cantines) on the dreadful life that awaited Ada as the wife of a black man, and ended the story with the words, "but she claims to be happy."

Happy she may have been, for in and near the hamlet of Lapala, in the hills west of Kingston to which the couple went to live in what the *Freeman* described as a "hut," there are still, it is said, a number of people who bear the name of Sampson, and may or may not be the descendants of Ada and Wesley Sampson.

And while Kingston people went on being stirred by tales of mixed marriages their City was being brought into wider attention in a very different way. Churches devoted to Christian sects favored by black people were doing well on Broadway. At the same time a neighborhood of black people was forming beside the Esopus Creek a bit beyond Higginsville where Catholic bluestone quarrymen on their way to the Wilbur waterfront refreshed themselves and were sometimes assaulted by Kingston Protestant toughs.

The blacks' land was in those days subject to floods, like that of the Schoharies, and so not valued by whites. It was now and then flooded by the Esopus Creek, sometimes disasterously. And so blacks formed a neighborhood called Mutton Hollow near where now Route 28 connects with Kingston. The name was given because white people saw a resemblance between the hair on the heads of black people and the wool on the heads of sheep or muttons—hence Mutton Hollow. The Artist de Lisser in his *Picturesque Ulster* photographed a group of shy young black girls,

"Lambs from Mutton Hollow"

with the caption "Lambs from Mutton Hollow."

One of the first public multi-racial events in Kingston was the "Grand Celebration" in honor of the one hundred and first anniversary of the birth of Abraham Lincoln held on February 14, 1910 at the Franklin Street A.M.E. Zion Church. The white Kingston school superintendant broke precedents, giving an address from the same platform as black speakers in a black church.

Grand Celebration

By the Colored Citizens of Kingston in honor of the One Hundred and First Anniversary of the birth of Abraham Lincoln at Franklin St. A. M. E. Z. Church,

Monday, February 14, 1910

Commencing at 8 P. M.

Program in honor of Abraham Lincoln's 100th birthday, February 14, 1910, in Kingston

3.
Ethnic Accommodations and Music
1870s

On October 19 1871, as the tumultuous seventies of railroad building, speculations and social and ethnic turmoil got underway, a reporter in the *Rondout Daily Freeman* touched on the state of music in Kingston in an article headlined "A Musical People." "There is hardly a house," the report began, "that does not own a piano, (parlor) organ or melodeon and when one walks through the streets at night sweet strains of music greet him at every step." Even making a reasonable discount for a reporter's occasional exaggeration, and the fact that the instruments mentioned were those most often advertised in Kingston newspapers, there is other ample evidence that music played a large part in Kingston life by whites and blacks even during a decade of economic stress. This was especially the case after the increased numbers of music-loving German emigrants reached Rondout after the mid-19th century.

Even before the pivotal year of 1848 when the failure of revolutionary movements on the continent of Europe plus the boost soon given to socialism by the *Communist Manifesto* of Marx and Engels had sent many Germans of the many German states to leave their homelands in the hope of a more friendly atmosphere for social reform as well as for economic betterment.

Wherever they went in many parts of the world and especially of the United States the Germans carried with them a decided love of the kind of music—vocal and instrumental—of their home background. Earlier Kingston had its own different musical culture with black domestic servants playing for dancing by the whites as well as blacks (as Calvinism eased), mothers lulling babies to sleep with traditional Dutch cradle songs; Yankee singing school teachers had come to Kingston. One time "great singer" Lewis Edson had settled in Woodstock as did his son Lewis, Jr. whose book, *The Social Harmonist* of 1800 was used by Edson to instruct local singers and those of the surrounding countryside. By the mid-nineteenth century Lowell Mason's book on singing in church services had edged out such texts as Edson's. A brass band, a Brass Temperance Band, several German bands and a cornet band were in active existence in Kingston. And the German bands and German singers were performing on a variety of occasions and teaching their music even to non-German Kingstonians and Rondouters. The *Freeman* reported that Kingston boys often followed German bands as they blew and banged their way from street to street. A trio of players of instruments invented by Germany's Adoplhe Sax was organized in Rondout a year before Sax had thought up the presently-popular saxophone. German emigrants tended to display in public a broader background in cultural matters than did other ethnic groups. This had been given emphasis by such public events as the celebration with much music in 1869 of the centenary of the birth of Friedrich von Humboldt, a path-breaking explorer and worker in the natural sciences, whose book *Cosmos* would become a classic of its time.

The proceedings of the centenary celebration held on the top of Golden Hill followed marching by massed celebrants to music from Rondout. There was music by members of several German singing societies, a gymnastic display by the Rondout Turnverein, and a variety of other tributes to German cultural achievements. There was the reading of an original local German poem in honor of von Humbolt and the unveiling of a portrait of von Humboldt. When the principal German language speaker chosen for the occasion proved unable to attend, the substitute chosen was Gen. George H. Sharpe, a non-German lawyer of broad intellectual and language background as well as an astute politician. Sharpe gave the German audience an appraisal of their hero in his own "characteristic style" and was enthusiastically applauded.

Through the century the various German immigrants in the Hudson Valley had built up their sense of brotherhood by singing society meetings, often held in Kingston, awarding prizes to those judged by such musical experts as Dr. Leopold Damrosch, father of the later well known Walter Damrosch. These contests were called Sängerfests. They became lively features of the Kingston year and were widely and even extravagantly praised in newspapers which however would count the number of barrels of locally brewed beer consumed, as well as praise the quality of the music to the skies.

When the Overlook Mountain House in Woodstock, largely financed by Kingston businessmen, opened in June 1872 the hotel band was a German one, Wagner's, from Rondout which played the "Overlook Waltz," a composition of their leader. And that July the Kingston *Daily Freeman* reported that black barber Jacob Arnold amused his customers by keeping time while lathering and shaving to the melodious trilling of the singing caged birds he kept in his shop. Some of the birds had benefitted as singers from centuries of musical training of their ancestors. And some local white barbers were themselves musicians who sang and played a variety of instruments when business was slack. Some of the immigrants of various ethnic sources, some musical and some not, rose to become prosperous leading citizens, active in business, professional and public affairs while continuing to be interested in music.

Notable among the Irish immigrants were Luke Noone and James J. Sweeney who rose to the very top of the bluestone industry. And notable too was George Francis Von Beck of lager beer brewing and Mansion House fame and who was perhaps once the richest man in Rondout—and in some ways the most puzzling and in some ways unfortunate.

4.
The Ups and Downs of Immigrant George Francis Von Beck

George Francis Von Beck emigrated from Germany in the early 1830s, and following a spectacular business success ended up before a lunacy commission on a claim that he was incapable of managing his own complicated affairs. His background in Europe and the United States, as known by the public, was largely based on bits and pieces which Von Beck revealed from time to time, and which sometimes were contradictory. But the legend he left behind appeared to be fascinating to Kingston people and remains so to this very day.

The legend began from his birth as the eighteenth century ended into an aristocratic French or German family. His father was an officer serving in Napoleon's army in Napoleon's doomed march on Moscow—the father died on the march. Young George Francis was left an orphan and was harshly brought up by strangers. He managed to acquire skill in civil engineering and became mayor of the town of Kayermayer in Germany. His taking the side of the people in a revolutionary movement led to harassing by the victorious conservative government of his German state. He was forced to emigrate to the United States. Almost penniless he trudged the American roads as a peddler and exhibitor of views of European scenery by means of a showman's box which he carried on his back and operated with a crank. Eventually he went on a selling trip along the D & H Canal cranking his showman's box for a small fee, and peddling odds and ends.

He settled down to work as a farmhand on a Canal-side farm for a man whom he soon persuaded to stake him to the captaincy of a coal-carrying D&H canal barge or boat. He took up life in the then commercially lively canal village of Eddyville located at the head of the Rondout Creek tidewater where he embarked on setting his acute business shrewdness loose in a succession of profitable ventures there and in adjoining Rondout. Speculating in the rapidly rising real estate market, setting up a pioneer lager beer brewery and a related malting house, and other ventures, made him one of the richest men in Rondout. He married Jane Denning of Eddyville by whom he had a large family. He became involved in firemanic and militia activities.

Most splendid to the eyes of the beholders of the three militia units he financed was the company of Guards, impressive for their fine horses, elegant uniforms and ostrich-plumed head-gear. Von Beck also managed the Rondout Mansion House built by James McEntee, a D & H engineer.

The Guards were said to have been modelled in their military precision and fine equipment on a famous German military unit. Although Von Beck was censured by Calvinistic and Sabbatarian Rondouters and Kingstonians for drilling his Guards on Sundays, he was popular enough to become elected the first president of the Village of Rondout when that governmental unit was formed in 1849. Soon he was also respected as owner as well as manager of the huge three-story cast iron balconied and cupolaed Mansion House, more elegant than any hostelry in old Kingston for the splendor of its furnishings and the quality of its service.

With George Von Beck's militia unit, the Jefferson Guards, gorgeously dressed with stage-coach to uptown Kingston outside the Mansion House, lithograph from State Library in Albany.

But fate in those greatest days of Von Beck's glory was nursing a heavy blow for him. On February 26, 1869 following a spell of failing health, he was felled by what he called "a stroke of palsy" and thereafter suffered periods of "lying senseless on my back" while his business records and other property were being stolen, Von Beck claimed. He was said by some to have become ill-tempered and to have suffered from "delusions of being robbed."

So Von Beck appeared before the Lunacy Commission. The hearing stirred much excitement and was even the subject of a report reprinted in a partly paraphrased shape by the conservative Kingston *Argus* from the scandal-loving (and politically conservative) The *New York Herald* in a first page story (as reprinted in the Kingston *Argus*), two columns to the right of another front page story headed "Ulster or Ulcer?" in which Ulster County was attacked (at a time of great political turmoil as Democratic quarrymen confronted their Republican Whig opponents violently around election days) as notorious for its abundant crimes. "Rondout," said the Herald as quoted by the Kingston *Argus* (formerly named the *Republican*, and still of strong right wing Whig views, and not to be confused with the Democratic Ulster *Argus*), "is a pest hole of incarnate demons in a county known for its criminality." The liberal Democratic (anti-Whig) Ulster *Argus* lustily sprang to the defense of his hometown of Rondout by quoting a reporter of James Gordon Bennett's scandal-spreading *Herald* who once confessed to him that his paper encouraged reporters to work "a thread of fact into a sensational novel."

The *Herald* (as reprinted in the Kingston *Argus*) under a headline of "The Von Beck Lunacy" printed what purported to be a biographical sketch of Von Beck which began as a confused version of its subject's early life, very different from the one circulated by Von Beck himself.

Clearly, the Whig columnists of the *New York Herald* and Kingston *Argus* had chosen an aging, ill man who was suspected of living as a victim, in the Whigs' political war against the Rondout Democrats. They charged Von Beck with not having been strictly honest in his dealings with the canal company, with having married Jane Denning when he clearly had left a wife and children in Germany. This last was true, but much of the rest of the biography was not. During the years that followed the attack on Von Beck, his German children, now grown, arrived to add their efforts in making life hard for the no longer very able old man. His children had him brought before the Lunacy Commission in Kingston. (Such a Commission was appointed for the purpose of determining whether an individual was of competent mind.) In spite of this, his local renown became restablished in Rondout where it flourishes to this very day.

For much of the rest of his life, Von Beck continued to be troubled by the Lunacy Commission and after his death the probating of his will was delayed by disputes between descendants on both sides of the Atlantic and while his legend as an immigrant hero went on being kept in circulation.

The treatment of the aging and infirm Von Beck was a good example of the power being gained by unscrupulous newspaper publishers like the elder James Gordon Bennett, and the publisher of the Kingston *Argus* (and an emigrant from Scotland), to destroy the reputations of chosen victims while using large staffs of good newspaper reporters—as Bennett did—whom he had set to work effectively covering the Civil War. Such unprovoked political assaults as that in the Kingston *Argus* on Von Beck and thus Rondout, were characteristic of the methods used by the elder James Gordon Bennett (then close to the end of his career) in building circulation for his paper, and he may have had no other reason of his own for launching his double bombardment against Von Beck and his home neighborhood of Rondout. The Kingston *Argus* as a conservative party upholder may have reprinted the *Herald* volley against Von Beck and Rondout for political reasons. But their assault appears to have left Von Beck's legend unimpaired and he remains a local hero to this day. His Mansion House was left largely untouched except for some restoration by the Urban Renewal Project of the 1960s which was to demolish so much of the Rondout of Von Beck's time.

Von Beck had advanced the accomodation of immigrants into the life of Kingston and Rondout by setting an example to show other immigrants that great material success was not out of the question for immigrants. As the nineteenth century entered its final decades many even recent Kingston immigrants had achieved success in many ways.

Most of the many immigrants who had chosen to live in Kingston, like people everywhere on our planet, had devoted their energies to making a living or aiming at accumulating a surplus that might make them rich and powerful. Yet there are fortunately always some others who choose to spend at least part of their lives in serving their fellows and their community in ways that can never make them rich. Outstanding in Kingston among these was a man named Richard Lalor Burtsell, born in 1840 of Irish and English emigrant ancestry who reached Rondout in 1891 as a not altogether willing emigrant from New York City to serve as pastor of the Catholic Church of St. Mary. Father Burtsell had been sent to Rondout, of which he knew nothing, by his bishop in order it was said to exile him from New York where he had openly supported the right of his friend, Father McGlynn to espouse the Single Tax doctrine of reformer Henry George. George who had been defeated for mayor of the City in 1886 was continuing to play a controversial part in New York. Already Burtsell had made a name for himself in New York by his energetic work among the less fortunate classes—he had founded the Church of St. Benedict the Moor, for Catholic blacks, among other projects.

In Rondout he threw his remarkable energies into building up St. Mary's and into taking a vigorous part in many Kingston and Rondout community secular as well as Catholic activities. He helped the Catholic Benedictine Sanitarium which was to become a big hospital, and he also helped the non-sectarian Kingston City Hospital then being founded. He served with distinction on the library and other boards.

In all of these his ability to rouse enthusiasm and stimulate contributions from others to worthwhile community causes came to be greatly valued and even indispensable. So much so that in 1902 he was honored at a reception in the Armory building sponsored by a committee of the most prominent men and women of the City and attended by cheering people of every religious belief known in Kingston.

Again in 1904 on Burtsell's return from Rome where he had been consulted by the Pope, he came back to St. Mary's as a newly created Monsignor. A procession in his honor along illuminated Kingston streets while fireworks crackled and blazed led to another reception at which many more testimonials as to what the Monsignor had accomplished for his city were a part of the hearty program of tribute.

Ethnic and religious prejudices had formed a part of life in Kingston from the days of first contact with the local Esopus people, and it was now publicly recognized that a long step toward removing this kind of prejudice had been taken. And that in this process Msg. Burtsell had played a remarkably significant role.

The History of Ulster County edited in 1907 by Judge A.T. Clearwater put Msg. Burtsell's place in Kingston well, concluding its account of the "spontaneous demonstration" of 1902 with this estimate of Burtsell's work in a remarkably multi-ethnic city once rent by religious and ethnic conflict: "He has been an instrument to break down barriers of prejudice and to unite the people of this city in common interests."

Ethnic and religious prejudice would recur in Kingston but never again on the scale they had shown before Msg. Burtsell had worked to dispell them. Old prejudices were stirred up on a substantial scale in the late 1800's and and early 1900's when it was proposed to unite the villages of Kingston and Rondout to form a single city, yet once united the two remain essentially united today, even as their ethnic mixture grows ever more complex. And this improvement was much due to the rigorous eforts of Msg. Burtsell.

5.
Kingston, the Rhine, the Catskills and the Hudson 1873

Once the Civil War had ended, and Reconstruction and the frenzied expansion and industrial tumult of the Gilded Age was having its own profitable way, Kingston and its surrounding region began to be written about as a place to which tourists came for adventure and pleasure as travel writers like Darby had earlier predicted they would. On August 20, 1873, (as copied from a recent number of the *Springfield [Mass.] Republican*, the Kingston *Daily Freeman* published an unsigned article in which it was stated that Kingston was "the base of operation for the (Catskill mountain) country for tourists." It characterized "Kingston on the Hudson" with its thriving river port of Rondout, known by "the high-sounding title of the City of Kingston" (in reference to the recent uniting of the two former villages) as a "queer medley of old Dutch sleepiness, Irish briskness and genuine New York culture." It was a fine compliment to Kingston. And more, it was a mixture of features with a very individual and attractive character of its own (like no other place on earth), even though the reporter added a none too favorable judgment of its whiskey-serving hotels, perhaps stimulated to his lively bit of characterization by his clever and noted editor Samuel Bowles (who was known as a connoisseur of American places).

By the 1870s, the Catskill Mountains were beginning to be written about as a rapidly growing summer resort for American urbanites and Southerners.

By 1886, Kingstonians had cause to brag when their city positively burst into print as a significant part of the long tourist-haunted, historic Hudson Valley. The Mid-Hudson region was now being judged worthy of being called by Europeans as well as Americans "the American Rhine," a designation which gave an added air of romance to Kingston. And this mention of Kingston and its relation to the Hudson Valley and the Rhine appeared, not in some obscure provincial publication but in a book by a "special correspondent" of that world renowned newspaper, *The Times of London,* then widely known from the power of its editorial voice as "The Thunderer."

The book was *A Visit to the States,* and in a chapter titled "The American Rhine" the Times man covered, in lively and very approving fashion, the charms of the Valley between Albany and Poughkeepsie. (Many Britons preferred at that time to avoid using the full name of the United States in order to avoid stirring up recollections of the losing of its colonial reign in the war of 1776-1783.) The *Times* man leaves Albany to descend the Valley with an effort at giving Albany a truly Rhenish touch. He writes of the Van Rensselaer family as having inhabited "a castle" called "Rensselaerstein," but Hudson River steamboats were also given their due by being referred to as "palatial" and the largest vessels of their sort in the world. Iceboating was mentioned as a special winter Hudson River sport.

The diligent Quakers who had moved to the City of Hudson and the celibate Shakers who had followed Mother Ann Lee from England to near the Valley are not overlooked. Nor is that east bank native of the Valley, former President Martin Van Buren or the Helderbergs of the west bank. As the Helderbergs fade away and the higher Catskill Mountains appear "in all their glory," the *Times* man finds it hard to restrain his enthusiasm for these heights facing the Hudson River from the West. From a majestic wall extending all the way to their visible ending, with Kingston "nestling" against the hills with Rondout beside it, extending for many miles before yielding to the Highlands and the Lower River (which the *Times* writer does not include under Chapter XLII), lies "The American Rhine." He exhibits in his ablest style the "cloves," and the waterfalls dashing down the mountain walls before he reaches his greatest Catskills enthusiasms—"one of the grandest mountain views in the Atlantic seaboard" he states. "Upon the tops of these mountains right at the verge, are perched two or three great summer hotels with chain cables to anchor them in the high winds. From the brink of the overhanging rocks, where it seems one could plunge thousands of feet into the valley below, the scene is unrivalled. At the distance of 10 or 12 miles the Hudson River stretches a silvery streak . . . which can be traced for almost 100 miles. . . . Its diminutive steamboats slowly move and, like a shining thread, as the sun strikes the car windows [of the railroad]. . . . The abrupt mountainside brings the valley almost beneath one's feet, the farm buildings looking like children's little toy houses, the trees like dwarfed bushes, and the alternating fields like the squares on a chessboard. Wagons crawl like little ants" upon the "dark blue Berkshire hills . . . 40 miles away. Behind them as a misty haze rises the White Mountains of New Hampshire."

To bring the reader down to the romantic and almost "Alpine" aspect of the Catskills, the Times writer assures his readers that "In earlier days the Catskills were the origin of most of the American native traditions." He gives as examples Washington Irving's Rip Van Winkle and novelist James Fenimore Cooper's Natty Bumpo. "Beguiled by Hudson's ghostly crew," he wrote, Rip "drank from the flagon and slept his sleep of 20 years."

Facing the wall of the Catskills southward until the wall appears to end behind Kingston, for many miles as far as Poughkeepsie lies the long, glamorous strip of land from which the view of the Catskills from the east bank and the glorious sunsets they provide may be enjoyed at their best. Here on well landscaped parks may be glimpsed the fine houses of members of the Livingston family, descendants of the Scottish "Earls of Linlithgow." The *Times* man gives as examples of these "noble estates" Rokeby (which is opposite Kingston) showing its tower rising above the "encircling trees" of its "undulating park," with the steam yacht *Nourmahal* of Rokeby's owner William B. Astor resting at anchor offshore.

The reporter always did his best to draw attention to features that might suggest similarities between the German and the American Rhines. He told how William Beekman, native of the German Rhineland, after accumulating much land in the Kingston vicinity, crossed the Hudson (to what would later on be called the rich man's or manorial side), married a Livingston daughter and built near the "Rhine Cliffe" an "ancient stone structure, which is still standing."

And the reporter went on to depict the remarkable region of which Kingston formed a part. A "noble estate" across the Hudson from Kingston the reporter described was Montgomery Place named for a scion of a noble Irish family, General Montgomery. He had died fighting on the anti-British side in the American Revolution. His widow was Janet Livingston of Clermont. Clermont, on its thirteen thousand acres detached from the manor of Livingston's, 165,000, (and known as the Lower Manor) had been the home of Chancellor Robert R. Livingston. Among these estates of heirs to old blood and old money were a few distinguished new money people, notably William Dinsmore who had made millions by building up the Adams Express Company which then had 5,000 wagons on the roads delivering packages to Americans, so the snobbish *Times* man wrote.

A few miles below Kingston, on the west bank, the 1,200 acre estate of Robert Livingston Pell arouses the wonder of the *Times* man. There fine apples, produced by Pell's orchard of 25,000 trees, are shipped to all parts of the world. A large vineyard of Isabella grapes is a feature of the place, (as are ten large ponds in which the new science of pisciculture is carried on, involving the growing of many varieties of fish). Ten miles of graveled roads and paths offered romantic drives and walks about the estate. (The mansion house, according to a 1871-72 Gazetteer of Ulster County, "is designed in the Roman style, and the large dining room ceiling is decorated with copies made at great cost of some of the most noted examples of Old Masters' art.") Mr. Pell also owned much landed property elsewhere and close by, including the summit of Woodstock's Overlook Mountain. This very desirable site for a mountain house (for paying guests), by pre-Civil War days was known to command the finest view of any summit in all the Catskills. Pell lost the Overlook mountaintop on what was once called in his honor Pell's Mountain because of the tragic death of his son and the onset of the turbulent seventies with their alternating triumphs and economic woes. Others acquired the Pell's Mountain site and there built the fashionable Overlook Mountain House, almost entirely with Kingston capital, designed and built by a Kingston architect builder named Van Wagenen, and leased to John Lasher of Palatine German Hudson Valley ancestry. Lasher for a while was the successful host of the elegant Rondout Mansion House, with its cupola and iron balconies. Many stockholders in the Overlook Mountain House were Kingston businessmmen who hoped to thrive by supplying the hotel with materials needed for its construction and operation.

Although the hotel entertained many notable people—among them author Herman Melville and his wife and children, and theater wizard Steele MacKaye author of the play *Hazel Kirke*, which had set a record for its long long run on the New York stage. MacKaye spent a miserable summer there trying in vain to write a successful sequel to *Hazel Kirke.* The hotel was not a consistent money-maker for Kingston, although in 1873, President U.S. Grant, accompanied by an aide of Grant's during the Civil War, Kingston's General George H. Sharpe, spent a day and a night at the Overlook Mountain House. His stay was widely reported in the newspapers and spread interest in the House. The ladies staying at the hotel had elaborately decorated the House for Grant's visit with mountain greenery inside and out (a form of decoration Grant was known to like). In the evening the young black waiters, all Civil War veterans and students at Lincoln University, sang Civil War songs for Grant. In the morning, under the direction of Abby Hutchinson, of the once famous Hutchinson family of singers for abolition, civil rights for women and other worthy causes, a mass chorus of 100 voices sang for Grant at the very top of Overlook Mountain. That night General Grant spent with the Sharpe family, in their mansard-roofed mansion facing what is now Academy Green Park in Kingston, shook hands with an estimated thousands and spoke at midnight from a balcony to many more Kingstonians who had not had a chance to shake hands with the hero.

The *Times of London* in 1873 had printed a report of Grant's visit to Overlook Mountain, which is visible from many parts of Kingston. The reporter of the 1888 reprint chose for his "Visit to the States" a variant of a tall story of a kind then being relished by Britons, as well as Americans. The tale dealt with the then President as having expressed wondering astonishment in 1873 when shown an immense rounded boulder poised on the very edge of the view-catching Overlook cliff as if in defiance of the the law of gravity and of common sense. Manager Lasher then formally presented the immense rock to the General, with the remark that it would make a good parlor ornament. The often photographed Rock is still poised on the edge of the cliff, facing Kingston. It has been known since 1873 as the "President's Rock" and Grant admirers still touch it in awe. And ladies of the past were seen kissing it.

President Grant's Rock, presented to him as a practical joke after he admired it. The manager of Overlook Mountain House made out over the rock to Ulysses S. Grant. The presentation of that rock was mentioned in the Times of London. From stereograph in collection of Alf Evers

6.
City Hall, an Armory and a Gerrymander 1872–79

BUILDING OF KINGSTON'S AMBITIOUS CITY HALL COULD HARDLY HAVE BEEN undertaken at a more cheerless time. City Hall construction began at the beginning of the first year of a five-year-long national economic recession. Many industries were paralyzed and the unemployed suffered while political corruption flourished in Washington under close friends of U.S. Grant himself; and in New York under Boss Tweed. In Ulster County the recession was helping bring disaster to the bluestone industry, and it saw (as a result of much agitation) by 1879-1880 the Gerrymandering of the boundaries of the town of Kingston in which the city of Kingston lies partially embedded—and the creation as well of the new town of Ulster (from part of the Town of Kingston) as an unsuccessful attempt at a cure for the Town's troubles, including unemployment in the bluestone industry and a benefitting of the local Republican Party, and a throttling of the Democratic Party's growing power in Ulster County.

In spite of the many obstacles of the troubled decade, construction and occupation of the proud and confident-looking City Hall had gone boldly ahead. On the commanding and still forest-covered elevation the imposing City Hall of the new city would stand and so too by 1880, in the freshly Gerrymandered city, would stand nearby the massive and deliberately intimidating Armory. Both the attractive City Hall and the grim Armory were built during the agitated years of 1870-1883 even as America suffered, while the City Hall arose, a prolonged economic recession and its first national railway strike when National Guardsmen were called out to intimidate and even to shoot strikers. There was also the fear that the supposed excesses of the modern Paris Commune which followed the end of the Franco-Prussian War would nimbly leap the Atlantic and taint America and cause the poorer classes to rise up against their betters and riot in the streets. Newspaper headlines in these years gave Americans in Kingston and elsewhere their first taste of a fear of "Communists," even as the building of the City Hall continued.

The Armory, of dull red brick on a dark bluestone base, completed in 1879-1880, and the nearby elegant new City Hall, built in 1873-1875, may well serve as good symbols of the two opposite sides of the decade—1873-1883. While the City Hall symbolizes civic pride even in hard times and the expectation shown by its ornamentation and Victorian exuberance and grandeur of a prosperous future for the united city, the Armory, with its crenellated tower equipped with slit windows for defense, symbolized the chilling fears of the civic riots then sweeping the country at the same time.

As the recession and the railway (the first one in the nation) strike ended (and the City Hall grounds were cleared and enlarged) there was an official New York State urge to safeguard dwellers in New York cities by building fortress-like state armories for the use of militia and to intimidate would-be rioters by the buildings' fierce appearance. There was local opposition in the seventies to building such an armory on Broadway (then newly

City Bonds For Sale.

By direction of the Common Council of the City of Kingston, there will be offered for sale on

TUESDAY, DEC. 8th, 1874,

At 10 o'clock A. M., at the Court House in said city,

$15,000 City of Kingston Bonds,

issued for the purpose of building the City Hall. **The Bonds** are coupon Bonds and bear **seven per cent. interest** payable semi-annually, on the 15th **days** of January and July. The principal is payable **as follows:**

10 Bonds	$100	each due Jan. 15,	1892
8 "	500	" " " "	1894
10 "	1,000	" " " "	1897

A bond of $100 will be offered for sale and the purchaser to have the privilege of taking $5,000 or any part thereof at price bid.

No bid less than par and accrued interest from July 15th, 1874 will be entertained.

CHARLES BRAY,
Chairman Finance Committee.

Kingston Armory, after it was later painted in a lighter shade after New York State ceased wanting it to appear foreboding, from post card in Alf Evers collection

named Union Avenue, to celebrate both the preservation of the national union in 1865 and the uniting of Kingston and Rondout). Nevertheless, the Armory, of dull red brick on a dark bluestone base and with a Medieval-looking crenellated tower rising above with slit windows, was built and still looks down since 1880 on passersby, although after some periods of disuse and deterioration the building would be converted with federal New Deal help during the Depression of the 1930s into a gentler and enlarged civic auditorium and recreation center, close to City Hall, the central High School and the Carnegie Library.

By the time the City Hall's designer, English-born Arthur Crooks of New York, had produced his plans for the City Hall, the earlier taste for civic structures that echoed ancient classical Greek and Roman models had run its course and Gothic Revival was reflecting a rise in Romantic tastes. Crooks' design reflected, not the churchly Gothic like that of the 1861 City Hall of New Haven, Connecticut, but the secular and urban Gothic of old public structures in northern Italy.

With its otherwise massive-looking red brick walls with their heaviness lightened by light-colored bands, City Hall inevitably invites attention by its appropriate site on the top of the hill almost on the boundary line between the former villages of Rondout and Kingston.

Above the third story of its tower the City Hall dramatically culminated in an ornamented corbelled stage which contained a large fire bell visible through openings all around.

Kingston City Hall, from brochure, "Hudson-Fulton Souvenir of Kingston" 1909

When a fire in 1928 required restoration, Gothic Revival and all things Victorian had become unfashionable. Guidebook author Bruce Wallace in his popular *The Hudson River by Daylight* would airily dismiss the City Hall as merely "aldermanic" in style as Georgian Revival was in vogue. It was then proposed by some to demolish the old City Hall after the 1928 fire and substitute a new one in the Georgian Revival manner as better suited to Kingston's "colonial" character. (The word "Colonial," so much detested in the 1770s, had by the late nineteenth century acquired in many American minds a romantic quality, with overtones of powdered wigs and courtly manners. But an attempt at restoration was judged less expensive than demolition and replacing by Georgian Revival. As a result a restoration with simplification of some Victorian Gothic Revival details was adopted and carried through as less costly.) Yet agitation to demolish the building went on even as the once sharp edge of anti-all-things-Victorian dulled. Then the enactment in the Congress of a Housing Authority in the 1940s added fuel to the urge to demolish much of Rondout as well as the old City Hall. But times had changed and the magnificent old City Hall found enough support from citizens who appreciated its quality to guarantee its restoration and its return to use as the proud center of Kingston government.

Meanwhile, as the City Hall was rising and being put to use, a phenomenon known as Gerrymandering came to Kingston as a by-product of the almost total unemployment of the bluestone quarrymen of that part of the Town of Kingston in which plentiful and relatively easily quarried layers of Devonian bluestone was found. These quarries had been worked by Irish Catholic workers now thrown into umployment by the recession of the 1870s, which lasted for more than five years.

The members of the Kingston Common Council sat down to work in their new chamber in the new City Hall while the recession of the '70s still gnawed at the City and the succession of other troubles that plagued the decade continued unabated. The year 1876 was to be marked by unprecedented violence at the local polls on the part of unemployed quarry voters in that part of the Town of Kingston and its suburbs where major bluestone quarries were located and where a decline in the prices of the stone swelled the ranks of the unemployed.

The Ulster County Board of Supervisors succeeded in gaining the approval of the Republican-controlled State Legislature, in which Kingston's General George H. Sharpe played a key role, to enact a plan for separating the quarry district from what its landowners called the "taxpayers district," which would ensure future Republican instead of previously Democratic political control of the town. The resulting clipping of some, and adding bits of others to neighboring towns and setting up the whole new Town of Ulster from what had been part of the Town of Kingston proved to be a masterpiece of the art of Gerrymandering.

The art of Gerrymandering is named in honor of Elbridge Gerry, a signer of the Declaration of Independence, Vice-President of the United States, and a clever New England politician (whose family had Livingston connections). One of Gerry's early efforts at boundary shifting in order to alter election results puzzled an observer who remarked that the result looked on the new map somewhat but not quite altogether like the shape of a salamander. No, he was told, that is "a Gerrymander"—and thus a new word soon became a useful addition to the American version of the English language.

The quarry workers had charged that there was a conspiracy on the part of bluestone dealers to keep the prices of bluestone flagging low, until they became so low that there would be no payment for the workers' labor. In actuality the demand for the flagging was dropping off because of the hard times and possibly the expected advent of artificial or Portland cement (invented in England back in the 1820s) for use in concrete sidewalks and walls instead of bluestone. Quarry workers were concentrated in such settlements as Jockey Hill, Hallihan's Hill and Stony Hollow, on land mostly owned by Kingston quarry developers who allowed workers to build shanties of their own or to rent very simple cottages on bluestone land. The creekside stoneyards at Rondout and Wilbur before the recession of the seventies had been crowded with hard (derby) hatted and red shirted workers. Derby hats protected workers' heads from flying fragments of stone the quarry workers called "spalts" which were sent flying off when hammers struck chisels and chisels struck bluestone. Now the stoneyards and quarries lay silent.

Elsewhere in parts of the Town which unlike the infertile quarry settlements, had been settled on deep and fertile land without quarry possibilities far back in the days of colonial Dutch and British rule, the land was worked by long established members of old colonial farm families who were doing well growing grain on good soil and now resented paying taxes to help the starving quarrymen on the "paupers' List" who paid no taxes directly because they owned no land and had no money because they were unemployed. The Town of Kingston expenses for poor relief one year in the '70s came, it was said, to amount to $15,975.99 per year while those of the rest of Ulster County were only $484. Local Democratic bosses that same year gave much needed help to the unemployed on the "Paupers' List." And some of those so helped gratefully responded by using violence to keep the opposing taxpaying Republicans from even voting. By 1876, election disorders were reaching a peak and were being widely reported in State newspapers.

An additional part of the Gerrymandering involved attaching to Woodstock the old, partly quarrying, pastoral Dutch-settled valley now known as Zena, which had previously been part of the Town of Kingston. The people of what is now Zena and some in its old stone houses had been among those complaining about the amount of taxes being levied on them while non-landowning quarrymen of the same town paid none.

The southern border of the City of Kingston became by the beginning of the twentieth century fairly regular, bounded by the once bustling Eddyville Canal and mill center (cotton, lumber and flour) which was a mere shattered shadow of its Canal days following the end of the great Canal times, plus a disastrous fire and a monstrous flood, both of which joined to smash Eddyville and destroy all signs of its one-time prosperity of the days when Von Beck and Cornell had been able to lay the foundation of their large fortune there.

7.
Birth Pangs of the City
1872

THE BIRTH OF THE CITY OF KINGSTON IN 1872 HAD NOT BEEN THE RESULT of a loving relationship between its parents, the Villages of Kingston and Rondout. The parents, as Judge A. T. Clearwater in 1907 would permit it to be put in the *History of Ulster County* he edited, were known as having had a "sub-acid feeling" for each other (a term well known to Ulster County apple growers as applied to fruit with a mixture of acid and sweet). It was a feeling which the birth of a civic offspring did little after 1872 to alter on the side of sweetness.

Rondout had been the first of the two Villages to realize that were the two to continue to exist side by side in the sub-acid spirit of rivalry, jealousy and fellowship they would not thrive. And searing commercial antagonisms would flourish. James G. Lindsley was the manager or "agent" of the Newark (N.J.) Limestone and Cement Company which had become (with bluestone) Rondout's leader in gnawing away at the bedrock of the region. Lindsley had been a leader in urging Rondout to become a separate city. With Lindsley as guide, a committee of Rondout male citizens was formed to apply to the State Legislature for a charter to incorporate their village as a city to be named Rondout. This would completely separate Rondout in name and government from Kingston. The principal reason for Rondout wanting to become a separate city was its much larger and faster-growing and differently based population and its industrial development in which Kingston at first shared only slightly.

Kingstonians at once saw the proposed City of Rondout—a separate city of larger population right beside them—as a busy rival and even a menace. Kingston citizens formed a committee which pushed for a charter under which Kingston and Rondout, different as they were, might work together to organize a single united city. A period of furious debate followed in the press, on street corners, in barrooms, at dinner tables. Rondouters made clear their belief that a Kingston clique of old family members, and a surplus of lawyers, bankers and real estate owners gave Kingston people no right to behave as autocrats and dictate policy in the proposed formation of a city.

The debates between the people of the two villages bristled with none-too-complimentary comments on each other. The Kingstonians stated flatly that Rondout's considerable superiority in population meant nothing because Rondout's recently acquired superabundance of mere children, hordes of immigrant non-citizens with great numbers of transients coming and going had made the number of Rondout residents seem much larger than it actually was. Fewer Rondouters owned real property or were properly qualified voters the Kingstonians asserted. Representatives of Rondout and Kingston journeyed to Albany and presented their cases to the appropriate legislative committee. The Legislative committee's members listened patiently to the heated demands of both sides and then advised the men in plain terms "to go home and cool off."

And then, having returned home and thought the matter over, the new joint Committeemen (from both villages) essentially cooled off enough to come up with an amended compromised and joint request. The names of the men—there were still no women—now appointed to the joint committee show a greater effort to combine people from various levels of the population. Kingstonians for example now included limestone and cement entrepreneurs and Irish immigrants and Wilbur quarry owner Luke Noone, who had grown prosperous enough to play an important role in Kingston's life. Noone had been among the first of all Irish immigrants in Kingston life as an enthusastic Democrat (and supporter of the Catholic church). Lindsley, of the original Rondout committee, was apparently still the most active of his group. He had overseen the burrowing of the Newark Limestone and Cement Company like moles into the Vleitberg—and had then demolished (and converted to saleable cement) the peak which had been a valued landmark to Hudson River pilots. Yet no one would deny that Lindsley had also brought new jobs and money to their hometown of Rondout and shown skill in managing the village's public affairs. As the new joint committee began work they were aware that immigrant son and dealer in real estate John O'Reilly had realized that money was to be made in the boom in real estate which the birth of the projected city would seem sure to bring. They must have been aware of the well known Rutzer Inn already doing well part way between Kingston and Rondout. O'Reilly had dickered to sell a tract of land almost at the very summit of the commanding rise between Rondout and Kingston, a site although then unsettled and forested but which seemed destined by nature itself to become the future civic center for the new city. It was a part of the land long scorned by the Dutch as the Armabowery or poor and even worthless land and by travel writer Darby as too rough to have any value or interest.

On the day that Kingston became a city the Rondout members of the organizing committee held what they felt was an appropriate meeting on O'Reilly's Hill, but without notifying a single Kingston member of the new Common Council of the new City about the event, which involved the laying of the City Hall cornerstone, with elaborate Masonic fraternal and other rites.

It was on the following evening that a very irritated Council member from Kingston proposed a resolution requiring the Council to lay a "half corner stone" to complete the dedication job performed without their attendance or ratification.

Above: Kingston fire company, postcard in collection of Alf Evers

Right: Horse drawn fire engine, Kingston, 1870s, from stereograph in collection of Alf Evers

Even after the City officials had begun to function in their fine new building in 1874, as the five-year recession still lingered, an air of crisis still hung over Kingston, especially at election time in 1876, during the incontrovertibly close vote for Samuel Tilden, a successful lawyer and Democrat for President against Rutherford B. Hayes. Hayes, an Ohio Republican devoted to Prohibition (it would be said of Hayes that while he was President, water flowed like wine in the White House) and the clearly needed adoption of Civil Service reform, was chosen as President over Tilden by the vote of the Congress, to which the close election decision had been referred, even though Tilden had a larger popular vote (against Haye's slight Electoral College majority).

Party hostility ran high that year of '76 in Kingston, with physical violence at the polls in the Town of Kingston between the unemployed Democratic bluestone workers and the conservative land-owning Republicans (among them farmers of the good agricultural parts of their shared voting district) who paid the property taxes and resented unemployed quarry workers who, owning no real property, paid no direct land taxes. The incidents of violence were widely reported, as the grand City Hall began to function, and this played a part in causing the later Gerrymandering of the whole Town of Kingston and a consequent loss thereafter of Democratic power in Ulster County and a new outline for the City of Kingston on maps.

8.
The West Shore Railroad Helps Set off Creation of an Industrial District 1883

By 1886 lawyer and judge Frederick Edward Westbrook would re-publish in his paperbound *Historical Sketches* (many of the sketches originally published in a Kingston newspaper) a fresh and triumphant hurrah for the arrival in 1883 at Kingston's Union Station of the first West Shore railroad train ever to whirl passengers directly between the great city of New York's station at Weehawken across New York harbor and the City of Kingston. On a "day forever to be remembered," as Westbrook would put it, 4,000 Kingstonians assembled to welcome that long hoped-for train. Then, church bells rang, cannons boomed, flags waved and whistles blew as the citizens cheered.

Kingston Station of West Shore Railroad, from souvenir album, "Views of the West Shore Route," from collection of Alf Evers

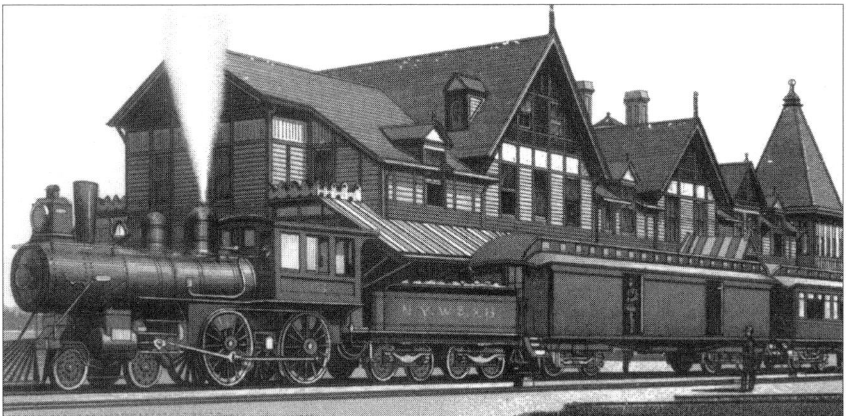

All this jubilation was especially justified, according to Westbrook, because on that day Kingston acquired (thanks to the West Shore Railroad," what Westbrook wrote amounted to "a year round port on the Hudson River" and an end to "Rondout's former sense of superiority." The united city then stood on the threshold of a glorious new era of prosperity as a railroad as well as a steamboat center with railroad tracks leading to and from it. However, as if fate had in mind balancing the triumphs of one decade by the troubles of the preceding one, the decade ending in 1883 had more than balanced with its troubles the glory proclaimed by Westbrook as the ten years began.

At the same time a branch railroad line from Kingston through Phoenicia and beyond had even penetrated the major summer resorts of the Catskills with their many popular farm boardinghouses and their immense, elegant summer hotels, all of which poured profits into Kingston. And all this, Westbrook wrote, was owed to the efforts of the "Honorable Thomas Cornell," the transportation wizard and by then Congressman of the district.

Westbrook proceeded in a truly boosterish vein to tell of how industry had been increasingly drawn to the new City of Kingston which was, in sober fact, then appearing also to have become the victor in the long battle with the other west bank Hudson River-side communities of Catskill and Newburgh for economic supremacy in the west bank of the mid-Hudson region. Its business people were now triumphantly claiming again with more justice this time the right to call their city the veritable "Gateway to the Catskills."

Westbrook did not forsee that the area stretching from the Strand Gate of the former stockade across the Plain to the beginning of the Armabowery of old and beyond the Plain to Rondout's shipyards, and continuing onward, thanks to the railroad, would become known as Kingston's industrial district, or that during the years when industry was prospering and then declining there would come a steady growth of awareness of the value of their City's historic assets. This awareness went on increasing even as the decline of the extractive stone industries in the 1890s and in the other industries later in the first and second decades of the twentieth century were in progress.

Some of the new railroad-inspired industries had been former sweatshops which had moved up from New York to avoid the rise of unions and strict control over working conditions, especially after the fatal fire at the Triangle Shirtwaist sweatshop in 1911.

The U.S. Lace Curtain Company set up a huge factory to cater to the lovers of a fashion in home decoration of the time. Jacobson's, Fessenden's and other shirt factories appeared as did factories producing pajamas, ladies' dresses, shirt waists, underwear and other products of the needle trades. Jacobson's provided a recreation room for its workers as a part of Kingston's attempt to attract formerly exploited workers.

The wage-earning women stitching and ironing such garments as shirts, pajamas and dresses, were numerous but not highly paid. Numerous too were the cigar-makers—working now in larger factories than the former cigar-selling shops which had made their own stock. Now, more than 1,000 of these left their jobs for a night's rest at home after a day's work at the big Powell and George Smith factory located for a time on mid-Broadway at Pine Grove Avenue, and returned to work each morning. This huge factory became part of the American Tobacco Corporation which came to dominate the once thriving Hudson Valley cigar-making factories and eventually, following different uses, the plant was demolished. George Smith became a Congressman while many other Kingston cigar making factories closed, as cigar smoking lost some popular favor as a male status symbol. The open space on Broadway and Pine Grove Avenue facing the side of the former huge cigar factory was a favorite place where political candidates such as Harry S. Truman and Averill Harriman appealed for support to the workers who could look down on the candidates from the factory windows and trade remarks with them.

Van Slyke and Horton manufactured the popular and historically named Peter Schuyler cigars in Kingston, but they also closed.

Van Slyke Cigar Company

Mullens Best chewing tobacco was long made in Kingston. Its bright yellow wrapper struck the eye from the hip pockets of overalls. Farmers of all degrees of poverty or wealth found common ground in chewing to avoid setting fire to barns with their mounds of inflammable hay and straw, because of sparks from corncob pipes or from cigars.

William Redin's drawing of the large Baldwin Foundry which first made cast iron parts for farm machinery and steamboats, at the edge of the Academy Green close to what had been the Strand Gate, from Tilson & Brink map, 1854

Better roads came to be called for in the 1890s as automobiles appeared, and a factory for making road building machines was built in the industrial district. And a very substantial factory for making magnetos came to Kingston for use in hydraulic control devices for airplanes, and plants turning out cardboard boxes and other containers took the place of the old-fashioned cooperages. The making of butchers' blocks, furniture and house-builders' timber and ornamentation drew its basic needs from nearby forests.

First of the users of Kingston's industrial district had been the James W. Baldwin foundry which made metal parts for farm machinery and steamboats, located at the very beginning of the Plains (at the edge of the Academy Green) close to the former Strand Gate. Many other plants which turned out machinery for an increasingly

The steamship *James Baldwin*

mechanized nation were built in the industrial district on what had been called the Plains, which reached beyond Baldwin's across the railroad backbone of the new industrial district and eventually across the Armbowery to link up with the ship and boat building district on the Rondout.

By the 1890s the extractive industries of the City were fading away while leaving their stony litter behind, while the shirt factories continued for a while and while some students of local history were making serious efforts to put the history of Kingston on a sounder and more factual basis.

Through much of the period of industrial increase in Kingston, awareness of the City's historical assets was also increasing and went on increasing even as the decline of the canal base and extractive industries in the 1890s and of the other industries after the second decade of the twentieth century were in progress, following the end of a brief World War 1 boom.

The City's brickyards formed a major industry—they molded and baked local clay from banks along the Hudson to help build up the City of New York. These Kingston bricks were often a base of New York City brownstones, which were only faced with more expensive brownstone.

A feature of Kingston during its period of industrial expansion was the use of flowers and foliage supplied by Valentin Burgevin. His greenhouses were located just to the east of Golden Hill. They were referred to as his hundred acres under glass. Valentin Bergevin played a valued part in Kingston's social and ceremonial life to an extent that surpassed any previous florist, even among many who had not previously felt they could afford the expense. He settled the habit of using flowers upon Kingston. In June during Burgevin's time, for instance, many people of Kingston went mountain laurel viewing for esthetic pleasure as the Japanese did plum blossom viewing. Many Kingston men hired architects and builders to place bay windows on the walls of their houses in which they themselves or their wives could grow flowers through the winters. This had not been done before Burgevin arrived. It was not unusual for a Kingston businessman in those days to wear a floral boutonniere on his lapel.

Burgevin's sons became prosperous businessmen in Kingston, serving on the boards of banks and other Kingston institutions.

In nearby Rhinebeck across the Hudson River the growing of fragrant English violets had so captured the imagination of Kingstonians that no lady was thought properly equipped for a social event without a corsage of the violets and every day freight car loads of the violets were shipped from Rhinebeck to New York City. The fashion, however, died out although Eleanor Roosevelt tried in the Depression of the 1930s to revive it in Rhinebeck.

The first and second World Wars brought increased growth to Kingston's industrial district, including the enlargement of the Apollo magneto plant, and that of nearby Electrol, which also made magnetos. The former Lorillard refrigerator factory gave way to the Peckham Industries which provided running gear for trucks and automobiles. Boatyards which had supplied boats for the Canal and had closed as the Canal declined in business now turned to making small vessels such as submarine chasers for the United States Navy during World War II.

The new West Shore Railroad did more for Kingston after 1883 than Westbrook had suggested. It made possible for a group of New Yorkers with a special interest to make what was called a Pilgrimage on a remarkably grand scale and at the expense of Thomas Cornell's heir Samuel D. Coykendall. The lavish Pilgrimage was like nothing that had ever before been planned for and carried out in Kingston.

9.
A Pilrimage to Kingston

ON SEPTEMBER 11, 1886 A SPECIAL TRAIN CARRYING 84 MALE PASSENGERS (no women), all claiming colonial Dutch ancestry and so rightful members of the Holland Society of New York, whizzed by special train up the West Shore Railroad tracks to Kingston from the Weehawken Station opposite the big City of New York. The Pilgrims reached their goal, as set down in their Society minutes, in the record time of only one hour and forty-five minutes. In Kingston the Pilgrims were joined by about thirty fellow members of the Holland Society from Albany. Ahead of the Pilgrims lay an exploration of the old stone houses of Kingston built by Dutch and some early English-ruled colonists. There was also the presentation of copies of Westbrook's *Historical Sketches.* (Westbrook was the preserver of the Kingston Senate House, which had been built by an ancestor of his in the late 1670's.)

A copy of the *Freeman and Journal* for September 23, 1881 was given to each and every Society Pilgrim. It contained a significant quotation from a pamphlet about the duty of Kingston's citizens "to preserve the ancient buildings erected on streets laid out by the friend of Kingston, Dutch colonial Governor Petrus Stuyvesant more than two hundred years ago as monuments to remind us of the early sufferings and privations of our heroic ancestors from savages and Christian foes. Preserve them as relics of a heroic and suffering period and as vestiges of our Country's glory and achievements."

These words were written by Frederick Westbrook, the man who had taken it on himself to preserve the Senate House built in part by a Dutch ancestor of his in the 1670s and to be admired by the Pilgrims that afternoon. Westbrook had been the first known of all Kingstonians to urge in print the preservation of the City's old stone houses.

The Senate House, from an old engraving

There was an excellent oration on the Dutch period of Kingston history given as was fitting in the Dutch Reformed Church by General George H. Sharpe, an astute politician and an eager gatherer of records and recollections of the city in its early pre-city years. In addition, there would be the next day a viewing of treasured relics and old documents including a remarkable collection of papers relating to Thomas Chambers and the early history of Rondout lent by a descendant of Chambers's stepchildren named Van Gaasbeek. The Pilgrims would be carried at the expense of Dutch-descended Samuel Decker Coykendall, the millionaire fellow member of the Society and soon to be manager and owner of the little railroad empire set up by his still-living father-in-law Thomas Cornell. The Pilgrims were taken by rail to the luxurious Hotel Kaaterskill high on the Catskill Mountains and there given a "sumptuous" dinner also believed to have been at Coykendall's expense, but possibly at Cornell's. The Hotel had been kept open for the Pilgrims' convenience about a week later than its usual late summer closing date—this also at Coykendall's expense.

The menu for the dinner at the hotel that night was printed on orange paper in honor of the historic Dutch House of Orange and a copy would be bound into the Society's elaborately designed and printed Yearbook for 1886-87. It was printed in Dutch, English and a smattering of French with a quotation from Washington Irving accompanying every course of the elaborate dinner. The secretary of the Society recorded that the food and wines were even better than those served at New York's famous Delmonico's and the Hotel Brunswick, at both of which epicurean resorts the Holland Society members had feasted.

After a night spent in rooms assigned to them in the immense mountaintop hotel the Pilgrims after breakfast rode on their chartered train down the mountain to a day of further sightseeing pleasure in old Kingston before taking their special train back to New York. Never before had Kingston people felt more honored and flattered than by the praise lavished on their city and by the money so freely scattered about by Coykendall. Congressman (and former Mayor) J.C. Lindsley, the big man of the Newark Limestone and Cement Company, felt stirred to write a plea in the *Daily Freeman* in which he urged the people of Kingston to honor the memory of their earliest white settlers. He began, "The entertainment given to the Holland Society has been the means of bringing to light many things that have slumbered in forgetfulness. They are now exhibited and commented upon."

He suggested that Kingston people honor Thomas Chambers whose bones, Lindsley lamented, lay in an unmarked grave in the Montrepose Cemetery, by establishing a fund to place over the grave a "properly inscribed" memorial stone. To this plea the then Democratic Ulster *Argus* which missed few opportunities to belittle the ideas of the conservative opposition party had pointed out that it had taken many years before even the Washington Monument could be completed by public contributions and that there was little likelihood of Lindsley's plea soon being responded to. The *Argus* was right. Twenty years would pass before a monument would appear above Chambers' grave, and then not as the result of individual contributions, but of city funds.

Yet the Pilgrims of 1886 and Congressman Lindsley had awakened Kingston to a new awareness of Chambers. The Congressman had written apologetically, "although Chambers was not a Hollander he cast his lot among them and shared their vicissitudes and set them an example of endurance and fortitude. Dying," the Congressman wrote (in error), "he left them his fortune." What neither Lindsley nor the *Argus* was aware of was that a stone "properly inscribed" already existed in 1886, but had been lost track of until its existence would be discovered in the late 1890s and be photographed as evidence. But of the whereabouts, its date or even the existence of the gravestone of the founding father of the City, hardly anyone in Kingston in 1886 seemed to have any notion. One rumor placed a stone in the custody of the Ulster County Historical Society. But after that Society's secretary and leader George W. Pratt died as a result of Civil War wounds suffered at the Second Battle of Bull Run, and the Society's possessions were scattered after it had disbanded.

Yet memories of the Pilgrimage of 1886 in the decades that followed stirred the people of Kingston into a realization of the value in dollars (in large part because of the great amount of money which Samuel Coykendall had spent on the Holland Society Pilgrimage) of their abundant historical assets in buildings, documents and traditions, and this awareness would ripen as the twentieth century dawned into a conviction that an image of Kingston as a major American historic city was worth presenting to the public. And little by little such a presentation would be made.

Yet it took even longer for Kingston people to realize that the Native Americans who had preceded them on their pleasant part of the earth had a rich culture of their own, which even included the singing of songs and the playing of games.

The Pilgrimage set Kingston people (who had Bibles which included pages of genealogical details of their ancestors) to turn to these pages and feel a new awareness of their heritage. Some of these peole maybe have felt amused by what they heard called ancestory worship by the Pilgrims of 1886. Yet when they gave the subject more thought they could not have helped seeing merit in tying American history to the deeds of their ancestors as recorded in the family Bibles. The expensive visit of New York City Pilgrims in 1886 may have been what prompted the women of Kingston to form the Wiltwyck Chapter of the Daughters of the American Revolution in 1895 and to use the organization as a means of commemorating events in Kingston's history, as well as the deeds of their own ancestors.

10.
Early Games, Sports, and Pastimes —Especially Baseball

NATIVE AMERICANS LIKE WHITES ALSO REQUIRE RELAXATION FROM THE rigors of life by indulging in the entertainment or amusement to be had in playing games and sports. This value of games to Natives was hinted at some years ago in a book on the "Games of North American Indians" by Stewart Culin. The book takes 845 pages to give accounts of these games and to list and comment on the objects used in playing them as recorded by ethnologists and anthropologists in American ethnic museums (excluding those used in play only by children). Not all of such games were known to have been played in Kingston, but many of them were recorded as once played by related Algonkian-speakers. Many of them probably were. Games and sports have long helped children of all peoples develop skills in using their minds, nerves and muscles. Among adults games provided occasions for indulgence in the betting which flourished among Native Americans as well as whites. Early writers on the history of Kingston have nothing to say about the games which their Native predecessors engaged in. As played by vigorous young men, games provided preparation for the deadly hostility which forms part of the art of war, as football does in our society. One game or sport of this sort which has left ample traces on the landscape of Kingston is the ball and stick game now, in modified form, called lacrosse, which has evolved among whites into a national game of Canada, as baseball is of the United States—and which was once played on the only sizable plateau which interrupts the steep slope from the top of the Weinberg (on the edge of the Armabowery) to Rondout Creek, as described earlier in this book. Tobogganing (the name derived from a Mic-mac word) was not usually thought of as a native game or sport although something similar was used by Natives to transport heavy goods and was known to the French of Canada and some Americans as a travois.

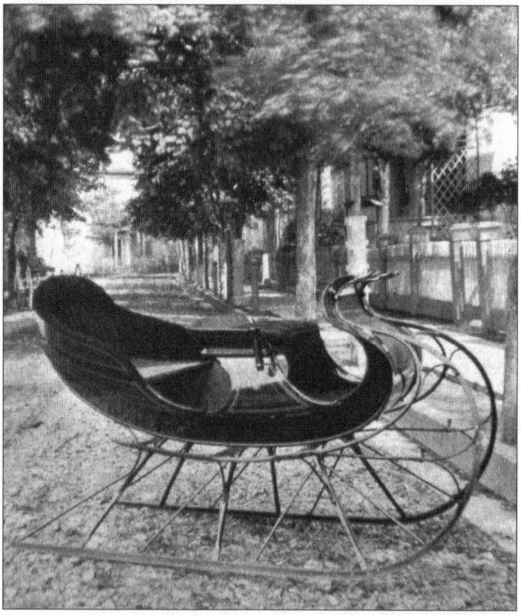

This elegant cutter was photographed for the maker in summertime to promote its sale for use the following winter, from a stereograph

The white colonists on their first arrival did not adopt the Native games and sports they found but adapted to new conditions those they had brought over in their minds from the homeland.

A variety of the ball games known in Europe since far back in Greek and Roman times was played by the Dutch and known as goff—the golf of today.

And, as back home in the Netherlands which was plentifully supplied with water resources, water sports were popular for pleasure and in competition by swimmers and boaters. And when winter turned the water of the creeks (or kills), ponds and the Hudson to ice, skating became popular among young and old on wooden skates with steel blades inserted. In the nineteenth century when more light and graceful horse-drawn sleighs were made locally, sleighing parties of young couples set out to the music of sleigh bells on the roads radiating out from Kingston with stops for refreshment at roadhouses of varying degrees of services and respectability. Children coasted down slopes on locally made sleds, threw snowballs and fashioned snow men.

Despite their Calvinistic code which discouraged many games and sports, others were permitted, if grudgingly, even by their clergy.

A winter sport enjoyed by some Kingstonians at the expense of the Cornell-Coykenall fortune, and a famous feature of the landscape in the late nineteenth century was tobogganing. The slide was well designed. It took off from the summit of the southern end of what had been known as the Weinberg which had been converted by then to Kingston's most elegant and expensive residential section for the monied citizens of Rondout and from which a fine panoramic view of Rondout might be enjoyed with its commercial and industrial assets punctuated by the 1890s by many impressive church steeples.

The toboggan slide was a source of entertainment of great appeal especially for the exclusive members of the toboggan club, in a place once noted for its strict Calvinism which also frowned on card-playing and, in its early years, on ballroom dancing.

Top, toboggan slide; *center*, coasting at Ponckhockie, *and below*, sleighing on Albany Avenue, all from *Picturesque Ulster*

Yet entertainment, as the nineteenth century rolled along, was becoming a feature of Kingston life, making itself felt in games and sports—except among such people as strict Methodists. There was interest in delving into colonial family genealogy and local history for family amusement and a pride in informing visitors of the City's colorful history—and this had become a modest part of Kingston culture, and was gaining in entertainment value. Mid-nineteenth century Kingston people would have entertaining and educational lectures supplied by a Hudson Valley Association which promoted the employment of popular performers and lecturers such as Abolitionist Wendell Phillips (whom his Kingston audience hissed when he advocated freeing the slaves), Dr. Oliver Wendell Holmes, eccentric Horace Greeley, blind pianists, midget General Tom Thumb, advocates of women's rights, talks on local history by such Kingston experts as General George H. Sharpe, William Lounsbery, and others, plus Lancashire Bell Ringers, midgets, giants and glass-blowers.

There were also circus performers and even the resident Hunt's circus, propagandists for off-beat Christian sects sometimes wearing appropriate robes and floating gowns, and salesmen of fish, menders of umbrellas with their cries of "Um-ber-*ell*as to mend!" all of whom made known their presence with characteristic and often entertaining "street cries."

Kingston had moved far fom the days when Moravian missionary (to both Natives and whites) Count Zinzendorf had been arrested for Sabbath-breaking for making notes for his sermons on Sunday in neighboring Hurley, although Sundays continued to be observed as days of prayer and quiet.

By the end of the 1890s and the early decades of the 20th century, Kingston people were even boarding the special open cars of the West Shore railroad to enjoy watching the inter-collegiate regattas held for years on the Hudson at Poughkeepsie and watching by winter the exciting racing by daring amateur ice-boaters on the Hudson.

To men of early Dutch colonial days, Calvinistic as they were, there were available the very different traditional "blood sports" which gave a kind of entertainment by treating animals with cruelty. One which was practiced by colonists on certain holidays was "pulling the goose" which was a feature of Fasteen, or pre-Lenten Mardi Gras in early spring of each year until denounced by the clergy as a relic of the pre-Reformation days of "Popery." Here, at Fasteen, a goose was hung by its feet from a branch of a tree with its head and neck well greased. Men and boys riding by on horseback tried as they rode by to seize the goose by the head and neck and pull it down.

Another blood sport was bear-baiting, known to have been indulged in as recently as the 1850s. A captured bear imprisoned in a pen was set upon by hunting dogs. The sport was the sight of the bear's attempt to defend himself against the fierce dogs. Hunting, fishing and trapping were indulged in for sport, as well as for food and to protect crops.

Painting of trapped bear, from collection of Alf Evers

The blood sport of cock-fighting was very popular in colonial days and though long outlawed still has it devotees. Game cocks, bred for their aggressiveness against fellow males and equipped with sharp steel spurs lashed to their shanks faced one another beak to beak in battle in small round cockpits surrounded by an audience of cheering and betting fanciers of the bloody sport. Fanciers arrived from a distance to watch such matches between well known gamecocks. New Paltz tradition tells of Kingston men going to Widow Wintje Hasbrouck's cellar kitchen in New Paltz to be present when famous cocks were fighting there.

A cock fight scheduled by a fancier and promoter named Armeter on the Sawkill Road near the Kingston city boundary line was reported as planned in 1943. It was raided by State Police, and prospective spectators saw the interior of the local police station instead of an exciting battle at Armeter's place. Cock fighting fanciers had a jargon of their own in which Maryland-born painter John Carroll liked to write on late in the 1920s in the *Woodstock Almanac.*

Cockfighting gadget from *Ulster County Gazette*, published by the Ulster County Historical Society, 1976. With steel spurs attached, game cocks fought each other for prizes for their owners.

Horses once filled a far larger part in daily life than they do today (now that there are motor vehicles.) It was not surprising that horse-racing (impromptu on the highways or well organized on race-tracks at Kingston or other Ulster County tracks) could attract great attention and lead to the maintenance of driving parks such as the well-kept one on Manor Avenue in Kingston.

Kingston people of the past found horse drawn carriages and sleighs as well as riding a fascination. Horses became an attraction to men who in their zeal for betting would wager with equal enthusiasm on the outcome of a race for President or on the victor in a street corner dog fight.

Hunting and fishing once relied on for food continued as sports and remain so today. In the mid-1790s the visiting Duc de la Rochefoucauld-Liancourt was roused from his bed in Kingston by smoky air caused, he was told, by hunters setting forest fires to round up deer to be shot. He did not indicate in his travel narrative whether the hunters were white or Native. They might have been either.

Old wills and inventories hint at the playing of board games such as the ones called tick-tack and backgammon. Chess was often played at taverns. A popular game involving dagger or knife play was called mumble-the-peg. It was played on a circle of cleared earth with a peg driven part way down in its center. Two players took their places beside the earthen ring and by turns tried to throw a well-sharpened dagger or pointed knife at the peg so as to cause the dagger or knife to stick there. The loser paid a penalty by being sometimes required to pull up the peg with his teeth. In a game of mumble-the-peg played in the early 1730s by a black man and a white Kingstonian, an awkward toss of the knife by the young black player caused the death of his young white opponent and the case was judged accidental by the Ulster County court. The surviving court record preserves the details of the fatal game.

In the booklet he sold from door to door in Kingston in 1839 eccentric wandering preacher William Boyse set down instructions for playing several of the old-fashioned ball and bat games which had for centuries been the pleasure of European boys, and which were fated to be merged into the American national game of baseball. In a section headed "Amusements at School" Boyse went back in his recollections first to a teacher who had a talent for "leaping." This he demonstrated in the school yard by having two boys hold a pole as high in the air as they could while he jumped over it. Next minister Boyse called back his recollection of playing in his boyhood in North Carolina of three of the ancient ball and bat games of "town ball," "cat" and the game called "baste" all of which contributed to modern baseball in various ways. Town ball, Boyse wrote, was played by two sides, one composed of townsmen and the other of out-of-townsmen played on a field marked off by two overlapping circles, the smaller being the town and the larger occupied by their out-of-town opponents.

First Boyse explained the still used way of choosing sides by putting one hand above the other on a bat. And then one side occupied the town and the other one the out-of-town field. "One got a bat and stood in the centre of the town; another standing at a suitable distance, threw him a ball" at which he aimed a blow. If one of the out-of-town side caught the ball or caught it on the first bounce the town-side was turned out of town. If no one caught it, the hitter ran to the first point on the outward circle (first base) and then clear around the circle if he could, and so on.

Cat used a square on the field with a hole at each corner in which a man stood with another behind (before) him. The man in the hole throws a ball over the head of the man standing before him toward the man at the right corner who aims with a bat at the ball as it comes toward him. If hit, all four men run to the next holes. If not hit after three strikes the side was turned out. "This was a fine exercise and healthy amusment," Boyse wrote. "It was better and less expensive than doctors' pills."

Another amusement was baste. "Two parties were arrayed as before stated. Each party was stationed at two pedestals or trees. When ready, one at one baste exclaimed,

> 'King, king Cantico'
> One from the other party,
> 'You're to come and I'm to go.'
> His alternate answered
> 'How many miles to barley bright"
> The answer was
> 'Three score and ten.'
> 'Can I get there by candle-light?'
> 'Yes, if your legs are long and light.'

Then one started out, and approached as near as he dared towards the other. If caught before he returned home, he was a captive among the other party, and increased their number. The side that were so taken was beat."

Boyse lists also "shooting popguns made out of elder" and wrestling of which his teacher disapproved. He presents as a change the words of a kissing game,

> "Oh brother Roger, how merry were we,
> When we sat under that Juniper tree,
> When we sat under that Juniper tree, hi O.
> Put that hat on his head,
>   Keep his head warm,
> And give him a kiss,
>   It will do him no harm"

Boyse wrote, "The ladies had something to do with that business."

He ended with the words, "Oh Lord, forgive the follies of my youth, and the greater follies of my riper years, for Jesus Christ's sake. Amen."

These same games reported by Boyse (some in a confused fashion) were probably also played by Kingston boys although Boyse doesn't clearly mention it.

By the 1840s after an attempt by elitists in the City of New York to boost English cricket as the national American game, Kingston Stockade elite followed suit by setting up the Eclipse Cricket Club in 1859, but it soon became clear that baseball, with roots in the old games whose instructions were written up by the Rev. William Boyse, had the vote of the American people. In New York City, baseball club after club sprang up in and after the 1850s, the game was organized and there its rules adopted. Kingston teams played each other and the many new teams throughout the Hudson Valley. By 1869 Frederick Fredenburgh, a Kingston graduate of Columbia College who had played on his college's baseball team and was later publisher of the Democratic *Kingston Daily Leader*, sponsored the city's first semi-professional baseball team, the Leaders, and accompanied the team to their games as far south as Washington and Richmond. Kingston, with the success of the Leaders, and after teams such as the Recreationals, and later still the Colonials, became recognized as "a baseball town." Through the 1880s and 90s, its teams won or lost many games against the Pittsburgh Pirates, the Boston Braves, and the Brooklyn Dodgers. The Leaders first home field was Donovan's Field on Washingston Avenue opposite the present George Washington School.

Some semi-professional Kingston players moved upward to fame on major league teams. Babe Ruth later on came to Kingston to give an exhibition of his batting skills which amazed his many Kingston fans. Baseball continued to have a firm grip on Kingston's affections—as it still does.

The success of the Leaders and other early Kingston baseball teams such as the Recreationals stimulated the interest in other sports. The Yellow Tigers professional football team gave up after a ten year try. Boxing was especially popular among Kingston's Irish immigrants with their homeland boxing traditions. Famous boxers visited Kingston to face opponents or demonstrate their skills, from Irish descendant John L. Sullivan (bareknuckle boxer who won his championship in 1892 from Paddy Ryan), and so on. The new Kingston High School built on Broadway opposite the City Hall, took up the new game of basketball (first played in 1891 in Springfield, Massachusetts) and played in the Armory after that once grim building's conversion to a city recreation center.

Sports and hobbies went on from the heyday of semi-professional baseball in the City together with many other newer sports and pastimes spawned by changing times. A diary kept by George Wood in 1915 when Wood was a student at the Kingston High School tells of how young Wood practiced and played football to a lesser extent than the baseball which had first place in his affections. And he also worked on his stamp collection. He spent winter afternoons "sleigh-riding" or coasting. He worked for pay at raking leaves, shoveling snow, and hand pumping the organ of his church in which he showed an interest that led to his adult career as a minister.

A downriver neighbor, bearded and famous John Burroughs, essayist on nature and grape grower who often visited Kingston, the "seer of Slabsides"[712] had encouraged a new kind of interest in the relation of humans to their environment. Because of this, young Kingston people like George Wood learned bird watching, and George had taken up the counting of varieties of birds he saw on bird day. Wood counted no fewer than twenty-nine varieties on the appointed day in 1915.

Interest in radio (its first Kingston broadcasts given by the local Boy Scouts) and later on television cut into the time once devoted to vigorous outdoor activity. And watching spectator sports took up much of the time once spent in playing sports, fastening its grip on an ever larger public.

By 1905, enough inquiry into Kingston's past had been done to persuade local historian Bejamin Myer Brink (who was beginning to publish his nine-volume monthly serial, *Olde Ulster*) to undertake climbing up the interior of the steeple of the old Dutch Church in order to check the truth of a familiar Kingston tradition. This tradition held that when a new bell for the church had been ordered to be made by bellfounder Kuk in old Amsterdam, the church people of Kingston and Marbletown had contributed silver spoons and coins to be melted and mixed with the ingredients of the bell metal for the bell. In spite of the arduous climb up the dusty steeple interior, Brink was unable to find any evidence on Mr. Kuk's bell of any contribution of silver. Yet he had shown that Kingston people were taking their traditional history more seriously than before and were taking pains to check its accuracy.

Part 10

Kingston Makes Progress Toward Becoming Accepted as a Truly Historic City of the USA

1890s-Present

1

The 1890s Bring Fast Change—Miss Stewart's Kirmesses Lead to the DAR's Historical Pageant; George Clinton's Remains are Brought to Kingston for Reburial; Coykendall's Amusement Park is Added to Kingston's Stock of Entertainments

STORES OR SHOPS FOR SELLING SUCH NECESSITIES OF DAILY LIFE AS FOOD AND clothing were almost unknown during the very early Dutch colonial days of Esopus and Kingston, but there were instead regular market days featuring trade in useful commodities amid much jollity. Such days were originally called kerkmasses in the Netherlands and "kermises" in Esopus, and originally in pre-Reformation European times, had featured only the celebration of a Christian mass to commemorate the founding of a local parish church. These once religious holidays had evolved over the years into market days at which goods and services were sold, and which were made attractive by much fun and jollity, including music and even very un-Calvinistic dancing in the streets and sometimes too much drinking. During the 1870s an event called a Kermis in a very much modified form was held to raise money to build a hospital for Kingston. It was not a success. Somewhat later other fundraisers for the same purpose did well, and the elaborate kermises (by the 1890s called "kirmesses") were continued year after year as entertainments during the 1890s and early 1900s, under the leadership of a talented and energetic dancer named Lila Stewart.

Miss Stewart's Kermises or Kirmesses had none of the simple, boisterous and often vulgar and rowdy air that marked similar events in old Holland as shown by familiar Dutch and Flemish painters or recalled from colonial Esopus days. Miss Stewart's amateur dances were suited to the 1890s when a lessening of Calvinism was

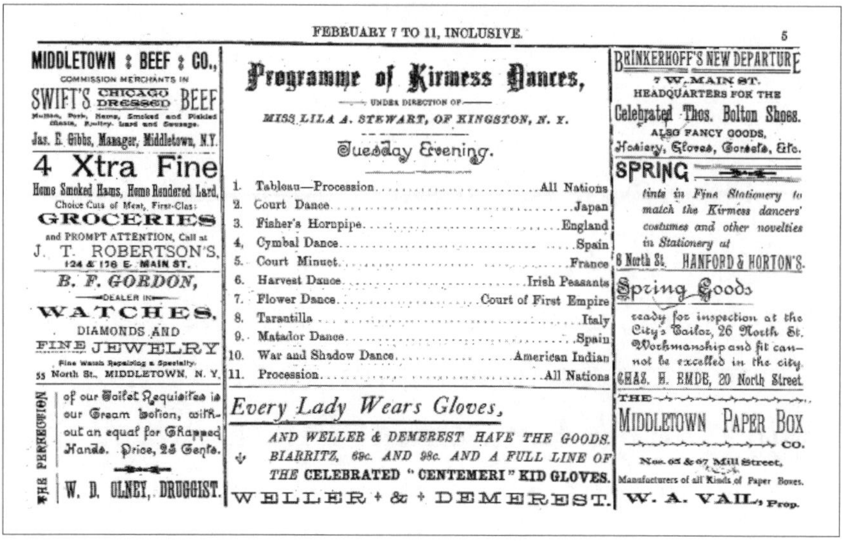

FEBRUARY 7 TO 11, INCLUSIVE. 5

MIDDLETOWN : BEEF : CO.,
COMMISSION MERCHANTS IN
SWIFT'S CHICAGO DRESSED BEEF
Mutton, Pork, Hams, Smoked and Pickled Meats, Poultry, Lard and Sausage.
Jas. E. Gibbs, Manager, Middletown, N.Y.

4 Xtra Fine
Home Smoked Hams, Home Rendered Lard,
Choice Cuts of Meat, First-Class
GROCERIES
and PROMPT ATTENTION, Call at
J. T. ROBERTSON'S,
124 & 126 E. MAIN ST.

B. F. GORDON,
DEALER IN
WATCHES,
DIAMONDS AND
FINE JEWELRY
Fine Watch Repairing a Specialty.
55 North St., MIDDLETOWN, N. Y.

THE PERFECTION of our Toilet Requisites is our Cream Lotion, without an equal for Chapped Hands. Price, 25 Cents.
W. D. OLNEY, DRUGGIST.

Programme of Kirmess Dances,
UNDER DIRECTION OF
MISS LILA A. STEWART, OF KINGSTON, N. Y.
Tuesday Evening.

1.	Tableau—Procession	All Nations
2.	Court Dance	Japan
3.	Fisher's Hornpipe	England
4.	Cymbal Dance	Spain
5.	Court Minuet	France
6.	Harvest Dance	Irish Peasants
7.	Flower Dance	Court of First Empire
8.	Tarantilla	Italy
9.	Matador Dance	Spain
10.	War and Shadow Dance	American Indian
11.	Procession	All Nations

Every Lady Wears Gloves,
AND WELLER & DEMEREST HAVE THE GOODS. BIARRITZ, 69c. AND 98c. AND A FULL LINE OF THE CELEBRATED "CENTEMERI" KID GLOVES.
WELLER & DEMEREST.

BRINKERHOFF'S NEW DEPARTURE
7 W. MAIN ST.
HEADQUARTERS FOR THE
Celebrated Thos. Bolton Shoes.
ALSO FANCY GOODS,
Hosiery, Gloves, Corsets, Etc.

SPRING
tints in Fine Stationery to match the Kirmess dancers' costumes and other novelties in Stationery at
8 North St. HANFORD & HORTON'S.

Spring Goods
ready for inspection at the City's Tailor, 26 North St. Workmanship and fit cannot be excelled in the city.
CHAS. H. EMDB, 20 North Street.

THE
MIDDLETOWN PAPER BOX
CO.
Nos. 65 & 67 Mill Street,
Manufacturers of all Kinds of Paper Boxes.
W. A. VAIL, Prop.

Program of Miss Stewart's Kirmiss held in 1893 in Middletown, N.Y., with local advertising

giving a vital change to American life. The dancers were elegantly and often expensively dressed and their dances often featured such elaborately costumed musical spectacles as "dances of the world" or "a court minuet" with such great imagination and verve as to lead Miss Stewart to be invited to duplicate them in other cities including New York at the elegant Waldorf Astoria hotel, as well as in Orange County's Middletown. She also gave lessons on dancing in New York City with marked success.

A "Grand Kirmess and Pardon" was put on at the Kingston Armory for 6 days in April of 1895, under the direction of Lila Stewart. The performances featured 300 dancers representing the various countries of the world, incorporating a Scottish hornpipe and other dances, and most striking of all, four Kingston ladies performed the Serpentine Dance which appeared to have been a favorite presentation of Miss Stewart. For a city in which Calvinism had reigned since its foundation by whites, it was an astounding week during which Kingston people enjoyed themselves immensely, and raised enough money to give their hospital a good start.

During the same years in Kingston there flourished a nostalgic yearning for the ambience of an earlier America as reflected in visions of a romanticized Kingston of the colonial past, and partly as a result Lila Stewart's evocations of the lovely but somewhat imaginary past of the colonial kermis, a historical pageant came to Kingston, one of the earliest put on in America.

In 1894 the members of the DAR in Albany staged a historical week or pageant in order, as they put it, to help educate the people of Albany and surrounding towns as to their history, and to stimulate them to patriotism.

On December 9-14, 1895, the Wiltwyck Chapter of the DAR presented at the Kingston Opera House as part of a week of "a historic pageant" featuring a reenactment of a Dutch wedding of the year 1676, with the bride a descendant of the 1676 bride and all those attending descendants of those who had attended the original wedding. Another feature was a George Washington Ball which was held at the Bogardus Tavern with the dancers dressed in a very different costume from 1676, featuring powdered wigs and courtly manners.

This historic pageant was among the very first such events to be given in America.

The 1890s were a time when Britons and Americans were throwing off the remnants of the Calvinism that marked high Victorianism in favor of trying new ways of seeing life in the ways given currence in the quarterly Yellow Book, edited and sometimes shockingly and feverishly illustrated by young Aubrey Beardsley, who would die in his twenties of tuberculosis. The Marquis of Queensbury during the '90s was pursuing Oscar Wilde through the courts, as Kingston watched,

GRAND KIRMESS AND PARDON
At the Kingston Armory
April 15, 16, 17, 18, 19, 20.
FOR THE BENEFIT OF THE
Kingston City Hospital
UNDER THE AUSPICES OF THE
14th SEPARATE COMPANY,
UNDER THE DIRECTION OF
MISS LILA A. STEWART.

Who successfully conducted the Kirmess at Kingston, Middletown, Monticello and and Port Jervis, N. Y., and Honesdale and Scranton, Pa.

National dances of France, Spain, Italy, Hungary, Germany, Russia, Scotland and England; also the American Indian dance. These dances will be interpreted by 300 people in costume. Hornpipe, Dew Drops and Leaves, Baby Reel and Carnival dance by children.

One of the Special Features of the Kirmess will be the beautiful

SERPENTINE DANCE

executed by four Ladies of Kingston.

A superb orchestra of talented home musicians, under the baton of Prof. William H. Reiser, will furnish music for the preliminary concert and for the dances. Ladies in National Costume will preside over the booths. Refreshments in abundance every afternoon and evening. Dancing every evening at the conclusion of the Kirmess.

Matinees Tuesday, Wednesday, Thursday and Friday at 4 P. M.
Saturday at 3 P. M.
General Admission 50 cents.
Reserved Seats 25 and 50 Cents.

Admission to Matinee 25 cents Reserved Seats 25 and 50 cents.
Doors open at 3 p. m. and 7 p. m. Curtain at 4 p. m. and 8 p. m.

Reserved Seats on sale at Winter's up and down town on Thursday morning, April 11th.

Right: the "Grand Kirmess and Pardon" from the Kingston *Daily Freeman*, April 15, 1895

Below: Kingston Hospital, 1886, post card in collection of Alf Evers

on the charge of having an improper sexual relationship with the Marquis's son Lord Alfred Douglas. Wilde ended up in prison where he wrote his enduring "Ballad of Reading Jail." Later Wilde exiled himself to France to face disgrace and an early death.

In the mid-'90s a rise in interest in the history of their city caused the placing of a bronze tablet in the honor of George Clinton, Kingston's adopted son. The tablet was placed with due ceremony on the front wall of the Ulster County Court House on Wall Street.

Colonialism however prettily presented, was a phase of the sometimes cruel exploitation of one people by another—a form of exploitation which had been thrown off in battle by the thirteen American colonial settlements in the bloody Revolution and which still exists elsewhere on the globe in the third world of today, though often in a modernized form involving low wages and child labor for those being exploited. In many Latin American countries under the leadership of such heroes as Bolivar and St. Martin, the people fought revolutions which looked back to the American Revolution and its resulting democratic Constitution as a model, and some were successes. It was as the nineteenth century ended that the word "colonial" began to be applied more and more to Kingston, for instance by local poet Henry Abbey, and used to entice Kingston consumers into local shops and other commercial enterprises presented as having an almost exotic and appealing colonial magic.

It was a phenomenon found throughout America. For instance, taking advantage of the rising national flood of colonial American obsessions, retired New England minister Wallace Nutting had expanded his hobby into a thriving business of producing and selling hand-tinted photographs and on into the production of books on the romanticized American past. And, beginning in 1914, Nutting would begin operating a half dozen genuine colonial New England houses which tourists might stay in amidst original and reproductions of colonial furniture and other artifacts.

In the 1890s and early 1900s as Lila Stewart was directing her kirmesses and the Kingston DAR presenting its colonial pageant, fashion-loving Americans around the nation began enjoying a pleasant flirtation with "colonial" living, with mock colonial houses being run up for them and furniture factories busily engaged in making machine-fashioned reproductions of old, once handmade colonial furniture. Many a man and his wife rid their house of ornate but comfortable Victorian dining chairs in exchange for not very comfortable new colonial chairs and turned off their gaslights and ate their dinners by the same sort of dim candlelight which had tried the eyes of their colonial ancestors (who had nothing brighter available). Such people in Kingston might rejoice in feeling that they were living stylishly.

Americans who could afford it furnished their new houses (of colonial design) with genuine antique colonial furniture similar to that pictured in Nutting's books and photographs. In Kingston as the colonial fashion took firm hold, the "old stone houses" and the other relics of the days of Kingston's colonial oppression, became ever more venerated. A few would become transformed into a charming atmosphere of fashionable colonial glamor and elegance for their occupants.

Miss Stewart's kirmesses would not have met with the approval they received at any earlier time in the history of Kingston when the stern Calvinist influence was shown not only in church matters but also in daily life. But times had changed and it had come about that the restored kirmesses with their emphasis on the enjoyment of visual beauty and graceful dance, however much frowned upon they would have been by stern John Calvin long centuries before, were well adapted to the more hedonistic spirit of the eighteen-nineties.

Lila Stewart's kirmesses and the "Historic Week" put on by the Wiltwyck Chapter of the DAR's in 1895, were elaborately costumed and rehearsed, presenting often romanticized scenes from their city's undeniably colorful past. Descendants of old local families rummaged in their attics in search of ancient costumes once worn in Kingston and when necessary sent to New York dealers in theatrical costumes to obtain costumes which seemed more appropriate than those in their attics. The successful historical pageant of 1895 marked a point at which their city's history and entertainment urges merged and gave the subject a wider interest and acceptance.

It was not until the celebratory atmosphere of the 1890s that it also became possible to stage the placing of the bronze plaque in honor of the city's great adopted son George Clinton on the front wall of the old courthouse built in 1819 on the same site as their colonial one burned by the British in 1777. There was a large assemblage at the unveiling, including members of the newly organized Wiltwyck chapter of the Daughters of the American Revolution, headed by Mary Isabella Forsyth as Regent, and the Colonial Dames of America, plus many members of the other "patriotic" organizations, as these were called, which had sprung into life following the example of the Society of Cincinnati (composed of officers who had served in the American Revolution and their descendents, including both George Washington and George Clinton) and which had given rise to a multitude of other commemorative patriotic organizations, many of which sent members to Kingston to attend the Clinton plaque unveiling.

For the coming was the celebration of what was believed to be the two hundred and fiftieth anniversary of the founding of Kingston as a white colonial community in 1657, and of the statewide and nationally-heralded Hudson-Fulton Celebration, marking the discovery of the Hudson River by Henry Hudson in 1609 for Dutch trading and colonization, as well as the celebration of Robert Fulton's first trip by the propulsive power of steam up the Hudson in 1807.

Dingman Versteeg, an emigre from Friesland in Holland had come to New York originally to translate Dutch documents for the Holland Society. Versteeg had recently completed making the first if not altogether adequate translation into English of the then earliest known official records of Dutch government in Kingston, and suggested to Benjamin Myer Brink of Kingston (the publisher of the historical serial called *Olde Ulster*) that it might be a favorable time to propose bringing the remains of Kingston Revolutionary hero George Clinton from the Congressional Cemetery in Washington to be reburied in the old Dutch burying ground at the corner of Wall and Main Streets among the graves of some of Kingston's very earliest colonial citizens.

Brink took notice of the proposal in his magazine and gave it his vigorous support. In fact, Brink was so greatly taken with Versteeg's suggestion that he plunged into making it a reality and with the help of others worked so hard at it as to cause the June 1908 number of *Olde Ulster* to reach subscribers a whole month late. A committee was formed and Chaplain R.R. Hoes, who had already shown much skill and industry in delving into Kingston's early history, shared with others the task of communicating with about 400 claimed descendants of Clinton, with the officials of the Congressional Cemetery and with the elders of the Old Dutch Church in Kingston, plus government officials in both Washington D.C. (including the Surgeon General of the United States) before the needed permissions were obtained to move the well-preserved body and the ten-foot-high stone monument which had stood over the original grave since Clinton's burial in 1812.

After all this work was done, the remains were transported, drawing the attention of large crowds through the streets of Washington and New York, to be placed aboard the United States Navy gunboat, *Wasp*, one of a flotilla of accompanying naval vessels which escorted the *Wasp* up the Hudson and stopped at the Highlands which had been the scene of Clinton's strenuous yet unavailing efforts at defending that point against British attack. And after ceremonies at West Point continued up the River to anchorage off Kingston Point. Up to this time the progress of the funeral cortege by land and water had the benefit of superb May weather, but on the morning after the *Wasp* had anchored off Kingston Point a violent rain storm drenched the city and vicinity, but this did not prevent thousands of Kingston citizens from enduring the drenching rain to pay their tributes along Broadway to George Clinton, as his coffin made its solemn way to the destined place in the old burial yard. There the body was reinterred with great care and elaborate ceremonies for the readopted son of Kingston. The stone monument from the Congressional Cemetery was finally uncrated and placed over the new grave—it displayed a circular portrait in carved stone made in 1812, to put Clinton's likeness on public view. From this time on George Clinton's grave has taken an honored place among the historic sites of the city of Kingston to which tourists are urged to visit.

The program of the first Ulster County Apple Blossom Festival of 1938 in its tribute to local history mentioned with pride that the great man had taken the oath of office as the first Governor of the State of New York in front of the court house on Kingston's Wall Street, as the program added, "within a stone's throw of his grave in the churchyard of the Old Dutch Church."

The July 1909 *Olde Ulster* (p. 215) published a poetic summation of what Clinton had come to mean to Kingston people (a poem modeled on the "Soldier, Rest! Thy Warfare O'er" section of Sir Walter Scott's *The Lady of the Lake*).

Soldier, rest! thy struggle over;
        Campaigns dreamed not of are won.
Statesman, sleep! the common people
        Thou didst champion have their own.
Yonder calm and peaceful mountains (the Catskills)
        Sprang to heights from nature's throes;
So from thy Titanic struggles
        Came thy native State's repose.
On thy mother county's bosom,
        With thy warriors round thee lying,
Camp once more forever with them—
        This is living! 'Tis not dying!

By the time the Clinton remains had found their hopefully final resting place, the glorious amusement park of Samuel D. Coykendall was establishing a resounding success out on Kingston Point (formerly the Indian Crossing and then Columbus Point) and by the '90s re-designed for only one purpose beside the further enrichment of Cornell heir-to-be Samuel D. Coykendall: that was to provide cheap amusement to all the people of Kingston and their visitors, rich and poor alike, at a small price of so much per amusement park feature, plus a modest general admission fee.

In the final decades of the nineteenth century, gay wit and playwright Oscar Wilde, famous illustrator Aubrey Beardsley and other swayers of taste were doing their best to introduce a yearning un-Calvinist atmosphere of greater enjoyment of life into the minds of Americans and Britons. Then much happened to change Kingston's Calvinistic past to make room for the enjoyment of a center for nothing else but amusement and even for presenting its City's history (as in the pageant of 1895) in a more pleasing and ever more profitable fashion for all and not only for the genealogically-minded descendants of the early colonists alone.

In 1893, Samuel D. Coykendall began putting together what was to become the Kingston Point Amusement Park, very seductively designed by Downing Olmsted, gifted son of the illustrious Frederick Law Olmsted, the designer, with Calvert Vaux, of New York's great Central Park. On this unique piece of Hudson Valley real estate projecting out into the River (and for that reason it had been used as the place where the large system of Indian trails met for the important Hudson crossing), Coykendall, son-in-law of soon to be deceased Thomas Cornell (who had been the city's outstanding and most aggressive entrepreneur), proposed constructing a public amusement park to be reached by uptown amusement-seeking Kingston people via Coykendall's recently electrified trolley line which would carry uptowners from their Washington Avenue station at Marius Street to the Park for a trifling fee.

Kingston horse-drawn trolley, from Tillson & Brink map of 1854

Kingston trolley, photo in author's archive

New York city people would reach the Park inexpensively on board the glorious "palatial" excursion steamboats of the Hudson River. The Ulster and Delaware Railroad (now controlled by Coykendall) would carry tourists enjoying a visit to the Catskills to the Park as well. Once the Park was in business this diverted the Hudson River steamboat owners from docking at Rhinecliffe to docking and unloading passengers across the River at the very busy Kingston Point Amusement Park Landing on Coykendall's west bank. Similar ventures involving both trolley lines and amusement parks on outlying and usually undistinguished parts of cities were being offered elsewhere in the nation at this time. This one however had its own special value and appeal—it offered a very great range of attractive, inexpensive amusement features at the very heart of the already magical Hudson Valley region celebrated worldwide by Washington Irving and many other gifted writers and artists and reachable now largely by Coykendall's various railroads as well as by his trolley and also by the elegant steamboats which enabled patriotic tourists to pleasantly educate themselves in their country's Revolutionary history while enjoying the scenic and famous Revolutionary War landmarks visible en route to and from the Park from the river steamboats' comfortable deck chairs, including those of Coykendall's famous *Mary Powell*, the "Queen of the Hudson."

The Kingston Point Park offered a shooting gallery, rowing on a picturesque lagoon, ambulatory tintype snappers, a Ferris wheel (just as soon as that new thrill

Kingston Point Park with Ferris Wheel, postcard in collection of Alf Evers

came on the market), a dance hall, a penny arcade, a bandstand, a merry-go-round, a bathing beach—and much, much more.

Kingston Point Park bandshell. Postcard from Alf Evers's Collection

There were also the facilities of the adjoining riverside Oriental Hotel, Chinese in decoration but German-American in cuisine and serving a famous Kingston-brewed lager beer. All this was set in an entrancing Hudson Riverside landscape of gardens boasting floral novelties, sinuous brick paths, flowering shrubbery, and artfully contrived walks and waterways for rowing. The Park proved to be so popular that on one Fourth of July over 3000 people sought—and found—amusement there. It proved a great money-maker for the Coykendall interests, especially as it was a major goal of its owner's profitable trolley line from uptown, until the Park's appeal dimmed with the rise of the automobile age in the 1920s, accompanied by the decline of the popularity of Hudson River steamboats, however palatial. In the early 1930s the Park went out of business and the large amusement-loving public found more up-to-date ways of enjoying itself (including the pleasures of movies, the automobile, phonographic records and radio) as the end of the Harding-Coolidge-Hoover cheery speculative dream began to fade into the sad realities of the Depression and the New Deal which sought to cure the economic ills which had caused the economic and societal collapse.

By the 1930s many sometimes tentative steps had been taken toward enabling Kingston to appear before the world as an attractive and educational historic City, one in which a growing awareness of the authentic part their city had played in American history would be made visible to tourists by the City's accumulation of charming buildings and traditions of its past. Its many features long neglected might now be brought to light and even restored in order to place Kingston and its relationship to the glorious Hudson Valley and the people's playground of the Catskills in the very forefront of places important to the entertainment of the nation, a part of American history largely and sadly neglected by some great national historians (usually from New England) of the past, including the merry but misleading history of Irving's Diedrich Knickerbocker. All this was interrupted by the Depression, a burst of what was called Urban Renewal, and the coming to the city of big industry, in the shape of IBM, and the construction of modern bridges and fast highways—yet the movement toward the realization of Kingston as a fascinating historic city moved relentlessly forward.

Earlier historic celebrations, from the first half-hearted one in 1826, to the State and national Centennial years of 1876 and 1877, to the 1886 well-financed private Pilgrimage of the Holland Society, and the Kingston and Hudson-Fulton celebrations of 1907 and 1909, had awakened a sense of great future possibilities, and had even turned a national spotlight on Kingston.

In the 1877 celebration the City's old stone houses had first been referred to as having been viewed with "awe and veneration" because of their having been ruined by the British and later rebuilt. And it was during the 1877 program of commemorative speeches that an orator first used the phrase, "historic city," as applied to Kingston, then only recently (in 1872) risen to the rank of a city.

The fervent appeal of Rear Admiral Higginson, added to other earlier appeals by others (including the appeal in the early 1880s by lawyer Frederick Westbrook urging the people of Kingston to preserve their old stone houses and Westbrook's efforts at making a modest showplace of the Senate House), had resulted after 1914 in increasing urgings to preserve the integrity of the city's historic legacy—an urge which in time caused excited protest whenever a hand was raised to threaten the integrity of one of the city's now undeniably precious "old stone houses" and other landmarks, including, as we have seen, the moving of George Clinton's remains to Kingston to remain there forever as a permanent asset to the city to whose history Clinton had contributed so much, and whose lead coffin is protected in the Old Dutch graveyard by being surrounded by a large mass enclosure of the artificial stone called concrete. An undated newspaper clipping on the Clinton re-burial had written that the mass of concrete in which Clinton's remains were placed could never be broken into until the sounding of the final trumpets as foretold in the Bible's Book of Revelation.

2.
Kingston Awakens to Its Own True History

THE FIFTIETH ANNIVERSARY OF THE INDEPENDENCE OF THE UNITED STATES had been celebrated by Kingston with little zest in 1826. Except for the lighting on South (now Overlook) Mountain in the Catskills of a bonfire clearly visible to Kingstonian eyes, and the cutting into a ledge beside the bonfire of the date of the 1826 anniversary of the Declaration of Independence. Such bonfires were usual that day on high and conspicuous spots up and down the Hudson Valley. Poems on Kingston's past occasionally appeared after that day in local newspapers, such as verses dealing with the burning of Kingston in 1777 by the British. In 1849 the Rondout *Courier* printed what purported to be a local legend, which involved more fancy than fact, and which also concerned the burning of Kingston and incidents connected with the now demolished Vleit Berg, the landmark which had once usefully marked the entrance of the Rondout Harbor in the days of sail.

By 1858 enough interest in the actual history of their county and villages had been aroused to warrant the organizing of the Ulster County Historical Society, devoted to bringing to light in research, discussion and print the true facts of the County's local history. Before that, Kingston and Rondout people had to rely on sometimes shaky oral history as recalled by oldtimers or hinted at in a very few family histories as in that of Abraham Hasbrouck and his descendants. Or by pondering the inscriptions on gravestones or the entries on the pages reserved for family genealogies in ponderous old brass-clasped Dutch Bibles. Or the jumbled facts and local stories offered by the authors of such gazetteers as those of Spafford, Barber and Howe, Disturnell, and under the heading of "Kingston."

The Historical Society, founded in 1858, prepared to go far beyond all this into a realm of true verifiable local history, probably stimulated by the publication by

New York State of huge volumes of translations of early Dutch colonial manuscript records which had remained until then unread in the Netherlands. The founding members of the Society were men (no women) of Dutch or Huguenot Ulster County ancestry, plus a few others, who prepared papers on a variety of local subjects which were read at meetings and then published by the Society as their *Proceedings.*

Notable among these papers was one by a newcomer to the community (with no Dutch ancestors), young George Watson Pratt, son of rich tanner and Congressman Zadock Pratt of Prattsville in neighboring Greene County. Young Pratt's scantily educated father had recognized his son's strong and inquiring intellect, had sent him in charge of a tutor to Europe for travel there and in Egypt and the Near and Middle East, and to study at a German University. Back home George Pratt had married and then moved to the congenial village of Kingston, bringing with him his extensive library devoted to American and other history he had accumulated.[721] Because of his knowledge of history, and his family's wealth, it is not surprising that Pratt was elected secretary (i.e., leader) of the new Ulster County Historical Society and submitted to its *Proceedings* an excellent paper on "The Expedition of General John Vaughan up the Hudson River in 1777 and the Burning of Kingston." Pratt's paper was well received because of the clarity of its exposition and the excellence of its sources, drawn from good American materials as well as those of official British naval records in London.

George Pratt found time in his busy life in Kingston to serve also as Colonel of the 20th Regiment or Ulster Guard of the County. Sensing the coming of the Civil War, Pratt had readied for service the militia regiment of which he was in command. While leading his men at the second Battle of Bull Run he was severely wounded, and before very long died.

A slim number of the Society's *Proceedings* was devoted to tributes to their leader but then the Society, without Pratt's informed and vigorous leadership, languished and died.

William Lounsbery, a lawyer in Kingston and owner and resident of the large and impressive gambrel-roofed Wynkoop house in Stone Ridge in which George Washington had once slept, demonstrated his knowledge of local history by writing about it for the 1856 William H. Boyd's (of Newburgh) *Directory of Kingston and Rondout*—it was the largest and best sketch of the history of the two communities up to then produced. (Brief sketches had already appeared in earlier gazeetteers.) In the sketch Lounsbery stated for the first time in print that following the end of adult slavery in New York State in 1828, the black population of Kingston had diminished—as indeed it had. But Lounsbery also put into print a witty and suggestive Kingston folk saying, "In Kingston every other house is a barn and every other white man is a negro." He also placed in his sketch one of the few known early references to the location and character of Thomas Chambers's "mansion house" on what is now Manor Avenue. Lounsbery, who may well have seen the house before its demolition, stated that the house had been square, of stone and as having holes in the walls for defensive musket fire.

As the one hundredth anniversary of the signing of the Declaration of Independence came close, the mayor of Kingston asked Lounsbery, as ex-secretary of the dying County Historical Society following George Pratt, to prepare an address on the City's history and Lounsbery complied. The address was delivered by Lounsbery on July 4, 1876, and was printed in pamphlet form to sell for twenty-five cents. It proved not to be the equal in quality of the same author's effort of 1856 since Lounsbery evidently used it in an effort to further his own political ambition by equating U.S. Grant (then politically active) and George Washington in character and achievements.

July 20, 1877 was an important milestone in Kingston's arousal of interest in its own history. This was the day chosen by the State of New York for a state-wide celebration to begin in Kingston of the hundreth anniversary of the adoption of the New York State Constitution in Kingston and the establishment of the revolutionary State government there.

There was that day in 1877 a huge assembly of celebrants on hand in Kingston, which had been busy since 5 a.m. that morning decorating Kingston houses and commercial buildings in an appropriate fashion with flags, bunting and streamers. Even roadside trees were decorated for the occasion, their trunks swathed in a similar fashion to the houses. In his brief introductory speech, Judge Frederick Westbrook, known as the protector of the old stone Senate house and for his knack of originating telling phrases, referred to Kingston as "historic ground" but ended his speech with a peroration which referred to Kingston as "our historic city" for the first time on record.

A major speech followed made by well-known speaker and railroad lawyer Chauncey Depew who began by using the rhetorical skill for which Depew was renowned, by relating "Kingston-on-the-Hudson" (then only five years old as a city) to the ancient city of "Rome-on-the-Tiber" in a way which brought cheers from his large audience. He went on in a long and able speech to deal well with the events which resulted in the Centennial Celebration of that day in Kingston, including a tribute to the great value of the New York State Constitution which had been adopted in Kingston on the same day in 1777, and Depew finally gave way to local history buff General George H. Sharpe.

Woodcut of Constitution House, later Bogardus Tavern, from Barber and Howe, *Historical Collections of the State of New York*, 1841

General Sharpe told of being in the company of General Van Buren a few days earlier when the two Kingstonians had carefully examined what he called the "old stone dwellings" of Kingston and determined there were forty-eight of them. He described some and spoke of their former owners, and then told his listeners that many of the largest stone houses which the British burned in October 1777 had been so large and had so much inflammable wood inside that they had burned with a flame so hot and destructive that no attempt was ever made to restore them, and the General spoke of having talked with old people who remembered that in their childhood they had played inside these old ruins and their "standing arches," in a sentiment of "awe and reverence." This was one of the first times that public attention had been drawn to the old stone houses of Kingston as historical assets or to Kingston as a historical city.

During the 1860s and 1870s Jonathan W. Hasbrouck had become a familiar figure on local highways and byways as he ransacked the brains and attic archives of oldtimers for help in gathering material for his history of the county which he was writing. And also at the same time he was asking for votes for a minor local office to which he hoped to be elected.

Although Jonathan W. Hasbrouck had been working for years on his history of Ulster County he apparently was not well enough to take part in the Centennial celebration and died in April of 1879. But the work he had completed in writing the early part of his history was sold by his widow to Nathaniel Bartlett Sylvester whose massive county history appeared in 1880 after much promotion, with credit for the early history given to Hasbrouck.

Sylvester's history is of the sort known in the trade as a "Mug Book," because it is embellished with up to full page portraits of those local worthies who could afford the expense. It was a better-than-average example of its class, with a good level of accuracy, reprinted in 1977 by Peter Mayer's Overlook Press.

In 1888, after long years of research, lawyer-politician-historian Marius Schoonmaker gave Kingston a substantial volume in which political, social and family history is treated against its background of state and national history. The book like that of Sylvester well deserves its recent reprinting.

Bringing the nineteenth century to an end with resounding tribute to Kingston's useful family and early history was the publication by Chaplain Randall Roswell Hoes, U.S.N., of his edition of the records of Kingston's Old Dutch Church, with its wealth of family and other useful data.

In 1905 Benjamin Myer Brink had undertaken, as a service to the rising interest in Ulster and Kingston history, the monthly publication, printed by Styles and Bruyn in Kingston in a handsome style, of *Olde Ulster*, a substantial serial collection of reprints of early records and freshly written material on the past of the County and City. Included were the results of much genealogical research, historical items gleaned from old newspapers, letters and manuscripts, traditional recollections and much else including a biography in several installments of George Clinton. The publication of *Olde Ulster* continued with only one interruption until 1914.

Kingston by then had shed some of its former air of a conservative traders and farmers market town and taken on an air of enough of a cultural and historical distinction to delight some well informed and discriminating tourists. The words "Colonial Band" even appeared, as a sign of the change, in large letters on the big bass drum which had once boomed for the former "Kingston Band."

Miss Julia MacEntee Dillon, daughter of a successful Rondout manufacturer of machinery, studied painting in Paris and London to such good effect as to win her admiration and prizes with her excellent paintings of peonies and roses, which were her specialty.

Miss Dillon restored and enlarged as her residence and studio an old stone house and likewise did Mrs. A. E. P. Searing, the author of a very elaborate and handsomely illustrated book on the region's lore and history called *The Land of Rip Van Winkle*. Julia Dillon and Mrs. Searing also took part in such community projects as helping found the Kingston Hospital. After inheriting the family machinery

The bass drum of the formerly Kingston band had the new name, "Colonial Band," painted on its head. Photo courtesy of Friends of Historic Kingston

Interior of the Dillon studio, courtesy of Friends of Historic Kingston

making business of Langworthy and Dillon upon her father's death, Julia Dillon undertook its management, but also went on painting. She was also active in managing the women's section of the great Columbian Exposition of 1893 held in Chicago, and she wrote a small book on Kingston gardens.

Mary Isabella Forsyth (while continuing life in her fine house on Pearl Street) wrote poems about Kingston's past and a song (for which she also wrote the music) to be sung on occasions of Kingston's historical celebrations. She also wrote a brief book on New York State and Kingston's history, published at her own expense as a contribution to the historic celebrations of 1907 and 1909. A Junior League came into being and the young women of the League took an active interest in local history, and worked hard later on compiling with professional help a published book on old houses of Ulster County worth preserving.

Mary Isabella Forsyth continued to give lavishly to charitable and historical causes and to share personally in their activities. Miss Forsyth and other family members gave to Kingston the land for Forsyth Park and Zoo. The zoo's first inhabitant was a black bear which wandered into the city and was first exhibited there in 1923.

Mrs. Forsyth also continued to preside as regent over the Wiltwyck chapter of the Daughters of the American Revolution while also being very busy in the Industrial Home for neglected and orphaned children.

The old Senate House, owned and managed after 1888 by the State of New York (part of it built near the end of the seventeenth century by an ancestor of former owner Frederick Westbrook who had done much toward preserving it), began to be spoken of as the oldest public building in the United States and the place in which much of the government of New York State was founded.

On the Senate House grounds the large modern (and inevitably bluestone) museum building was years later (1927) to arise on the spacious grounds of the Senate House (from which long before a barn and a medley of lesser farm structures had been removed) and which would contain the finest collection in existence of paintings and other works of the City's own John Vander Lyn plus a good regional historical library with a substantial ever-increasing stock of regional books, antiques, manuscripts and mementoes. The Library is much used by workers in regional and local history.

The curved wall of the entrance space of the Museum was planned by its architects to accommodate a small part of the John Vander Lyn *Panoramic View of the Palace and Gardens of Versailles* which is now a pride of the American Wing of New York City's Metropolitan Museum of Art. (See page 428 for an account of the *Panorama*.)

Adjoining the Senate House Museum and under the same management is the local red brick Loughran House, a nineteenth century Kingston doctor's house marked from the street by two large and imposing gateposts crafted of unusual ornamental local limestone.

A dark, appropriately ash gray volunteer firehouse of the characteristic classically inspired design of the 1870s with its collection of heirloom volunteer fire fighting equipment and volunteer gear has become a unique museum on Fair Street. Its collections shed a fascinating light on the large part which fire-fighting by volunteers played in Kingston culture of the past, in a community that had more than a fair share of fires partly because of its thatched roofs, straw bedding for man and beast, and wooden palisades of early times.

The pride of volunteer fire companies was made evident by their dress or parade uniforms. The Cornell Hose Company, for example, wore wine-colored brass buttoned frock coats with fawn-colored trousers. Fawn-colored caps bore the name Cornell in purple letters. Dress uniforms like these were features of firemen's conventions and parades. Some dress uniforms were special versions worn with firefighting equipment like the the four-wheeled hose carriages with mirrored sides and silver ornamentation. Sponsors of such glorious uniforms and parade equipment were often politicians and entrepreneurs like Thomas Cornell whose Cornell Hose Company won awards at firemanic conventions. Working uniforms and equipment, of course, were strictly practical and so went unsponsored.

Judge Alphonso Trumpbour Clearwater who had become the first official historian of Kingston edited a stout history of the County of Ulster published in 1907.

In 1934 the Ulster County Historical Society, which had been disbanded following the Civil War which caused the death of the Society's leader and secretary Col. George W. Pratt, was revived and began in the early 1930s once again to publish its *Proceedings* (as the *Ulster Gazette*) which still continues to explore and present many interesting aspects of County and Kingston history. The County Society also maintains a county museum in the early stone Bevier House in Marbletown, which has a fine collection of materials relating to Kingston.

With the decline of the extractive industries, the obsolescence and final abandonment of the D&H Canal and the failure to maintain the ambitious regional railroad system of Thomas Cornell against competition from more modern transportation by motor cars and trucks on new and higher-speed highways and time-saving Hudson River bridges, and unable to make up entirely for its loss of productive, profitable industries, Kingston lost a measure of its prosperity. And so too ended the festive share of Kingston prosperity going back to Colonial days by reason of its brewing of paricularly strong beer and a good bit of distilling both of which were ended by Prohibition in 1919, and the failure of some Kingston breweries to adapt to the making of the "near beer," which was legal but weak. Nor did Kingston participate on a large scale in the booming soft drink industry of today.

The City, except for interest in its history, entered a period of decline. Yet at the same time pride in the City's history and in the old stone houses once protected from Native attack by a log stockade was growing, and extending to include the eloquent architectural vestiges of its more recent history (such as handsome Victorian mansions, cast iron painted commercial facades and balconies and many other surviving romantic relics of a growing city), but except to prospering dealers in local antiques, this pride had little value for a time to the local economy. It was sometimes said then that local history was becoming Kingston's major industry as its other industries faltered, but little by little that industry was paying larger dividends.

At this time in the early twentieth century the Allen brothers had given Kingston somc hopc of bccoming involvcd in thc manufacturc of a promising automobile, the Allen-Kingston. In New York City the brothers had first imported and sold European automobiles. The one they proposed manufacturing in Kingston had a good deal of the elegant look of European models, which would have relied on a greater use of handicraft methods rather than the mass production methods that were coming into use in Detroit.

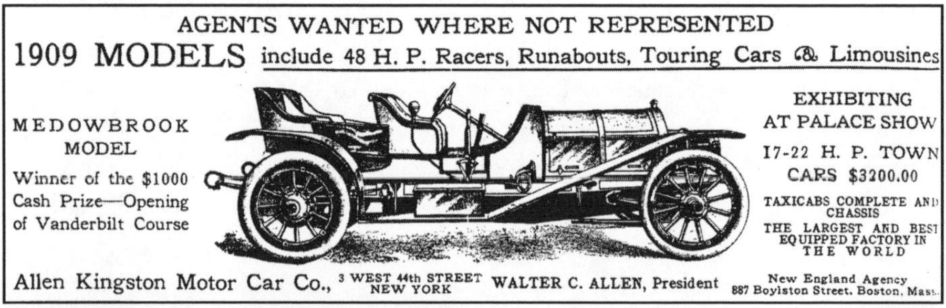

Top: Ad showing the sporty model and showing some of the promotion hype at which the Allen brothers were skilled. *Bottom:* Driving an Allen-Kingston automobile

Yet despite the occasional winning of a notable automobile race, and its unfounded claim to have the largest automobile factory in the country, the attractive looking Allen-Kingston was sued, as were many other automobile makers, by those outside Kingston who claimed to have the basic patent for the automobile engine, under the "Selden patent rights" and the Allen-Kingston automobile faded away.

By then, it had become obvious even to the once hopeful few that Kingston even with its good transportation facilities was not going to become an "automobile city" like Detroit or Indianapolis. And the Allen-Kingston became extinct probably in part because of its makers' inability to adopt the mass industry methods which were rushing the U.S. automobile industry into world leadership.

Light industries including needle trades (some of which lasted in Kingston for decades and did well) had arrived, some from New York City, in the hope of escaping the growing strength there of effective unionization. And the manufacturing of a variety of wood-using or mechanical devices in demand in an ever more mechanized society, among them tall post beds considered a suitable product of a "colonial city," were not sufficient to restore Kingston's prosperity to the height it had once attained in the years of reliance on substantial income from its three big and bedrock-removing extractive industries and the Canal, which had resulted however in a mauling of the earth and its bedrock from its excavations and from digging tributary ponds and streams to keep the Canal filled with water as well as from its creation of sometimes shoddy workers' housing on parts of the land unsuited to such use.

The First World War had given Kingston a strong economic boost when boatyards and shipyards were reopened to make small craft such as submarine chasers for the U.S. Navy and a variety of other war-related products were made in the city. Yet the boost did not become a boom and once the war ended so too did many war-related new manufacturing industries, with a few valued exceptions.

Early in the 1920s the Kingston Chamber of Commerce (perhaps concerned by the post-war dip in the economy and about the time of the failure of the once promising Allen-Kingston automobile, and such blows as the rejection as a factory site by General Electric, in favor of Schenectady) commissioned a Chicago firm of business analysts to undertake a study of Kingston which might help the discouraged Chamber's members find a way to a renewed prosperity. The study delved with intelligence into many levels of Kingston life. Among other things it suggested that the City (as based on official census figures) had become a very multi-ethnic place which had drawn upon a surprising number of countries for its working population. Here is a brief summary of that revealing population study.

Among ethnic groups living in Kingston by 1920 were people born in Armenia, Austria, Belgium, Czecho-Slovakia, Canada, Cuba, Denmark, England, Finland, France, Germany, Hungary, Ireland, Italy, Yugo-Slavia, Lithuania, Norway, Poland,

Netherlands, Roumania, Russia, Scotland, South America, Spain, Switzerland, Sweden, Egypt, Wales and various islands in the West Indies.

The majority of Kingston's people were still native-born, but 679 had been born in Germany, 399 in Italy, 346 in Ireland, 486 in Roumania, 39 in Scotland, 173 in Austria, and smaller numbers down to only one person born in the Netherlands. This last figure was in sharp contrast with the numbers in the early years of colonialization. The large number born in Central Europe, it might be added, represented women in the needle trades; the people from Italy were largely brickyard workers or former railroad or Ashokan Reservoir construction workers.

Taken as a whole, Kingston's population of 26,688 in 1920, in its multi-ethnicity was not altogether unlike that of some other American cities, yet it had its own characteristic mix which added varied spices to the City's already multi-ethnic quality.

In January of 1993 George Allen, then the reference librarian of Kingston's Carnegie Library, would organize an exhibition of the family histories of eight typical immigrant families arrived in the past century or less. The exhibition was the subject of a detailed full-page review in the *Kingston Daily Freeman* by a sympathetic reporter. Based on family records and photographs, and interviews with family members, the article dealt with immigrants of a few generations which had arrived in Kingston with limited means to make good places for themselves and to serve the city well. A member of one Polish family of the eight was a wood carver and cabinet-maker who had left visible signs of his skill in the City's buildings. A member of another of the eight had established a successful bakery and given the City entertainment each December by driving his horse-drawn wagon on city streets while he handed out gifts of cookies and cakes while dressed as Santa Claus.

COUNTRY OF ORIGIN, OF FOREIGN-BORN

POPULATION OF KINGSTON

Nativity of the Foreign-born Whites.

Armenia,	13
Austria,	172
Belgium,	2
Canada-French,	19
Canada, other,	74
Cuba,	4
Czecho-Slovakia,	7
Denmark,	10
England,	141
Finland,	7
France,	22
Germany,	675
Greece,	11
Hungary,	51
Ireland,	399
Italy,	346
Jugo-Slavia,	15
Lithuania,	1
Netherlands,	5
Norway,	12
Poland,	190
Roumania,	2
Russia,	486
Scotland,	39
South America,	1
Spain,	3
Sweden,	11
Switzerland,	11
Syria,	24
Wales,	1
West Indies,	--

A page from the Survey dealing with multi-ethnicity of Kingston

One early immigrant had been so pleased with what he had found in Kingston that he did without food for one day of every week during his first year in the strange new City in order to save enough money to bring his parents and siblings to join him. This family eventually owned a successful fur store on North Front Street. Another of these families produced a young woman who was the first Kingston woman to graduate from a law school. Still another family had produced a member who became the sportscaster of Kingston's first radio station which was operated by the local Boy Scouts from the very topmost stage of the Kingston City Hall tower. Another, who was black, became the first of his color to own his own business (in the insurance field), and to be active in the Kingston Elks Club which was led by a black immigrant woman called the "Exalted Ruler."

Yet another member of the eight exhibiting families did well in real estate; and others did well in a variety of other occupations. Of course, there were some immigrants who did not find Kingston congenial, and there was one of the eight who was rejected at Ellis Island on his first try, but tried again and was accepted, and became a mule driver manager on the Ashokan Reservoir project, and whose son became a well known Kingston surveyor. Another became an outstanding trial lawyer and a judge.

Adding to Kingston's ethnic diversity were the people from Europe, Jewish in their religion and culture who began turning up as immigrants in Kingston, driven from their homelands by violent hostility and hoping for a better and more hospitable place to live and work in America. Some had been victims of the organized anti-Semitic efforts called pogroms; others merely by a lack of opportunity for Jews.

Many of these people and other emigrants had interesting stories to tell of why they emigrated and how it was they chose Kingston. One man who was an outstanding success as a Kingston dentist liked to tell of leaving his native Poland to avoid their compulsory military draft in which Jewish soldiers were treated with particular lack of respect. The man escaped Poland while hiding in a load of hay and making his way to New York while his brother settled in England where he studied oriental languages at a British university after which he became a professor. The New York man earned his way through dental school by working in a mechanical dentistry place and once he had his degree in dentistry turned down an offer to teach dentistry in a good South American dental college in favor of setting up as a practicing dentist in Kingston, after being assured in New York that Kingston was a "good place for Jews" with no record of the kind of persecution which had led him to flee from Poland.

3.
Thomas Chambers Revived
1886-1905

While Thomas Chambers had been a big man in the Esopus and the Wiltwyck of his day, later generations of Kingstonians for many years seldom mentioned him after his death in 1694 until the Pilgrimage of the Holland Society members of 1886 drew grateful if temporary attention to him as the true City founding father even though he was not even a real Dutchman, as the Pilgrims would have preferred. (And so would not have been welcomed into membership in the Holland Society.) The strong appeal of Congressman Lindsley for contributions to pay for a marker above Chambers's unmarked grave in Montrepose Cemetery did not bring any results at all, as far as it can be learned, and it would not be until the publication in *Picturesque Ulster* in 1896 that a suprising chain of events took place which would lead to the placing above Chambers's grave by the anniversary year of 1907, of a handsome monument suggesting a Roman sarcophagus on which Chambers was promoted without any evidence whatever to the rank of an English knight or baronet by placing the word "Sir" before his name. This probably occurred because of someone supposing (in error) that as the lord (or landlord) of a manor Chambers was entitled to it.

The belated bringing to a place of honor but not of knighthood among Kingston's heroes was stimulated unintentionally by two men, Richard Lionel de Lisser and U.S. Navy chaplain R. R. Hoes. Richard Lionel de Lisser was a descendant of a Portuguese Jewish family which had emigrated to Jamaica, B.W.I. from Portugal in the late 1500s. De Lisser's work of the late 1890s was fortified by the work in the first five years or so of the twentieth century by Chaplain Randall Roswell Hoes (pronounced Hoose), U.S.N., of colonial Dutch antecedents and a meticulous delver into Kingston's past. Hoes was also the son of a former Dutch Reformed Kingston minister.

De Lisser, married to a Kingston woman, had set himself the task of clearing up a few of the many gaps and discrepancies in what was known of Chambers's Kingston career. In this he had the help of Abraham Hasbrouck, grandson of the sloop-owning and operating Abraham who had settled in Rondout from a southern Ulster County farm in the 1790s. Hasbrouck generously offered de Lisser, as de Lisser wrote in his "Rambles of an Artist" (included in his *Picturesque Ulster*), the use of his family chest containing old Rondout documents and maps, and additional information from his own considerable personal recollections. (One of the maps, part of which is shown on page 217, and found in the Hasbrouck chest, shows the house of the Chambers's heirs, the Van Gaasbeeks, with the site of the "redoubt" (the redout or rondout, once a fortified place) close by.

The Indian "tennis court" was a short distance above this map and to the left. De Lisser, who was an excellent photographer as well as a painter, took or commissioned pictures of old maps of Rondout showing the now vanished "Vault (or Burial) Lot" (swept away long ago in Rondout's hasty growth) in which Thomas Chambers and some of his Van Gaasbeek heirs had been buried, the stone on which was cut his monogram, TC, made into one, with the T superimposed over the C, and the year and day of Chambers death, April 9, 1694, all done in typical late seventeenth century script cut into the stone.

In addition de Lisser produced in his *Picturesque Ulster* a photo of the then still living ancient pear tree said to have been planted by Chambers and long used, de Lisser wrote, as a witness tree by surveyors. (A pear preserved in a sealed glass jar may be seen at the Senate House or its Museum today, labeled as a product of the long lived Chambers pear tree.) The pear tree stood on the edge of the Vault Lot with a good view of the new frame house which the father of the second Rondout Abraham, Janson Hasbrouck, had caused to be built at or close to the site of the Hasbrouck stone house of the 1790s, with the Chambers gravestone carefully moved from the Vault Lot and visibly embedded in the stone foundation at the south end of the long veranda of the much admired new and then fashionable frame house. (A similarly placed pear tree is remembered to have been planted close to the grave of Peter Stuyvesant in Manhattan, perhaps in

The pear tree, from *Picturesque Ulster*

The gravestone of Thomas Chambers, from *Picturesque Ulster*

both cases to suggest the hope of Christian immortality; for the pear is a notably long lived tree.) The old stone house and later on the more fancy frame or "Yankee" one (and the vestiges of the Vault Lot as well) had become victims of Rondout's almost frantic expansion in response to the arrival of the limestone mining, bluestone quarrying, cement making and D & H Canal (and the going out of fashion of stone dwellings).

Chambers's gravestone was moved about with due respect yet without leaving a clear trail until, with even the frame Hasbrouck house torn down as Rondout boomed, the gravestone after further still secret wanderings finally found safekeeping in the Senate House Museum (and not on exhibition), and not above the grave in the Montrepose Cemetery to compete in its simplicity with the more elegant new monument of 1907.

Chaplain Hoes also had gone ahead in his research and established that Chambers had owned at least two houses, one at Rondout at the Strand (or Kingston Landing), and another (the one mentioned as Chambers's "mansion (or manor) house" in the manor grant on what is now Manor Avenue close to the boundary line between Kingston and the present gerrymander-created Town of Ulster). Hoes obtained good information about the appearance of the Manor Avenue manor or mansion house from sixty-odd year old Miss Van Leuven who had lived there as a girl and had a good memory. From interviews with Miss Van Leuven, Hoes made notes of the building's appearance and character. After approval by Miss Van Leuven, he showed the notes to Kingston restoration architect Myron S. Teller who then made an architectural rendering based on Van Leuven's verbal representations. This rendering the lady carefully studied and agreed that it conformed very well to her memory of what the building had looked like in her girlhood. It resembled when first built the small square fortified manor houses once built (in perilous pre-Tudor days) in Britain, of stone with small openings for defense by musket fire against attackers—a design well suited some time later to the settlement of Esopus where attacks not only from Natives but also from the French of Canada were frequently anticipated. It had later been remodeled to suit more settled days but still showed continuing visible evidence of its original design. (Miss Van Leuven's recollection also conformed to the description of the building, which he probably saw before it was demolished, in William Lounsbery's published statement in 1857 that it was of stone and square with musket holes.) An account of the late 19th century tearing down of the old manor house and the inclusion of some of the stones to form the walls of the rectory of the Episcopalean Church on Albany Avenue will be found in the *People's History* of onetime City historian W. C. de Witt.

Hoes's notes of his interviews with Miss Van Leuven and the renderings of the old house by Myron Teller have been carefully deposited in the library of the Kingston Senate House Museum where they may be studied today for the light they may shed on future researches into the history of Foxhall Manor and Chambers. Also there deposited are some lists of objects excavated from the site which are unlikely to have any relevance to the appearance of the original manor house, but may date from Revolutionary War days and hint at preparations for military use of the place then. The design of the "mansion house fortified for defense" as Lounsbery had said in 1857 in repetition of the old grant, seems to have been settled by the work of Hoes, Teller and Miss Van Leuven and is likely to remain so unless further evidence comes to light.

Of permanent value in recording the "old stone house" aspect of Kingston's later history are the many very excellent and well reproduced photographs of old houses once within and outside the stockade walls and shown in de Lisser's *Picturesque Ulster*, first published in 1896 by Styles and Bruyn of Kingston. Many excellent photographs of the stone houses as well as other later houses outside the stockade limits were taken by de Lisser and some by Cornelius Hume, a bank teller of Kingston. The excellent photographic renderings of these houses as of the late 1890s are a priceless part of the assets of the City. The original glass plates of de Lisser's photographs were contributed to a wartime scrap drive by a forgotten but ill-inspired patriot, after they were taken from hoped-for safety in a vault in a Saugerties bank.

Rendering of Thomas Chambers' Manor House (or Mansion House) drawn by Myron Teller from a description by Miss Van Leuven, original in Senate House Museum Library

4.
"Kingston Not Included?" in the Hudson-Fulton Celebration 1909

The years during which the nation was headed from the White House by Presidents William McKinley and Theodore Roosevelt were those when the United States first strongly emerged to international eyes as a world power with well defined colonialist and even hints of what are called imperialist ambitions. They were also the years of growing expressions of patriotism and spells of flag-waving which led to the creation of Flag Day by Congress, to be celebrated annually on June 14. And they were years when Americans felt an ever increasing awareness of having a historical heritage. Kingston by then had already moved a long way from its early rigidly Calvinistic (if also rowdy) phase into a city modestly notable for the variety of lively entertainment features it had come to provide for its citizens young and old and for the tourists who visited it as pilgrims to the homes of their ancestors, as the Holland Society members of 1886 had been, but also for its ability to engage and stir the visitors' interest in the distinctive character of the American past as so well presented by Kingston. The entertainment in what more and more Kingstonians by then liked to call their "Colonial City" ranged from baseball games to comic music hall or vaudeville acts and the occasional tryout of a sympathetic Irish-American play by actor and director Dan Sully whose summer rehearsal and summer headquarters were in nearby Woodstock, or of the touring New York acting groups.

In 1908, Kingston expected to draw an unparalleled throng of visitors by an elaborate staging of a celebration of the 250th anniversary of the founding of their colonial community (by white colonists) believed to have been led by now better known Thomas Chambers, later on of Foxhall Manor. They also gladly looked forward to taking part in the great statewide patriotic celebration of 1909 of the 300th anniversary of English explorer Henry Hudson's discovery for European trade and colonizing the river and banks of the Atlantic estuary which has come to bear his name, and the first successful trip on his pioneer steam-powered boat by Robert Fulton up the Hudson in 1807. The great entertaining event was called the Hudson-Fulton Celebration, in enthusiastic national promotional efforts. But here, as the Kingston *Daily Freeman* ruefully headlined it's story, "Kingston is not included."

Upstate-downstate rivalries and jealousies had already by 1909 been hard facts of New York provincial and state life (as far back as the seventeenth century New York days of the Boulting Act)—the threatened exclusion of Kingston and other upstate Hudson Valley localities from the proposed joyous and profitable festivities, and their restriction to the vicinity of the City of New York alone, was strongly protested. The State Hudson-Fulton Committee responded to upstate protests by naming one day of the week long celebration to be at the disposal (for local purposes) of each of the counties past which Hudson and Fulton had recorded sailing, one in 1609 by the force of wind and the other in 1807 by the power of steam. Ulster County's Day was set as June 5. This appeared to be a good compromise, yet the Kingston Committee added a new log to the fire that had been ignited by the slight upon the City of Kingston. In referring to Chambers, he was named "Sir Thomas" as if he had been an English knight or baronet and not a simple commoner, a mistake probably caused by the fact that he was a "lord" or "landlord" of a manor.

The Kingston committee for the two celebrations announced through its chairman Judge A. T. Clearwater that it had set aside $2,000 (from public funds) to pay for the erection of a monument over Chambers's grave to be dedicated on June 5 and the publication of a memorial volume for the entire Kingston celebration. No mention was given of any contribution made back in 1886 at Congressman Lindsley's suggestion. The Judge (who was of Dutch descent), and at that time the accepted City spokesman in local historical matters, always emphasized the decided Dutchness of the place and loved to orate on the glorious past of what today we know as Holland (while saying nothing of the multi-ethnic nature of the City which census figures had shown to have developed from the very beginning of Esopus as a white man's colony and even earlier.) Yet someone on the Committee, said to have been the Judge himself, had made an egregious error in providing an incorrect handle for the adopted Dutchman now accepted even by Clearwater as "our founding father."

Chaplain R. R. Hoes, U.S. Navy, like Richard De Lisser had well understood Chambers's publicity value as a civic founding father of the first importance, and had already devoted skill and energy to clearing up some blank and muddy spots in Chambers' slife story. Hoes now positively exploded in a letter to Kingston mayor and leading Rondout citizen Walter C. Crane.

In his reply to the mayor Hoes stated that in all his "extensive research" into the "romantic notions" which he implied had been mistakenly seen as parts of

Kingston's history he had never once seen any mention of the dubbing of Chambers into knighthood or as his being a baronet. He further denounced the shaky state into which he believed the City's history had fallen, as deplorable.

The mayor gave Hoes' letter a chilly and testy reply, as if reluctant to soil his fingers by meddling with what might be taken as an attempt to deprive Chambers (even in death) of a deserved official honor. He advised the Chaplain to take up the matter with the local celebration committee. When Ulster County Day finally dawned with its crowning event the long delayed dedication of the handsome new Chambers's tomb in Montrepose Cemetery, the word "Sir" still preceded his name. The "Sir" was all the more egregious because it was now boldly carved on the memorial stone above Chambers's grave. It continued to remain there, as if in open defiance of all doubters, during two long years of wrangling before better sense prevailed and it was chiseled into deserved oblivion. And a degree of peace reigned once again among Kingston's historically-minded on the question of what the *Freeman* had scornfully called "the Chambers Myth."

With its failure to be included in the original Hudson-Fulton Celebration forgiven and forgotten, Kingston went ahead to celebrate the two events with vigor. Newspapers did a great deal of pointing with pride to Kingston's past and that of its Rondout Landing, and orators did their hopefully informing and entertaining best. Shopkeepers on Wall Street and on Broadway decorated their windows in an appropriate fashion—one shop filled its window on the street with a good model of the steamboat *Clermont* as Kingstonians preferred calling it, but officially known as the *North River Steamboat*, beneath a full display of Christmas tree ornaments which would not be on sale until that fall.

There were many speeches and Kingston people were reminded that the first skipper of Fulton's steamboat had been a member of their own city's Brink family of undoubted Dutch origin.

The people too were reminded that Chancellor Robert R. Livingston had become a partner of steamboat perfecter Fulton (who was to marry a Livingston daughter), once the 1807 trip proved successful. The Chancellor had been a good friend and neighbor of Kingston. Hadn't Fulton's partner the Chancellor demonstrated his friendship as well as his patriotism by his giving each owner of a Kingston house burned by the British in 1777 fifty acres of Livingston land in the Great or Hardenbergh Patent? (Later the entire tract given to the Kingstonians would receive its present name of New Kingston. It is located off Route 28, past Margaretville, in a charming and agriculturally good countryside.) And hadn't the people of Kingston shown their appreciation of the Chancellor after he came home from distinguished duty as the American minister to France in 1804 by honoring their good neighbor with a lively parade and a testimonial banquet?

1909 Hudson-Fulton display in Woolworth's shop window in Kingston, with steamship models, photo from collection of Alf Evers

The two Celebrations, that of the approximately 250th anniversary of the founding of Kingston largely by Dutchmen led by English Chambers, and that of the 300th Anniversary of English Henry Hudson's discovery of the Hudson for what turned out to be both Dutch and English commerce and colonialism, had been notable points in the recognition of the beginning of the Village as a well-known Hudson River port. The Celebrations also emphasized the value of the history of the Village and the Hudson River not only to New York State but also to national history, to which, it was being recognized, the Dutch had contributed so much more than the early New England writers of American history were yet willing to admit, and which Irving's Knickerbocker history had presented in a charming and yet not exactly accurate light which had been taken seriously by too many who had been enchanted by Irving's seductive prose.

5.
A Rear-Admiral Deplores Destroying Historic Buildings in 1914

AS AN INDICATION OF THE GROWTH IN KINGSTON OF AN INTEREST IN THEIR City's colorful past and of their ancestors' accomplishments, the Wiltwyck chapter of the Daughters of the American Revolution had been founded in 1892. Their Kingston chapter house would be bought in 1907, the year of the celebration of the City's approximately 250th year since its settlement by white colonists. Mary Isabella Forsyth was named first Regent. Members of the organization were required to prove their descent from a soldier of the American Revolution. This resulted not only in a considerable local flurry in genealogical research, but in the purchase and restoration in that historic year of the old stone Sleght-Tappen house in which Jesse Buel had published his newspaper, the *Ulster Plebeian.* The Daughters made historically correct attempts to commemorate some events in Kingston's history. One of these attempts paid tribute to Kingston's Revolutionary War veterans (from whom the DAR members were descended) by means of a handsome bronze tablet dealing with the burning of Kingston by the British on October 17, 1777 and by the deeds of their Revolutionary forebears.

The tablet was placed on their building's outside south wall. This was a memorable event, for only once before had any local group taken any similar commemorative step in honor of the deeds of their heroic ancestors.

As principal speaker at the dedication ceremonies in 1914, the members chose Rear-Admiral Francis J. Higginson, a Bostonian by birth living with his wife in dignified retirement in the river port City after serving in the U.S. Navy and commanding the battleship Massachusetts during the battle of Santiago in the Spanish-American War.

Higginson was a respected Naval veteran and the only one of his rank to then live in Kingston. (A rear-admiral ranks just below an admiral and above a captain and may display two stars.) Whenever Higginson spoke in public, he commanded attention and respect. The Admiral first complimented the ladies on the high quality of their tablet and then provided a brief history of similar commemorative efforts going back to ancient Egypt. He deplored the lack of visible tributes to the honor of Kingston's other heroes. He pointed out that, lacking such tributes, these heroes and their deeds were in danger of slipping from memory and being "wiped out." And he warned that because of the recent pulling-down of some old stone structures associated in the public mind with George Washington's visit to Kingston on November 16, 1782, memory of such visits would grow dim, and a vital part of Kingston's past might be irrevocably lost. Judge A. T. Clearwater then spoke in agreement with the Admiral's gloomy admonitions suggesting the possibility of a history-less future for Kingston with sites of historical importance destroyed forever.

1908 and 1909 had been years of heightened historical sensitivity for the City because of the holding of Kingston's major historical celebrations. The warnings against the folly of damaging their historical heritage by tearing down the very buildings that did so much to help keep alive that heritage had an effect. (Back in 1883, a similar warning by Frederick Westbrook against the tearing down of historic buildings had had little effect.)

On June 5, 1909 (a day of the Hudson-Fulton Celebration) ninety Kingston businessmen assembled in the new and glorious Renaissance inspired marble and granite Central Post Office on Broadway to protest against the destruction of two undistinguished postal sub-stations of no outstanding historic value located at two opposite ends of the city and the recent construction of the magnificent building (in which they met) to take the place of both the uptown postal sub-station in Kingston and the downtown one in Rondout. The meeting would have a result (but not until about sixty years later) in the tearing down of the glorious Central Post Office, no matter how much it had been praised year after year by competent connoisseurs of architecture. The Central Post Office had been an outcome of the sudden realization by the federal government (which had built and paid for it) that they might save $2,600 a year for taxpayers by combining their Kingston operations. Many Kingston people by 1909 had learned to venerate their old stone houses once surrounded by a stockade but were not able to appreciate the architectural quality of the very sophisticated Renaissance inspired Central Post Office. The protest meeting of 1909 was called because of the belief of the ninety businessmen (six of whom had never before entered it and called it, as many others did, the "mausoleum" or "the folly").

The handsome 1907 Central Post Office builoding, built for and paid for by the Federal Government and demolished by Kingston, post card in collection of Alf Evers

The reason for the placing of the two sub-stations "at opposite ends of the town" was the result, it was being said, of the "geographical situation." When plans to merge the villages of Kingston and Rondout were being debated in the 1870s, the geographical situation had recognized two centers of population connected by the former Strand Road, a long, ill-kept, largely unbuilt-up road (now known as Broadway) giving the City the nickname, used by the scornful, of "dumbell city." The placing of the City Hall on Union Avenue (later Broadway) at the height of O'Reilly's Woods in the Armabowery between the two united villages, and the later clustering of the architecturally ambitious City Hall, the grim Armory, the Kingston Hospital, the High School and the City's Carnegie Library and other civic services of the future on this height were intended to provide a Civic Center that would help truly to unite the two separate centers. (The road known today as Broadway had been renamed Union Avenue to promote a hoped-for recognition of the union of the two former villages into a single united city, and the continued union of the nation after the Civil War.)

With further future means of faster transportation—streetcars (first horse and then electric), bicycles, buses and automobiles—available, Central Broadway and the future industrial district dependent on it and the West Shore Railroad, would need no longer be regarded as the handle of a dumbell and the derogatory nickname was forgotten as was the name of the Armabowery. A satisfactory method of handling mail was worked out following the 1909 meeting. Yet prejudice against the fine Central Post Office lingered on and became insistent.

With the agreement of the Mayor and the Common Council, and the business community, the visibly splendid Central Post Office of marble and granite which added stately beauty to the region was offered by Postal authorities to the City for one dollar and when the City refused the building was put on the real estate market, and then the "mausoleum" was demolished without significant public protest, but with great difficulty caused by its excellent construction. The site was bought by a chain of fast food purveyors who erected a tawdry little sales ediface for hamburger eaters. The venture failed, several similar successors also failed to lure hamburger or hotdog eaters, and once again demolishing had given a temporary apparent solution to a problem.

After the demolition of the Central Post Office, a flood of protests finally arose, and the loss of so fine a part of the City's stock of structures of historic and cultural value came to be widely and regretfully understood. Among the protestors at the destruction of what had been a magnificent part of Kingston's architectural heritage was talented Leslie Bender, a Woodstock painter who had been charmed by the character of Kingston and had moved her studio there. She, with wide public approval, planned an outdoor mural painting to face the badly-used site, to display scenes which would celebrate Kingston's historic heritage, and to do what it could to celebrate the memory of the splendid old Post Office in which after it had been destroyed more and more Kingstonians felt a nostalgic pride, and thought of appropriate uses for.

6. The Time they Shook the PlumTree, 1905-1915

THE CONSTRUCTION OF THE NEARBY ASHOKAN RESERVOIR BETWEEN 1905 and 1915 brought a period of golden prosperity to the lawyers (and many others) of Kingston and some others who were engaged in the enormous amount of legal work involved, in transferring titles and options to the land to be used for the great Catskill Mountain water system of New York City, especially the nearby Ashokan Reservoir. A photograph taken during these years shows Judge and City Historian A. T. Clearwater sitting alone at one end of what is called "the largest law office in Ulster County" with a long central table heaped with legal books and documents relating to Reservoir work awaiting his attention.

The period came to be known in Kingston as "the time they shook the plum tree" for those of the legal profession, as well as for others who profited from the New York water supply project.

Most of the rough hard labor for the Reservoir was done by Italian workers hired from contractors or padrones (who were dealers supplying Italian laborers they brought to the United States often from the padrones' own hometowns in Italy which were sometimes almost depopulated by their efforts, to build railroads, canals—and also water supplies such as the Ashokan Reservoir). Many of these Italian laborers, once their Reservoir work was ended, settled to the South of Kingston along the Hudson. Many became fruit farmers and are said to have given local people a lasting love for Italian cooking and wine.

Kingston lawyer Alphonso T. Clearwater, attorney for Samuel D. Coykendall of the Ulster and Delaware Railroad, at first worked with enormous energy against constructing the proposed Reservoir. This stimulated many local people to a rigorous opposition to the Ashokan project in ways that have continued to be expressed to the present day through opposition in the region to New York City influence in relation to its eventual Catskill Mountain watershed.

Judge Clearwater thundered in the Kingston and other courtrooms against New York City's choice of the Catskills as a source of its water supply, and instead proposed the far more distant Adirondacks as a better site. The expensive moving of miles of the tracks of Coykendall's Ulster and Delaware Railroad then gave Judge Clearwater ample opportunity to display the kind of oratory which he also used on happier occasions in praising the Dutch roots of Kingston history. In the case of the courtroom dispute over the value of Mrs. Cudney's ginseng farm, much public interest was caused because, it was claimed, the value was placed so high by the lady because of the Chinese belief in the youth-restoring and aphrodisiacal qualities of the herb.

Lesser legal fry drove aboard horse-drawn buggies from house to house over the lands that they hinted might be flooded, even to an impossible distance from the proposed site, carrying ink-bottles, pens and forms ready for landowners to sign options which would give New York City the right to purchase at substantially increased prices under the guidance of the eager lawyers. Poor farmlands that had been almost valueless before, were now judged to be valuable, thanks to these attorneys' advice, because they had landscape features hitherto unnoticed which might appeal to land-ignorant summer boarders, if properly presented.

A bright young local man who had walked all the way to a Midwestern college to get his education now used his education to guide him in the business of buying houses condemned by the City of New York, to move and resell in surrounding communities. Some were sold to Woodstock artists to use as studios, and a church migrated to be used as a summer home by a reporter for a New York city newspaper. And some of these once Esopus Valley houses are said to have turned up as residences in Kingston. And some of the dispossessed inhabitants of the reservoir site came to live in Kingston. One took up living in Mexico City. Another was met as a fellow guest at a Paris hotel.

The vast number of legal papers associated with the Ashokan Reservoir were stored in Kingston where they remained year after year, and some became part of the historical collection of the new Ulster County Community College, but after years of use were reclaimed by government and other authorities.

After the huge Reservoir sufficiently filled with pure mountain water in 1915 and the results of a few heavy rains were held back in its moist embrace, Kingston people realized that the Reservoir which many of its citizens had opposed, had a positive value to them because it retained the rushing waters of Esopus Creek floods, which formerly had damaged (or fertilized) their uptown flatlands, but now no longer did so. The Esopus Creek now comes to an end in the Reservoir. A reconstructed creek of mixed water flowing from the Reservoir is known now as the lower Esopus.

There hasn't been a serious flood in uptown Kingston since 1915, and this helped give the flatlands a new use as the ideal site for a large flood-free shopping center. Included in the area now protected from flooding was the once a flood-prone Mutton Hollow, located within a black section of Kingston across which a steel bridge carried Route 28 as it entered Kingston.

Mutton Hollow (near the current Route 28 traffic circle) in Distress, due to flooding that stopped with the building of the Ashokan Reservoir, from *Picturesque Ulster*.

7.
"Old Stone Houses" Come into Their Own 1920s

SPURRED ON BY THE ROSE-TINTED COLONIAL DREAM WHICH HAD BEEN AROUSED up to and through the 1920s with the aid of retired clergyman and New Englander Wallace Nutting's hand-tinted photographs and cheerful, popular books on Colonial life around the nation, the market value of Kingston's old stone houses of Colonial days was steadily rising, as the twentieth century advanced, in response to a growing interest in restoring a few of them as desirable residences. Local Kingston architect Myron S. Teller (of Dutch descent) came to specialize in restoration and he set up a Wiltwyck Forge where accurate reproductions of old Kingston door latches with crosses (meant, old timers said, to keep witches away), hinges and andirons of wrought iron were hammered out by skilled traditional blacksmiths of the Van Kleeck family and others. The growing interest in these old Dutch buildings of the 17th century stockade, so different in character and charm, as tourists remarked, from those of other historical parts of the nation (and still maintaining their old village relationship to each other) was helping build up a pride in what had come to be more and more often called "Colonial Kingston" which helped to give rise to the widespread use of the word "Colonial" even in the names of modern commercial enterprises (such as that of the successful baseball team called the Leaders or the Colonials, a game unheard of in colonial days), as noted in the preface to this book. Dealers in and eager collectors of regional antiques multiplied and so too did the publications about Kingston and Ulster County history locally and elsewhere and most memory of the unpleasant meaning of "colonial" as understood by American Revolutionists of 1776, and bragged about by Governor Lord Edward Cornbury in 1705, faded away.

As the plans for including the Esopus Valley Reservoir in New York City's enlarged system of water supply were completed and construction began in 1905, New England minister Wallace Nutting was giving up the pulpit in favor of producing for sale hand-tinted photographs of an idyllic American past in which the resistance of American natives played no part and the soil cheerfully welcomed European notions of managing it for profit and pleasure in spite of its wolves, unwilling Natives and rattlesnakes. Nutting wrote and illustrated books on the furniture of the colonial past. He set up in 1914 a little chain of restored colonial houses in which touring Americans might put up in and play at being happy colonists.

But as the First World War began, some Ulster County residents of German background ran up German flags and their boys in schoolyards shouted "Hoch der Kaiser" or "raise up the Kaiser high." And sons and daughters of Irish emigrants recalled their elders' tales of rack-rent (that is, exorbitantly high) absentee English landlords of Irish farms and hoped these heartless landlords would get their just desserts. But as this war settled down into an unprecedented era of cruelty, a dramatic change came over Kingston people of all ethnic origins.

As the war had begun in 1914 in Europe, recently immigrant-descended Kingston people were shocked, in part because of their own multi-ethnic European origins, by the reckless destruction of human lives (some of them their own relatives) and of many historic European buildings extending to beautiful ancient cathedrals, palaces and the pretty villages of their own ancestors. Kingstonians of many ancestral stocks became shocked enough to cause them to pay added attention to the preservation of the simple treasures of their old stone houses, and this helped them become more willing to take steps to preserve them for future community benefit. There was a realization that these unique and irreplacable old stone symbols, charmingly simple as they were, had come to have a value in the marketplace that led to a further rise in their prices.

Following the conclusion in victory of the United States and its allies in the First World War, a wave of pride in its history and its triumph in war had rolled over the Nation and Kingston. And by the mid-1920s some of the old houses were even being proudly lived in by a few more prominent citizens of Kingston (not all of whom were of Dutch ancestry) and were undergoing a simple sort of restoration. The old stone house in which the first New York State Senate had met in 1777 had come into the ownership of the State of New York back in 1888 after having been taken care of by early stone house enthusiast Frederick Westbrook who welcomed tourists to what he regarded as the house's "hallowed precincts." It then about 1888 began operating as a local historical showplace under State management and was later in 1927 joined on the same grounds by a large inevitably bluestone historical museum, drawing both interested tourists and locals.

In Williamsburg, Virginia by the end of the twenties, Hudson Valley Rockefeller millions had helped make an instant success of the charming large scale restoration of Williamsburg, once the Colonial provincial capital of Virginia. This success would lead the way to ambitious plans for restoring other places which had acquired glamor as relating to the American colonial and federal past, and some were even reaching reality. One was Henry Ford's nostalgic attempt at recreating the atmosphere of his boyhood in the form of Greenfield Village in Dearborn, Michigan. Others created more sophisticated Colonial village restorations in New York and New England. In Kingston, simple picture postcards (those sure signs of tourist presence) and some showing the Senate or other old stone houses, had been on sale for some time. By the twenties, Louis E. Jones, a Woodstock artist, was selling his fine photographic post cards in a series soon-to-be-copyrighted as "Beautiful Catskills," "Beautiful Woodstock," and "Beautiful Kingston."

Among Kingston people who had restored old houses and worked in them were painter Julia Dillon and Mrs. A.E.P. Searing, author of the elaborately illustrated *The Land of Rip Van Winkle*, which dealt with the lore and legends of the region.

During the 1920s, Mrs. Helen Wilkinson Reynolds of Dutchess County had been hard at work researching and writing a book to be named *The Old Dutch Houses of the Hudson Valley up to 1776*. This handsome book was published in hardcover in 1929, with a perceptive introduction by President-to-be Franklin Delano Roosevelt. The book contained informative pages about the old stone houses of Kingston. Helen Reynolds attributed the development of a special type of old stone house in early Ulster County and Kingston to the conservatism of the Dutch colonists and to the special characteristics of their Colonial landscape. Her book was well received nationally and was followed by a paper edition, and a smaller paper-covered one devoted to the old stone houses of Ulster County, including Kingston, and written and illustrated by Kingston architect and restoration specialist Myron S. Teller who included information that would be useful to local owners of these houses who had restoration in mind.

Among enthusiasts for the old stone houses of Ulster County, and especially of Kingston, was State Governor Franklin D. Roosevelt of Hyde Park who now and then enjoyed taking guests from his splendid Hyde Park estate, on which he practiced forestry, to Kingston to admire these simple old stone houses. Roosevelt traced his ancestry to early occupants of some of these houses in one of which, the Hoffman House, his ancestors Martinus Hoffman and Martinus's wife Emerentje de Witt had lived, and he encouraged architect friends like Henry. J. Tombs to use the old stone buildings as inspiration for such new ones as, for example, the Rhinebeck Post Office.

In Kingston such people as County judge Joseph Fowler and Dr. Henry Bibby lived in well-restored old stone houses of which they were proud.

In 1938, Henry J. Tombs drew plans from a rough sketch by President Roosevelt for Top Cottage, which the President first planned as a retreat in which he might write his memoirs once his Presidency was ended. The sketch was based on the old stone houses of Kingston. The cottage, located on the 74-acre high wooded hilltop site above the old Roosevelt family home at Hyde Park, came to be used during the Second World War as a safe and secluded place where the President discussed policy and military matters with consultants. One of these, who had stayed overnight at Top Cottage, once stepped out into the woods to stretch his legs while walking Roosevelt's dog and in the spy-fearing atmosphere of wartime questioned a woman whom he met in the Roosevelt woods as to her name and reason for being there. The man was satisfied that the woman was no spy and the two went their separate ways. It was only then that the woman realized she had heard the gentleman's distinctive voice on the radio and seen his picture in books and newspapers—he was Winston Churchill. The President had formed a habit of appearing on Kingston's Academy Green Park in his open car on the evening before every day in which he ran for office, and there greeted his Kingston supporters (of whom there were not enough to carry the County for him) and reminded them of his ancestral connections with the city and its old stone houses.

By the 1920s, with the increasingly publicized historic celebrations of 1826, 1872, 1876, 1907 and 1909 behind it, the status of Kingston as a historic American place was widely accepted, and Kingston had been the subject of much newspaper writing and orating which sought to capture in words the City people's colorful heritage. And with the Pilgrimage of the Holland Society members having given a strong stimulus to the City's pride in the unique Dutchness of its early heritage, and the moneys spent by Coykendall in 1886 in support, it might have been time to capitalize on their unique background as made evident by many visible and tangible signs of its past. Yet, as the Great Depression of the thirties struck the nation and the City, there was no attempt known to apply for federal funds to put the City's history, for business purposes, into a more usable and profitable shape, as a bait for history-hungry visitors with money in their pockets.

Yet, in the federally funded *Guide to New York State* of 1946, Kingston was given some pages (with photographs), by the New Deal Writers Project (which wrote the book). The *Guide* contains a photo of the Senate House and a brief summary of the City's history with decorative designs by artist Harry Tedlie, a close relative of then popular film actress Shirley Temple, and a resident of Woodstock, borrowed from Woodstock's New Deal Artists' Project. The *Guide* depicted Kingston as a serious historic City rather than following the stereotype of extreme and extravagant Dutchness contained in Washington's Irving's romanticized if amusing history of Diedrick Knickerbocker.

In Rondout of the 1930s the harsh hand of the Depression had struck a particularly severe blow to add to those suffered in that part of the City since the collapse of the D & H Canal plus those of the bedrock-depleting extractive bluestone, limestone and cement industries, and in the ending of the bustle of the waterfront yards to which the stone had for many years been shipped to be prepared for sale and being floated away for use.

As the Depression years battered Rondout, Father Divine, black evangelist and social reformer, chose a reluctant Ulster County as the "Promised Land" for his people known to the members as angels. And some Harlem followers were among those who took to living in then deteriorated and largely vacant Rondout tenements, as Rondout took on the look of an albatross hung on the neck of uptown Kingston, as poet S.T. Coleridge had sung of one hanging around the neck of his Ancient Mariner. The city fathers commissioned the city planning firm of Raymond & May to study the Rondout albatross and recommend measures to restore Rondout's (and Kingston's) existence as vital communities.

There was not much immediate citizen protest against the resulting Plans, and it was decided to put them into action. There was some protest from owners of Rondout lots who believed they were not being well paid for their lots once buildings were gone, and in part because of approval of the demolition as being a way of ousting the growing black and other poor population. It was, for uptown Kingston, so it seemed at first to the shopowners in the old trading district of Wall and North Front Streets, an effective way of assuring them a prosperous future.

The condition of Rondout Harbor, which had once filled visitors with delight by its cheerful crowding with boats under sail and steam, ringing of bells and shrilling of whistles, had given way to a silent and melancholy scene abounding in rotting barges, crumbling docks and boats left to their own uncared-for fate, and a lighthouse no longer tended and an overall air of a once happy river port now given up to ruin.

In March 1923, in the pre-Depression age, the General Organization Company of Chicago, Illinois had completed a 210-page *Promotional Survey* of Kingston-Rondout commissioned by the Kingston Chamber of Commerce, struck by a slight post-war slump. In this well written and sturdily bound typescript the Organization analyzed the business aspect of the City and recommended means by which Kingston might be improved to the benefit of the business community. The *Promotional Survey*, besides dealing with the commercial and industrial ventures of Kingston and their future possibilities, supplied an almost lyrical burst of praise of Kingston, beginning with "It is Kingston's fortune to be the principal gateway to the Catskill-Shawangunk mountain region. This is a land of wonderful natural beauty in mountain views, lakes and forests. It is equally rich in historic traditional and legendary lore." The report goes on to tell of the historic links of the City with early Revolutionary events, frontier raids and clashes with the Natives that sometimes led to massacres, torture and captivity in the course of white colonial settlement. It reminded the Chamber of Commerce members of the part played by Washington Irving and Fenimore Cooper in drawing valuable attention to the pleasant land now so easily reached by water and by rail, and of the multitudes of tourists who had already found it irresistible as an enjoyable goal. And it made it plain that this remarkable region needs only something it had neglected—advertising and a more cooperative relationship with the farming people of Ulster County from whom the Chamber members had previously stood too much apart.

The Chicago experts submitted a lengthy questionnaire to the members of the Chamber, who indicated in their answers that they wanted very much a first class hotel.

The Chicago men agreed to the need for a hotel but claimed that financing such a hotel would not attract New York City capital, since the adoption in 1919 of the national Volstead Act, outlawing the sale of liquor. It was now impossible for such hotels as they had in mind to rely on their barroom to turn a profit, and that compelled them to charge what the public saw as excessively high prices for rooms and meals.

The Chicago experts pointed out that if Kingston wanted a first class hotel, they must themselves supply half the capital needed for the building.

The Kingston businessmen therefore built the first-class hotel, mindful of the Chicago experts' praise of Kingston's scenic and historic past and named it the Governor Clinton to honor their most historically famous figure, now buried among them. To emphasize the hotel's historic relations, it included in its coffee room (of colonial design) two mural paintings by Kingston and Rondout painter Emily Hoysradt, one of which showed Kingston's historic assets on a pictorial map.

The Governor Clinton Hotel was an imposing red brick Georgian Revival structure, with a white portico, facing the historic Academy Green Park from the Clinton Avenue site of the former General George H. Sharpe mansion which the hotel project had first rolled to the back of the lot and later demolished, to be replaced by the hotel. On the rear of the hotel well-furnished in colonial style was attached a spacious veranda from which guests might admire a splendid view of the Catskill mountains of historic Rip Van Winkle's world famous twenty year sleep.

The monument to General Sharpe's horse on the hotel grounds—a horse which had carried the general through his duties as a member of General Grant's staff during the Civil War, vanished, no one knows to where.

In 1950, Mrs. Emily Crane Chadbourne, well known Kingston philanthropist, was able to secure from a junkyard in which they had been resting three ten-foot-high bronze statues, well made by distinguished sculptor E. Massie Rhind, of George Clinton, Henry Hudson and Peter Stuyvesant. Mrs. Chadbourne offered these to the City of Kingston and they were placed directly across Clinton avenue from the hotel's white porticoed entrance on a specially landscaped area designed by skilled landscape architect Albert Gaffert, Jr., in which the three statues stand on three lofty granite

The Governor Clinton Hotel

pedestals facing a number of elegant and gracefully curved benches on which guests at the hotel, their friends and nursemaids with their charges might sit and admire these historic works of art made even more historic by their remarkable rescue from the junkyard. The statues had been made around 1890 by the distinguished sculptor during a period when such architectural works of art were having a brief spurt of fashion as they ornamented commercial buildings. They had graced an important office building on lower Broadway in New York City before being discarded as the fashion for such ornaments waned in perceived usefulness to business enterprises.

The Governor Clinton hotel, in spite of being managed by a chain which also managed similar hotels throughout the eastern United States, was not able to withstand the rise of a new feature of American society which the Chicago experts had not seen coming—the motel, and it was converted into an apartment house which, although with no special appeal to the tourist trade, continues to serve Kingston well. (The older Hotel Stuyvesant, located at John and Fair Street, and named for the colonial Dutch governor of New Netherland, had been Kingston's best hotel before the Governor Clinton was built. It also succumbed to the powerful wave of motels and it was converted to a residence hotel for elderly and infirm people.) The statue of Stuyvesant still stands beside those of Clinton and Hudson in the Academy Park or Green.

Yet all the efforts made by Kingston people to tie together the hotel and their history were of no avail against the coming into use of a flood of motels which made many hotels such as the Governor Clinton obsolete. Social historians like Asa Briggs, however, agree that a city is made of up of its neighborhoods. The handsome Governor Clinton Hotel, with its many links to Kingston's history, has acted to maintain the good quality of the neighborhood it helps keep charming by serving the City as a much needed good apartment house—a service which it still gives.

8. Depression, the New Deal of F.D.R., Urban Renewal and IBM Have their Effect on Kingston's History 1930s–1960s

The First and Second World Wars, like previous wars, had their effects on Kingston in military service, battle wounds and deaths and domestic shortages, and also in an initial increased sympathy for their fatherlands on the part of German and Irish and other immigrant descendants. And in the growth of the building of many small vessels in Rondout's shipyards to be used for war purposes—shipyards had revived after their decline accompanying the demise of the barge and boat Canal and the extractive industries which departed but left behind not always pretty mementoes of their past on the once lovely natural landscape in the form of shattered bedrock and ugly heaps of quarry waste or yawning holes in the ground.

Previously, small industries making gunpowder had been enlarged in the Kingston area as wars raged and many shipped their dangerous war products through Rondout Harbor (an activity always accompanied by a certain risk of explosion).

Yet the City suffered hard times through the Depression of the 1930s after its wartime mini-booms until the construction of the New York Thruway forged a modern and faster link between Kingston and the great city of New York, and by the construction of the Rhinecliffe and other bridges, both of which together promised a measure of economic relief, and increased income-producing population. The movement of modern industry up the Hudson Valley to avoid urban problems sent the main frame computer plant of IBM partly into Kingston in 1955 and more into the bordering gerrymander-created Town of Ulster. The huge and prosperous IBM effort radiated some of its benefits and its losses to Kingston in the form of increased population and a greatly expanded shopping center on Albany Avenue and Route 9W which also detracted from the older shopping area on Wall Street in the old city of

Above: Typical small Hudson Valley powder mill

Right: Climbers in old bluestone quarry, showing continuing use of the past, photo from collection of Alf Evers

Kingston (largely planned by General Joseph S. Smith and aides in the late 1820s and the 1830s to accommodate the expected D. & H. Canal boom). These new shopping centers eventually came to be largely owned outside of Ulster County and were often branches of huge and distant corporate giants, and were sometimes franchised by them to local operators. Many IBM employees lived in Kingston or on the City's outskirts or suburbs (which had not been previously visually damaged by extractive industry) and patronized its businesses and utilized its social, entertainment and cultural services while enjoying Kingston's unique character and outdoor recreational opportunities.

Finally, as the computer age took firm hold on the Valley, the nation and the world, the judgment of corporate IBM managers found it more profitable to move their huge plant southward from Kingston, but still remain in the Hudson Valley which they expected to boom—to the detriment at first of Kingston. The City was threatened with a substantial population loss estimated at 7000.

Above: Eleanor Roosevelt in Kingston in 1945, Henry Morgenthau, Jr. second from right

Left: Franklin Roosevelt at May 30, 1932 Memorial Day event in Kingston; photos courtesy of Franklin D. Roosevelt Library

After the dealing of this blow, another one had been dealt to Kingston by its adoption of a federally funded Urban Renewal plan for seriously deteriorated Rondout, where the removal of the picturesque Vlight Berg, the construction of an almost mile long Island Dock in the Rondout Creek for storing and handling canal-born coal, and the transformation (largely by blasting) of a steep and rocky Rondout creek-side slope into a site for limestone mining and cement-making and crowded helter-skelter human habitations sometimes barely fit for workers—all to the profit of industrialists—was threatening all its hard-sought new economic and human values. This part of the unplanned City had blossomed, like an exotic yet unkempt tropical garden in which good and bad were mingled during the Canal and extractive industry boom in which industrial needs alone were considered by those in power. The dust of extractive industries had damaged workers' lungs and those of family members and led to a tuberculosis hospital appearing on Golden Hill.

Rondout had inevitably lost a large part of its over-crowded low-income population because of its loss of industry and prosperity. Other low income people, some of them Afro-Americans from New York City, were moving to Rondout's half-deserted and ill-kept slum-like buildings. A similar situation prevailed in Newburgh and other Hudson River cities and towns, but in the case of Rondout, the Urban Renewal plan was designed to tear down much of the shoddily boom-built Rondout without adequate attention being paid at first to the needs for housing of the modest number of inhabitants who had clung on in the area, many of whom were newly arrived poor.

In 1966, as Rondout demolition was underway, it had been predicted in print by specialists in planning and land use who had been much impressed by the City's location amid the fine transportation facilities in and west of the Hudson Valley, that a splendid future lay ahead for Kingston by the year 2000. By then, they predicted, Kingston would have become a thriving trade and manufacturing center with a population of over 200,000. Later that forecast took on the look of a bad joke.

As part of the Urban Renewal plan it was proposed to demolish the majestic City Hall built on the hilltop in the 1870s and substitute a new and much smaller one somewhat in the style of Georgian Revival buildings popular at the time (and seen by some as fitting in a "colonial Kingston"), in the previously demolished part of Rondout. This urge to tear down the old City Hall was prompted in part by the demand of New York State authorities that better space for courtrooms be provided than were offered in the old City Hall. The proposed new City Hall would therefore act as a diminished city facility, but would have new courtrooms and a new police station. It was planned to provide better housing for the refugees of old purposely-destroyed Rondout, but the kind of housing looked forward to was thought of with little understanding of the needs of working people. In some larger cities, many-storied apartment houses had been provided as part of Urban Renewal plans, and these before too long were torn down because they did not establish a favorable environment for low income people and instead provided secluded spaces such as elevators, often empty interiors and parts of halls which proved favorable for the increased commission of violent crimes and the selling of illegal drugs. Some of these high risers were later replaced by housing more hospitable to the welfare, and needs and desires of low-income workers and were easier and less costly for these people to maintain.

As a corollary to the original Rondout Urban Renewal Plan a proposal was set up for uptown Kingston, designed to modernize the Wall Street and North Front Street business and shopping area from its pleasantly old-fashioned look to one better suited to the needs of the age of the automobile and the corporation-friendly consumer economy. A seductive rendering of part of the proposed uptown shopping area was put into circulation in the hope of winning approval from both uptown business people and consumers.

There seemed to be urgency for taking action uptown because the uptown shopkeepers and other uptown business people were only too well aware of a menace which was just beginning to arise very near them. In and around other towns and cities there had been a huge expansion of units of chain retail merchandising business centers which drained the life blood from older urban shopping areas such as theirs. And right beside the uptown shopping center (as established in the 1820s

A building, *left*, in 1967 just before it was demolished, and *right*, as it was being demolished, thanks to Urban Renewal. From slides in author's collection

and '30s) and along the Esopus Creek there lay a large tract ideally suited to the needs of giant shopping centers operated by large well-financed corporations, with shops leased or franchised to local people or newcomers.

Once the construction of the Ashokan Reservoir was completed in 1915, the chances of catastrophic floods along the fertile floodplain of the Esopus Creek flatlands had been ended. The periodic flooding had deposited fertile silt giving the creeklands great richness. After 1915, flooding ceased and the flatlands became ideal for development on the former floodplain of a shopping center.

It was proposed to convert uptown Kingston into a profitable modern shopping and commercial center, with widened and straightened streets and much additional parking areas, to encourage well-trained modern consumers to do business there. Under this plan Clinton Avenue would be widened and extended across Uptown and other steps taken, in the hope of solving Uptown's traffic problem caused by its narrow, however attractive old streets, many going back to Stockade times.

Kingston under this plan would be converted into a modern looking, efficient auto-friendly community while some of its historic buildings, it was hoped, might be retained. The plan was received favorably at first by Kingston people, even by some well aware of their rich historical heritage. A few old stone houses on North Front Street were demolished before rising public howls of protest caused the cancellation of this part of the project. And, for example ,the old stone Hoffman House, which stood at what had been the important northwest corner of the Stockade, was spared, and federal funds intended for its demolition were spent on restoring a badly sagging wall so that it could endure for centuries to come. (In Dutch colonial days, the house had been lived in by President Franklin D. Roosevelt's ancestors Martinus Hoffman and his wife Emerentje de Witt.)

Spared too was the handsome Dr. Kiersted House, the earliest frame structure within the Stockade.

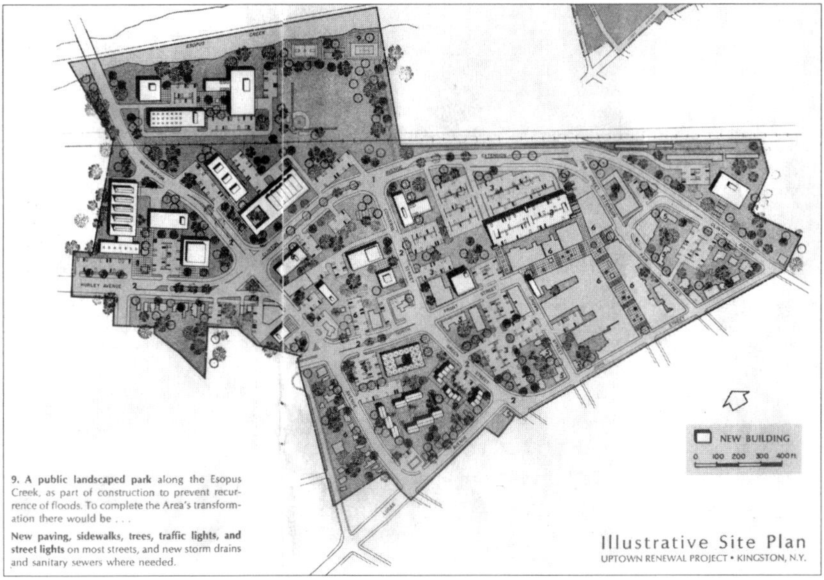

9. **A public landscaped park** along the Esopus Creek, as part of construction to prevent recurrence of floods. To complete the Area's transformation there would be . . .
New paving, sidewalks, trees, traffic lights, and street lights on most streets, and new storm drains and sanitary sewers where needed.
NEW BUILDING
0 100 200 300 400 ft
Illustrative Site Plan
UPTOWN RENEWAL PROJECT • KINGSTON, N.Y.

Clinton Avenue was not sent slanting (as had first been planned) across uptown Kingston by means of an extension, but wherever a deteriorated building appeared to be likely to offend the eyes of shoppers bent only on compulsive consuming, these facades were modernized to make them more appetizing.

Meantime, the flatlands beside the Esopus Creek were being cleared by their Kingston owners, preparing for the huge shopping center to come. This land was the one on which white Kingston's predecessors, the Native Asian-descended Americans, had grown their tangled crops of beans, corn, squash, and tobacco and pitched their easily moved wigwams made of poles and bark. Later, early white settlers used the dark, deep fertile soil to grow the fine and profitable crops of wheat, rye and other European grains which were to become a mainstay of early Kingston's white economy.

The flatlands, regardless of their remarkable fertility, were bulldozed and tar-

Artist John Pike's rendering of the plan for uptown Kingston, courtesy of Stanley London Collection

macked and landscaped with ornamental shade trees, shrubs and exotic flowers to become ideal parking spaces for the eager shoppers who were already flocking to the center's first mostly unfinished one story buildings. Native chipped stone tools and fragments of Native clay cooking pots and the charcoal of old cooking sites were sealed beneath the tarmac.

Uptown, the Wall Street and North Front Street merchants were aroused by what was going on right beside them, and commissioned Woodstock artist and designer John Pike to design canopied sidewalks for Wall Street and North Front somewhat in the manner of those in some English resort towns. These canopies were permanent fixtures covering sidewalks of upper strata light gray bluestone and local brick (with flower boxes beside them) to provide shade for shop windows and protection from rain and snow for consumers.

The canopies however were hastily and not very well built and when they developed leakage and other problems, so devoted had the uptown merchants become to them that they pitched in, some with their own hands, to repair and to paint them.

In spite of the visual appeal of the widely acclaimed Pike Plan, it was not entirely able to compete well with the large chain retail stores, with their lower prices and greater variety, plus unlimited free parking spaces, on the flatlands bordering Kingston and once said to have been favored for the production of Kingston's famous wheat which was so plentiful it could be used in making malt for the well known strong Kingston beers, and favored in making bread by fastidious housewives like faraway Martha Washington.

9.
A Promised Land in Ulster County during the 1930s

Along with feeling the impact of the reformist New Deal of the nineteen thirties, Kingston and all of Ulster County felt the impact of another plan for social betterment in the shape of Father Divine's Peace Mission's attempt to convert the county into a "Promised Land."[781] This second plan was the brainchild of the energetic, charismatic combined evangelist and utopian prophet of almost heavenly life on earth, born in Maryland as George Baker, but better known under his assumed name of Father Divine, which Baker took up after he claimed himself to be an immortal earthly embodiment of God.

As a Utopian reformer with some similarities to Marcus Garvey who offered a promised land in Africa to blacks, Father Divine offered to lead his followers, known as angels, into a Promised Land of equal opportunity and of the civil rights for all promised by the American Constitution and its amendments but still denied in practice to those who were Afro-Americans. Guided by Father Divine's fervent preaching and his unquestioned ingenuity, groups of angels pooled their scanty assets and drew upon some other yet undisclosed resources to buy land in Ulster County and there under their Peace Mission strove to create a place where peace and joy might reign for all believers. Some assumed names seen as more fitting to residents of a Promised Land—Holiness Love, Satisfied Love, Sweet Angel being among those noted in County records in 1937. Some were later listed under such names in Ulster County telephone directories.

Well established local real estate agents cooperated in selling land to angel groups. A sale which drew much publicity was that of the large estate of Howland Spencer, lying across the Hudson from that of President Franklin D. and Eleanor Roosevelt at Hyde Park. Spencer hated President Roosevelt in part as "a traitor to his class" and made no bones about selling his own place at a low price to Divine's angels out of "spite."

The Roosevelts, however, did not rise to Spencer's bait, and did not speak publicly of it. Another sale of 1937 was to a group of twenty-six angels, this one being that of the Greenkill Hotel, a big resort place near Eddyville with many outbuildings. Among the angels in this deal was Sweet Angel, a blonde, pretty, intelligent and able young Canadian woman who would become more closely linked to Father Divine some years later. This hotel would have become a school for the angels' children but it was soon destroyed by fire, rumored to have been the result of arson.

Farm after farm passed into the hands of angels (with the help of eager local real estate agents) and all were industriously managed. Roadside property, once in the hands of Divine's angels, was used as restaurants and filling stations at which meals and gasoline were sold at below the usual prices. Factories or workshops for making clothing and other items of daily use were set up, especially at High Falls, which became a center of much angelic activity. Many Ulster County people were initially aghast at the arrival of the angels. The Ulster County clerk proclaimed from his office in Kingston that "the setting up of a Promised Land" would utterly destroy Ulster County's prospering summer boarding industry. Throughout the county similar fears of doom to result from the angels' presence proved groundless. The newcomers worked hard, did not commit crimes, or behave in a disorderly fashion.

After 1937, once the Greenkill Resort was purchased by some angels and burned, the group's momentum began to be checked.

A prominent feature of Father Divine's impact on the public had been the large and luxurious "banquets" staged under his auspices. At these affairs all, including the poorest, were made to feel welcome. The Father himself carved roasts, filled and passed out heaped-up plates of excellent foods while expounding his ideas. Beside him his wife Peninnah or Mother Divine formed a portly and reassuring presence radiating an air of hearty good will as she welcomed all the guests. She now and then delivered a brief sermon at the banquets, although that was usually left to Father.

Father Divine with horses in Ulster County

But now, in 1937 Mother Divine no longer appeared at the banquets. The couple was said to be living in a mansard-roofed mansion in Kingston (actually in Wilbur) built by James Sweeney, and occupied by three generations of bluestone barons who also had offices in New York, Brooklyn and Philadelphia, in addition to the large Sweeney stoneyards at Wilbur. There was no explanation from the Father of Peninnah's continuing absence. There were plenty of rumors. She lay seriously ill at home or in the Kingston Hospital—even that she had died. And death, as the Father had assured his angels, was something which would not touch their God on earth or his wife.

In 1941, Father Divine announced in Philadelphia from Woodmont, the elegant estate on which he had been living more and more often, that he and Sweet Angel had married three months before. This shocked many of his angels, not only because there had been no word of Peninnah's death or divorce, but because the Father had made it plain that he was in favor of chastity. And when marriage did occur it should not be between blacks and whites. Sweet Angel was a Canadian white.

In the Promised Land to which Father Divine was no longer paying much attention, and while Marcus Garvey was under an increased legal assault which ended his hopes, there was definitely a lessening of drive. Father Divine's movement of combined religion and social reform had by the late thirties become almost entirely an organized church run by a bureaucracy as Father Divine aged and suffered from the infirmities incident to prolonged diabetes. The Church bureaucracy was headed with great skill by his blonde new wife, Sweet Angel.

By then, many but by no means all of the New Deal measures had passed into law or seemed soon to do so and perhaps this accounted for Father Divine's growing lack of interest in his once cherished social reforms. However, he remained active in his interest in full civil rights for all, and when, later on, President Lyndon B. Johnson made a stirring speech in favor of civil rights for all Americans in the 1960s the Father wrote the President a letter thanking him and also reminding Johnson of his own role in promoting acceptance of these same rights by all.

Father Divine died in his 80s, in 1965, with the church he had founded still resolutely holding its head above water with its Promised Land fading as Marcus Garvey's African hopes had done. Father Divine deserves a prominent place in the history of social reform in the period, although many do not relish the bizarre embellishments or the luxurious lifestyle which he brought to his efforts in the joining of Christian religion with civil rights for all while claiming to have a special divine relationship to his God.

10.
Hudson River Pollution Fears Increase and Restoration Begins 1930s-onward

Many American and European tourists, enamored of what Washington Irving had called "the lordly Hudson," came to enjoy its wonders, only to find the Hudson River's waters and its banks grown ever more polluted by industrial and human use. Yet, to a growing number of sensitive people of the nineteenth century, this fouling of a great river famed in art, legend and history had to be confronted and dealt with. Yet it was not until late in the nineteenth century when a substantial group of Americans could be brought together to take an active stand against the fouling of the Hudson River so many had come to love.

During the decades of Kingston's late nineteenth century slump in population, these aroused citizens were continuing to take vigorous steps to check the pollution of the Hudson River and its Valley, while as yet still ignorant of the harmful effects of the pollution of the atmosphere beginning to be caused by growing use of coal in industry. Since early in the 19th century the hard, columnar trap rock of which the scenic Palisades are formed, and which rise on the west bank of the lower Hudson opposite the City of New York, had been quarried here and there (to the loss of some of their remarkable visual appeal) to be used in road-building and for other mundane purposes. Bankside factories had been allowed to pour their plentiful and often poisonous wastes into the once-clear Hudson and their tall factory chimneys sent their dark clouds of soot and gases aloft into the increasingly polluted atmosphere.

Mid- and upper Hudson ice harvesters had built immense uncouth and unpainted riverside storehouses to hold ice pending demand in hot weather but which had destroyed the charm of river banks. Once mechanical refrigeration had begun to be used about 1914, as pollution increased, these ice storehouses became useless and burned in spectacular often nighttime blazes. Influential and monied

Hudson River admirers had organized, as the twentieth century was nearing, to protect the River and the Valley they loved (and in which their estates lay), which some of them admired only from the decks of their yachts. First to be effectively protected, under law, in the 1890s, were the Palisades, saved by the efforts of the largely upper class members of the American Scenic and Historic Preservation Society in a notable legal victory. By the 1960s, the proposed pumped-up storage plant proposed to be hewn out of the side of Storm King mountain would lead to a torrent of sometimes successful protest by well-organized middle-class citizens which eventually led to the appearance on the Hudson of the lovely sloop Clearwater, as part of a movement largely organized by singer Pete Seeger and others with large followings which symbolized for thousands of young Americans of all classes the enduring struggle to clean up the Hudson and its tributary streams.

Kingston agents by post-Civil War days had been exploring Catskill Mountain streams in order to use them as future sources of pure water to replace the unreliable springs and scattered, shallow wells they had relied on until then but which were giving clear signs of occasional pollution.

As the nineteenth century ended Kingston had a fairly good sewage system for that day and after 1942, thanks to the New Deal's Clean Air and Water Act, a federal grant resulting from that Act assured that the City would no longer pour its untreated human sewage into the Hudson, as so many Hudson Valley towns and cities continued to do. Kingston had a good, reliable filtered water supply by then based on Catskill mountain streams.

The pollution poured into the Hudson by manufacturing above Albany continued to be an important factor in the serious contamination of the Hudson.

Water pollution was not so easily lessened (as lower yields and quality of Hudson River spawning shad and other fish testified). Citizens had organized successfully in protest against such environmental disasters as the proposed pumping up of storage water planned for Storm King mountain to supply electric power to New York City.

The time for vigorous action to stem industrial and human sewage pollution of natural resources such as those of the Hudson lay a few decades in the future. Meanwhile in Kingston after its awakening to the value of its scenic and historic assets, a keen awareness of air and water pollution slowly grew while the Hudson River went on acting as a cheap dumping place for industrial scrap metals, old cars and often toxic wastes from factories up and down the River which poured through pipes into the Hudson's waters by day and night. This last meant death sentences to many desirable birds, fish, plants and other living things which had made their homes seasonally or year round in the great estuarial river. Commercial and sport fishing of affected species had to be outlawed as food to protect the public health. Boating in the foul water became unattractive and bathing lost its appeal as every high tide brought and deposited visible and hidden sewage on what had once been clean and inviting beaches. New and less attractive plants and animals which did well in polluted water were taking over the Hudson and causing it to lose some of its former charm and usefulness to humans. Elsewhere in the nation as the industrial age gained hard-to- resist strength, rivers and lakes were reacting as was the Hudson. The deterioration from human use of the land and water brought not only local protesting organizations into being but more effectively actions by the national Congress of the New Deal years, which provided funding for the protection of water, soil and air.˙ A prolonged battle to protect their claimed right to pollute the Hudson was lost in theory by corporate America. Yet healing all the great River's wounds will not occur quickly nor will it be easy.

There are three major components of our planet that for centuries defied all human attempts to bring them into the marketplace and become easily defended private property—these are the air that forms the atmosphere we breathe, the oceans and the rivers which are the great storehouses of our planet's water supply and send their waters into the ownerless ocean. Therefore all of these rivers, including the Hudson, might be used, some supposed, to dispose of the waste products of human activity.

PCBs were poured into the Hudson and on its banks, but instead of being carried down to poison those living at the River's lower reaches or in the ocean, they obligingly sank down and became incorporated within the stream beds. This could work very well, except when a catastrophic flood would upset the River's water, or an accident like the sinking of a ship might send poisonous PCBs charging downstream. The General Electric corporation spent millions in advertising to persuade the public that their method of disposing of PCBs was not the creation of a tragedy about to happen. But the increasingly conservation-minded public refused to be persuaded, and General Electric at last agreed to abandon their policy and to permit (and pay for under Federal law) the dredging of the River's bottom near Albany with proper precautions.

A river like a plant or an animal reacts almost like a living thing to the stresses that are placed upon it whether by man or by nature. And the time for humans to restore the Hudson to its former cleanliness and beauty is here.

In his State of the State message of January 2004, Governor George Pataki spoke of progress having been made in ridding the Hudson from pollution and he mentioned the number of communities which had agreed to take part in the Greenway project. He reported that since Kingston had joined Governor Cuomo's appeal of 1989, 200 other Hudson Valley communities had followed the early leadership of Kingston.

11.
Kingston Men Join the U.S. Navy and Make History on the Seas

Because Kingston and Rondout were located on the estuarial Hudson which flows into the Atlantic Ocean, it owed much of its importance as a river port to this fact. And many Kingston boys enlisted in the United States Navy. Others after appointment to Annapolis began careers as officers in the Navy. Among these were a good many who became known as inventors of improvements of equipment for use in naval warfare. Washington Irving Chambers was a native of Kingston and a graduate of the U.S. Naval Academy at Annapolis who invented improvements in adapting the gyroscopic principle to directing torpedoes toward the hulls of enemy ships.

Another Kingston navy officer played a part in devising means of making possible the development of naval vessels that served as aircraft carriers.

Serving as commander of a variety of naval vessels the son of historian Marius Schoonmaker, Cornelius Shoonmaker took part in the dispute between a British, German, and his own flagship in 1888 over control of certain parts of island places in the Pacific such as a port on the island of Samoa. While the three ships were in the Coral-reef-ringed harbor at Samoa a severe typhoon struck the island and put them in peril in the cramped quarters. The commander of the British ship, with his engines at full steam, made for the exit from the harbor and successfully steamed out into the relative safety of the Pacific. The Commander Schoonmaker's flagship, however, was severely damaged by the typoon and sank, with the loss of the Commander and most of his men.

Another Naval officer who was assigned to take part in northern Polar expeditions was Lieutenant Charles Chipp. Chipp was an officer aboard the *Jeannette*, a sturdily built vessel intended to withstand the pressure of pack ice in polar waters.

The ship took off from San Francisco in 1881 to make a kind of reverse attempt at solving the riddle of the Northwest Passage, by approaching it from the Pacific Ocean end, and to determine whether a German theory that the North Pole was surrounded by open water held true. The *Jeannette,* however, became jammed in pack ice which threatened to crush it, and Captain DeLong, who was in command, ordered two of the ship's longboats to set out with the crew divided between them, with himself in command of one and Lt. Chipp in command of the other. The boat commanded by DeLong, after a grueling passage to the point at which the Siberian river Lena enters its delta, reached safety. However, the boat commanded by Lt. Chipp was wrecked by a violent storm with the loss of the Lieutenant and his men and the records of the expedition carried aboard. The *Jeannette* had been financed by the younger James Gordon Bennett, owner of the *New York Herald.* The only result of the expedition was the naming of a bleak island Herald Island, in honor of Bennett's newspaper. However, Lt. Chipp remains a hero to Kingston and followers of polar exploration. The Northwest Passage mystery was eventually solved in 1906 by Danish Roald Amundsen who did further polar exploration aboard a dirigible which he believed to be safer but, in a rescue attempt by his dirigible, Amundsen met his own end too.

Kingston became a favorite place for quiet retirement for naval officers, those in rank up to Rear-Admiral Higginson, and including Captain Andrew S. Hickey who used his retirement days to write a useful 1952 history of Kingston which includes topics not previously well touched upon by other historians of the City.

12.
Early Kingston Housewives and a Fashion Model Turned Aviator Serve the City Well

KINGSTON WOMEN ALSO HELPED GIVE KINGSTON A REPUTATION BY REASON of their skill in butter-making. Henry James in his *Transatlantic Sketches* of 1874 wrote of watching a Dutch housewife vigorously scrubbing a stoop which was already so clean that it really required no further scrubbing. This Dutch passion for household cleanliness crossed the Atlantic and appeared in Kingston and was inherited in the 19th and early 20th century by farmers' wives in surrounding agricultural country .

This passion on the part of Dutch women for extreme house cleanliness having found its way across the Atlantic to New Netherlands, it enabled Dutch housewives of Kingston to add cash to the family income, because their good butter was a valued staple in the Dutch diet, and had a ready sale at a good price.

Well into the twentieth century on Ulster and Delaware County farms, the old Kingston way of making butter by farmwives was continued. The fresh milk was set in pans on well-scrubbed hanging wooden shelves in the well scrubbed cellar to permit the cream to rise to the top and be skimmed; then put into well-cleaned wooden churns from which it emerged as fragrant butter after being churned. The butter, placed in a very clean wooden bowl, was then thoroughly washed of all remnants of whey by being kneaded with a clean wooden paddle scrubbed to whiteness. When the dealers in farm products came out from Kingston to buy butter and other farm products, they would raise the crock in which the farmwife kept her butter in her well-scrubbed cellar to their noses, explaining in apology to a new farmwife, "Sometimes butter smells of the cellar." If that were the case, the butter brought a lower price because butter easily takes on the odor and taste of its surroundings.

Woman were also active in other ways in distinguishing Kingston in the late nineteenth and early twentieth century. Some Kingston women studied medicine and some like Dr. Kitty Gage, successfully practiced in Kingston.

In 1959, the year of the celebration of the three hundred and fiftieth anniversary of the discovery of the Hudson River, Miss Gale Brownlee, a fashion model turned aviator, was asked to act the role of a witch on board a small road-travelling and amusing version of Hudson's ship, the *Half Moon.* Instead she designed a fetching blue naval officer's uniform for herself and under the name of Miss Henry Hudson, boldly captained the little ship, once she had persuaded the Ulster County motor vehicle bureau to grant a license for such a strange vehicle to roll on the public highways. Under so novel if unexpectedly attractive a captain, she helped arouse much interest in the historical Celebration by her charming and whimsical impersonation.

Left to right: Gale Brownlee, Assemblyman Ken Wilson, Joseph Fitzsimmon, John Pike, and Alf Evers aboard the *Half Moon*

In 1975, the local power company, Central Hudson, proposed building a coal-fueled power plant with a tall smokestack to dispose of its polluting fumes—this on the former Terry Brickyard site too close for safety to the Rhinecliff Bridge and the new Kingston Airport of the time. Miss Brownlee flew over Ulster and the surrounding area with her camera and took photographs which demonstrated that the

Photomontage from air of proposed power plant smoke stacks near Kingston-Rhinecliffe Bridge. Photo courtesy of Gale Brownlee

pollution-dispensing smokestack proposed by the power company would be much taller and more polluting than they had said. In addition she and a graphic artist at IBM made a mock-up of what the smoke stacks and gadgetry would be like to arouse public interest. All this led to the eventual refusal of officials to permit the power plant to be built.

Had the power plant been built it would have dealt a blow to Kingston's ever growing appeal as a historic city and a popular place for tourists to visit because of the fouling of the City's atmosphere and the hazards presented to air travel.

13.
Charles Lang Freer Thinks Internationally About Art and Founds a Unique Art Museum

KINGSTON, DUTCH INFLUENCED AS IT WAS, WAS NEVER ENTIRELY ISOLATED from the major currents of American life. It was located more than a mile across the estuarial Hudson River opposite what is now Rhinebeck, from Dutchess County's northern edge and not very far above that from Columbia County and the great Livingston Manor which its first owner had stretched to some 165,000 acres. Rhinebeck lay opposite the mouth of the Redout or Rondout Kill or Creek at the place once known as the "Indian Crossing" from its pre-historic use as a link in a great system of extensive interrelated Native trails for the use of runners. When the winter cold froze the Hudson River sufficiently well enough to enable the ice to bear the weight of white men and their horses, then the ice would permit the frequent passage of pedestrians, skaters and sleighs quickly back and forth across it almost as if the River had vanished.

In the absence of a church at Kipsbergen (now Rhinebeck), white babies born there were carried across the River to be baptized at Kingston's Dutch Church where their parents' marriages had been solemnized and recorded. The earliest deeds to land in what is now Rhinebeck were put on record in the Ulster County clerk's office in Kingston. They were so-called Indian deeds which conveyed land rights to buy a substantial amount of the east bank by several brothers of Kingston's Dutch family named Kip, from two Esopus sachems who claimed a right to the Hudson's east bank.

Gilbert Livingston, a younger son of Robert Livingston, the first lord of the immense manor named for him, crossed the Hudson and settled down in Kingston where he became Ulster County clerk to keep track of land ownerships while his equally land-obsessed cousin Henry served new Dutchess County in a similar capacity. William Beekman, the owner of much Ulster land, moved across the river from Kingston to marry a member of the land-rich Livingston family. The newly wed Beekmans at first built a small stone house on their east bank land much like those across the River at Kingston, but which was later much enlarged and modified to fit the dignity of the manorial Livingstons.

Children of the east bank manorial families were educated at the Kingston Academy which from its beginning in 1774 had done much to help bridge the original social and cultural gap between the Dutch-flavored culture of the west bank of Kingston and that of the east bank with the British-oriented and aristocratic pretensions of its dominant class and its German or High Dutch tenant farmers (in contrast to the Low Dutch or Holland Dutch who had been the colonists on the west bank and had come from the Netherlands). As a Latin school the Kingston Academy was a suitable place for the secondary education of the sons of the manorial class. Many a son of the manorial class who would rise to prominence in the State of the future had been a product of the Kingston Academy. General John Armstrong, a member of George Washingston's Revolutionary staff and later American minister to France, for instance (his wife was a Livingston), took up residence in the old stone Senate House in Kingston in order to keep an eye on his sons who were students at the Academy, and he had a wooden mantel in one of the major rooms of the building he lived in, they say, replaced by one of French marble to enable him to feel more at home.

When Chancellor Livingston returned to the United States in 1804 from a very successful tour of duty as our minister to France (during which he negotiated the Louisiana Purchase which more than doubled the area of the United States and at a cost of less than four cents an acre paid to France), Kingston welcomed him home like a favorite son by parading through flag-draped Kingston streets and tendering him a fancy testimonial banquet. In his role as an American version of a British enlightened Whig landlord, but with the interests of his many tenants on both sides of the Hudson River at heart, Judge Robert Livingston (father of the Chancellor) set up a mill in what had been a part of the Kingston Commons near what is now Saugerties, to supply local farmers with ground limestone which was becoming popular then among knowledgeable farmers as a soil or agricultural amendment, and he or his son gave his many tenants at his Woodstock lands a ram with superior wool from the royal flock of merino sheep at Rambouillet in France to improve the breed of Woodstock sheep.

Kingston was indeed in some ways a lingering outpost of old Dutch sleepiness yet at the same time it had its valued ties to the world of the great American landlords who followed the latest things in scientific agriculture and in fashionable life. So the people of the village kept in touch with a more elegant side of American life by reason of their connection with the people of the Hudson Valley's "manorial" or rich man's or gentleman's side of the Hudson River.

After the death of Chancellor Livingston in 1813, his son-in-law Robert L. Livingston proposed lumbering his late wife Margaret Maria's share of the Hardenbergh Patent in the Catskill Mountains, with wood processing plants at work at Kingston Point prior to shipping finished products out to market down the Hudson. But this visionary scheme (for its period) called the Esopus Creek Navigation Company failed, in part through the reluctance of Livingston's many Woodstock tenants to work off their back rents by serving as raftsmen on the sometimes rough and always narrow Esopus, and as well by the sharp economic downturn of the 1830s.

As Robert L. Livingston was manfully pursuing his lumbering schemes, he was also trying to educate his nine motherless children after his wife's death, and then sending them off for a proper finishing to Europe with letters of introduction to the aristocratic friends Robert L. had made in Paris when he had served there as the Chancellor's official secretary.

Robert L.'s son, Montgomery, who had become a landscape painter, and socially ambitious Eugene, made an appearance at the Kingston Courthouse in support of their fellow Ulster County landlords' side in the trial of revolting Hardenbergh Patent tenant farmers in the late 1840s. Around 1849, an amendment to the New York State constitution (as a result of the tenants' Anti-Rent War) forbade the writing of any more of the old manorial kind of leases, and with that the attempt to put a manorial stamp on the Kingston side of the Hudson came to an end and Hardenbergh Patent lands were sold to tenants.

Among creative native sons of whom Kingston could be proud as contributing much to its somewhat unconsiously cosmopolitan air after the final decades of the 19th century was Charles Lang Freer, descended from an old local Huguenot family, one of the first of these to reach Kingston as immigrants in the seventeenth century. Born in 1854, Charles Lang Freer was the son of a struggling keeper of a livery stable. Charles was one of six brothers and sisters, who during his great success in a railroad-related and art collecting career, remained strongly attached to his hometown of Kingston and his siblings living there, and enjoyed visiting the place and renewing old acquaintances from time to time from his rooms in the Stuyvesant Hotel on the corner of Fair and John Streets.

At the age of fourteen following the death of his mother young Freer dropped out of the seventh grade of elementary school to help support his family. He soon took a job with the Rondout & Oswego (later the Ulster & Delaware Railroad) where his skill with figures and his command of bookkeeping elevated him into a good job as a paymaster and accountant.

In the period of frenzied railroad building following the Civil War, U & D Superintendent Col. Frank J. Hecker took Freer along as a partner when he went West. In Indiana before too long the pair was able to combine three small and struggling railroads into a single profitable one. Hecker and Freer next moved to Detroit where they built much-needed wooden railroad freight cars. In this they were so successful that by the time Freer was forty-five he and his partner were independently rich.

Following the example of other newly rich American industrialists adjusting to a chance at more elegant lives, Freer had already developed his latent feeling for art. He collected prints and paintings by Americans and others, and lived in a relatively modest home stylishly designed in the then current "aesthetic" manner Freer may have first learned of by hearing a lecture in Detroit by poet, playwright and wit Oscar Wilde who spoke on aesthetics and handicrafts in Detroit on his first American tour in 1882.

In the construction of his own Detroit home, in collaboration with his gifted architect Wilson Eyre, Freer used bluestone shipped from Freer's hometown of Kingston as a strong base below an upper story which was faced with wooden shingles as siding. Masons brought from Freer's hometown handled the laying of the bluestone. Freer's house was much admired for having a sophisticated esthetic simplicity in contrast, it was said, to the adjoining 80-room mock chateau of his partner Hecker.

Freer and Hecker managed their business affairs so shrewdly that before the hard times of the early 1890s arrived, they had organized the big American Car and Foundry Company which gave them a virtual (and still legal) monopoly of the freight car making industry.

Freer's expanding interest in art led him at first to buy examples of the etchings and the paintings of some then safely well known Americans. Later he became impressed by the etchings of expatriate American master James Abbot McNeil Whistler.

Ever since Captain Matthew Perry had opened the door to long secluded Japan in 1850, Japanese culture and art had been trickling into America and Europe. By the 1870s and '80s the trickle had become a stream which showed effects in the work of artists Mary Cassatt and James Whistler. Charles Freer with his innate sensitivity became deeply influenced by the work of Whistler. He called upon the brilliant if eccentric Whistler at his London home, ventured to become his patron and accumulated the largest collection of Whistler's etchings, in all their states, in existence as well as many of his paintings. Eventually he bought the Whistler-influenced and Japanese influenced controversial Blue or Peacock Room, then regarded as a shocking and dangerously exotic aberration. The room with its vibrant blue walls with large gilded peacocks flying above, was all in a taste too much influenced by the Japanese to please the Liverpool shipping magnate who had commissioned it to display his collection of pottery and had not seen it in progress because he was away on business as it was created; nevertheless the industrialist reluctantly paid for it. By this time Freer had acquired a passionate devotion to the art of the Orient. English imperialist poet Rudyard Kipling had written in 1880 that "East is East and West is West and never the twain shall meet." Freer, like his good friend the orientalist Ernest Fenellosa heartily disagreed, and saw common elements at the roots of both which produced harmonious results.

When Freer decided to sell (to be delivered after his death) his huge collection of Oriental and American art to the Smithsonian Institution (which had shown little interest in art up to this time) for one dollar, his many conditions made the completion of the proposed sale difficult, and President Theodore Roosevelt was called in to straighten things out. Before the offer was accepted, Freer, completely released from his industrial cares, had already traveled widely in the Orient, Near and Middle East and Egypt studying old pottery, porcelain and paintings with his museum-to-be in mind. He had become very learned in some branches of oriental art then little explored by Americans. By then Freer had become a suave and polished gentleman who favorably impressed all he met. He had never been entirely well, for he was believed to have inherited an ailment which stayed with him throughout his life and caused him to have frequent periods of debilitation. In spite of this, he made his first trip to the far distant interior of China in search of early Chinese scroll paintings, and he was carried there aboard a rickshaw by two dedicated oriental men whom he liked to say were capable of making over thirty miles in a day. He also hiked in the Catskills with American artist friends.

Freer assembled a fine library of art history and artists' books which he zealously studied when he was not traveling.

During his final years, Freer seemed to be determined to make sure that his future museum containing his art collection would be exactly what he wanted, both in the building's exterior appearance and character and even in the grouping of the exhibits within. These included carefully chosen examples of contemporary American art as well as what is considered the largest and finest collection of works by the often Orient-influenced Whistler and an immense collection of Oriental art and such objects as pottery. He had expected his famous friend Stanford White, partner in the prestigious architectural firm of McKim, Mead and White to design his museum. White also designed special simple but elegant picture frames for Freer, which contrasted favorably to modern eyes with the heavy and sometimes gaudy frames in fashion at the time. When White became the victim in a sensational murder by railroad-enriched Harry K. Thaw (in a dispute over the affections of model and showgirl Evelyn Nesbit), he chose White-influenced Charles Platt to take charge of designing his museum. He had come to believe that the museum he envisioned would be so planned as to reflect his belief that the same universal impulses lay behind and harmonized the art of East and West.

While engaged in work related to plans for the museum he was giving to the nation he did not fail to keep up with Kingston and his relatives living there. He ordered built a striking house, designed by Wilson Eyre, with a bluegreen roof on Kingston's Albany Avenue for his widowed sister Emily. He gave a Kingston church an organ and presented the Kingston Carnegie Library with a pair of large antique Chinese vases which are brought out and displayed at the Library on important occasions. In September of 1919 he had moved to the very fashionable Gotham Hotel in Manhattan after suffering a stroke—this in order to be close to the medical help he needed. He stipulated in his will that he be buried in his family plot in Kingston's well-landscaped Wiltwyck Cemetery, and so he was after his death in early autumn of 1919, and his burial under a plain local bluestone slab in contrast with the plain but sophisticated memorial to him created in Tokyo by Japanese friends and admirers.

The Charles Lang Freer Museum of Art, the first of its kind in America, was opened close to the Smithsonian on the Mall in Washington, D.C. in 1923 to the vigorous applause of both the art world and the public.

In recent years, because of the increase of interest in Oriental art in America as well as in the work of Whistler, the trustees of the Smithsonian responded by enlarging the Freer museum (to include two stories underground for students of the art displayed above and for maintenance of the exhibits) and by bringing many more of Freer's paintings and art objects out of storage and put on display. The new gallery and its exhibits were received by the art world with enthusiasm when the new museum opened a few years ago, amplified by some additions to the original collections.

No other native born person of Kingston has achieved a greater international fame than did Charles Lang Freer, whose gift to the nation becomes more and more treasured as time goes by, and the value of his special sensitivity to art and art's place in life becomes ever more appreciated.

14.
John Burroughs and Others Who Brought Renown to Kingston

WIDELY ADMIRED JOHN BURROUGHS DID NOT LIVE IN KINGSTON, NOR was he born there, but lived on a ten acre farm in its suburb of West Park on the Hudson River where he grew grapes for the market, wrote essays on many aspects of nature, entertained many literary notables and others. Burroughs inspired thousands, many of whom he had previously met only in the pages of his works, toward a deeper understanding of the mysteries of nature, and built a rustic retreat to work in, completed in 1895 which he named Slabsides. Slabsides, built and furnished largely with Burroughs' own hands, is now listed on the National Register of Historic Places as a distinctive Burroughs-built place to which the many admirers of that lucid exponent of nature's ways thronged—and still do, to express their admiration of the man and of his work.

Students at the Kingston High School as well as those at Vassar College in Poughkeepsie and the New Paltz Normal School (now State University College at New Paltz) were among those who made frequent pilgrimages to West Park to enjoy walks with the "Seer of Slabsides" and to benefit from his intimate knowledge, insights and understanding of the natural world and its relation to man.

Burroughs was a sensitive and popular writer who had taught Americans not only to watch birds flying and nesting, flowers opening or to wonder at other natural phenomena but to take thoughtful pleasure in all aspects of nature. President Theodore Roosevelt, Thomas A. Edison, Henry Ford, and West Park neighbor Civil War General Daniel Butterfield (the composer of the bugle call, "Taps") were among the many eminent admirers who visited Burroughs at West Park. Burroughs' long time and close friend, the great poet Walt Whitman, (who was the subject of one of Burroughs' many books) had been a visitor long before Slabsides was built. Whitman wrote striking vignettes of the West Park woods where the owners of its many estates took pains to give the place an special added charm by landscaping and maintaining its roads and edging them with local cobblestones.

Thousands of pilgrims came to Slabsides almost as if to a shrine at which the worship of nature in company with nature's priest was celebrated. It was in honor of his simple life style too in which as he had matured he showed the influence of Charles Darwin's thinking and that of the "Creative Evolution" of Henri Bergson, as well as for the simple grace and insight of his prose that Burroughs had so great a number of followers, including even fastidious Henry James who praised Burroughs' lucid style (as shown especially in his essays on his visit to England).

At a discouraged moment in his youth, Burroughs, then studying medicine in an Ulster County doctor's office (before he became an Ulster County school teacher), wrote a simple poem in which he gave utterance to the faith of his parents in the very conservative Old School Baptist Church. They and other people in his native Roxbury in the western Catskills believed with John Calvin and others in a predestination in which God was thought to have thoughtfully ordained every event of every human life at the very moment of conception. It was a simple belief which had comforted many in difficult moments. Burroughs, brought up in an Old School Baptist home, retained throughout his life a few bits of his childhood teachings such as an unwillingness to celebrate Christmas with gifts and Christmas decorations.

Burroughs's poem, called "Waiting" begins:

> "Serene, I fold my hands and wait,
> Nor care for wind, nor tide, nor sea;
> I rave no more 'gainst Time or Fate,
> for lo! my own shall come to me."

and continues through several stanzas to express faith in a confidence-inspiring personal destiny. The poem is included in many anthologies including the authoritative John Bartlett's *Familiar Quotations* (on p. 770).

Burroughs was so often asked by discouraged Americans to write personal copies for them of the poem "Waiting" that, patient as he usually was, he sometimes in late life expressed a passing irritation. Copies of the hand-written poem in his own characteristic script are treasured to this day in Ulster County and other households to be read at times of doubt and stress. One was once owned by a nature loving and Burroughs-admiring wood-turner in Woodstock named Shaffer Vosburgh (whose mill is now on the National Register of Historic Places), who refused to allow the felling of a stand of mature native hemlock trees on his land, noting "The birds love those trees and I love the birds."

"Waiting" was once said by Burroughs' companion and biographer Dr. Clara Barrus to be the most often quoted of any poem by an American author.

Among prosperous New York people who were West Park residents, along with celebrity John Burroughs, was John V. Buckman, believed to have amassed a fortune by operating about fifty trading vessels out of New York's spacious harbor. Judge Alton B. Parker, who practiced law in Kingston, brought a passing sort of national fame to his West Park home of Rosemount and Kingston too in 1904 when he ran for President as a Democrat against doughty Theodore Roosevelt. During that campaign, little West Park buzzed with the coming and going of reporters and Democratic politicos while Burroughs quietly continued to raise grapes for the market on his modest little farm and continued to write his beguiling essays, jotting down copies of "Waiting" when asked, even though he had long before given up the ideas of the Old School Baptists in which he had been raised.

From expressing a simple joy in observing nature Burroughs moved on as as he matured to telling in his essays of his serious searching for the significance of nature and of the universe in which we live.

After Burroughs, there were many Kingstonians who added to the City's history. For instance, outstanding among the first American promoters of a national health plan for all Americans, was Kingston-born Arthur Flemming who spent a long and useful life as a government official and advocate for issues such as national health care for all. Born in Kingston in 1905, Flemming became a journalist who covered President Franklin Roosevelt's bi-weekly press conferences for a national magazine, and later served as Secretary of Health, Education and Welfare in the Cabinet of President Dwight Eisenhower. Flemming was also chair of the U.S. Civil Rights Commission, but was fired in 1982 by President Reagan after Flemming was critical of the Reagan administration's civil rights record. In 1994, President Bill Clinton awarded Dr. Flemming the Presidential Medal of Freedom. Flemming left behind an inspiring legacy of strong advocacy of the need for a national program of health care and equal civil rights for all.

A Kingston painter who brought fame to his hometown was Jervis McEntee, son of a Delaware and Hudson Canal engineer. He is usually classed as a member of the Hudson River School of landscape painters. Jervis McEntee (known to Kingston friends as Jeddy) passed most of his life between a charming summer studio (now demolished) of romantic Victorian design on the Weinberg with extensive views of the Catskills, the Rondout and the Hudson Valley, and a New York City studio in a well known studio building crowded with major painters of the time who were among his good friends. His often somber paintings of fall and winter landscapes evoke a haunting and yet charming melancholy. He was a friend of the great tragedian Edwin Booth who visited McEntee at his studio on the Weinberg, as did other people notable in the world of the various arts. McEntee was also an active member of the influential National Academy of Design.

Sharing McEntee's New York studio for a while was a Rondout friend Joseph Tubby, an English-born landscape painter of a very distinctive style of his own in design and color who painted local houses and bridges for a living. The two painters made sketching trips together into the Adirondacks and Catskills. Tubby had some modest recognition as a landscape painter and exhibited with the National Academy and elsewhere in New York. In his very lengthy and detailed journals, McEntee recorded details of much activity in the New York City art and theater worlds of his time and so shed an important light on an interesting period in the history of American art as well as that of Kingston.

McEntee married the sister of architect Calvert Vaux who had emigrated from England to become a partner of A.J. Downing, the influential landscape designer and writer on gardening and rural architecture of Newburgh. It was Vaux who designed the now vanished McEntee studio-residence on the Weinberg.

Another creative person but of another kind was Rondout watchmaker and jeweler G. Rahmer who invented a remarkable grandfather's clock a bit over 6 feet high which had a novel horizontal movement. An example of this clock stood in a Rondout bank for many years. It featured a window in its walnut case through which its elaborate working mechanism could be studied in action. The clock was known among clock experts as an outstanding invention and an example is now a prized part of a large collection of time keepers.

There were many other inventors in Kingston's industrial period—one of these creative people was shown at work in his cluttered workshop in de Lisser's *Picturesque Ulster*, in a picture captioned "A Wall Street Edison." This inventor has not yet been identified.

The "Wall Street Edison" from de Lisser's *Picturesque Ulster*

Local creatively-minded veterinarian Dr. Philip Poley specialized in treating the eyes of animals, wrote professional papers on the subject and earned so fine a reputation that he was consulted to treat the eyes of one of the dogs of England's royal family. He invented instruments to be used in surgery on animals' eyes, one of which was adapted to human cases—all this in a relatively short life span.

Shingle planing invention, from an 1864 *Scientific American*

A Rondout writer, Ernest Jarrold, who became a reporter for the *New York Sun*, achieved popularity with his Mickey Finn tales dealing with the adventures of a fictional and mischievous Rondout boy, using a name for his title character already well known as that of a knock-out drink. The Mickey Finn stories were published first in *Harper's Magazine* and other magazines, and then in book form. The stories affectionately showed the Irish with kindly humor, and are still read with praise by Kingston people. A distinctive Ponckhockie Street was named for Jarrold's family, which developed it with creative taste but at a loss.

Kingston people who wrote, painted or acted often gravitated to the art colony growing up in Woodstock after 1902. One of these was playwright Howard Koch whose 1937 radio play version of H.G. Wells' *War of the Worlds* produced by Orson Welles proved so overly realistic when broadcast that it persuaded many thousands of frightened Americans that an actual war with invaders from space was being waged against them.

A man with strong local roots and who achieved a substantial acceptance as a gifted worker in the field of serious contemporary arts was musician Robert Craft. Craft became acquainted with the avant-garde and other musicians of the nearby art colony of Woodstock. He became an orchestra conductor, lecturer and writer on music and secretary to and close associate of Igor Stravinsky in the great Russian composer's later life after he had settled in the United States. Craft is credited with having influenced Stravinsky in his later serialist compositions as well as in his writings.

Craft made many trips to Europe to act as guest conductor of orchestras in performances of such works as those of Arnold Schönberg, the Austrian composer who had devised, by 1914, a 12-tone musical scale in which all twelve tones were given equal importance. Schönberg's innovation roused great controversy among musicians and Craft sided with the followers of Schönberg's ideas.

Kingston, unlike Catskill to the north has had no Afro-American to serve as his or her people's local historian and so the contributions of Afro-Americans are not easy to unearth beyond some newspaper references, for instance, to troubles in Kingston during the New York City draft riots in which black people were victimized and caused to leave Kingston. But in recent years Kingston was chosen as the site of a remarkable novel of life among its black people. It is a fascinating work dealing with the mingled subconscious thoughts and conscious actions of blacks in the city, written in a deft and sophisticated style. The black author is Richard Perry, and the title is *Around the Corner*, published by William Morrow.

It was not only in the field of the arts and inventions that Kingstonians brought credit to their city. One of the lawyers who went back and forth from Kingston to New York City to carry on a large legal practice was MacDonald De Witt. This man who usually spent his weekends at his old family home in Kingston earned the reputation of being an expert in the law of libel and slander by his work in the Andy Gump case. Andy Gump was the title character in a very popular comic strip syndicated in 309 newspapers. The suit involved the use by comic strip artist Sidney Smith of a sketch the artist had made of a man from Canandaigua, New York, who had lost his lower jaw and had grown a heavy mustache to help hide his loss. The Canandaguian whose sketch Smith had made sued, and was awarded $150,000 damages, but had not been pleased with the size of the award, and took the suit to the Court of Appeals with MacDonald De Witt's firm as his lawyers. The case was hard fought and brought fame to attorney De Witt. The case became a often cited precedent in other similar legal tussles involving creative properties.

All these native Kingstonians and many others associated with the City played parts in the elevation of the place from its former undeserved provincial reputation to a City which deserved recognition in the nation—and made it worthy of inclusion in the air of fame and glamor which had long hung over the Hudson Valley—a region which for years had attracted Americans and Europeans by its scenic beauty, the achievements of its people, and its legendary and historic connections. And now by the novel ideas of its inventors and lawyers, and by the deeds of local men and women who had chosen life in the U.S. Navy as a career.

15.

Vander Lyn's Versailles *Panorama*, painted mostly in a Kingston barn, and a New Museum of Decorative Arts Make News in its History for Kingston

IN 1988 A MOST SIGNIFICANT PART OF JOHN VANDER LYN'S LASTING LEGACY IN art to Kingston and to the nation was put on modern view. Kingston's own John Vander Lyn, who had died in 1852, burst in 1988 into a greater national fame when his magnificent, newly restored *Panoramic View of the Palace and Gardens of Versailles* (most of it painted in a Kingston barn belonging to a member of the old Huguenot Hasbrouck family) was opened to the public as a stellar attraction of the ambitious new American Wing of the great Metropolitan Museum of Art in New York City.

The *Panoramic View* had been well cared for during many years after Vander Lyn's death by his dedicated niece Catherine (or Kate as her friends called her) and then after Catherine died by the Kingston Senate House Associates until a better appreciation of Vander Lyn arrived. It had been hoped once to restore the huge *Panoramic View* and place part of it on display on the curved wall of the entrance room to Kingston's Senate House Museum, but when this proved inadvisable or impossible, the panorama had lain safely in a folded-up condition in the Senate House Museum attic for years. After all hope of restoring it and putting it on view in Kingston had been considered and given up by the Senate House museum, it was at last turned over to the Metropolitan Museum with the help of Kingston's generous Emily Crane Chadbourne, who in addition helped pay for some of the expensive restoration and preparation for display in the Metropolitan Museum's ambitious new American Wing.

John Vander Lyn (1776-1852) *Self-Portrait,* The Metropolitan Museum of Art, Bequest of Ann S. Stephens in the name of her mother, Mrs. Ann S. Stephens, 1918.

The final decades of the eighteenth century and the earliest ones of the nineteenth were a time when much effort went into extending the limits of the human eye to deal with the visual arts. Among them were the huge circular oil paintings to be seen from a central point in an almost magical reality by means of a novel method patented by Irish artist James Barker in 1787, and soon put to use in London and Paris to satisfy a public craving for almost super-realistic views of famous places as well as such history-changing events as famous battles. The panoramic pictures were seen by even so respected an authority as famous painter Sir Joshua Reynolds of the Royal Academy of England as important examples of a new kind of then much esteemed historical painting. John Vander Lyn, newly returned to Paris from a visit to America, became captivated by the thought of creating a Panoramic View of the beautiful and world-renowned palace and gardens of Versailles by means of James Barker's ingenius invention.

Vander Lyn may well have agreed with the opinion of Sir Joshua Reynolds that the panorama form offered a new opportunity for the kind of historical painting to which he knew many great artists aspired.

In the author's possession is an print, from the early 19th century, showing pre-French Revolutionary Bourbon courtiers enjoying the pleasures of the Versailles gardens. This print contrasts sharply with the gardens as opened to the public in the reign of constitutional Bourbon monarch Louis XVIII, restored to the throne after the fall of Napoleon. Here is a bit of the gardens under the absolutist pre-Revolutionary Bourbon monarchs:

Courtiers enjoying Versailles, a painted print, circa 1818, once owned by John Vander Lyn, from the collection of Alf Evers, who acquired it from a descendent of Vander Lyn

And here as seen when Louis XVIII gave the convincing impression of being a constitutional monarch of post-Revolutionary times, historically correct in every detail of its era.

The Panorama with pleasure-seekers of about 1819, appropriately dressed for people of their time as shown by Vander Lyn. The Metropolitan Museum, Gift of the Senate House Association, 1952

Vander Lyn began making sketches with the aid of a lens-using device called the camera obscura as well as more conventional freehand and correctly measured drawings of the ordinary public taking their pleasure amid the visual glories of the historic restored Royal Versailles gardens and in sight of its huge palace. (Some of these sketches are now on view in the Senate House Museum of Kingston.) This was in the hope of presenting the place to Americans by means of what seemed to be a magical view (correct in every detail even to the special charm given to the place by the flattering September afternoon sunlight). By 1819 the painter had been hard at work on the huge *Panorama* in a great barn he used as a studio in his hometown of Kingston lent to him by a friend of the old Kingston Hasbrouck family. He painted it in sections. One-fourth of the 12 foot x 165 foot painting was hung at a time on an improvised easel which faced a scaffold in the barn on which Vander Lyn and an assistant worked painting the palace and the gardens but reserving some of the figures, it is believed, and some other details until after the canvas could be shipped down the Hudson River to New York and installed in the cylindrical building called the Rotunda in City Hall Park on the recently cleared site of the former City Alms House. The Rotunda would also serve, Vander Lyn hoped, as the City's first art gallery and museum.

The giant panoramic canvas, probably formed of many normal sheets of canvas, had first been carefully stitched together. In the capacious old barn Vander Lyn worked with his collection of notes and images of the Palace and Gardens together with his measurements and the memories of lovely September afternoons spent there in careful observations and renderings of the scene and the many varied people who frequented it, to give a haunting depiction of the place as it had looked on a September afternoon of 1819.

Month after month the painting of the huge canvas went on in hot weather and cold, consuming a vast amount of paint (John's father was a dealer in paint as well as a wagon painter) until at last the first stage of the essay in painting a contemporary but also historical subject was ended and the nearly finished work was to be made ready for exhibition by the addition in its New York City exhibition place of some masterly finishing touches to architectural and historical details but above all by the great assembly of human beings who would give animation to a slice of French life as beautifully documented on that long-vanished sunny September afternoon. Vander Lyn had included, as he worked in the barn, people ranging in the social scale from restored Bourbon King Louis XVIII to a carefree boy intent only on chasing a butterfly, as well as a group of *citoyens* and *citoyennes* driving care away by playing a lively game of blind man's buff. The *Panorama* showed the King himself standing on a porch, looking out on a group of visiting heads of allied nations which supported his rule, including the Czar of Russia and the king of Prussia—all attired in their most impressive uniforms. There were tall Grenadiers on guard duty in the huge park and loving couples intent mostly on each other. The male member of one of these couples, however, is extending his walking stick to point out to his lady love an especially fine feature of the gardens. Glittering fountains embellished with sculptures threw sprays of crystalline water into the air to sparkle in the brilliant sunlight. And peeping out from behind a wall is what is believed to be Vander Lyn himself, gazing with earnest eyes to make sure perhaps that he had missed nothing historically significant in the lively scene laid out before him, and thanks to his skill, for posterity.

The Rotunda in New York's City Hall Park where the *Panoramic View* was first exhibited was a plain cylindrical window-less structure. In order to highlight and illuminate the painting, the rotunda's top was probably surrounded by artfully arranged openings at the eaves plus a small ocellus at the top of the gently slanting roof's central peak. In addition, artificial lighting may have helped out when needed.

Vander Lyn's *Panoramic View* when exhibited however did not bring him more than moderate renown and the need to pay for the lease of the Rotunda at the New York City Hall Park kept him obliged to gain support by painting the portraits he did so well, and showing his own historic panorama as well as those created by other less masterly painters of European cities and battles in exhibitions in Charleston and Philadelphia. Today, his superbly restored *Panorama* in the American Wing of the Metropolitan Museum is a resounding success to an American public with a better appreciation of the visual arts and history than was possible in the early days of the American Republic; such as realizing that the treaty which brought the Revolution to a end with the help of France had been signed in the palace of Versailles (which is visible in the *Panorama*) in 1783. Vander Lyn's stature from the appreciation of his Panorama helps add to the rise of his native place to the status of a historic city, in which a great American painter played a part in the evolution of the wide screen magical reality of the films of our own time.

In 1997 a splendid museum, not devoted specifically to Kingston history but to that of American taste in the decorative arts, opened on the corner of Wall and Main Streets boldly facing the Old Dutch Church and its moldy and mossy old churchyard from which rises the monument above the grave of George Clinton. It was opened to the public by the Friends of Historic Kingston to whom it had been bequeathed by Fred J. Johnston for that purpose. Johnston had grown from a modest career as a young local antiques expert and dealer to distinction as a trusted consultant to Henry F. Dupont in the formation of Dupont's now famous Winterthur Museum in Wilmington, Delaware. The handsome early frame house built in 1812 for State Senator John Suydan had had such notables as Washington Irving and President Martin Van Buren as overnight guests of the State Senator. When the building had been threatened with demolition to be replaced by a filling station, Johnston had borrowed money to buy it and preserve it, using it as the location of his antiques business. He had furnished the building with American and some relevant European antiques chosen and arranged in accordance with his impeccable taste, and added a charming small garden and a room for the display of Kingston artifacts.

Henry Dupont on a visit to Johnston's museum had referred to it, in tribute to its fine decoration by Johnston, as a "Winterthur-on-the-Hudson." This was choice praise indeed.

On May 3, 1997, the Museum opened and has been a popular and rewarding place for Kingstonians and their tourists ever since. It is a welcome addition to the city's other historic assets which charm an ever greater number of visitors each year.

The exterior and interior of the Johnston Museum, courtesy of Friends of Historic Kingston

16.
The Old City Hall Restored
1990s–2000

IT WAS AS THE TWENTIETH CENTURY ENDED AND A NEW MILLENNIUM DAWNED on Kingston that a new and very preservationally and historically perceptive mayor came into office and saw the demolishing of the Central Post Office as having positive value even in its rubbled state as a good example of what NOT to do. He suggested that the City fathers (the members of its Common Council) might learn a lesson from the sense of loss since 1969 felt by so many citizens at the unnecessary destruction of their architecturally distinguished Central Post Office building. "We have to learn from our mistakes," said Mayor T. R. Gallo. "I'm happy that our city fathers are not making that same mistake with Old City Hall."

1975 demonstration to save City Hall, photo courtesy of Friends of Historic Kingston

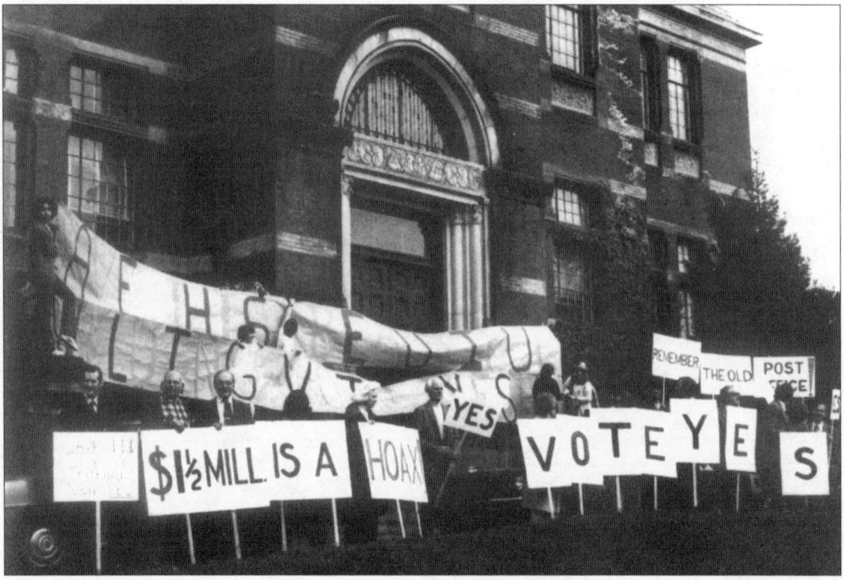

By voting to restore the old City Hall, the Mayor continued, "From a tourism perspective, we have to look at all our buildings and try to protect them. That should be our niche. They make us stand apart and give us our identity." Gallo told how people who raised money for the City Hall restoration by selling a wide variety of items, from brownies to umbrellas, often mentioned how they loved the project. "They point one block down the street (Broadway)," Mayor Gallo, said, "where we lost another historic building, the old Post Office, and it's very fresh in their minds."

Gallo then wisely encouraged Kingston people to use even a painful loss to spur themselves into vigorous action in what under the mayor's active leadership was becoming a true united community effort to prevent the old City Hall from going the way into destruction of other priceless historic assets.

Kingston from time to time in recent years had been swept by waves of enthusiasm for preserving for proud display the historical treasures of old buildings and other visible and tangible assets set so nobly in the legendary and scenic landscape of the Catskills and the Hudson River Valley. This occured in 1886, when the Holland Society pilgrims were stirred to such a pitch of rapture by the generosity, (surprising for that time), of Samuel D. Coykendall, a fellow member who was of course also Dutch descended; in 1907, 1909 and 1914 and in the explosion of national pride evoked in the 1920s. But now at last their old city, under the leadership of a historically minded mayor (who also was keenly aware of the value in dollars of tourism to his city), appeared to have realized the full power of the City's special historical identity. Then in January of 1989, Governor Mario Cuomo asked the State Legislature to empower Hudson Valley communities (each with its own special charm) to organize a Greenway project which would unite all the many attractions of the long famous and glamorous region into a convenient and unified system for enjoyment by tourists as well as by Valley dwellers. Kingston's important place in the Valley especially with the great River approaching a cleansing from its industrial and human waste pollution on the verge of nearing a reasonable degree of completion, the time had come for the City to burst its former restraining bounds and display with an eager new pride its historical identity to historically minded tourists whose visits would be made more convenient and enjoyable by the automobile-friendly Greenway. A Greenway could be expected to have wide public acceptance because it is an adaptation to the use of the automobile age of the proven European canal system which had long been popular (and still is) among European tourists for pleasant recreational travel as well as the shipping of goods. In 1796, John Vander Lyn's friend and fellow painter Robert Fulton, in his notable book of that year, *A Treatise on the Improvement of Canal Navigation*, had looked ahead to a time when similar canal systems could be of use by both tourists and inhabitants of American valleys. The Greenway would translate Fulton's vision into the age of the automobile.

The restored City Hall, 2000, photo by Michael Saporito

With the Common Council's backing, the new vision of the City's future compellingly presented by Mayor Gallo before 1998 when restoration of the old City Hall was approved, with a substantial preliminary budget alotted. And in a spirit of undertaking the project in the best possible style the City took a bold step into the future, as bold a step as that which had led the Kingston Common Council of the 1870s to plan and build a City Hall larger and much more elegant than some laggard citizens had expected but expressing a brighter vision of a bigger and better Kingston to come.

The best restoration architect obtainable, John G. Waite Associates, was commissioned. Mr. Waite would comment later on that the restoration had been undertaken in the spirit of the restoration of a masterpiece of a great painter, with old accretions often peeled away to return to the structure's original high quality. Care was taken to employ dedicated Kingston artisans wherever possible. An example of the mayor's determination to harness community spirit and zeal was the creation of a club of Kingston High School students to work at research into the hidden details of the building as of earlier days. A part of the students' efforts was research leading to the restoration of the (semicircular) lunettes in plaster on the upper part of the walls of the Common Council chambers. The lunettes had been destroyed in part by water damage. They had not been a part of the original City Hall architect's plan but had been added as an element of the repairs following a fire in 1928. The lunettes, featuring scenes and other images relating to Kingston's early history had a decided value because they brought to the City Hall of 1929 in what is now mid-Broadway a good sense of early uptown Kingston of the seventeenth century. These were the days when the ridge in O'Reilly's Woods from which the City Hall now asserted its command of the entire new City had been part of the wilderness of the useless armabowery of the early Dutch. And so the lunettes, it was hoped, would help unify the City formed by the disparate and sometimes quarreling villages of Kingston and Rondout and not yet accepted as a well unified municipality in all its details. It was hoped back in 1929 that the City Hall lunettes would aid Kingston in acquiring the sense of unity many felt it had lacked ever since it became a single city, and had shown earlier in the days when its very productive wheatfields and its good Landing Place on the Rondout Harbor had worked together in mutually profitable harmony.

By 1969 too the position of the Native Americans in the City's history had modified to a milder one which aroused interest in the designating on City-owned land (once used by the Natives) of a remarkable profile rock known locally as an image of Chief Ponckhockie. In 1969, a member of the Common Council had proposed dedicating the profile rock as a monument in honor of Chief Ponckhockie, but after it was discovered that there was never a chief by that name (Ponckhockie is a place name of uncertain but probably Native origin) the project was dropped. Recently, in view of the better relationship which has developed between white and Native Americans, there is sentiment in Kingston for designating the very impressive rock as a memorial to the place in Kingston's history of displaced Native predecessors of the Kingstonians of the present. This proposal has gained approval among Native American scholars as well.

Neither the 1929, nor the present restoration of the old City Hall had aimed at an exact replication of the building that had been completed in 1875, but as one which combined restoration to the state of the mid-1870s with adaptations for use in the age of the silicon chip and the computer. A good example of this dual nature of the restoration was the replacing not only of the damaged lunettes but also of the desks for the Common Councilors which were originally made with skill

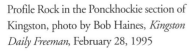

Profile Rock in the Ponckhockie section of Kingston, photo by Bob Haines, *Kingston Daily Freeman*, February 28, 1995

about 1875 by Wachman, the Rondout maker of fine furniture. These had been made for the age when the steel pen point was beginning to replace the quill pen usually made from the sharpened feather of a goose, but now desks large enough to accommodate laptop computers would be installed.

To conform with the concerns for safety and convenience of modern building codes, marble steps had taken the place of wooden ones (beginning in 1929), and accommodations for modern heat, plumbing and a water system had to be made, as well as the provision for use of the restored Hall by handicapped persons of whose needs society was becoming more aware.

The elaborately detailed and open topmost original stage of the tower had been restored in 1929, after its destruction by the fire, but in a simpler, somewhat Romanesque mode, and without the impressive corbelled base of the original stage.

As a restoration combining a returning to the building's original style with minimal concessions to render it able to give many years of use as a center of efficient city government, the Hall of today, as completed in the spring of 2000, was hailed as a masterpiece while still deserving its listing on the National Register of Historic Places as a notable example of the state of American municipal architectural design of 1875—and as a tribute to the drive and enthusiastic leadership of the late Mayor T. R. Gallo in rallying the people of his City into a community effort helping move Kingston onward toward becoming ranked more firmly than ever among the most distinctive historic cities of the Nation.

17.
Into the Future

IN 1968 JOHN S. DYSON IN HIS GUIDEBOOK NAMED *OUR HISTORIC HUDSON*, with a foreword by former Secretary of the Interior Morris Udall, deplored the destruction of some fine old buildings of Rondout's great days as a Hudson River port and suggested that Urban Renewal funds planned for further demolition of Rondout's historic buildings be used to create instead a historic waterfront park with features that would entertain tourists. By 1979 this advice had been heeded by Kingston enthusiasts organized in the Friends of Historic Kingston.

The *Newsletter* of the Preservation League of New York State for November-December 1979 had headlined its report on what was going on in Kingston, "Preservation Invigorates Kingston Renewal Efforts." The report told of how Kingston people were acting together in handling the results of an over-zealously destructive Urban Renewal Plan by connecting their Rondout waterfront, once the third in importance of all Hudson River ports (behind only New York City and Albany) with historic uptown Stockade Kingston. Kingston's efforts of 1979 called for Rondout to be given the feeling of a living and innovative waterfront museum highlighting a historic period in the Hudson Valley when Rondout Harbor had served well as the busy Kingston Landing Place.

The site of the Kingston stockade on the height above Rondout with its old blue limestone houses (of traders and farmers of the fertile Esopus creekside flatlands) had already been "recognized as architecturally important" and had earlier been placed on the National Register of Historic Places. Fortunately not all of the old Rondout buildings were torn down which had first served the needs of the Harbor area, of the Dutch farmers and traders of the once protectively stockaded village above, and then those of the Delaware and Hudson Canal at its terminal on the Hudson at Rondout Harbor.

Torn down were the indisputably handsome Rondout bank and business buildings which had served the canal and Rondout's former extractive and other industries.

The people of Kingston interceded through the Friends of Historic Kingston, founded in 1965, (and later also through S.C.O.R.E., Strand Community Organization to Rehabilitate the Environment) to halt the destruction of buildings which they felt had historic value. Among the buildings they saved was the elegant Mansion House. To quote again the *Newsletter of the Preservation League*: "With the strong support of local civic and preservation agencies, the City has used federal funds to improve the partly demolished area. A 1975 Community Development Block Grant provided for initial planning. To date, approximately $872,000 in federal funds have provided for a variety of projects and it is projected that the total public investment in the Rondout will exceed $2 million."

West Strand had not been included in the Renewal Project, because it was less run down, and was therefore largely left standing. "Here Victorian commercial facades, some of cast iron, on the west side of Broadway have been restored and foundations stabilized." A charming row of small old commercial buildings of the heyday of the Rondout waterfront was restored on Abeel Street, one ornamented with a cast iron balcony across its front. These buildings now appropriately house an art gallery, a restaurant and an antiques shop in the place of old-fashioned Smitty's barbershop (once favored by rivermen) and dealers in ropes for ships' rigging and other nautical goods. The small old creekside waterfront open spaces facing these Abeel Street buildings were preserved and adapted to modern uses for tourists as a waterfront park with benches. Among the remaining waterfront buildings listed to be restored was the one on that site which had housed on its first floor the Sampson family shoe store and upstairs the Sampson's Rondout Opera House where "divine Sarah Bernhardt" had once graced the stage. Nearby today on the Rondout Harbor bulkhead stands the new Hudson River Maritime Museum with its many fascinating exhibits and lectures by old and new rivermen recalling the great days of Hudson River travelling by canoe, sail and steam. Close by, on the very edge of the bulkhead the mighty 72-foot-long steam tugboat *Matilda* rests in retirement but ready to welcome the inspection of tourists. The open dock space between the *Matilda* and the Maritime Museum is often used for festivals such as that celebrating the Hudson River's famous shad which is cooked and served to large and appreciative crowds according to several delicious traditional recipes. Pumpkin festivals featuring old-fashioned pumpkin pies are held there with the help of the graceful sloop *Clearwater* docked alongside the Harbor's bulkhead loaded with pumpkins, and to be boarded by local and visiting people who learn the sloop's urgent message of conservation and of the progress of cleaning up the Hudson and where Pete Seeger himself sometimes sang and played his banjo.

A few steps away from the Maritime Museum stands another appropriate museum —this one celebrates the trolley cars of the past (which for years linked uptown Kingston and the waterfront) and now sends out on a regular schedule a gasoline powered trolleycar-like vehicle to carry visitors to Kingston Point, once the thronged site of Samuel Coykendall's fantastic Amusement Park and a terminal for his trolleys and one of his railroads. Kingston Point of today (long ago the old Indian Crossing of the Hudson River used by speedy Native runners on the former network of well-worn intersecting Native trails) now offers a bathing beach, a playground and other riverside attractions of the present age, under the direction of the Kingston Rotary Club.

Recreational craft, both sailboats and motorboats are available for boarding or charter at the creekside, or to take passengers on scheduled sightseeing trips, or for nighttime dining and dancing enjoyment or for meetings of clubs while moving up and down the historic Hudson.

The almost three mile length of Rondout Harbor is alive these days (except in winter) with private recreational sailing, motor craft, and canoes. Instructions in the art of sailing and the maintenance of all sorts of pleasure boats may be had at various marinas along the Rondout all the way to no longer bustling but now picturesque Eddyville where tidewater ends and above which stone canal lock ruins (once skillfully fashioned of local stone) may be seen.

On the steep slope above the creek below Eddyville romantic remnants of the extractive and industrial age of Rondout remain to be glimpsed. Entrances to former limestone kilns or mineshafts now being partly and picturesquely masked by vines are among the sights. This part of the Rondout Creek was once also the scene of great activity by builders and maintainers of barges, schooners, sloops and other vessels at shipyards once resounding with the hammer and mallet strokes of ship and barge craftsmen.

In 1979, the *Newsletter* of the Preservation League stated of Kingston that "City officials and local citizens are understandably hopeful about the City's future. The recent influx of federal and state funds combined with a preservation-conscious city administration seems to justify the optimism. There are obstacles admittedly still to be overcome. . . . But . . . Kingston's future looks bright."

Since this was written in 1979 many of these obstacles have been surmounted and the Rondout waterfront, as we have seen, in renewed cooperation with the uptown old Stockade area with its four distinctive museums and its unique little village of seventeenth and early eighteenth century Dutch stone houses (one of them, the Persen house, recently professionally restored to the condition of its youth) have become popular goals for historically-minded Americans from all parts of the nation and of all ethnic roots. With this acceptance came appreciation of Kingston as a place of more than three and a half centuries of white human existence and development from being already a many centuries old creekside cluster of wigwams and Native gardens whose unwritten history had been sketchily handed down only in the brain cells of successive generations of Natives and by the symbols of their ancestral deeds hinted at only on a few surviving wampum belts, through years of Dutch Company and British government exploitations, to a multi-ethnic and literate American city still set in the scenic and historic yet forward-looking valley of the Hudson River.

Will the people of Kingston now move on to face the new challenges of the future in the light of its rich variety of experiences of its past to grapple well with the problems that will surely face it in a restless and contentious world? Hopefully the people will.

AN APPENDIX
William Redin, American Painter who Painted Kingston and Drew Kingston Places

IN THE EARLY 1850S THE HIGH HILL FORMERLY CALLED THE KIJKUIT IN DUTCH days from its use as a lookout by Native Americans of a previous time and then by the Dutch of the Village Kingston became Golden Hill and the site of an early Kingston real estate development, part of an extensive promotional scheme. A painter named William Redin who had lived in New York City where he had exhibited a portrait at the National Academy of Design, was commissioned, it was reported, to undertake a painting of a panoramic view of the landscape including the Village of Kingston and the Catskills beyond as seen from the side of what soon would be called Golden Hill.

Painter William Redin may have had scene-painting experience for he showed the land between the verge of Golden Hill and the houses of the Village of Kingston in a way that emphasized pleasing illusion rather than strict reality. And he used almost a half dozen mowers to harvest a golden crop on a midget field and so gave a picturesque base to the hill. Beyond this stood what some have called a "ghost house" of pure white which may have been a later addition, for it was never given the glaze which would tie it to the rest of the landscape.

On the Tilson and Brink map of Ulster County, published in 1854, Redin created a number of excellent drawings, in the margins, of Kingston buildings, and a view of the new and bosky Wiltwyck Cemetery with a little railroad chugging along its lower boundary—a railroad which would not arrive in anything like that approximate position for almost twenty years. A Golden Hill School for Girls flourished for a while and then closed. The Redin drawings for the Tillson and Brink map were in most cases the first ever published of any Kingston buildings. The surveys for the map were made with none-too-great accuracy by youthful Jay Gould before the became known as a speculator in railroad construction and management.

A further search of Ulster County newspapers is likely to reveal more about Redin. The painting below repays careful study. The mowers in the foreground are cutting the common flag reed which grows in damp places and formerly had value when cured for being woven into the common seats of rush-bottom chairs of every local household. These chairs were displaced before long by the cane-seated chairs produced in shops and factories among the Catskill Mountains shown in the distance of the painting. The surveyors shown with considerable accuracy may well be those who were subdividing the Golden Hill tract into building lots. The Golden Hill real estate project was launched at a time when the American economy was leading up to the Wall Street crash of 1855.

Details of Redin's life may be had in the New York Historical Society's *Dictionary of American Painters to 1860,* by Groce and Wallace. There Redin is described as a portrait painter and also a resident of New York City for a time, and a photographer and an architect.

William Redin's 1851 painting of Golden Hill, used by permission of the owner

Acknowledgments

My early background in Ulster County put me in touch with many people who contributed to my knowledge of Kingston and the County to which it is the county seat. It began the day in August 1914 when I walked down the gangplank of the Hudson River nightboat, *Benjamin B. O'Dell* and from there was driven in a surrey to the small Ulster County farm near Kingston on which my parents hoped to bring up their children close to nature after we had lived for some time close to the City of New York on the lower west palisaded banks of the Hudson. My architect/painter father Ivar Evers encouraged me to use his fine library with its many books on psychology, folklore and history.

Among the people who helped me to understand the Ulster County and Kingston backgrounds were doctors, dentists and shopkeepers in Kingston, and the workers on the family farm, including Charlie Wood from whom I learned how to use old fashioned farm tools and to care for farm animals.

I learned too that a belief in witchcraft still existed in the County and Kingston from the past, and that the way in which Ulster people and those of Kingston (frequently still called Sopus) spoke to one another had a special flavor, with a few hints of the Dutch that had once been the language of Kingston.

After six years on the farm the time came for my older sister and I to attend high school. We considered Kingston and New Paltz, but chose the New Paltz school as somewhat closer, but commuting proved difficult, so my parents gave up the farming venture and bought the old stone house in New Paltz known then as the Abraham Hasbrouck house and began the first stage of its restoration. During my high school years, my Sunday School teacher was Ralph LeFevre, who was the author of *The History of New Paltz and its Old Families,* and helped give me a taste for exploring the history of Ulster County and Kingston.

Others who helped in my boyhood days to direct my attention to history included Byron Terwilliger, a simple country school teacher who collected Native artifacts and copied inscriptions from mossy old gravestones for genealogists, and whom I helped decipher early Ulster and Kingston French and Dutch documents for historical purposes.

I came to be close to New Paltz psychologist Dr. Margaret K. Smith, whose interest in local history led her to contribute a fine paper on the lives of the women of the colonial Hudson Valley to the Dutchess County Historical Society publication and to encourage me in my growing interest in the history of Kingston and Ulster County. Dr. Smith helped give me a useful grounding in psychology and hoped I would have chosen a career in that discipline.

I left New Paltz in 1925 to attend Hamilton College for a year during which I became a close friend of fellow student B. F. Skinner who went on to achieve fame as a behavioral psychologist. I did not return to Ulster County until after a period of studying painting and after marrying and earning a living as an investigator of people doing business with life insurance companies.

It was an occupation in which I learned basic techniques of research. After turning to successful writing of my children's books in collaboration with my illustrator wife, we moved to Ulster County and there I took up again the interest in the county and the past, which I had felt in my boyhood.

I wrote for local newspapers, and began accumulating files on the past, which helped when the time came in the writing of a book on the Catskills and of a book on Woodstock, and of the present book on Kingston. In my writing of *Kingston: City on the Hudson* I was interrupted by total loss of sight in one eye, and much of the sight in the other, and by other illnesses including cancer. At this time, Ulster County friends came to my aid and made possible the completion of this book. Chief among the friends who came to my rescue when my eyesight was failing was poet Ed Sanders, who faithfully transcribed my handwriting, illegible to others, and supplied me with many drafts of the manuscript since the late 1990s printed in 18 point type, as well as scanning images and assembling the bibliography.

I own deep thanks especially to my caregiver Thomas O'Brien, who has given me daily, and even round the clock help for the last seven years.

Others who helped were Fred Steuding of Hurley, who organized my large collection of 3x5 note cards, and the alphabetical files for the book. Steuding also took photos for the book, performed library research, and located and organized many of the images. My gratitude to Ulster County Historian and good friend Karlyn Knaust Elia for her generous support and her assistance in locating material from 19th and 20th century sources. In addition, there were a host of other Ulster County and Kingston people who answered queries and helped perform research which made it possible to write the present book.

I want to express my thanks also to the many members of the staffs of the libraries whose collections I drew upon for Kingston material. Among these were the Senate House Museum library, the Adriance library in Poughkeepsie, the New York State Library in Albany, and the New York Public Library at 42nd Street and Fifth Avenue with its inter-library services. My gratitude also to my hometown Woodstock Library.

I owe thanks to Peter Mayer who asked me to write this book, and to Maureen Nagy who kept me in touch with the publisher at Overlook Press. And I want to thank my son Christopher for letting me examine materials of use as sources which came into his bookshop in Saugerties—source material I might otherwise have missed.

To all those old friends, going back to my boyhood at the age of nine I owe my deep thanks.

Regarding the Bibliography and Source Notes

Over the decades, Alf Evers gathered in his house on Hutchin Hill Road, located in the hamlet of Shady in the town of Woodstock, New York, a large library of books, maps, periodicals, photographs, stereographs, photocopies, posters, ephemera and pamphlets on the regional history of New York, and United States history in general. It was from this remarkable personal historical archive that Alf Evers wrote the great bulk of *Kingston-on-Hudson.*

For his books, Alf created source notes on 3x5 cards. For *Kingston-on-Hudson* he made literally thousands of 3x5 cards note cards on his sources which were alphabetized by Fred Steuding and put into small filing cabinets. In addition, there were two open topped hanging file boxes on wheels with alphabetical source files, also organized by Fred Steuding.

In working on his book on Kingston, beginning in 1989 and continuing steadily up till his death, Alf put together also a collection of newspaper articles, many of them from 19th century sources, which were on hand and available to him, thanks to his accumulative skills and persistence. He also collected an extensive archive of slides, photos and images relating to Kingston's history, which were stored in a small chest of drawers.

I began typing for Alf in 1997, when his eyesight had weakened to the point of not being able to type or work a computer. We worked steadily together through those years until the book began to take its final shape in 2002. Beginning then, he would make extensive handwritten changes in the printouts, which were done in 18 point type to enable him to read it more easily, and then I would enter the changes into the computer, often consulting with him whenever his handwriting was difficult to decipher, and then I would print out new versions of the manuscript In this way, I printed over 20,000 pages of revisions. His memory remained photographic up till his final days, and when I could not read his handwriting, he could recall the text.

Beginning in 2003, Alf and I created the basic bibliography of the book. To do this, I brought all books and publications relating to Kingston, Ulster County, New York State and regional history from various shelf systems in his house to a large set of shelves next to the desk where he worked. These I alphabetized, and he decided which belonged in the bibliography.

Around the summer of 2004, the book was obviously close to being completed. Alf was eager to begin his next book, a biography of Hervey White, and we had gathered in boxes by his desk a considerable amount of written material on White. Alf had begun dictating ideas for the book into a digital tape recorder which the Woodstock Guild had given him.

At the same time Alf began selecting images for *Kingston-on-Hudson.* He instructed me on what images he wanted to examine, and I brought them to him from the many books in his library, and from his archive of Kingston images in the small chest of drawers nearby. He looked at each with a magnifying glass, and made decisions on which he wanted to use. As he worked on further drafts of the manuscript, he would note where he wanted specific images to be placed in the text. A number of images I had to search for outside the house. Alf's friend, Ulster County Historian Karlyn Knaust Elia, helped obtain some of them.

Alf also began paying attention to the source notes for *Kingston-on-Hudson.* I had divided the book into five 3-ring notebooks, in large bold-faced type, so that he could more easily work on revisions, and could even drop a notebook by accident and the manuscript would stay in place. For the notes, we worked out a system where he would jot down sources on the back sides of previous pages. He worked assiduously on the source notes during the final months of his life. Often he would recall the exact name and author of the source, or refer me to the extensive 3x5 card files, or the alphabetized hanging files to locate the sources. One source he asked me to locate was in a book he recalled from 1932, and apparently hadn't read since!

Alf Evers completed the manuscript of *Kingston-on-Hudson* in the fall of 2004, after 15 years of work, and submitted the manuscript to his publisher, Peter Mayer, who soon sent a letter of praise which buoyed Alf's spirits, and he began final work on the book just a few months from his hundredth birthday. Even in his final weeks, with his health in a precipitous ebb, he was a perfectionist. Polishing a sentence was always on his mind. He would wake up in the middle of the night with an idea on how to improve a paragraph. He kept on perfecting *Kingston-on-Hudson* right up to his final afternoon, which was December 29. Just hours after he passed away, I found voluminous hand drawn corrections to the manuscript, including an entire chapter which he wanted re-sequenced.

During his final months Alf jotted down hundreds of sources for the text onto the backs of facing pages. Other sources he dictated to me, or brought up during our sessions. In the week before he passed away, he asked me to check some sources for the manuscript in some regional libraries. Unfortunately, he was still at work on the source notes when he died.

After Alf was gone, I began assembling and sequencing the source notes based on his handwritten and dictated instructions. I spent several months checking his notes against the books, newspapers, pamphlets, and ephemera in his vast library. Karlyn Knaust Elia provided valuable help in locating some additional images that Alf wanted to use in the book, and she also did source note research in 19th century newspapers and other publications. Kathy Longyear, co-president of the Woodstock Historical Society, read through the numerous letters of Kingston Civil War soldier Samuel Schepmoes, which Alf owned, to check the quotes Alf utilized. Deana Preston of the Senate House Museum Library also provided useful assistance during this time, as she had during the years Alf was writing *Kingston-on-Hudson.* Assemblyman Kevin Cahill provided Alf some useful material on Kingston native Arthur Flemming. Austin Metze helped scan some of the images. In addition, during the months before and after Alf's passing, Ursula Carrie worked on behalf of Carla Smith and the Woodstock Byrdcliffe Guild to list Alf's extensive library and files on historical subjects onto a computer. During her work, she was able to help locate several images Alf had chosen for inclusion in the book. The Guild will house Evers historical archives in a special library at White Pines in the Byrdcliffe Colony in Woodstock.

Everything in the book is the creation of Alf Evers—I typed it exactly the way he wrote or dictated it, in his mature, late-life sentence structures. He brought to this book his enormous knowledge of world history and American history. He was a brilliant historian, and uniquely so, for no other writer in all of recorded time has written a book in his late 90's, especially of the quality and complexity of *Kingston-on-Hudson.*

—EDWARD SANDERS

Bibliography

Abridgement of the Debates of Congress from 1789 to 1856, Volume XVI, 1846-1850, D. Appleton & Company, NY 1861

Randolf G. Adams, *Political Ideas of the American Revolution,* Barnes & Noble, 3rd edition, 1958

Melvin L. Adelman, *A Sporting Time, New York City and the Rise of Modern Athletics, 1920-1870,* University of Illinois Press, 1990

H.G. Alsberg, editor, *The American Guide,* New York, Hastings House, 1949 *(Fourteenth Annual Report of the) American Scenic and Historic Preservation Society,* Albany, 1909

America Visited, (Oscar Wilde section), Edith I. Coombs, Book League of America, NY, n.d.

Tyler Anbinder, *Nativism & Slavery, The Northern Know Nothings & the Politics of the 1850s,* Oxford University Press, 1992

Archives of American Art, Smithsonian Institution, R.W. Bowker Co., NY, 1972

Automobile Blue Book of 1906, American Automobile Association, NY, 1906

Kevin J. Avery and Peter L. Fodera, *John Vanderlyn's Panoramic View of the Palace and Gardens of Versailles,* NY, The Metropolitan Museum of Art, 1988

Charles Baird, *History of the Huguenot Emigration to America,* Vol. 1, NY, Dodd, Mead & Company, 1885

William A. Baker, *Sloops & Shallops,* University of South Carolina Press 1966

John W. Barber and Henry Howe, *Historical Collections of the State of New York,* S. Tuttle, 1841

Gilbert Hobbs Barnes, *The Anti-Slavery Impulse— 1830-1844,* American Historical Society, 1933

Walter Barrett, *The Old Merchants of New York City,* 5 Volumes, NY, Greenwood Press, 1968

Clara Barrus, *The Life and Letters of John Burroughs,* two volumes, Russell & Russell, New York, reissue 1968

Allen Beach, *The Centennial Celebrations of the State of New York,* Albany, 1879

Charles and Mary Beard, *The Rise of American Civilization,* 1930, MacMillan, New York

Carl Lotus Becker, *The History of Political Parties in the Province of New York, 1760-1776,* Madison, University of Wisconsin Press, 1960

Lucius Beebe, *The Big Spenders, the Epic story of the Rich Rich, the Grandees of America and the Magnificoes, and how they Spent their Fortunes,* Doubleday, 1966

Iver Bernstein, *The New York City Draft Riots,* Oxford University Press, 1990

Gerald M. Best, *The Ulster and Delaware Railroad Through the Catskills,* San Marino, Calif., 1972.

John Bierhorst, *The Way of the Earth, Native Americans and the Environment,* New York, William Morrow & Co., 1994

James H. Billington, *Fire in the Minds of Men— Origins of the Revolutionary Faith,* Basic Books, New York, 1980

Charles L. Blockson, *The Underground Railroad,* NY, Berkley Books, 1989

Stuart M. Blumin, *The Urban Threshold— Growth and Change in a Nineteenth-Century American Community,* 1976, U. of Chicago Press, Chicago

Patricia Bonomi, *A Factious People— Politics and Society in Colonial New York,* Columbia University Press, 1971

Daniel J. Boorstein, *The Americans— The National Experience,* Random House, 1965

Robert Boyle, *The Hudson River,* NY, W.W. Norton, 1979

William Boyse, *The Writings of William Boyse,* New York, 1838

Anna R. Bradbury, *History of the City of Hudson,* Hudson, NY, 1908

William Aspenwall Bradley, *Dutch Landscape Painters of the Seventeenth Century,* Yale University Press, 1908

John Brand, *Observations on Popular Antiquities,* London, Chatto and Windus, 1888

Carl Bridenbaugh, *Cities in the Wilderness— Urban Life in America, 1625-1742,* Capricorn, NY, 1955

Carl Bridenbaugh, *The Colonial Craftsman,* New York University, 1966

Bridging the Years— 1712-1962 (250th Anniversary of Schoharie), Schoharie, NY, 1962

Benjamin Myer Brink, *The Early History of Saugerties, 1660-1825,* Kingston, R.W. Anderson & Son, 1902

John Romeyn Brodhead, *History of the State of New York, First Period, 1609-1664,* New York, Harper and Brothers, 1859.

Roger Burlingame, *March of the Iron Men,* Charles Scribners, 1938

John Burroughs, *Camping & Tramping with Roosevelt,* Boston, Houghton Mifflin, 1907

John Burroughs, *My Boyhood,* NY, Doubleday, 1924

John Burroughs Talks, as reported by Clifton Johnson, Houghton Mifflin, 1922

John Burroughs' Grandaughter, Elizabeth Burroughs Kelley, West Park Books, 1993

Ethel Bussy, *History and Stories of Margaretville and Surrounding Area,* 1961 (references to founding of New Kingston, p. 91)

Carl Carmer, *Rivers of America— the Hudson,* NY, Rinehart and Company, 1939

Sean Dennis Cashman, *America in the Gilded Age— from the Death of Lincoln to the Rise of Theodore Roosevelt,* NYU Press, 1984, second edition

Bruce Catton, *The Centennial History of the Civil War— The Coming Fury,* Doubleday, 1961

J.D. Chambers and G.E. Mingay, *The Agricultural Revolution 1750-1880,* Schocken Books, New York, 1966

Thomas D. Clark, *Frontier America— the Story of the Westward Movement,* 2nd edition, Charles Scribners, NY, 1969

Alphonso T. Clearwater, Editor, *The History of Ulster County New York,* Kingston, W.J. Van Deusen, 1907

A.T. Clearwater, *Kingston, a Tribute,* Sept. 12, 1929

Public Papers of George Clinton, 10 volumes, Albany, 1911

Floyd Clymer, *Treasure of Early American Automobiles, 1877-1925,* NY, Bonanza Books, 1950

Cadwallader Colden, *The History of the Five Indian Nations of Canada,* Two volumes, NY, New Amsterdam Book Co., 1902

The Public Papers of George Clinton, 3 volumes, NY and Albany, 1899

Thomas Cochran and Thomas Brewer, *Views of American Economic Growth: the Agricultural Era, Volume One,* McGraw-Hill, New York, 1966

Thomas Condon, *New York Beginnings, The Commercial Origins of New Netherland,* NYU Press, 1968

James Fenimore Cooper, *Notations of the Americans,* 2 volumes, NY, Frederick Ungar, 1963

Edward Tanjore Corwin, *A Manual of the Reformed Church in America,* NY, Board of Publication of the Reformed Church in America, 1879

Edward Countryman, *A People in Revolution, the American Revolution and Political Society in New York 1760-1790,* Johns Hopkins University Press, Baltimore, 1981

The Craftsman in Early America, edited by Ian M.G. Quimby, published for the Henry Francis du Pont Winterthur Museum, NY. W.W. Norton, 1984

Stewart Culin, *Games of the North American Indians,* Dover Publications, NY 1975

George Dangerfield, *Chancellor Robert R. Livingston of New York— 1746-1813,* Harcourt, Brace, NY 1960

Jaspar Dankers and Peter Sluyter, *Journal of a Voyage to New York,* Readex Microprint, 1966

William Darby, *A Tour from the City of New York to Detroit,* New York, 1819

John Darrow, "A Remarkable Clock Mechanism by G. Rahmer of Rondout, New York," *The National Association of Watch and Clock Collectors Bulletin,* October 2000

Edmond Demolins, *Les Grandes Routes des Peuples— Essai de Géographie Social, Comment la Route Crée le Type Social, Les Routes deL'Antiquité*

William C. DeWitt, *People's History of Kingston, Rondout and Vicinity, 1820-194*3, New Haven, 1943

Lorenzo Dow's Life and Works Complete, Cinncinati, Applegate and Company, 1860

Ruth Alden Doan, *The Miller Heresy, Millennialism, and American Culture,* Philadelphia, Temple University Press, 1987

Documents Relative to the Colonial History of the State of New York, particularly Vol. 13, on Hudson Valley and Kingston history, Vol. 13, 1881

Documents Relative to the Colonial History of the State of New York, E. B. O'Callaghan, editor, Albany, Vol. 1 1856; Vol. 2 1858; Vol. 3 1853; Vol. 4, 1854; Vol. 5 1855; Vol VI (the London Documents, 1734-1755) 1855; Vol. 8 (the London Documents 1768-1782) 1857; Vol. 9 (the Paris documents 1631-1744) 1855; Vol. 10 (the Paris documents 1745-1774) 1858; index volume 1861.

A.J. Downing, *A Treatise on the Theory and Practice of Landscape Gardening,* reprint of 1859 edition, NY, Funk & Wagnalls, 1967

Richard Drinnon, *Facing West: The Metap;hysics of Indian-Hating and Empire-Building,* University of Minnesota Press, 1980

Frances E. Dunwell, *The Hudson River Highlands,* Columbia University Press, 1991.

Timothy Dwight, *Travels in New England and New York.* 3 volumes, Cambridge, Belnap Press, 1969

John S. Dyson, *Our Historic Hudson,* Introduction by Stewart Udall, 1968, James Adler, Roosevelt, NY

Alice Morse Earle, *Colonial Days in Old New York,* Empire State Book, NY, 1926 reprint of 1896 Charles Scribner's edition.

F. S. Eastman, *History of the State of New York,* published by Augustus K. White, 1832

Ecclesiastical Records, State of New York, edited by Edward T. Corwin, 7 volumes, Albany 1901-1716

David Ellis, James Frost, Harold Syrett, Harry Carman, *A Short History of New York State,* Cornell U Press, 1957

Louis C. Elson, *The National Music off America and its Sources,* Boston, L.C. Page, 1900

Encyclopedia of American Biography, Second Edition, John A. Garraty, Jerome L. Sternstein, editors, HarperCollins, 1996

Town of Esopus Story— 3000 B.C.-1978 A.D. Town of Esopus Bicentennial Committee, 1979

George Ewart Evans, *Tools of Their Trade: An Oral History of Men at Work,* c. 1900, NY, Taplinger, 1970

William R. Ferris, Jr., "The Collection of Racial Lore: Approaches and Problems, *New York Folklore Quarterly,* September 1971

John Fiske, *The Dutch and Quaker Colonies in America, Vol 1 and 2,* Boston, Houghton Mifflin, 1900

Charles Flagg and Judson Jennings, *Bibliography of New York Colonial History,* Bulletin 56, New York State Library, 1901

Robert M. Fogelson, *America's Armories—Architecture, Society, and Public Order,* Harvard University Press, 1989

Paul E. Fontenoy, *The Sloops of the Hudson River,* Mystic Seaport Museum, 1994

Mary Isabella Forsyth, *The Beginnings of New York: Old Kingston, the First State Capital.* Boston, 1909

Joseph Frese, Jacob Judd, *Business Enterprise in Early New York,* Tarrytown, Sleepy Hollow Press, 1979

Marc B. Fried, *The Early History of Kingston & Ulster County, N.Y.,* Ulster County Historical Society, Kingston, 1975

James Arthur Frost, *Life on the Upper Susquehenna 1783-1860,* Columbia University, NY 1961

Paul W. Gates, *The Farmer's Age: Agriculture, 1815-1860,* Harper Torchbooks, NY, 1960

Gazetteer of the State of New York, Albany, 1813

Gazetteer of the State of New York, Albany, 1842

Gazetteer and Business Directory of Sullivan County, 1872-1873

Gazetteer and Business Directory of Ulster County, New York, 1871-72, Hamilton Child, Syracuse, NY

Margaret Gibbs, *The DAR,* NY, Holt, Rinehart and Winston, 1969

Ann Gilchrist, *Footsteps Across Cement, a History of the Township of Rosendale, New York,* 1976

J.L. and J.B. Gilder, editors, *Authors at Home,* New York, 1902

Ruth R. Glunt, *The Old Lighthouses of the Hudson River,* Moran Printing Company, 1969

Maud W. Goodwin, *Dutch and English on the Hudson River.*

W. R. Gordon, *The Life of Henry Ostrander,* NY, Board of Publication of the Reformed Church in America, 1975

P. Douglass Gorrie, *Churches and Sects of the United States,* New York 1850

Anne Grant, *Memoirs of an American Lady*, Albany, Joel Munsell, 1876

Brian Greenberg, *Worker and Community—Response to Industrialization in a Nineteenth-Century American City, Albany, New York, 1850-1884*, State University of New York Press, 1985

Greene County Directory, 1886

George C. Groce and David H. Wallace, *The New York Historical Society's Dictionary of Artists in America, 1564-1860*, New Haven, Yale University Press 1957

Edward H. Hall, *Water for New York City*, Hope Farm Press, 1993

H.A. Haring, *Our Catskill Mountains*, NY, G.P. Putnam's Sons, 1931

Harper Dictionary of Modern Thought, Alan Bullock and Oliver Stallybrass, editors, Harper & Row, 1977

James D. Hart, *Oxford Companion to American Literature*, 3rd edition, Oxford University Press 1956

Harvard Guide to American History, Cambridge, Mass., revised edition, 1974, vol. 1 and vol. 2

Gilbert D.B. Hasbrouck, *The Reformed Protestant Dutch Church of Kingston, New York*, Kingston, NY 1928

Laurence M. Hauptman, *The Native Americans: a History of the First Residents of New Paltz and Environs*, Etting Memorial Library, New Paltz, 1999

Ulysses Prentiss Hedrick, *A History of Agriculture in the State of New York*, New York, Hill and Wang, 1933

Andrew S. Hickey, *The Story of Kingston, First Capitol of New York State—1609-1952*, Stratford House, New York, 1952

Brooke Hindle, editor, *Material Culture of the Wooden Age*, Tarrytown, Sleepy Hollow Press, 1981

C. G. Hine, *The Old Mine Road*, Rutgers University Press, 1963

Historic Walkill and Hudson River Valleys, Walkill Valley Publishing Association, Walden, NY, 1909

History of the State of New York, in ten volumes, Alexander C. Flick editor, published by Columbia University Press for the the New York State Historical Association, 1933-1937

History of Ulster County, With Emphasis upon the Last 100 years, compiled by the Historians of Ulster County for the Tercentenary Year, 1983

R.R. Hoes, *The Old Court Houses of Ulster County, New York*, Freeman Publishing Company, Kingston, 1918

The Diary of Philip Hone 1828-1851, edited by Allan Nevins, Dodd, Mead, New York 1927

S.C. Hutchins, *Civil List and Forms of Government of the Colony and State of New York*, Albany, Weed, Parsons & Co., 1869

George V. Hutton, "The Zenith and Sudden Decline of the Great Hudson River Brick Industry," *The Hudson Valley Regional Review*, March 2002

J.H. Innes, *New Amsterdam and Its People*, NY, Charles Scribner's Songs, 1902

Inventory of the Church Archives in New York City, Reformed Church in America, Historical Records Survey, Work Projects Administration, New York City, 1939

Washington Irving, *A Book of the Hudson*, G. P. Putnam, NY, NY 1949

Kenneth T. Jackson, *Crabcrass Frontier, the Suburbanization of the United States*, Oxford University Press, 1985

Washington Irving, *History of New York*, NY, The University Society, ND

Joseph Jackson, *Development of American Architecture*, Philadelphia, David McKay Co., 1926

J. Franklin Jameson, *Narratives of New Netherland, 1609-1664*, NY, Charles Scribner's Sons, 1909

Thomas A. Janvier, *In Old New York*, Harper & Brothers, NY 1894

The Jesuit Relations and Allied Documents: Travels and Explorations of the Jesuit Missionaries in North America (1610-1791), Edna Kenton, Editor, Albert & Charles Boni, NY 1925

John P. Kaminski, *George Clinton—Yeoman Politician of the New Republic*, Madison, Wisconsin, 1993

Michael Kammen, *Colonial New York, a History*, Charles Scribner's Sons, NY, 1975

Allan Keller, *Life Along the Hudson*, Sleepy Hollow Restorations, Tarreytown, 1976

Elizabeth Burroughs Kelley, *John Burroughs: Naturalist*, Exposition Press, New York, 1959

Frank Bergen Kelley, *Historical Guide to the City of New York*, Frederick A. Stokes Co., NY, 1913 (p. 91 mentions Peter Stuyvesant's pear tree)

Isabel Thompson Kelsay, *Joseph Brant 1743-1807, Man of Two Worlds*, Syracuse University Press 1984

Edna Kenton, editor, *The Jesuit Relations and Allied Documents: Travels and Explorations of the Jesuit Missionaries in North America (1610-1791)*, NY, Albert and Charles Boni, 1925

Sung Bok Kim, *Landlord and Tenant in Colonial New York*, University of North Carolina at Chapel Hill, 1978

Charles P. Kindleberger, *Manias, Panics, and Crashes—A History of Financial Crises*, NY, Basic Books, 1978

Kingston Directory, 1947, Price & Lee Co., New Haven

Kingston Directory, 1958, Price & Lee Co., New Haven

Kingston, Rondout & Ellenville Village Directory for 1871-72, J.H. Lant, 1871

(Kingston) *Common Council Proceedings, City of Kingston*, 1873-1874.

Kingston's 350th Anniversary, 1609-1959, Hudson-Champlain Souvenir Booklet, Kingston 1959

Kingston New York Tercentenary 1652-1952, Souvenir Booklet, 60 pp.

Spencer Klaw, *Without Sin—the Life and Death of the Oneida Community*, Penguin Books 1993

Edward H. Knight, *Knight's American Mechanical Dictionary*, J. B. Ford, New York, 1874

Michael Kudish, *Vegetational History of the Catskill High Peaks*, PhD thesis, 1971, Syracuse University

Jack Larkin, *The Reshaping of Everyday Life—1790-1840*, New York, HarperPerennial, 1988

Peter Laslett, *The World We Have Lost—England Before the Industrial Age*, NY, Charles Scribner's Sons, 1965

Laws of the State of New York, Volume 3, Albany, 1797

Laws of the State of New York, Volumes 1 & 2, Albany, 1798

Laws of the State of New York, 2 volumes, Albany, 1802

Laws of the State of New York, Volume 1, Albany, H.C. Southwick & Co., 1813

Laws of the State of New York, Vol. 3, Albany, 1815

Gail Leggio, "Japanism in America," *American Arts Quarterly*, Summer 2003

Legislative Manual for the Use of the Legislature of the State of New York, 1937

Legislative Manual for the Use of the Legislature of the State of New York, 1964-65

Letters about the Hudson River, 1835-1837, reprint of 1837 edition, Hope Farm Press

Ralph Le Fevre, *History of New Paltz, New York and its Old Families, 1678 to 1820*, Generalogical Publishing, Baltimore, 1973

Benson J. Lossing, *The Hudson from The Wilderness to the Sea*, NY Birtue and Yorston, 1866

Carl Lumholtz, *Unknown Mexico— Explorations in the Sierra Madre and Other Regions, 1890-1898*, Two Volumes, NY, Dover, 1987

Ferdinand Lundberg, *America's 60 Families*, Vanguard Press, 1937

Henry Nobel MacCracken, *Blithe Dutchess*, Hastings House, New York, 1958

William H. MacLeish, *The Day Before America—Changing the Nature of a Continent*, Boston, Houghton Mifflin, 1994

Patrick M. Malone, *The Skulking Way of War—Technololgy and Tactics Among the New England Indian*, Baltimore, Johns Hopkins, 1991

A Marbletown Album 1669-1977, Stone Ridge Library 1977

Albro Martin, *Railroads Triumphant, the Growth, Rejection & Rebirth of a Vital American Force*, Oxford University Press, 1992

Peter Mathias, *The First Industrial Nation—An Economical History of Britain 1700-1914*, Charles Scribner's, NY 1969

Memorial History of the City of New York, James Grant Wilson, editor, New-York History Company, NY, 4 volumes, 1892

H.L. Mencken, *The American Language*, Afred Knopf, NY, 1949

Merriam-Webster's Collegiate Encyclopedia, 2000

C. Blackburn Miller, *Hudson Valley Squire*, New York, Frederick A. Stokes Co., 1941

John C. Miller, *Origins of the American Revolution*, Boston, Little Brown, 1943

Minutes of the Court of Fort Orange and Beverwyck, 1652-1660, Arnold J.F. Van Laer editor, 2 vols., Albany, 1922

Lewis Mumford, *Technics and Human Development, The Myth of the Machine*, Volume One, NY, Harcourt Brace Jovanovich, 1967

Munsey's Magazine, Vol. XV, #2, May 1896, long article "The World Awheel—the Story of the Bicycle."

Narrative and Critical History of America, Vol. IV, edited by Justin Ward, Houghton, Mifflin, Boston, 1884

Narrative of Sojourner Truth, Nell Irvin Painter, editor; Penguin Books, 1998

(New Paltz) *The Story of the Paltz—Being a Brief History of New Paltz*, 1915

New York—A Guide to the Empire State, Writers Program of the WPA, 1940, Oxford University Press.

New York State Historical Association; Proceedings of the Thirteenth Annal Meeting with List of Members, Volume XI, 1912, contains "Wiltwyck Under the Dutch" by Ausustus H. Van Buren, and "The Palantine Settlement," by Benjamin Myer Brink.

New York State Museum, Forty-Seventh Annual Report, for the Year 1893, Albany, James B. Lyon, 1894

History of the State of New York, 10 volumes, NY, 1933, Columbia University Press.

Marjorie Hope Nicolson, *Mountain Gloom and Mountain Glory: The Development of the Aesthetics of the Infinite*, Ithaca, Cornell University Press, 1959

Richard Nicolls, *Esopus Indian Treaty 1665*, Ulster County Clerk's Record s Management, Archives Division, 2002

Thomas Elliot Norton, *The Fur Trade in Colonial New York—1686-1776*, University of Wisconsin Press, 1974

The Official Maps of New York, National Survey Co., n.d., nineteenth century

One Hundred Fiftieth Anniversary of he Founding of the Government of the State of New York, Souvenir Program, Kingston, September 10, 1927

One Hundred Years of the History of the Ulster County Historical Society 1859-1959, Marbletown, NY 1959

John W. Osborne, *The Silent Revolution, the Industrial Revolution in England as a Source of Cultural Change,* Charles Scribner' s, New York, 1970

Nell Irvin Painter, *Sojourner Truth— a Life, a Symbol,* New York, W.W. Norton, 1996

Robert Allerton Parker, *A Yankee Saint—John Humphrey Noyes and the Oneida Community,* G.P. Putnam's Sons, NY, 1935

Hertha Pauli, *Her Name was Sojourner Truth,* NY, Appleton-Century-Crofts, 1962

J.H. Perry, *The Establishment of the European Hegemony: 1415-1715,* NY, Harper Torchbooks, 1966

E. C. Pielou, *After the Ice Age—the Return of Life to Glaciated North America,* University of Chicago Press, 1992

Mary De Peyster Rutgers and McCrea Conger (Vanamee), *New York's Making—Seen Through the Eyes of My Ancestors,* London, Methuen & Co., 1938

Will Plank, *Banners and Bugles, a Record of Ulster County, New York and the Mid-Hudson Region in the Civil War,* Centennial Press, Marborough, NY, 1963

Proceedings of the Huguenot Society of America, Volume 2, pp 231-232, an account of the annoyance of the Indians over "trespass of white people's cale and dogs upon their patches of maize and beans." And an account of the Indian massacre of June 6, 1663 at the village of Esopus.

Proceedings of the New York State Historical Association, Volume XI, New York State Historical Association, 1912

Proceedings of the New York State Historical Association, Volume XL, New York State Historical Association, 1912

Proceedings of the New York State Historical Association, Volume XVI, New York State Historical Association, 1917

A Promotional Survey of Kingston New York for the Chamber of Commerce by the General Organization Company Chicago, Illinois, March 1923, 210 pp.

James E. Quinlan, *History of Sullivan County,* Liberty, New York, 1873, reprinted, South Fallsburgh, New York, 1965

Max J. Herzberg et al, *Reader's Encyclopedia of American Literature,* Thomas Crowell, NY 1962

Helen Wilkinson Reynolds, *Dutch Houses in the Hudson Valley Before 1776,* Dover edition, 1965, reprint of original edition of 1929

William B. Rhoads, *Kingston, New York—The Architectural Guild,* Black Dome Press, Hensonville, NY, 2003

Donald C. Ringwald, *Steamboats for Rondout—Passenger Service Between New York and Rondout Creek, 1829 through 1863,* Steamship Historical Society of America, 1981.

Donald C. Ringwald, "When the Steamboats Reigned," Kingston's 350th Anniversary, 1609-1959, Kingston, NY, 1959.

William A. Ritchie, *The Archaeology of New York State,* Natural History Press, Garden City, NY 1965

William A. Ritchie, *Indian History of New York State,* Part III, The Algonkian Tribes, New York State Museum and Science Service, Albany, New York

William A. Ritchie, *An Introduction to Hudson Valley Prehistory*, New York State Museum and Science Service, Bulletin #367, Albany, NY 1958

William A. Ritchie, Robert E. Funk, *Aboriginal Settlement Patterns in the Northeast*, SUNY State Education Department, Memoir 20, 1973

James A. Roberts, Comptroller, *New York in the Revolution as Colony and State*, Albany, Brandow Printing Co., 1898

Michael Robbins, *The Railway Age*, Routledge & Kegan Paul, London 1962

E.M. Ruttenber, *History of the Indian Tribes of Hudson's River*, Albany, 1872

Charles Rockwell, The Catskill Mountains and the Region Around, NY, Taintor Brothers, 1867

Will Rose, *The Vanishing Village*, Citadel Press, NY 1963

Ernst Samhaber, *Merchants Make History*, NY, John Day Company, 1964

Jennifer Saville, *Jervis McEntee (1828-1891) Artist of Melancholy*, Master of Arts Thesis, 1982, University of Delaware

Simon Schama, *The Embarassment of Riches—An Interpretation of Dutch Culture in the Golden Age*, 1988, University of California Press

Marius Schoonmaker, *The History of Kingston, New York from its Early Settlement to the Year 1820*, NY, Burr Printing House, 1888

Marius Schoonmaker, *John Vanderlyn, Artist 1775-1852*, Kingston, Senate House Association, 1950

Leon Sciaky, "The Rondout and its Canal," *The Quarterly Journal of the New York State Historical Association*, Vol. XXII, No. 3, July 1941

A.E.P. Searing, *The Land of Rip Van Winkle*, G. P. Putnam's Sons, New York 1884

John F. Sears, *Sacred Places—American Tourist Attractions in the Nineteenth Century*, Oxford University Press, 1989

William Sewel, Egbert Buys, *A Compleat Dictionary of English and Dutch*, Amsterdam, 1796

Harold Seymour, *Baseball, the People's Game*, Oxford University Press, 1990

Paul Shepard, *Man in the Landscape—a Historic View of the Esthetics of Nature*, Alfred A. Knopf, New York 1967

Jeffrey Simpson, *The Hudson River 1850-1918, a Photographic Portrait*, Sleepy Hollow Press 1981

Philip H. Smith, *General History of Dutchess County, 1609 to 1876*, Pawling, New York, 1877

Richard Smith, *A Tour of the Hudson, the Mohawk, the Susquehanna, and the Deleware in 1769*, Purple Mountain Press, 1989

William Smith, Jr., edited by Michael Kammen, *The History of the Province of New York*, in two volumes, Harvard University Press, 1972

(Sojourner Truth) *Narrative of Sojourner Truth; a Bondswoman of Olden Time, with a History of her Labors and Correspondence*, Penguin Books, 1998

Souvenir Program and Historical-Civic-Industrial Survey of the City of Kingston, Kingston, June, 1936

Horatio Gates Spafford, *A Gazetteer of the State of New York*, Albany, H.C. Southwick, 1813

Horatio Gates Spafford, *A Gazetteer of the State of New York*, Albany, H.C. Southwick, 1824, reprint, Interlaken, N.Y., 1981

Richard A. Spears, *Dictionary of American Slang and Colloquial Expressions*, National Textbook Company, Chicago, 1990

Timothy B. Spears, "Circles of Grace: Passion and Control in the Thought of John Humphrey Noyes," *New York History*, January 1989, NY State Historical Association

Lorenz von Stein, *The History of the Social Movement in France, 1798-1850*, 1964, Bedminster Press, Totowa, NJ

Bob Steuding, *Rondout—A Hudson River Port*, Fleischmanns, NY, Purple Mountain Press, 1995

John R. Stilgoe, *Common Landscape of America, 1580 to 1845*, Yale University Press, 1982

The Story of Anthracite, The Hudson Coal Company, New York, 1932

William Strickland, *Journal of a Tour in the United States of America, 1794-1795*, New-York Historical Society, 1971

Nathaniel Bartlett Sylvester, *History of Ulster County, New York, with Illustrations and Biographical Sketches of the Prominent Men and Pioneers* (with early history by Jonathan W. Hasbrouck), reprint of 1880 edition, Overlook Press, 1977

The Sullivan-Clinton Campaign in 1779, Chronology and Selected Documents, Division of Archives and History, University of the State of New York, Albany, 1929

Charles Swain, interview by Sandra Thompson-Hopgood. Swain is Greene County Minorities historian, from *City of Kingston 350th Anniversity Souvenir Book*

George Rogers Taylor, *The Transportation Revolution, 1815-1860*, Harper Torchbooks, 1951.

John Tebbel, *The American Magazine—a Compact History*, NY, Hawthorne Books, 1969

James Thacher, *The American Revolution*, Hurlbutt, Kellogg & Co, Hartford 1860

David C. Thurheimer, *Landmarks of the Revolution in New York State*, New York State American Revolution Bicentennial Commission, Albany, 1972

Robert Titus, *The Catskills in the Ice Age*, Purple Mountain Press, Fleischmanns, New York 1996

G.M. Trevelyan, *English Social History*, London, Longmans, Green and Company, 1943

Yi-Fu Tuan, *Topophilia, a Study of Environmental Perception, Attitudes, and Values*, Prentice-Hall 1974

James Turner, *The Politics of Landscape*, Harvard University Press, 1979

Ulster County Data Book, Ulster County Planning Board, Kingston, New York, 1984

Ulster County Directory, D.S. Lawrence & Company, Newburgh, N.Y., 1880

The Ulster & Delaware Railroad, Rondout, NY, 1903

Ulster County Committee for the Prevention of Tuberculosis, Minutes 1909-1918, bound volume

Ulster County, N.Y. Wills, in two volumes, translated and edited by Gustave Anjou, NY 1906.

C. Van Benthuysen, *A Summary View of the Millennial Church or United Society of Believers, Commonly Called Shakers*, 2nd edition, Albany, 1848

The Van Bunshoten or Van Benschoten Family in America—a Genealogy and Brief History, West Park-on-Hudson, NY 1907

Augustus H. Van Buren, *A History of Ulster County under the Dominion of the Dutch*, Kingston, New York, 1923

Carl Van Doren, *Secret History of the American Revolution*, 1941, Viking Press

A.J.F. van Laer, translator and editor, *Van Rensselaer Bowier Manuscripts*, Albany, University of the State of New York, 1908

C. Van Santvoord, *The Hundred and Twentieth Regiment—New York State Volunteers*, Hope Farm Press, 1883

William E. Verplanck and Moses W. Collyer, *The Sloops of the Hudson*, Port Washingston, Ira. J. Friedman, Inc., 1908, 1968

Thomas Vennum, Jr., *American Indian Lacrosse, Little Brother of War*, Smithsonian Institute, 1994

Clarence L. Ver Steeg, *The Formative Years, 1607-1763*, NY, Hill and Wang, 1964

Bernard H.M. Vlekke, *Evolution of the Dutch Nation*, NY, Roy Publishers, 1945

Manville B. Wakefield, *Coal Boats to Tidewater, the Story of the Delaware & Hudson Canal*, revised edition 1971, Wakefair Press, Grahamsville, New York

Everett Webber, *Escape to Utopia, The Communal Movement in America*, NY, Hastings House, 1959

Charles H. Weidner, *Water for a City, a History of New York City's Problem from the Beginning to the Delaware River System*, Rutgers University Press, 1974

Robert Weisbrot, *Father Divine, The Utopian Evangelist of the Depression Era who Became an American Legend*, Beacon Press, Boston 1983

Peter C. Welsh, *Tanning in the United States to 1850*, Washington, Smithsonian Institution, 1964

Thomas S. Wermuth, *Rip Van Winkle's Neighbors—the Transformation of Rural Society in the Hudson River Valley, 1770-1850*, SUNY NY press, 2001

Edgar A. Werner, *Civil List and Constitutional History of the Colony and State of New York*, Albany, 1888

James McNeil Whistler, *The Gentle Art of Making Enemies*, John W. Lovell, NY 1890

Austin Willey, *History of the Antislavery Cause in State and Nation*, Negro Universities Press, NY, reprint 1969 of 1860 edition

Rufus Rockwell Wilson and Otilie Erickson Wilson, *New York in Literature*, Primavera Press, Elmira, New York 1947

A.J. Williams-Myers, *Long Hammering—Essays on the Forging of an African American Presence in the Hudson River Valley to the Early Twentieth Century*, 1994, Africa World Press, Trenton, NJ

Paul Wilstach, *Hudson River Landings*, Indianapolis, Bobbs Merrill, 1933

Ron Woods, *Kingston's Magnificent City Parks*, 1992

Year Book of the Holland Society of New York, 1887

Louise Hasbrouck Zimm, Joseph W. Emsley, Rev. A. Elwood Corning, Willitt C. Jewell, *Southeastern New York, a History of the Counties of Ulster, Dutchess, Orange, Rockland and Putnam*, 2 vols. Lewis Historical Publishing Company, New York

Source Notes

Preface

For Kingston-on-the-Hull see the *Columbia-Viking Desk Encyclopedia,* Volume 1, p. 612. Ralph Radcliffe Whitehead's description of Kingston-on-Hudson is in "A Plea for Manual Work," in *Handicraft,* June 1903, p. 1

See Merriam-Webster's *Collegiate Encyclopedia,* 2000, page 1393, on various European rivers; also the definition of myth in the same *Encyclopedia,* page 1121.

The phrase "barbaric burning" was first printed in an unknown American newspaper (not in Kingston), at the time of the actual fire, and then used over and over.

Charles Safford's (later in business as Safford and Scudder) unpaged pamphlet is in the library of the Senate House Museum.

Sacred Places is the title of a book by John F. Sears, the director of the Franklin and Eleanor Roosevelt Institute in Hyde Park, N.Y.

The author recalls the quote beginning "No city or landscape" as from the art historian Allen Staley.

Concerning the spelling of Vander Lyn. The Vanderlyn family has been known by a number of variations of the one I have used here for the most famous of them. It was an old variant used by his grandfather Pieter, also a painter, and by the famous John himself in a sketchbook, circa 1790, now in the collection of the Kingston Senate House Museum, and sometimes in signing a painting.

PART 1

1. The Fertile Place Where the Three Valleys Meet

Lincoln's Second Annual Message to Congress, December 1, 1862, is found in *Bartlett's Familiar Quotations,* John Bartlett; Little, Brown & Co., p. 638

For the full text of the quote from *Olde Ulster, an Historical and Genealogical Magazine,* see Vol. 1, No. 4, April 1905, p. 97

On the ice mass that once covered Kingston, see Robert Titus, *The Catskills in the Ice Age,* Fleischmanns 1996, Chapter 10, "The Spillways of Olive."

Early Native immigrants, see William A. Ritchie, *The Archaeology of New York State,* Natural History Press, Garden City, NY 1965, Chapter 1, "The Earliest Occupants— Paleo-Indian Hunters (c. 7000 B.C.)"; and the Natives with ways of life adapted to milder regions, see William A. Ritchie, *An Introduction to Hudson Valley Prehistory,* New York State Museum and Science Service, Bulletin #367, Albany, NY 1958

On spirits associated with inanimate objects and the need to propitiate the spirits, see John Bierhorst, *The Way of the Earth, Native Americans and the Environment,* New York, William Morrow & Co., 1994

See William A. Ritchie, *The Archaeology of New York State,* Natural History Press, Garden City, L.I. 1965, p. 13, on how a post glacial lake developed in from of the recessional Port Huron ice. "Through a channel at Rome this water body drained Eastward into Lake Albany in the eastern Mohawk and Hudson Valley.... around 10,000 B.C." Also, p. 97.

2. NATIVES AND INTRUDERS TRY TO LIVE TOGETHER LIKE BROTHERS

Natives in the Hudson Valley used the word "Brother" in their formal intertribal agreements and also in formal agreements with the Dutch. See, for example, Documents Relating to the Colonial History of New York, Vol. 13, 1881, p. 112, in a "Final Answer Given to the Mohawks," dated September 24, 1659, where the hortatory "Brothers" is used eight times, such as "Brothers, sixteen years have now passed, since we made the first treaty of friendship and brotherhood between you and all the Dutch, whom then we joined together with an iron chain."

For the quote from Robert Juet, see "The Third Voyage of Master Henry Hudson," 1609, in J. Franklin Jameson, *Narratives of New Netherland,* 1609-1664, NY, Charles Scribner's Sons, 1909, p. 22.

For the fur-abundant Esopus area, see for instance the unpublished history of Jonathan Hasbrouck, as quoted in Nathaniel Bartlett Sylvester's *History of Ulster County,* New York, Overlook Press reprint, 1977, p. 28.

On the fur trade monopoly, see, for instance, John Romeyn Brodhead, *History of the State of New York, First Period, 1609-1664,* NY, Harper and Brothers, 1859, p. 155.

An attempt by the author to locate records of mining among the charred remains of Company records damaged in the Library fire of 1911 was without success. "I went through ashes of the documents at the New York State Library, and I found enough to get the mention of the high Catskills with respect to some Dutch speculators who were hoping to find gold," said Alf evers, August 9, 2004. See Chapter 3 of the author's *The Catskills from Wilderness to Woodstock,* 1973, tracing the efforts of the early Dutch for veins of metal in the Catskills and Hudson Valley.

The writer on what the Dutch brought to the Hudson Valley, see Maud Goodwin, *Dutch and English on the Hudson River,* p. 120

The Jesuit Relations and Allied Documents: Travels and Explorations of the Jesuit Missionaries in North America (1610-1791), Edna Kenton, Editor, Albert & Charles Boni, NY; this book has information on Fr. Isaac Jogues, who wrote *Novum Belgium,* "a description of the Dutch colonies in the Hudson." Jogues was killed by Natives on October 18, 1646.

On the 18 different languages in Manhattan, p. 259 Jameson, op. cit., Father Isaac Jogues, 1846, *Novum Belgium.*

The text of the February 1650 letter of the Directors to Stuyvesant is found in *Documents Relative to the Colonial History of New York,* Vol. 13, p. 26; the March 21, 1851 letter is found in *Documents Relative to the Colonial History of New York,* Vol. 13, p. 27

Piet Heyn "captured (for the Dutch West India Corporation) a vast booty in the Spanish treasure ships," *Encyclopedia Britannica*, 11th edition, 1910-11, Vol. 8, pp. 734-735

The original Chambers deed is at the Senate House Museum Library in Kingston. See article, "The Indian Deed to Thomas Chambers," *Olde Ulster*, Vol. 1, number 3, March 1903; See Marc B. Fried, The Early History of Kingston & Ulster County, N.Y., Ulster County Historical Society, Kingston, 1975, pp. 14-15.

For examples of Indian Deeds, see *Documents Relative to the Colonial History of New York*, Vol. 13, pp. 397-403.

See in Jameson, *Narratives of New Netherland*, for "The Representation of New Netherland, 1650;" also *The Memorial History of New York*, Vol. 1, p. 200 for an account of Kieft's ordering of uncalled-for attack on Raritan Indians in July, 1640.

The Representation is found in E.B. O'Callahan, ed. *Documents Relative to the Colonial History of the State of New York*, Vol. 1, pp. 294-295; Albany: Weed, Parsons and Company, 1856

Athar-Hacton, see *Ecclesiastical Records, State of New York*, Vol. 1, p 398

3. A Trio of Very Bold Men

Chambers fined for speaking abusively, see *Minutes of the Court of Fort Orange and Beverwyck*, Vol. 1

Jurisdiction over Esopus in early years, see A.J.F. van Laer, translator and editor, *Van Rensselaer Bowier Manuscripts*, Albany, University of the State of New York, 1908, p. 835

For Thomas Morton and Merrymount, see information in W. Bradford, *Plymouth Plantation, 1620-1647*

On Davitz as selling liquors to the Natives from a sloop, see *Minutes of the Court of Fort Orange and Beverwyck*, Vol. 1, p. 88.

For Jacob Clomp and Kit Davitz's sale of brandy for beaver, see *Minutes of the Court of Fort Orange & Beverwyck (1652-1656)*, Vol. 1, Albany, 1920.

Many entries in *Documents Relative to the Colonial History of New York*, Vol. 13, 1881 are marked as from Great Esopus or Great Aesopus; also, Lorenzo Dow's book

In the author's lifetime, he heard Sopus used in daily speech.

For "Kingston-Sopus," see *Lorenzo Dow's Life and Works Complete*, Cincinnati, Applegate & Co., 1860, p. 56

Biographic information on Johan and Johanna de Hulter in Vol. 13, *Documents Relative to the Colonial History of New York*, in the Court Records of Fort Orange; also Mary De Peyster Rutgers and McCrea Conger (Vanamee), *New York's Making— Seen Through the Eyes of My Ancestors*, London, Methuen & Co., 1938 about the history of NY

On de Laet's "promotional enticements, see sections from Johan de Laet's "New World," in Jameson, *Narratives of New Netherland*, p. 31 et seq.

De Hulter's brick and tile venture are referenced in the Court Records of Ft. Orange and Beverwyck.

See index to the *Minutes of the Court of Fort Orange & Beverwyck (1652-1656)*, 2 vols, Albany, 1920, and see for instance, p. 158 of Volume XIII, where he's referred to as "Honble Johan de Hulter."

For de Hulter's petition on controlling servants, see *Minutes of the Court of Fort Orange &*

Beverwyck (1652-1656), 2 vols, Albany, 1920, Vol. 1, p. 228 De Hulter's petition was dated July 14, 1655

PART 2

1. When Natives Attack New Amsterdam, 80 Long Miles to the South, the Colonists at Esopus Flee to Fort Orange, Forty Miles to their North.

On Native warfare techniques, see William Smith, Jr.'s *The History of the Province of NY, Vol. 1 & 2*, Patrick Malone's *The Skulking Way of War— Technology and Tactics Among the New England Indians;* Cadwallader Colden, *The History of the Five Indian Nations of Canada;* Drake on Pequot Wars, or Michael Kammen's *Colonial New York, a History.*

Natives attacking while Dutch were trying to oust the Swedes, see Vol. 13, *Documents Relative to the Colonial History of New York*, on Hudson Valley and Kingston history; E. M. Ruttenber, *A History of the Indian Tribes of Hudson River.*

Full text of de Hulter's letter to get the Esopus lands legally granted to her in *Documents Relative to the Colonial History of New York*, Vol. 13, p. 71

For wealth of Ebbingh, see tax table, p. 352, *The Memorial History of New York*, Vol 1

See *Documents Relative to the Colonial History of New York*, Vol. 13, 1881, p. 177 on the 1,000 acres subdivided to de Hulter; Ebbingh getting two years to cultivate the 1,000 acres, p. 158

Indian deeds are discussed in Sung Bok Kim, *Landlord and Tenant in Colonial New York*, University of North Carolina at Chapel Hill, 1978. For Esopus Indian deeds see *Olde Ulster*, Volume 1, p. 77, and Vol. 3, p. 149. For abstracts of deeds in the Fort Orange Records, see p. 572 of Vol. 13, *Documents Relative to the Colonial History of New York*

See *Documents Relative to the Colonial History of New York*, Vol. 13, 1881, regarding Ebbingh getting two years to cultivate the 1,000 acres, p. 158; for "six wagon loads of grain," see p. 352

2. The Two Cultures Start to Mingle and the Colonial Farming Community Begins to Take Shape

For "Hendrik, the sewant reyger," see *Proceedings of New York State Historical Association*, Vol. XI, 1912, "The Dutch Records of Kingston," p. 3; plus a note from Alf Evers on his knowledge about wampum: "help in learning about wampum was had from Dr. Edward Nel, an economist in the graduate department of the New School of Social Research of New York." Hendrik is named "Henry Zeewant ryger (Wampummaker)" on p. 230 of *Documents Relative to the Colonial History of New York*, Vol. 13.

Source for children's clothing made by Natives is the inventory of possessions left behind after the death in 1665 of Gysbert Van Imborch, printed in *Ulster County, N.Y. Wills*, edited by Gustave Anjou, New York, 1906, Volume 1, p. 24. Also see Augustus H. Van Buren's *Ulster County Under the Dutch*, Kingston, NY 1923, pp. 138-140

3. A Protective Stockade against the unhappy Natives is Built, a Prospective Minister Comes and Goes, and an Ambush at the Indian Tennis Court Leads on to more Conflict

The shooting of Bamboes, see *Documents Relative to the Colonial History of New York,* Vol. 13, 1881, pp. 77-78; for nickname Bamboes, see p. 80. For Bamboes as a "fugitive from justice," see *Minutes of the Court of Fort Orange and Beverwyck, 1652-1660,* Vol. 2, p. 52.

For Native reparations to Rondout colony, see *Documents Relative to the Colonial History of New York,* Vol. 13, 1881, pp. 93-94, "Proposals Made to the Esopus Indians and their Answers," October 15, 1658; also see letter, p. 284, July 30, 1663 from Director Stuyvesant to Capt. Krieger, urging Krieger to "give (the Esopus Natives) no rest, but they must be pursued and attacked upon every information received, as much as possible."; also see "Journal of the Esopus War," Captain Krieger, starting at p. 323 of *Documents.*

Peter Stuyvesant's justification for mounting a fierce war against the Esopus Natives, see his letter, dated February 9, 1660, at p. 137, *Documents Relative to the Colonial History of New York,* Vol. 13

Golden Hill, see ad promoting the real estate proposal in *The Republican* (a Kingston paper), December, 1853; also see *The Journal,* October 15, 1851.

For Stuyvesant's close supervision of the construction of the Kingston stockade, see Peter Stuyvesant's journal of his visit "to the Esopus," May 20-June 25, 1658, pp. 81-87, *Documents Relative to the Colonial History of New York,* Vol. 13; also see John Romeyn Brodhead, *History of the State of New York— 1609-1664,* New York 1859, p. 649.

Hermanus Bloem (often spelled Blom) coming to Esopus as dominie, see *History of the Dutch Reform Church;* and E.T. Corwin's *Ecclesiastical Records of the State of New York,* Albany 1916; and also Corwin's *A Manual of the Reformed Church in America,* NY, 1902; Chaplain Roswell Randall Hoes, "Preliminary Sketch of the Old Dutch Church of Kingston, N.Y., and of Some of its Ministers," in *Proceedings of the New York State Historical Association,* Vol XI, 1912, pp. 186-230

Regarding Stuyvesant's challenge to the Esopus Natives to engage in a staged fight, there is no documentary source so it must be regarded with suspicion— yet feelings between whites and Natives at this time were certainly not very friendly as their actions at this period showed.

On the court at Wiltwyck, and Swartwout's appointment as Schout; and on Thomas Chambers charged for kniving a man, see "The Dutch Records of Kingston," 1658-1684, revised translation by Samuel Oppenheim, in *Proceedings of the New York State Historical Association,* Vol XI, 1912; for instance for the Chambers knifing accusation, see pp. 5-6; for the court deciding in favor of Westercamp's "sexual service," see pp. 57-58; for the fundament cleansing advise of Aeltje Roeloffson, see p. 83

4. THE RONDOUT INDIAN TENNIS COURT AND ITS PLACE IN NATIVE LIFE

See Augustus H. Van Buren, *A History of Ulster County under the Dominion of the Dutch,* Kingston, New York, 1923, p. 9, on the "'Tennis Court' near the corner of Hone and Pierpont streets" which was mentioned by Thomas Chambers in a letter of 1658, and Chambers mentioning of a game played at the Court.

Another level plain across the Greene County line, on which a church stands, is also called the Katsbaan. The church is known as the Katsbaan Church. It is not known as a native site. See deed from Town of Kingston, 1804, selling land to William Swart, mentioning "the lot of land called Cautsbaim, belonging to the said Wm Swart," located where the author has placed the Esopus Native Katsbaan. See also the "Indenture" made on August 5, 1814, between John Inhel of New York City and William Swart of Kingston, mentioning "that certain piece or parcel of land lying on the west side of the Kings Highway that leads to the Stand called the Caatsbaan, beginning at a stone set in the ground near the west side of the path, where it ascends, a small rising ground and first enter on the Kaatsbaan (sic)." For Mary Isabella Forsyth's error, see her *The Beginnings of New York: Old Kingston, the First State Capital*, 1909.

The "tennis court near the strand" is mentioned in a letter to Stuyvesant, from Esopus, September 29, 1659, *Documents Relative to the Colonial History of New York,* Vol. 13, p. 115

On Esopus stick and ball games, see Thomas Vennum, Jr., *American Indian Lacrosse, Little Brother of War*, Smithsonian Institute, 1994; and Stewart Culin, *Games of the North American Indians,* Dover Publications, NY 1975

Stoll's hay barracks fired by arrows, see *Documents Relative to the Colonial History of New York,* Vol. 13, p. 115.

For the full text of Cadwallader Colden's 1759 letter criticizing the Dutch, see Vol. 1, pp. 287-291, of William Smith, Jr., *The History of the Province of New York,* Harvard University Press, 1972

Chambers as English soldier of fortune for the Dutch, see the 1857 *Kingston and Rondout Directory,* p. 165

103. Stuyvesant having difficulty raising troops to go to Esopus, see *Documents Relative to the Colonial History of New York,* Vol. 13, pp. 123-124

PART 3

1. THE ESOPUS WARS DRIVE THE NATIVES FROM THEIR HOMELAND

Stoll as wife-beater, see *Minutes of the Court of Fort Orange & Beverwyck (1652-1656)*, 2 vols, Albany, 1920, Vol. 1, Nov. 30, 1655; more on Jacob Stoll, see A.J.F. van Laer, translator and editor, *Van Rensselaer Bowier Manuscripts,* Albany, University of the State of New York, 1908, p. 835

Stockade-dwellers who reported that Stoll had opened fire first, *Documents Relative to the Colonial History of New York,* Vol. 13, pp. 118-119; for the Catskill Indians' report on the incident see pp. 119-120; proposition by Mohawk Sachems, see p. 122.

2. TIMES OF PEACE, TIMES OF WAR ARE CAUSE FOR GAINS IN LAND FOR WHITES AND TEMPORARY DESTRUCTION OF THEIR SOCIETY FOR NATIVES

For the Company directors' letter on the "barbarous Esopus tribe," March 9, 1660, see *Documents Relative to the Colonial History of New York,* Vol. 13, pp. 149-150

The murder of Esopus sachem Preumaker, see *Documents Relative to the Colonial History of New York,* Vol. 13, p. 171

Dominie Bloem's activities in Esopus, see *Ecclesiastical Records, State of New York,* edited by Edward T. Corwin, Albany 1901-1916

On the name Sopus, the author recalls it used by Charlie Wood on Evers Farm up to 1919.

CHAPTER 3. HORROR IN THE STOCKADE

Dominie Bloem's report on the "horror in the stockade," see his account in *Ecclesiastical Records, State of New York,* edited by Edward T. Corwin, Vol. 1, pp. 534-535

Another account of the June 6, 1663 attack on the Stockade is in *Proceedings of the Huguenot Society of America,* Volume 2, pp 231-232, plus an account of the annoyance of the Indians over "trespass of white people's cale and dogs upon their patches of maize and beans."

For the full text of the magistrates letter to Stuyvesant, June 10, 1663, see *Documents Relative to the Colonial History of New York,* Vol. 13, p. 245

Martin Krieger's Journal is found in *Documents Relative to the Colonial History of New York,* Vol. 13, pp. 323-354.

The treaty signed May 15, 1664 in Fort Amsterdam is covered in Marius Schoonmaker's *History of Kingston,* p. 46; the treaty text is in *Documents Relative to the Colonial History of New York,* Vol. 13, pp. 375-377

For the subsequent treaty of October, 1665, where some of the renewals of the treaty are noted, see *Richard Nicolls Esopus Indian Treaty 1665,* "An Agreement made between Richard Nicolls Esq. Governor Under his Royal Highness the Duke of Yorke and the Sachems and People called the Sopes Indyans," published by the Ulster County Clerk's Records Management Program, 2002. Also see Scott and Baker, "Renewal of Governor Nicolls Treaty of 1665 with the Esopus Indians at Kingston, N.Y.," in *New York Historical Society Quarterly,* July 1953, pp. 268-270.

4. Wiltwyck Comes out of its Stockade— a Poem about Esopus is Written

For dominie Bloem inveighing against Wiltwyckians celebrating Fastenseen or Mardi Gras, see "The Dutch Records of Kingston," pp. 126-127, in *Proceedings of the New York State Historical Association,* Vol. XI, 1912

Henricus Selyns' poem, "Bridal Torch," is found in Henry C. Murphy, *Anthology of New Netherland or Translations from the Early Dutch Poets of New York,* Ira J. Friedman, Inc., Port Washington, NY, nd.

PART 4

1. When Changing Loyalties were Expected of Kingston

For fur trading issues, see Thomas Elliot Norton, *The Fur Trade in Colonial New York—1686-1776,* University of Wisconsin Press, 1974

Other sources for this chapter, *History of the State of New York,* in ten volumes, Alexander C. Flick editor, published by Columbia University Press for the the New York State Historical Association, 1933-1937; Edward Tanjore Corwin, *A Manual of the Reformed Church in America,* NY, Board of Publication of the Reformed Church in America, 1879; *Ecclesiastical Records, State of New York,* edited by Edward T. Corwin, Albany 1901-1916; Patricia Bonomi, *A Factious People—Politics and Society in Colonial New York,* Columbia University Press, 1971; Michael Kammen, *Colonial New York, a History,* Charles Scribner's Sons, NY, 1975 ; Marius Schoonmaker's *History of Kingston,* which the author has found to be helpful and accurate.

For the Kingston/Wiltwyck complaints against Brodhead, see *Documents Relating to the Colonial History of New York,* Vol. 13, pp. 406-414; the court proceedings are to be found on pp. 414-415

For information on Gisbert (or Gysbert) Van Imborch (sometimes Van Imbroch), see *Ulster County, N.Y. Wills,* edited by Gustave Anjou, New York, 1906, Volume 1, pp. 22-29. (*Documents,* Vol. 13— spells it Van Imborgh.)

2. In a Time of Conflict, Captain Chambers Rises to Become the Lord of Foxhall Manor 1672

On manors, see *History of the State of New York*, III, Columbia University Press, 1933, "The Courts and the Law in Colonial New York," by Julius Goebel, Jr., p.16, ".....(Governor) Nicolls made a deliberate effort to import into New York a familiar English institution... This was the introduction of the manorial system."

Full text of Lovelace's granting Chambers the right to be lord of the Manor, *Documents Relative to the Colonial History of New York*, Vol. 13, p. 468

Chambers' will, see *Ulster County, N.Y. Wills*, edited by Gustave Anjou, New York, 1906, Volume 2, p. 107

3. A TIME WHEN BRITAIN GAINS CULTURAL STRENGTH IN THE LIFE AND LAND OF KINGSTON

For the stationing and activities of Captain Daniel Brodhead and the English in Wiltwyck, see numerous entries in *Documents Relative to the Colonial History of New York*, Vol. 13.

4. LABADIST CULTISTS COME AND GO AND REPORT FAVORABLY ON THE CONDITION OF KINGSTON 1679

On the Labadist visit to Kingston, see Jasper Dankers and Peter Sluyter, *Journal of a Voyage to New York and a Tour in Several of the American Colonies in 1679-80*, Readex Microprint Corp., 1966; see also *Olde Ulster*, Vol. 5, p. 71

For the Huguenots settling in New Paltz, see Charles Baird, *History of the Huguenot Emigration to America*, Vol. 1, NY, Dodd, Mead & Company, 1885, pp. 190-200; also *Proceedings of the Huguenot Society of America*, Vol. 3, Part 1, James Le Fevre, "The Huguenot Pantentees of New Paltz," pp. 80-91

5. THE BOULTING ACT ANGERS KINGSTON, WILLIAM LEISLER STEPS FORWARD AS THE "GLORIOUS REVOLUTION" PLACES WILLIAM OF ORANGE AND QUEEN MARY STUART, ELDEST DAUGHTER OF KING JAMES II ON THE THRONE OF ENGLAND

For sources on the Boulting (or Bolting) Act, and William Leisler, see Michael Kammen, *Colonial New York, a History*, Charles Scribner's Sons, NY, 1975 p. 113; biographic sketch p. 121; see *Memorial History of the City of New York*, James Grant Wilson, editor, 1892, Vol. 1, p. 605, on "1678 Bolting Privilege granted to New York City." Leisler's biography, see *Memorial History*, Vol. 1, pp. 462-463

Cadwallader Colden's report on flour and bread is quoted in Michael Kammen, *Colonial New York, a History*, p. 170

State seal changed in 1691 to feature kneeling natives, see *Memorial History*, Vol. 1 p. 478

PART 5

1. 18TH CENTURY KINGSTON PEOPLE ENDURE BRITISH COLONIAL RULE

On de Lancey ordering the blockhouse in Kingston to be built, see *Olde Ulster*, Vol. 6, 1910, p. 312. For articles on Kingston during the French and Indian Wars, see *Olde Ulster*, Vol. 5, p. 15; Vol. 6, p. 312

On a line of blockhouses along the frontier, see Andrew Hickey, *The Story of Kingston, First Capitol of New York State— 1609-1952,* Stratford House, New York, 1952, p. 196.

On Mink Hollow being named after a run away slave from Kingston named Andrew Mink, see Anita Smith, "Stories of Mink Hollow, Hearsay and History Number 2," *Publications of the Woodstock Historical Society,* Vol. 8, p. 20, August 1932.

2. Slavery for Some and Prosperity for Others

For the text of Gov. Cornbury's 1705 report to London, see p. 76, Vol. 2, *Memorial History of the City of New York,* James Grant Wilson, editor, New-York History Company, NY, 1892, where Cornbury writes: "I declare my opinion to be that all these collonys, which are but twigs belonging to the same Tree (England), ought to be kep entirely dependent upon and subservient to, England...."

As for Cornbury's crossdressing, there is a picture of him in drag, p. 86, Vol. 2, *Memorial History of New York.*

For the full text on the burning of Jack, see Hoes, *The Old Court Houses of Ulster County, New York,* p. 6.

3. Life in 18th Century Kingston among White Colonists

The kermis was to have a good place in Kingston history. It's a Dutch word, initially spelled kermis, but by the end of the 19th century, it was called a kirmess.

For the Kinderhookers and the Wolverhookers, see Jonathan Hasbrouck's account in his *History of Ulster County, New York,* pp. 179-180, in A. C. Clearwater's book of the same name.

The piepowder (or pypowder) court mentioned also in Schoonmaker's *History of Kingston,* p. 91

Source for slave cemetery in Kingston later being the location of a lumberyard is Harry Siemsen, historian of the Town of Sawkill.

On Jacob's Valley as a place of misfits, see the *Rondout Courier,* January 1864.

Information on the life of Chancellor Robert Livingston, see George Dangerfield's *Chancellor Robert R. Livingston of New York— 1746-1813, Harcourt, Brace, NY 1960*

On the rousing welcome Kingston gave Livingston, see Marius Schoonmaker, *History of Kingston,* p. 433

4. The Huguenot Touch

Huguenots settling in New Paltz, see *History of New Paltz and its Old Families,* Ralph LeFevre; also "The Huguenot Patentees of New Paltz, New York," James LeFevre, in *Proceedings of the Huguenot Society of America,* Vol. 3, Part 1, New York, 1896 pp. 80-91

The author has a copy of the journal of Abraham Hasbrouck, from which he has derived much of the Huguenot material.

5. Ann Moore, Quaker Missionary

For information on Ann Moore, see copy of her diary made by Chaplain Hoes in the Senate House Museum Library.

For grudging toleration of Quakers in British-controlled New Amsterdam, see John Fiske's *The Dutch and Quaker Colonies in America.*

6. "COETUS AND CONFERENTIA"

Sources for "Coetus and Conferentia" controversy, see Corwin's *A Manual of the Reformed Church in America,* 1879; also *Ecclesiastical Records, State of New York,* edited by Edward T. Corwin, 7 volumes, Albany 1901-1716— he author has found the latter to be quite accurate.

Also see Marius Schoonmaker's *History of Kingston,* pp. 214-221

PART 6

1. GEORGE CLINTON AND THE PRELUDE TO REVOLUTION

Sources on George Clinton include *George Clinton—Yeoman Politician of the New Republic* by John Kaminski; and the 10-volume set, in the author's archives, *Public Papers of George Clinton,* Albany, 1911

Charles De Witt's letters are to be found in the Senate House Library in Kingston. On Cadwallader Colden, Jr. opposing Clinton for the Assembly, see...

Marius Schoonmaker's *History of Kingston* has much to say on De Witt, Clinton, and Kingston leading up to the Revolution.

A number of articles on Clinton are to be found in *Olde Ulster.* On Clinton as Clerk of the Court of Common Pleas, see *Olde Ulster,* Vol. 1, p. 62.

2. THE YEARS OF REVOLUTION BEGIN

On the families of Lt. Gov. Colden and De Lancey see *History of the State of New York,* Vol. III, p. 149-50, 152.

On Clinton defending MacDougal, see *Olde Ulster,* Vol. 4 p. 40

Kaminski's biography of George Clinton; and Edward Countryman, *A People in Revolt.*

on pre-Revolutionary factions, see Patricia Bonomi's *A Fractious People: Politics and Society in Colonial New York.*

For George Clinton's military career, see a group of articles in *Olde Ulster,* Vols. 4, 5, 6.

3. GENERAL VAUGHAN FORCES THE HUDSON AND ATTACKS KINGSTON

For Vaughan's movements before the burning, see *Olde Ulster* Vol. 4, pp. 47, 71, 77, 115.

Kingston becoming State Capital, an account is in Schoonmaker, *History of Kingston,* Chapter 16, pp. 259-276.

For the inauguration of George Clinton in Kingston, see...

For prisoners of war in cellar of Kingston Courthouse,

For more on Kingston during Revolutionary War, see Journals of Blatchley Webb, who wrote about arriving in Kingston while the ruins were smoking.

An account of the 1777 burning is in Benson Lossing's *Field Notes of the Revolution.*

George Clinton's letters are contained in *The Public Papers of George Clinton,* 3 volumes, NY and Albany, 1899

4. TRIAL BY FIRE

For the burning of Kingston, see *Olde Ulster,* Vol. 1, p. 33; Vol. 4, pp. 12, 47, 71, 77, 106, 115, 157, 169, 198, 232, 267; Vol 10, p. 209; see also Schoonmaker's *History of Kingston,* Chapter 17, pp. 277-302; also General George H. Sharpe, "The Burning of Kingston," in De Lisser's *Picturesque Ulster,* beginning at p. 46.

On the *Lady Washington,* see *Ulster County Gazette,* Ulster County Historical Society, Vol. 3, Num. 4, April 1966

Material on the burning in the Hasbrouck family journal, a copy of which is in the author's archives; see also Chapter X of Benson J. Lossing, *The Hudson from The Wilderness to the Sea,* NY Birtue and Yorston, 1866

More on Kingston during the Revolution, A.T. Clearwater, ed., *The History of Ulster County,* pp. 120-213

5. Clinton-Sullivan, Tories and "Monster" Brant

For Washington's letter to Sullivan urging "total destruction," see James Arthur Frost, *Life on the Upper Susquehanna 1783-1860,* Columbia University, NY 1961, p. 5.

For Charles Inglis's refutation of *Common Sense,* see E. B. O'Callaghan, *Documentary History of the State of New York,* Albany, 1850, Vol. III, Inglis's "State of the Anglo-American Church," dated Oct. 31, 1776, p. 1059, in which he describes how in Feb. 1776 he had written an answer to *Common Sense,* "one of the most virulent, artful, and pernicious pamphlets I ever met with."

On Samuel Seabury's pamphlets, see *History of the State of New York,* Alexander Flick, editor, New York State Historical Association, Columbia University Press, 1931, Vol. 3, pp. 330-331

On Joseph Brant as "Monster," see the biography by Isabel Thompson Kelsay, *Joseph Brant 1743-1807, Man of Two Worlds,* Syracuse University Press 1984

Catskills tenants serving as British soldiers, see chapter, "War Divides the Catskills," in Evers' *Catskills*

On tarring and feathering of Ulster County Tories, the Senate House Museum Library archives has an extract of a letter, dated Oct. 22, 1783, describing the headshaving and tarring of a Wallkill Tory.

More on Joseph Brant in Evers' *Catskills,* Ch. 25, and p. 173, end note 1

See Richard Drinnon, *Facing West: The Metaphysics of Indian-Hating and Empire-Building,* University of Minnesota Press, 1980, p. 332, relating that the Seneca Cornplanter in 1792 had told Washington that to his face.

On the roads into the back country proposed by Kingston Trustees, see Evers, *Woodstock: History of a Town,* pp 81-82

For the text on party feeling between Republicans and Federalists, see Marius Schoonmaker's *History of Kingston,* p. 389

Kingston offering a square mile for the U.S. capital, see Schoonmaker, p 369 et seq.

See chapter XX of Schoonmaker's *History of Kingston* for a tracing of the history of the Kingston Academy; also letters of Charles De Witt in the Senate House Museum library

6. George Washington Visits Kingston

Note from author: on Washington's Kingston visit, see Marius Schoonmaker's *History of Kingston* and related mss. in Kingston Senate House Library. See also *Olde Ulster* Vol 1, p. 116; Vol. 3, p. 6, 11; Vol. 6, p. 113; Vol. 7, p. 367; and A.T. Clearwater, ed., *The History of the County of Ulster,* p. 213

PART 7

1. After the War Was Won

On Chancellor Livingston's gift of land to victims of the burning of Kingston, see Sylvester, *History of Ulster County,* Part 1, p. 196

On speculators buying up Continental paper from former Revolutionary soldiers on the sly, then making large profits, see Leonard L. Richards, *Shays's Rebellion, The American Revolution's Final Battle,* University of Pennsylvania Press, 2002, pp. 78-80

2. The Beginning (and the Ending) of the Kingston Commons

On the "rights of estover in the commons," see Evers *Catskills,* p. 395

For the English enclosure movement, see John W. Osborne *The Silent Revolution, The Industrial Revolution in England as a Source of Cultural Change,* Charles Scribner's, 1970, pp. 33-34; also Peter Mathias, *The First Industrial Nation, an Economic History of Britain 1700-1914,* Charles Scribner's 1969, pp. 72-74; and E. P. Thompson, *The Making of the English Working Class,* Vintage Books, 1966, pp. 216-221.

The ending of the Kingston commons is mentioned in Benjamin Myer Brink, *The Early History of Saugerties, 1660-1825,* Kingston, R.W. Anderson & Son, 1902

For land parcels sold by Kingston Trustees beginning in 1804, see for instance the deed of sale to William Swart in the County Clerk's office, dated Feb. 22, 1804, for a parcel contiguous to the Rondout Katsbaan (also owned by Mr. Swart).

More on dividing the Kingston commons or "Plains" in Clearwater's 1907 *History of Ulster County,* p. 214.

For Kingston acreage dedicated for the benefit of the Kingston Academy, see chapter 45, "The Schools of the County," in Clearwater *History of Ulster County,* p. 524, where in early 1804, the Trustees applied for permission to establish a college, were turned down, and then deeded to the Kingston Academy 800 acres; map of Kingston Commons, in *Olde Ulster,* Vol. 1, 1905, p. 147, article on patent of Commons, article beginning p. 145

3. Kingston Academy's Success

See chapter XX of Schoonmaker's history of Kingston for a tracing of the history of the Kingston Academy; also letters of Charles De Witt in the Senate House Museum library.

Also, "Kingston Academy," by C.M. Ryon, in De Lisser's *Picturesque Ulster,* beginning at p. 64. In the author's archives is "The Spectator," Annual Issue for Commencement Week, 1909, 50 pp.

4. John Vander Lyn

On Burr and Vander Lyn, see *John Vanderlyn, Artist 1775-1852,* Marius Schoonmaker, Kingston, Senate House Association, 1950.

See *American Painters in Paris,* Yvon Bizardel, Macmillan, NY 1960, pp. 50-58; pp 80-96, esp. p. 94 on Vander Lyn growing indignant at "the arrogance of the rich."

Newspaper articles on Vander Lyn, see *Democrat Journal,* July 25, 1850; *Art News,* November 1956; *Daily Freeman,* July 15, 1996; "Recollections of John Vanderlyn, the Artist," in *The Atlantic Monthly,* February 1867; *Kingston Daily Freeman,* Sept. 23, 1873; October 14, 1886.

Article on Pieter Vanderlyn, John's grandfather, in *Antiques,* Vol XLI, no. 6, Dec. 1942; also Vol. LXXV, No. 6, June 1959

For an article on Vander Lyn's picture of the Vlight Bergh, see *Rondout Courier,* June 30, 1848; biographic article in the *Courier,* May 28, 1848.

See article in *Antiques,* December 1990, where his name is spelled Vander Lyn, and it is noted that Vander Lyn himself spelled it that way until 1836; article on Vander Lyn's oil painting of Niagara Falls.

PART 8

1. Sojourner Truth

For general source information on the chapter on Sojourner Truth, see books in Alf Evers' library, *Sojourner Truth, A Life, a Symbol,* by Nell Irvin Painter, NY, W. W. Norton, 1996; *Her Name was Sojourner Truth,* by Hertha Pauli, NY, Appleton-Century-Crofts, 1962; and *Narrative of Sojourner Truth,* Nell Irvin Painter, editor; Penguin Books, 1998

For black slaves in Kingston, see Hasbrouck's history of Kingston as printed in A. T. Clearwater's *History of Ulster County New York;* for owners of slaves in Ulster County, see *Olde Ulster,* Vol. 6, p. 257; also "Slavery in Ulster County," Augustus Van Buren, *Kingston Freeman,* Sept. 4, 1933.

Andrew Hickey, *The Story of Kingston,* pp. 191-192, quote from ordinance of Kingston Trustees of 1757 regulating treatment of slaves.

Copy of John Addison's speech opposing the bill for the gradual abolition of slavery is in the author's Kingston archive.

Pinkster or Pinxster, see Marius Schoonmaker, p. 427; Clearwater, p. 180

Popple is a local name for the poplar, a tree which springs up in reforested land but with almost no market value. Hence a place not worth much.

On Dow being denied the right to preach at the Kingston Courthouse, see *Lorenzo Dow's Life and Works Complete*, Cincinnati, Applegate and Company, 1860

The text of John Addison's speech to the New York Legislature against the bill for the gradual abolition of slavery is in the author's Kingston archive.

Chapter 2. Steam, Scenery and the Effects of Rumors of a Canal to Come

On the boy's exclamation upon seeing the steamboat, see Schoonmaker, p. 414

For more background on Kingston and Rondout's steamship businesses, see Donald C. Ringwald, *Steamboats for Rondout— Passenger service between New York and Rondout Creek, 1829-1863,* 1981, Steamship Historical Society of America.

For information on General Joseph S. Smith, see N.B. Sylvester, *History of Ulster County,* pp. 204, 286-287; *Kingston Daily Freeman,* July 30, 1878; Aug. 21, 1879; *Kingston Daily Leader,* Mar. 30, 1906.

The author finds Donald C. Ringwald's "When the Steamboats Reigned," *Kingston's 350th Anniversary, 1609-1959,* Kingston, NY, 1959, a good account of the transition from sloops to steamboats.

3. An Army of Diggers Advances on Rondout

For mistreatment and impact of Irish workers, see James Quinlan, *History of Sullivan County;* Irish workers on the D&H Canal, see *History of the State of New York,* Vol. 7, pp. 25-27; Stuart Blumin, *Urban Threshold,* pp. 78-79.

A history of the Delaware & Hudson Canal, see pp. 47-49, Louise Hasbrouck Zimm, "Ulster County" section of *Southeastern New York,* Vol. 1, Lewis Historical Publishing Co. NY 1946.

Another source for the author was Manville B. Wakefield, *Coal Boats to Tidewater, the Story of the Delaware & Hudson Canal,* revised edition 1971, Wakefair Press, Grahamsville, New York

On the treatment of Canal workers and diggers, see Peter Way, "Evil Humors and Ardent Spirits: the Rough Culture of Canal Construction Laborers," *The Journal of American History,* Bloomington, Ind., March 1993, 1397.

See also Leon Sciaky, "The Rondout and its Canal," in *New York History,* the Quarterly Journal of the New York State Historical Association, Vol. XXII, No. 3, pp. 272-289; and articles on the building of the D & H, in *Olde Ulster,* Vol. 5, p. 363; Vol. 6, pp. 231, 289; Vol. 9, p. 250

4. The Stourbridge Lion Takes a Ride on the D&H Canal as a Trial

Information on the *Stourbridge Lion,* see *The Americans,* Daniel Boorstin, p. 105; see pp. 51-52, Louise Hasbrouck Zimm, "Ulster County" section of *Southeastern New York,* Vol. 1, Lewis Historical Publishing Co. NY 1946

The author finds a good account of the *Stourbridge Lion* in *The Story of Anthracite,* pp. 83-86; *Railroads Triumphant,* pp. 254-255; *Proceedings of the Ulster County Historical Society, 1947-1953* pp. 55-56; D.C. Ringwald, *Steamboats for Rondout,* p. 15; Manville B. Wakefield, Coal Boats to Tidewater, the Story of the Delaware & Hudson Canal, revised edition 1971, Wakefair Press, Grahamsville, New York, pp. 9-11; also Arlo Martin, *Railroads Triumphant,* Oxford University Press, 1992, pp 254-255,

5. Temperance, Abolition, the End of Time, and the Reign of Peace

On the strength of Kingston's beer, see Jaspar Dankers and Peter Sluyter, *Journal of a Voyage to New York,* Readex Microprint, 1966, p. 325; Henry Vanderlyn's diary up through 1832 is in the Senate House Museum Library; his diary after 1832 is to be found at the New York Historical Society.

For background on the Millerites see Ruth Alden Doan, *The Miller Heresy, Millennialism, and American Culture,* Philadelphia, Temple University Press, 1987; also Nell Irvin Painter, *Sojourner Truth,* W. W. Norton, 1996, p. 79-88.

For information on Kingston's Rev. John Lillie, a "firm and outspoken opponent of Souther slavery," see pp. 570-571 of Edward Tanjore Corwin's *A Manual of the Reformed Church in America.*

For Boyse in Ulster County and witchcraft in Woodstock, see p. 561, *The Writings of William Boyse,* New York, 1838; the "Stack your arms!" quote, p. 594

The diary of Wilbur storekeeper Nathaniel Booth, 1844-1857, 2 vols., is in the Senate House Museum Library.

6. "Free Love" on the Rondout

See articles in the *Rondout Courier,* On Oneida, Noyes, Cragin, et al., Aug 8, 1851; Sept. 5, 1851; Sept. 12, 1851, Nov. 24, 1851, Nov. 25, 1851; Nov 28, 1851; Dec. 26, 1851; on the Rebecca Ford, Sept. 26, 1851; Oct. 3, 1851; on Perfectionism in Rondout, see Nathaniel

Booth's diary. For articles and letters on Mary Cragin, see *Rondout Courier*, Nov. 24, 1851; also Robert Allerton Parker, *A Yankee Saint— John Humphrey Noyes and the Oneida Community*, G.P. Putnam's Sons, NY, 1935, Chapter IV, "Mary Cragin"; and more background, Spencer Klaw, *Without Sin, the Life and Death of the Oneida Community*, Viking Penguin, New York, 1993; chapter, "Oneida and the Perfect Race," in Everett Webber, *Escape to Utopia, The Communal Movement in America*, Hastings House, New York, 1959

7. Rondout Transformed

On the Children's Church, see pp. 215-252 of Sylvester's *History of Ulster County, New York*.

8. "Where is the Vlight Berg?"

For collapse of Minister's Face, see *Ulster Palladium*, Oct. 26, 1831

See *Rondout Courier*, Feb. 11, 1848 ("Where is the Vlight Berg?"); February 18, 1848 (Revolutionary War legend at the Vlight Berg); Feb. 24, 1848 (where it is spelled Vlight Berg); June 30, 1848; May 11, 1849; May 18, 1849; July 20 1866 (the gun-powder disaster); also p. 71 of Donald C. Ringwald's *Steamboats for Rondout— Passenger Service Between New York and Rondout Creek, 1829 Through 1863*, Steamship Historical Society of America, 1981; *The Rondout Courier*, Jan. 20, 1849 has a small article on how the Newark Lime and Cement Co. was "making its way into the bowels of the Vlight Bergh." Extinction of passenger pigeons, see A. W. Schorger, *The Passenger Pigeon, its Natural History and Extinction*, University of Oklahoma Press, 1955

9. North River Bluestone

Material on Kingston bluestone business can be found in De Lisser's *Picturesque Ulster*, for instance at p. 77; also for bluestone and quarrying, see Sylvester's *History of Ulster County*, pp. 278-279; for brickmaking, see pp. 280; for opening up of stone businesses, see Marius Schoonmaker, *History of Kingston, New York* p. 414; also article, "Hudson River Brick Industry" in *Kingston Freeman and Journal*, Sept. 29, 1909.

On Ben Snyder's recollection, see Evers, *Woodstock*, p. 353; for Lucius Lawson, ibid. p. 535

10. Politicians Appeal to the Irish of Wilbur

For the quotes from Nathaniel Booth, see his diary of 1844-1857, 2 vols., in the Senate House Museum Library, Kingston

The praise for Mike Walsh is from Daniel Patrick Moynihan; information on Mike Walsh is also found in Daniel Boorstin, *The Americans, The Democratic Experience*, Random House, NY, 1973, p. 258; and pp. 248-252 for the background of Irish arriving in the United States; Irish machine politics, p. 255-256.

11. A Utopian Dream for Jacob's Valley

See long article on Jacob's Valley in *Rondout Courier*, Dec. 25, 1863; also *The Journal* (Kingston), May 1850, a description of the Valley; *Rondout Courier* April 2, 1850; Nathaniel

Booth's diary also has entries, such as Nov. 2, 1850, on Jacob's Valley, and on Booth's "long walk in Jacob's Valley" with his daughter Elly, "she was delighted," Vol. 2, p. 108; also see W. C. DeWitt, *People's History,* p. 158; a poem about Jacob's Valley, see *Olde Ulster,* Vol. 8, pp. 318-319; on young people hanging out in Jacob's Valley, N.B. Sylvester, *History of Ulster County,* p. 180; also see Stuart M. Blumin, *The Urban Threshold— Growth and Change in a Nineteenth-Century American Community,* 1976, U. of Chicago Press, Chicago, pp. 116-117

See also Marius Schoonmaker's *History of Kingston,* p. 425-426; and *Kingston Journal,* Wednesday, October 24, 1849, an article, "The True Free Soil Party" and Locofocracy.

12. Know-Nothings, Soft-Shells and Hard-Shells

Reverend Philips' pamphlet of his Nov. 30, 1854 sermon, "The Benefits of Foreign Immigration," is in the author's archives, published by J. P. Hageman, Rondout, 1854

Text of Henry Backus's ballad, see chapter XLIII, "The Saugerties Bard," in Brink's *The Early History of Saugerties.*

For the gathering at Rondout on April 19, 1861 at Washington Hall in Rondout see the *Ulster Republican,* April 17, 1861.

For the spontaneous gathering the same night at the Kingston Courthouse after the telegraph told of the attack on Ft. Sumter, and the resolution the meeting issued, see the *Rondout Courier,* April 26, 1861. Information on the Know Nothings, see Tyler Anbinder, *Nativism & Slavery, The Northern Know Nothings & the Politics of the 1850s,* Oxford University Press, 1992; also Stuart M. Blumin, *The Urban Threshold— Growth and Change in a Nineteenth-Century American Community,* 1976, U. of Chicago Press, Chicago, pp. 147-148; and the *Rondout Courier,* Feb. 22, 1856, how at the State elections, "the Know Nothings swept every one of the 18 towns in the County"; also, "Know Nothing Officials of Ulster," *The Republican,* January 9, 1856.

13. Canoes to Sloops to Steamboats

For an interesting account of Kingston area Native elm bark canoe making, see Marius Schoonmaker's *History of Kingston,* pp. 330-331

On the bewitched sloop *Martin Wynkoop,* see Evers *Catskills,* ch. 31, "Finger Doctors, Stick Doctors and Prottle."

14. The Supreme Court Frees the Steamboat

For the story of the *Congress,* see Chapter 2, "The Beginnings of Passenger Steamboats out of Rondout Creek," in Donald C. Ringwald, *Steamboats for Rondout— Passenger Service Between New York and Rondout Creek, 1829 Through 1863,* Steamship Historical Society of America, 1981; also Ringwald for an account of the *Santa,* pp. 48-52, 80-82, 124-126; on the building of the *Santa* see William E. Verplanck and Moses W. Collyer, *The Sloops of the Hudson,* Ira J. Friedman, NY, 1968 reissue, p. 78; Cornell purchasing the *Santa,* see Ringwald, *The Hudson Day Line,* p. 45; see *Rondout Courier,* Apr. 19, 1861.

On harvesting of Christmas trees for New York City, see Evers, *Catskills,* p. 442

As for the scent of the Christmas trees shipped on steamers, the author remembers the balsam fir fragrance which heralded the approach of Christmas in late fall trips on Hudson River steamboats.

Don Foster's *Author Unknown: On the Trail of Anonymous,* Henry Holt, NY, 2000, has demonstrated that "A Visit from St. Nicholas" was probably written by Major Henry Livingston, Jr.

15. A Competition in Church Building

On the Presbyterian Church in Rondout and the Wurts brothers, see Alfonso T. Clearwater, *History of Ulster County,* pp. 462-463.

For $32.02 to begin St. Mary's Church "high above Rondout," see page 427, "The Roman Catholic Church," Rev. Richard Lalor Burtsell, in A. T. Clearwater's *History of Ulster County.*

The Fair Street Reformed Church of 1849, see *Clearwater,* p. 414. For Minard LeFever as architect, see pp. 22-23, Gilbert D. B. Hasbrouck, *The Reformed Protestant Dutch Church of Kingston, New York,* Kingston 1928

Steeple falling, December 1853, see DeWitt, *People's History of Kingston,* pp. 97-98;

Children's Church in East Rondout in 1870, see pp. 215-252 of Sylvester's *History of Ulster County, New York.*

16. Business Ethics and a Vanishing Judge

Sources of "Ethics and a Vanishing Judge," see Van Slyke's "Reformed Protestant Dutch Church" and also the journal of Nathaniel Booth.

A biographic sketch of Judge James C. Forsyth is in Clearwater, *History of Ulster County, pp. 604-605;* see articles in *Rondout Courier* on Forsyth, Sept. 16, 1853; Sept. 30, 1853.

Articles on Judge Forsyth and his flight or disappearance, see *Ulster Republican,* Sept. 21, 1853; October 12, 19, 1853; and the auction of his possessions, Dec. 21, 1853

17. Railroad Hopes

There is much material on Thomas Cornell as local railroad baron, and hauler of anthracite in Gerald M. Best, *The Ulster and Delaware Railroad Through the Catskills,* San Marino, Calif., 1972.

On the bonding scandal regarding the U & D bonds, see Brink, Benjamin Myer, "Bonding Towns and Corrupt Politics," *Olde Ulster,* Vol. VI, November, 1910, No. 11, Kingston, New York, pp.. 321-329

Article on "shrinking" of value of bonds, *Kingston Freeman,* Feb. 18, 1892

On the Cornell hose carriage, see the *Rondout Courier,* Apr. 9, 1869

Obituary of Thomas Cornell, *The (Albany) Argus,* March 31, 1890

Information also contained in ten page Alf Evers typescript, "The Two Faces of Thomas Cornell," in author's Kingston archive.

Article, "The Rise and Fall of the U & D," by Alf Evers, Catskill Center for Conservation and Development, 1983; a typescript of the same article is in the author's Kingston archive

Also, in the New York State Library, see *Genealogy of the Cornell Family,* New York, T.A. Wright 1902

On full text of resolution on exposure of coffins in Sharpe Burial Ground by the digging of Cornell's U & D through Kingston, see *The Journal,* January 1, 1871

On archeological digs at Ponckhockie, see *Kingston Freeman,* November 26, 1989; also, "The Henrickson Site; a Late Woodland Indian Village in the City of Kingston," Leonard Eisenberg, in *Man in the Northeast,* Num. 38, 1989, pp. 21-53

18. Bloody Civil War Years

The author has the full 1860 *Ulster Republican* Carrier's Address in his Kingston archives.

For Lincoln's proclamation, see *Rondout Courier,* April 19, 1861; for the packed meeting at the Kingston Courthouse, and the ensuing resolution, and on the resolution adopted at a Rondout meeting on April 19, 1861, see the *Rondout Courier,* April 26, 1861; also *Ulster Republican,* April 24, 1861. On the departure of the 20th Regiment from under Colonel Pratt, see *Ulster Republican,* May 1, 1861

For accurate information on Kingston during the Civil War, the author recommends the book *Banners and Bugles* by Will Plank, subtitled *A Record of Ulster County, New York and the Mid-Hudson Region in the Civil War,* published in 1963.

"Jobunckers" is mentioned in Marius Schoonmaker's *History of Kingston,* p. 433. It's a word the author could not find in dictionaries or in H.W. Mencken's *The American Language.* Susan Davis, in *Parades and Power, Street Theater in the Nineteenth Century,* Philadelphia, 1986, notes how mock militias of the 1820s through the 1840s paraded in opposition to the "corruptions of the militia system" and "burlesque military parades became expressions of poor working class protest over the rampant inequalities of duties and rank within the local brigades (in Philadelphia)."

Biography of George W. Pratt in *Olde Ulster,* Vol. 8, p. 105; further biographic information on Pratt, see *Proceedings of the Ulster County Historical Society,* 1862, Ch. 4, pp. 38-39; and *Collections of the Ulster County Historical Society,* Vol. 1, Part 4, 1862, presentations in honor of the memory of Colonel Pratt. Detailed 7 page biography by Seward R. Osborne, "Colonel George Watson Pratt, New York Patriot," in author's Kingston archives.

The original Samuel Schepmoes letters are in the author's archives. There were 20 letters in 1862, 51 in 1863, 49 in 1864, and 14 in 1865. The letter, to his parents in Kingston, in which he felt he was doing his duty to the "good old flag," is dated Sept. 21, 1862. The letter in which he wrote that the "war will last until the officers have made enough money....." was written from Falmouth, Va., dated Dec. 29, 1862. The letter about his hunger ("I want you to have a whole hog killed for me") is dated Oct. 12, 1862. On sleeping with "one eye open," and marching through cold rain, see letter dated Dec. 29, 1862. Schepmoes finding Gen. Grant "a real Hoosier," see letter, July 25, 1864. For Schepmoes support of McClellan in the 1864 election, see letter dated Sept. 4, 1864. Schepmoes promising to tell his parents of his first battlefield experience upon returning home is in an undated letter.

Schepmoes is listed in Sylvester, *History of Ulster County,* p. 294, as "Samuel H. Schepmoes, enl. Aug. 18, 1862, 120 Regt., Co. I." From an analysis of his letters, it is clear that on Sept. 18, 1864, he was struck by a ball while on picket duty, and taken to a hospital, and then taken to New York. Schepmoes, however, is listed with the following entry "Schepmoes, Samuel H. 20. August 14, 1862. Kingston. June 3, 1864. Wounded September 20, 1864. Died at Kingston, 1893," on p. 313, C. Van Santvoord, *The One Hundred and Twentieth Regiment, New York State Volunteers,* Hope Farm Press, 1983; an alphabetical listing of those buried in Wiltwyck Cemetery has Samuel Schepmoes born Feb. 3, 1842, and passing Dec. 14, 1892. See Schepmoes Family Tree, in *Old Dutch Post-Star,* Dec. 2, 1976.

For further material on Kingston in the Civil War, see De Witt's *People's History of Kingston,* pp. 145-159; and the chapter, "Ulster in the Rebellion", in Sylvester's *History of Ulster County,* pp. 155-166; also William Lounsbery, "The Ulster Regiment in the 'Great Rebellion,'" in *Collections of The Ulster Historical Society,* Vol. 1, Part 4, 1862, pp. 210-228.

PART 9

1. THOMAS CORNELL THINKS BIG

Kingston Daily Freeman, Feb. 18, 1892, article on bond troubles with Rondout and Oswego bonds, reorganized under Ulster and Delaware Railroad Company.

For material on Thomas Cornell, see his obituary, *The Argus,* Albany, Mar. 31, 1890; article "Cornell Victory," in *Kingston Daily Leader* Aug. 24, 1888; see also Gerald M. Bert, *The Ulster and Delaware Railroad Through the Catskills,* San Marino, Calif., 1972, which the author found to be a good source; Cornell seeking to become a Congressman, see *Kingston Journal,* Nov. 2, 9, 1882

2. THE SCHOHARIE AND OTHER ETHNIC MIXES 1856-1880

For a lengthy, useful description on the Schoharies and the "Binnewater Class" see the *Rondout Courier,* Nov 7, 1851; also Stuart Blumin, *The Urban Threshold,* pp. 101-102.

Material on Schoharies and Vly Yonders in Evers, *Woodstock: History of an American Town,* pp. 364-365, 398.

3. ETHNIC ACCOMMODATIONS AND MUSIC

Information on the Edsons, and on Dan Sully, see Anita M. Smith, *Woodstock History and Hearsay,* Woodstock, New York 1959, pp. 21, 117; for a history of the Overlook Mountain House, see Evers, *The Catskills from Wilderness to Woodstock,* Ch. 4, pp. 470-480

For the celebration in Kingston of von Humboldt's centenary, see the *Rondout Courier,* September 10, 1869.

4. THE UPS AND DOWN OF IMMIGRANT GEORGE FRANCIS VON BECK

See article, "The Von Beck Lunacy Case," in *The Argus,* July 6, 1870; Von Beck as the first president of the Trustees of the newly incorporated Rondout in 1849, see Clearwater's *History of Ulster County,* p. 226. Also, a piece on "Major Von Beck," *Camp Ward Journal,* August 22, 1855; see also *Kingston Weekly Leader,* July 18, 1896; and printed brochure "The History of the Wolfer Children in Connection with their Grandfather, G.F. Von Beck"; also Von Beck's will in Ulster County Surrogate's office, Nov. 2, 1874, pp. 797-799; and more on Von Beck in Bob Steuding, *Rondout, a Hudson River Port,* Purple Mountain Press, Fleischmanns, New York, 1995, pp. 77-81

For Father Burtsell, see Burtsell's long tracing, "The Roman Catholic Church," in Clearwater's *History of Ulster County,* Ch. 36, pp. 416-450; also Clearwater, pp. 565-566, for a biography of Burtsell, including the reference to his establishing the Church of St. Benedict the Moor in New York City.

5. Kingston, the Rhine, the Catskills and the Hudson

For Robert Livingston Pell, see *Gazetteer and Business Directory of Ulster County, New York, 1871-72,* Hamilton Child, Syracuse, NY, pp. 82-84; history of Overlook Mountain House, see chapter 64 of Evers' *The Catskills from Wilderness to Woodstock.*

6. City Hall, an Armory and a Gerrymander 1872-1879

Article on laying of corner stone of Kingston City Hall, *Argus,* April 15, 1874.

For an analysis of the wave of armory building that began with the railroad strike of 1877, and the fears of class warfare and the French Commune, see the chapter, "Fears of Class Warfare," in Robert M. Fogelson, *America's Armories— Architecture, Society and Public Order,* Harvard University Press, 1989; articles on the railroad strike, see *Kingston Daily Freeman,* July 8, 17, 19, 21, 23, 24, 25, 1877; also the *Argus,* July 25, 1777.

See Sylvester's *History of Ulster County,* p. 296, "The part of Kingston annexed to Woodstock"; for the "New Town of Kingston," see pp. 285-286; also on the creation of the Town of Ulster, see beginning p. 334; on Town of Ulster, see p. 227 of Clearwater's *History,* the author notes, "from a very Republican point of view of the Gerrymander." Another history of the Irish quarrymen becoming a strong political machine on Jockey Hill, and the division of Kingston, see Kathleen Burton Maxwell, "The Town of Kingston," in *History of Ulster County, With Emphasis upon the Last 100 years,* compiled by the Historians of Ulster County for the Tercentenary Year, 1983, pp. 140-152.

The 1879 Kingston expenses for assistance to the poor, see *Kingston Daily Freeman,* Feb. 13, 1879.

The author salutes the help of historian and folksinger Harry Siemsen for his clippings and recollections regarding this chapter.

7. Birth Pangs of the City

In the author's Kingston archives is *Common Council Proceedings, City of Kingston,* 1873-1875, of use in the writing of this chapter.

On the "dumbbell" see Andrew S. Hickey, *The Story of Kingston,* p. 119

See article on difficulties of the two villages' committees, *The Press,* Feb. 23, 1871; also Clearwater's *History of Ulster County,* "The City of Kingston," by Howard Hendricks, pp. 225-227 on the politics in Kingston that led to the Gerrymander.

On the incorporation, see *The Argus,* Oct. 24, 1877

Stuart M. Blumin has a chapter, "New Town," on the differences and connections between Kingston and Rondout leading up their unification, in *The Urban Threshold— Growth and Change in a Nineteenth-Century American Community,* 1976, U. of Chicago Press, Chicago;

Articles on Rondout City charter, see *The Press,* Jan. 26, Feb. 2, 1871; for the committee to join Kingston and Rondout, and the charter, see *The Press,* Feb. 16, Mar. 2, 9, 1871; see too the Kingston *Argus* (formerly *The Republican)* Jan. 1, 1870.

Article on John Lindsley, see *The Press,* Oct. 20, 1870

8. The West Shore Railroad Sets off Creation of an Industrial District

Information on Frederick Westbrook in A.T. Clearwater, *History of Ulster County,* p. 488.

Article on West Shore Railroad in *The Leader,* August 30, 1883

Gerald M. Best, *The Ulster and Delaware Railroad Through the Catskills,* San Marino, Calif., 1972; article listing thriving Kingston factories (such as the Powell, Smith & Co. cigar factory), *The Leader,* Nov. 14, 1896; List of Kingston textile, forest, iron and steel, paper, cigar, knit goods, etc., see De Witt, *People's History of Kingston,* pp. 337-339; Kingston as shirtmaking center, see Louise Hasbrouck Zimm, "Ulster County," in *Southeastern New York,* Vol. 1, p. 192; a sketch of industry in Kingston serviced by the railroads, pp. 126-127, "Kingston," in *History of Ulster County, With Emphasis on the Last 100 Years,* 1983. See the extensive list, "Industries in Kingston whose products are found throughout the United States and Foreign Lands," p. 42, *Souvenir Program and Historic/Civic/Industrial Survey of the City of Kingston,* June 1936, in the author's Kingston archives.

9. A Pilgrimage to Kingston

See the Holland Society's detailed publication of its pilgrimage to Kingston in its *Year Book of the Holland Society of New York,* 1886-7, in the author's Kingston archive.

For articles on the Holland Society's 1886 pilgrimage to Kingston, see *Kingston Daily Freeman,* Sept. 16, 19, 23; Oct. 7, 1886.

10. Games, Sports and Pastimes—Especially Baseball

See the chapter "Baseball in Kingston," pp. 181-207, in William C. DeWitt, *People's History of Kingston, Rondout and Vicinity, 1820-1943,* New Haven, 1943; paragraph on the Rondout Baseball Club in *Rondout Courier* March 29, 1861; another article, "Baseball in Rondout," in the *Courier,* Sept. 17, 1869; *Kingston Daily Freeman,* July 21, 1877; also Harold Seymour, *Baseball, the People's Game,* Oxford University Press, 1990.

"Pulling the goose," see Alice Morse Earle, *Colonial Days in Old New York,* Empire State Book, NY, 1926 reprint of 1896 Charles Scribner's edition, pp. 189-190

Article, "Cockfighting in Ulster County," by Bob Lasher, *Ulster County Gazette,* Vol. 15, No. 2, 1986.

Articles on Kingston Driving Park, *Weekly Freeman,* August 6, 1875; *Freeman,* Sept. 14, 1888; half mile track at the end of Manor Avenue, *Kingston Daily Freeman,* Sept. 14, 1925.

Quotes from William Boyse from *The Writings of William Boyse,* New York, 1838, in the author's Kingston archives.

On Brink climbing the steeple's interior in 1905, see William C. DeWitt, *People's History of Kingston, Rondout and Vicinity, 1820-1943,* p. 394

PART 10

1. The 1890's Bring Fast Change—Miss Stewart's Kirmesses and Historical Pageants; George Clinton's Remains are Brought to Kingston for Re-Burial; Coykendall's Amusement Park is Added to Kingston's Stock of Entertainments

Webster's New American Dictionary spells it "kermis or Kermess, a celebration formerly held each year in the Low Countries, accompanied by feasting, processions, and sports; in U.S., an indoor entertainment usually for charitable purposes"; *Brewer's Dictionary of Phrase and Fable,* Centenary Edition, NY, 1970, p. 603, spells it "Kermesse, Kermis, or Kirmess," from Kirkmass or church mass held in most towns of the Low Countries on anniversary of dedication of parish church; accompanied by processions, feasting, sports and games "often of a somewhat riotous nature"; see Breughel's painting *The Kermess.* More on Kermises, see John Romeyn Brodhead, *History of the State of New York, First Period, 1609-1664,* New York, Harper and Brothers, 1859, pp. 489, 748; Andrew S. Hickey, *The Story of Kingston, First Capitol of New York State— 1609-1952,* Stratford House, New York, 1952, p. 171; for early "Pardon and Kirmess" see *Kingston Daily Leader,* Jan. 29, 1891.

On Lila Stewart, see William C. DeWitt, *People's History of Kingston, Rondout and Vicinity, 1820-1943,* "Dramatics in Kingston— Miss Lila Stuart," pp. 357-358;

Articles in the *Kingston Freeman* on Kirmesses, April 2, 3, 1894; April, 5, 15, 16, 17, 1895; on Stewart's Kirmiss in New Paltz, *Kingston Daily Leader,* Oct. 9, 12, 1895; *Kingston Freeman,* Oct. 9, 1895; on the "Historical Pageant" of the Wiltwyck Chapter of the D.A.R., see *Kingston Freeman,* Sept. 10, 16, 23, 1895; Oct. 13, 1895; *Kingston Daily Leader,* Oct. 30, 1895.

For the City of Kingston Hospital, see *Organization, History, Work and Purposes,* published on the occasion of the formal opening of the hospital, Nov. 27, 1894, 41 pp., in the author's Kingston archives; also "The City of Kingston Hospital," by Rev. R. L. Burtsell, in *Picturesque Ulster,* pp. 51-54.

On Coykendall's business career, see De Witt's *People's History of Kingston,* Chapter XI, "Back to Rondout," pp 66-71; the trolley and Coykendall, Clearwater's *History of Ulster County,* pp. 224-225

On Kingston Point, see Clearwater's *History of Ulster county,* on Coykendall's trolley to the Point. Also Marius Schoonmaker on the history of the Point; and DeWitt's *People's History of Kingston,* pp 4-5; De Lisser's *Picturesque Ulster,* p. 77: and *Kingston Daily Freeman,* "Kingston Point Park For Sale," Aug. 17, 1925

2. Kingston Awakens to Its Own True History

For the full William Lounsbery's text, "A Brief Historical Notice of Kingston and Rondout," see *The Kingston and Rondout Directory,* William H. Boyd, publisher, 1857, pp. 160-174; for the "every other white man is a negro" quote see p. 163.

See the *Rondout Courier,* February 18, 1848 for the Revolutionary War legend at the Vlight Berg.

See memoir of Julia McEntee Dillon by Mabel Burgevin in *Ulster County Gazette,* Ulster County Historical Society, Vol. 16, No. 1, 1987

Mary Isabella Forsyth's poem, "The Homeless Children," is found in DeWitt's *People's History of Kingston, Rondout and Vicinity, 1820-1943,* p. 387

3. Thomas Chambers Revived as Founding Father 1886-1905

On ex-Mayor Lindsley pointing out that Chambers was buried in Montrepose Cemetery without a marker, see *The Argus,* September 22, 1886; Letter from Lindsley suggesting a stone for Chambers, *Weekly Freeman,* Sept. 23, 1886; see letter from Myron Teller to "My dear Dr. Hoes" on the sketch of Chambers house from the memory of Mary Van Leuven, Nov. 23, 1906, copy in author's Kingston archives, original in Senate House Museum Library; "Chambers Monument Will be Erected," *Kingston Daily Freeman,* June 25, 1909; "Thomas Chambers Monument Erected," *Kingston Daily Freeman,* Sept. 25, 1909.

On the Chambers foundation at Colonel Kiersted's place, see *Weekly Freeman,* Apr. 6, 1877

On Chambers reinterment and monument, see *Old Ulster,* Vol. 5, p. 327; also the author found a good account of Chambers and Fox Hall in Lionel de Lisser, *Picturesque Ulster,* pp. 55-57.

4. "Kingston Not Included?" in The Hudson-Fulton Celebration 1909

Many details of Hudson-Fulton Celebration are in W. C. De Witt's *People's History of Kingston, Rondout and Vicinity, 1820-1943,* New Haven, 1943

See article in *Kingston Daily Freeman,* Dec. 21, 1906, "Kingston Should be Included."

In the author's archives is the "Hudson-Fulton Souvenir Program" of 1909; see also Andrew S. Hickey, *The Story of Kingston,* 1952, pp. 171-172; on the unveiling of the Thomas Chambers monument in 1909, see *Olde Ulster,* Vol. 5, p. 333

5. A Rear-Admiral Deplores Destroying Kingston's Historic Buildings in 1914

The *Kingston Daily Freeman,* Oct. 16, 1914, quotes Admiral Higginson at length urging preservation of Kingston's old houses and history. Biographic information on Higginson in DeWitt's *People's History of Kingston, Rondout and Vicinity, 1820-1943,* p. 406.

Wiltwyck DAR Chapter, organized on Feb. 12, 1892, chartered Nov. 2, 1892, incorporated Feb. 15, 1906— see Louise Hasbrouck Zimm, "Ulster County," in *Southeastern New York,* Vol. 1, p. 167. History of DAR chapter house, *Olde Ulster,* Vol. 7, pp. 33, 125

6. The Time They Shook the Plum Tree, 1905-1915, and Ended Flooding for Kingston

For Judge Clearwater's "immense" office on Wall Street in Kingston, see DeWitt's *People's History of Kingston,* p. 103; the photo of Clearwater in his office is in the Senate House Museum Library; for "the time they shook the pear tree" see Chapter 78, "The Ashokan Reservoir is Built" in Evers' *The Catskills from Wilderness to Woodstock.* For Clearwater's representation of Mrs. Cudney and her "ginseng plantation," see p. 594 of Evers. See also the chapter "Water Supply," in the Ulster County section, written by Louise Hasbrouck Zimm, in *Southeastern New York,* Lewis Historical Publishing, New York, 1946, Vol. 1, pp. 101-110.

For an overall view, the the book in the author's Kingston archive, *Water for a City, a History of New York City's Problem from the Beginning to the Delaware River System,* Charles H. Weidner, Rutgers University Press, 1974.

7. "Old Stone Houses" Come into Their Own 1920's

On the blacksmith shop in Kingston of Myron Teller, and information on his life, see Louise Hasbrouck Zimm's "Ulster County," in *Southeastern New York,* Vol. 1, pp. 146-147.

On the history of the Senate House, see brochure, "Senate House Historic Site," Office of Parks, Recreation and Historic Preservation, 2004

The Early Stone Houses of Ulster County, Myron S. Teller, Ulster County Historical Society, 2nd printing, 1974.

Franklyn Roosevelt in Kingston, see *Kingston Daily Freeman,* May 30, 1932; De Witt's *People's History of Kingston, Rondout and Vicinity,* p. 412

The 1923 *Promotional Survey* of Kingston-Rondout is in the author's Kingston archives.

8. Depression, the New Deal of F.D.R., Urban Renewal and IBM Have their Effect on Kingston's History

775. A note from the author, "Source for some of this, Douglas Braik, chairman of the Design Section of the Philadelphia Housing Authority, working during Depression and New Deal days on urban and workers housing." p. 1026

On Urban Renewal in Kingston, the author found useful the account in the *History of Ulster County, With Emphasis upon the Last 100 years,* compiled by the Historians of Ulster County for the Tercentenary Year, 1983, pp 131-132

On the saving of the remains of the Low-Bogardus house from Urban Renewal, see *Ulster County Gazette,* Vol. 8, Num. 2, May 1978.

Brochure, "Kingston's Uptown Renewal Project," proposing a pedestrian mall on John and North Front Streets, in author's Kingston archives.

Articles on the Pike Plan completed in 1975, *Kingston Daily Freeman* Nov. 19, 1989; Dec. 29, 1999.

9. A Promised Land in Ulster County during the 1930s

Father Divine material is to be found in Robert Weisbrot's *Father Divine— The Utopian Evangelist of the Depression Era Who Became an American Legend,* Beacon Press, Boston, 1983

Also, see *Kingston Daily Freeman,* Mar. 19, 1937, article on "Greenkill Park Bought by 26 Divine Angels"; also *Freeman* article, Mar. 20, 1937, "Greenkill Park to be Private School for Divine Children"; *Ulster County Townsman,* July 30, 1992, article by Charles Tiano on Father Divine; *The Weekender,* Spring 2001, article on Father Divine.

10. Hudson River Pollution Fears Increase and Restoration Begins

On protecting the Palisades, see Frances E. Dunwell, *The Hudson River Highlands,* Columbia University Press, 1991, p. 144

For a history of the proposed pumped-storage electric plant at Storm King see Robert Boyle, *The Hudson River, a Natural and Unnatural History,* W.W. Norton, 1979, pp. 153-181.

As of 1936, all of Kingston's sewage was discharged into the Rondout Creek, but by 1940 all cities bordering the Hudson River were required to treat their sewage before discharging it into the River— see p. 29, "Sewerage and Drainage," *Souvenir Program and Historical, Civic, Industrial Survey of the City of Kingston,* June, 1936.

PCBs placed by GE in the Hudson, see Robert Boyle, *The Hudson River, a Natural and Unnatural History,* W.W. Norton, 1979, Epilogue, pp. 295-302.

Overall historic pollution of the Hudson River, see Boyle's *The Hudson River,* pp. 94-104; and Allan Keller, *Life Along the Hudson,* pp. 259-262.

The author notes the image of the smokestacks of the West Point Foundry at Cold Spring, printed in 1841, p. 449, in John W. Barber and Henry Howe, *Historical Collections of the State of New York,* S. Tuttle.

11. Kingston Men Join the U.S. Navy and Make History on the Seas

Washington Irving Chambers, see pp. 353-354 of De Witt's *People's History of Kingston, Rondout and Vicinity.*

Commander Cornelius Schoonmaker, see pp. 354-355 of De Witt's *People's History of Kingston, Rondout and Vicinity.*

The author is grateful for information on Lt. Charles Winans Chipp provided by Mabel Chipp, wife of former Ulster County coroner Arthur Chipp, a descendant of Lt. Charles Chipp.

12. Early Kingston Housewives and a Fashion Model Turned Aviator Serve the City Well

Material in this chapter from author's personal experience; correspondence from Gale Brownlee, Jan. 2003; see "Gale Brownlee 'Flying Fashion Model,'" in *The Woodstock Week,* Sept. 30, 1965; *Hudson Valley* magazine, Jan. 1975, cover story, "Nuclear Power Plants: Kingston? Poughkeepsie? Newburgh?"; *Kingston Daily Freeman* articles on proposed power plant near Kingston-Rhinecliff Bridge: June 7, July 6, Aug. 2, Nov. 26, 30, 1972; Feb. 8, 22, Oct. 19, 1973; May 28, 1974; *Old Dutch Post-Star* Sept. 26, 1972; *New York Daily News,* Oct 29, 1973*Woodstock Times* Sept. 28, 1972; for Brownlee's work in helping set up the Benedictine Hospital Heliport, see *Kingston Daily Freeman,* \, Oct 21, 1970; photos courtesy of Gale Brownlee.

13. Charles Lang Freer Thinks Internationally about Art and Founds a Unique Art Museum

On babies from Rhinebeck being baptized in Kingston, see....

Gilbert Livingston as Ulster County clerk, see Evers, *Woodstock: History of an American Town,* p. 27; there is considerable additional material on the Livingstons in Evers' *Woodstock,* and also in his *The Catskills from Wilderness to Woodstock.*

Information on Charles L. Freer, see *The New York Times,* "The Freer Makes the Old New once More," Sun. May 9, 1993; obituary in *Kingston Daily Freeman,* Sept. 26, 1919; and in *The New York Times,* Sept. 26, 1919;

14. John Burroughs and Others Who Brought Renown to Kingston

Alton Parker conducting his race for the Presidency in 1904 from Rosemount, see Louise Hasbrouck Zimm, "Ulster County," p. 197, in *Southeastern New York.*

For material on Arthur Flemming, see obituary in *Kingston Daily Freeman,* Sept. 9, 1996; for his stance on National Health Care, see *Kingston Daily Freeman,* Aug. 15, 1985; additional biographic information provided by Assemblyman Kevin Cahill, in the author's Kingston archives.

Jervis McEntee: biographic sketch in Sylvester's *History of Ulster County,* part 1, p. 204; "Jervis McEntee's Diary," *Archives of American Art,* Vol. 8, Nos 3 and 4, pp. 1-23; obituary of McEntee, *Kingston Daily Leader,* Jan. 28, 31, 1891; auction of McEntee's paintings, *Kingston Weekly Leader,* March 26, 1892; in the author's archives is exhibition book, "A Selection of Drawings by Jervis McEntee from the Lockwood DeForest Collection," Hirschl and Adler Galleries, New York, 1976

Joseph Tubby: see entry in George C. Groce and David H. Wallace, *The New York Historical Society's Dictionary of Artists in America, 1564-1860,* New Haven, Yale University Press 1957; exhibit of his paintings at Dodge's hardware store, *Kingston Daily Freeman,* Apr. 7, 1875; more May 4, 1875; praise of his landscape paintings, *Rondout Courier,* Oct. 24,

1851; brochure of exhibition of paintings of Tubby, 1821-1896, at Senate House Museum, Dec. 1953; biographic 7 page typescript on Tubby in the author's Kingston archives.

Calvert Vaux: see Kenneth T. Jackson, *Crabgrass Frontier, the Suburbanization of the United States,* Oxford University Press, 1985, pp. 66-67.

G. Rahmer' clock is described in John Darrow, "A Remarkable Clock Mechanism by G. Rahmer of Rondout, New York," in National Association of Watch and Clock Collectors Bulletin, October 2000, p. 623.

Dr. Philip Poley

Ernest Jarrold: see biographic sketch in Andrew Hickey, *The Story of Kingston,* p. 168; *Kingston Daily Freeman,* July 6, 1876.

Robert Craft, article on traveling with Ivor Stravinsky in Europe, *Kingston Daily Freeman,* Aug. 8, 1957; entry in Grolier Encyclopedia on Craft.

MacDonald De Witt/Andy Gump: brief biographic entry on DeWitt in De Witt's *People's History of Kingston,* p. 187; a tracing of the Andy Gump comic strip suit, see *People's History,* pp. 351-352.

15. Vander Lyn's Versailles Panorama, Painted Mostly in a Kingston Barn, and a New Museum of Decorative Arts Make News in History for Kingston

See *John Vanderlyn, Artist 1775-1852,* Marius Schoonmaker, Kingston, Senate House Association, 1950.

For a print of the Rotunda, and information on the mounting of the Panorama, see *John Vanderlyn's Panoramic View of the Palace and Gardens of Versailles,* Albert H. Vela Company, NY, 1956. Also, *John Vanderlyn's Panoramic View of the Palace and Gardens of Versailles,* Kevin J. Avery, Peter L. Fodera, Metropolitan Museum of Art, 1988

p. 1103, In Joshua Reynolds, *Discourses on Painting and the Fine Arts,* London, 1821 (or 1837)

16. The Old City Hall Gets Restored.1990s-2000

Gallo quotes, "one block down the street," *Kingston Daily Freeman,* Dec. 29, 1999; City Hall booklet, 30 pp., *Kingston Daily Freeman,* May 9, 2000; "More than 650 attend the reopening of a Broadway landmark," *Kingston Daily Freeman,* May 22, 2000.

Article on Ponckhockie Rock, *Freeman,* Feb. 28, 1995

Possible origin of name Ponckhockie, see *Weekly Freeman,* May 10, 1878.

17. Into the Future

S.C.O.R.E. stands for Strand Community Organization for Rehabilitating the Environment

Friends of Historic Kingston founded in 1965?

Appendix

William Redin, American Painter who Painted Kingston and Drew Kingston Places

See entries on Redin in George C. Groce and David H. Wallace, *The New York Historical Society's Dictionary of Artists in America, 1564-1860,* New Haven, Yale University Press 1957,

p. 528. His name was also spelled Reding, and in a Kingston newspaper, Reddin. One of the original large Ulster County maps by Oliver J. Tillson and P. Henry Brink, dated 1853, featuring illustrations and views sketched by W. H. Redin, is in the author's Kingston archive.

See material on Golden Hill in the *Gazetteer and Business Directory of Ulster County,* New York, 1871-72, Hamilton Child, Syracuse, NY; advertisement for lots for sale, *Ulster Republican,* Dec. 1853; "View of Kingston," in *The Journal,* Oct. 15, 1851; and De Witt's *People's History of Kingston,* p. 87.

Index